THE PSYCHOLOGY OF LEARNING AND MOTIVATION

Advances in Research and Theory

EDITED BY GORDON H. BOWER

STANFORD UNIVERSITY, STANFORD, CALIFORNIA

Volume 13

1979

ACADEMIC PRESS **New York • San Francisco • London**

A SUBSIDIARY OF HARCOURT BRACE JOVANOVICH, PUBLISHERS

ACADEMIC PRESS, INC.
111 Fifth Avenue, New York, New York 10003

United Kingdom Edition published by
ACADEMIC PRESS, INC. (LONDON) LTD.
24/28 Oval Road, London NW1 7DX

LIBRARY OF CONGRESS CATALOG CARD NUMBER: 66–30104

ISBN 0–12–543313–1

PRINTED IN THE UNITED STATES OF AMERICA

79 80 81 82   9 8 7 6 5 4 3 2 1

CONTENTS

MEMORY STORAGE FACTORS LEADING TO INFANTILE AMNESIA

Norman E. Spear

LEARNED HELPLESSNESS: ALL OF US WERE RIGHT (AND WRONG): INESCAPABLE SHOCK HAS MULTIPLE EFFECTS

Steven F. Maier and Raymond L. Jackson

ON THE COGNITIVE COMPONENT OF LEARNED HELPLESSNESS AND DEPRESSION

Lauren B. Alloy and Martin E. P. Seligman

A GENERAL LEARNING THEORY AND ITS APPLICATION TO SCHEMA ABSTRACTION

John R. Anderson, Paul J. Kline, and Charles M. Beasley, Jr.

SIMILARITY AND ORDER IN MEMORY

Robert G. Crowder

STIMULUS CLASSIFICATION: PARTITIONING STRATEGIES AND USE OF EVIDENCE

Patrick Rabbitt

IMMEDIATE MEMORY AND DISCOURSE PROCESSING

Robert J. Jarvella

LIST OF CONTRIBUTORS

Numbers in parentheses indicate the pages on which the authors' contributions begin.

Lauren B. Alloy, Department of Psychology, University of Pennsylvania, Philadelphia, Pennsylvania 19104 (219)

John R. Anderson, Department of Psychology, Carnegie-Mellon University Pittsburgh, Pennsylvania 15213 (277)

Charles M. Beasley, Jr., Department of Neurology, Yale University School of Medicine, New Haven, Connecticut 06520 (277)

Robert G. Crowder, Department of Psychology, Yale University, New Haven, Connecticut 06520 (319)

Raymond L. Jackson, Department of Psychology, University of Colorado, Boulder, Colorado 80309 (155)

Robert J. Jarvella, Projektgruppe für Psycholinguistik, Max-Planck-Gesellschaft, Berg en Dalseweg 79, Nijmegen 6522 BC, The Netherlands (379)

Paul J. Kline, Department of Psychology, Carnegie-Mellon University, Pittsburgh, Pennsylvania 15213 (277)

Janice A. Lawry, Department of Psychology, University of Minnesota, Minneapolis, Minnesota 55455 (1)

Steven F. Maier, Department of Psychology, University of Colorado, Boulder, Colorado 80309 (155)

J. Bruce Overmier, Department of Psychology, University of Minnesota, Minneapolis, Minnesota 55455 (1)

Patrick Rabbitt, Department of Experimental Psychology, University of Oxford, Oxford, England OX1 3UD (355)

Jonathan Schull, Department of Psychology, University of Pennsylvania, Philadelphia, Pennsylvania 19104 (57)

Martin E. P. Seligman, Department of Psychology, University of Pennsylvania, Philadelphia, Pennsylvania 19104 (219)

Norman E. Spear, Department of Psychology, State University of New York at Binghamton, Binghamton, New York 13901 (91)

CONTENTS OF PREVIOUS VOLUMES

Volume 5

Volume 6

Volume 7

Volume 8

Volume 9

Volume 10

Volume 11

Volume 12

THE PSYCHOLOGY OF LEARNING AND MOTIVATION

Advances in Research and Theory

VOLUME 13

PAVLOVIAN CONDITIONING AND THE MEDIATION OF BEHAVIOR[1]

J. Bruce Overmier and Janice A. Lawry

UNIVERSITY OF MINNESOTA
MINNEAPOLIS, MINNESOTA

I. Introduction

Since the clear recognition that behaviors may be acquired by either of two operationally distinct paradigms, one arising from the experiments of Pavlov (Pavlovian conditioning) and the other from the early work of Thorndike (instrumental training), the study of learning has been stimulated by the question of whether these two paradigms represent different learning processes. As yet, this question has not been fully adjudicated. Increasingly, psychologists are noting that many of the traditional bases for making process distinctions (Kimble, 1961) are being eroded (Hearst, 1975; Rescorla & Solomon, 1967). Yet, discovery of manipulations of the central nervous system which seem to dissociate learning under the two paradigms serves to maintain the viability of the

[1]Preparation of this manuscript and conduct of the research reported herein was supported in part by grants to J.B.O. (MH 13558 and BNS 77-28161), to the Center for Research in Human Learning (NICHHD-HD 01136, NICHHD-HD-00098, and BNS-7503816, and by an Eva O. Miller Fellowship to J.A.L.).

ISBN 0-12-543313-1

process distinction (e.g., DiCara, Braun, & Pappas, 1970; Flood, Overmier, & Savage, 1976; McCleary, 1960). It is not obvious how the issue of one versus two learning processes will be finally resolved. Retention of the distinction between Pavlovian conditioning and instrumental training may well be more dependent upon conceptual utility than upon scientific validity.[2]

One class of theories has relied heavily upon this process distinction and has invoked Pavlovian conditioning as a central explanatory entity in accounting for behavior resulting from instrumental training (e.g., Amsel, 1958; Konorski, 1964; Logan & Wagner, 1965; Mowrer, 1947; Spence, 1956; Rescorla & Solomon, 1967; Trapold & Overmier, 1972). The basic common tenet among these "two-process theories" is that a Pavlovian conditioning process serves to mediate the behavior observed under the three-term contingency of instrumental training (stimulus–response–reinforcer, S–R–S^R). This tenet relies upon the observation that imbedded within the instrumental paradigm itself are the necessary and sufficient conditions for Pavlovian conditioning, that is, predictive stimulus–reinforcer pairings.

II. Assessment of the Two-Process Approach

A. Direct Assessment: Concurrent Measurement

One line of research undertaken to support two-process mediational theories was to search for direct evidence of a Pavlovian conditioned response being established concurrently with and/or covarying with the instrumental behavior. Following Konorski and Miller (1937a, 1937b), Schlosberg (1937), and Mowrer (1947), it was assumed that autonomic effectors either were the mediating event or at least provided a direct index of the mediating event which somehow modulated the instrumental behavior.

Many experiments using this strategy have been reported (for reviews, see Overmier, 1979b; Rescorla & Solomon, 1967). For example, Soltysik (1960; Soltysik & Kowalska, 1960) compared conditioned heart rate acceleration with concurrent acquisition and differentiation of instrumental avoidance, while Shapiro (Shapiro & Miller, 1965) compared anticipatory salivation with concurrent instrumental responding for

[2]It would appear that tenability of two-process theories would depend upon the confirmation of the existence of two separate learning processes under the two paradigms. This is not necessarily the case. It can be argued that the two-process distinction is superfluous to the basic theoretical notion of an independently manipulable mediator by means of which S–R behavior can be altered through associative experiences which do not involve running off of the S–R sequence (cf. Logan, 1959; Meehl & MacCorquodale, 1951; Trapold & Overmier, 1972).

food, both found close covariation between the two classes of response. However, many other experiments have provided specific examples of noncorrelation and/or dissociation between autonomic conditioned responses (CRs) and amplitude of the instrumental behavior (e.g., Black, 1959; Ellison & Konorski, 1964; Overmier, 1966a, 1968a). Any thorough review of the existing data reveals that the necessary invariant relations to qualify autonomic CRs as mediators of instrumental responding have not been consistently obtained (Overmier, 1979b). This inconsistency, coupled with the findings that instrumental contingencies can exert control over autonomic functions (e.g., DiCara & Miller, 1968; Shapiro and Herendeen, 1975), has led to the abandonment of this concurrent measurement strategy for evaluating two-process theories. Interestingly, however, there has been no concommitant abandonment of two-process theories per se, perhaps because they continue to offer a consistent account of a variety of instrumental phenomena, particularly those in which response-noncontingent reward manipulations modulate performance (see, e.g., Gray, 1975).

B. Indirect Assessment: Transfer of Control

Having given up the quest of direct assessment of the embedded mediational process, one is left with the tasks of (1) providing a body of evidence which confirms the existence of a mediational process and (2) understanding how it operates. These tasks have been approached by ascertaining empirically whether Pavlovian conditioned stimuli (CSs) have observable influences upon instrumental responding in the absence of changes in the instrumental contingencies. Such influences are expected under the assumption that Pavlovian conditioning is, indeed, responsible for generating a mediational process. This reasoning has been referred to as "the essential postulate of two-process theory" by Rescorla and Solomon (1967, p. 170).

Efforts to explore the potential influences of Pavlovian conditioned stimuli upon the performance of instrumental acts have typically used an experimental paradigm which we have come to refer to as the *transfer-of-control* paradigm. This paradigm follows directly from two learning process theories. In transfer-of-control experiments, a stimulus, in the presence of which an animal has never before performed a selected instrumental response, immediately assumes some degree of control over that response as a result of certain response-independent Pavlovian condition. The importance of this class of experiments is that it *(a)* separates the two associative relationships thought to be important, *(b)* provides a strong test for two learning process theories by providing empirical evidence as to whether Pavlovian stimuli can and do influence instrumental responding, and *(c)* provides a means of manipulating variables important to the Pavlovian "process" relatively unconfounded by the possibility of concurrent alteration of the instrumental "process."

To standardize terminology and to illustrate the rationale and logic of this class of experiments, which has been central to our research program, we will describe in outline form one prototypic transfer-of-control experiment. The prototype experiment involves three distinct phases: (1) a Pavlovian *pairing phase* in which, with the target instrumental response somehow precluded, some stimulus is established as an excitatory or inhibitory CS (CS + or CS−) for a reinforcer event (this reinforcer may be the same or as different from the reinforcer employed in the instrumental training phase); (2) an *instrumental baseline training phase* in which a specific response is established by conventional positive reinforcement or avoidance methods; and (3) a transfer-of-control *test phase* in which, with the instrumental response free to occur, the CS+ or CS− is tested for its power to evoke or modulate the instrumental performace. In our dog experiments, the first two phases are typically carried out in different apparatus units. The rationale for conducting the different operations in different apparatus units is presented in detail by Trapold and Overmier (1972). Stated briefly, this strategy maximizes the opportunity to see the effects of any mediational process unconfounded by (or at least minimizing) operant response interaction.

The basic finding from such experiments (e.g., Solomon & Turner, 1962) is that a CS+, a stimulus never before associated with the instrumental response, acquires the capacity to influence or "control" the instrumental response during the test phase. Other experiments have established that these effects are based upon the associative histories of the CS (Bull & Overmier, 1968; Rescorla & LoLordo, 1967). Thus, the transfer to the CS of control over the instrumental response is attributed directly to the response-independent Pavlovian conditioning process and is interpreted as constituting strong confirmation that instrumental performance is normally modulated by a second response-independent process over and above any basic S–R associative process (Rescorla & Solomon, 1967; Trapold & Overmier, 1972).

We should note that there are many variations on this prototype experiment. For example, one can reserve the order of the first two phases as given in the prototype. The presentation order of the first two phases is critical neither to the concept underlying the transfer-of-control experiment nor to the qualitative outcome obtained (Overmier & Leaf, 1965). The Pavlovian conditioning and the instrumental test phase may even be run concurrently as in the traditional "on-baseline" CER procedures, which are one instantiation of the transfer-of-control paradigm.

In yet another variation, testing and instrumental training proceed concurrently; here transfer of control is seen not as immediately enhanced capacity of the CS+ to control the instrumental response but as facilitation or interference of instrumental response acquisition when the CS is employed as a discriminative stimulus, S^D (e.g., Overmier & Payne, 1971).

C. Overview of Pavlovian and Instrumental Interactions

To set the stage for subsequent theoretical analyses, let us briefly characterize the pattern of data that has been generated from the classes of simple transfer-of-control experiments. Rescorla and Solomon (1967) provided a systematic review of the early transfer-of-control data. In it they organized the experiments by reference to whether *(a)* the Pavlovian conditioning was appetitive or aversive, or *(b)* the instrumental reinforcer was a positive or a negative one. This yielded four major classes of interactions depending upon whether the US and the reinforcer were hedonically similar (homogeneous case) or hedonically opposite (heterogeneous case).

The psychological literature now leaves little doubt that Pavlovian conditioned CSs can and do modulate the performance of instrumental behaviors. For example, aversive Pavlovian CSs (AvCS) have been shown to exert striking control over instrumental avoidance responding; Rescorla and LoLordo (1965) and Bull and Overmier (1968) demonstrated that a CS+ for shock increases the rate of avoidance responding when superimposed upon Sidman avoidance or when compounded with the discriminative stimulus for avoidance (AvS^D). Such acceleration is typically a positive function of the severity of the Pavlovian US (Grossen & Bolles, 1968; Martin & Riess, 1969; Overmier, 1966a, 1966b, 1968a). Perhaps more importantly for the strongest forms of mediational theory, such an AvCS+ will also elicit avoidance responses previously trained to other stimuli (Solomon & Turner, 1962) and will do even when the original response-controlling stimulus (AvS^D) no longer does so (Overmier & Bull, 1969), a point to which we shall return later.

Aversive Pavlovian CSs also exert strong control over instrumental reward responding. Presentations of AvCS+s result is marked decreases in the rate of ongoing responding; this is the well-known CER phenomenon (Brady & Hunt, 1955; Estes & Skinner, 1941; for reviews, see Blackman, 1977; Davis 1968).

A number of experiments also suggest that an appetitive Pavlovian CS+ (ApCS) results in an increase or facilitation of instrumental reward responding (Estes, 1943, 1948; Henton & Brady, 1970; Herrnstein &

Morse, 1957; LoLordo, McMillan, & Riley, 1974; Meltzer & Hamm, 1974, 1978; Shapiro, Miller & Bresnahan, 1966).[3] Analogously, prior appetitive Pavlovian conditioning as a CS+ or CS− reliably results in facilitation and interference, respectively, of instrumental reward learning wherein the Pavlovian stimulus is used as the discriminative stimulus in the instrumental task (Bower & Grusec, 1964; Trapold & Winokur, 1967).

At the time of the review by Rescorla and Solomon, the effect of appetitive Pavlovian CSs upon instrumental avoidance responding had not been investigated. Since then, however, several studies have established that superimposing an ApCS+ upon instrumental avoidance performance results in suppression (Bull, 1970; Bull & Overmier, 1969; Davis & Kreuter, 1972; Grossen, Kostansek, & Bolles, 1969).

This brief characterization of the data may be summarized in tabular form: Summary I provides a simplified presentation of the basic effects of Pavlovian CSs upon instrumental responding:

SUMMARY I

TRANSFER-OF-CONTROL INTERACTIONS

	Baseline		Baseline		
	R_{Av}	R_{Ap}	R_{Av}	R_{Ap}	
AvCS+	↑	↓	↓	↑	ApCS+

Note that the summary does not incorporate the effects of a CS−. One thing that becomes clear upon review of the transfer-of-control literature is that precious little attention has been given to the effects of Pavlovian CS−s. This may have been merely a by-product of our ignorance of the pattern of effects to be obtained with CS+s. Alternatively, it may reflect less well-developed general theorizing as to what mediational effects might be predicted for CS−s (exception is Mowrer, 1960).

Given that Pavlovian CSs were demonstrated to be powerful modulators of instrumental performance, a well-explicated account for these complex interactions between Pavlovian conditioning and instrumental training was needed. Several tentative theories of mediation were available (e.g., Konorski, 1964, 1967; Mowrer, 1947; Rescorla & Solomon, 1967; Spence, 1956). Before these theories can be seriously addressed,

[3]There is considerable controversy over this effect (Azrin & Hake, 1969; Baum & Gleitman, 1967; Hyde, 1969; see Wielkiewicz & Lawry, 1979 for review).

however, the "less glamorous" possibility that interactions of operants might simulate mediational effects has to be treated.

D. Operant Interaction Hypothesis

This is really a methodological problem of ruling out "simple" instrumental response interactions as a basis for explanation of the transfer effects observed. This problem will be treated here only to illustrate strategies, including our own, for dealing with this problem. A more thorough treatment has been provided elsewhere (Trapold & Overmier, 1972).

In general, the problem arises from the potential for the US to reinforce instrumentally any behaviors occurring during the Pavlovian pairings (Black, 1971; Maier & Schneirla, 1942; Perkins, 1968). Those wishing to account for Pavlovian–instrumental interactions in terms of operants argue that operants (unspecified) could be learned during the pairing phase. These operants, acquired perhaps superstitiously and presumed to be under CS control, could then be evoked during the transfer test phase and, through inherent mechanical compatibility or incompatibility with the target response, cause the observed facilitation or interference, respectively. Moreover, it must be recognized that just such interactions could, indeed, produce transfer effects, although why a consistent pattern of effects within each class of interaction experiment should be obtained despite wide variation in Pavlovian and instrumental procedures is unclear.

Given the general nonspecific nature of the operant analysis, it is almost impossible to completely eliminate the potential for such effects. However, several strategies have been used to obviate the operant account; some are more adequate than others, yet taken together they represent a reasonable basis on which to assess the viability of the operant account. Let us discuss the strategies used in our laboratory.

One strategy has been to minimize the opportunity for our subjects to learn an instrumental response during the Pavlovian phase. This has been accomplished by physically restraining the animals and delivering the USs in such a way that the subjects' actions cannot modulate the delivery of the US (e.g., directly attached electrodes). This "restraint" strategy has also been supplemented by carrying out the Pavlovian pairings in an apparatus very different from that in which the transfer testing is to take place (e.g., Bull, 1970; Bull & Overmier, 1969; Overmier & Payne, 1971; Overmier & Starkman, 1974); the rationale for the apparatus shift is that the degree to which any learned operant may later be manifest is a function of the similarity of stimulus conditions and that the greater the apparatus difference the greater the operant response generalization decrement. The most extreme form of our effort to prevent learning of "operants" during the pairing phase followed the procedure of Solomon and Turner (1962) and Leaf (1964). It involved complete pharmacological blockage of the skeletal motor system using curariform drugs (Overmier, 1966a, 1968a; Overmier & Seligman, 1967).

A second strategy has been to show that the degree of transfer observed is a function of the hedonic relationship between the UCS and the instrumental reinforcer, is independent of the opportunity to learn an operant during the pairing phase, and is independent of variations in the particular form of the target instrumental response. Our use of this strategy (Overmier & Brackbill, 1977; Overmier & Bull, 1969, 1970; Payne, 1972) followed its earlier use by Waller and Waller (1963) and by others working with appetitive reinforcers (Trapold & Carlson, 1965; Trapold & Fairlie, 1965), where the strategy continues to be popular (e.g., Hearst & Peterson, 1973).

A final strategy has been to insure that a specific operant is learned rather than leaving to chance the possibility that our dogs may learn a response during the pairing phase. Following this strategy one trains the same response under stimulus control in two groups but for hedonically different reinforcers, relying upon embedded pairings for the "Pavlovian" conditioning. Then, in a different apparatus, both groups learn the identical baseline behavior, and finally test presentations of the "Pavlovian" stimuli are carried out. If the transfer effects obtained to Pavlovian stimuli here are primarily due to evoked operant behaviors acquired in the pairing phase, then the baseline behavior of both groups should be affected in the same way independent of the reinforcer with which the stimuli had been paired. If the stimuli produce different results in the two groups, then operant response mechanical interaction must be considered an inadequate account of the observed phenomena. Using just this approach, Overmier, Bull, and Pack (1971a) showed that a cue for pedal pressing had opposite effects upon a hurdle-jump shuttle avoidance response depending upon whether the stimulus had cued an appetitive response (ApS^D) or an avoidance response (ApS^D). A control stimulus, which was not associated with either US but in the presence of which pedal pressing did occur, had no effect upon the baseline shuttle avoidance during transfer tests. These results are shown in Fig. 1; clearly, this pattern of effects cannot be explained by reference to operant response interaction.

Others have obtained results consistent with this analysis (e.g., Grossen *et al.*, 1969). Thus, even if a simulus is an S^D for some operant response

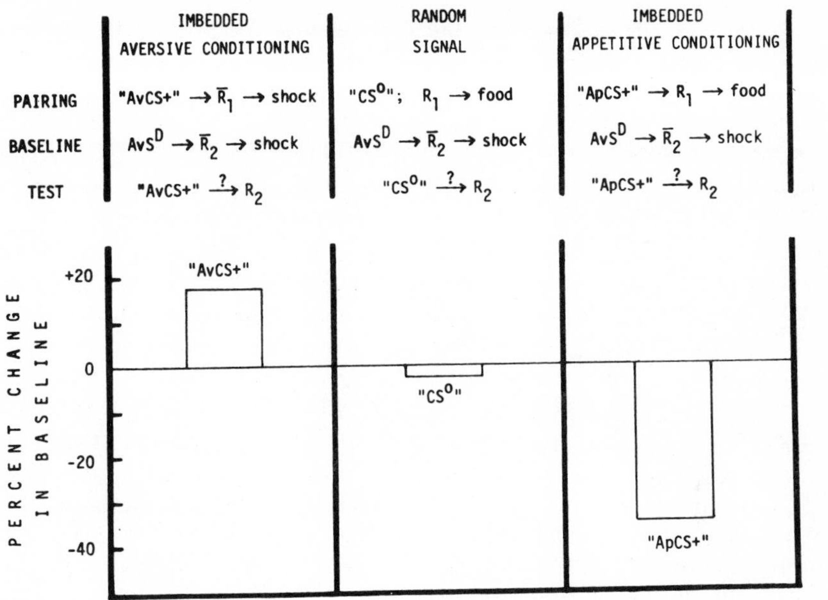

Fig. 1. Percentage change in baseline rate of shuttlebox avoidance responding produced by superimposing stimuli with histories of functioning as AvS^D, ApS^O, or ApS^D for pressing a pedal in a small booth. Because the experiment was designed to test whether the effects of Pavlovian CSs exercise their control in transfer experiments by virtue of coming to control some operant, we have labeld the test stimuli as "AvCS+," CS^O, and ApCS+" even though the Pavlovian pairings were imbedded in instrumental training for three groups.

different from (orthogonal to) the target response, in a transfer test the pattern of obtained effects is the same as if the stimulus had been a true Pavlovian CS+. This is captured in Summary II.

Overall, we feel that the available data obtained from several laboratories using a variety of strategies inveigh against the hypothesis that mechanical interaction of operants is the predominant process underlying transfer-of-control phenomena. What then are the alternatives?

SUMMARY II

Transfer-of-Control Interactions

	Baseline		Baseline		
	R_{Av}	R_{Ap}	R_{Av}	R_{Ap}	
AvCS+	↑	↓	↓	↑	ApCS+
AvS^D (orthogonal R)	↑	↓	↓	↑	ApS^D (orthogonal R)

III. Mediational Approaches

Invocation of mediational mechanisms is not at all new; indeed, it has a long, venerable history among behaviorists (Hull, 1930; Watson, 1913; see Goss, 1961, for a historical review). There have been a variety of mediational approaches. These differ with respect to whether or not they invoke a second learning process. Mediational approaches also differ in whether or not the mediation is a parallel response-controlling mechanism. Finally, they differ with respect to the recognized mediational properties and their functions. One's decisions on each of these questions is important in making predictions about the effects of Pavlovian stimuli upon instrumental behavior.

A. Common Elements

The traditional uniprocess S–R associational approaches relied upon acquired stimulus similarity for explanation of complex behavior phenomena (Osgood, 1953) and used as the empirical prototype Shipley's (1933) "mediated stimulus generalization" experiment. This mediated stimulus generalization was seen as a way to account for the "anticipatory" behavior seen in the early experiments in "signaled escape" tasks (N.E. Miller, 1948; Warner, 1932a). Here the observed avoidance responses that occurred during the S^D were attributed to the S^D's elicitation of a mediator, the properties of which were fractional components ("detachable reactions," Osgood, 1953, p. 396; "fractional anticipatory goal reactions," Hull, 1930, 1931) of the shock; these, in turn, evoke the same responses as the shock through stimulus generalization. Thus, the mechanism for producing avoidance behaviors was simply shock escape behavior generalized to the S^D. This view has been a persistent one, rather broadly accepted (cf. Kimble, 1961; Schoenfeld, 1950). May's (1948) transfer-of-control experiment is purported to be a demonstration of just this and has been commonly cited as evidence for mediation via common elements generalization yielding avoidance behavior (Kimble, 1961; Steward, 1970). The experiment and analysis are as follows:

Phase 1. Train to escape shock: Shock $\rightarrow R_p \rightarrow S_p \rightarrow R_{escape}$

Phase 2. Conditioning: Buzzer $\rightarrow$ Shock $\rightarrow R_p \rightarrow S_p$ (escape prevented)
$\dashrightarrow (r_p\text{–}s_p)$

Phase 3. Avoidance test: Buzzer $\rightarrow (r_p\text{–}s_p) \rightarrow R_{\text{"escape"}}$

where r_p–s_p are the detachable components of shock-elicited pain (R_p) and its feedback (S_p).

There are several sources of difficulty for this analysis. For example, it is now well known that escape behavior is not a prerequisite to avoidance learning (e.g., Overmier, 1968b, 1979a); and Bolles (1969) has shown that the avoidance response need in no way resemble the escape behavior. Neither does the avoidance trained animal exercise that response when the US is applied under escape contingencies (Fonberg, 1962). Thus, we have come to have serious doubts about textbook explanations of avoidance which rely upon mediation by common elements and generalization as the explanatory entities. Our doubts were initially based upon the above observations plus an intuition that "fear" was an anticipatory state with potential mediating functions that had little if anything in common with pain per se. The evidence for this abounds: For example, Warner (1932b) early observed that while shock led to escape responding, the signal for it led to freezing. Other researchers have long been puzzled by why rats press levers during shocks but not during "fear" (e.g., D'Amato & Schiff, 1964). Indeed, we think we now have good evidence that the mechanisms for the evocation of escape and avoidance responses are qualitatively different—sufficiently so as to make the common elements account of transfer of control clearly inapplicable.

If our intuition that fear has very little in common with pain were correct, the May (1948) experiment as described above should not have yielded immediate transfer of control as was reported. Careful rereading of May's detailed description of his procedures reveals that the experiment is not, in fact, as commonly described. May administered successive escape trials in the shuttlebox on a fixed-time schedule unless the rat had recently performed a "spontaneous" response, in which case the fixed-time interval was reset! He also notes that sometimes he had to wait several minutes before he could administer the next scheduled escape trial. In current day perspectives (and jargon), we can readily see that May's animals were given Sidman *avoidance training* (R–S = 60 sec, S–S = 0 sec) in phase 1 and that they learned to avoid.

Given this background, Ehrman and Overmier (1976) undertook to provide the test of the common elements hypothesis that May had intended. Two groups of dogs were placed in a shuttlebox. One group received 90 pure escape-training trials in which a light stimulus and shock came on simultaneously; while the termination of the shock was response dependent, there was no shock avoidance contingency. In contrast, the second group received 90 avoidance-training trials in which a light came on 10 sec before the shock and responses during either the light or light-plus-shock terminated the trial. Then, these two groups received discriminative, aversive Pavlovian conditioning with two tone CSs (CS+ and CS−) while penned in a small compartment. Finally, with the instrumental response free to occur again, test presentations of both tones and the light were given. If the textbook common elements account were correct, both groups should have behaved similarly during testing. However, that is not what they found; the escape group did not respond to either of the tone CSs or to the light by crossing the barrier. The avoidance group, in contrast, showed immediate transfer of control by jumping the barrier to each presentation of the tone CS+ (and, of course, the light) but did not respond to the tone CS−, indicating that the responding to the CS+ was not due simply to enhanced stimulus responsivity, sensitization, or cross-modal generalization. These data are shown in Fig. 2. We must therefore conclude that having learned a response under aversive reinforcement does not by itself insure that it is available for transfer of control to stimuli which signal shocks; the

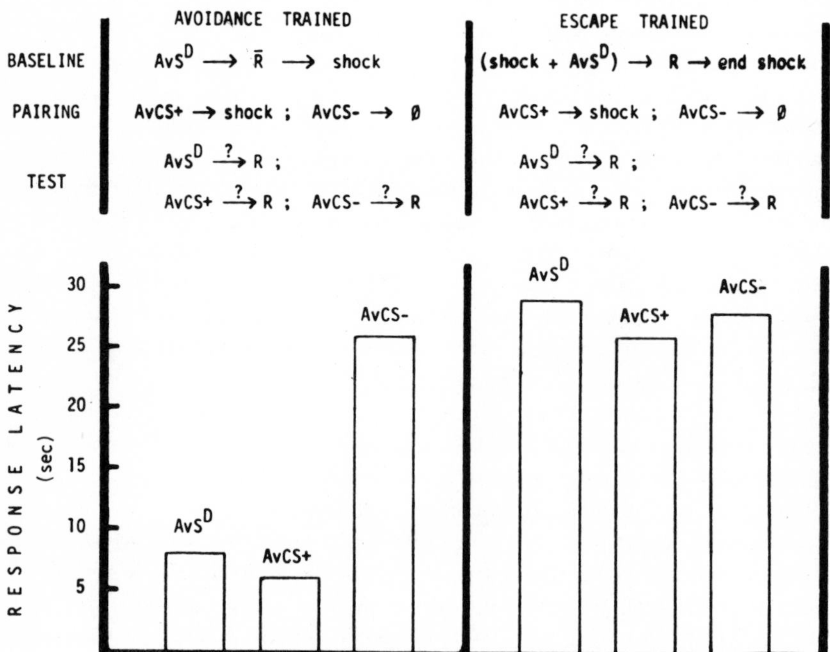

Fig. 2. Effectiveness of aversive Pavlovian CSs in eliciting *de novo* an instrumental response previously trained as either an avoidance response (left) or an escape response (right). Maximum latency was 30 sec. Note that while the white noise "S^D" in the escape group did not by itself control responding, during escape training the dogs all responded within a very few seconds to it in compound with the shock. Simultaneous onsets of a stimulus and a reinforcer do not endow the stimulus as an S^D (e.g., Schoenfeld, Antonitus, & Bersh, 1950).

response must also have been established as an anticipatory one under mediational control.

It follows from these results that our intuitions about the mediational state being very different from that elicited by the shock were well founded. Furthermore, the data indicated that the response-evoking mechanisms of escape and avoidance behaviors are fundamentally different, with only the latter being controlled via mediational processes. The development of the conditioned mediational process must occur under specific, limited stimulus and training arrangements which allow for the development of anticipatory states.

The absence of empirical support for—and indeed substantial evidence against—mediated stimulus generalization via common elements as an account for transfer-of-control phenomena leaves us with lacunae we must fill. The lacunae have to do with the nature of mediators operating in avoidance tasks and their modus operandi. The common elements view provided a conceptually simple solution to this problem: Because the mediator was assumed to be a fractional anticipatory component of the US event, the nature and properties of the mediator were exactly those of the US itself but of reduced strength, their mechanisms of behavior modulation essentially identical to that of the US. As we lay aside the "common elements" explanation, however, we also must forego the conceptually (deceptively?) simple solutions it offered to the difficult questions surrounding the nature and properties of the mediator.

Are there alternatives to the common elements view? Certainly Tolman's theorizing on "expectancies" did not rely upon the intervening variable having the same properties or regulating behavior in the same way as the US event. In two-process theory, moreover, Mowrer (1947) took a full step away when he inferred that a Pavlovian CS acquired only the affective/emotional properties of the US. In contrast, Hull's (1952) version of the "pure stimulus act" focused upon the stimulus properties of the US produced response and upon the mediator as a "self-stimulating" process (cf. also Osgood, 1953).

Perhaps we ought to begin a reanalysis. In doing so, we can usefully review the assumptions that earlier "two-process theorists" have made about the mediating process and representative data that bear on their validity. One might well note that relatively few have actually pursued a course of empirical "validation" of the assumptions about the mediator and its modus operandi. The notable exceptions are *(a)* Mowrer's (e.g., 1950) efforts to establish that the Pavlovian conditioning associative process is different from the instrumental response selection associative process, *(b)* Spence's, Miller's, and Solomon's searches for the fractional antedating response (e.g., N.E. Miller & DeBold, 1965; Spence's students Patten & Deaux, 1966; Wynne & Solomon, 1955), *(c)* Rescorla and Solomon's (1967) and Konorski's (1967) analyses of transfer data showing the generalized drive (so-called "big-D") mediation account to be inadequate, and *(d)* Amsel's (1967) thorough empirical efforts to demonstrate both the energizing and stimulus properties of the mediational state arising from the omission of a regularly presented reward (i.e., "frustration").

B. Two-Process Models

Although two-process theories share the basic idea that a Pavlovian conditioned mediator modulates instrumental responding, these theories can be seen to differ with respect to where in the behavior stream the mediator "resides" and how it functions. Regarding the first problem of "locus," Mowrer (1939, 1947) viewed the mediator (fear, in this case) as being elicited by the stimulus, with the mediator in turn evoking the response in a *serial* chain (i.e., S–M–R)—a conception similar to that in verbal mediation paradigms (Jenkins, 1963). In contrast, Hull (1931), Konorski (1964), and Spence (1956) viewed the mediator as being established in *parallel* to the instrumental S–R chain (i.e., $S \nearrow^{M} \searrow R$). We could refer to this first distinction as one of mechanism with the mediator operating either sequential within or parallel to the S–R chain.

Turning to the second problem, two-process theories differ with respect to what properties the mediator has that allow it to modulate the instrumental behavior (Osgood, 1953). Two distinctive positions have been adopted. One early view (e.g., Hull, 1931) was that the mediator has stimulus properties which could function as discriminative cues in response selection. A more recent view has been that the mediator has affective/hedonic properties which function to energize the organism and activate response systems appropriate to the affective/hedonic state (Konorski, 1964; see also Bindra, 1974; Bolles, 1970). Additionally, some theories have suggested that the mediator has both affective/hedonic properties which energize responses and stimulus properties which cue responses (e.g., Amsel, 1958; Spence, 1956).

These two distinctions, between mechanisms and between properties and functions, are set out in Table I and suggest six distinctive mediational models. Consideration of these models is the stimulating speculative framework within which we have been working most recently.

One is tempted to try to determine the correctness of the alternatives in each dimension of Table I taken separately. This cannot really be done, however, because the predictions about the outcomes of any particular experiment in fact are the joint product of one's assumptions (choice of an alternative) on both dimensions. That is to say that Table I is an artificial fractionation of the dimensionality of the components

TABLE I

DISTINCTIONS CONCERNING THE MEDIATIONAL PROCESS

Mediational mechanisms	Properties and functions of mediators		
	Stimulus: cue	Hedonic: energize	Dual
Parallel	P/S	P/H	P/S + H
Sequential	S/S	S/H	S/S + H

of mediation, yet a useful heuristic. It should not be assumed that we believe this heuristic exhausts the alternative properties of elicited mediators. For example, it is possible—indeed, likely, given the demonstrations of Overmier and Payne (1971) and Dickenson (1976, 1977) of enhanced aversive conditioning to previously established appetitive CS + s —that mediators serve general attention alerting functions, too, independent of any hedonic-energizing and/or stimulus-associative cueing functions. (See Fowler, Fago, Domber, & Hochhauser, 1973; Ghiselli & Fowler, 1976, for further support of a separate, general attention directing property.) However, a focus on the alternatives already incorporated into Table I will suffice to organize the remaining discussion of our research.

While it is relatively easy to "pigeonhole" some theorists according to Table I, it is difficult if not impossible to do so with others because they often have not been very explicit about their assumptions with respect to one or the other dimension. Clear recognition of both aspects is often missing. This problem is not unique to the concept of mediation but arises whenever intervening variables are invoked (Brown, 1961).

IV. Sequential versus Parallel Mediators

Among two-process theories, at least two views regarding stimulus control over instrumental responding are found. One of these states that a stimulus only affects a response via the mediational state it elicits. This sequential position is characterized by a single pathway of response influence; the stimulus elicits the mediator and the mediator then elicits the instrumental response (i.e., S–M–R). Alternatively, a second position proposes that a direct stimulus–response link operates in parallel with the mediational pathway (i.e., S<M>R). Depending upon the nature of the mediator's properties, affective/hedonic or stimulus cueing, the mediator would function respectively to energize the S–R link or contribute directly to the cueing of the instrumental response.

An example of the parallel process is to be found in the model offered by Konorski (1964, 1967). Konorski maintained that conditioning establishes a stimulus–response association (CS+ or S^D directly connected to the response via an associative bond) and the stimulus also elicits a mediational state which influences responding. Konorski assigned separate functions to these two paths and strongly stated that both were "indispensable" for response execution. The S–R connection was characterized as "telling" the animal which response to make in order to satisfy the acting drive or need state. In essence, the S–R "link" is seen as serving a "response-cueing" function. The M–R influence (also elicited by the stimulus) was said to provide the necessary "response energization" for the performance of the response.

Although Konorski made it quite clear that both sources of influence were thought to be necessary for the formation and elicitation of the instrumental response, he did suggest that compensation for one "weak" pathway could occur by increased strength of the other. He also stated that one pathway could be selectively strengthened while leaving the other unaltered, which suggests a certain independence between links. Konorski was not, however, very specific about what kinds of operations would result in the selective strengthening or weakening of either connection. While Konorski focused his discussions upon two "links" (M–R and S–R), it is clear that this model really involves three such links (S–M, M–R, and S–R).

Before one accepts any parallel model, the rules of parsimony suggest that one ask if an S–R link is truly necessary, or if the S–M–R pathway will suffice. Indeed, Mowrer's (1947) account of avoidance learning can be considered a prototype example of such a purely sequential model. In the case of signaled avoidance, the discriminative stimulus (AvS^D) was said to elicit some "conditioned emotional reaction" (i.e., affective mediational state) usually referred to as "fear." As is characteristic of two-process theories, the S–M link was attributed to Pavlovian pairings between AvS^D and shock, embedded within the early instrumental training trials. The M–R connection, "fear–R_{Av}" in this case, was said to be established via instrumental reinforcement contingencies in that the R_{Av} led to a reduction in the fear state. In this model, the avoidance response is viewed as a reaction to the "motivational" properties of the fear mediator. We might note that Mowrer (1947) assumed that the affective mediator served not only a response energization function, but also a reinforcing function.

While we have already challenged those interpretations of Mowrer's model which rely upon common elements between the fear mediator and shock-produced pain (see discussion above), the data cited (e.g., Ehrman & Overmier, 1976) do not attack the validity of two-process theory or a sequential model, per se. In fact, the data clearly support the notion that mechanisms of avoidance response evocation and control are closely related to Pavlovian processes. Consequently, some sort of two-process theory continues to be viable.

Thus we see that both the sequential and the parallel two-process models suggest that the observed behavior is the product of conceptually independent links or pathways which are operationally separable. The transfer-of-control paradigm has, of course, been refined to exploit this separability feature (Rescorla & Solomon, 1967; Solomon & Turner, 1962). To the extent such experiments are successful, they provide results congruent with theory. Moreover, as we have seen, they have been successful in showing that given an S^D → fear mediator → avoidance response "linkage," the Pavlovian conditioning of an additional CS+ → fear associative link enables the CS+ to modulate and control the avoidance response (cf. Bull & Overmier, 1968; Martin & Riess, 1969; Overmier & Leaf, 1965; Rescorla & LoLordo, 1965; Riess, 1969; Solomon & Turner, 1962; and in appetitive analogs: Bower & Grusec, 1964; Henton & Brady, 1970; Hyde, Trapold, & Gross, 1968; Mellgren & Ost, 1969; Trapold & Winokur, 1967). These do not, however, show the independence of the elements in the hypothetical pathways. Independence of the links is critical to the viability of a sequential process model. Therefore, we sought to provide evidence for this.

Our general approach to demonstrating independence was to show that one could selectively "break" one mediational link (either the S–M or the M–R) while leaving the other intact. This intactness was to be demonstrated by integrating the unbroken link with a new link to establish a functionally new behavior competence. Both the details and the logic of these experiments are sufficiently complicated to warrant our detailed presentation.

In one of our efforts (Overmier & Brackbill, 1977), we wished to show that in a stimulus–mediator–response (S–M–R) pathway, one could break the mediator–response (M–R) link while leaving the stimulus–mediator (S–M) link intact and unaltered. From the outset it seemed that the procedures required to break the M–R link without interruption of the S–M link would be difficult to work out because they were (hypothetically) established by a single operation, discrete-trial avoidance training. A second problem arises from the question of how we are to know the S–M link is intact if we have broken the M–R link. The resolution to the second problem was found in using two different avoidance responses trained in different apparatus units, one established under discriminative stimulus control to which we can apply the M–R link elimination procedure and one to use for assessing the S–M link using a transfer-of-control procedure. With respect to the first problem, one must eliminate the M–R link of the S^D–M–R pathway without presenting the discriminative stimulus; this is because operations breaking the M–R link that also involve presentations of the S^D would risk being accounted for in terms of changes in the S–M link. We followed the implications of Davenport's suggestion (Davenport & Olson, 1968)—and experimental confirmation (Davenport, Spector, & Coger, 1970)—that the most appropriate avoidance response elimination procedure (in the sense of being directly analogous to the extinction of appetitive responses) was simply to remove the response shock–omission contingency (see also Meyer, 1970).

There were four phases to Overmier and Brackbill's (1977) experiment. First, dogs were given free-operant avoidance training (Sidman, 1953) in a shuttlebox until avoidance was reliable and stable. Then, in a separate apparatus, they were trained in a discrete-trial, discriminative-avoidance task; in the presence of one tone (S^D) they had to press a panel with their heads to prevent shock delivery, while a second tone was never followed by shocks and functioned as an S^Δ. The third phase was the critical one for the experiment group. During it, the second avoidance response was "extinguished" by presenting a series of unsignaled, response-independent shocks of fixed duration; occasional probe trials with the S^D revealed when the S^D no longer controlled panel pressing. However, in the fourth phase, when the S^D was superimposed upon ongoing free-operant avoidance responding, the S^D markedly facilitated this other avoidance behavior while the S^Δ depressed it.[4] These data are shown in Fig. 3. Importantly, the facilitation observed in the experimental group was equivalent to that observed in a group in which the panel-press avoidance had not been extinguished (i.e, no phase 3 treatment) as well as to that observed in a group which received only an equivalent Pavlovian conditioning treatment during phase 2. This pattern is consistent with Payne's (1972) earlier demonstration in our laboratory that if S^Ds for panel-press avoidance and Pavlovian CS+s are equated in number of pairings and nonpairings, the degrees of transfer of control of a shuttlebox avoidance response are equivalent.

On the basis of Overmier and Brackbill's data, it was concluded that elimination of the avoidance response to a stimulus does not impair that stimulus's ability to elicit fear and modulate the performance of a second independent avoidance response. In terms of the model, clearly, breaking the M–R_2 link did not impair the strenght of the S–M link as was revealed in the transfer-of-control test. Further, we believe that the

[4]The perceptive reader cannot help but observe the similarity of this operation to the "learned helplessness" treatment (Overmier & Seligman, 1967). Yet, as will be seen in the next few paragraphs, these dogs were not helpless in any other sense than they would no longer perform the previously trained R_2 as either an escape or an avoidance response yet would perform R_1 in another situation. Perhaps "helplessness" training is the process of breaking the preexisting (as in SSDRs) mediator–response links.

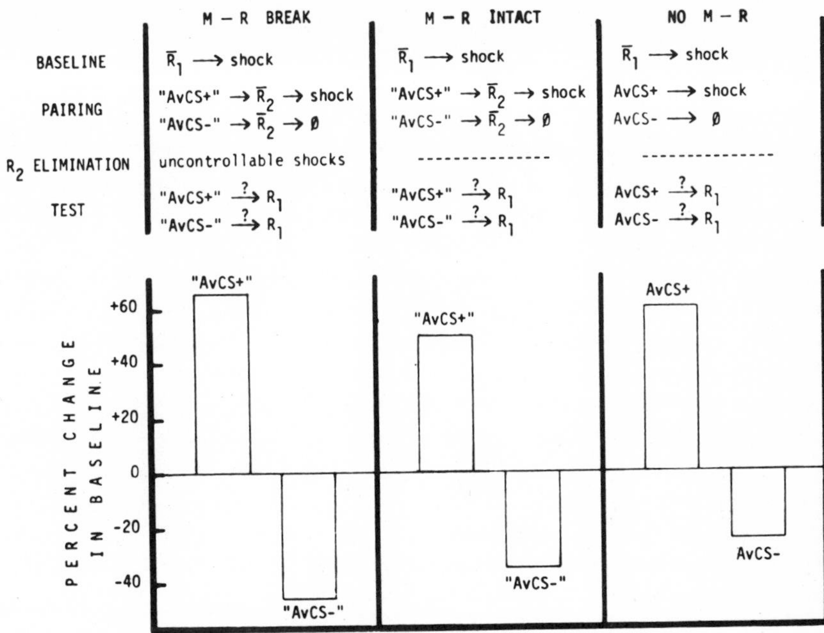

Fig. 3. Effects of various histories of instrumental response control (established but broken, established and continuing, and Pavlovian conditioning only) upon the extent to which an aversive stimulus controls a separately trained free operant avoidance response. The "Av CS+" was the S^D for R_2 while "AvCS−" was the S^{Δ}.

present data also can bear on the question of parallel versus sequential process. Because phase 4 indicated that the S–M link was intact, yet phase 3 which operated only on the M–R_2 link revealed through the test probes that S^D could not evoke R_2, it follows that there is not a direct S–R_2 link paralleling the S–M–R_2 pathway. If there were, then, despite our manipulation of the M–R_2 link, the S^D which activates the still strong S–M link should have also evoked the trained panel-press avoidance response since both a stimulus–response and a stimulus–mediator link would have been available. This did not happen, however, indicating that there was no S–R_2 link for the elicited mediator to modulate in phase 3.

Another of our experiments nicely complements this result in that whereas Overmier and Brackbill have focused upon manipulating the M–R link, Overmier and Bull have focused upon the S–M link. They set themselves the task of showing that it is possible to break the S–M link while leaving the M–R link intact. In their experiment (Overmier & Bull, 1969), dogs were first trained in a discrete-trial instrumental avoidance training in a shuttlebox until they were reliably avoiding in the presence of the S^D, a visual cue. In the second phase, the subjects were confined in a small chamber preventing exercise of the avoidance response and given a series of Pavlovian conditioning trials designed to manipulate the S–M link and a new CS–M link. During the Pavlovian conditioning phase, the S^D was presented repeatedly but never followed by shocks (Pavlovian extinction); additionally, a new tone (CS+) was presented always followed by shocks, while a second tone (CS−) was presented never followed by shocks. Finally, the dogs were replaced in the shuttlebox situation and transfer-of-control test trials with all three stimuli were given. During these tests, neither the S^D nor the CS− evoked the avoidance response previously trained to the S^D. The CS+, however, immediately and reliably evoked the avoidance response with latencies equivalent to those of original learning. These results are shown in Fig. 4. It is clear that transfer to a Pavlovian CS+ of control of an avoidance response is not dependent upon the continued control of that avoidance response by the original training stimulus. In terms of the two-process model, the Pavlovian processes eliminated the S^D–M link and established a new CS–M link, which later in testing allowed the CS+ to evoke the avoidance response by virtue of the CS–M–R mediated pathway. That the CS+ evoked the avoidance response at full strength

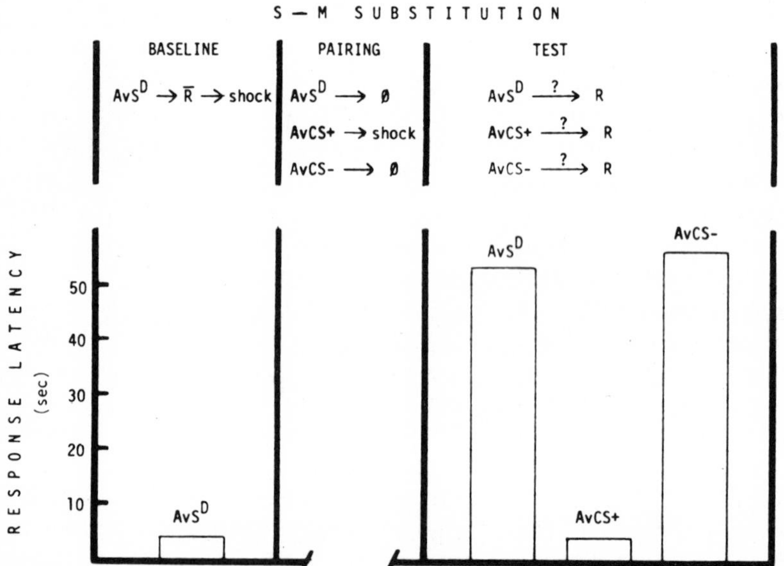

Fig. 4. The degree to which an avoidance response can be evoked by an aversive Pavlovian CS after the S^Ds power to evoke that response has been eliminated through Pavlovian extinction of the S^D.

while the S^D no longer did so at all indicates that the S–M and M–R links are separably manipulable and fully independent.

Taken together, the two experiments confirm the separability and independence of the S–M and M–R elements of an S–M–R pathway in the control of avoidance behavior. Furthermore, these studies indicate that not only is a direct S–R pathway unnecessary but, in fact, it may not exist. If it is the case that concatenations of S–M and M–R links are to fully account for behavior, then it appears to be necessary that the mediator have some stimulus properties to cue the requisite response. Otherwise only nonspecific energization (perhaps of only selected classes of behavior; however, see Bindra, 1974) should be seen in transfer tests. For example, in the Overmier and Bull (1969) experiment where the CS+ was shown to evoke the avoidance response no longer evoked by the S^D, we may ask how the particular response could be immediately "selected" since the CS+ had never been directly associated with this response. The Overmier and Brackbill (1977) experiment showed that the discrete-trial avoidance procedure did not yield direct S–R associative control, else the S^D probes in that experiment would have yielded the response. How is it that a simple schedule of unsignaled, inescapable shocks can lead to no further avoidance responses to an S^D in the absence of exercise of the response in the presence of the S^D, especially given that we know through later tests that the S^D does continue to evoke "fear"? The most parsimonious account is to assign not only response-energizing properties to the mediator but response-cueing properties as well. Indeed, it might even be argued that an associative cueing view of the mediator may be sufficient to account for the full range of transfer effects without referring to motivation at all (see Trapold & Overmier, 1972, for discussion). We must, then, seek (1) to assess the adequacy of motivational accounts of transfer of control, and (2) to provide evidence for stimulus properties of mediators.

Before we turn to these tasks, however, an aside on the implications of the present evidence for the two-process feature of two-process theories is called for. The demonstration of the separability and independence of the two links does not necessarily imply that the links depend upon two distinct learning processes. At best, all we can say is that there are two links or two "units" of learnings which are separate and can be manipulated independently of one another and that this is accomplished through different procedures. The independence of the units and differences in the procedures used to manipulate them may or may not reflect different processes. However, as we suggested earlier, whether they do or do not is quite inconsequential to the predictive power of the model and its usefulness in accounting for existing transfer data.

V. Properties and Functions of Mediators

Having supported a mediational model that hypothesizes control over behavior via two independent sequential links, we now must ask just how it is that the mediator exerts control. What are the properties of the mediator and how do these function? The properties commonly attributed to mediators have been "motivational." Actually, so far, we have eschewed the word "motivational" because of the wide variety of ways in which the word has been used and the variety of functions assigned to "motivators" (Bolles, 1967); for example, Spence (1956) assigned both energizing and stimulus properties to his construct "incentive motivation." In the present analysis, we wish to differentiate the several possible functions of mediators and therefore shall continue to avoid the word "motivational" as much as is practicable in our further discussions.

A. Hedonic Energizing

By far the most common notion has been that elicited affective/hedonic states serve to activate the organism and to energize responses. Substantial controversy, however, has surrounded the "breadth" of this activation and the rules of interaction during simulatenous elicitation of two (or more) such affective/hedonic mediators.

1. *Nonselective*

One common early hypothesis about the Pavlovian conditioned mediator was that it exerted its behavioral influence primarily by means of "motivational" mechanisms (N.E. Miller, 1948; Mowrer, 1939; Sheffield, 1954; Spence, 1956). While each of the several theories differed in their focus and in their details, in general they agreed that elicitation of the mediator (or mediational state) resulted primarily in simple, nonselective energization of the ongoing behavior. Brown (1961) has taken some care to unclutter the uses of "motivation" and has provided the most clear presentation of motivation as nonselective energization—or "big-D theory," as it is sometimes called. Tests of this hypothesis were promptly undertaken. A classic example of this line of research is the Brown, Kalish, and Farber (1951) superimposition of an aversive Pavlovian CS+ upon startle responding which yielded increased response magnitudes.

While much of the research generated was consistent with big-D concepts, all such tests were not uniformly supportive of the nonselective energization hypothesis. For example, Trapold (1962) superimposed an appetitive Pavlovian CS+ upon startle responding and did not observe increased magnitudes of response; in similar experiments, others (Armus & Sniadowski-Dolinsky, 1966) even observed decreases in response magnitudes, and, of course, the classic experiment by Estes and Skinner (1941) demonstrating that an aversive CS+ suppressed pressing of a lever for food is inconsistent with the nonselective energization hypothesis. In part, because of failures such as these to support the "big-D theory," we think it fair to suggest that other views of the hedonic energization process have recently gained considerable acceptance at the expense of the nonselective energization hypothesis.

2. *Selective Energization*

Konorski and Szwejkowska (1956) observed that prior aversive conditioning with a CS+; retarded subsequent transformation of that stimulus into an appetitive CS+; similarly, they reported that prior appetitive conditioning also retarded subsequent aversive conditioning with the same CS. These observations have been subsequently confirmed by others (e.g., Scavio, 1974; although there are exceptions, e.g., Dickenson, 1977). Based upon his experiments, Konorski (1964, 1967) argued persuasively that Pavlovian conditioned mediational states were of at least limited specificity rather than sources of generalized response energization. Furthermore, Konorski theorized that the mediational state conditioned with aversive outcome events is functionally different from the mediational state conditioned with appetitive events and that there is a reciprocal antagonism between these two mediational states. Such antagonistic interactions between appetitive and aversive mediational processes would account for the difficulties Konorski and Szwejkowska (1956) encountered in achieving heterogeneous transformations of CS+s.

Rescorla and Solomon (1967) were led to much the same conclusion based upon a thorough review of transfer-of-control experiments which we summarized earlier (see Section II,C). Importantly, they detected a systematic empirical pattern: facilitation when homogeneous reinforcers were used in the Pavlovian and the instrumental phases, and interference when heterogeneous reinforcers were used (refer back to Summary I). On the basis of this pattern, Rescorla and Solomon suggested that an inhibitory "reflex interrelation" exists between the appetitive and the aversive mediators and that this feature supplemented "motivational" principles, resulting in a viable motivational hypothesis about the *modus operandi* of conditioned mediational processes. According to this analysis, CS-elicited "fear" would combine synergystically with any "fear" already present to facilitate ongoing avoidance responding but would reflexly depress any appetitive "incentive motivation" to result in suppression of bar pressing for food, while an inhibitor of fear would have the opposite effects. Similarly, CS-elicited "hope" would combine synergystically with any incentive already present to facilitate appetitive responding but would reflexly depress fear to suppress avoidance responding, while an inhibitor of incentive would have the opposite effects of these two states. This view found support not only in the behavioral research literature but also in the physiological (Phillips & Olds, 1969; Stein, 1964) and the clinical (Wolpe, 1958) literatures as well.

Thus, several lines of evidence have led to a mediational model in which the central explanatory entities are two classes of reciprocally inhibitory conditioned affective states which modulate behavior through "motivational" mechanisms. Although what is meant by "motivational" has typically not been precisely explicated, the implicit assumption has been clear that the function of these affective mediational processes is one of response energization with additivity within hedonic classes and antagonism between them. The suggestion has further been that the functional strength of the affective processes is monotonic with UCS intensity, duration, number of pairings, and other such variables.

It might be interesting to speculate on whether the growth parameters of these monotonic functions are similar for appetitive and aversive mediators. Psychophysical scaling experiments may give one clue (Stevens, 1966, 1970). In general, perceptions of aversive stimuli are magnified so that perceived differences are greater than physical differences between stimuli, while the opposite seems to be true for appetitive stimuli. This, coupled with Wilder's law of initial value (Wilder, 1957) applied to instrumental responding, suggests that detecting the hypothesized additivity would often be difficult given injudicious parameter selection and even more so in the case of homogeneous appetitive interactions than in homogeneous aversive interactions. Furthermore, heterogeneous interactions ought to provide an especially good testing ground for such a theory.

3. *Empirical Problems*

Despite the broad base of empirical support for a hedonically specific (restricted) energization model and its power to correctly predict the outcomes of a heterogeneous interaction undetermined at the time (e.g., Bull, 1970; Grossen *et al.*, 1969), an increasing number of studies have been yielding results inconsistent with the model. For example, a careful review of the homogeneous appetitive transfer experiments reveals that suppression is reported more often than facilitation (e.g., Azrin & Hake, 1969; see Wielkiewicz & Lawry, 1979, for review). Moreover, within the homogeneous aversive domain, reports of AvCS+s paired with very intense UCSs having suppressive effects upon avoidance are appearing (e.g., Bryant, 1972, Scobie, 1972, 1973). Indeed, in the homogeneous aversive case, Brackbill and Overmier (1979) have been able to systematically obtain either facilitation or suppression of the avoidance baseline by simply carrying out the Pavlovian pairings off baseline or on baseline, respectively, with the magnitudes of these effects increasing linearly with UCS intensity.

Outcomes inconsistent with prediction have also been obtained with heterogeneous interactions as well. In some cases, an AvCS+ has not been successful in supressing instrumental appetitive responding (e.g., Blackman, 1968a, 1968b), and Fowler *et al.* (1973) have shown that such a Pavlovian stimulus may facilitate the acquisition of appetitively reinforced choice behavior when presented contingent upon correct choices. Also inconsistent with predictions from the model is the observation that an ApCS+ is facilitated in becoming an AvS^D (Bacon & Bindra, 1967; Braud, 1971; Overmier & Payne, 1971).

It is hardly surprising that an occasional transfer-of-control study would fail to support the model. However, a set of failures forming a consistent pattern is a clear sign that the model has failed to incorporate some important feature(s) of the mediational process. Whether it be some general attentional property (Fowler *et al.;* 1973; Overmier & Bull, 1970) or stimulus properties with associative functions (Hull, 1931; Logan & Warner, 1965; McHose & Moore, 1976; Staats & Warren, 1974) is to be determined. Our view is that the potential stimulus properties have until recently received inadequate empirical testing, especially in the aversive case.

B. Associative Model of Response Mediation

In view of the limitations on a motivationally based mediator, the potential stimulus properties and response-cueing function of Pavlovian conditioned mediators will now be considered. We argued that the demonstrations of the separability and independence of the sequential S–M and M–R links in avoidance conditioning (Bull & Overmier, 1969; Overmier & Brackbill, 1977) implied a response-cueing function of the mediator. That is, the central mediational state was said necessarily to possess distinct stimulus attributes which became associated with responses. This view is hardly a new one. Indeed, this idea was at the core of Hull's (1930, 1931) postulation of the "r_g–s_g" mechanism. As Hull described it, the function of the fractional goal response was to produce a "critically useful stimulus" as part of the total stimulus complex available to the subject during training which served to evoke the appropriate locomotor responses leading to the goal.

In his analysis of this mechanism, Hull (1952) eventually came to compare it with Tolman's concept of expectation. Tolman (1932) had defined expectation as "an immanent cognitive determinant aroused by actually presented stimuli." Based upon this definition, Hull suggested that an s_g might be a "concrete case" of a covert expectation. Following this line of reasoning, an "expectation" or "expectancy" is to be viewed as an internal state of affairs in anticipation of a highly probable event (e.g., a UCS). Defined in this way, an "expectancy" is no more than another word for what has so far been referred to as a mediator. Indeed, Rozeboom (1958) has argued that mediation theory is formally identical to expectancy theory. Expectancy does not, however, imply a cognitive awareness of this state. The core feature of expectancy theory in operational terms is that the probability of a response in the presence of an S^D ought to be manipulable by operations that do not involve running off the S–R sequence (Meehl & MacCorquodale, 1951). It is exactly this feature that is exploited by the transfer-of-control paradigm.

The concept of certain internal states providing potentially useful stimuli which would come to control responding was further elaborated upon by Logan and Wagner (1965) in their analysis of incentive learning. This notion has also played a key role in those theories which have viewed frustration as a mediational state with unique stimulus properties, such frustration arising from interference with an ongoing behavioral sequence (Brown & Farber, 1951) as well as conditions of nonreinforcement in a previously reinforced situation (Amsel, 1958; Amsel & Ward, 1954, 1965). Ross (1964) and Galbraith (1973) have, in fact, provided evidence consistent with the hypothesis that "frustration" has stimulus properties.

Demonstration of Stimulus Properties

Our search for evidence for stimulus properties of mediators which can function as cues for response selection has relied upon a discriminative choice paradigm. The special feature of this paradigm is that the *outcomes* of the discriminated correct choices can be manipulated so as to produce mediators which are differentially associated with the correct responses. This differential consistent outcome condition is then compared to one in which the outcomes for both responses either are always the same (nondifferential consistent) or are randomly mixed (mixed outcome). Figure 5 illustrates one instantiation of the paradigm. Of interest is the relative accuracy of choice under these conditions.

If mediational stimuli are a function of the features (qualitative, quantitative, or both) of the outcome events, then in the differential consistent outcome case the mediators elicited by the choice stimuli, S_1 and S_2, would have unique stimulus characteristics that could cue the individual correct responses. The availability of such supplementary cues would enhance accuracy of choice. In contrast, the mediators elicited by S_1 and S_2 in the control conditions would be identical and their stimulus properties equally associated with both responses. The presence of these mediational stimuli then would be a source of interfering cues and should impair accuracy of choice. Thus, in experiments of this kind, faster learning and superior performance by the differential consistent outcome group than by control groups is taken as evidence both for distinctive stimulus properties of mediators and for associative response-cueing function of these stimulus properties.

Trapold (1970) pioneered the use of this discriminative choice paradigm with rats, using food pellets and sucrose solution as the outcome events. This experiment demonstrated the functional importance of qualitatively different outcomes for the two responses. He observed that the differential consistent outcome group acquired the discrimination faster and to a higher asymptotic level of performance than did nondifferential outcome control groups. This result was confirmed and extended in the appetitive domain by others (Brodigan & Peterson, 1976; Carlson, 1974; Carlson & Wielkiewicz, 1972).

Overmier, Bull, and Trapold (1971b) also promptly applied the paradigm to avoidance learning. Their goal was to demonstrate that the qualitative features of the shock US in an avoidance task result in an S^D-elicited mediator with unique stimulus properties which can associatively influence avoidance responding. They trained dogs in a conditional choice avoidance task in which the two alternative response panels were located on either side of the dog's head. In the presence of S_1, only a response on the right panel (R_1) would avoid or terminate shock, while in the presence of S_2, only a response on the left panel (R_2) would avoid or terminate shock. For one differential consistent group, failure to avoid in the presence of each stimulus, S_1 and S_2, led to a qualitatively unique shock stimulus, a steady shock to the left rear foot (O_1) or a pulsed shock to the right foot (O_2), respectively. A second differential consistent group (crossed) simply had the specification of O_1 and O_2 reversed. Both of these groups learned this conditional choice avoidance task faster than did a control group (mixed), which experienced mixed outcome events wherein failures to avoid in S_1 and S_2 were each followed by steady left foot shocks on half the trials and by pulsed right foot shocks and the other half. These data are shown in Fig. 5.

It now seems clear that there is substantial evidence from both the appetitive and the aversive domains that mediators do have stimulus properties and that these can function to cue response selection. It is

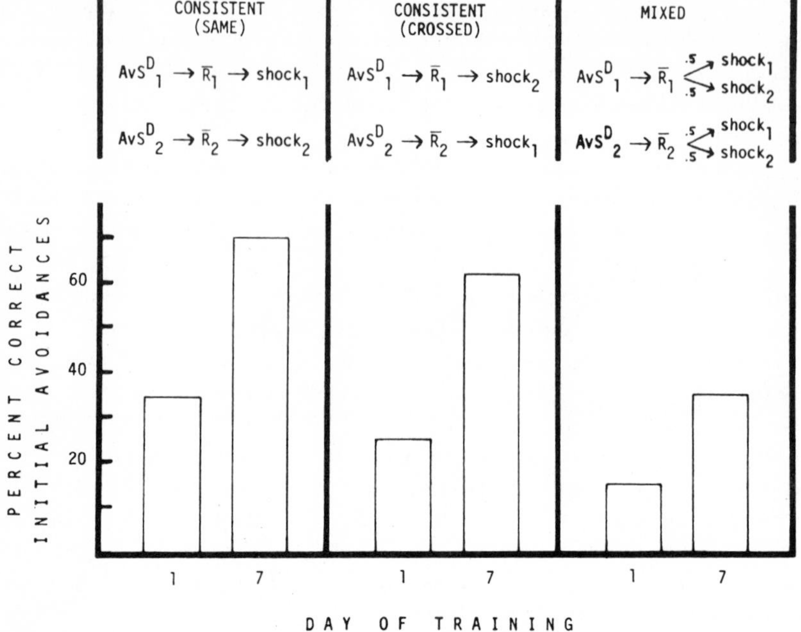

Fig. 5. Percentages of initial correct avoidance responses in a discriminative choice avoidance task. The groups differ with respect to the reinforcers associated with the two choices: For two groups (left and center panels) the two choices were consistently followed by different reinforcers, while in the control group (right panel), the two choices were both followed by both reinforcers in a mixed order. Shown are performances on training days 1 and 7.

possible, however, even likely, that the relative functional strength of the stimulus properties of the conditioned mediators may differ somewhat between the appetitive and aversive paradigms.

Having accepted the evidence for stimulus properties and their potential for response cueing, we need note that such a cueing function is only established when instrumental responses occur (and are reinforced) in the presence of these or similar mediational stimuli. This "caveat" is important because in many transsituational transfer-of-control experiments based upon hedonically heterogeneous reinforcers (e.g., Anderson, O'Farrell, Formica, & Caponigri, 1969; Bull, 1970), one mediator is established through response-independent Pavlovian conditioning procedures. Thus, when such Pavlovian CS+s are subsequently tested and observed to modulate the instrumental performance, the effect is not to be accounted for in terms of mediator-based stimuli associatively evoking (i.e., cueing) some instrumental response that mechanically interacts with the target instrumental response. (And earlier we dismissed direct operant interaction, too.) How then can one account for pure Pavlovian-to-instrumental interaction effects based upon the stimulus properties to the mediators in such cases? The question is whether such stimulus properties by themselves are sufficient to explain known mediational effects.

Trapold and Overmier (1972) have suggested that mediational stimulus properties could provide a viable alternative to a "motivational" account of transfer-of-control phenomena. They argued that any external stimuli which elicit mediational states with the same stimulus properties by virtue of having been paired directly (i.e., Pavlovianly) or indirectly (i.e., in instrumental training) with the same reinforcer should tend to evoke the same instrumental responses. Thus, in a transfer-of-control study, a CS+ for shock comes to evoke an instrumental avoidance response because of the shared stimulus properties of its elicited mediator with those elicited by the S^D for avoidance. Similarly, a CS+ for food is expected to suppress avoidance responding because it elicits a mediator with stimulus properties discriminatively different from those controlling the avoidance response. The facilitation is seen as an instance of stimulus additivity (Weiss, 1972); the impairment is seen as an instance of stimulus generalization decrement.

Clearly, this analysis can be readily applied to the full range of transfer-of-control data only if we can identify what features of reinforcers (or other outcome events) result in discriminably different mediational stimulus attributes. Trapold and Overmier (1972) suggested, for a beginning, we might hypothesize that every variation in a UCS (quantitative as well as qualitative) resulted in the conditioning of different mediational stimuli. It follows that those mediational stimuli derived from UCSs more similar to one another would, of course, be closer to one another along some stimulus dimension, with degree of generalization being inversely proportional to the dimensional distance between. The analysis here is closely patterned after E. J. Capaldi (1967).

This associative mediational stimulus account anticipated (correctly, as it has turned out) that in homogeneous interactions the CS+ will typically yield facilitation of the baseline behavior except when the magnitude of the UCS is "markedly" different from that maintaining the baseline. This is just the result Scobie (1972) obtained in the aversive case, and E. D. Capaldi, Hovancik, and Friedman (1976) obtained the parallel result in the appetitive case: When the CS was paired with a UCS the magnitude of which was similar to that maintaining the baseline behavior, responding was enhanced by the CS+, but when the magnitudes were substantially different, responding was depressed by the CS+.

Interestingly, the magnitude difference required to yield depression seems somewhat smaller in the appetitive domain than in the aversive. The implications of this are not fully clear, but it may imply a difference in the relative steepness of the generalization gradients, these being less steep in the aversive case. Alternatively, there may be a fundamental difference between the sensitivities of appetitive and aversive responding to mediational stimulus control. One could also note that this depression effect when the CS+ is paired with a quantitatively deviant reinforcer is, apparently, asymmetrical in the aversive case. That is, while AvCS+s paired with more intense shocks can depress baseline responding, pairings with weaker shocks do not have such an effect. This asymmetry is not consistent with predictions of the associative model and suggests that we cannot explain all the transfer data without some recourse to energization concepts. Perhaps under some aversive conditions affective energizing properties are prepotent over stimulus properties of mediators.

It seems clear that neither the energizing function nor the response-cueing function of mediators can independently account for the full range of existing data. Indeed, the discrepancies between the appetitive and aversive studies have led us to consider that mediational states may serve both functions, creating the potential for a dual source of influence on the final behavior output.

It should be emphasized that the inclusion of stimulus properties of the mediational state in no way precludes the possibility of concurrent affective energizing properties, and vice versa. Both may coexist and simultaneously interact to influence the final behavioral outcome. That mediational states can and do possess both kinds of properties in an assumption central to theories of frustration (Amsel, 1958, 1967; Brown & Farber, 1951) and incentive (Spence, 1956). Assuming this possibility of dual sources of influence, the task then becomes one of trying to evaluate the relative importance of the different mediational functions in controlling behavior under various conditions.

VI. Interaction of Affective and Stimulus Properties

In the previous discussion of energizing and stimulus accounts of mediational function, it was made clear that neither model can successfully handle all the relevant data. However, given the strong evidence uniquely supporting each view, it was assumed that mediators serve both affective-energization and response-cueing functions with respect to instrumental behaviors. Thus, a single elicited mediator would have at least two distinct properties, affective and stimulus, which then separately function to energize and cue, respectively.

There are not many experiments which clearly indicate the simultaneous influence of both properties. One reason for this is that, in many experiments, both would be expected to have similar effects on the response indices measured. Consider the case where a CS+ for shock is superimposed on a Sidman avoidance response. Typically, this produces response facilitation measured either as an increase rate relative to the average rate just prior to the CS+ presentation or as a decreased latency to jump in the presence of the CS+ relative to that measured during a CS− or some control stimulus. Such facilitation can be consistent with both the affective and associative views, but for different reasons. In the first case, a CS+-elicited mediational state is thought to further energize the S–R association controlling the response. In the second case, the mediational state is thought to contribute to the stimulus complex which evokes the response. This is because of the mediational stimuli's hypothesized similarity with those stimuli already associated with responding via the instrumental contingencies. Either one of the mediational functions, or both, may be operating to produce the facilitation evaluated with rate or latency measures. Hence, many of the early transfer-of-control studies have used procedures which do not discriminate between different mediational influences.

The evidence discussed so far that supports the inference of stimulus properties of mediators has come from the discriminative choice paradigm. Indeed, this paradigm was chosen because it should be particularly sensitive to response-cueing functions and generally insensitive to "motivational" influences of mediators (Reynolds, 1949). What seems needed is a demonstration experiment that provides additional support for response-cueing functions but does so *(a)* using methodology commonly used to test the reflex interrelation energizing model, and *(b)* in the face of opposite predictions from that model.

This line of argument led us to design an experiment in which we pitted the reflex antagonism of the affective energizing function of conditioned mediators against their possible cue function. In this experiment, we again relied upon the Pavlovian contingency embedded within discrete-trial instrumental training to condition a mediator elicitable by a stimulus under our control; this technique had previously been successfully used in our laboratory (Overmier *et al.*, 1971a) to obtain evidence for the reflex interrelation energization model and against simple operant interaction as explaining transfer-of-control effects. The advantage of this technique in the present case is that if conditioned mediators do have stimulus properties and these stimulus properties can get "hooked up" to responses reinforced in the presence of these mediational stimuli, then reliance upon the embedded contingencies should establish the mediational stimuli as cues for the response.

We reasoned that if an instrumental response were first established to a specific stimulus (S_1) using an aversive reinforcer, and then the topographically identical response was established under a second set of stimulus conditions (S_2) using now an appetitive reinforcer, test presentations of the S_1 superimposed upon S_2 (in essence compounding S_1 and S_2) would achieve an assessment of the relative contributions of the affective-reflex–interrelational and response-cueing mechanisms of the mediators elicited by the two stimuli. The hypothesis of reciprocal antagonisms between conditioned energizing properties of mediators based upon antipodean reinforcers leads one to expect the rate of responding to be less during the compound than during either of the individual stimulus conditions. According to the associative model, however, the two distinctively different mediators would both cue the same response; thus, with concurrent elicitation of both mediators one might expect the rate of responding to be greater during the compound than during either of the individual stimulus conditions.

Overmier and Schwarzkopf (1974), using hurdle jumping in the shuttlebox, tested these conflicting expectations. A group of dogs (AvS^D on Ap-baseline) initially was trained to discriminatively jump a hurdle on an operant schedule in which a variable number of responses (mean = 3) were required (VR-3) during a tone S^D to avoid shocks. A contrasting S^Δ tone was never followed by shocks, nor were any ever administered during the intertrial interval conditions. After the avoidance discrimination was well established, the dogs were shifted to appetitive training; jumping the hurdle was reinforced with food on a variable-interval (VI) 15-sec schedule in the presence of only the houselight. Finally, in test trials, the avoidance S^D was superimposed upon the ongoing appetitive baseline behavior. The result was that rate of jumping increased dramatically during the AvS^D presentations—a result more consistent with the predictions of the associative model.

Further confirmation of this pattern was found in a second group which was treated similarly except the roles of the reinforcers were switched. This group (ApS^D on Av baseline) initially was trained to jump the hurdle discriminatively on a VR-3 to obtain food. Only jumps in the presence of the tone S^D were reinforced, while jumps in the presence of the S^Δ tone and the intertrial interval were never reinforced. After mastery, the dogs were shifted to training on a temporal avoidance schedule (R–S = 30 sec) under the control of the houselight. Finally during test trials the appetitive S^D was superimposed upon the avoidance baseline behavior. Again, the result was that rate of jumping increased during the ApS^D presentations as predicted by an associative model. The results from both of these groups are shown in Fig. 6.

What makes the results of this experiment more interesting is the observation that the present experiment has many features in common

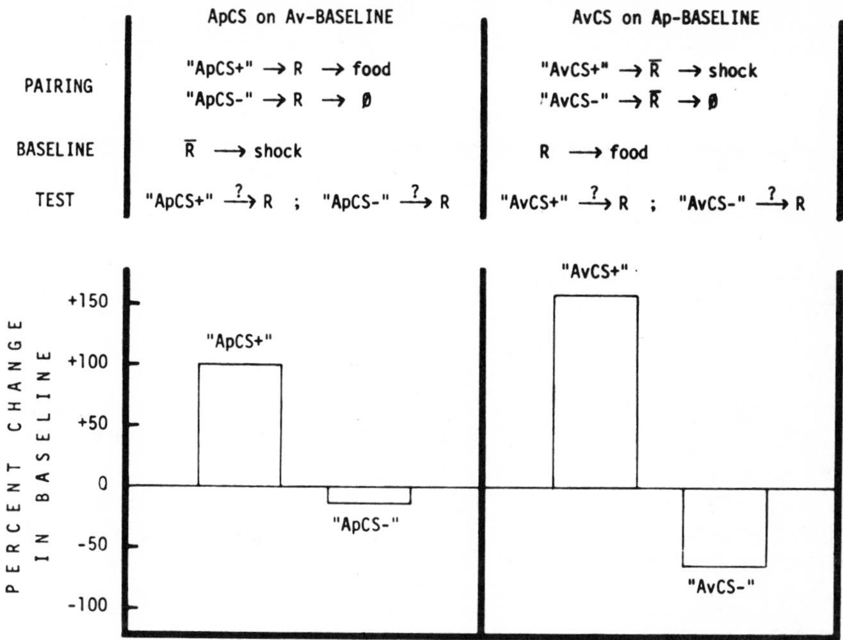

Fig. 6. Effects of superimposing a stimulus upon a given baseline of responding (summation test) when the stimulus was established as a discriminative cue for a response topographically identical to the baseline response but using a reinforcer hedonically opposite that of the baseline reinforcer.

with the conditioned suppression experiments. In the latter, when a stimulus which has previously signaled shock is superimposed upon positively reinforced operant behavior, responding is suppressed (Estes & Skinner, 1941); similarly, when a stimulus which has previously signaled food is superimposed upon free-operant avoidance responding, responding is also suppressed (Bull, 1970). Furthermore, such suppression is also observed when an S^D for shuttlebox avoidance is superimposed upon free-operant bar pressing for food (Kamin, Brimer, & Black, 1963) and when an S^D for pedal pressing for food reinforcement is superimposed upon shuttlebox barrier-jumping avoidance (Overmier *et al.*, 1971a). The results of these conditioned suppression experiments, where the superimposed stimulus is a CS+ or is an S^D for behavior topographically orthogonal to the baseline behavior, are opposite to the results of Overmier and Schwarzkopf (1974) experiment, where the superimposed stimulus is an S^D for behavior topographically similar to the baseline behavior. This is despite the great communality of operations and of the stimulus–reinforcer relationships in the two experiments. This implies that explanations of conditioned suppression which invoke subtractive interactions of reflexly interrelated motivational states (Dickenson & Pearce, 1977; Millenson & deVilliers, 1972; Rescorla & Solomon, 1967) are not entirely satisfactory. At the very least, such views must recognize that the discriminative functions of the S^Ds with respect to responses can overwhelm the effects of the motivational interactions, if any.

The findings of Overmier and Schwarzkopf (1974) directly contradict the motivational theory's prediction that a stimulus eliciting an affective mediational property which is antagonistic to the affective property supporting the target response should impair performance.[5] However, consistent with an associative viewpoint, adding stimuli that cued the target response enhanced performance. Similar "response summation" effects have been reported when two S^Ds for the same appetitive instrumental response are compounded (Weiss, 1964; Wolf, 1963) as well as when two S^Ds for the same avoidance response are compounded (Emurian & Weiss, 1972; L. Miller, 1969). Cross-motivationally, O'Neill and Biederman (1974) found that an ApS^D facilitated the acquisition of an avoidance response when used as an AvS^D only if the appetitive and avoidance tasks were topographically similar. The pattern leads us to yet another revision of Summaries I and II, as can be seen in Summary III.

A. New Experiments

A careful analysis of the heterogeneous additive summation experiment of Overmier and Schwarzkopf (as well as those showing homogeneous summation) reveals that, while inveighing against a simple affective reflex interaction model, they do not provide as strong support for the cue-function analysis of mediators as one may like. This is because the hypothesized mediator was being elicited by the S^Ds and, therefore, the exteroceptive S^D function was perfectly confounded with mediational cue function. To demonstrate more satisfactorily that such response enhancement can result from mediational effects, it is necessary to test with Pavlovian stimuli that have not been directly associated with the target response. However, if these CSs elicit mediational stimuli that have been associated with the target response via separate relevant instrumental training, then the CSs too should facilitate performance of the target response. Thus, the necessary strong tests for mediational stimulus-cueing functions and assessment of their relative strength in

[5]It is also possible that one might use the Overmier and Schwarzkopf data to argue for summation of motivations across hedonic states. However, our experiments that follow rule out this possibility.

SUMMARY III

TRANSFER-OF-CONTROL INTERACTIONS

	Baseline		Baseline		
	R_{Av}	R_{Ap}	R_{Av}	R_{Ap}	
Av CS+	↑	↓	↓	↑	Ap CS+
AvS^D (orthogonal R)	↑	↓	↓	↑	ApS^D (orthogonal R)
AvS^D (same R)	↑	↑	↑	↑	ApS^D (same R)

behavior control can be achieved by "simply" adding a pure Pavlovian conditioning stage to the designs of Overmier and Schwarzkopf and then, in the final stage, testing the direction and degree of transfer of control exercised by these CSs, both absolutely and relative to the S^D which has been associated with the same reinforcer.

Let us present a theoretical analysis of this new class of experiment. Both avoidance and appetitive instrumental training are conducted using the topographically identical responses. During the appetitive instrumental training, S_1 comes to elicit a particular mediational state (M_{Ap}) as a result of its temporal pairings with food reinforcement. M_{Ap} has specific affective and stimulus attributes, the latter of which are associated with the response and hence are part of the stimulus complex which controls the response. During avoidance training, S_2 comes to elicit M_{Av} due to the S_2–shock pairings. The mediational state, M_{Av}, differs from M_{Ap} with respect to both its affective and its stimulus properties, although the stimulus attributes of M_{Av} are also associated with and control the topographically identical response. In the Pavlovian conditioning phase, a new stimulus (S_3) is established as a CS+ by pairing it with one of the reinforcers, therefore giving rise to either the M_{Ap} or the M_{Av} state. Thus S_3 elicits a mediator the stimulus attributes of which are associated with the instrumental response, even though S_3 itself has never directly been associated with the response. In the test phase, the effect of S_3 on performance is evaluated by presenting it on the instrumental baseline whose reinforcer is affectively opposite to the reinforcer used in the Pavlovian condition. Thus, the mediator elicited by S_3 has affective properties which should depress (deenergize?) responding and stimulus properties which should cue and facilitate responding.

Three such experiments were conducted in our laboratory. Each involved two distinct instrumental-training phases, a separate Pavlovian conditioning phase, and then an appropriate series of tests. Linder explored the effects of AvCSs upon appetitive responding and Ehrman explored the effects of ApCSs upon aversive responding. We shall consider each experiment in turn.

The first experiment used a within-subjects design. Dogs were first given discrete-trial hurdle-jumping, appetitive discrimination training in a dimly illuminated two-way shuttlebox. Food was available during a clicker (ApS^D) but not during its absence (ApS^{Δ}) or during the intertrial interval. Upon achieving stable performance on this task, subjects were then given free-operant avoidance training in the same apparatus, but now in the presence of bright lights (AvS). Each hurdle-jump response postponed shock for a period of 30 sec. In the third phase, discriminative, appetitive Pavlovian conditioning was conducted while each subject was restrained on an elevated platform in a separate, distinctive sound-attenuating cubicle. Here, two tones of different frequency were presented such that one tone (ApCS+) was always followed by the delivery of a dry food pellet (like that used to reinforce responding during the instrumental appetitive training) and the second tone was never followed by food (ApCS−).

After stable instrumental performance was reestablished on the original instrumental tasks, testing began. Presentations of the ApCS+, ApCS−, and ApS^D were each superimposed on the avoidance baseline. As illustrated in Fig. 7, the ApS^D produced a marked increase in the

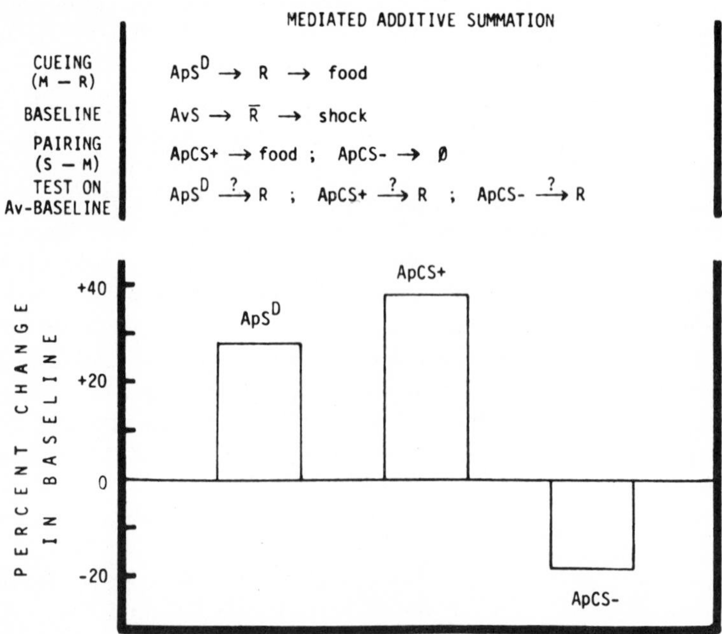

Fig. 7. Effects of appetitive stimuli of different histories (i.e., as S^D, CS+, CS−) upon the performance of ongoing avoidance responding. Each dog experienced all three stimuli.

rate of responding, thus replicating the earlier findings of Overmier and Schwarzkopf (1974). Most importantly, however, the ApCS+ also produced an increase in baseline rates, while the ApCS− tended to produce a decrease. As previously discussed, this facilitation during the ApCS+ cannot be attributed to direct stimulus control since this CS have never occurred in the presence of the response (or even the apparatus) prior to testing. Instead, the facilitation must reflect mediational effects, and ones which result from the common stimulus attributes of the mediational states elicited by the ApCS+ and ApS^D. During the appetitive instrumental training, these mediational stimuli became associated with the hurdle-jump response and hence "cue" this response whenever elicited—either by the ApS^D or by the ApCS+.

It is interesting to note that the degree of facilitation observed during the ApCS+ and ApS^D trials was approximately equal. This suggests that the direct ApS^D–R association, if any, plays a lesser role than the M_{Ap}–R association in controlling the response. (Based upon the earlier experiments of Overmier and Brackbill, 1977, we had previously called into question the existence of any direct S–R link. The present results are consistent with such rejection of an S–R link.) The observed effect of facilitation by ApCS+ (and not ApCS−) equivalent to that produced by ApS^D provides strong support for an associative stimulus-cueing relation between the mediator and the response.

A second experiment contrasted the ApCS+ facilitation of avoidance responding with two different control conditions using a between-subjects design. For one control group, the appetitive instrumental training phase was omitted so that the M_{Ap} could never become associated with the target response. As previously demonstrated by Bull (1970), the ApCS+ in this group is expected to suppress avoidance responding rather than facilitate it. The second control received instrumental training identical to that of the experimental group, but during Pavlovian conditioning food was delivered independently of CS presentations. This truly random control condition was included to evaluate nonassociative effects of the test CS on performance (Rescorla, 1967).

Using the same apparatus as before, the appetitive Pavlovian conditioning phase was conducted first. The experimental and the first control groups received a tone (ApCS+) followed by food, while the truly random control group received random presentations of the tone (CS^0) and food. Next, the experimental and truly random control subjects were given discriminated appetitive instrumental training in the shuttlebox. Hurdle jumping was reinforced on a VI 15-sec schedule in the presence of a clicker (ApS^D) and not in its absence (ApS^Δ). As previously noted, this phase was omitted for the second control group.

Subsequently, all groups were given free-operant avoidance training in the shuttlebox similar to that of the earlier experiment. Finally, the effects of the ApCS stimuli were measured over 2 days of testing by presenting them while the dogs were responding on the avoidance baseline.

The response to all test stimuli are illustrated in Fig. 8. Consistent with the previous study and the predictions for associative mediational effects, the ApCS+ produced a substantial increase in the response rate of the experimental group. In contrast, the control group that had no appetitive instrumental training showed a decrease in responding during the ApCS+, thus replicating the earlier findings of Bull (1970). The truly random control group also showed a tendency to increase responding during the CS⁰ presentations, although the magnitude of this effect was less than that shown by the experimental group to ApCS+. We might also note that in follow-up tests with the experimental subjects,

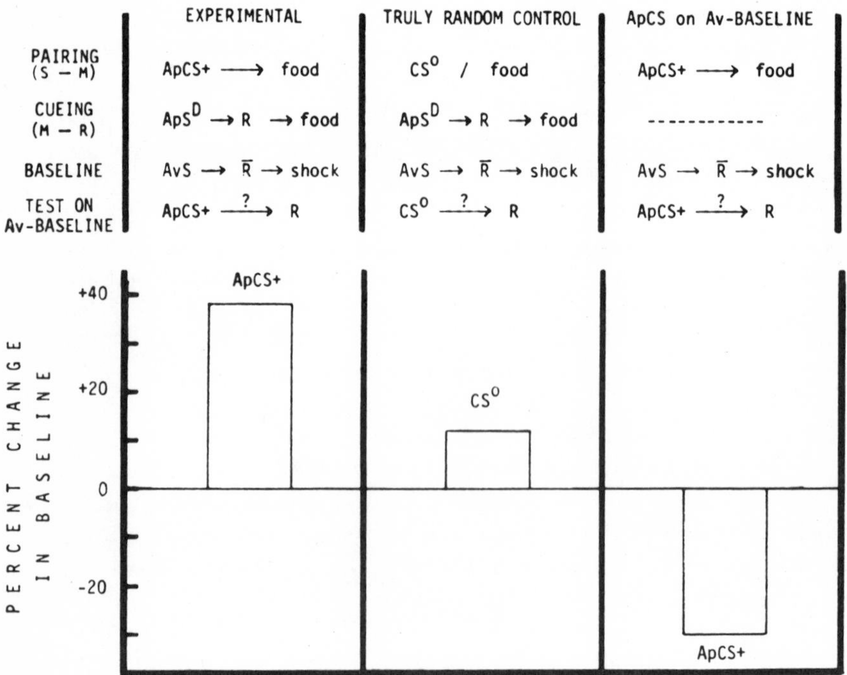

Fig. 8. Effects of appetitive CSs upon the performance of ongoing avoidance responding in groups of dogs with different histories. These differences were with respect to Pavlovian pairings with food (left and right panels) or not (center panel) and with respect to whether they had had instrumental appetitive training on the target response (left and center panels) or not (right panel).

the ApS^D produced pronounced increases in responding, once again replicating the original findings of Overmier and Schwarzkopf (1974).

An analysis of the relative amounts of facilitation produced by the ApCS+ and CS^O versus the ApS^D also reveals a difference between experimental and truly random control subjects. As in the previous study, comparable levels of facilitation were observed during ApCS+ and ApS^D presentations in experimental subjects (ApCS+/ApS^D > 80%). However, the CS^O in the truly random control subjects produced about 20% of the facilitation observed during the ApS^D. Therefore, the ApCS+ facilitation cannot be due to simple nonassociative effects. As before, these data suggest that ApCS+ facilitation is largely due to mediational stimulus control over responding exerted via an M_{Ap}–R association.

In summary, these two appetitive transfer studies (ApCS on Av baseline) strongly suggest that mediational stimuli, when given the opportunity to become associated with the target response, do so and may predominate over opposing motivational effects arising from the interaction of two antagonistic affective states.

Having provided both a within- as well as a between-subjects demonstration of ApCS+ facilitation of avoidance responding, we next sought to provide a parallel demonstration of AvCS+ facilitation of an appetitively reinforced response (AvCS on Ap-baseline). Slightly different procedures were used, however.

In this multiphase study, dogs were first given discriminated free-operant training. Hurdle jumping was reinforced with food during a light stimulus (ApS^D) but not during its absence (ApS$^\Delta$). After this discrimination was mastered, the experimental subjects received discrete-trial, discriminated-avoidance training in the shuttlebox. A white-noise stimulus (AvS^D) was used to signal trial onset. In the third phase, Pavlovian fear conditioning was conducted in our distinctive, sound-attenuating cubicle where dogs were secured in a rubber hammock suspended from a metal frame. Two tone frequencies were presented; one (AvCS+) was always followed by shock, and the other (AvCS−) was never followed by shock. Shock was delivered via stainless steel electrode plates attached to the subject's footpads.

The control group in this study received appetitive instrumental training and Pavlovian conditioning identical to that of the experimentals. In phase two, however, these subjects received escape training rather than avoidance training. For these subjects the white-noise (AvS^D ?) and shock onsets were simultaneous events. We have previously shown that an AvCS+ will not elicit the escape response under transfer-of-control conditions (Ehrman & Overmier, 1976). Since the AvCS+ gains no mediated control over instrumental escape responding, then in tests the

AvCS+ is not expected to facilitate the appetitive instrumental response even though the dogs have learned to hurdle the barrier under direct aversive control. Rather, the AvCS+ should lead to response suppression in this group; this is the familiar CER effect (Estes & Skinner, 1941).

Testing on the appetitive baseline involved a series of trials in which the ApS^D was presented alone or in combination with either the AvS^D, the AvCS+, or the AvCS−. The percentage change in response speed measured relative to the ApS^D is illustrated for each of the combined cue tests in Fig. 9. In the avoidance-trained subjects, the AvS^D and AvCS+ stimuli both resulted in a pronounced increase in response speeds relative to the ApS^D alone. The AvS^D facilitation observed here again replicates the findings of Overmier and Schwarzkopf (1974).

As in the appetitive transfer case, the AvCS+ is thought to have its

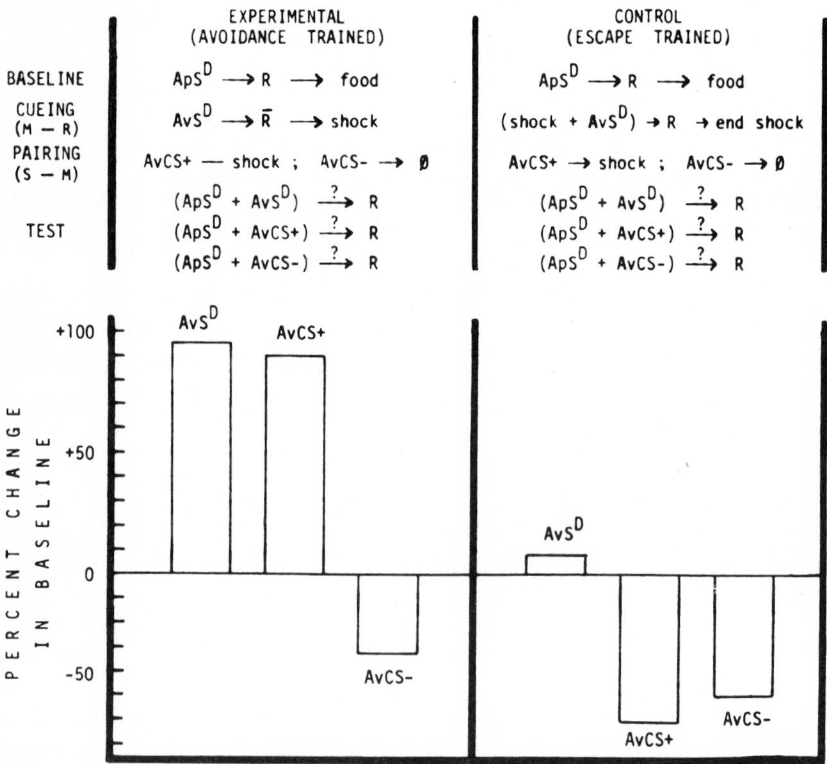

Fig. 9. Effects of aversive stimuli with varying histories (i.e., S^D, CS+, and CS−) in two groups upon the latency of discrete trial appetitive responding. The groups differ in whether the instrumental aversive training phase was under avoidance contingencies (thus establishing the response under mediated control) or under escape contingencies.

facilitative effect because of the similarity in the mediational state it elicits with that elicited by the AvS^D. In each case, stimulus–shock pairings gave rise to a mediational state (M_{Av}) which has particular stimulus properties as well as affective ones. These mediational stimulus attributes had the opportunity to become associated with the target response during the avoidance training. Hence, both the AvCS+ and AvS^D facilitate the hurdle-jump response during testing via this M_{Av}–R associative link, in spite of the affective properties of the M_{Av}, which are in opposition to those of the M_{Ap} being elicited by ApS^D.

In the escape-trained control subjects, a different pattern emerged. As expected, here the AvS^D had little effect on response performance, while the AvCS+ produced a substantial decrease in the speed of responding relative to the ApS^D alone. This suppressive effect of the AvCS+ we may attribute to the interaction of the affective properties of the M_{Av} and M_{Ap} states, which are here unconfounded by any countervailing effects of response cueing. However, as previously discussed, this invocation of a motivational interpretation could be superfluous. Relying only on associative processes, the M_{Av} could interfere with responding via a stimulus generalization decrement by adding stimuli dissimilar to those controlling the appetitive response. Which of these explanations best characterizes the data is considered in more detail later (p. 42–43).

These last three experiments lead to a final revision in our summary schedule of transfer-of-control interaction effects (Summary IV). Of special interest in this last revision is the contrast between the first and last lines of the schedule of interactions. This contrast is between stimuli of identical histories, yet their effects in heterogeneous interactions upon identical baselines are quite reversed. This reversal is a function of an additional, separate instrumental-training phase with an independent stimulus, which has in common with the Pavlovian CS only its response-contingent outcome event. This overall pattern fairly demands

SUMMARY IV

TRANSFER-OF-CONTROL INTERACTIONS

	Baseline		Baseline		
	R_{Av}	R_{Ap}	R_{Av}	R_{Ap}	
AvCS+	↑	↓	↓	↑	ApCS+
AvS^D (orthogonal R)	↑	↓	↓	↑	ApS^D (orthogonal R)
AvS^D (same R)	↑	↑	↑	↑	ApS^D (same R)
AvCS+ (given AvS^D → same R)	↑	↑	↑	↑	ApCS+ (given ApS^D → same R)

a mediational interpretation. Furthermore, it does not admit of explanation through reference to affective mediational properties—either simple additive energization (i.e., big D) or reflex antagonism between hedonically different energizers (i.e., algebraic summation). A mediational state with stimulus properties which can function to cue responses is minimally necessary. Whether a mediational model invoking only these stimulus properties is sufficient is as yet not fully determined.

In part, resolution of the "sufficiency question" will revolve about coming to understand the mediational properties of signals for the omission of events, that is, CS−s. If it proves to be the case that such stimuli do elicit mediational states which have distinctive stimulus properties similar in salience to those of CS+s, then affective mediational properties will be strongly implicated. This is because rarely in transfer-of-control experiments are the effects of Pavlovian CS−s even directionally similar to those of CS+s, much less quantitatively similar. Yet a mediational model relying solely upon stimulus properties would have to predict that in basic heterogeneous transfer-of-control experiments the CS+ and CS− stimuli would have to produce at least directionally similar effects. This has not been the usual pattern (Grossen *et al.*, 1969; Hammond, 1966; Overmier & Bull, 1970; Ray & Stein, 1959).

B. Summary of Studies Contrasting Affective and Stimulus Components

Our recent studies provide strong support for mediational stimulus properties; furthermore, when these stimulus properties are given the opportunity to serve a response-cueing function they may even override affective influences of the mediator. This is not, however, to claim that affective mediational properties did not influence subjects' behavior in some manner undetected in these experiments. In both sets of experiments, testing was conducted only on the baseline whose reinforcer was affectively opposite that used during Pavlovian conditioning. It would have been useful to also have presented transfer tests on the baseline whose reinforcer was affectively compatible with that used during Pavlovian conditioning. Perhaps the test CS+ stimuli would have produced an even greater facilitation under these conditions. If so, then motivational effects of the mediator could have been shown to be modulating the degree of facilitation observed across the two baseline conditions.

There is no question that a comparison of this sort would have been theoretically informative; yet practically it would have been quite difficult to obtain. At the very beginning of these studies, it became quite obvious that pitting the mediation functions against one another created a highly stressful situation for our subjects. This "stress" was most often revealed by the frequent and complete collapse of either or both the appetitive and the aversive instrumental baselines. In such cases, there was usually little or no recovery in spite of the prolonged shaping efforts of the experimenters. This problem was more than a little reminiscent of the often reported experimental neuroses seen under motivational conflict (Masserman, 1943; see Mineka & Kihlstrom, 1978, for review). Because of these problems, many of the subjects never reached the testing phase of these experiments. Such problems may indicate a more significant affective role than has been measured. However, it is important to point out that whatever impact affective influences may have had, there were no instances in Ehrman's and Linder's work reported here in which the CS+ produced response effects inconsistent with an associative model's predictions. The only instances of suppression observed were in those control groups where the stimulus attributes of the CS+-elicited mediational state had no prior opportunity to become associated with and cue the target response.

While these data argue for the prepotence of the response-cueing function of the mediator over a motivational function, it would be premature to conclude that this would always be the case. It seems especially risky to assume a particular mediational influence had no effect simply because it did not affect a particular response measure in the way it might have if it were the only influence operating. If we accept the existence of multiple mediational influences, then more sophisticated methods of measuring them may be required. This might call for multiple behavioral measures or for more complex comparisons, such as testing stimuli against various baseline conditions.

Other empirical evidence for dual mediational functions.

Fowler and his associates reported experiments using multiple behavioral measures which also seem to provide evidence for the simultaneous operation of both mediational functions. His procedure involves testing rats on a brightness discrimination task for food reinforcement in a T maze. The ease with which this discrimination is acquired can be influenced by presenting various stimulus events contingent on a correct choice. These stimuli have included shock (Fowler, 1971), a CS+ for shock (Fowler, Goodman, & Zanich, 1977), or a CS− for food (Zanich & Fowler, 1978). Without going into the details of these experiments, it can be argued that the addition of some salient affective stimulus, such as one of those mentioned, should lead to an expectancy with distinctive stimulus properties. These mediational stimulus properties would be in addition to those already supported by the food and no-food outcomes. The additional mediational stimuli should come to exert stimulus control over choice behavior in the T maze, thus facilitating discrimination performance much the way differential outcomes were thought to facilitate performance in the two-choice discrimination experiments.

What is particularly interesting about these experiments, however, is that the choice behavior and running speeds are not always correlated across groups. For example, a group which received an AvCS+ contingent on a correct response acquired the discrimination faster than a group which received an AvCS− or a CS^0 (Fowler *et al.*, 1977; Ghiselli & Fowler, 1976). If the UCS had been a relatively high shock intensity, then the AvCS− subjects ran faster than did AvCS+ subjects, even though the latter had a higher percentage correct responses. This depressed running in the group receiving a CS+ for a high-intensity shock suggests a motivational component at work. The AvCS+ should elicit an affective state which opposes that elicited by the expectancy of food reward, an interaction expected to decrease the amount of response energization, thus accounting for slower running speeds. However, a CS+ for a high-intensity shock is also likely to elicit more salient mediational stimulus properties, which may become associated with and exert increased control over the choice behavior, thus accounting for the superior discrimination performance. Together, the studies of Fowler and his associates demonstrate that both mediational functions considered here may play a role simultaneously, and, further, that these functions may be detected via different aspects of behavior.

VII. Conclusions and Commentary

A stimulus paired with a UCS is thought to give rise to some "mediational state" or "expectancy." The focus of our research has been on the various properties and functions of these mediators and the mechanism(s) through which they modulate instrumental behavior.

One series of our experiments used Pavlovian procedures to manipulate the hypothesized mediational links. These experiments led us to assert that there are S–M and M–R links in the regulation of behavior and that these are sequential and independent of one another. Furthermore, we were even led by our experiments to suggest that only these two links are involved and that invocation of a separate, parallel, direct S–R link was not only unnecessary but likely incorrect.

While we are satisfied with our conclusions as based upon our research, we wish to point out that there exist data which pose a serious challenge to any effort to reject a direct S–R link. These data come from discriminative choice experiments in which the reinforcer for both responses is the same (S_1–R_1–O_1; S_2–R_2–O_1). Learning of such differential correct responses to S_1 and S_2 cannot be accounted for by reference to S-elicited mediators alone, because these should be identical since both S_1 and S_2 signal the same reinforcer. Konorski (1964) early recognized this problem, and while often little or no evidence for mastery is obtained under such conditions (Lawicka, 1964; see the control group in Overmier *et al.*, 1971b; see also Fig. 5 in this paper), such problems can be learned (Friedman & Carlson, 1973; Peterson, Wheeler, & Armstrong, 1978; Trapold, 1970). That mastery can be achieved when the outcomes are the same implies than at S–R link must exist. However, the lack of reliable learning under these conditions implies that it must often be a weak contributor to response selection.

A second series of our experiments focused upon the properties of mediators and their functions. We first considered affective mediational properties and their response-energization function. Also, like earlier researchers, we were led to argue that if this were the only property of mediators, then mediational states arising from appetitive and aversive reinforcers must be said to be mutually inhibitory. Still, review of relevant experiments, including some of our own, revealed data inconsistent with such a model. This led to consideration of potential stimulus properties of mediators which could serve an associative response-cueing function. We adduced data which we believe compel the conclusion that different reinforcers produce mediators with different stimulus properties and that these stimulus attributes can function as discriminative cues for particular responses.

One might speculate that the salience of the stimulus properties of mediators is some positive function of the hedonic value of the reinforcers upon which they are based. This would imply that mediators based upon hedonic events would be superior in gaining control over response to those mediators based upon neutral events. However, in this regard, it is necessary to note that the omission of reinforcers is likely not a neutral event (even though no stimulus change occurs) but a hedonically significant event. Such considerations lead naturally to the as yet unexplored question of whether the stimulus properties of the mediators based upon the omission of differing reinforcers are themselves different.

Because neither the affective-energizing nor the stimulus-associative views of the mediational process could account for all of the data, one is led to argue that both functions operate concurrently, much as others have suggested. However, now we have more definitive data. Additionally, some of our experiments assessed the relative strength of these two functions. In our transfer-of-control experiments, when the motivational and associative influences were pitted one against the other, the associative mediational function appeared to exert greater control over responding.

Is there more to be researched? We have already suggested the possibility that these two mediational functions are weighted differently in appetitive and aversive tasks. In the aversive case, it is possible that the energization function overrides mediational stimulus influences except when those stimulus properties are very salient or cue a specific response. In the appetitive situation, by contrast, it may be that the stimulus properties, and any associations to them, are always more influential than the affective properties. This could account for some of the nonparallelisms between the two for some transfer effects (e.g., magnitude of UCS manipulations: Martin & Riess, 1969, versus Hyde *et al.*, 1968).

It is even possible that different mediational functions may exert differential degrees of influence as a function of training and/or conditioning. For example, in a study by Ghiselli and Fowler (1976), evidence for motivational effects occurred only on early trials; thereafter, stimulus-associative effects seemed to be more dominant. Moreover, Ost and Mellgren (1970) reported that the facility with which an ApCS+ gains control over appetitive discriminative performance is a U-shaped function of the number of CS–UCS pairings. Additionally, Soltysik, Konorski, Holownia, and Rentoul (1975) have proposed a model that suggests fluctuations in which mediational property will be prepotent within a single CS presentation as a function of time until the UCS.

Finally, while the thrust of this paper has been demonstration and analysis of the energizing and response-cueing mediational functions, this should not be taken to imply that these two items exhaust the list of functions. A recent potential addition has been a general "signaling" function (Overmier & Bull, 1970). Fowler and associates (e.g., Fowler *et al.*, 1973) invoked just this function to account for the enhanced T-maze acquisition for food when AvCS+ was contingent upon correct choices and when AvCS− was contingent upon incorrect choices. The nature of this signaling function was thought to depend upon the correlation that the CS previously had with some UCS—any UCS. Such a signaling function would be useful in understanding such findings as those wherein an ApCS+ is facilitated in becoming an AvS^D (Braud, 1971; Overmier & Payne, 1971).

The idea of multiple mediational functions may be gainfully related to differing classes of *information* useful in modulating an animal's learning and performance. For example, mediational signaling properties provide information on stimulus *validity,* which regulates attention. Mediational affective properties provide information on the *value* of the expected event, and this is realized as an energizing function. Mediational stimulus properties provide information *guiding* the organism in the selection of the requisite response. Access to these classes of information would enhance the adaptive flexibility of the organism seeking to cope with a fluctuating environment.

Clearly, much research on the established and potential mediational processes is yet required for full understanding. Our work and speculations represent one small positive step toward this goal.

References

Amsel, A. The role of frustrative non-reward in non-continuous reward situations. *Psychological Bulletin*, 1958, **55,** 102–119.

Amsel, A. Partial reinforcement effects on vigor and persistence: Advances in frustration theory derived from a number of within-subjects experiments. In K. W. Spence & J. A. Taylor (Eds.), *The psychology of learning and motivation: Advances in research and theory*. New York: Academic Press, 1967.

Amsel, A., & Ward, J. S. Motivational properties of frustration: II. Frustration drive stimulus and frustration reduction in selective learning. *Journal of Experimental Psychology*, 1954, **48,** 37–47.

Amsel, A., & Ward, J. S. Frustration and persistence: Resistance to discrimination following prior experience with discriminada. *Psychological Monographs*, 1965, **79,**(4, Whole No. 597).

Anderson, D. C., O'Farrell, T., Formica, R., & Caponigri, V. Preconditioning CS exposure: Variations in place of conditioning and presentations. *Psychonomic Science*, 1969, **15,** 54–55.

Armus, H. L., & Sniadowski-Dolinsky, D. Startle decrement and secondary reinforcement stimulation. *Psychonomic Science*, 1966, **4,** 175–176.

Azrin, N., & Hake, D. F. Positive conditioned suppression: Conditioned suppression using positive reinforcers as the unconditioned stimuli. *Journal of the Experimental Analysis of Behavior*, 1969, **12,** 167–173.

Bacon, W. E., & Bindra, D. The generality of the incentive-motivational effects of classically conditioned stimuli in instrumental learning. *Acta Biologiae Experimentalis*, 1967, **27,** 185–197.

Baum, M., & Gleitman, H. "Conditioned anticipation" with an extinction baseline: The need for a disinhibition control group. *Psychonomic Science*, 1967, **8,** 95–96.

Bindra, D. A motivational view of learning, performance, and behavior modification. *Psychological Review*, 1974, **81,** 199–213.

Black, A. H. Heart rate changes during avoidance learning in dogs. *Canadian Journal of Psychology*, 1959, **13,** 229–242.

Black, A. H. Autonomic aversive conditioning in infrahuman subjects. In F. R. Brush (Ed.), *Aversive conditioning and learning*. New York: Academic Press, 1971.

Blackman, D. E. Conditioned suppression or facilitation as a function of the behavioral baseline. *Journal of the Experimental Analysis of Behavior*, 1968(a), **11,** 53–61.

Blackman, D. E. Response rate, reinforcement frequency and conditioned suppression. *Journal of the Experimental Analysis of Behavior*, 1968, **11,** 503–516. (b)

Blackman, D. E. Conditioned suppression and the effects of classical conditioning on operant behavior. In W. K. Honig & J. E. R. Staddon (Eds.), *Handbook of operant behavior*. Englewood Cliffs, N.J.: Prentice-Hall, 1977.

Bolles, R. C. *Theory of motivation.* New York: Harper, 1967.

Bolles, R. C. Avoidance and escape learning: Simultaneous acquisition of different responses. *Journal of Comparative and Physiological Psychology*, 1969, **68,** 355–358.

Bolles, R. C. Species-specific defense reaction and avoidance learning. *Psychological Review,* 1970, **77,** 32–48.

Bower, G. H., and Grusec, T. Effect of prior Pavlovian discrimination training upon learning an operant discrimination. *Journal of the Experimental Analysis of Behavior,* 1964, **7,** 401–404.

Brackbill, R. M., & Overmier, J. B. Aversive control of instrumental avoidance as a function of selected parameters and kind of Pavlovian conditioning. Under review, 1979.

Brady, J. V., & Hunt, H. F. An experimental approach to the analysis of emotional behavior. *Journal of Psychology,* 1955, **40,** 313–324.

Braud, W. G. Effectiveness of "neutral," habituated, shock-related, and food-related stimuli as CSs for avoidance learning in goldfish. *Conditional Reflex,* 1971, **6,** 153–156.

Brodigan, D. L., & Peterson, G. B. Two-choice discrimination performance of pigeons as a function of reward expectancy, pre-choice delay, and domesticity. *Animal Learning and Behavior,* 1976, **2,** 121–124.

Brown, J. S. *The motivation of behavior.* New York: McGraw-Hill, 1961.

Brown, J. S., & Farber, I. E. Emotions conceptualized as intervening variables with suggestions toward a theory of frustration. *Psychological Bulletin,* 1951, **48,** 465–495.

Brown, J. S., Kalish, H. I., & Farber, I. E. Conditioned fear as revealed by magnitude of startle response to an auditory stimulus. *Journal of Experimental Psychology,* 1951, **41,** 317–328.

Bryant, R. C. Conditioned suppression of free-operant avoidance. *Journal of the Experimental Analysis of Behavior,* 1972, **17,** 257–260.

Bull, J. A. An interaction between appetitive Pavlovian CSs and instrumental avoidance responding. *Learning and Motivation,* 1970, **1,** 18–26.

Bull, J. A., & Overmier, J. B. The additive and subtractive properties of extinction of inhibition. *Journal of Comparative and Physiological Psychology,* 1968, **66,** 511–514.

Bull, J. A., & Overmier, J. B. The incompatibility of appetitive and aversive conditioned motivation. *Proceedings of the 77th Annual Convention of the American Psychological Association,* 1969, **4,** 97–98.

Capaldi, E. D., Hovancik, J. R., & Friedman, F. Effects of expectancies of different reward magnitudes in transfer from noncontingent pairings to instrumental performance. *Learning and Motivation,* 1976, **7,** 197–210.

Capaldi, E. J. A Sequential hypothesis of instrumental learning. In K. W. Spence & J. T. Spence (Eds.), *The psychology of learning and motivation* (Vol. 1). New York: Academic Press, 1967. Pp. 67–156.

Carlson, J. G. Preconditioning the effects of shock-correlated reinforcement. *Journal of Experimental Psychology,* 1974, **103,** 409–413.

Carlson, J. G., & Wielkiewicz, R. M. Delay of reinforcement in instrumental learning of rats. *Journal of Comparative and Physiological Psychology,* 1972, **81,** 365–370.

D'Amato, M. R., & Schiff, D. Long-term discriminated avoidance in the rat. *Journal of Comparative and Physiological Psychology,* 1964, **57,** 123–126.

Davenport, D. G., & Olson, R. D. A reinterpretation of extinction in discriminated avoidance. *Psychonomic Science,* 1968, **13,** 5–6.

Davenport, D., G., Spector, N. J., & Coger, R. W. The redefinition of extinction applied to Sidman free-operant responding. *Psychonomic Science,* 1970, **19,** 181–182.

Davis, H. Conditioned suppression: A survey of the literature. Psychonomic Monographs, Supplements, 1968, **2**(14, Whole No. 30), 283–291.

Davis, H., & Kreuter, C. Conditioned suppression of avoidance response by a stimulus paired with food. *Journal of the Experimental Analysis of Behavior,* 1972, **17,** 277–285.

DiCara, L. V., Braun, J. J., & Pappas, B. A. Classical conditioning and instrumental learning of cardiac and gastrointestinal responses following removal of neocortex in the rat. *Journal of Comparative and Physiological Psychology*, 1970, **73,** 208–216.

DiCara, L. V., & Miller, N. E. Changes in heart rate instrumentally learned by curarized rats as avoidance responses. *Journal of Comparative and Physiological Psychology*, 1968, **65,** 8–12.

Dickenson, A. Appetitive–aversive interactions: Facilitation of aversive conditioning by prior appetitive training in the rat. *Animal Learning and Behavior*, 1976, **4,** 416–420.

Dickenson, A. Appetitive–aversive interactions: Superconditioning of fear by an appetitive CS. *Quarterly Journal of Experimental Psychology*, 1977, **29,** 71–83.

Dickenson, A., & Pearce, J. M. Inhibitory interactions between appetitive and aversive stimuli. Psychological Bulletin, 1977, **84,** 690–711.

Ehrman, R. N., & Overmier, J. B. Dissimilarity of mechanisms for evocation of escape and avoidance responding in dogs. *Animal Learning and Behavior*, 1976, **4,** 347–351.

Ellison, G. D., & Konorski, J. Separation of the salivary and motor responses in instrumental conditioning. *Science*, 1964, **146,** 1071–1072.

Emurian, H. H., & Weiss, S. J. Compounding discriminative stimuli controlling free-operant responding. *Journal of the Experimental Analysis of Behavior*, 1972, **17,** 249–256.

Estes, W. K. Discriminative conditioning. I: A discriminative property of conditioned anticipation. *Journal of Experimental Psychology*, 1943, **32,** 150–155.

Estes, W. K. Discriminative conditioning. II: Effects of Pavlovian conditioned stimulus upon a subsequently established operant response. *Journal of Experimental Psychology*, 1948, **38,** 173–177.

Estes, W. K., & Skinner, B. F. Some quantitative properties of anxiety. *Journal of Experimental Psychology*, 1941, **29,** 390–400.

Flood, N. C., Overmier, J. B., & Savage, G. E. Teleost telencephalon and learning: An interpretive review of data and hypothesis. *Physiology and Behavior*, 1976, **16,** 783–798.

Fonberg, E. Transfer of the conditioned reaction to the unconditioned noxious stimuli. *Acta Biologiae Experimentalis*, 1962, **22,** 251–258.

Fowler, H. Suppression and facilitation by response contingent shock. In F. R. Brush (Ed.), *Aversive conditioning and learning*. New York: Academic Press, 1971.

Fowler, H., Fago, G. C., Domber, E. A., & Hochhauser, M. Signaling and affective functions in Pavlovian conditioning. *Animal Learning and Behavior*, 1973, **1,** 81–89.

Fowler, H., Goodman, J. H., & Zanich, M. L. Pavlovian aversive to instrumental appetitive transfer: Evidence for across-reinforcement blocking effects. *Animal Learning and Behavior*, 1977, **5,** 129–134.

Friedman, G. J., & Carlson, J. G. Effects of a stimulus correlated with positive reinforcement upon discrimination learning. *Journal of Experimental Psychology*, 1973, **97,** 281–286.

Galbraith, K. Fractional anticipatory goal responses as cues in discrimination learning. *Journal of Experimental Psychology*, 1973, **97,** 177–181.

Ghiselli, W. B., & Fowler, H. Signaling and affective functions of conditioned aversive stimuli in an appetitive choice discrimination: US intensity effects. *Learning and Motivation*, 1976, **7,** 1–16.

Goss, A. E. Early behaviorism and verbal mediating responses. *American Psychologist*, 1961, **16,** 285–298.

Gray, J. A. *Elements of a two-process theory of learning*. New York: Academic Press, 1975.

Grossen, N. E., & Bolles, R. C. Effects of a classical conditioned "fear signal" and "safety signal" on nondiscriminated avoidance behavior. *Psychonomic Science*, 1968, **11,** 321–322.

Grossen, N. E., Kostansek, D. J., & Bolles, R. C. Effects of appetitive discriminative stimuli on avoidance behavior. *Journal of Experimental Psychology*, 1969, **81,** 340–343.

Hammond, L. J. Increased responding to CS− in differential CER. *Psychonomic Science,* 1966, **5,** 337–338.

Hearst, E. The classical–instrumental distinction: Reflexes, voluntary behavior, and categories of associative learning. In W. K. Estes (Ed.), *Handbook of learning and cognitive processes,* (Vol. 2). Hillsdale, N.J.: Lawrence Erlbaum Associates, 1975.

Hearst, E., & Peterson, G. B. Transfer of conditioned excitation and inhibition from one operant response to another. *Journal of Experimental Psychology,* 1973, **99,** 360–368.

Henton, W. W., & Brady, J. V. Operant acceleration during a pre-reward stimulus. *Journal of the Experimental Analysis of Behavior,* 1970, **13,** 205–209.

Herrnstein, R. J., & Morse, W. H. Some effects of response-independent positive reinforcement on maintained operant behavior. *Journal of Comparative and Physiological Psychology,* 1957, **50,** 461–467.

Hull, C. L. Knowledge and purpose as habit mechanisms. *Psychological Review,* 1930, **37,** 511–525.

Hull, C. L. Goal attraction and directing ideas conceived as habit phenomena. *Psychological Review,* 1931, **38,** 487–506.

Hull, C. L. *A behavioral system.* New Haven: Yale University Press, 1952.

Hyde, T. S. *Effects of Pavlovian conditioned stimuli on discriminative instrumental baseline respondings.* Unpublished doctoral dissertation, University of Minnesota, 1969.

Hyde, T. S., Trapold, M. A., & Gross, D. M. Facilitative effect of a CS for reinforcement as a function of reinforcement magnitude: A test of incentive motivation theory. *Journal of Experimental Psychology,* 1968, **78,** 423–428.

Jenkins, J. J. Mediated associations: Paradigms and situations. In C. N. Cofer & B. S. Musgrave (Eds.), *Verbal behavior and learning.* New York: McGraw-Hill, 1963. Chap. 6.

Kamin, L. J., Brimer, C., & Black, A. H. Conditioned suppression as a monitor of fear of the CS in the course of avoidance training. *Journal of Comparative and Physiological Psychology,* 1963, **56,** 497–501.

Kimble, G. A. *Hilgard and Marquis' conditioning and learning* (2nd ed.). New York: Appleton, 1961.

Konorski, J. Some problems concerning the mechanism of instrumental conditioning. *Acta Biologiae Experimentalis,* 1964, **24,** 59–72.

Konorski, J. *Integrative activity of the brain.* Chicago: University of Chicago Press, 1967.

Konorski, J., & Miller, S. On two types of conditioned reflex. *Journal of General Psychology,* 1937, **16,** 264–272. (a)

Konorski, J., & Miller, S. Further remarks on two types of conditioned reflex. *Journal of General Psychology,* 1937, **17,** 405–407. (b)

Konorski, J., & Szwejkowska, G. Reciprocal transformations of heterogeneous conditioned reflexes. *Acta Biologiae Experimentalis,* 1956, **17,** 141–165.

Lawicka, W. The role of stimuli modality in successive discrimination and differential learning. *Bulletin of the Polish Academy of Sciences, Biological Science,* 1964, **12,** 35–38.

Leaf, R. C. Avoidance response evocation as a function of prior discriminative fear conditioning under curare. *Journal of Comparative and Physiological Psychology,* 1964, **58,** 446–449.

Logan, F. A. The Hull–Spence approach. In S. Koch (Ed.), *Psychology: A study of science* (Vol. 2). New York: McGraw-Hill, 1959. Pp. 293–358.

Logan, F. A., & Wagner, A. R. *Reward and punishment.* Boston: Allyn & Bacon, 1965.

LoLordo, V. M., McMillan, J. C., & Riley, A. L. The effects upon food-reinforced pecking and treadle-pressing of auditory and visual signals for response-independent food. *Learning and Motivation,* 1974, **5,** 24–41.

Maier, N. R. F., & Schneirla, T. C. Mechanisms in conditioning. *Psychological Review*, 1942, **49,** 117–134.

Martin, L. K., & Riess, D. Effects of US intensity during previous discrete delay conditioning on conditioned acceleration during avoidance extinction. *Journal of Comparative and Physiological Psychology*, 1969, **69,** 196–200.

Masserman, J. H. *Behavior and neurosis.* Chicago: University of Chicago Press, 1943.

May, M. A. Experimentally acquired drives. *Journal of Experimental Psychology*, 1948, **38,** 66–77.

McCleary, R. A. Type of response as a factor in interocular transfer in the fish. *Journal of Comparative and Physiological Psychology*, 1960, **53,** 311–321.

McHose, J. H., & Moore, J. N. Expectancy, salience, and habit: A non-contextual interpretation of the effects of changes in the conditions of reinforcement on simple instrumental responses. *Psychological Review*, 1976, **83,** 292–307.

Meehl, P. E., & MacCorquodale, K. Some methodological comments concerning expectancy theory. *Psychological Review*, 1951, **58,** 230–233.

Mellgren, R. L., & Ost, J. W. P. Transfer of Pavlovian differential conditioning to an operant discrimination. *Journal of Comparative and Physiological Psychology*, 1969, **67,** 390–394.

Meltzer, D., & Hamm, R. J. Conditioned enhancement as a function of the percentage of CS-US pairings and CS duration. *Bulletin of the Psychonomic Society*, 1974, **4,** 467–470.

Meltzer, D., & Hamm, R. J. Differential conditioning of conditioned enhancement and positive conditioned suppression. *Bulletin of the Psychonomic Society*, 1978, **11,** 29–32.

Meyer, P. A. Role of unavoidability procedure in eliminating avoidance behavior in humans. *Journal of Experimental Psychology*, 1970, **86,** 337–340.

Millenson, J. R., & deVilliers, P. A. Motivational properties of conditioned anxiety. In R. M. Gilbert & J. R. Millenson (Eds.), *Reinforcement: Behavior analysis.* New York: Academic Press, 1972. Pp. 98–128.

Miller, L. Stimulus compounding with an instrumental avoidance response. *Psychonomic Science*, 1969, **16,** 46–47.

Miller, N. E. Studies of fear as an acquirable drive. I. Fear as motivation and fear reduction as reinforcement in the learning of new responses. *Journal of Experimental Psychology*, 1948, **38,** 89–101.

Miller, N. E., & DeBold, R. C. Classically conditioned tongue-licking and operant bar-pressing recorded simultaneously in the rat. *Journal of Comparative and Physiological Psychology*, 1965, **59,** 109–111.

Mineka, S., & Kihlstrom, J. F. Unpredictable and uncontrollable events: A new perspective on experimental neurosis. *Journal of Abnormal Psychology*, 1978, **87,** 256–271.

Mowrer, O. H. A stimulus-response analysis of anxiety and its role as a reinforcing agent. *Psychological Review*, 1939, **46,** 553–565.

Mowrer, O. H. On the dual nature of learning: A re-interpretation of "conditioning" and "problem-solving." *Harvard Educational Review*, 1947, **17,** 102–148.

Mowrer, O. H. *Learning theory and personality dynamics.* New York: Ronald Press, 1950.

Mowrer, O. H. *Learning theory and behavior.* New York: Wiley, 1960.

O'Neill, W., & Biederman, G. B. Avoidance conditioning as a function of appetitive stimulus pretraining: Response and stimulus transfer effect. *Learning and Motivation*, 1974, **5,** 195–208.

Osgood, C. E. *Method and theory in experimental psychology.* London and New York: Oxford University Press, 1953.

Ost, J. W., & Mellgren, R. L. Transfer from Pavlovian differential to operant discriminative training: Effect of amount of Pavlovian conditioning. *Journal of Comparative and Physiological Psychology*, 1970, **71,** 487–491.

Overmier, J. B. Instrumental and cardiac indices of Pavlovian fear conditioning as a function of UCS duration. *Journal of Comparative and Physiological Psychology*, 1966, **62,** 15–20. (a)

Overmier, J. B. Differential transfer of control of avoidance responses as a function of UCS duration. *Psychonomic Science*, 1966, **5,** 25–26. (b)

Overmier, J. B. Differential Pavlovian fear conditioning as a function of the qualitative nature of the UCS: Constant versus pulsating shock. *Conditional Reflex*, 1968, **3,** 175–180. (a)

Overmier, J. B. Interference with avoidance behavior: Failure to avoid traumatic shock. *Journal of Experimental Psychology*, 1968, **78,** 340–343. (b)

Overmier, J. B. Avoidance learning. In M. E. Bitterman, V. M. LoLordo, and J. B. Overmier, & M. E. Rashotte (Eds.), *Animal learning: Survey and analysis*. New York: Plenum, 1979. Chap. 10. (a)

Overmier, J. B. Theories of instrumental learning. In M. E. Bitterman, V. M. LoLordo, J. B. Overmier, & M. E. Rashotte (Eds.), *Animal learning: Survey and analysis*. New York: Plenum, 1979. Chap. 11. (b)

Overmier, J. B., & Brackbill, R. M. On the independence of stimulus evocation of fear and fear evocation of responses. *Behaviour, Research, and Therapy*, 1977, **15,** 51–56.

Overmier, J. B., & Bull, J. A. On the independence of stimulus control of avoidance. *Journal of Experimental Psychology*, 1969, **79,** 464–467.

Overmier, J. B., & Bull, J. A. Influences of appetitive Pavlovian conditioning upon avoidance behavior. In J. H. Reynierse (Ed.), *Current issues in animal learning*. Lincoln: University of Nebraska Press, 1970. Pp. 117–141.

Overmier, J. B., Bull, J. A., & Pack, K. On instrumental response interaction as explaining the influences of Pavlovian CSs upon avoidance behavior. *Learning and Motivation*, 1971, **2,** 103–112. (a)

Overmier, J. B., Bull, J. A., & Trapold, M. A. Discriminative cue properties of different fears and their role in response selection in dogs. *Journal of Comparative and Physiological Psychology*, 1971, **76,** 478–482. (b)

Overmier, J. B., & Leaf, R. C. Effects of discriminative Pavlovian fear conditioning upon previously or subsequently acquired avoidance responding. *Journal of Comparative and Physiological Psychology*, 1965, **60,** 213–217.

Overmier, J. B., & Payne, R. J. Facilitation of instrumental avoidance learning by prior appetitive Pavlovian conditioning to the cue. *Acta Neurobiologiae Experimentalis*, 1971, **31,** 341–349.

Overmier, J. B., & Schwarzkopf, K. H. Summation of food and shock based responding. *Learning and Motivation*, 1974, **5,** 42–52.

Overmier, J. B., & Seligman, M. E. P. Effects of inescapable shock upon subsequent escape and avoidance responding. *Journal of Comparative and Physiological Psychology*, 1967, **63,** 28–33.

Overmier, J. B., & Starkman, N. Transfer of control of avoidance in normal and forebrainless goldfish. *Physiology and Behavior*, 1974, **12,** 605–608.

Patten, R. L., & Deaux, E. B. Classical conditioning and extinction of the licking response in rats. *Psychonomic Science*, 1966, **4,** 21–22.

Payne, R. J. Alteration of Sidman avoidance baselines by CSs paired with avoidable or unavoidable shock. *Psychological Reports*, 1972, **31,** 291–294.

Perkins, C. C., Jr. An analysis of the concept of reinforcement. *Psychological Review*, 1968, **75,** 155–172.

Peterson, G. B., Wheeler, R. L., & Armstrong, G. D. Expectancies as mediators in the differential reward conditional discrimination performance of pigeons. *Animals Learning and Behavior,* 1978, **6,** 279–285.

Phillips, M. I., & Olds, J. Unit activity: Motivation-dependent responses from midbrain neurons. *Science,* 1969, **165,** 1269–1271.

Ray, O. S., & Stein, L. Generalization of conditioned suppression. *Journal of the Experimental Analysis of Behavior,* 1959, **2,** 357–361.

Rescorla, R. A. Pavlovian conditioning and its proper control procedures. *Psychological Review,* 1967, **74,** 71–80.

Rescorla, R. A., & LoLordo, V. M. Inhibition of avoidance behavior. *Journal of Comparative and Physiological Psychology,* 1965, **59,** 406–412.

Rescorla, R. A., & Solomon, R. L. Two-process learning theory: Relationships between Pavlovian conditioning and instrumental learning. *Psychological Review,* 1967, **74,** 151–182.

Reynolds, B. Acquisition of a black-white discrimination habit under two levels of reinforcement. *Journal of Experimental Psychology,* 1949, **39,** 760–769.

Riess, D. Pavlovian phenomena in conditioned acceleration: Stimulus summation. *Conditional Reflex,* 1969, **4,** 257–264.

Ross, R. R. Positive and negative partial-reinforcement extinction efforts carried through continuous reinforcement, changed motivation and changed response. *Journal of Experimental Psychology,* 1964, **68,** 492–502.

Rozeboom, W. W. "What is learned?"—an empirical enigma? *Psychological Review,* 1958, **65,** 22–33.

Scavio, M. A. Classical–classical transfer: Effects of prior aversive conditioning upon appetitive conditioning in rabbits. *Journal of Comparative and Physiological Psychology,* 1974, **86,** 107–115.

Schlosberg, H. The relationship between success and the laws of conditioning. *Psychological Review,* 1937, **44,** 379–394.

Schoenfeld, W. N. An experimental approach to anxiety, escape, and avoidance behavior. In P. H. Hoch & J. Zubin (Eds.), *Anxiety.* New York: Grune & Stratton, 1950. Pp. 70–99.

Schoenfeld, W. N., Antonitus, J. J., & Bersh, P. J. A preliminary study of training conditions necessary for secondary reinforcement. *Journal of Experimental Psychology,* 1950, **40,** 40–45.

Scobie, S. R. Integration of an aversive Pavlovian conditioned stimulus with aversively and appetitively motivated operants in rats. *Journal of Comparative and Physiological Psychology,* 1972, **79,** 171–188.

Scobie, S. R. The response-shock interval and conditioned suppression of avoidance in rats. *Animal Learning and Behavior,* 1973, **1,** 17–20.

Seward, J. P. Conditioning theory. In M. H. Marx (Ed.), *Learning: Theories.* New York: Macmillan, 1970. Pp. 49–120.

Shapiro, M. M., & Herendeen, D. L. Food-reinforced inhibition of conditioned salivation in dogs. *Journal of Comparative and Physiological Psychology,* 1975, **88,** 628–632.

Shapiro, M. M., & Miller, T. M. On the relationship between conditioned and discriminative stimuli and between instrumental and consummatory responses. In W. F. Prokasy (Ed.), *Classical conditioning: A symposium.* New York: Appleton, 1965. Pp. 269–301.

Shapiro, M. M., Miller, T. M., & Bresnahan, J. L. Dummy trials, novel stimuli, and Pavlovian-trained stimuli: Their effect upon instrumental and consummatory response relationships. *Journal of Comparative and Physiological Psychology,* 1966, **61,** 480–483.

Sheffield, F. D. New evidence on the drive-induction theory of reinforcement. Colloquium presentation, 1954. In R. N. Haber (Ed.), *Current research in motivation.* New York: Holt, 1966. Pp. 111–122.

Shipley, W. C. An apparent transfer of conditioning. *Journal of General Psychology,* 1933, **8,** 382–391.

Sidman, M. Avoidance conditioning with brief shock and no extroceptive warning signal. *Science,* 1953, **118,** 157–158.

Solomon, R. L., & Turner, L. H. Discriminative classical conditioning in dogs paralyzed by curare can later control discriminative avoidance responses in the normal state. *Psychological Review,* 1962, **69,** 202–219.

Soltysik, S. Studies on avoidance conditioning: II. Differentiation and extinction of avoidance reflexes. *Acta Biologiae Experimentalis,* 1960, **20,** 171–182.

Soltysik, S., Konorski, J., Holowina, A., & Rentoul, T. The effect of conditioned stimuli signaling food upon the autochthonous instrumental responses in dogs. *Acta Neurologicae Experimentalis,* 1975, **36,** 277–310.

Soltysik, S., & Kowalska, M. Studies on the avoidance conditioning. I. Relations between cardiac (type I) and motor (type II) effects in the avoidance reflex. *Acta Biologiae Experimentalis,* 1960, **20,** 157–170.

Spence, K. *Behavior theory and conditioning.* New Haven: Yale University Press, 1956.

Staats, A. W., & Warren, D. R. Motivation and three-function learning: Food deprivation and approach–avoidance to food words. *Journal of Experimental Psychology,* 1974, **103,** 1191–1199.

Stein, L. Reciprocal action of reward and punishment mechanisms. In R. Heath (Ed.), *The role of pleasure in behavior.* New York: Harper, 1964. Pp. 113–139.

Stevens, S. S. Matching functions between loudness and ten other continua. *Perception & Psychophysics,* 1966, **1,** 5–8.

Stevens, S. S. Neural events and the psychophysical law. *Science,* 1970, **170,** 1043–1050.

Tolman, E. C. *Purposive behavior in animals and men.* New York: Century, 1932.

Trapold, M.A. The effect of incentive motivation on an unrelated reflex response. *Journal of Comparative and Physiological Psychology,* 1962, **55,** 1034–1039.

Trapold, M. A. Are expectancies based upon different positive reinforcing events discriminably different? *Learning and Motivation,* 1970, **1,** 129–140.

Trapold, M. A., & Carlson, J. G. Proximity of the manipulation and foodcup as a determinant of the generalized S^D effect. *Psychonomic Science,* 1965, **2,** 327–328.

Trapold, M. A., & Fairlie, J. Transfer of discrimination learning based upon contingent and noncontingent training procedures. *Psychological Reports,* 1965, **17,** 239–246.

Trapold, M. A., & Overmier, J. B. The second learning process in instrumental learning. In A. H. Black & W. F. Prokasy (Eds.), *Classical conditioning II: Current theory and research.* New York: Appleton, 1972.

Trapold, M. A., & Winokur, S. Transfer from classical conditioning and extinction to acquisition, extinction, and stimulus generalization of a positively reinforced instrumental response. *Journal of Experimental Psychology,* 1967, **73,** 517–525.

Waller, M. B., & Waller, P. F. The effects of unavoidable shocks on a multiple schedule having an avoidance component. *Journal of the Experimental Analysis of Behavior,* 1963, **6,** 29–37.

Warner, L. H. The association span of the white rat. *Journal of Genetic Psychology,* 1932, **41,** 57–90. (a)

Warner, L. H. An experimental search for the "conditioned response." *Journal of Genetic Psychology,* 1932, **41,** 91–115. (b)

Watson, J. B. Psychology as the behaviorist views it. *Psychological Review,* 1913, **20,** 158–177.

Weiss, S. J. Summation of response strenght's instrumentally conditioned to stimuli along different sensory modalities. *Journal of Experimental Psychology,* 1964, **68,** 151–155.

Weiss, S. J. Stimulus compounding in free-operant and classical conditioning. *Psychological Bulletin,* 1972, **78,** 189–208.

Wielkiewicz, R. M., & Lawry, J. A. *The interaction of appetitive Pavlovian stimuli with positively reinforced instrumental behavior.* Unpublished manuscript, under review, 1979.

Wilder, J. The law of initial vaues in neurology and psychiatry. Facts and problems. *Journal of Nervous and Mental Disease,* 1957, **125,** 73–86.

Wolf, M. M. Some effects of combined S^Ds. *Journal of the Experimental Analysis of Behavior,* 1963, **6,** 343–347.

Wolpe, J. *Psychotherapy by reciprocal inhibition.* Stanford: Stanford University Press, 1958.

Wynne, L. C., & Solomon, R. L. Traumatic avoidance learning: Acquisition and extinction in dogs deprived of normal autonomic function. *Genetic Psychology Monographs,* 1955, **52,** 241–284.

Zanich, M. L., & Fowler, H. Transfer from Pavlovian appetitive to instrumental appetitive conditioning: Signaling versus discrepancy interpretations. *Journal of Experimental Psychology: Animal Behavior Processes,* 1978, **4,** 37–49.

A CONDITIONED OPPONENT THEORY OF PAVLOVIAN CONDITIONING AND HABITUATION[1]

Jonathan Schull

UNIVERSITY OF PENNSYLVANIA
PHILADELPHIA, PENNSYLVANIA

I. Introduction

Animals' reactions to hedonic stimuli and to signals of those stimuli change with experience. Sometimes hedonic stimuli evoke intense affective reactions and cause changes in conditioned reactions to signals,

[1]This work was supported in part by an NSF predoctoral fellowship awarded to me, and by USPHS grant #1 RO1 MH-29187-91 to R.L. Solomon. Special thanks to Paul Rozin, Martin G. P. Selisman, and Richard L. Solomon for their counsel and sponsorship. For discussion and criticism of earlier versions of this paper, I also thank David Burdette, Ronald Ehrman, Beatrice Hillsberg, Hillard Kaplan, Joseph Livan, Robert A. Rescorla, Burton Rosner, Jerry Rudy, Barry Schwartz, Stephen Seaman, David Starr, and Alan R. Wagner.

THE PSYCHOLOGY OF LEARNING
AND MOTIVATION, VOL. 13

ISBN 0-12-543313-1

sometimes they do not. Prediction, description, and explanation of such phenomena are continuing concerns of students of learning and motivation. What determines the topography, strength, and affective quality of conditioned and unconditioned reactions to hedonic stimuli and to their signals? Under what conditions do such reactions change? What processes underlie the changes? What are the biological functions of the learning abilities which underlie the behavior changes we study?

The present paper addresses these questions. It argues that Pavlovian conditioning occurs when hedonic stimuli disrupt affective equilibrium, and that an important function of the learning which occurs on such occasions is to reduce the disruptiveness of subsequent exposures to the same hedonic stimulus. The theory presented here modifies Solomon's and Corbit's (1974) opponent-process theory of motivation, by postulating the existence of endogenous conditioned responses which function to oppose and counteract disturbances of affective (and perhaps perceptual) equilibrium. The properties of these conditioned regulatory processes, generically called "conditioned opponents," may account for recent findings on conditioned tolerance and habituation and on preference for signaled or unsignaled reinforcement. Furthermore, the "conditioned opponent theory" extends Solomon's and Corbit's account of affective habituation in a way which can explain many Pavlovian conditioning phenomena, including those encompassed by the Rescorla-Wagner (1972) theory of conditioning. That theory specifies (but does not explain) the conditions under which reinforcement and nonreinforcement will be more or less effective. In recent years, it has become common to explain such phenomena in terms of attentional, memorial, and rehearsal processes. The present argument is very different. It suggests a new interpretation of the successes and failures of Rescorla's and Wagner's theory, and it generates new experimental predictions of its own.

The plan of this paper is as follows. First, opponent-process theories, and opponent-process phenomena, are introduced to support the notion that conditioned compensatory reactions play a role in behavior, physiology, and experience. Then, the conditioned opponent theory is stated in the form of two postulates which extend Solomon's and Corbit's theory from the domain of affective regulation to that of Rescorla's and Wagner's theory of Pavlovian conditioning. The next two sections unpack the experimental implications of these two postulates and review the relevant experimental literatures. Finally, the discussion argues that the theory makes sense in the context of instrumental learning and natural selection and considers the prospects for extending the theory. There is a summary, and we conclude that the conditioned opponent theory, though speculative, could help organize theory and research in several areas of psychology.

II. Opponent Processes

When one views a red light, the hue first appears intensely saturated and then fades. A drug, such as morphine, produces an initial "rush" of euphoria (and/or nausea) and then the effects wane. When a long-lasting electric shock is applied to the feet of a dog, heart rate and general arousal rapidly rise to a peak and then subside back toward normal levels. Such phenomena can be explained in terms of opponent-process principles of organization: Adaptation to prolonged stimuli is due to the recruitment of an endogenous "opponent-process" which opposes and neutralizes direct effects of these stimuli.

According to such accounts, the opponent-process is seen most clearly when the adapted-to stimulus is withdrawn: When the red light is terminated, a green afterimage reveals itself; the removal of morphine can cause an afterreaction (withdrawal) which is anything but euphoric; and the termination of footshock causes heart rate to drop below normal levels. With time these negative afterreactions fade and equilibrium is restored. Opponent-process color theory (Hering, 1920/1964; Hurvich & Jameson, 1974; cf. Gibson, 1937) notes that when green is superimposed upon red, it detracts from the perceived saturation of red; therefore, an endogenous "green" opponent process may be responsible for adaptation to red as well as for the negative afterimage. Analogously, Solomon and Corbit's theory suggests that adaptation and negative afterreactions to affect-arousing stimuli are caused by affective opponent processes which oppose and outlast direct effects of those stimuli.

The pattern of reaction described above is illustrated at the top of Fig. 1A (after Solomon and Corbit, 1974, p. 128). Soon after the onset of the hedonic stimulus event (or "reinforcer"), the animal's manifest affective response (terror in response to shock, euphoria to morphine) peaks and then adapts. When the reinforcer is terminated, a negative afterreaction emerges and then fades. This is the "standard pattern of affective dynamics" (Solomon & Corbit, 1974).

Solomon and Corbit explain this pattern as follows (see the middle diagram of Fig. 1A). An animal's reaction at any moment manifests the interaction of a reinforcer-produced "*a* process" and an endogenous opponent "*b* process." These two processes are postulated to have different time courses; whereas the *a* process is aroused immediately by the stimulus and dies away as soon as the stimulus is terminated, the *b* process takes longer to recruit and longer to decay. Furthermore, the

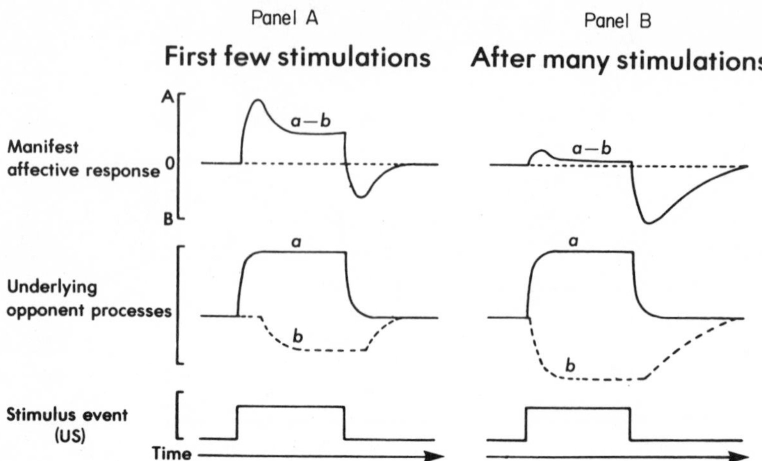

Fig. 1. The consequences of subtracting the *b* process from the *a* process when the *b* process is small and when it is large. When $a > b$, the manifest affect response reflects an A state; B states occur when $a < b$. According to Solomon and Corbit, the *b* process grows nonassociatively through exercise. The conditioned opponent account is different. (After Solomon and Corbit, 1974.)

two processes are postulated to have opposite effects upon affect; while the *a* process produces the primary reaction to the reinforcer called the "A state" (e.g., the pleasurable "high" of morphine), the *b* process that subsequently emerges reduces the intensity of the primary reaction and also produces hedonically an opposite B state (e.g., withdrawal) when it overpowers or outlasts the *a* process. As shown in Fig. 1, these notions about underlying processes account for the "standard pattern" of affective states. The animal's state is given by the quantity $(a - b)$: when the *a* process is greater than the *b* process, an A state results, and when *b* is greater than *a*, the animal experiences a B state.

For our present purposes, the most important feature of the opponent-process theory is shown in Fig. 1B. In their paper, Solomon and Corbit noted that animals commonly "get used to" repeatedly presented reinforcers. Successive stimuli yield ever smaller primary reactions and yield increasingly large afterreactions. For example, repeated doses of morphine induce highs that are less and less pleasurable, and withdrawal states that are more and more aversive. As shown in the middle diagram of Fig. 1B, this pattern can be explained simply by the hypothesis that repeated exposure to the reinforcer somehow causes the *b* process to grow, while the *a* process remains fixed.

III. Conditioned Opponents

A. The Conditioned Opponent Hypothesis

What elicits the *b* process and why does it grow? Here is where the present theory differs from Solomon's and Corbit's. Although those authors allow for conditioning of A states and B states, they postulate that the *b* process is a slave process, elicited by the *a* process, "strengthened by use, and weakened by disuse. These changes are nonassociative in nature," (Solomon & Corbit, 1974, p. 144). In contrast, the present theory is based upon the hypothesis that the rules which govern the growth and expression of the *b* process are those which govern Pavlovian conditioned responses. The "conditioned opponent" process, like other conditioned responses (CRs) putatively comes to be elicited by conditioned stimuli (CSs) which have been repeatedly paired with the affective disturbances caused by the reinforcer (or "unconditioned stimulus", US). This is the conditioned opponent hypothesis.[2]

There are good empirical reasons to suppose that opponent processes can be triggered by stimuli other than those they oppose. Even in the visual system, opponent color responses can come to be elicited by achromatic stimuli which have been paired with chromatic unconditioned stimuli (McCullough, 1965). If, for example, one spends a few minutes viewing black vertical stripes (the CS) superimposed upon a bright red background (the US), the stripes acquire a long-lasting ability to elicit an opponent response (the CR): hours or days later, long after simple afterimages have dissipated, when one views vertical black and white stripes they appear black and light green. The McCullough effects, and other contingent negative aftereffects in visual perception (Skowbo, Timney, Gentry, & Morant, 1975; cf. McCarter & Silver, 1977; Murch, 1976, 1977), lend plausibility to the hypothesis that opponent-process systems which regulate affect might learn when and how to oppose hedonic stimuli more effectively.

[2]By the present hypothesis, Pavlovian conditioning is responsible for changes in the strength and elicitation of opponent processes, and the *b* process is subject to many of the same influences as other CRs. The hypothesis does not (and need not) specify how conditioned opponents (or any other CRs) are created. Some systems may have to learn how, as well as when, to oppose novel disturbances. Other systems are undoubtedly equipped with innate opponent reactions to disturbances; through conditioning these reactions may grow and come to be elicited by CSs. It is also probable that some opponent processes (be they innate or acquired) are strengthened nonassociatively by mere exercise as Solomon and Corbit supposed. Although this notion is compatible with the hypothesis that opponent processes are conditioned responses, the two ideas lead to some differential predictions which are taken up again in sections V.H. and V.I.

A second, more compelling reason for modifying Solomón's and Corbit's theory comes from Shepard Siegel's work which indicates that morphine tolerance is a conditioned response (Siegel, 1975, 1977a, 1979). Siegel finds that tolerance (as claimed by Solomon and Corbit) results from an endogenous compensatory response which opposes the direct effects of morphine. However, he also finds that this compensatory response is elicited by environmental cues which have previously been associated with experience of the drug. As we shall see, Siegel's rats show tolerance to morphine-produced analgesia only in environments which had previously been paired with morphine injections. Furthermore, when given saline injection in those environments, the rats are hyperalgesic (especially sensitive to pain), as if the *b* process which opposes morphine analgesia is indeed elicited by conditioned, non-pharmacological, contextual cues. By adopting the conditioned opponent hypothesis, such results as these can be accommodated within opponent-process theory.

B. The Conditioned Opponent Theory

When added to Solomon's and Corbit's theory, the following two postulates constitute the "conditioned opponent" theory. They embody the general hypothesis that the *b* processes to many kinds of hedonic stimuli are (at least sometimes) conditioned responses. The virtues of this particular formulation should soon become clear.

Postulate One: *When a conditioned stimulus is paired with an A state, its ability to elicit conditioned opponents and other CRs increases.*

Postulate Two: *When a conditioned stimulus is paired with a B state, its ability to elicit conditioned opponents and other CRs decreases, and/or its ability to inhibit these CRs increases.*

The first postulate is illustrated in Fig. 2.In the left panel, a neutral stimulus is paired with an A state for the first time. The A state is large because there is no conditioned opponent to oppose the *a* process produced by the US. The right panel shows that as a result of such pairings the CS has become what is conventionally called a conditioned excitor.[3] As follows from the first postulate, it has acquired the ability to elicit anticipatory CRs of the sort usually measured in conditioning experiments (anticipatory fear, salivation in advance of food, etc.), as well as

[3]Following convention, CSs that elicit anticipatory and compensatory CRs because they have been paired with A states will be called "conditioned excitors." CSs that have been paired with B states and that can therefore inhibit CRs (including conditioned opponents) will be called "conditioned inhibitors." Conditioned excitation should not be confused with the *a* process, nor conditioned inhibition with the *b* process. Identity is not assumed here.

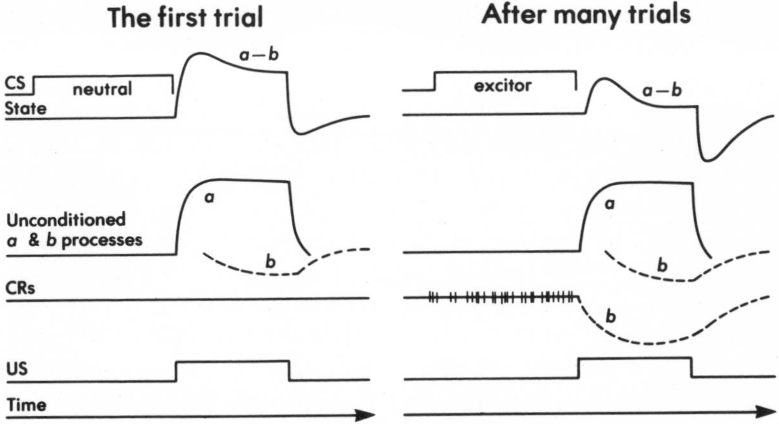

Fig. 2. The first postulate: When a conditioned stimulus is paired with an A state, its ability to elicit conditioned opponents and other CRs increase. Left: A netural stimulus is paired with a large A state. Right: After many such pairings the stimulus has become a conditioned excitor which elicits anticipatory CRs (indicated by vertical lines) in advance of the US, and compensatory CRs (conditioned opponents, "*b*") when the US is due. (Unconditioned opponents are not assumed to grow.)

the compensatory conditioned opponent ("*b*"). That is why the *b* process grows, and why the A state produced by the US has diminished.

In the present theory, it is the growth of conditioned *b* processes rather than unconditioned *b* processes that putatively cause habituation to the US. Nonetheless in many situations (including those emphasized by Solomon and Corbit) the conditioned opponent hypothesis changes the implications of opponent-process theory only slightly. Note that when environmental signals invariably precede the US, the conditioned opponent behaves just like Solomon's and Corbit's nonassociative slave process of Fig. 1. Functional considerations suggest, and the present theory assumes, that the *b* process is a well-timed CR which emerges at the moment the US is due to be presented, rather than at the onset of the signal (cf. Sears, Baker and Fry, 1979). Note also that in situations lacking reliable environmental signals of the US, the conditioned opponent should again act as in Solomon's and Corbit's figure: in this case, the onset of the *a* process, or of some other stimulus feature of the US acting as a CS, could come to elicit the *b* process; the *b* process would grow with repeated exposure to the US, and would produce habituation and afterreactions (c.f. Stein, 1966). Indeed, for our present purposes it is unnecessary to postulate the existence of nonconditioned opponent processes. They undoubtedly exist in many systems, but for the remainder of this paper their contribution will be ignored.

However there are many situations in which the conditioned opponent hypothesis does generate new predictions. When the contingency between environmental CSs and hedonic USs is variable (as in many conditioning experiments and in life), the strength of the *b* process should depend upon the animal's past experience with the CSs present on a given trial, not just upon past experience with the US. For example, if the US is presented in the absence of the previously conditioned stimuli which elicit the *b* process, then the US's ability to produce large A states should be restored (as shown in the left panel of Fig. 2) and as instanced when Siegel finds that morphine tolerance vanishes in the absence of morphine-paired stimuli. Conversely, if the US is omitted in the presence of a CS which has previously been paired with the US, the conditioned opponent should be elicited even though the US is absent. This is illustrated in Fig. 3, left panel. A CS which had previously been paired with A states is now presented in the absence of the US: Since there is no *a* process, the conditioned opponent produces a B state (e.g., hyperalgesia).

Figure 3 illustrates the second postulate of the present theory. In the first panel the CS is being paired with a B state of its own making. That is why (according to the second postulate) the conditioned opponent and the anticipatory CRs extinguish. Another implication of the second postulate will be elaborated later; viz.; when neutral CSs are paired with B states they acquire the ability to inhibit the *b* process and other CRs.

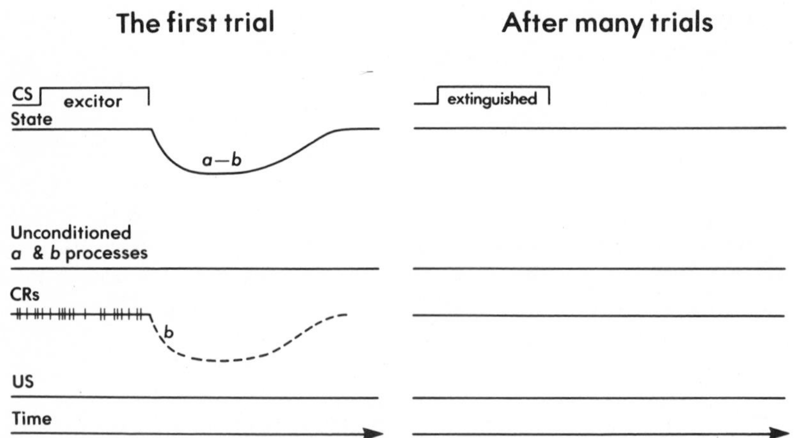

Fig. 3. The second postulate: When a conditioned stimulus is paired with a B state, its ability to elicit conditioned opponents and other CRs decreases, and/or its ability to inhibit these CRs increases. Left: as in the previous figure, a conditioned excitor is presented and the conditioned opponent is elicited when the US is due. However, on this trial the US is omitted for the first time. The CS is therefore paired with a B state. Right: after many such pairings, the CS has lost its ability to elicit CRs.

(It should be remembered that conditioned inhibitors inhibit the *b* process.)

These postulates merit consideration for several reasons. First, they make sense for systems designed to minimize states of affective disequilibrium. In the presence of stimuli that have previously been associated with A states, the *b* process is elicited; therefore, when the US occurs in its usual context, the *a* process is opposed. The conditioned opponent enables animals to prepare for and thereby minimize predictable disturbances of equilibrium. Furthermore, suppose that environmental contingencies change and the US in unexpectedly omitted in the presence of conditioned stimuli which elicit the *b* process. Because no *a* process would occur, a B state would be experienced. The second postulate ensures that the animal learns to prevent such self-produced states of disequilibrium because conditioned stimuli that precipitate and are automatically paired with B states lose their ability to do so, and neutral stimuli that are present when B states are precipitated acquire the ability to inhibit the *b* process. Thus, conditioned stimuli regulate the strength of the *b* process and other conditioned responses in an adaptive manner.

Another virtue of the two postulates above is that they bring Pavlovian conditioning phenomena squarely into the domain of opponent-process theory. The postulates imply that it is A and B states, not USs per se, which instigate Pavlovian conditioning. They imply that the effectiveness of a US on any conditioning trial will depend upon the ability of CSs present on that trial to elicit or inhibit the *b* process. Moreover, they specify the conditions under which CSs should gain or lose the ability to elicit or inhibit not only the compensatory *b* process, but more conventional anticipatory CRs as well. With one caveat, therefore, it will be possible to apply the two postulates of the conditioned opponent theory to Rescorla's and Wagner's mathematical model of Pavlovian conditioning.

C. A Caveat

To avoid confusion it should be recognized that the present theory specifies when CSs gain or lose conditioned excitatory or inhibitory abilities, but not how CRs are elicited or inhibited. Nor does it predict the particular form of any conditioned responses other than conditioned opponents. These are important but difficult problems. Perhaps conditioned excitors and inhibitors have opposite effects upon "central motive states" (e.g., fear) which are derived from US-produced A states. One might assume, for example, that CSs which have been paired with A-states aquire the ability to evoke conditioned A-states (e.g., fear) which stimulate anticipatory CRs (such as freezing) and also trigger the conditioned opponent when the US is imminent. However the existence of conditioned A states or conditioned *a* processes is not assumed in the present theory, and for now the conditioned opponent is postulated to oppose only unconditioned *a* processes produced by the USs. An alternative assumption is that CSs activate expectations or memorial representations of the states which they precede, and that these anticipatory states (which are neither A nor B) generate or suppress CRs. It is also possible that CSs evoke some CRs "directly" without conscious, cognitive, or affective mediation (as may be the case for the contingent negative aftereffects and for some kinds of affective habituation, where CS, US, and CR are all confined to the same perceptual system). We do not know yet. The present theory assumes no particular mechanism of CR elicitation, nor does it assume that the same mechanisms underlie all CRs (or all conditioned opponents).

IV. The Rescorla and Wagner Theory of Pavlovian Conditioning

In an extensive series of experiments measuring conditioned emotional reactions to formerly neutral stimuli, Kamin (1968, 1969) paired a tone CS with a shock US in the presence of another CS (a light) which had previously been associated with shock. He found that when the shock was presented in the context of the light the shock was unable to reinforce conditioning of the tone. Why, and how, does the previously conditioned light stimulus render the US ineffective and "block" conditioning of the tone? Kamin proposed that blocking reflects a general principle: only unexpected or "surprising" USs can reinforce conditioning. No less than his empirical findings, Kamin's theoretical interpretations in terms of memorial and attentional mechanisms have proved extremely influential.

Wagner (1969a, 1969b) and Rescorla (1969a) subsequently extended Kamin's theoretical suggestions and developed a mathematical model based upon the notion that the size of the discrepancy between expectations and outcomes determines the amount of learning which occurs on a given trial (Rescorla & Wagner, 1972; Wagner & Rescorla, 1972). Their associative theorem $\Delta V_x = k(\lambda - \bar{V})$ states that on each conditioning trial ΔV_x, the change in associative value of a target CS "X," (i.e., the amount of learning which occurs), is proportional to the discrepancy between λ and $\bar{V}$. λ is a constant which stands for the asymptotic level of conditioning that a given US can support. The variable $\bar{V}$ is equal to the sum of the associative strengths of all the CSs present during the trial in question ($\bar{V} = V_x + V_y + \ldots$). ($k$ is a learning rate parameter ($0 < k < 1$) which handles such factors as the salience of the CS and the associability of the US.) Because λ reflects the magnitude of the US and because the CSs which summate to yield $\bar{V}$ are often supposed to activate memorial representations or expectations of the US, the equation is usually interpreted as representing the relation of outcome to expectancy (e.g., Rescorla, 1973; Wagner, 1978).

However, the model's predictions do not depend upon that interpretation. The Rescorlà-Wagner equation $\Delta V_x = k(\lambda - \bar{V})$ predicts blocking no matter how one interprets the symbols λ and $\bar{V}$: there will be no change in the associative strength of a CS_x ($\Delta V_x = 0$) on trials in which other CSs contribute to a V which equals λ.

It is important to realize, therefore, that these equations make virtually no statement about the psychological and physiological mechanisms underlying the phenomena they model. The underlying processes could be cognitive and/or affective, they could be conscious and/or nonconscious. Similarly, the Rescorla–Wagner model is silent on the question of how adequate levels of expectation can render a potent physical stimulus impotent as a reinforcer in Pavlovian conditioning experiments. And it says nothing about how animals should react to the reinforcers used in such experiments. The conditioned opponent theory speaks to just these issues.

The present theory arose from the observation that in function and in form Solomon's and Corbit's opponent-process theory of affective habituation is remarkably similar to Rescorla's and Wagner's theory of Pavlovian conditioning. The domains of the two theories are strikingly complementary: one theory addresses variations in the magnitude of reactions to repeatedly presented reinforcers (given by the quantity of $a - b$); the other addresses variations in the effectiveness of those same reinforcers in Pavlovian conditioning experiments (the effectiveness of the reinforcer is proportional to the quantity $\lambda - \bar{V}$). A formal similarity is also apparent: Each theory invokes an entity (b or $\bar{V}$) whose variable magnitude subtracts arithmetically from the fixed strength of the reinforcer (a or λ). So perhaps the "affective arithmetic" of a and b processes described by Solomon and Corbit is responsible for the variations in reinforcement modeled by Rescorla and Wagner. Assume, then, that on a given trial the associative strength of CS_x increases or decreases in direct proportion to the A or B states with which it is paired. The size of these states is given by the quantity $(a - b)$; therefore this assumption yields the formula $\Delta V_x = k(a - b)$, where the terms ΔV_x and k serve the same functions as in Rescorla's and Wagner's equation, and a and b represent the strength of the two opponent processes on a given trial.

This equation captures the two postulates stated earlier. If a CS_x is presented on a trial in which $a - b$ is positive (this is the definition of an A state), its associative value increases, signifying its increased ability to elicit CRs. If CS_x is paired with B state (when $a - b$ is negative), its associative value will decrease, signifying either a decreased ability to elicit CRs (if V_x is decreased toward zero), or an increased ability to inhibit CRs (if V_x is decreased below zero and has a negative value). Also, if CS_x is presented on a trial in which another CS elicits a *b* process which is strong as the *a* process produced by the US, then $\Delta V_x = k(a - b) = 0$, and blocking should be the result.

Compare the equation $\Delta V_x = k(a - b)$ to Rescorla's and Wagner's $\Delta V_x = k(\lambda - \bar{V})$. Since *a*, like λ, is a constant that reflects the magnitude of the US, the formula would yield the same predictions as Rescorla's and Wagner's associative theorem when the strength of *b* is equal to $\bar{V} = V_x + V^y + \ldots$. The two postulates work here too. Because the magnitude of a conditioned response on a given trial typically reflects the summed effects of excitatory and inhibitory CSs present on that trial, the hypothesis that the *b* process is like other CRs (elicited by conditioned excitors and inhibited by conditioned inhibitors) implies that *b* should indeed approximate $\bar{V}$. The two terms would be equal under the assumptions (1) that excitatory and inhibitory CSs are the sole determinants of the strength of the *b* process, and (2) that the associative strengths of those CSs summate linearly.

The conclusion is that Rescorla's and Wagner's equations should accurately predict both changes in associative strength and the intensity and quality of affective and behavioral reactions to USs, when the above assumptions are safe. However, when those assumptions are demonstrably unsafe[4] (and we will examine some situations of this sort) the Rescorla–Wagner model may generate false predictions which the present theory can avoid.

Thus, while the conditioned opponent theory necessitates only slight modifications in the theories from which it stems, it promises to organize a larger body of data than does either parent theory, to raise new questions, and to suggest a new interpretation of the mechanisms underlying a number of associative and habituative phenomena. These are explicated in the following sections.

V. Habituation and Limits to Excitatory Conditioning

This section focuses on the conditioned opponent's putative ability to reduce the magnitude of A states. I will argue that when a US is pre-

[4]Rescorla and Wagner made these assumptions somewhat less dangerous by using their model's quantitative results to generate only ordinal predictions about performance. The same tack is taken here (but see Frey & Sears, 1978).

sented, the magnitude of the A state it produces can be, and has been, assayed a number of ways in a variety of settings. A states may be assayed relatively directly in experiments on tolerance and habituation in which animal's reactions to USs wane with successive presentations. They are assayed somewhat less directly in experiments which offer animals a choice between signaled USs (which should be attenuated by conditioned opponents elicited by the signal) and unsignaled USs (which should be relatively unopposed). Finally, A states are assayed least directly, but perhaps with most precision and sophistication, in Pavlovian conditioning experiments which measure the animal's conditioned responses to CSs that have previously been paired with A states. Results for each type of experiment may be explained by the action of conditioned habituative processes which are affected by the same manipulation as other CRs, and whose strength varies as predicted by the present theory.

A. The Excitatory Asymptote

To see how the present theory relates habituative and associative phenomena, consider the simple case in which a CS is repeatedly paired with a novel US. The common result of such an experiment is that the CS comes to elicit new anticipatory responses, which gain strength rapidly on early trials and then gradually approach their asymptotic strengths on later trials. Why?

The excitatory asymptote requires explanation. It often cannot be attributed to ceiling (or floor) effects: If the magnitude of the US is increased, CR magnitudes often increase commensurately. Nor can the asymptote be explained by limits in the amount of anticipation supportable by a given US: animals will often show superasymptotic CRs when two CSs which have previously been separately conditioned to asymptote are presented simultaneously as a compound. What, then, limits excitatory conditioning? The growth of the conditioned opponent.

Because the *b* process is small during the first few pairings of CS and US, the A states produced by the US will be relatively large (as in the first panel of Fig. 2). Therefore, the CS paired with those A states will show correspondingly large gains in its ability to elicit conditioned opponents (and other CRs). That is why the *b* process grows, why affective habituation occurs to the US, and why excitatory conditioning slows and then stops. Because the *b* process is larger on each successive trial, the US-produced A states experienced on each trial are smaller, and the CS paired with those A states shows smaller and smaller gains in excitatory strength. Excitatory conditioning and the growth of habituation should stop when the strength of the *b* process matches that of the *a* process [formally, when $a = b$, $\Delta V_x = k(a - b) = 0$].[5,6]

Thus the present theory, like Rescorla's and Wagner's, predicts the negatively accelerated learning curve. However, it does so by invoking a hypothetical process whose properties may explain a number of correlated empirical phenomena.

B. Habituation and Tolerance

The preceding account implies that reactions to USs should diminish over the course of Pavlovian conditioning experiments and should rebound when the US is presented unsignaled. This result has been reported in a number of conditioning preparations (see reviews in Kimmel, 1966; Kimmel & Burns, 1975). Similarly Siegel (e.g., 1976, 1978) has found that tolerance to the analgesic and hyperthermic effects of morphine is manifested only in the presence of those environmental stimuli which had previously been paired with morphine. When tested elsewhere, no tolerance was observed. Analogous phenomena can be demonstrated in the visual system: A red stimulus field (US) appears less intensely saturated when superimposed upon a black and white grating (CS) whose orientation had previously been paired with red; the same physical stimulus appears more red in the context of gratings of other orientations (Schull & Ollove, in preparation).

[5]It would seem to follow that all anticipatory and compensatory conditioned responses must reach asymptote on the same trial. However, this is not necessarily so. Suppose that morphine evokes several *a* processes (say, one responsible for analgesia, another for hyperthermia). Also, suppose that the *b* process which opposes hyperthermia grows faster than does the *b* process for analgesia. Then, conditioned responses which are related to hypothermia wiil reach asymptote sooner than those reinforced by analgesia. If this did turn out to be true, experimental analysis of the physiological subsystems involved might become possible. Different systems activated by the same US might attend to different kinds of cues, each system might achieve effective compensation at its own rate, or each system might affect different aspects of behavior or physiology.

[6]After the asymptote has been reached, should not some anticipatory CRs wane, since the CS is no longer followed by an affectively potent A state? Perhaps (Sherman & Maier, 1978). However, even on trials in which $a = b$, the animal's experience of the US could still be quite intense; it depends upon the simultaneity of the opponent processes. For example, the second panel of Fig. 2 depicts a trial in which the total strength of the *a* process is exactly matched by the combined strength of the conditioned and unconditioned *b* processes. While no excitatory conditioning should occur on that trial, this is not a neutral experience, and CRs may still be maintained.

C. Signaled versus Unsignaled Reinforcement

The notion that excitatory CSs elicit conditioned opponent processes implies also that, in general, unsignaled USs (i.e., USs which are not preceded by well-conditioned CSs) would be of greater affective potency than signaled USs. Support for this claim comes from a number of sources.

In experiments designed to elucidate memorial mechanisms in animal conditioning, Wagner and his colleagues have shown that unsignaled USs occupy and persist in short-term memory more than signaled USs do (see Wagner, Rudy, & Whitlow, 1973; see also reviews in Wagner, 1976, 1978). Such results are consistent with the view that signals elicit compensatory processes which attenuate the A states produced by the US. Of course, they are also consistent with Wagner's explanations in terms of the priming in short-term memory of a US representation by the signal.

D. Preference for Signaled versus Unsignaled USs

From the present perspective, signaled aversive USs should not only be less salient than unsignaled, they should be less aversive. By the same token, signaled rewards should be less pleasurable than are unsignaled ones. Animals' preferences should, and apparently do, reflect these differences. Given the choice in a shuttle box, rats do reliably prefer signaled over unsignaled shock. (Lockard, 1963; see review in Seligman & Binik, 1977). Although there is no shortage of theories about this phenomenon (cf. Badia and Harsh, 1977; Furedy & Biederman, 1976; Perkins, Seymann, Levis, & Spencer, 1966; Seligman & Binik, 1977), the preferences may emerge because signaled shocks are more effectively opposed than unsignaled shocks.

Do conditioned opponents also render signaled rewards less pleasurable? Perhaps. While experiments using electrical brain stimulation reward have shown preferences for signaled over unsignaled reinforcement (Cantor & Lolordo, 1970, 1972; not the result predicted by the present theory), in other experiments using liquid food reinforcement rats clearly preferred "pleasant surprises" to signaled rewards, as the present theory predicts (Hershiser & Trapold, 1971; Schull, Fullerton, & Neuringer, 1975). The nature and determinants of preference for signaled or unsignaled reward require further investigation (cf. Hershiser & Trapold, 1971; Perkins, 1955; Seligman, Maier, & Solomon, 1971, pp. 385–386); certainly there is no reason to assume that preferences are solely determined by affective habituation (Schull, Neuringer, & Fullerton, 1977).

E. Blocking and US Preexposure Effects

Kamin's blocking effect is perhaps the most important demonstration of the impotence of signaled USs; this may be "just" another instance of conditioned tolerance. If a US is presented in the context of strong excitatory CSs which elicit the *b* process, the US should produce a smaller A state, as in the second panel of Fig. 2. Neutral stimuli paired with the US on such occasions should show little increase of excitatory strength. Originally considered quite surprising, blocking has now been demonstrated in a variety of experimental settings, with conventional aversive USs, such as shock, pharmacological aversive USs, such as lithium chloride (Gillan & Domjan, 1977); and with food reinforcement (Allaway, 1971; Tomie, 1976).

Current research and theory about blocking and blockinglike effects may be converging on a view similar to the one suggested here. Tomie (1976) recently argued that blocking by contextual cues provided by the experimental setting may account for a large literature on "US preexposure effects" which shows that prior experience with a US reduces its ability to reinforce excitatory conditioning. In a recent review of that literature, Randich & LoLordo (1979) concluded that accounts based upon context blocking or upon "central habituation of the emotional response to the UCS" remain the most viable. Moreover, Gillan and Domjan (1977) and Braveman (in preparation) have independently suggested that blocking and US preexposure effects in taste-aversion learning could be due to the action of conditioned *b* processes. Each of these suggestions foreshadows the argument made here, that not only blockinglike effects but many other phenomena reviewed in this paper may parsimoniously be accounted for by a theory of central habituation based upon the concept of the conditioned opponent process.

F. Proximal US Effects

Another blockinglike effect may be due to the same mechanism. In rabbit eyelid conditioning (Terry, 1976) and in taste-aversion conditioning (Domjan & Best, 1977), it has recently been shown that presentation of a "proximal US" shortly before a CS is paired with a "conditioning" US attenuates the latter US's potency. As Domjan and Best suggested, this effect may occur because a *b* process lingers after the proximal US, and reduces the potency of the A state produced by the conditioning US. If the mechanism underlying this effect is in fact the conditioned opponent, then presenting an additional excitatory CS along with the proximal US should enhance the effect. This is a unique prediction of the present theory and should be tested.

G. Further Experimental Predictions and Corroborative Evidence

The following sections explicate some important experimental possibilities raised by the present theory. If the conditioned opponent theory is to be fully exploited and critically tested in the laboratory, new experimental designs will be required. Measures of affective and behavioral habituation to US presentations should be related to measures of the amount of conditioning which results from such presentations. It will then be possible to see whether, from experiment to experiment and from trial to trial, manipulations which enhance habituation also attenuate excitatory conditioning (as follows from the postulate that excitory conditioning is reinforced by A states) and whether manipulations which enhance excitatory conditioning also enhance long-term habituation (as follows from the hypothesis that the process underlying habituation is a conditioned response).

I will also identify the kinds of manipulations which should theoretically be particularly important. Insofar as the present theory is correct, such phenomena as habituation and conditioned tolerance, preferences for signaled or unsignaled reinforcement, limits to excitatory conditioning, blocking, and related effects will all be systematically affected by psychological and physiological manipulations which affect the strength of conditioned opponent processes.

H. Massed versus Distributed Trials

Varying the length of the intertrial interval is an example. The analysis applied to the proximal US effect implies that the shorter the time since the last US, the more likely it is that each US will overlap with the slowly decaying *b* process from the previous trial. The A state produced by each US will therefore be attenuated, and that may be why habituation is more complete when assayed during massed trials, while excitatory conditioning is less complete after massed trials.

The present theory posits that the *b* process is a CR and, like other CRs, it should be elicited more strongly after distributed trials. Therefore chronic habituation and tolerance should be strongest following spaced trials, provided that habituation is assayed in the presence of excitatory cues (e.g., in the experimental setting), after "proximal" *b* processes from previous USs have dissipated. (This is one point where the present theory can be pitted against Solomon's and Corbit's. In their formulation, the *b* process is strengthened nonassociatively, through exercise; therefore greater habituation should result from massed rather than spaced trials.) The best evidence on this point comes from studies on habituation of startle responses (Davis, 1970a, 1970b). The results were consistent with the conditioned opponent analysis: Startle to auditory USs showed more habituation during massed trials than during spaced, but when measured after training, spaced trials yielded more habituation.

I. The *b* Process as a Conditioned Response

By the hypothesis that the *b* process is a conditioned response, it is reasonable to ask whether other manipulations which reduce the strength of more conventional CRs also reduce the strength of the conditioned opponent.

Associative manipulations, such as extinction of the environmental CSs which elicit the conditioned opponent, should cause USs to regain their potency. Extinction has been shown to attenuate conditioned diminution of the UR in humans (Morrow, 1966), morphine tolerance in rats (Siegel, 1975, 1978), habituation to auditory stimuli in rabbits (reported in Wagner, 1976), and blocking (Kamin 1968; Tomie, 1976). By the same token, the presentation of conditioned inhibitory CSs, which inhibit CRs, should inhibit the conditioned opponent and again cause USs to produce larger A states. It has already been shown that excitatory Pavlovian conditioning is enhanced in the presence of conditioned inhibitors (Rescorla, 1971; Taukulis & Revusky, 1975); the present theory uniquely predicts that conditioned inhibitors should also attenuate habituation, tolerance, and other manifestations of the conditioned opponent. These predictions have not been tested (they apply also to backward inhibitory CSs, discussed in Section VI, D).

It might be possible to retard the growth of the conditioned opponent, like that of other CRs, by reducing the salience of conditioned stimuli. This can be done by latent inhibition, in which animals are preexposed to the nominal CSs which will subsequently be paired with the US. This manipulation has been shown to retard development of morphine tolerance in rats (Siegel, 1977a), of conditioned diminution of the UR in humans (Baxter, 1966), and of the McCullough effect in humans (Schull & Ollove, in preparation). Whether preexposure to situational cues routinely impairs other supposed manifestations of conditioned opponent processes remains to be seen.

If the *b* process behaves like a CR, it might be strengthened by various nonassociative procedures which strengthen other CRs. If so, there are habituative and blockinglike phenomena awaiting discovery. It might be possible to generate "conditioned" opponents through pseudoconditioning (see, e.g., Sheafor, 1975), or perhaps extinguished conditioned opponents can be rejuvenated through spontaneous recovery over time, or through disinhibition by novel stimuli.

J. Dishabituation and Deblocking

The present theory also suggests that one could disrupt blocking and enhance excitatory conditioning by using procedures which are known to disrupt habituation. Dishabituation commonly occurs on trials in which a novel stimulus is introduced (e.g., Thompson & Spencer, 1966), or when some parameter of the habituated-to US is changed (Graham, 1973). Now, Mackintosh and his colleagues have recently shown that blocking fails to occur (1) during the first few ("compounding") trials in which the novel target stimulus and the previously conditioned blocking stimulus are both paired with shock (MacKintosh, 1975a), and (2) on the trial following the unexpected addition or omission of a second shock (Dickinson, Hall, & Mackintosh, 1976). Consistent with Mackintosh's (1975b) attentional theory, they argue that blocking or deblocking occurs in such experiments when CSs lose or retain their salience. But perhaps deblocking occurs when the US regains salience through dishabituation. In the case (1) above, deblocking might occur during compounding because the novel CS acts as an external inhibitor of the conditioned opponent, just as it sometimes disrupts other CRs (see, e.g., Kamin, 1968). In the case (2), adding or omitting shocks might similarly disrupt the expression of the conditioned opponent on subsequent trials, perhaps by upsetting expectations. To evaluate these possibilities, Mackinstosh's procedures should be replicated in experiments designed to detect dishabituation as well as deblocking. By the present account, the two phenomena should be found to occur on the same trials as a result of the same manipulations. (A similar reinterpretation of Mackintosh's experiments has recently been made by Randich & LoLordo, 1979.)

K. Physiological Manipulations

It may also be possible to use physiological techniques to inhibit the conditioned opponent to some USs. Consider the (rather simplistic) hypothesis that the newly discovered endogenous opiates of the brain (e.g., Snyder, 1977) constitute a physiological mechanism for the conditioned opponent to painful or aversive USs. Given that opiates are notorious for their ability to reduce the aversiveness of painful stimuli and to produce pleasurable psychological states (the right characteristics for an opponent to pain), it is quite plausible that endogenous opiates would be released when conditioned stimuli signal impending electric shocks. The notion has clear implications: Opiate receptor blockers, such as Naloxone, could be used to nullify the conditioned opponent and affect fear conditioning and affective habituation in a systematic manner.

We (Ehrman, Josephson, Schull, & Sparich, 1979) have recently obtained some support for these speculations. Animals given naloxone when CSs are being paired with shock subsequently show a much larger conditioned emotional response to the CSs than do animals given saline during conditioning. Furthermore, in two blocking experiments we found that Naloxone substantially reduced or abolished the ability of a previously conditioned light to block conditioning of a tone; for animals given Naloxone during compound conditioning, the shock remained effective. Those results could simply mean that the effect of Naloxone is to increase general pain sensitivity as if shock intensities had been increased, whereas we might hope that Naloxone inhibits the actual mechanism of blocking. However, we are encouraged by the results from one group of animals given Naloxone during the light–shock pretraining as well as during compound conditioning; if Naloxone simply increase shock intensity, this would just be like conducting a blocking experiment with more intense shocks. While blocking was obtained, we also observed substantial conditioning of the tone.

Further evidence against a simple pain enhancement account of our results comes from shock escape experiments which show that rats do not behave when given the drug the way they behave when shock intensities are actually increased (Ehrman *et al.*, 1979; Goldstein, Pryor, Otis, & Larsen, 1976). Moreover, in an experiment reported before our own results were in, Fanselow and Bolles (1977) found that the rat's preference for signaled over unsignaled shock could be abolished by Naloxone. These results are consistent with the hypothesis that endogenous opiates are differentially released during signaled as opposed to unsignaled shocks, and they lend credence to the present theory.

Certainly it is too early to draw any conclusions about the relation (if any) between endogenous opiates and opponent processes, but the matter deserves further study. As I have tried to show in this section, the conditioned opponent theory and the animal conditioning paradigms discussed in this paper could provide useful tools for investigating psychological and physiological mechanisms of conditioning and affect.[7]

[7]This may be a good place to mention an important problem confronting proponents of opponent-process theory. While it may be that expected morphine injections do not produce analgesia, it is probably not true that fully expected shocks do not hurt. What exactly does the theory claim? The answer, frankly, is not clear. The theory refers to A and B states. Physiological and behavioral reactions to those states and to signals of those states can be specified, and changes in those reactions can be predicted with reasonable accuracy by the theory. The fundamental nature of A and B states is not specified, however, nor is it clear how *b* cancels *a*. (In the case of painful USs, the opiates may provide a clue: Users of opiate pain killers report that the "sensation" of pain is still there, it just does not bother them; see Mansky, 1978.) The answer will surely be different from reinforcer to reinforcer and from one stimulus dimension to another. For now the question remains open.

VI. Opponent States and Inhibitory Conditioning

So far we have considered situations in which the *b* process attenuates A states and so causes habituation and limits excitatory conditioning. In this section we are concerned with cases in which the *b* process is putatively stronger than the *a* process and so causes B states and inhibitory conditioning. The conditioned opponent theory suggests that B states occur on two occasions: (1) when excitatory CSs elicit the *b* process, but the US and therefore the *a* process do not occur, and (2) when the US is withdrawn, before the *b* process has died out (this is the B state emphasized by Solomon & Corbit, 1974).[8] Because the *b* process which predominates on such occasions is the opponent of the *a* process, animals' affective and behavioral reactions during B states should often be the opposite of their reactions during A states. And, according to the second postulate of our theory, conditioned stimuli paired with B states should undergo associative changes which are opposite of those undergone by CSs paired with A states.

A. Conditioned Opponent States.

Siegel's research provides compelling evidence that B states can be evoked by conditioned excitatory stimuli. To test the notion that the process responsible for morphine tolerance is a conditioned response, Siegel gave rats placebo injections in morphine-paired environments (i.e., he presented the CS, and omitted the US). Whereas in naive rats morphine increased body temperature and decreased pain sensitivity (A state), animals given placebo injections showed decreased body temperature and increase pain sensitivity (B state). With continued trials in which the morphine US was omitted, these conditioned opponent states extinguished, so that when morphine injections were resumed, animals were no longer tolerant (Siegel, 1975, 1978, 1979). Those results follow from the present theory.

How common are conditioned opponent reactions? Although it is usually assumed (and often observed) that CRs resemble URs, such results as Siegel's are not uncommon. Siegel (1975, 1979) has summarized 40 years of pharmacological conditioning literature which provides many examples of conditioned compensatory responses to insulin,

[8]Using excitatory CSs, it should also be possible to produce B states even without omitting or withdrawing the US. If two asymptotically conditioned excitors were presented, a double-sized conditioned *b* process might find itself opposing a single-sized *a* process. The resulting B state could cause the CSs to lose excitatory strength and could cause a neutral stimulus with which it is paired to gain inhibitory strength. These predictions also follow from the Rescorla-Wagner model and have been confirmed by Kamin and Gaioni (1974) and by Kremer (1978).

epinephrine, and other drugs. More recently Domjan and Gillan (1977) and Braveman (in preparation) have shown that compensatory CRs are evoked by stimuli paired with lithium chloride injections. Conditioned compensatory responses have also been reported for nonpharmacological disturbances. Cardiac deceleration is often the CR to shock-paired CSs, whereas the UR to shock is cardiac acceleration; presumably the compensatory CR mediates heart rate habituation to shock (Obrist, Sutterer, & Howard, 1972). In humans, adaptation of vestibular nystagmus to rotation is mediated by compensatory eye movements. These eye movements cancel the normal ("nontolerant") nystagmus reaction, are elicited by rotation-paired "ready signals," and persist for some time after rotation is terminated (Wendt, 1931). Finally, as has been noted, the McCullough effect can be considered a paradigmatic case of compensatory conditioning, albeit within the visual system. Consistent with the second postulate of the present theory, the conditioned opponent response, seen when the CS is presented and the chromatic US is omitted, is extinguished by repeated testing (Jones & Holding, 1975).

The present theory generalizes such observations; the same conditioned opponents responsible for habituation when USs are presented, and for afterreactions when USs are withdrawn, are also responsible for conditioned opponent states when the US is omitted in the context of excitatory CSs. This generalization applies to many kinds of USs. When the US is aversive, very similar opponent states (relief, joy) should be seen whether the US is withdrawn or unexpectedly omitted. Similarly, affective reactions when rewarding USs are terminated (frustration, disappointment) should be very much like reactions when expected rewards are omitted (cf. Amsel, 1958; Wagner, 1969c). Such opponent states from unfulfilled expectations do seem to exist, and to jibe neatly with Solomon's and Corbit's theory. The occurrence of such states follows from the hypothesis that the *b* process is elicited by conditioned excitatory stimuli.[9]

The conditioned opponent theory further postulates that such B states, whether produced by withdrawal or by omission of the US, are potent casual agents in conditioning experiments. By acting as endog-

[9]However, CSs do sometimes elicit what appear to be conditioned A-like states. When should we expect to observe which kinds of CRs? Siegel (1977b) discusses this problem in the context of pharmacological conditioning, in which for undetermined reasons, similar experiments have yielded conflicting results; he concludes that a solution awaits further research (see also Lynch, Stein, & Fertziger, 1976). Little more can be said here, but perhaps the present theory could aid such investigations by specifying a set of experimental operations which putatively affect conditioned opponents, and by indicating associative and habituative phenomena which can be used as indicators of the conditioned opponent's behavior.

enous "reinforcers" they are putatively responsible for extinction, conditioned inhibition, and backward inhibitory conditioning.

B. Extinction

In theory, as in practice, extinction is the opposite of acquisition. Whereas during acquisition a neutral CS is paired with an A state produced by the US and therefore gains excitatory strength, in extinction an excitatory CS is putatively paired with a self-produced B state and therefore loses excitatory strength. Similarly, whereas the conditioned opponent grows during excitatory conditioning, it shrinks during extinction as the CS loses its ability to elicit conditioned responses. Extinction must stop when the extinguished CS is no longer able to elicit the *b* process and produce a B state.

Note that our formal models do not differentiate between an extinguished CS and a neutral CS which has never been conditioned: Both have associative values of zero and neither can elicit CRs. Still, the conditioned opponent theory does not necessarily claim that extinction "undoes" a CS's association with the A state; rather, extinction establishes "counterassociations" with the B state. It could be these latter associations that are somehow upset in the phenomenon of "disinhibition."

Note also that the theory implies that stimuli paired with B states can lose the ability to elicit the *b* process (cf., Solomon & Corbit, 1974, p. 133). While this may seem inconsistent with the Pavlovian notion of stimulus substitution, it is consistent with the literatures reviewed above, and it makes adaptive sense. When the US is omitted, the *b* process is no longer functional; B states tell animals that they have overcompensated, and so during extinction, animals learn to stop overcompensating and producing B states.

C. Conditioned Inhibition

According to the conditioned opponent theory, when neutral stimuli are paired with a B state they putatively gain conditioned inhibitory properties. The properties of conditioned inhibitors are often found to be opposite to those of conditioned excitors, as would be expected if excitors and inhibitors acquired their properties through association with opposite states (cf. Hearst, 1972; Rescorla, 1969b; Rescorla & Holland, 1977). Thus, conditioned inhibitors reduce the strength of CRs which would otherwise be elicited by excitors ("summation"), they require more excitatory conditioning to reach a criterion level of response elicitation ("retardation"), and, as mentioned earlier, they can enhance a USs ability to reinforce excitatory conditioning. (This is just the opposite of blocking, in which conditioned excitors elicit the conditioned opponent; here, conditioned inhibitors putatively act by inhibiting the conditioned opponent.)

These properties of conditioned inhibitors can be captured by the simple statement that their associative values are opposite in sign to those of excitors, and it is a major virtue of Rescorla's and Wagner's model that it automatically assigns positive associative values to excitors and negative associative values to inhibitors. While the same can be said of the present theory [during B states the quantity $(a - b)$ is by definition negative, so the equation $\Delta V_x = k(a - b)$ yields negative changes in associative value for stimuli paired with B states], the conditioned opponent theory also gives some psychological meaning to these mathematical conventions and relates them to other opponent-process phenomena.

Furthermore, B states should be able to endow the CSs with which they are paired with properties beyond those implied by negative associative values. For example, the active preferences observed for conditioned inhibitory stimuli in taste-aversion experiments (e.g., Best, 1975) do not follow in a simple manner from the notion of associative negativity, though they do not make sense if those flavors are being associated with a pleasurable opponent state opposite to the lithium-produced malaise (cf., Domjan & Gillan, 1977).

D. Backward Conditioning

Since there are putatively two ways to produce B states, there should be two ways to produce an inhibitory conditioned stimulus. One way is to present a neutral stimulus on trials in which an excitatory CS but no US is presented; the B state produced by the excitor will then be paired with the neutral stimulus. This is the kind of manipulation emphasized by Wagner and Rescorla (1972).

Another inhibitory conditioning procedure was suggested by Solomon and Corbit. If a neutral CS is presented when the US is withdrawn, the CS will be paired with the post-US B state. Solomon and Corbit predicted that the properties of such "backward" CSs should be very different from those of CSs paired with A states. The present theory concurs: Such stimuli should acquire conditioned inhibitory properties.

The existing literature on backward conditioning can support many interpretations (Moscovitch & LoLordo, 1968; cf. Maier, Rapaport, & Wheatley, 1976; Wagner & Terry, 1975). Some evidence suggests that the first trials of backward conditioning yield excitation, not inhibition (Mahoney & Ayres, 1976). While the reasons for excitation are not clear (a lingering *a* process on early trials is a possibility), the absence of inhibition follows from both associative and nonassociative opponent process theories: On early trials the *b* process (and the post-US B state necessary for inhibitory conditioning) should be weak or nonexistent.

Whereas Solomon and Corbit attribute this weakness of the *b* process to lack of exercise, however, the conditioned opponent theory attributes it to the absence of CSs with the excitatory strength to elicit the *b* process. An experiment by Wagner and Terry (1975) favors the present account: Rats with equivalent prior exposure to shock had backward CSs paired with signaled or unsignaled shocks. Only the unsignaled USs supported backward excitatory conditioning.

After enough presentations of the US, backward inhibitory conditioning apparently does occur, and the sooner the CS follows the US, the more inhibitory strength it acquires (Maier *et al.*, 1976; Moscovitch & LoLordo, 1966). This result is consistent with the notion that a transient, post-US B state "reinforces" backward inhibitory conditioning.

Several unique and as yet untested predictions about backward conditioning also follow from the conditioned opponent theory. First, inhibitory conditioning should be more effective with signaled rather than unsignaled USs (the signal should optimally elicit the *b* process). Second, a backward CS should acquire inhibitory strength most rapidly if it is introduced when animals have already been preexposed to signaled shocks (so that the conditioned opponent is already strong when backward conditioning begins). Third, to the extent that a conditioned opponent causes the B state which promotes inhibitory conditioning, removal of the excitatory CSs which elicit the *b* process should prevent backward inhibitory conditioning. Finally, backward inhibitory CSs, like conditioned inhibitors should be able to inhibit the *b* process and its various manifestations.

E. Extinction of Inhibitory CSs

A significant failure of the Rescorla–Wagner model has proved to be its prediction that repeated nonreinforced presentations of conditioned inhibitors should cause them to lose their inhibitory properties. The prediction follows simply from the model; on such trials $\lambda = 0$ because no US is presented, and $\bar{V}$ is equal to V_x, which is negative for conditioned inhibitors. Therefore $\lambda - \bar{V}$ is positive, and the equation $\Delta V_x = k(\lambda - \bar{V})$ yields positive increments of V_x on each trial, until $V_x = \bar{V} = 0$. Yet in three experiments by Zimmer-Hart and Rescorla (1974), nonreinforced presentations of conditioned inhibitors had no extinctive effects.

The theory offered here does not generate the spurious prediction that conditioned inhibitors should be extinguishable in this manner: An inhibitor presented alone would be followed by neither an A state nor a B state, and so its associative strength should not be changed. However, this case is also worth examining for the light it sheds on the difference between the conditioned opponent theory and the Rescorla–Wagner theory. Throughout this paper it has been argued that the predictions of the Rescorla–Wagner model are often borne out because the intervening variables λ and $\bar{V}$ usually approximate the strength of the hypothetical *a* and *b* processes which actually underlie conditioning and habituation. In the present theory the *b* process is assumed to be an actual endogenous conditioned response whose behavior is often predicted by Rescorla's and Wagner's equations, but which is also subject to nonmathematical constraints which apply to other CRs. In the present case, if we were to assume that $b = \bar{V}$ when a conditioned inhibitor is presented alone, we would be faced with a conditioned opponent response of negative strength. For an actual conditioned response, this makes no sense,[10] and that may be why the Rescorla–Wagner model's prediction is not borne out.

Thus, while a theory such as the present one is necessarily speculative, it may have heuristic advantages over strictly mathematical models of conditioning. One virtue of the Rescorla and Wagner model is that it makes straightforward, unambiguous predictions about the behavior of a black box. It is also true, however, that the mathematical structure of a model need have no direct relation to the actual mechanisms operating within the box. And so when a formal model breaks down (as the Rescorla–Wagner model does in the MacKintosh deblocking experiments and the Zimmer-Hart and Rescorla experiments), it may say little about what is going on inside the black box. The conditioned opponent theory claims that inside the black box modeled by Rescorla's and Wagner's equations are the potentially measurable, manipulable *a* and *b* processes which are actually responsible for conditioning. The present theory thus manages to retain the formal structure and the predictive power of the Rescorla–Wagner model and to extend it to new phenomena. It might also let us peer into the black box.

[10]The concept of a negative *b* process might make sense in systems in which conditioned inhibitors did not simply inhibit the *b* process (as postulated here, and as would seem most efficient), but mobilized another antagonistic process which counteracted the conditioned opponent. (That antagonistic process could be the *a* process, or it could be some other kind of "anti-*b* process.") In systems organized that way, solitary conditioned inhibitors might in fact elicit something like an A state (or an anti-B state) which could cause the conditioned inhibitor to extinguish.

VII. Discussion

Is it reasonable to suppose that animals might be designed as the present theory suggests? I think so. The idea that nervous systems are designed to counteract disturbances of physiological and neural equilibria is by no means new. Cannon showed that compensatory mechanisms maintain physiological variables within limits necessary for survival; he also suggested that some of the "wisdom" of the body is acquired through "exercise and training" (Cannon, 1932/1963, p. 301). It also appears that nervous systems react to, and compensate for, stimuli whose internal effects range from the purely sensory (as in the visual system) to the intensely hedonic (as in the painful shocks, aversive illnesses, and pleasurable rewards used in conditioning experiments). It has been argued that the brain could be organized no other way (Ashby, 1960; Powers, 1973).[11] But one can also argue that learned regulation of affective equilibrium has a certain logic of its own.

While it is hard to prove, there seems little doubt that natural selection has endowed animals with intense hedonic reactions to particular aspects of experience. Animals (including humans) apparently experience intense positive reactions toward stimuli which relate to enhanced survival and reproduction (food when food deprived, warmth when chilled, mates and offspring, etc.); stimuli which relate to danger are often experienced as aversive (pain is usually a reaction to tissue damage, etc.). It therefore seems reasonable to suppose that affective reactions, in coordination with learning mechanisms serve to guide animals through life. Pleasurable experiences instigate behaviors and behavior changes which maximize the animal's commerce with survival-enhancing events. Aversive experiences steer the animal clear of risky situations.

However, a related aspect of intense sensation or affect is that it dominates experience, can be distracting, and can be disruptive of organized adaptive behavior. Hedonic experience, like sensory experience, must be regulated in such a way as to minimize intense deviations from neutrality without making animals insensitive to environmental contingencies. I suggest that conditioned opponent processes may serve to optimize the effects of intense hedonic stimuli upon instrumental behavior. They may serve remarkably well to ensure that animals habituate to just those hedonic stimuli which are constants in a given environment and are either under control or uncontrollable.

Consider aversive learning first. The present theory suggests that

[11]Indeed, those arguments suggest that some "conditioned" and "unconditioned" opponents might be learned "instrumental" responses which are "reinforced" by returns to equilibrium. The Pavlovian framework we have been using does not preclude this interesting possibility.

animals should react with maximum vigor and rapid learning to aversive stimuli which are novel to the particular situations in which they occur (conditioned opponents should be weak on such occasions). Until habituation occurs, aversive events would instigate strong withdrawal reactions and effectively punish behaviors which cause them. Animals should habituate to aversive stimuli only in those situations from which they have repeatedly been unable to extricate themselves (Pavlovian conditioning experiments are of this type; if our subjects had their way, they would never be exposed to aversive USs). Conditioned opponents may serve to reduce stress in such situations without precluding the possibility that the animal could learn to improve its objective situation: If a change in environmental contingencies or a new behavior pattern were to terminate or prevent an expected aversive stimulus, pleasurable conditioned opponent states (relief) would occur and could reinforce escape and avoidance behaviors (cf. Denny, 1971).

In the case of positive reinforcement, instrumental learning will promote habituation to pleasurable stimuli because animals will learn to administer reinforcers to themselves whenever possible. Instrumental learning should slow and performance should stabilize as conditioned opponents elicited by situational and response-produced stimuli come to coincide with the reinforcer. The animal's behavior should then settle into a relatively workaday routine; still, conditioned opponents will produce frustrative opponent states if expected reinforcers are unexpectedly omitted, and the animal could learn from these experiences (cf. Amsel, 1958; Wagner, 1969c).

Thus, conditioned opponent processes, in coordination with processes of instrumental learning, may minimize the disruptive effects of affect upon organized behavior, while maximizing the ability of survival-relevant hedonic events to shape behavioral propensities in a biologically adaptive manner. Natural selection may have ensured that pleasure-seeking animals methodically work to enhance their own survival by equipping its creatures with appropriate hedonic reactions to survival-relevant stimuli, with stimulus–stimulus and response–stimulus learning abilities, and with endogenous opponent processes which reduce hedonic reactions to familiar hedonic stimuli.

Less speculatively, the preceding argument also suggests that the interaction of Pavlovian and instrumental conditioning might profitably be studied using the present theory. The effects of conditioned opponents should influence the potency of hedonic stimuli as reinforcers and punishers; their effects should be witnessed when expected versus unexpected USs (and omissions of USs) are administered to reward or punish new behaviors. It is also possible that manipulation of response–reinforcer contingencies would affect the growth and elicitation of conditioned opponents and thus influence the progress of habituation and Pavlovian conditioning (see, e.g., Alloy & Ehrman, 1978). With more empirical and theoretical work on these matters, it may be possible to develop the argument sketched above so as to integrate the results of operant as well as Pavlovian conditioning experiments within an opponent-process framework (cf., Donahoe, 1977).

VIII. Summary and Conclusions

The conditioned opponent hypothesis—that endogenous compensatory responses are elicited by conditioned stimuli associated with states of disequilibrium—has far-reaching implications. It renders opponent-process theory consistent with findings that habituation and tolerance to sensory, pharmacological, and hedonic USs are context specific, and with indications that perceptual, behavioral, and psychological reactions opposite those produced by the direct effects of USs can be produced by omitting USs in the contexts in which they have been experienced before. With the postulate that A states reinforce excitatory conditioning, the conditioned opponent hypothesis suggests a new explanation for the excitatory asymptote, for blocking and blockinglike phenomena; it predicts that such phenomena will be found to be intimately related to habituation. With the postulate that B states reinforce inhibitory conditioning, the present theory indicates that the same procedures which produce opponent states should produce extinction, conditioned inhibition, and backward inhibitory conditioning.

Furthermore, with the assumption that the strength of the conditioned opponent is influenced by many of the same factors which are known to influence other conditioned responses, the present theory generates new predictions, suggests new experiments, and leads to a novel reinterpretation of the successes and failures of Rescorla's and Wagner's mathematical model of conditioning. Finally, with the assumption that A and B states can reinforce or punish instrumental responses, the conditioned opponent theory may be made applicable to instrumental-learning experiments.

The conditioned opponent theory is speculative. Nevertheless, it parsimoniously organizes a surprisingly large set of experimental findings with considerable success and raises a number of questions worthy of future investigation. The theory could therefore provide a useful conceptual framework for the study of the relations between affective habituation, Pavlovian conditioning, and instrumental learning, and perhaps also for manipulating and determining the physiological mechanisms underlying opponent-process phenomena in a number of domains.

REFERENCES

Allaway, T. A. *Attention, information, and auto-shaping.* Unpublished doctoral dissertation. University of Pennsylvania, 1971.

Alloy, L. B., & Ehrman, R. *Response-reinforcer independence interferes with subsequent acquisition of stimulus—reinforcer contingencies: Learned helplessness?* Paper presented at the 19th annual meeting of the Psychonomic Society, San Antonio, November 1978.

Amsel, A. The role of frustrative non-reward in noncontinuous reward situations. *Psychological Bulletin,* 1958, **55,** 102–119.

Ashby, W. R. *Design for A brain.* New York: Wiley, 1960.

Badia, P., & Harsh, J. Preference for signaled over unsignaled schock schedules: A reply to Furedy and Biederman. *Bulletin of the Psychonomic Society,* 1977, **10,** 13–16.

Baxter, R. Diminution and recovery of the UCR in delayed and trace classical GSR conditioning. *Journal of Experimental Psychology,* 1966, **71,** 447–451.

Best, M. R. Conditioned and latent inhibition in taste-aversion learning: Clarifying the role of learned safety. *Journal of Experimental Psychology: Animal Behavior Processes,* 1975, **104,** 97–113.

Braveman, N. S. The role of blocking and compensatory conditioning in the treatment preexposure effect. In preparation, 1979.

Cannon, W. B. *The wisdom of the body.* 1932 (revised 1939). Republished: New York, Norton, 1963.)

Cantor, M. B., & Lolordo, V. M. Rats prefer signaled reinforcing brain stimulation to unsignaled ESB. *Journal of Comparative and Physiological Psychology,* 1970, **71,** 183–191.

Cantor, M. B., & Lolordo, V. M. Reward value of brain stimulation is inversely proportional to uncertainty about its onset. *Journal of Comparative and Physiological Psychology,* 1972, **79,** 259–270.

Davis, M. Effects of interstimulus interval length and variability on startle-response habituation in the rat. *Journal of Comparative and Physiological Psychology,* 1970, **72,** 177–192. (a)

Davis, M. Interstimulus interval and startle response habituation with a "control" for total time during training. *Psychonomic Science,* 1970, **20,** 39–41.

Denny, M. R. Relaxation theory and experiments. In F. R. Brush (Ed.), *Aversive conditioning and learning.* New York: Academic Press, 1971.

Dickinson, A., Hall, G., & Mackintosh, N.J. Surprise and the attenuation of blocking. *Journal of Experimental Psychology: Animal Behavior Processes,* 1976, **2,** 313–322.

Domjan, M., & Best, M. R. Paradoxial effects of proximal unconditioned stimulus pre-exposure: Interference with and conditioning of a taste-aversion. *Journal of Experimental Psychology: Animal Behavior Processes,* 1977, **3,** 310–321.

Domjan, M., & Gillan, D. J. Aftereffects of lithium-conditioned stimuli on consummatory behavior. *Journal of Experimental Psychology: Animal Behavior Processes,* 1977, **3,** 322–334.

Donahoe, J. W. Some implications of a relational principle of reinforcement. *Journal of the Experimental Analysis of Behavior,* 1977, **27,** 341–350.

Ehrman, R. N., Josephson, P. J., Schull, J., & Sparich, C. Behavioral effects of the endorphin systems within instrumental and classical conditioning paradigms. Paper presented at the 50th meeting of the Eastern Psychological Association, Philadelphia, 1979.

Fanselow, M. S., & Bolles, R. C. *Naloxone attenuates rats' preference for signaled shock.* Paper presented at the 18th annual meeting of the Psychonomic Society, Washington, D.C., November 1977.

Frey, P. W., & Sears, R. J. Model of conditioning incorporating the Rescorla–Wagner associative axiom, a dynamic attention process, and a catastrophe rule. *Psychological Review,* 1978, **85**(4), 321–340.

Furedy, J. J., & Biederman, G. B. Preference for signaled shock phenomenon: Direct and indirect evidence for modificability factors in the shuttlebox. *Animal Learning and Behavior,* 1976, **4,** 1–5.

Gibson, J. J. Adaptation with negative aftereffect. *Psychological Review,* 1937, **44,** 222–244.

Gillan, D. J., & Domjan, M. Taste-aversion conditioning with expected versus unexpected drug treatment. *Journal of Experimental Psychology: Animal Behavior Processes,* 1977, **3,** 297–309.

Goldstein, A., Pryor, G. T., Otis, L. S., & Larsen, F. On the role of endogenous opiate peptides: failure of Naloxone to influence shock escape threshold in the rat. *Life Sciences,* 1976, **18,** 599–604.

Graham, F. K. Habituation and dishabituation of responses innervated by the autonomic nervous system. In H. V. S. Peeke & M. J. Herz (Eds.), *Habituation* Vol. I. New York: Academic Press, 1973.

Hearst, E. Some persistent problems in the analysis of conditioned inhibition. In R. A. Boakes & M. S. Halliday (Eds.), *Inhibition and learning.* New York: Academic Press, 1972.

Hering, E. [*Outlines of a theory of the light sense*] (L. M. Hurvich & D. Jameson, trans.). Cambridge, Mass.: Harvard University Press, 1964. (Originally published, 1920.)

Hershiser, D., & Trapold, M. A. Preference for unsignaled over signaled direct reinforcement in the rat. *Journal of Comparative and Physiological Psychology,* 1971, **77,** 323–328.

Hurvich, L. M., & Jameson, D. Opponent processes as a model of neural organization. *American Psychologist,* 1974, **29,** 88–102.

Jones, P. D., & Holding, D. H. Extremely long persistence of the McCulloch effect. *Journal of Experimental Psychology: Human Perception and Performance,* 1975, **1,** 323–327.

Kamin, L. J. Attention-like processes in classical conditioning. In M. R. Jones (Ed.), *Miami symposium on the prediction of behavior: Aversive stimulation.* Miami, University of Miami Press, 1968.

Kamin, L. J. Predictability, surprise, attention, and conditioning. In B. Campbell & R. Church (Eds.), *Punishment and Aversive Behavior.* New York: Appleton, 1969.

Kamin, L. J., & Gaioni, S. J. Compound conditioned emotional response conditioning with differentially salient elements in rats. *Journal of Comparative and Physiological Psychology,* 1974, **87,** 591–597.

Kimmel, H. D. Inhibition of the unconditioned response in classical conditioning. *Psychological Review,* 1966, **73,** 232–240.

Kimmel, H. D., & Burns, R. A. Adaptation in conditioning. In W. K. Estes (Ed.), *Handbook of learning and cognitive processes* (Vol. 2). *Conditioning and behavior theory.* Hillsdale, N.J.: Lawrence Erlbaum Associates, 1975.

Kremer, E. F. The Rescorla–Wagner model: Losses in associative strength in compound conditioned stimuli. *Journal of Experimental Psychology: Animal Behavioral Processes,* 1978, **4,** 22–36.

Lockard, J. S. Choice of warning signal or no warning signal in an unavoidable shock situation. *Journal of Comparative and Physiological Psychology,* 1963, **56,** 526–530.

Lynch, J. J., Stein, E. A., & Fertziger, A. P. An analysis of 70 years of morphine classical conditioning: Implications for clinical treatment of narcotic addiction. *Journal of Nervous and Mental Diseases,* 1976, **163,** 47–58.

Mackintosh, N. J. Blocking of conditioned suppression: Role of the first compound trial. *Journal of Experimental Psychology: Animal Behavioral Processes,* 1975, **1,** 335–345. (a)

Mackintosh, N. J. A theory of attention: Variations in the associability of stimuli with reinforcement. *Psychological Review,* 1975, **82,** 276–298. (b)

Mahoney, W. J., & Ayres, J. J. B. One-trial simultaneous and backward fear conditioning as reflected in conditioned suppression of licking in rats. *Animal Learning and Behavior,* 1976, **4,** 357–362.

Maier, S. F., Rapaport, P., and Wheatley, K. L. Conditioned inhibition and the UCS-CS interval. *Animal Learning and Behavior,* 1976, **4,** 217–220.

Mansky, P. A. Opiates: Human psychopharmacology. In L. L. Iversen, S. D. Iversen, & S. H. Snyder (Eds.), *Handbook of psychopharmacology* (Vol. 12). *Drugs of abuse.* New York: Plenum, 1978.

McCarter, A., & Silver, A. I. Letter to the editors. The McCullough Effect: A classical conditioning phenomenon? *Vision Research,* 1977, **17,** 317–319.

McCullough, C. Color adaptation of edge-detectors in the human visual system. *Science,* 1965, **149,** 1115–1116.

Morrow, M. C. Recovery of conditioned UCR diminution following extinction. *Journal of Experimental Psychology,* 1966, **71,** 884–888.

Moscovitch, A., & LoLordo, V. M. Role of safety in the Pavlovian backward fear-conditioning procedure. *Journal of Comparative and Physiological Psychology,* 1968, **66,** 673–678.

Murch, G. M. Classical conditioning of the McCullough effect: Temporal parameters. *Vision Research,* 1976, **16,** 615–619.

Murch, G. M. Letter to the editors. A reply to McCarter and Silver. *Vision Research,* 1977, **17,** 321–322.

Obrist, P. A., Sutterer, J. R., & Howard, J. L. Preparatory cardiac changes: A psychobiological approach. In A. H. Black & W. F. Prokasy (Eds.), *Classical conditioning II.* New York: Appleton, 1972.

Perkins, C. C., Jr. The stimulus conditions which follow learned responses. *Psychological Review,* 1955, **62,** 341–348.

Perkins, C. C., Seymann, R., Levis, D. J., & Spencer, R. Factors affecting preference for signal shock over shock signal. *Journal of Experimental Psychology,* 1966, **72,** 190–196.

Powers, W. T. *Behavior: The control of perception.* Chicago: Aldine, 1973.

Randich, A., & LoLordo, V. M. Associative and non-associative theories of the UCS pre-exposure phenomenon: Implications for Pavlovian conditioning. *Psychological Bulletin,* 1979, **86,** 523–548.

Rescorla, R. A. Conditioned inhibition of fear. In W. K. Honig & N. J. Mackintosh (Eds.), *Fundamental issues in associative learning.* Halifax: Dalhousie University Press, 1969. (a)

Rescorla, R. A. Pavlovian conditioned inhibition. *Psychological Bulletin,* 1969, **72,** 77–94. (b)

Rescorla, R. A. Variation in the effectiveness of reinforcement and nonreinforcement following prior inhibitory conditioning. *Learning and Motivation,* 1971, **2,** 113–123.

Rescorla, R. A. A model of Pavlovian conditioning. In V. S. Rusinov (Ed.), *Mechanisms of formation and inhibition of conditional reflex.* Moscow: "Nauka," 1973.

Rescorla, R. A., & Holland, P. C. Associations in Pavlovian conditioned inhibition. *Learning and Motivation,* 1977, **8,** 429–447.

Rescorla, R. A., & Wagner, A. R. A theory of Pavlovian conditioning: Variations in the effectiveness of reinforcement and nonreinforcement. In A. H. Black & W. F. Prokasy (Eds.), *Classical conditioning II: Current theory and research.* New York: Appleton, 1972.

Schull, J., Fullerton, A., & Neuringer, A. *Rats prefer unsignaled over signaled reward.* Paper presented at the Western Psychological Association Convention, Sacramento, April, 1975.

Schull, J., Neuringer, A., & Fullerton, A., *Rats prefer unsignaled over signaled reward.* Unpublished manuscript, 1977.

Schull, J., & Ollove, M. In preparation.

Sears, R. J., Baker, J. S., & Frey, P. W. The eye blink as a time-locked response: implications for serial and second order conditioning. *Journal of Experimental Psychology: Animal Behavior Processes,* 1979, **5,** 43–64.

Seligman, M. E. P., & Binik, Y. M. The safety signal hypothesis. In H. Davis & H. Hurvitz (Eds.), *Pavlovian-operant interaction.* Hillsdale, N.J.: Lawrence Erlbaum Associates, 1977.

Seligman, M. E. P., Maier, S. F., & Solomon, R. L. Unpredictable and uncontrollable aversive events. In F. R. Brush, (Ed.), *Aversive conditioning and learning.* New York: Academic Press, 1971.

Sheafor, P. J. "Pseudoconditioned" jaw movements of the rabbit reflect associations conditioned to contextual background cues. *Journal of Experimental Psychology: Animal Behavior Processes,* 1975, **104,** 245–260.

Sherman, J. E., & Maier, S. F. The decrement in conditioned fear with increased trials of simultaneous conditioning is not specific to the simultaneous procedure. *Learning and Motivation,* 1978, **9,** 31–53.

Siegel, S. Evidence from rats that morphine tolerance is a learned response. *Journal of Comparative and Physiological Psychology,* 1975, **89,** 498–506.

Siegel, S. Morphine analgesic tolerance: Its situation specificity supports a Pavlovian conditioning model. *Science,* 1976, **193,** 323–325.

Siegel, S. Morphine tolerance acquisition as an associative process. *Journal of Experimental Psychology: Animal Behavioral Processes,* 1977, **3,** 1–13. (a)

Siegel, S. Learning and psychopharmacology. In M. E. Jarvik (Ed.), *Psychopharmacology in the practice of medicine.* New York: Appleton: 1977. (b).

Siegel, S. The role of conditioning in drug tolerance and addicition. In J. D. Keehn (Ed.), *Psychopathology in animals.* New York: Academic Press, 1979.

Siegel S. Tolerance to the hyperthermic effect of morphine in the rat is a learned response. *Journal of Comparative and Physiological Psychology,* 1978, **92,** 1137–1149.

Skowbo, D., Timney, B. B., Gentry, T. A., & Morant, R. B. McCullough effects: Experimental findings and theoretical accounts. *Psychological Bulletin,* 1975, **82,** 497–510.

Snyder, S. H. Opiate receptors and internal opiates. *Scientific American, 1977,* **236**(3), 44–56.

Solomon, R. L., & Corbit, J. D. An opponent-process theory of motivation: I. Temporal dynamics of affect. *Psychological Review,* 1974, **81,** 119–145.

Stein, L. Habituation and stimulus novelty: A model based on classical conditioning. *Psychology Review,* 1966, **73,** 352–356.

Taukulis, H. K., & Revusky, S. H. Odor as a conditioned inhibitor: Applicability of the Rescorla–Wagner model to feeding behavior. *Learning and Motivation,* 1975, **6,** 11–27.

Terry, W. S. The effects of priming US representation in short-term memory on Pavlovian conditioning. *Journal of Experimental Psychology: Animal Behavior Processes,* 1976, **2,** 354–369.

Thompson, R. F., & Spencer, W. A. Habituation: A model phenomenon for the study of neuronal substrates of behavior. *Psychological Review,* 1966, **73,** 16–43.

Tomie, A. Interference with autoshaping by prior context conditioning. *Journal of Experimental Psychology: Animal Behavior Processes,* 1976, **2,** 323–334.

Wagner, A. R. Stimulus validity and stimulus selection. In W. K. Honig & N. J. Mackintosh (Eds.), *Fundamental issues in associative learning.* Halifex: Dalhousie University Press, 1969. (a)

Wagner, A. R. Stimulus selection and a "modified continuity theory." In G. H. Bower & J. T. Spence (Eds.), *The psychology of learning and motivation* (Vol. 3). New York: Academic Press, 1969. (b)

Wagner, A. R. Frustrative nonreward: A variety of punishment. In B. A. Campbell & R. M. Church (Eds.), *Punishment and aversive behavior.* New York: Appleton, 1969. (c)

Wagner, A. R. Priming and STM: An information processing mechanism for self-generated or retrieval generated depression in performance. In T. J. Tighe & R. N. Leaton (Eds.),

Habituation: Perspectives from child development, animal behavior, and neurophysiology. Hillsdale, N.J.: Lawrence Erlbaum Associates, 1976.

Wagner, A. R. Expectancies and the priming of STM. In S. H. Hulse, H. Fowler, & W. K. Honig (Eds.), *Cognitive processes in animal behavior.* Hillsdale, N.J.: Lawrence Erlbaum Associates, 1978.

Wagner, A. R., & Rescorla, R. A. Inhibition in Pavlovian conditioning: Application of a theory. In R. A. Boakes & M. S. Halliday (Eds.), *Inhibition and learning.* New York: Academic Press, 1972.

Wagner, A. R., Rudy, J. W., & Whitlow, J. W. Rehearsal in animal conditioning. *Journal of Experimental Psychology,* 1973, **97,** 407–426.

Wagner, A. R., & Terry, W. S. Backward conditioning to a CS following an expected *vs* a surprising UCS. *Animal Learning and Behavior,* 1975, **3,** 370–374.

Wendt, G. R. Negative adaptation as an active positive antagonism. *Psychological Bulletin,* 1931, **28,** 681–682. (Abstract)

Zimmer-Hart, C. L., & Rescorla, R. A. Extinction of Pavlovian conditioned inhibitors. *Journal of Comparative and Physiological Psychology,* 1974, **86,** 837–845.

MEMORY STORAGE FACTORS LEADING TO INFANTILE AMNESIA[1]

Norman E. Spear

STATE UNIVERSITY OF NEW YORK AT BINGHAMTON
BINGHAMTON, NEW YORK

I. Introduction

Humans are notably deficient in remembering events of their early childhood, a phenomenon that Freud referred to as "infantile amnesia." Animal models of infantile amnesia permit, potentially, a wide-ranging

[1]Preparation of this article was supported by grants from the National Science Foundation (BNS 74-24194 and BNS 78-02360). Completion of this paper depended upon the excellent secretarial assistance of Teri Tanenhaus and technical assistance of Normal G. Richter and I am most grateful for it. I wish also to express my gratitude to those colleagues who generously provided their astute professional advice concerning the content of this paper: Linda Patia Spear, Robert I. Isaacson, Richard G. Bryan, Gayle Solheim, and Robert Infurna. In this respect I am especially indebted to Ralph R. Miller for his extraordinarily thorough editorial and general suggestions.

ISBN 0-12-543313-1

experimental analysis of the phenomenon. Like the exaggerated forgetting of infancy that seems to occur among humans, tests with a variety of animals indicate that specific episodes learned during physiological immaturity are also forgotten more rapidly than those learned in adulthood (Campbell & Coulter, 1976; Campbell & Spear, 1972; Spear, 1978; Spear & Campbell, 1979). There is little need to defend the application of animal models for understanding biomedical problems of importance to human welfare, in view of the successful history of this practice. Of more significance are specific advantages in using the rat to analyze the problem of infantile amnesia. These include: the relatively rapid maturation of the rat which compresses the interval between infancy and adulthood to the order of 1 or 2 months rather than the 15 or 20 years required with the human; the extensive knowledge of ontogenetic changes in neurophysiological features of the rat's central nervous system and their close parallel with those of other altricial mammals, such as man; and the relatively rich learning episodes that ethically may be presented the rat for later tests of infantile amnesia, including levels of emotional stress that could not possibly be implemented in experimental investigations of the phenomenon with humans.

When I refer to infantile amnesia in this chapter, it is with regard to the established difference in rate of forgetting by immature compared to mature animals; and "forgetting" is used in an operational sense to refer to the decrement in learned performance that occurs between learning and a later test for retention. This broadens the concept a good deal relative to the original Freudian term, where reference was restricted to retention intervals of several years usually encompassing a sizable portion of a human's life span (for elaboration of the Freudian view, see White & Pillemar, 1979). The infantile amnesia with which we are dealing is described merely as more rapid forgetting by immature than by mature animals.

The simplicity of this definition should not obscure the difficulty in achieving satisfactory experimental tests of infantile amnesia. For instance, to account for differences in forgetting in terms of differences in maturation, we must be certain that level of maturation is not confounded by other factors that also might alter rate for forgetting, such as degree of learning and motivation. The point has been repeated to a tiring degree in analytical papers on infantile amnesia, but it is a fundamental feature of experimental design and cannot be evaded. Negligence of this issue is all right only if one is content to conclude that differences observed in the test of forgetting are due either to difference in the age of the animal, or to the degree of learning attained prior to the retention interval, or to differences in conditions of motivation; but such a conclusion would hardly be suitable for building theories about the effect of age on forgetting.

I emphasize this point of experimental design because the present contribution considers features of information processing that appear to be correlated with age and may contribute to exaggerated forgetting of the events of ones infancy. These features often concern differences in the quality of learning. At this time the intention is to employ such differences as explanatory factors in respect to infantile amnesia. However, as these factors become better understood and are perhaps shown to alter the rate of forgetting, separable from the influence of age, they will become sources of experimental confounding rather than sources of explanation. This is mentioned not as an unnecessary lesson in elementary experimental design but to place some perspective on the present level of understanding of infantile amnesia and the scope of the present paper. In short, we are dealing with a subject variable (age) which, like sex differences or differences in skin pigment, includes a vast array of correlated features. The task of determining which features are and which are not necessary or sufficient for influencing rate of forgetting may be expected to be lengthy and tedious.

The central idea of this chapter is that age-related differences in forgetting may depend on age-related differences in what is stored as the memory of a particular learning episode. By a "memory" is meant the organism's multidimensional record of a particular set of events or "episode."

To evaluate this idea I will begin with a brief categorization of a variety of theories of infantile amensia, and their evaluation. This provides the rationale for the major section concerning the potential importance of the stage of initial formation of memory, termed here, "memory storage," for determining infantile amnesia.

What is the likelihood that in comparison to adults, immature animals learn different things, and perhaps fewer things, about a task that is to be remembered—even when the experimenter's best measures of learning indicate that degree of learning is equal for animals of all ages? What is the possibility that immature animals are especially "prepared" to learn certain things? Quite beyond sensory and perceptual limitations, might immature animals simply store some events more readily than others as part of a cohesive memory, because of the animals' developmental status? If so, does this imply that the laws of the ontogeny of learning and retention *must* be essentially task-specific? In considering these questions I will present evidence that such a requirement of task specificity for the ontogeny of learning and retention would be quite premature.

The overall attempt is to provide an alternative to the physiological–psychological dichotomy suggested by Campbell and Spear (1972) as a framework for studying infantile amnesia. This earlier view considered two general sources of infantile amnesia: (1) the physiological limitations or peculiarities of immature animals and (2) the animals' age-specific behavioral dispositions and experiences. It was presented as an idealized model for the study of infantile amnesia and has led to some useful experiments (e.g., Campbell, Misanin, White, & Lytle, 1974). However, the value of such a model ultimately is limited because a dichotomy between physiological and psychological factors cannot, of course, be genuine. Furthermore, recent advances in the field have suggested new approaches that may be more fruitful. I propose that the study of infantile amnesia focus on the consequences of immaturity during original memory storage and the effects of growth, broadly defined, interceding between this storage and the retention test.

II. Alternative Theories of Infantile Amnesia

Why the events of infancy should be more susceptible to forgetting than those of later life has been the subject of frequent theoretical speculation. The topic cannot really be said to have undergone genuine theoretical debate because this would imply a somewhat more systematic set of theoretical issues and structure than has been the case. So rather than as "debate," theoretical consideration of the topic is better characterized as "speculation," and rather free-wheeling speculation at that, because so little experimental analysis has been completed.

Freud's stimulating ideas represent the first theoretical views of infantile amnesia to be influential. As White and Pillemer (1979) have documented, the Freudian viewpoint encompasses two explanations of infantile amnesia: (1) Events of infancy no longer are accessible to the adult because, upon emergence of the reality principle, memories representing the child's formerly basic hedonic existance were repressed; (2) the adult is impaired in reconstructing the events of childhood because the adult's representation of reality is so disparate from that used by an infant.

To Freud's view may be added a number of other readily generated and plausible notions as to why infantile amnesia occurs; they are of interest here because they may be distinguished in terms of two characteristics. The first concerns the permanence of infantile amnesia. While one group of theories expects that memories for events of infancy ultimately would be retrievable under relatively innocuous experiential or environmental circumstances, another expects that without drastic physiological intervention, infantile amnesia could be neither prevented nor alleviated. As to the first group: The Freudian interpretation based on repression expects that with the proper psychotherapy, infantile amnesia will be alleviated; Tompkins (1970) emphasized the exaggerated change in stimulus context between infancy and adulthood as the source of infantile forgetting and suggested that if the context of infancy could be reinstated, so would the memories of infancy; for those views holding that specific aspects of an episode are represented by infants and adults in terms of such different words or concepts that the infant version cannot be translated by the adult (e.g., Allport, 1937), the expectation must be that memories of infancy are retrievable if one could only "break the code." In contrast to these notions are those holding that the infant has inadequate neurophysiological equipment to store and maintain memories or that subsequent morphological development in the growing brain precludes retrieval of a memory due to the complex overlay of additional synapses; such theories would expect that access to infantile memories could be gained only through abnormal alterations in the central nervous system. For example, the view that encephalization includes active inhibition of the expression of early memories traceable to development of the forebrain, suggests that extirpation of the forebrain might be expected to permit retrieval of these memories and hence, alleviation of infantile amnesia.

The second characteristic dividing theories of infantile amnesia is the locus of its fundamental source. While one set of theories emphasizes subsequent growth of any of several types as the fundamental reason for infantile amnesia, another set identifies immaturity during memory storage (i.e., during original learning, when the information is acquired) as the cause of the more rapid forgetting. Freudian repression of infantile memories, for instance, concerns ontogenetic changes that may be characterized simply as the product of postacquisition growth. Examples of other views that fit in this category emphasize the "amnesic" consequences of growth-induced changes in the organism's perception of learning episodes and the context in which they occur, or of the increasing inaccessibility of stored memories as a consequence of morphological development in the central nervous system, or indeed of any other aspect of development, such as neurochemical changes that occur during growth. The alternative grouping of theories that accounts for infantile amnesia by immaturity during memory storage is illustrated by each of the following hypotheses: (1) Stored memories will be manifested to the extent that they are represented redundantly in the central nervous system, and the limited storage capacity of the immature animal precludes or limits such redundancy. (2) The immature animal is limited in the amount of information it can process with respect to any given episode and so does not store a sufficient number of contextual memory attributes to support later retrieval of the target memory. (3) The general physiological and neurochemical capacities of the immature animal are basic limitations to permanent memory storage due to the competing demands of growth (e.g., a notion that so much protein synthesis is required for basic physiological growth that little can be spared for the process of storing memories).

These two distinctions among theories of infantile amnesia are significant. With regard to the first distinction—the permanence of infantile amnesia—if the experimental analysis of infantile amnesia is to proceed at the behavioral level at all, it will be necessary to identify treatments that do not require traumatic physiological intervention but nevertheless prevent or alleviate infantile amnesia. If the effect is invariant regardless of experiential differences, however, then we will be directed not only to a particular kind of theory but also to an experimental analysis dealing with neurophysiological and neurochemical variables rather than with acquired conflicting memories, perceptual change, retrieval cues, and so forth. As to the second distinction—whether infantile amnesia is primarily due to immaturity during initial storage of the memory (memory storage) or to events that accompany subsequent growth—an equal significance is seen in how the experimental analysis of infantile amnesia will help us understand more general issues in the processing of memories. For instance, with "physiological growth" essentially a once in a lifetime experience and somewhat restricted in its time course, we can expect that if infantile amnesia could be understood solely in terms of this parameter, study of this phenomenon would tell us relatively little about other aspects of forgetting and retention.

Broad explanatory factors such as growth and immaturity during memory storage encompass a great deal, but they are neither sufficiently precise, nor do they exhaust the potential explanations for infantile amnesia. For instance, both of these factors assume that the exaggerated forgetting of infancy is caused by a mechanism unique to immature animals and not shared by adults. This assumption may be inappropriate. It is entirely possible that forgetting in immature animals is caused by precisely the same basic mechanisms as in adults but the immature animals are simply more susceptible to them. While these alternatives cannot be clearly dissociated on the basis of the evidence and experimental methods developed so far, and while they are certainly not mutually exclusive, the distinction is at least useful for organizing what is known and what might be learned about infantile amnesia. That immature animals may be especially susceptible to adult sources of forgetting will be discussed in a moment. For now, we consider the alternative, that the exaggerated forgetting among immature animals is uniquely determined.

III. Unique Mechanisms of Forgetting among Immature Animals

If infantile amnesia reflects a unique mechanism of forgetting among immature animals, what is it? Toward an answer, I choose to emphasize the two broad theories of the phenomenon discussed previously.

The first possibility, you will recall, is that for the purpose of later remembering, the immature animal is simply deficient in original storage of the memory relative to adults. It is convenient to consider issues of retention and forgetting by viewing the "memory" representing a given episode as multidimensional, including a set of attributes that represent discernible events constituting the episode (Bower, 1967; Spear, 1971, 1973, 1976; Underwood, 1969). From this view we might expect that immature animals store too few attributes to support later retrieval of the memory; alternatively, they might store those memory attributes that happen to be most susceptible to forgetting, while those stored by adults are better suited to resist the forces of forgetting and support subsequent retrieval of the target attribute of the memory.

For the second possibility, a unique mechanism associated with growth has seemed appealing. This appeal arises chiefly from the context of the classical definition of infantile amnesia, where the nominal source of forgetting is a long interval between learning and the demand for retrieval of the memory. In terms of characteristics of the brain that have been linked to learning and retention, substantial physical growth occurs during the interval between infancy and adulthood (for a brief review, see Campbell & Spear, 1972). It should be appreciated also that in addition to a retention interval, a variety of other experimental operations qualify as "sources of forgetting" and these too might interact with features of growth to exaggerate forgetting (Spear, 1978). Implicit here is the related appreciation that the interval between learning and testing cannot itself be directly responsible for forgetting and as the underlying forgetting mechanisms correlated with the interval become identified, some but not others may be found to interact with growth.

The structure of this discussion will proceed from this point in three basic sections. The first will consider evidence bearing upon growth as a mechanism of forgetting possibly unique to immature animals. The next discusses whether immature animals are more susceptible to the same sources that cause forgetting in adults. The final and major section considers evidence addressing the possibility that immature animals are uniquely deficient in initial memory storage in such a way as to accelerate later forgetting.

Although the possibility is not ignored here, the present analysis does not consider in detail whether memory retrieval might be deficient in immature animals. There are two reasons for this. First, the conventional experimental paradigm for assessing infantile amnesia tests adults for retention of infantile or adult memories; for those animals presented the critical episode-to-be-learned as infants or adults, the retention interval is sufficiently long that all are adults at the time of the memory retrieval (even though one set of adults may be a bit younger than the other). While we might expect the effectiveness of memory retrieval to change ontogenetically, especially if the nature of the stored memory differs as a function of age and if the efficacy of retrieval depends ultimately on what is stored ("encoding specificity"), there would seem to be no a priori basis on which to expect the *process* of memory retrieval to differ among young and middle-aged adults. The second reason, largely a consequence of the first, is that there are insufficient data to apply to this issue of retrieval differences. The question of how the process of retrieving memories for specific episodes might differ as a function of age is an important one and surely will be studied extensively in the future. Our present analysis of age-dependent forgetting may have to be modified considerably when such data are in, especially with respect to tests of age dependency in forgetting over relatively short intervals, where animals differ significantly in level of maturity at the time of the retention test as well as during original learning. Until more is known about maturation of the retrieval process, however, we must proceed on what is known about other aspects of memory processing.

IV. Does Growth Produce Forgetting?

If some aspect of the animal's growth during a retention interval is responsible for the exaggerated forgetting observed at the end of that interval, then the amount of forgetting should change in accord with the growth that takes place. By modifying thyroid activity or the secretion of growth hormone from the pituitary, it is possible in principle to systematically control the amount of growth between learning and the test for retention. While studies of this kind are in at least a preliminary stage in our laboratory and others (Murphy & Nagy, 1976), analytical problems are enormous. For instance, the multiple action of drugs used to alter growth patterns by modifying the finely tuned endocrine system includes effects that potentially could affect retention performance, whether or not growth were altered. In short, clear evidence about infantile amnesia is not yet available from studies of this kind. Three other experimental strategies have addressed whether growth induces forgetting, two rather directly through manipulation of subject variables and the third by applying reactivation treatments intended to alleviate forgetting in accord with the growth that occurs between learning and testing.

A. Altricial versus Precocial Animals

Mammalian species differ markedly in the level of neurophysiological maturity found at birth, even within limited classes such as the rodent. Like the human, the newborn rat has a thoroughly undeveloped central nervous system at birth and so is quite dependent on parental care and its own neurophysiological maturation for survival to adulthood. In contrast, the guinea pig emerges from the womb with a central nervous system that is essentially adultlike and with an appearance and behavioral repertorie that make it seem within minutes of birth as merely a scaled-down, miniature adult. Campbell and associates Campbell, Misanin, White, & Lytle, 1974) capitalized on this striking species difference in their empirical assessment of how neurophysiological growth between learning and testing (or immaturity during memory storage) contributes to infantile amnesia. Their reasoning was this: If the difference in forgetting by immature compared to mature rats is greater than that found for immature and mature guinea pigs, one could infer that it is the rats' initial immaturity or subsequent growth of their central nervous systems during the rentention interval that is responsible for their infantile amnesia; but if infantile amnesia were as great in the guinea pigs as in the rats, then experiential (psychological) factors would seem of more importance to infantile amnesia. The results were really quite clear: After learning of either of the two tasks, discriminated escape or passive avoidance, forgetting after a long interval was greater among immature rats (15–25 days old) than adults, but forgetting of the same tasks by immature guinea pigs (5 days old or less) did not differ from that shown by adult guinea pigs, even after intervals of longer duration than those used for the rats.

Interpretation of behavioral differences between species is notoriously difficult and subject to question. Campbell *et al.* (1974) were of course fully aware of the interpretive limitations in their study and we need not dwell on these. For our present purposes, however, the confounding of growth during the retention interval by degree of maturity during memory storage (also noted by Campbell *et al.*) is notable here because of the example it provides: The central nervous system of the young guinea pigs not only undergoes less growth during the retention interval than that of the young rats but also is more mature during the original storage of the memory. Is it possible to unravel and eliminate this common confounding? I believe the answer is yes, but moreover, to the extent that memory storage is found to differ in immature and mature animals, separation of the consequences of this factor from that of growth will be absolutely necessary if we are to analyze infantile amnesia properly. We consider this in more detail later.

B. Metamorphosis

If growth causes forgetting, then in the normal animal periods of accelerated growth should be accompanied by acclerated forgetting. Can one confirm this by identifying such periods and observing exaggerated forgetting when they occur? Unfortunately, while spurts of growth of many varieties can be identified within individual animals, this ordinarily cannot be accomplished until well after the beginning of the spurt. Also, such spurts are unlikely to be at all uniform in duration. Within some species, however, a special period of dramatic growth—metamorphosis—is relatively uniform and immediately obvious. Memory theorists often have speculated that forgetting might be especially marked when, for example, a creature acquires a memory as a green, crawling caterpillar and is tested for it as a white-winged, airborne moth.

The fundamental question is whether forgetting during metamorphosis is any different than if the same interval had elapsed without metamorphosis. Certain theories predict more forgetting during metamorphosis due to the contextual change between memory storage and memory retrieval. Others expect less forgetting during metamorphosis, because at this time the animal's general activity lessens and so the probability of interpolated acquisition of conflicting memories (and hence, retroactive interference) should also be lessened. The study that comes closest to a thorough test of the alternatives is that of Miller and Berk (1976; see also Alloway, 1972). These investigators studied the African frog, *Xenopus lacuis*, comparing its forgetting during metamorphosis with that by the premetamorphosis tadpole or the postmetamorphosis frog. All animals were given an equally long retention interval. Although forgetting was greater when these animals were trained and tested as tadpoles than when trained and tested as frogs, thus verifying infantile amnesia for this species, forgetting over the period of metamorphosis was no greater than that for the older animals.

These results imply that either the relative inactivity during metamorphosis reduced infantile amnesia in the metamorphizing animals or these animals were sufficiently mature to be spared infantile amnesia;

but there is no indication from these results that growth per se is conducive to forgetting. The issue cannot be said to be closed because during its metamorphosis, the African frog does not undergo a particularly drastic change in either its general activity levels or the development of its central nervous system. However, these results do suggest that it would be unwise to ignore experiential factors in favor of brain growth as a major contributor to infantile amnesia.

C. Reactivation Experiments

If animals are reexposed following a retention interval to selected aspects of a learning episode, forgetting of that episode may be alleviated (Haroutunian & Riccio, 1977; Spear, 1973, 1976). From the view that reexposure to selected fractional portions of the learning episode can cause the stored memory of the episode to be restored to an active state, such reexposure has been termed a "reactivation treatment." The reactivation-treatment technique has been applied by Spear and Parsons (1976) to test certain certain theories of infantile amnesia including one hypothetical consequence of growth—hence its discussion here.[2]

Suppose that following a long retention interval, a reactivation treatment were presented to animals that had been immature when they acquired the target memory. Would alleviation of forgetting be any greater or less than that found for adults given the same treatment? This question is pertinent because different theories of infantile amnesia provide different answers.

As mentioned earlier, at the most general level some theories simply do not provide for the retrieval of the memories of infancy without drastic physiological intervention, while others would predict that relatively innocuous reactivation treatments could aid remembering about infancy. Before reviewing specific theoretical decisions that may be reached through the reactivation paradigm, it is useful to note how, empirically, alleviation of infantile amnesia must be defined.

An effective reactivation treatment would be expected to alleviate forgetting in adult as well as in immature animals; therefore to show *alleviation of infantile amensia*, one must show that forgetting of infantile

[2]It is notable that technical and conceptual innovation by Carolyn Rovee-Collier and her associates has permitted the initiation of similar tests with human infants, 2–3 months old, as subjects. The experiments by Rovee-Collier, *et al.*, to date, have established the following: (1) operant conditioning and good retention over 24 hours (Rovee & Fagin, 1976); (2) forgetting that seems maximal after a week (Sullivan & Rovee-Collier, 1979); and (3) alleviation of this forgetting after as long as 4 weeks have passed since conditioning, when a reactivation treatment is introduced 24 hours prior to the retention test (Rovee-Collier, 1978).

memories is alleviated more than that of adult memories. It is insufficient to show that the forgetting of infantile memories is reduced. Stated in this way, we shall see that with a few debatable exceptions, there are no firm indications at present that infantile amnesia can be either prevented or alleviated.

As there exists no systematic theory of infantile amnesia, the answers provided by reactivation experiments are limited to theoretical issues of a more general nature. At this level of analysis the question is the degree to which forgotten infantile memories remain present in storage but inaccessible as opposed to their becoming totally unavailable (i.e., are lost from storage). If forgetting of infantile memories is lessened through application of reactivation treatments, then we may infer that storage had remained at least partially intact pending retrieval.

It may also be possible to draw from reactivation experiments a weak inference as to precisely which aspects of the learning episode are stored but become inaccessible during the retention interval and which either were simply not stored originally or were rendered irreversibly unavailable. For instance, suppose the pretest presentation of a particular stimulus element (reactivation treatment) was found to alleviate forgetting after a long interval but not after a shorter one. From this we might infer that the memory attribute representing that particular stimulus was fully active after the shorter interval (because its arousal by the reactivation treatment did not alter retention) but became inactive or inaccessible as the interval between training and reactivation lengthened. This inference would be weak because, for example, retrieval of the target memory attribute after the shorter interval may have proceeded independently of the reactivated memory attribute if a large number of alternative attributes were accessible at that point to aid retrieval.

Another possible inference from reactivation experiments concerns what is stored. Assuming the encoding specificity principle (Tulving, 1972), the elements of a reactivation treatment that alleviate forgetting can be inferred to be identical, or at least sufficiently similar, to some of those represented in memory storage as memory attributes of the learning episode. Now suppose that for animals given a learning episode as infants or as adults, a particular reactivation treatment alleviates the forgetting of adult memories more than for the infant memories, while a different reactivation treatment has the opposite effect, i.e., greater alleviation in forgetting of the infant memories. Such a result can lead to the inference that the immature and adult animals differ either in what is stored originally or in what is forgotten during the retention level.

The latter inference emerges from several assumptions within the theoretical framework (Spear, 1971, 1973, 1978) that has guided research in my laboratory. In this view, retrieval of a target attribute of a memory is the direct consequence of the arousal of a sufficient number or proportion (or kind) of the memory attributes that had been stored with the target in the representation of the learning episode. Presentation of a particular aspect of the original learning episode is assumed to arouse the attribute representing that aspect, if the animal notices this presentation. When a reactivation treatment is effective in alleviating forgetting, it may be assumed that the treatment stimuli correspond to those represented as memory attributes and that these attributes are otherwise inaccessible at the time of the reactivation treatment. So, an ineffective reactivation treatment could mean that the corresponding events of the learning episode were either not stored originally, or were not forgotten, or were permanently lost after acquisition. The primary inference therefore is that the reactivation treatment effect for a particular age of subject but not for another age identifies either a difference in what was stored originally to represent the learning episode or a difference in what has become permanently unavailable or inaccessible over time. The inference is weak because of the large number of questionable assumptions that lead to it, but it does provide testable outcomes.

The experimental paradigm that would lead to the above inferences requires systematic variation in age and the presence or absence of each of several kinds of reactivation treatments, plus comparisons in each age and reactivation condition between trained animals that have been given the reactivation treatment and those that have not, and between untrained animals given the reactivation treatment and those not. It is perhaps not surprising, therefore, that a complete study of this kind is rare. A few years ago, in our laboratory, Patricia Parsons and Norman Richter conducted such a study in terms of retention of Pavlovian fear conditioning (some of these data are presented by Spear & Parsons, 1976), but it was not published because the results indicated no notable differences between immature and mature animals in the effectiveness of particular reactivation treatments.

An example of potential interest, however, has arisen recently in a doctoral dissertation completed by Dr. Paul Sussman of Carleton University. In the experiment of particular interest, Sussman compared the influence of a reactivation treatment on long-term retention (28-day interval) in rats given avoidance conditioning when 19 days of age or 47 days of age (Sussman, 1978, Experiment 6). Prior to the test for retention of either passive avoidance or one-way active avoidance, the animals given the reactivation treatment were first reexposed briefly to the training apparatus and then 1 hr later, we administered an inescapable and unavoidable footshock in a quite different apparatus. We need not consider in detail the control conditions included in Sussman's experiment except to assert that the results of these seem to permit this important conclusion: The reactivation treatment was more beneficial to retention by immature animals than by mature animals for both avoidance tasks. This is of interest because with a nearly identical active-avoidance task and retention test, but a different reactivation treatment, our results have been the opposite of Sussman's, with animals trained as adults benefiting more from the reactivation treatment than those trained when immature (Spear & Parsons, 1976, p. 162). Whereas Sussman's reactivation procedure involved the rat's reexposure first to the apparatus and then later to unsignaled, inescapable footshock, the reactivation treatment we had used was a signaled and escapable (but not avoidable) footshock given in the training apparatus (see also Spear, Gordon, & Martin, 1973). At the moment I have not the slightest idea why Sussman's treatment had more benefit for the relatively immature animals while ours had less, but it is these sorts of differences (preferably compared within a single experiment, of course) that may provide some insight as to what is stored or forgotten by immature animals in comparison to adults.

With the exception of the above results by Sussman (1978, Experiment 6), studies of the influence of reactivation treatments on retention by rats of differing ages have, to date, indicated a tendency for reactivation treatments to be more effective among more mature animals (Spear & Parsons, 1976; Spear & Smith, 1978). It should be clear, however, that the evidence does not yet permit a firm general conclusion on this matter.

A final prediction emerging from the reactivation treatment paradigm is that immature animals should benefit more when such treatments are distributed throughout the retention interval than when a single treatment is given at the end of the interval. This expectation was developed from a few tentative assumptions: (1) that the manner in which the infant perceives its environment or organizes it through concepts of mnemonic categories (or "schemata," "structures," or whatever) differs from that used by the same animal as an adult, and the difficulty in translation impedes retention; (2) that when a memory is converted from a passive to an active state (as presumably caused by a reactivation treatment, for example), it becomes susceptible to modification in accord with the animal's contemporary perceptual and organizational dispositions; and (3) that such modification or "accomodation" of the memory aids in the translation between the form of the memory stored as an infant and what is to be remembered as an adult.

So far, there has appeared only one test of such a prediction, reported by Spear and Parsons (1976), and this was really not adequate to permit a firm decision on the matter. Spear and Parsons reported that following forgetting of classical fear conditioning, a single reactivation treatment presented just 24 hr prior to the retention test was as effective as several reactivation treatments distributed throughout the retention interval of several weeks, and this relationship did not change whether the animals had received their original conditioning as infants, weanlings ,or adults. That only a single task was represented in these tests, and this a simple one involving no instrumental responding and with little control to be acquired by discrete stimuli (and so perhaps little requirement for special perceptual or conceptual organization), enhances the usual hesitancy to accept the null hypothesis for this problem. To the extent that the assumptions are viable, therefore, the need for thorough testing of the above prediction is obvious.

V. Are Immature Animals Especially Susceptible to Adult Sources of Forgetting?

Before proceeding to a discussion of how memory storage factors might contribute to infantile amnesia—the primary topic of this paper—one more possibility must be considered: Perhaps infantile amnesia is not due to mechanisms unique to maturing animals. Perhaps, instead, the same underlying mechanisms are responsible for both infantile and adult forgetting, but infants are more susceptible to them. A predominant source of forgetting among adults is interference, retroactive and proactive; we now consider whether retention of immature animals is more susceptible than that of adults to such interference arising from acquired conflicting memories.

Relatively few studies have addressed the topic of age-related susceptibility to interference in retention. The best of these studying retroactive interference was recently conducted by Berk (1978) of Brooklyn College, and for proactive interference, by G. S. Smith (1978) of SUNY, Binghamton. The results of both studies indicate that immature animals are more susceptible to interference-induced forgetting than adults. While both are thorough, well-controlled studies that warrant careful attention, they are considered only briefly here because they are not central to the major topic of this contribution.

Berk (1978) presented thirsty rats with contingent pairings of a specific tone and a footshock and later assessed retention by the extent to which these animals suppressed their drinking of sweetened condensed milk on exposure to that tone or similar tones (an index of "conditioned emotional response," CER). Training parameters were carefully adjusted so that rats were equated in level of original conditioning, whether conditioned at age 19 days or in adulthood. With a retention interval of eight or more days, the rat pups displayed infantile amnesia. For the tests specifically addressed to retroactive interference, however, a short interval was used that yielded no age differences in forgetting without an interference treatment between conditioning and testing. To provide a source of retroactive interference, the fundamental manipulation was introduced between conditioning and the retention test. Animals were exposed to interpolated presentations of a tone in the absence of shock. Some animals were given the conditioning tone and others either no tone at all or one of several tones that deviated systematically from the frequency of the conditioning tone. The question was whether the degradation of original conditioning caused by this source of retroactive interference (i.e., primary or generalized extinction) would differ for the immature and mature animals in terms of a subsequent retention test. The basic results indicated that relative to comparable animals not given interpolated exposure to tones, their occurrence caused more retroactive interference for the infant than for the adult rats. This conclusion agreed with that from another good experiment by N. Smith (1968).

To test for ontogenetic differences in the influence of proactive interference on forgetting, G. S. Smith (1978) compared retention of a discriminated escape response by infant (16 days old) and adult rats exposed, prior to learning the critical discrimination, to one of five levels of conflicting escape–response contingencies. The two extremes of these levels of prior contingencies were no experience with any aspect of the task (except handling) and the exact reversal of the critical discrimination. The three remaining conditions included: (1) a sequence of footshocks identical to that given the basic reversal condition and presented in the same apparatus later used for discriminated escape learning, but with no regular contingency between any stimulus or response and termination of footshock; (2) the same footshocks but with termination of footshock upon entry into one of the goal boxes of the discriminated-escape apparatus, with the "correct" goal box varied randomly from trial to trial; (3) the same footshocks as in the other conditions but on an entirely noncontingent basis presented in an apparatus quite different from that used for discriminated escape learning.

Following learning of the critical discriminated-escape task, retention tests were given to independent groups of animals after intervals of 2 min, or 1, 7, 30, or 65 days (the two longer intervals given only to adults). The results of the retention test—where entry into either of the two alternative goal boxes yielded escape from the footshock—may be seen in Fig. 1. The results were quite simple. Forgetting by infant animals was enhanced by sources of proactive interference, while that of adults was not. The latter finding with adult animals—no enhancement of

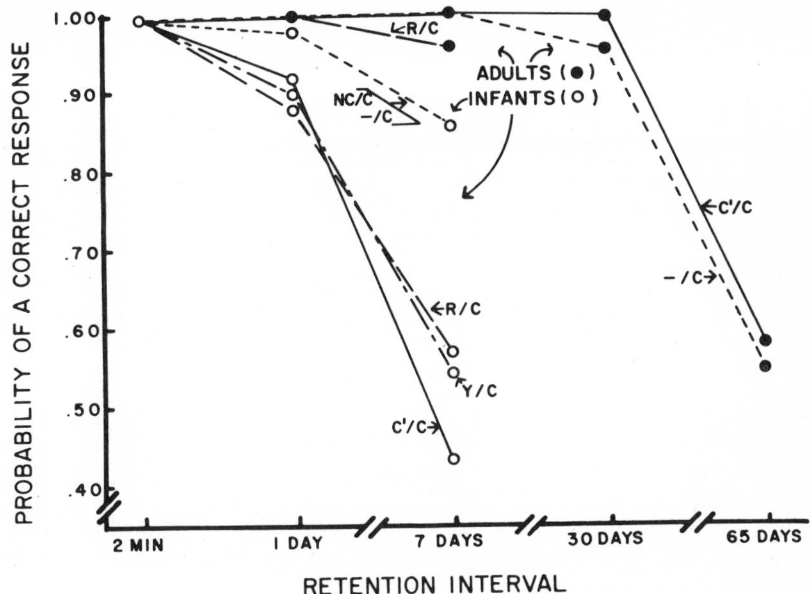

Fig. 1. Probability of a correct response during critical discrimination learning (C) is shown as a function of length of the retention interval, age during learning (infants were 16–17 days old, adults were about 80 days old), and the treatment that preceded critical learning as the source of proactive interference. Prior to critical learning, five independent groups of rats received either: the reverse discrimination (C′/C); footshock in the same apparatus as critical learning but termination contingent upon entry into either of the two goal boxes, with the correct goal box on any given trial determined at random (R/C); footshock in the same apparatus with termination not response dependent but equated in duration on each trial with that of a yoked subject in the basic control condition (Y/C); noncontingent footshock given in an apparatus quite different from that of discrimination learning (NC/C); or no prior treatment at all, the basic control condition (–/C). Because of their relatively rapid forgetting, infant subjects represented in this figure were given no retention interval longer than 7 days.

forgetting a simple position discrimination over a long retention interval, due to the prior conflicting learning—is consistent with a large number of previous experiments from our laboratory and others (e.g., Zentall, 1970; for reviews, see Gleitman, 1971; and Spear, 1971). Relative to other infants given no prior conflicting contingencies, proactive interference is seen in terms of enhanced forgetting across a 7-day period among infants given any one of the three conflicting contingencies in the apparatus that later was used for the critical discrimination learning. Comparable prior experience with footshock in a different apparatus did not affect their forgetting. Because the level of learning the critical discriminated-escape task was held constant and the rate of this learning was not systematically related to the degree of forgetting associated with a particular contingency, and because there was no significant interaction between age and prior contingency in terms of rate of learning, it can be stated that the phenomenon shown here is one of forgetting and does not merely reflect differential degrees of learning.

These results lead collectively to the conclusion that age-related differences in susceptibility to interference remain a viable source of age-related differences in forgetting. On this basis, any theoretical view of infantile amnesia treating the phenomenon exclusively as due to sources of forgetting unique to immature animals would be at least premature, and possibly in error.

VI. Do Immature Characteristics of Memory Storage Produce Forgetting?

The present section emphasizes a single point: Beyond age-dependent differences that may exist in the forgetting of a common set of memorial representations, infantile amnesia might occur because the memorial representations held by neonates or infants are different from those held by older animals exposed to the same learning episode. This could be so in spite of measured equality in how much learning took place originally.

I take the view that immature animals notice different events than adults notice presented the same episode. Also, immature animals probably store fewer memory attributes than adults to represent an episode. Therefore, both what is stored and how much is stored may differ.

Although my conjectures are plausible, there is not much solid evidence to support them. For children, a deficiency in the number of attributes stored can be inferred from their consistent deficiency relative to adults in standard memory-span tests, and there is reasonably good evidence for an age-related difference in what is learned, at least for verbally oriented tasks (e.g., Bach & Underwood, 1970; Melkman & Deutsch, 1977). For animals there has been still less evidence, even though the learning episodes on which they are tested may be said to include a wider variety of separable events than is represented in a list of words.

We now consider recent evidence that may be brought to bear on this topic.

A. How Might Forgetting Be Related to Memory Content?

The issues detailed previously are important for interpretation of infantile amnesia. From the basic assumption that retention will be an increasing function of the number of events processed during testing that correspond to those represented in the originally stored memory, two simple implications emerge. First, if immature animals store fewer memory attributes than adults, then the probability of a match-up between these stored attributes and the events of the retention test will be lower than for memories acquired by adults. Second, a similar deficiency in this match-up would occur if the memory attributes of the infant were different from those stored by older animals for the same episode. By definition, tests for infantile amnesia occur when the infants are significantly older. It is notable that such a mismatch between stored memory attributes and events noticed during the retention test would be greatest when the test requires relearning. Under this condition, the test fully incorporates the earlier episode. Infantile amnesia has seemed most evident in terms of a relearning test (Spear, 1971).

Before I elaborate further on such implications, it should be made clear that I am *not* saying that infantile amnesia is merely a matter of poorer learning by immature animals rather than greater forgetting. If so, the issues would be trivial for the purpose of understanding infantile forgetting. The phenomenon is of interest precisely because the infant memories can be manifested so clearly in behavior shortly after they are acquired. Rather, discussion here is directed at the possibility that age-related differences in precisely what is learned about a particular episode interact with the subsequent occurrence of a long retention interval to yield differences in amount forgotten. A parallel may be found in recently evolving explanations of the effect of proactive interference on the forgetting of verbal memories. Here, emphasis has shifted from previously suspected interactions between length of the retention interval and accessibility of prior conflicting memories, to the prior memories' influence on qualitative differences in what is actually learned (stored) and the consequential differences in subsequent forgetting as the retention interval lengthens (Hasher & Johnson, 1975; Spear, 1978, p. 214).

The simple observation most central to this discussion is that there is not a perfect correspondence between what is learned (the content of a memory) and the behavior manifest as a consequence. Basically, this is no different than the classical distinction between learning and performance. However, because the content of a memory may interact with a source of forgetting to determine performance on a retention test, the implications go further. For instance, the number or kind of memory attributes stored originally by an adult may be largely redundant and unnecessary for behavioral manifestation of the target memory attribute shortly after learning and yet crucial for its retrieval at a later time. In like fashion, but more relevant at this point, while storage of a particular number or kind of memory attributes may be quite sufficient for manifestation of appropriate behavior shortly after learning, it might be inadequate to promote the retrieval of that memory and the occurrence of that behavior at a later time; and this may provide the prototypic circumstances for memories acquired in infancy.

In summary, it is to be understood that the experimental operations that make up the learning episode—and hence, the "nominal content" of the memory to be stored—are assumed to be held constant for immature and mature animals. Also assumed held constant is degree of learning, defined as the probability of manifesting that memory in terms of the target behavior prior to the introduction of the source of forgetting (operationally, the long retention interval). The question is whether age-related differences in the actual content of the stored memory interact with the source of forgetting to yield age-related differences in forgetting. It may be anticipated that this question is not readily answerable because the basic influence of the content of a memory on forgetting is largely uncertain and has been found to be of relatively little importance (Spear, 1978, pp. 437–466).

B. Toward an Empirical Analysis of Memory Content

It is useful to consider the two major forms that an age-related difference in memory content might take. The first is that, relative to adults, infants might simply store too few attributes to the exclusion of those which although redundant for initial manifestation of the memory, are important for its later retrieval. The second possibility is that immature animals may store as many attributes as adults but the "wrong" ones, specifically those attributes that happen to be most susceptible to the detrimental forces of the source of forgetting and hence not accessible at the long-term retention test.

An implication from each of the above is that perhaps, by age-specific disposition, immature animals store and retain certain attributes as well as adults but fail to store those most critical for later retention. As an illustration, rat pups could store quite different information than adults to represent a common learning episode, but so long as they have in common one item of information that is sufficient for accuracy (e.g., follow odor A), their performance on an immediate test may be identical to that of adults that had actually learned a good deal more than merely to follow A. Adults may also have learned, for instance, to follow odors B, C, and D that happen to be at the same locations as A, and they may have learned as well to turn left at the corner, enter the brighter alley, and so forth; although unnecessary for performance immediately after learning, this initially redundant information may be critical for support of later memory retrieval. In one sense, this is an indictment of the ambiguity of our measurement technique and our behavioral units of analysis, and ultimately we must address this issue by determining more fully what is stored as the memory representing a particular episode. A recent Ph.D. Thesis by James Wolz in our laboratory served as a preliminary attempt to do so empirically while studying the specific influence on forgetting of age-related differences in what was stored in a memory.

The general purpose of Wolz's study was to determine whether neonatal rats (11-day-old) compared to infants (16-day-old) differed in the information they employ in learning a simple discrimination and in remembering it over a long interval. The learning episode required performance of a discriminated escape in a T maze in which spatial and odor differences between the two alternatives were perfectly correlated and consequently redundant. Following acquisition of the discrimination to a common criterion, a test given a short time (40 min) later assessed the extent to which the odor and spatial information had been employed during learning by the 11-day-old compared to the 16-day-old rats. To permit assessment of the relative forgetting of these sources of information, identically trained rats were tested 5 days after the original learning. Although the analysis of these data is not yet complete, it appears that so far as forgetting is concerned, the present study added little to our knowledge simply because, in contrast to the indications of pilot experiments, forgetting after 5 days was essentially maximal in all conditions for both age groups.

Two differences of interest did emerge. Both concerned the short-term tests of which stimuli were processed by the 11- and 16-day-old rats in solving the discrimination. For this assessment, four experimental test conditions are of primary importance. In one condition, animals were simply retrained on the original discrimination, which indicated essentially perfect retention for both age groups. In another condition, both odor and spatial location of the correct alternative were reversed to provide another indication of simple retention, this time in terms of negative transfer. For this index, too, there were no differences in the performance of the 11- and 16-day-old pups (both showed a great deal of negative transfer).

The important conditions for our purpose involved partial reversal shifts; in one, only the odors (but not the spatial locations) paired with the correct alternative were reversed and, in the other, only the spatial location (but not the odors) of the correct alternative was reversed. Both of these treatments thoroughly disrupted performance among the 16-day-old animals. At this age, discrimination performance during the early part of reversal did not differ from that of animals previously trained on the spatial discrimination. In contrast, the 11-day-old animals behaved as if they had learned nothing about the spatial dimension; they continued to respond to the odor that previously had been paired with escape, regardless of its spatial location. When the 11-day-olds had only the odors reversed, their transfer performance was equal to that found when both odor and spatial location were reversed. However, when only spatial location was reversed, these 11-day-old animals persisted in running to the previously safe odor and so, during the early portions of reversal, made many more errors when only the spatial location of the correct alternative was reversed than when the odor dimension was reversed. Results from other conditions included by Wolz to assess the relative importance of the correct and incorrect odors, an issue not of direct relevance to the present discussion, also agreed with the general conclusion that the 11-day-old animals learned only about odor while the 16-day-old animals learned about odor and spatial location.

More precisely, the evidence indicated that both the 11-day-olds and the 16-day-olds employed the odor dimension in solving the discrimination and employed it with about equal effectiveness; but the 16-day-old animals also employed the spatial discrimination, and as effectively as the odor discrimination, while the 11-day-olds did not. One possible implication is that in comparison with the 11-day-old rat, the 16-day-old is more capable of developing associations involving stimuli redundant to acquisition of a discrimination. If this were so, the next question would be whether this acquired redundant information might be responsible for better retention by 16-day-old than 11-day-old rats. Unfortunately, the limitations on measurement of forgetting in the Wolz experiment preclude an answer to this question. It is important to be cautious, however, in noting that this is not the only implication. Rather than age-related differences in capacity for redundant information processing, what may be reflected instead are only age-related differences in attentional dispositions or, even more basically, sensory capacities. However, to the extent that older animals emerge from a learning episode with more information, there remains a possibility that it is this extra information that is responsible for their better retention after longer intervals.

C. Episodes (Learning Tasks) Consistent with the Ecology of the Immature Rat

The preceding suggestions imply that infantile amnesia might not occur as strongly for some episodes as for others. For instance, simple episodes with only a few separable events, or those with events to which immature and mature animals attend equally, might show no more susceptibility to forgetting by the younger than by the older animals. To test such a notion requires consideration of how the immature animal's world compares with that of the adult. What does the immature rat do in its nest and to what does it attend there that might lead to our construction of experimental episodes that would be represented equally in memory storage by the immature and mature rat? This approach is becoming increasingly common, as illustrated in a recent volume (Spear and Campbell, 1979; see especially chapters by Rosenblatt and by Blass *et al.*). The present section briefly illustrates the spirit of this approach.

The ontogeny of learning and retention is best viewed with careful consideration for the natural requirements of adjustment among immature animals. The alternative, to treat immature animals as mature ones that happen to be incompletely formed and smaller, is not only misleading but also is likely to cause underestimation of the animal's potential for learning at young ages. This was the case, for example, with Fuller's (Fuller, Easler & Banks, 1950) and Scott's (1958) influential work several years ago with dogs; on the basis of failures to show that neonates could be conditioned readily with techniques applied to adults, it was concluded that associative processes did not contribute much to the adaptation of the neonate. The fact is that, helpless and protected though the rat may be as a neonate, there are specific environmental pressures that tax its dispositions for behavioral plasticity. In terms of responding to those specific events most crucial to its normal adaptation, there is now evidence that the neonate as young as 1 or 2 days of age clearly can adjust its behavior to the environment by learning to respond differently than before to certain stimuli, and can show retention for this learning over surprisingly long periods.

Within the last few years, close observation of neonates in the nest through simulated ethological techniques has been combined with improved experimental techniques to teach us more about the behavior of these animals (Blass, Kenny, Stoloff, Bruno, Teicher, & Hall, 1979; Rosenblatt, 1979). Beginning at about 3 days old postnatal, rats begin to show more activity in the home nest than elsewhere, essentially limited to head lifting at this age. By days 5 and 6, the rat will approach the home nest shavings as opposed to clean shavings. Conceivably this could be on the basis of thermal gradients, but more probably it is on the basis of odor. Rats distinguish maternal odors as early as day 3 and use the odor of the mother as a basis for returning from a distance after day 10, when they begin to leave the nest. Whereas 8-day-old rats will settle in the nest when placed there, beginning at about day 10, rat pups tend to leave it when placed there.

Behavioral effects of stimuli associated with the home nest are rather profound. General activity in isolated rats peaks at day 15 but is curtailed sharply by the presence of home nest objects. We will see that a variety of other behaviors are also modified rather drastically when the rat pup detects the presence of objects associated with the home nest. Incidentally, the enhanced general activity found in isolated rats away from the home nest seems clearly to be a consequence of stress or fear and not curiosity or exploration.

Attachment to the nipple in newborn animals seems dependent on the initial presence on the nipple of the mother's amniotic fluid and later of saliva from the rat pup, thus implicating odors and tastes as important features of environmental control. It is known that to some extent rat pups, as other animals, orient to and find nipples also on the basis of thermal gradients, although absolute temperature of the mother does not seem particularly important until relatively late in the neonate's life. It is not until about the age of 11 or 12 days that rat pups will respond adversely to a lowered temperature of the mother's ventrum.

Internal regulation of the intake of nutrition through stomach loading, cellular dehydration, or cholecystokinin (a hormone in the gut believed to inhibit feeding in adults) does not begin until day 15, obtaining adult levels at about day 21. Prior to day 15, for example, rat pups will suckle without regard to whether the nipple is lactating. Indeed, such neonates will go to a good deal of effort in order to suckle on a nonlactating nipple in the same way they will strive to be close to an adult rat whether or not the opportunity to suckle is present.

Such considerations, derived from recent work by Amsel (1979), Blass *et al.* (1979), Campbell and his associates (Campbell & Raskin, 1978; Randall & Campbell, 1976) and Rosenblatt (1979; see also, e.g., Almli & Fisher, 1977; Altman & Bulut, 1976), tell us that the world of the neonatal rat is dominated by tastes, odors, temperature differences, and ultrasounds, yet with suckling and crawling its only notable instrumental behaviors. With the onset of what we will call "advanced infancy" in rats (say, 15–20 days of age), visual stimuli and noises of lower frequencies than before appear to gain in importance. Also, items of a somewhat new texture are consumed, although because the food and liquids available at the nest site are those also taken in by the mother, the tastes are probably not different than those present from birth in its mother's milk. The empirical question to be addressed is, for an episode consisting primarily of elements frequently processed by immature animals—such as odors, tastes, sounds, and suckling—how will learning and forgetting by neonatal and infant rats compare with that by adults? The *apparent* answer is that the learning by immature rats is more rapid and the forgetting less than expected from earlier evidence.

D. Evidence Suggesting that the Nature of the Episode-To-Be Remembered (Memory Content) Affects Neonatal Learning and Forgetting

Prior to a few years ago, learning and retention by neonatal and infant rats was assessed with tests modeled largely on those employed to test adults. Aside from scattered attempts to study classical conditioning in very young rats, the most extensive investigation in altricial neonatal rodents was that conducted in the laboratories of James Misanin and Z. Michael Nagy (for a review of these studies, see Nagy, 1979; Spear, 1978, pp. 222–227). In general terms, their work indicated that the rat became capable of 24-hr retention of a simple escape response at about 9 days of age, although capable of showing some indices of learning it a few days earlier and of learning and retaining a spatial discrimination a few days later. The emergence of comparable capacities in the mouse was found to occur in roughly similar fashion. It was especially notable, therefore, when Rudy and Cheatle (1977, 1979) reported that if rats only 2 days old were made ill in the context of a specific odor, they manifested a conditioned aversion to that odor 6 days later, at an age of 8 days. At about the same time as Rudy's and Cheatle's initial experiments, Blass and his colleagues reported evidence for the learning of a position discrimination and significant retention 48 hr later among rats only 7 days old, when the reward for entering the correct goal box of the Y maze was suckling from an anesthetized female. Equally striking, Kenny and Blass (1977) reported that this 48-hr retention by the 7-day-old rat was equal to that found in rats as old as 21 days! Also during this period, Amsel and his colleagues found that 10- to 12-day-old rats responding to obtain access to an anesthetized adult female readily learn to increase their running speeds with practice in a straight alley, and to decrease their speeds with surprising abruptness when such access is removed. Under similar conditions, rats of this age also were found quite capable of learning a successive discrimination when one floor texture led to the anesthetized female and the other did not (Brake, 1978). Moreover, when rats 12–13 days old were reinforced (i.e., given access to the adult female) on less than 100% of the acquisition trials, they later showed conditioned persistence in traversing the alley during extinction trials (Amsel, 1979). Finally, as Altman and his colleagues have shown, rats 6 days of age seem capable of learning a position discrimination in order to return to their home nest (e.g., Altman & Bulut, 1976).

Do these instances of remarkable learning and retentive capacities in the neonatal rat merely reflect age-dependent "preparedness" (see Seligman & Hager, 1972)? Are we to find in these results the implication that when certain contingencies involve circumstances of special importance to the neonate's adjustment and adaptation, learning and retention may proceed at adultlike levels almost independently of the animal's level of maturity? Is it the case that infantile amnesia does not really reflect a less effective system for memory processing among immature or growing animals, but that these systems are simply not prepared to deal with the specific content of the episodes typicably tested? While these alternatives may ultimately be confirmed, they are not inevitable. It is possible, for example, that the particular contents of the episodes to be learned in the previous examples were not processed with special effectiveness by immature rats and, instead, some nonassociative aspect of these training circumstances was especially conducive to their learning and retention. In the next section, evidence favoring this last possibility will be addressed.

E. Effects of the Home Environment on Learning and Retention

The above cases of surprisingly rapid learning or good retention in very young rats share a procedural aspect not ordinarily found in such studies: The tests for learning or retention were all conducted in the presence of objects associated with the pups' home nest. For the studies of Rudy and Cheatle, littermates were present during conditioning; for the studies of Altman and his colleagues, access to the actual home nest was provided; for the studies of Amsel, Brake, and Kenny and Blass, approach to an anesthetized adult female rat was permitted. Although not necessarily the pup's actual mother, the similarity is obvious, and it is likely that odors from other pups or littermates also were on this adult female. Whether stimuli similar to those of the home nest may significantly alter the hormonal or behavioral consequences of "isolation stress" in the young rat is not entirely clear; neither are the precise mechanisms known through which this might be accomplished to affect learning. There are, however, sufficient hints of both a phenomenon and potential mechanisms (e.g., Campbell & Raskin, 1978; Leon & Moltz, 1972; Randall & Campbell, 1976; Shapiro & Salas, 1970) to justify the study of the influence of home environment on learned behavior. One such series of experiments was conducted in our laboratory by Gregory Smith.

1. *Home Objects (Odor) Alter the Inhibitory and Associative Behaviors of Infants*

This study by Smith began by examining the behavior of infant and adult rats in the presence of home litter shavings in which the animals had lived for 7 days. In comparison to the adult, the infant rat at 16 days of age is known to appear less affected by experience in either of two simple testing situations: passive avoidance, in which the animal must learn not to go into a compartment in which a mildly painful footshock was previously given; and spontaneous alternation, which labels the characteristic tendency of adult rats not to enter the most recently experienced of two compartments having relatively neutral consequences. In brief, innumerable experiments have shown that 16-day-old rats require more training than the adult to learn passive avoidance; furthermore, they exhibit less spontaneous alternation. The infant rat at this particular age (16 days old) is a convenient subject because mother rats with pups of this age release a pheromone that their pups find attractive (Leon & Moltz, 1972). This provides at least one plausible vehicle for an effect of the home litter shavings, namely, an odor that the 16-day-old rat is likely to notice.

The results of these experiments may be described quite simply. The age-related deficit in passive avoidance learning was drastically reduced in the infant pups when home litter shavings were present, and so was the age-related deficit in spontaneous alternation (see Fig. 2). The presence of clean shavings (shavings not previously used as nesting material) affected the behavior of these infants, whereas the behavior of the adults was unaffected regardless of the nature of the shavings.

The effect of the home litter shavings therefore appeared to act only on the behavior of the younger rats. It remained uncertain, however, whether the effect was to alter the actual processing of memory for this episode. The effect of the litter shavings on spontaneous alternation in the infant rats minimized the possibility that it had facilitated their passive avoidance performance merely by making them less active generally (Campbell & Raskin, 1978). Still, both passive avoidance and spontaneous alternation often are categorized as requiring inhibitory tendencies (or more generally, "withholding behaviors"). Further experiments were therefore designed to test the influence of the presence of home litter shavings using other types of learning tasks.

One set of experiments tested discriminative escape learning. For this task, the rat is required to enter the correct goal box in a T maze in order to escape an otherwise ubiquitous footshock. Although 16-day-old rats eventually can achieve a level of mastery in this task equal to that of adults, they typically require more training trials to do so. When home litter shavings were placed underneath the T maze, learning by the adult rats was unaffected, but we (Gregory Smith and I) were somewhat surprised to find that the rate of learning was significantly improved for the infants, to a level that was no different from that for adults.

Before concluding that the learning process was affected in this ex-

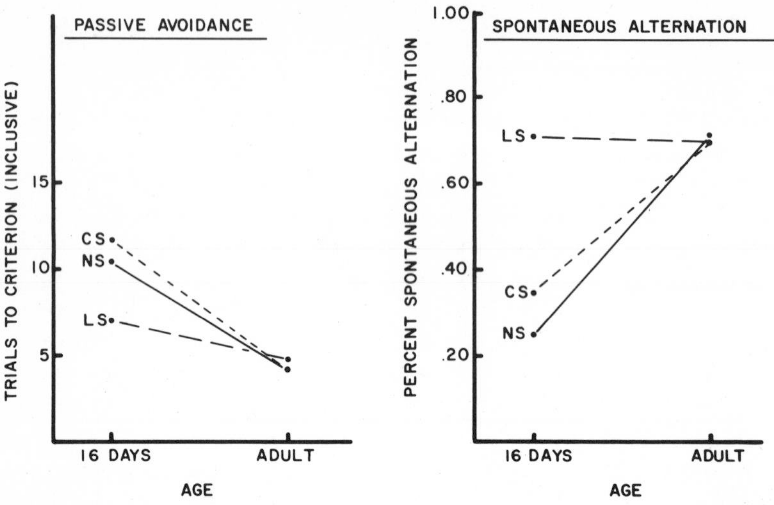

Fig. 2. Relative rates of learning to passively avoid one of two compartments and percentage trials in a T maze on which an animal alternated its choice from that of the previous trial, are shown for 16-day-old rats and adult rats. The animals differed in what was strewn immediately under the apparatus in which they received their experimental treatment—either wood shavings that had served as the floor of the home litter cage for the previous 7 days (LS), clean shavings of the same kind (CS), or no wood shavings at all (NS). Copyright 1978 by the American Association for the Advancement of Science. Smith, G. J. and Spear, N. E., *Science*, Vol. **202,** pp. 327–329, Fig. 1. 20 October 1978.

periment, we felt that additional control conditions were necessary to ensure that we had not changed a trivial aspect of what was learned. These conditions, which could apply also to the spontaneous alternation experiment, were intended to address the possible cue value of the shavings. In conducting these experiments we tried to spread the litter shavings uniformly underneath the apparatus, but it seemed vaguely possible that the immature rats might identify some discrete portion of the litter shavings with a particular alternative in the T maze and so benefit from the special cue value of this kind of shavings rather than from some nonassociative process. As we found no evidence for cue value of the home litter shavings, I will not describe how such cue value might have led to our initial results. For these control conditions an additional variable was introduced orthogonal to type of litter shavings (none, clean, or home litter): For half the animals in each of these conditions the pans holding the litter shavings under the apparatus were rotated every third trial, and for the other half a particular bit of litter shavings remained in the same position throughout all of training. Rotating the litter shavings made no difference, thus indicating no special benefit from the litter shavings for "guiding" the infants to particular locations in the T maze (see Fig. 3).

The final experiment in this series assessed the effect of home litter shavings on the rate of learning one-way active avoidance. This task also is ultimately mastered by 16-day-old animals, but such infants require more trials to do so than do adults (Klein & Spear, 1969). Two experiments were conducted in which a total of 38 rats learned the active avoidance with the home litter shavings present and 40 learned with clean shavings. For this task, the results indicated that the learning by 16-day-old animals was not facilitated when home litter shavings were present under the apparatus; with home litter shavings 17.7 trials were required before completion of the criterion of five consecutive avoidances, and with clean shavings 17.3 trials were required.

Because we had been surprised to observe any effect of home litter shavings on the learning of 16-day-old rats in these experiments, we cannot say we were surprised not to find the effect with the active avoidance task. We cannot at this stage offer principles to account for the configuration of results obtained in these experiments. What can be asserted is that the presence of home litter elements may have important

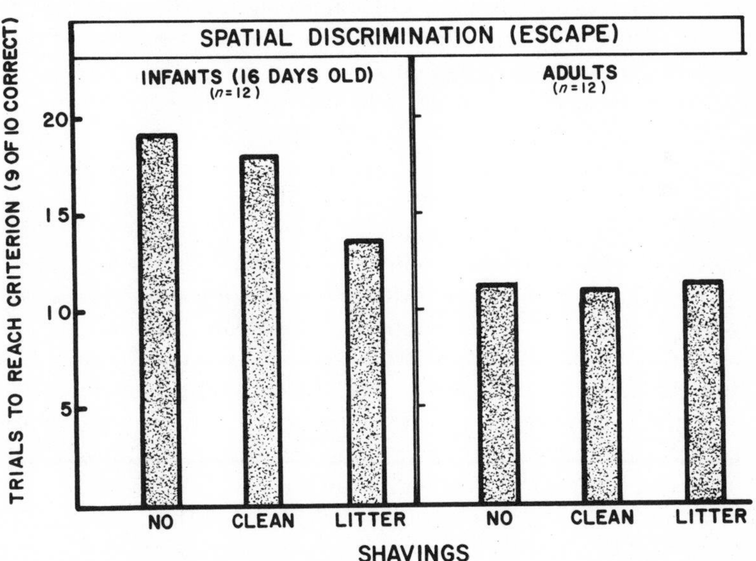

Fig. 3. Number of trials required to complete the criterion of learning is shown for 16-day-old and adult rats that differed in what was strewn underneath the T maze used for this discrimination task. Wood shavings strewn there either had served as the floor of the home cage for the previous 7 days (litter), or came straight from the bag (clean), or no shavings at all were present (no).

effects on associative processes and these effects are, apparently, due to nonassociative consequences of these elements. I refer to "nonassociative" to indicate that the cue value of the home litter element does not seem critical to the effect. We turn now to two further sets of experiments addressing this common issue with quite different procedures. In doing so, we will find the picture becoming more complicated, although continuing to support the notion that subtle aspects of the environment during memory storage can affect learning or retention in immature animals. The first involves another series of experiments by Gregory Smith in our laboratory.

2. *An Effect of Home-Environmental Stimuli on Conditioning in Neonates*

Rudy and Cheatle (1979) placed a set of several 2-day-old rat pups together in a container in which they were exposed to a particular odor, such as lemon. Most often the animals were littermates, frequently an entire litter. After 5 min the pups were removed, some injected with Lithium chloride (LiCl) and some with saline, and then they were returned together to the same odor in the same container. Those pups made ill by LiCl in the presence of the lemon odor showed a conditioned aversion to that odor when tested six days later, a dramatic effect replicated frequently by Rudy and Cheatle in an extensive series of creative experiments. The new experiments by Smith asked two questions: First, is this conditioning in 2-day-old neonatal rats influenced by the procedure of exposing them to the critical stimuli when huddled together with other littermates (as is their practice in the nest at this age) in comparison to the same exposure when isolated from their littermates? Second, if such an effect does occur, is it because the animals conditioned together with a group of littermates are warmer than those isolated?

The results, shown in Fig. 4, indicate that in contrast to the significant conditioned aversion to the odor among neonates made ill when exposed to the odor in a group, animals given identical exposure to the odor and the illness in isolation from other neonates showed no evidence of conditioning whatsoever. Figure 4 indicates also that this is not a matter of differential warming, because the same relationship held whether the container was brought to nest temperature with a warming pad or left at the somewhat colder room temperature. While I was as startled as anyone to find that neonates in isolation conditioned more poorly than those trained while in close contiguity with other neonates, what I found most surprising was that the effect could not be attributed to differential warming. Throughout the history of its psychobiological investigation, the processing of memories has often seemed sensitive to differences

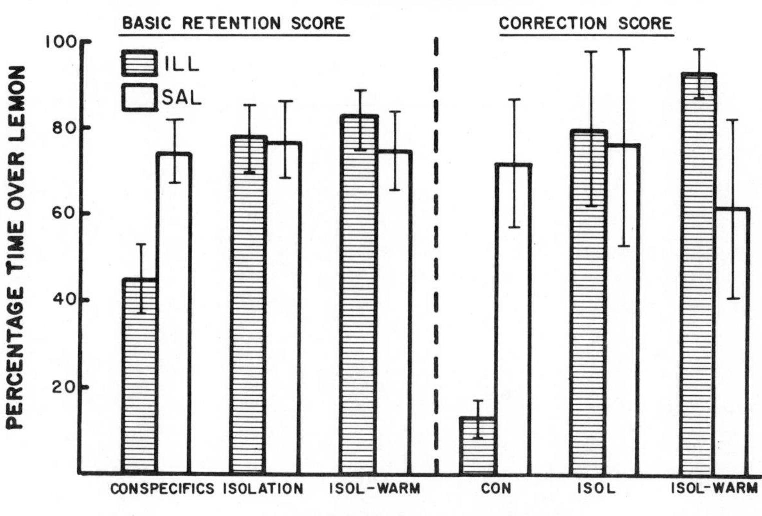

Fig. 4. Percentage time spent over a lemon odor (relative to time over the alternative, garlic, odor) is shown for rats exposed, when 2 days old, to lemon odor in association with either an injection of LiCl to induce toxicosis or an injection of physiological saline. The initial exposure to lemon in association with the injection was given either to isolated individual animals or to a group of four littermates (conspecifics) simultaneously, or to individuals in isolation but with temperature maintained at that of the home nest rather than the somewhat cooler room temperature. The "correction score" is based exclusively upon data from littermates of animals conditioned with conspecifics, whose test scores met a special criterion of learning (use of this correction score did not alter the conclusions).

in body temperature (Gleitman, 1971; Riccio, Hodges & Rohrbaugh, 1968) and, with perhaps some stretch of one's imagination, it had seemed possible to account generally for an influence of home nesting elements on learning and conditioning by effects of the heat generated from these elements. The strength of this effect in the neonatal rat would be expected because these animals are essentially poikilothermic and, even at 16 days of age, the rat is not regulating its body temperature at adult levels (Adolph, 1968). These results were also surprising because, while the effects of home litter elements on 16-day-old rats conceivably could be mediated by the sort of maternal pheromone identified by Leon and Moltz as affecting rats at this age, Leon and Moltz found that younger rats were not so affected. It therefore seems unlikely that this same pheromone could be influencing the behavior of the 2-day-old rat pups. Although not clarifying with respect to explanation, it is notable that our recent experiments indicate that the presence of home-nest odors may facilitate instrumental discriminated-escape learning in rats as young as 7-days old (Smith, Greenfield & Spear, 1979).

This is not to suggest that maternal pheromones and alterations in body temperature can be dismissed as important mediators of the influence of the home nest environment on behavior. These factors certainly would seem, in my opinion, to remain primary candidates as mediators of the effects. Instead, I take the varied circumstances of the above experiments to reflect a fundamentally complex, multidetermined set of phenomena that may be ordered not only in terms of varied causes but also in varied manifestations of the effects. I refer here to the likelihood that home environmental cues are unlikely to influence all learning in the same way. As an extreme example, conditioning an infant rat to decrease intake of its mother's milk by inducing illness following feeding would seem less likely to be effective in the home nest than elsewhere. It is known that prior exposure to a taste detracts from the probability of an acquired aversion to that taste, especially when the prior exposure is given in the same context as that in which the animal is to acquire the aversion to the taste (e.g., Domjan, 1972; Lubow, 1973).

3. *Impairment of Conditioning by Stimuli of the Home Environment*

Robert Infurna and Pamela Steinert have conducted in our laboratory an extensive investigation of a powerful, though unexpected, effect of the home environment on infantile conditioning of a taste aversion. The phenomenon was discovered in attempting to develop a methodologically rigorous paradigm for comparing the long-term retention of a conditioned taste aversion for infant and adult rats. Realizing that a change in context between original conditioning and a retention test is known generally to influence test performance differently after long and short intervals (Spear, 1978), it seemed important that immature and mature animals not be treated differently in this respect. It also seemed that if the adult animals were to be conditioned in a cage identical to that of their home cage, so should the immature animals. Yet, it was clear that the immature animals could not be left in their home (maternal) cage for a long retention interval because they would simply outgrow it. Therefore, Infurna and Steinert conducted the following experiments.

As an initial test in this series, 18-day-old rats were conditioned in either their home cage or in a relatively novel environment (a standard, hanging wire cage for rats) and then were tested for the conditioned aversion in either the same location as conditioning or in the alternative environment. Throughout this series of experiments, what is meant by the "home cage" is the plastic maternity box in which the animals were born and in which they had spent their entire lives prior to the conditioning episode. Wooden inserts during conditioning and testing created individual cubicles for each rat, to permit individual measurement in this type of group home cage. For all experiments in this series a six-day interval between training and testing was interpolated to ensure full recovery from the induced illness that served as the unconditioned stimulus.

A few other details of method also will hold for all experiments described in this series: (1) The subjects always were water-deprived rats, 18 days old during conditioning unless specified otherwise. (2) For conditioning, the rats were permitted access to a 15% sucrose solution for 1 hr and immediately afterward were injected with LiCl (typically a 3.0 molar equivalent dose, quite sufficient to induce significant illness). (3) For each experimental (conditioned) group in each experiment, there were two corresponding control conditions. One of these was injected with only saline after access to the sucrose solution; the other was given access to only water and then injected with LiCl. (4) Conditioning was always assessed by a two-bottle test, one bottle containing tap water and the other filled with the 15% sucrose solution. (5) The data reported here are in terms of percentage preference for the sucrose solution at the test, but it should be understood that for these experiments, the same conclusions hold with absolute sucrose intake as the response measure.

The original concern in the first experiment was, as mentioned earlier, the extent to which a shift in location between conditioning and testing might affect the degree of conditioning manifested on the test day. However, instead of finding a statistical interaction between place of conditioning and place of testing, we found a main effect of location of conditioning, an effect to be replicated in persistent fashion throughout this series of experiments. In short, lesser aversion to the sucrose solution was acquired by the immature animals conditioned in their home cage than for those conditioned elsewhere; there was no effect of location of testing and no interaction between location of conditioning and location of testing. Results from the control conditions indicated that the experimental treatments did not alter sucrose preferences for animals that were either not made ill or made ill without prior access to sucrose solution, but were otherwise treated the same as conditioned animals. Incidentally, in comparison to these baseline control conditions, it was verified statistically that animals conditioned in the home cage did acquire an aversion, a conclusion that holds also for every other experiment in this series. The major point remains, however, that degree of conditioning was less for these rats than that for those conditioned in a relatively novel environment.

Is this an ontogenetic effect, a phenomenon unique to immature animals? An identical experiment completed with adult animals indicates that it is. For this experiment, animals remained housed in their plastic litter cages from birth until adulthood (70 days of age, in this case; after weaning, they were housed with animals of the same sex, four per cage). The same experimental design was applied as for the infants, with the animals conditioned in either their home cage or the novel environment and then tested in either the same or the alternative environment. The results were quite different than those for the infants, but they may be stated as simply: Conditioning of these adults was not affected by the location of conditioning or by the interaction between location of conditioning and that of testing; the only significant effect was in terms of where they were tested. Those tested in the home cage manifested less conditioned aversion to the sucrose than those tested in the novel cage. The results for both the infants and adults are shown in Fig. 5. For now we can ignore the test-location effect with the adults; of primary concern here is that the location of conditioning seems to affect only infants.

Infurna and Steinert carried out further experimental procedures toward analyzing this effect on the conditioning of infant rats. The first step was to identify which aspect of the conditioning procedure was most sensitive to the location of its occurrence. Three separable events of conditioning seemed most likely to be of importance: consumption of the sucrose solution that served as the conditioned stimulus (CS); onset and duration of the illness that served as the unconditioned stimulus (UCS); and experience during the remainder of the interval following pairing of the CS and UCS until the test for conditioning. To test whether the location in which the former two events occurred was important for conditioning, infant rats differed in where they drank the sucrose concentration and in where they spent the 1-hr period that followed their postdrinking injection of LiCl. In a two-way factorial design, drinking occurred in either the home cage or the novel environment and the immediate postdrinking illness phase occurred in either the same location as the drinking or in the alternative environment. All animals were tested in the environment where their initial drinking of the sucrose solution had occurred. The results indicated that only the site of drinking was important; where the animal became ill did not affect the magnitude of the conditioned aversion. Collapsing across the latter variable, animals previously given their sucrose solution in the home cage showed a percentage preference for sucrose of 26% on the test day. As before, this indicates a significant aversion relative

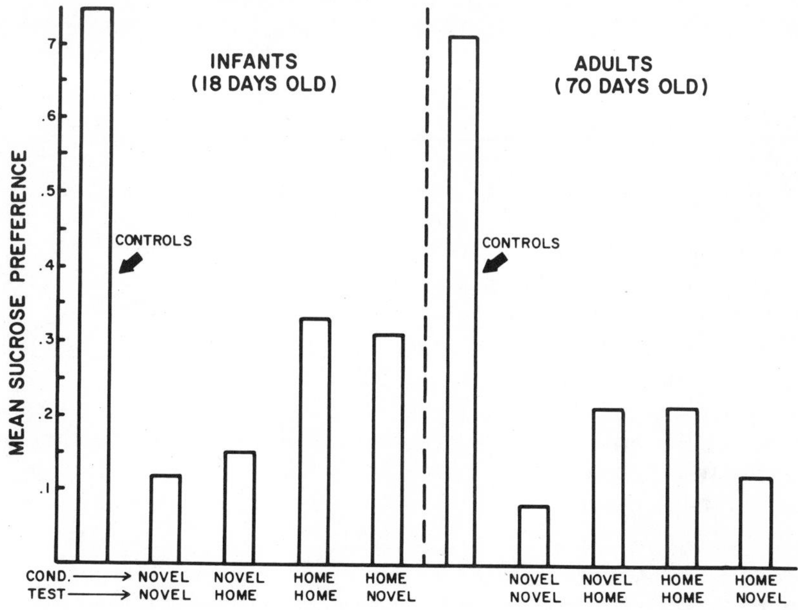

Fig. 5. Percentage preference for sucrose solution is shown for 18-day-old or adult rats made ill following ingestion of sucrose solution in either their home cage or a relatively novel environment (the lower the score, the greater the conditioned aversion to sucrose solution). Place of drinking did not alter sucrose preference for any of the 12 control conditions. For simplicity, these control conditions are combined for representation in this figure.

to each of the two control conditions, which consistently had a sucrose preference of about 70% throughout these experiments; yet, this mild aversion among rats made ill after drinking in their home cage contrasts with the significantly lower percentage preference (stronger aversion) for sucrose of 12% shown by animals that had consumed the sucrose in the novel environment before their illness.

A small point worth mentioning is our concern that the temporal patterns of drinking might have differed in the familiar and novel environments, leading to a systematic difference in the delay between the taste and the illness. On the basis of correlational analysis between these temporal patterns and degree of conditioning, and because of the results of other experiments that need not be discussed here, we rejected this possibility.

The next experiment was a small one, varying only site of conditioning, which again was the same as that of testing, but with the entire interval between conditioning and the test spent by the rat in the novel environment. For previous experiments this interval of 6 days was always spent in the home cage, so it was unclear whether the effect of where the sucrose solution was originally consumed would remain if this period were spent in the alternative environment, the novel wire cage. The results indicated that where the animals spent the retention interval was unimportant. Those pups that originally consumed the sucrose solution in their home environment again showed an attenuated conditioned aversion, with a percentage sucrose preference on test day of 24% in comparison to 7% for the animals that had consumed their solution in the novel environment.

The attenuation of the conditioned taste aversion for infants given the taste in their home cage seemed likely to be a special case of "latent inhibition," the decrement in conditioning caused by prior exposure to stimuli sufficiently similar to some critical aspect of the conditioning episode. Nearly always, this "critical aspect" had been the CS, and as noted earlier, prior exposure to a taste does indeed attenuate conditioning of an aversion to that taste. Generally, such attenuation can be lessened or eliminated when the context of the prior exposure differs from that of conditioning (Domjan, 1977). Perhaps the present phenomenon represented an instance of generalized latent inhibition due to the similarity between the sucrose solution and the mother's milk (which includes, for example, the sugar lactose and had been the only liquid previously consumed in the lifetime of these infants). This latent inhibition might be lessened in the context different from that of the nest. It seemed reasonable, however, to first test the simpler possibility that the present effect was a simple consequence of the novelty of the context of the drinking (cf. Rudy, Rosenberg & Sandell, 1977). The question was whether a limited amount of prior familiarization with the novel environment would attenuate conditioning there also. The design was a two-way factorial in which infant rats were given 1 hr of confinement in the novel environment for 1 or 5 days immediately prior to conditioning. Conditioning took place in either the home cage or the novel environment.

The results indicated that these levels of familiarization made no difference in conditioning. Also, combining levels of familiarization, the relative attenuation of conditioning in the home cage remained about the same as before, with a mean sucrose preference of 31% for all these rats and 6% for those conditioned in the "novel" environment. To determine whether the influence of familiarization might have been greater had the animals been given an opportunity to drink something during that period in the novel environment, other infant rats were given access to either water or an almond-flavored solution, or to no liquids at all during each of three daily, 1-hr periods of familiarization in the novel wire cage preceding conditioning there. Access to a liquid during familiarization did not alter the effect of that experience on conditioning; mean preference for sucrose solution was 8% for all rats combined, about the same level of conditioned aversion regularly obtained with conditioning in this novel environment.

The last experiment in this series emphasized the ontogenetic aspect of this conditioning phenomenon. For this experiment, the influence of conditioning environment on acquired taste aversions for 18-day-old infants was compared with that for 21-day-old rats. The latter is the usual age of weaning in our laboratory and for most commercial suppliers of rats. Half the animals in each age group received their conditioning experience in the home cage and half in the novel environment, and all animals were tested in the same location as their conditioning. The procedures were exactly as before except that a third control condition was added to those that typically accompanied each of the experimental conditions; animals received only the LiCl injection with no prior drinking experience for this condition, the relevance of which is unimportant for the present discussion. As in all previous experiments, the experimental variables had no influence on the sucrose preference of animals in any of these control conditions. For the conditioned animals the basic result, simple but dramatic, was that while the environment of conditioning had the same effect on the 18-day-olds as before (sucrose preference of 24% for those conditioned in the home and 12% for those conditioned in the novel environment), there was no significant effect among the 21-day-old animals (sucrose preference of 15% and 12%, respectively, for those conditioned in the home and novel environments).

How is this series of experiments important for understanding how factors of memory storage might lead to infantile amnesia? I feel the phenomenon identified and analyzed in this study exemplifies in striking fashion that what is learned or how much is learned when immature animals are exposed to a particular episode may depend importantly on the context of the episode, and more so than for adults or even slightly older but still immature animals. I am suggesting that although special age-dependent influences of context on memory storage may differ for different episodes, such effects may be a general fact of life, not restricted to the acquisition of aversions to taste. The special influence of context seems likely to be manifested most plainly in comparisons between home context and nonhome context, if only because for immature organisms, there is a very special magnitude in the difference of familiarity between these two. Having spent an entire lifetime in a single relatively restricted space that occupies nearly all of one's sensory-perceptual activity is, after all, rather uncommon for adults, although practically uniform among altricial infants. Yet, the fact that the home-environment conditioning effect did not seem to occur among animals 21 days old or in adulthood suggests that mere confinement to the same place throughout a lifetime is not sufficient for the conditioning effect (this may be sufficient for the *testing* effect with adults, however). Perhaps among older animals, even those in cages, access to more distant, extra-nest events through sharpened capacities for vision, hearing, and olfaction mitigates the experiential constraints of confinement to the home environment.

We cannot be certain at this time whether the present phenomenon is a consequence of "learned safety" in terms of context or is due to context-dependent latent inhibition of taste generalized through those sugars in the mother's milk that may decrease in quality or concentration as weaning approaches, or whatever. What we can expect, however, is the discovery of further cases in which the processing of memories for episodes experienced in the home environment may have quantitative or qualitative differences from those for nonhome episodes in the infant's life. Such effects seem inevitable in view of the far greater potential for specific or nonspecific transfer from previous memories in the home environment and for nonassociative environmental effects of novel compared to home environments on altricial infants. I suspect that such effects on memory storage are sources of infantile amnesia.

F. Further Indication that Infantile Amnesia May Depend on Content of the Stored Memory

Two important series of experiments from the laboratory of Professor Byron Campbell at Princeton University have indicated that for certain training episodes, infantile amnesia does not occur among rats in the upper ranges of infancy (say, 18–20 days of age), although somewhat younger infants do show infantile amnesia in these cases. As with the extraordinary learning and retention by neonates discussed earlier, we must ask whether the present "unusual" cases reflect a special infantile propensity for more effective processing of certain classes of information than others. Moreover, as with the earlier cases, we will see that factors other than the particular content of the stored memory seem to provide equally likely explanations.

The first series (Coulter, Collier, and Campbell, 1976) assessed retention in terms of a conditioned emotional response measured after the animals had been given pairings of a tone (CS) and a footshock (UCS). The most significant feature of their technique is that conditioning to the tone was conducted in a different apparatus than was used for testing, conventionally termed an "off-baseline" procedure. For both immature and adult animals, therefore, there was no advantage in remembering contextual features of the conditioning situation and no disadvantage in forgetting it. In one sense, this could be said to simplify the analytical situation by limiting the elements tested for retention; at least ideally, the only relevant memory attributes were those representing the tone, the footshock, and their contingent relationship. Coulter *et al.* felt there should be less infantile amnesia with this task than with the previously applied instrumental conditioning tasks that seem to require the animal to remember special motor behaviors or locations as well as contextual features of an apparatus or other aspects of training. They reasoned that if growth-induced changes in perception and motor behaviors caused greater forgetting in the infant animals after they were mature, less infantile amnesia should be observed by minimizing the influence of such changes. Their prediction was confirmed; with their procedures, animals conditioned when 17–22 days of age showed no more forgetting over a long interval than did adults (although as mentioned before, infantile amnesia was observed in still younger rats).

The implication that infantile amnesia may depend on what is to be remembered also seems supported in another series of experiments by Campbell and Alberts (1979). These experiments found no infantile amnesia for an acquired taste aversion among rats conditioned when 18–20 days of age, although again, the effect was found among still younger rats. In view of the complex, age-related effects of nonassociative context on conditioned taste aversions discussed in the previous section, we should be cautious about any definite conclusions concerning special age-related amnesic characteristics of this kind of conditioning. At the present time there seems no clear demand that the results of Campbell and Alberts be qualified on this basis; however, there is a good reason to believe that the results of Coulter *et al.* are due not to the particular content of memory tested in those experiments, but to the conditions under which the memory was stored. In particular, the conditioning procedure used by Coulter *et al.* required that training be distributed over 3 days. We turn now to evidence indicating that such distribution of practice not only reduces long-term forgetting, but it may do so more effectively for immature animals than for adults.

1. The Effect of Distribution of Practice and Age on Long-Term Forgetting

To test whether the distributed-practice procedures used by Coulter *et al.* (1976) were responsible for the absence of infantile amnesia in their preweanling rats, Pearl Kessler (1976) conducted four thorough experiments in Dr. Coulter's laboratory as part of her doctoral dissertation. Essentially, the experiments by Kessler (1976) tested forgetting by preweanling and adult rats as a function of either of two kinds of variation in the distribution of conditioning trials. Conditioning involved the pairing of a tone and footshock, the tone to be tested later for its capacity to elicit a disruptive emotional response. For one set of experiments, variation was in number of minutes separating conditioning trials within a daily conditioning session; this variable did not affect forgetting and we will say no more about it. A clear effect of distribution of practice emerged, however, when varied in terms of the number of separate days on which conditioning trials were given. When all trials were given to the younger rats within a single day (at age 20 days), forgetting over more than a month's time was considerably greater than if the same number of conditioning trials had been distributed across either a 2-day period (at age 19 and 20 days) or across a 3-day period (at ages 18, 19, and 20 days).

Adult forgetting was not similarly affected by this variation in trial distribution. Was it infantile amnesia per se that was affected? A firm conclusion on this matter was not possible because of a measurement problem with the adult animals. The problem is a common one in experiments using the conditioned emotional response as an index of retention: Under no condition did the adults show any forgetting, and moreover, the conditioned emotional response was essentially maximal in all conditions, thus permitting the possibility that there was actually better retention by the adults than the infants after the shorter interval (and so perhaps a higher degree of learning originally), although it was impossible to decide from these data.

Kessler and Spear (1979) assessed the generality of the Kessler (1976) finding and the possibility that infantile amnesia per se might be sensitive to differences in distribution of practice. For this study, a different kind of conditioning task and several levels of conditioning were used to prevent ceiling effects on the measurement of conditioning after short intervals. Infant rats 17–19 days of age and adults (about 80 days of age) were given 3, 9, or 15 pairings of an odor (lemon or peppermint) with footshock in conjunction with the same number of presentations of the alternative odor without footshock. To test retention either 1 day or 28 days following the last conditioning trial, we measured the extent to which the rats preferred a spatial location scented with lemon compared to one scented with peppermint. Distribution of the conditioning trials was varied orthogonally to the other variables; the rats were given either all their conditioning trials on a single day or one-third on each of three consecutive days. For example, the younger animals either received all their conditioning trials at 19 days of age or one-third when 17 days, one-third when 18 days, and one-third when 19 days of age.

The results indicated clearly that when conditioning for the immature rats had been distributed across days, forgetting between 1- and 28-day tests was attenuated in comparison to when conditioning had been on a single day (see Fig. 6). It was not so clear, however, that infantile amnesia was attenuated by distributed practice. Although retention performance was not at a ceiling for the adult animals in any condition, thus avoiding the problems of the Kessler (1976) study, there nevertheless was no measurable forgetting by the adults in any condition. Indeed, the adults showed some indications of reminiscence (better retention after long than short intervals), although this would appear to be due to factors that depressed performance after the shorter interval for the adult (Spear, 1978, Chap. 4). Although it is unclear what caused this initial depression of performance, it probably is age dependent because the immature animals tended to perform even better than the adults after the short retention interval. If one were willing to ignore the baseline provided by the 1-day retention test it may be seen in Fig. 6 that performance after the long interval tended to benefit more from distributed training among the infants than the adults, but such a practice is too risky to provide a firm conclusion. What we can say is that widely spaced practice reduces forgetting over long intervals by immature animals and may also reduce infantile amnesia as well.

2. *Why Does Distributed Practice Reduce Forgetting by 19-Day-Old Infants?*

To explain this effect of distributed practice, four major facts must be considered: (1) We have learned from Kessler's work that distributing conditioning trials across 2 or 3 days for infant animals about 20 days of age yields better retention a month later than if all conditioning trials were massed within a single day. The effect is not seen after a short interval and so may be assumed to represent an influence on forgetting during the longer interval. (2) Kessler also determined that, if variation in intertrial interval is on the order of several minutes in length and the infants remain in the experimental situation during the intertrial interval, the better retention following more distributed practice does not occur. (3) Subsequently, Coulter (1979) found that if the rat was removed from the experimental situation between trials, its long-term retention was facilitated regardless of the length of the interval that elapsed between trials (within the ranges tested, from 5 min to 24 hr). (4) It cannot yet be determined whether the benefit to infantile retention from distributed practice is any different than would be found in mature animals;

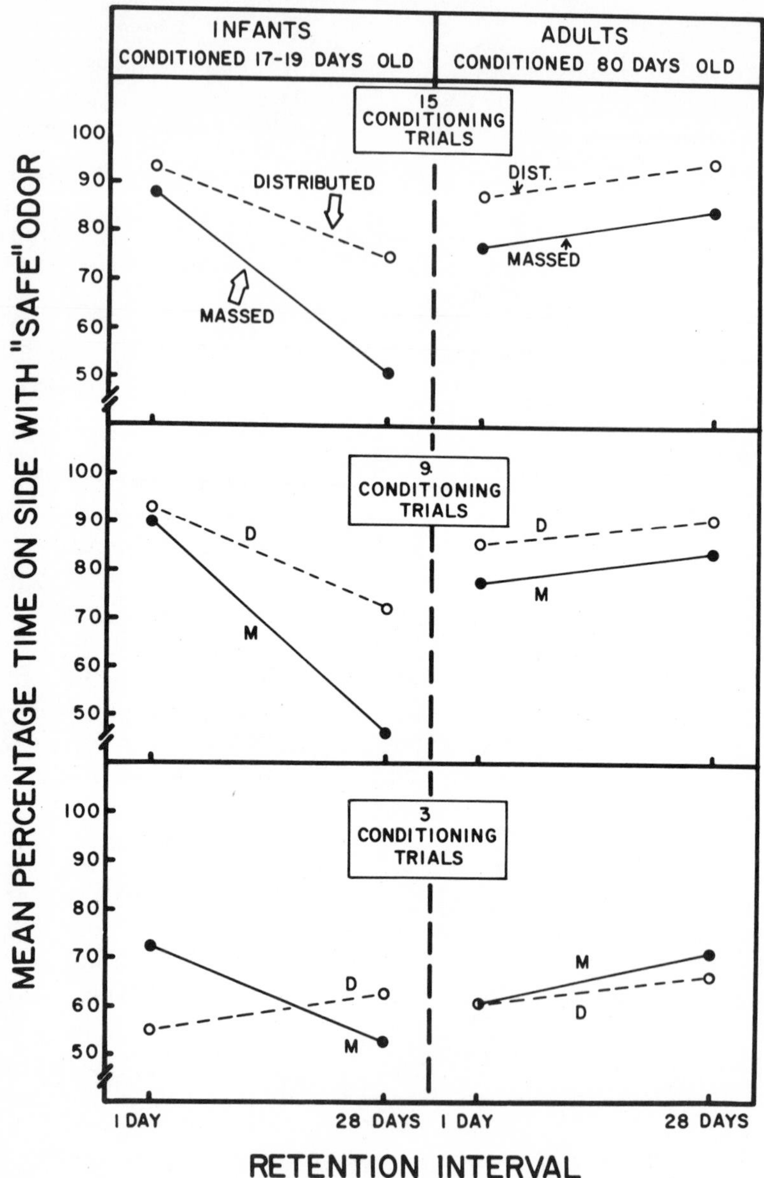

Fig. 6. Mean percentage preference for an odor not previously paired with footshock relative to that for the alternative odor paired with footshock, is shown for animals 17–19 days old (19 days old for massed training) or about 80 days old during the conditioning trials. Independent groups of rats of each age were tested either 1 or 28 days after they were conditioned with either 3, 9, or 15 presentations of the odor–shock contingencies given under either massed (all trials in a single day) or distributed (one-third of the trials on each of the 3 days) conditions.

the relevant studies so far have yielded too little forgetting under massed conditions among the adults to permit a decision as to how much distributed practice might reduce it.

What testable explanation can accommodate these facts? Let us suppose for a moment that one general device for preventing forgetting is to store redundant information about an episode—information unnecessary for performance after a short retention interval but nevertheless important for promoting retrieval of the memory after a long interval. Perhaps the effect of removing the subject from the conditioning situation during an intertrial interval is to encourage the incorporation of additional redundant memory attributes; each time the animal is reintroduced to the conditioning situation, its new perspective leads to its noticing additional events and so to storage of additional memory attributes to represent these events. If a single conditioning trial is sufficient for near-maximal learning (as happens to be so for the paradigm used by Kessler and Spear), further trials would lead to the acquisition of redundant attributes to the extent that new (to the animal) aspects of the episode are noticed during these trials. The indications that the distributed-practice effect is stronger among infants than adults lends support to such an interpretation. Immature animals would be expected to be especially deficient in acquiring redundant memory attributes during massed training relative to during distributed training for two reasons: (1) the presumably limited information-processing capacity of the infants that leaves them at a general disadvantage in processing redundant information relative to adults; (2) the general habituation deficit in infants (assuming such a deficit exists) leaves them less likely to switch their processing to additional aspects furing massed trials.

Is there any evidence that relative to massed practice, distributed practice facilitates memory storage of multiple elements among immature animals? If so, are there any indications that this facilitation is any greater than would be found among adult animals? I have not been able to find such evidence in the literature. The work on this problem in our laboratory is incomplete, but one of these studies, although not originally intended as a direct test of this kind of theory, does address it tangentially and is worth brief mention here.

For one experiment (conducted by Galye Sòlheim, Pamela Steinert, and Jean Hamberg), infant rats were given either distributed or massed conditioning trials that included pairing of a compound conditioned stimulus (CS) with a footshock (UCS). The compound CS consisted of a simultaneous tone and flashing light, and conditioning was assessed in terms of transfer to an active avoidance task that included this same compound CS and the same footshock as the UCS. When infants were presented their conditioning trials in distributed fashion, with six per day given at each of ages 17, 18, 19, and 20 days, conditioning was significantly more effective than when 24 massed conditioning trials were given at age 20 days.

Now suppose that as implied by the above theory, the better conditioning by these infants given distributed practice is because, relative to those given massed practice, they are more likely to sample and process additional elements of the conditioning episode, due to the "new perspective" provided them by their removal and return to the conditioning situation after an intertrial interval. Together with the assumption that the infants are limited in their processing capacity and so process only a subset of all elements on each trial, the implication is that these animals need not be presented with the entire compound on each trial for full effect of conditioning. So if only a single element on which the animal could "concentrate" were presented each trial under distributed practice—for example, only footshock on some trials, only the light-plus-footshock on others and only the tone-plus-footshock on still others—conditioning might equal that found when all elements are presented in compound on each trial, even though there is less overall exposure to the elements in the former case. Furthermore, even if presentations of the individual elements were massed, but a change in the particular element presented were introduced very few trials or so, then possibly the "new perspective" provided by distributed practice could be approximated under conditions of massed practice. The latter two predictions received some support in another experiment by Solheim, Steinert, and Hamberg. When the conditioning elements were presented to infant rats either as a compound or in component fashion (e.g., first six trials of shock only, then six trials of light-plus-shock, then six trials of tone-plus-shock), conditioning with the component and compound procedures was equal among animals given distributed practice and this degree of conditioning was matched by animals given the component procedure with massed practice. Moreover, conditioning under all three of these conditions was significantly superior to that obtained when the compound procedure was given with massed conditioning trials. Although the data are still incomplete, comparable tests with adult subjects do not appear to yield this pattern of effects.

G. Does Distributed Practice Benefit Retention among Infants Younger than 19 Days Old?

If it is indeed true that distributed practice benefits the long-term retention of 19-day-old rats more than that of adults, is retention aided even more among younger animals? Richard Bryan, who had developed the conditioned odor aversion paradigm applied by Kessler and Spear for the test with 19-day-old rats, applied this paradigm in our laboratory seeking a possible distributed-practice effect on retention among still younger rats.

For the present topic there is particular value in Bryan's extension of the ontogenetic study of a distributed-practice effect on forgetting. First, although conditions of memory storage may have profound effects on learning, they rarely have been found to influence subsequent forgetting (Spear, 1978). Distribution of practice qualifies as one such condition of memory storage that can affect both learning and forgetting and so its study could provide insight into the general relationship between memory storage and later forgetting. Second, the suggestion that this variable might have a greater effect on forgetting among immature than among adult rats encourages the notion that age-dependent characteristics of memory storage can account for infantile amnesia. Third, examination of the effect of distributed practice on forgetting by neonates—animals a good deal younger than the infants tested by Kessler—may lead to the discovery of functional differences in memory processing among these different age groups. Differences of this kind are predicted by the Campbell and Spear (1972) hypothesis that infantile amnesia among older infants may be based on different factors than those responsible for infantile amnesia in neonates. We will see that Bryan's study lends some support to the Campbell–Spear hypothesis.

1. *Procedure and Basic Phenomena*

The procedure that Bryan selected for this series was quite simple. The consequence of conditioning was to be a conditioned aversion to a specific odor. For the conditioning trial, the rat was first placed for 20 sec in the "safe" compartment of a two-compartment apparatus. This compartment was scented with one of two alternative odors (typically, lemon or peppermint). The rat was then placed in the alternative compartment, scented with the alternative odor, and left there for 10 sec, the last 3 sec of which were accompanied by a shock to the rat's feet. The rat was then placed back in the safe compartment (no footshock here) for 20 sec more, which concluded the "conditioning trial." Bryan determined that immediately after a single conditioning trial of this kind, rats 15 days of age showed essentially complete avoidance of the odor paired with footshock in preference for the safe odor, and rats 7 days of age showed comparable avoidance after only a few such trials. For the typical retention test for the latter animals, the 7- or 8-day-old rat was merely placed in a rectangular enclosed area, half of which was scented with lemon and half with peppermint. The time spent in either of these two odorized halves was measured throughout a period of 150 sec. The testing apparatus for the 15-day-olds was somewhat larger and Y-shaped like that used by Kessler and Spear for the 19-day olds, to provide more measures of retention with these relatively mobile animals. These procedures were developed through many months of intense experimentation by Bryan.

It was during this preliminary experimentation that Bryan determined that significant retention after 24 hr occurred for the 7-day-old rat given five conditioning trials, only if the trials were distributed (intertrial interval of about 30 min) and not if they were massed (intertrial interval of only a few seconds). In contrast, however, retention by 15-day-old rats after intervals of 1, 7, or 28 days was no better if the conditioning trials had been distributed than if given in massed fashion.

Although the experiments by Kessler (1976) and by Kessler and Spear (1979) had indicated that retention by 19- to 20-day-old rats over a long interval benefited considerably from distributed practice, and the Kessler–Spear study had employed procedures almost identical to Bryan's, the failure to find a similar effect among animals conditioned at 15 days of age was not a complete surprise. Such a possibility had been suggested by the results of Coulter *et al.* (1976). Using only distributed-practice procedures, Coulter *et al.* found that animals conditioned when about 15 days old showed substantial infantile amnesia relative to adults while those conditioned at age 20 days did not. Although not demanded by their data, a possible implication was that retention by the 15-day-old animals does not benefit from distributed practice. In this context, therefore, we found the finding of an analogous distributed practice effect at a still younger age, 7 days old, far more exciting because it seemed to reflect a discontinuity between the processes governing forgetting in neonates and those governing forgetting among older but still preweanling infants.

An ontogenetic discontinuity of this kind had been proposed by Campbell and Spear (1972) to explain infantile amnesia. Physiological or behavioral characteristics that disappear and then reappear during ontogeny do not demand postulation of an ontogenetic discontinuity in basic processes, but they do suggest it. Finding the distributed-practice effect in the 7-day-old neonates also seemed to bolster this suggestion because the sort of explanation proposed above for the distributed-practice effect among 20-day-old rats just did not seem a particularly plausible one for neonates. If only because of their relatively limited sensory capabilities, it seemed that a different set of processes might be responsible for the neonatal effect. So, Bryan set about to analyze the basis of the distributed practice effect in the 7-day-old rat.

Before reviewing these tests of 7-day-old rats, it is important to describe in somewhat more detail the critical experiments indicating that retention by the 15-day-old rat does not benefit from distributed practice in the same manner as that for the 19- or 20-day-old.

2. *Absence of the Effect in 15-Day-Old Rats*

Bryan conducted three experiments for this portion of the study, all testing retention of the conditioned odor aversion. In the first of these experiments, distributed practice consisting of giving conditioning trials at ages 13, 14, and 15 days, one trial given at age 13 days and two at each of 14 and 15 days, and then the retention interval was introduced. Animals given massed practice received all five of their conditioning trials on day 15 separated by an interval of only the few seconds required to remove and replace the rat in the same manner as occurred for those given distributed practice. Figure 7 shows the results of a retention test given to independent groups of animals either a few seconds after the final conditioning trial (immediate test), or 1, 7, or 28 days afterward. The response measure of primary interest is the percentage of time spent by the rat in avoidance of the odor previously paired with shock (for the present technique, this is the same as percentage preference for the safe odor or, more simply, percentage correct responding; time spent in ambiguous preference is discounted in these scores). It can be seen in Fig. 7 that in spite of very drastic forgetting, from a score of about 100% on the immediate test to about 60% 28 days later, forgetting by animals given distributed training trials occurred at a rate no different than for animals given massed training trials. It can also be seen that this absence of a distributed practice effect is not due merely to limitations on measurement (i.e., ceiling or floor effects).

Variation in distribution of practice was applied for these 15-day-old animals in the same manner as that by Kessler for the 20-day-old animals, with a 24-hr period separating blocks of massed conditioning trials. In contrast, distributed practice for Bryan's 7-day-old animals had included presentation of all five training trials in a single day with a half-hour interval interpolated between trials. Because it was clear that no measurable retention could be found after a 24-hr interval for 7-day-old animals given several massed trials, it seemed unreasonable at that time to vary distribution of practice with the 7-day-olds in the same manner as Kessler had for the 20-day-olds. However, it was possible that dis-

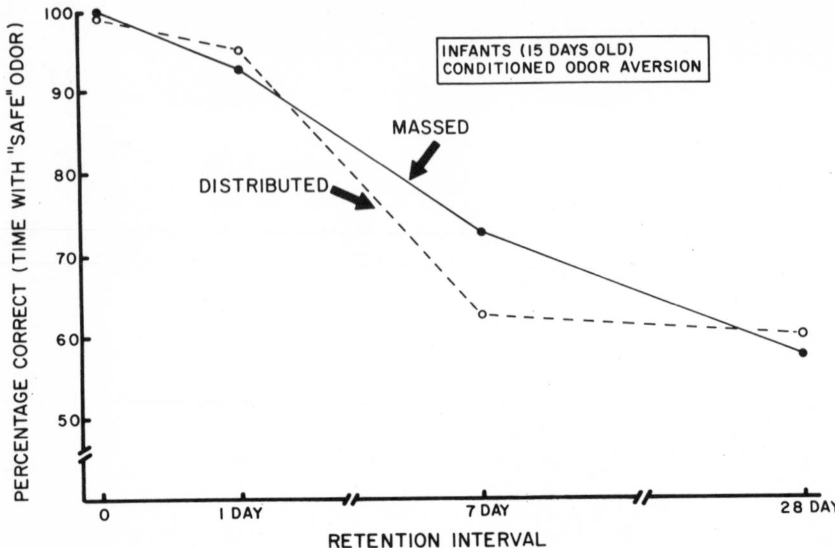

Fig. 7. Percentage preference for an odor previously presented in the absence of shock relative to an odor previously paired with shock. Either all conditioning trials were given at age 15 days (massed) or one-third were given at each of ages 13, 14, and 15 days (distributed). Retention tests were given either immediately or 1, 7, or 28 days following the conditioning trials.

tributed training of the type found effective at age 7 days might facilitate retention of animals at age 15 days. To test this, Bryan's second experiment used a retention interval of 7 days for the 15-day-olds because, with a percentage correct of about 70% after this interval (see Fig. 7), measurement was safe from either ceiling or floor effects. The results indicated that again, retention after 7 days did not differ between 15-day-olds given one-half hour between each conditioning trial and those given only a few seconds between each trial; percentage correct responding for those in the former condition was 81% and for those in the latter, 89%. Finally, a third experiment by Bryan included distributed practice with an intertrial interval of 2 hr, together with other modifications of procedure, and here again, no better retention occurred for the 15-day-old animals after distributed than after massed practice.

H. Initial Analysis of the Distributed-Trials Effect with 7-Day-Old Rats

At this point, attention was focused totally on analysis of the distributed trials effect among 7-day-old animals. An initial question was whether in spite of the apparent ontogenetic discontinuity suggested by the 15-day-old animals, there might exist functional similarities between the distributed practice effects on retention by 7-day-old animals and those about 19 days old. We have already mentioned the important finding by Coulter (1979) that for infants in the age range of 18–20 days, retention was facilitated when animals were merely removed from the conditioning episode between conditioning trials, regardless of length of the interval between trials. Bryan asked whether a similar effect would also be found among 7-day-old animals.

In designing this experiment, the question arose as to how one could "remove" a 7-day-old animal from an experimental situation in a manner comparable to removal of a 19-day-old rat. Some of the differences between such animals can be appreciated in terms of their appearance, shown in Fig. 8. Among the most obvious behavioral differences, the 7-day-old crawls to encounter events while the 19-day-old scurries about on its paws with quick, coordinated movements. Although precise differences in sensory capacities are still unclear and we know that animals of both ages do well in discriminating certain odors, it does not take a great deal of imagination to expect relative deficits in audition and vision for the 7-day-old because its eyes and ears are closed while those of the 19-day old are open. From even the most superficial consideration, then, it was clear that the type and magnitude of the sensory consequences of removal from an episode would be at a different level for the 7-day-old and 19-day-old rats. Another problem was how the neonate could "remain" in the present experimental situation with neutral effect. This was possible in the Coulter study where conditioning was exclusively to a discrete tone that could be readily removed, whereas removal of odors remains a classical difficulty of the present procedures. Bryan's decision was to compare 24-hr retention by 7-day-old animals when they were removed from the experimental apparatus and taken to a holding cage in a different room during a half-hour intertrial interval, with that when they remained in the presence of the safe odor (CS –) during this period. Examination of the data showed the latter animals had slightly better retention than the former, a result in the direction opposite that predicted from Coulter's effected with older animals.

Another way to test the Coulter effect with 7-day-old animals might be to treat the animals during a very short intertrial interval in exactly the same manner as those given a long (half-hour) intertrial interval. For the typical massed-practice procedure, Bryan had permitted only a second or two to elapse as the interval between successive trials, just long enough to pick the rat up and replace it to equal the handling given the distributed practice animals, and during this time the rat of course remained in the experimental situation. For the next experiment,

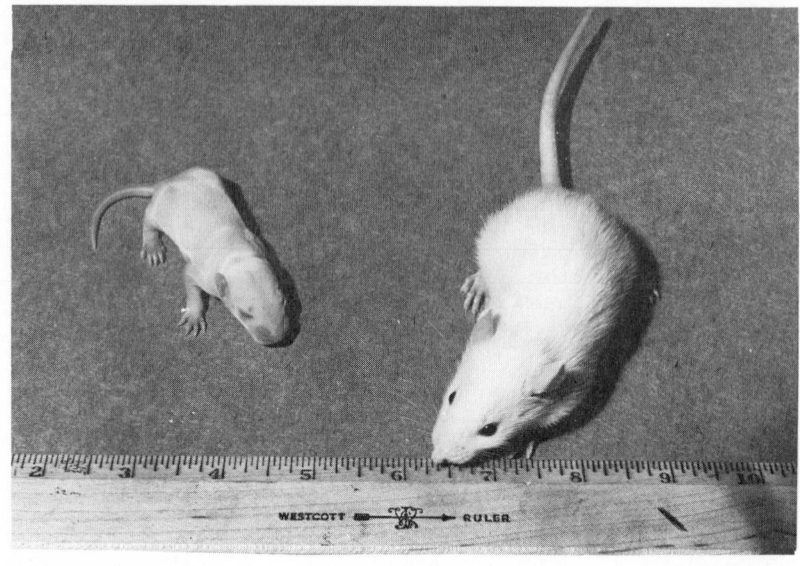

(A)

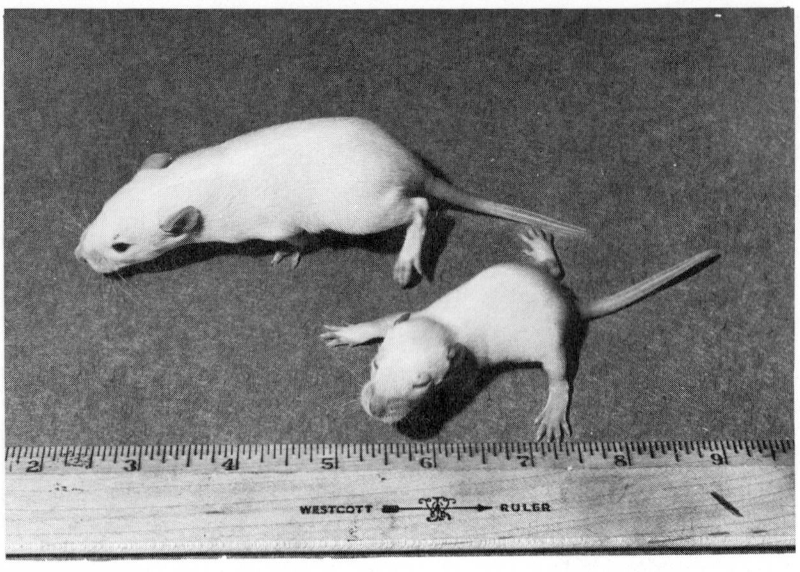

(B)

Fig. 8. These are pictures of rats of the type and age used for experiments reported in this chapter. (A) A 21-day-old rat and a 7-day-old rat; (B) a 14-day-old rat and a 10-day-old rat.

massed practice was defined by a 30-sec intertrial interval during which the neonate was placed in its home cage or in isolation in the same manner as comparable groups given a 30-min intertrial interval. This did not change the result; as before, those given the "massed" procedures did not show retention 24 hr later, while those with the more distributed training had significantly better retention than both random choice and the massed practice animals. Furthermore, a subsequent parametric investigation of the effect of length of intertrial interval, with animals spending the intertrial interval away from the apparatus in each case, indicated a progressive increase in retention with intertrial intervals of 17 sec, 100 sec, 10 min, and 1 hr.

While not totally conclusive because of the conceptual difficulties in paralleling Coulter's experiment, this evidence was sufficient to confirm our disposition to pursue an explanation of the distributed practice effect in 7-day olds possibly quite different from that used to explain the analogous effect in 19-day-olds.

1. *Control Experiments*

The first step at this stage was to test explanations based on trivial factors. To save the space required for a full description of these studies, suffice it to say that Bryan conducted a thorough set of experiments confirming that the benefit from distributed practice for 7-day-old pups could not be attributed to greater sensory adaption to odors in the massed than in the distributed conditions, to differential familiarity with the CS− and CS+ odors, or to differences in the time of day at which animals given massed and those given distributed practice received their initial or their final training trial.

2. *Learning or Forgetting?*

Is this distributed practice effect in 7-day-old animals due to differences in original learning or to differences in subsequent rate of forgetting? This basic consideration pertinent to all investigations of infantile amnesia was tested by Bryan in a number of experiments. The basic question was whether performance on a retention test in the absence of the 24-hr interval yields the same differences as are found with the 24-hr interval; in other words, would a distributed practice effect be found with a test given immediately following conditioning?

When a test was given 30 sec after completion of five trials of distributed or massed conditioning, no differences in performance were observed. It could not be concluded that learning was equal, however;

measurement was impaired by a ceiling effect, as animals in both conditions responded with about 97% accuracy. To reduce the ceiling effect, the next experiment employed only two conditioning trials, the minimum required for manipulation of distribution of practice. Again there was no significant difference after a 30-sec retention interval for animals given two massed trials compared to others with two distributed trials (percentage correct was 78% and 89% respectively), but, as before, a ceiling effect was possible because many subjects performed with 100% accuracy. To further reduce the ceiling effect (although complicating interpretation), two massed or two distributed conditioning trials were followed by a 1-min period of extinction (shock-free exposure to the CS+), with the retention test given 30 sec later. Again, there was no significant difference attributable to distribution of practice, and this time measurement was not constrained at the upper limit. The direction of the difference (66% for massed, 75% for distributed) prompted a replication experiment, but once again, no significant differences were found. Finally, Bryan tried a different, perhaps more sensitive response measure, latency to escape the CS+ odor. This test was given 30 sec after presentation of five conditioning trials, either massed or distributed. Again no significant differences occurred.

Because the slight numerical differences always favored the distributed condition, it remained conceivable that in spite of the considerable negative evidence statistically, a difference in initial learning might exist. A final answer seemed to depend on the development of more sensitive measurement techniques. In the meantime it appeared that the distributed practice effect after the 24-hr interval was too large to be accounted for by differences in how much was learned. The next experiments asked whether differences in what was learned might be responsible for the retention effect.

3. *Does Distribution of Practice Affect Memory Content?*

The hypothesis was that for animals given distributed in comparison to massed practice, the memory attribute representing the CS− (safe odor) is stored so as to promote more effective retention 24 hr later. The reasons for this hypothesis will soon become evident.

The first step was to assess the role of the CS−, if any, in conditioning of the 7-day-old. An experiment established that the CS− was neccessary for significant retention 24 hr after distributed trials; the neonates showed a higher percentage correct responding with the typical trials (CS− without shock and CS+ with shock) than when trials included only a single odor accompanied by shock. No retention was evident at all in the latter condition. This did not seem due to a perceptual benefit from simply having an odor to compare with CS+ during conditioning, because retention was found only if the *same* "CS−" were present during testing as in conditioning.

Because effective retention after a 24-hr period following distributed practice in the 7-day-old infant seemed to require that the memory have incorporated within it an attribute representing CS−, the next step was to determine whether the distributed practice effect itself is caused by greater learning about CS− under distributed than massed conditions. To test this Bryan employed a 2 × 3 factorial design with animals given either massed conditioning trials, distributed trials, or no conditioning trials, and a retention test either immediately thereafter or 24 hr later. At the retention test the pup chose between CS− and a third odor not present during conditioning. There is no need to elaborate the details of these results and their significance beyond this simple answer to the present question: The numerical direction of the results indicated that over the 24-hr interval, animals given distributed practice showed, if anything, poorer retention of the characteristics of CS− than did the massed-practice subjects, precisely the opposite to the original hypothesis. It appears that the advantage of distributed practice is not gained through differential storage of information about CS−.

4. *Learning to Retrieve*

Attention was turned to the forgetting that may occur during a long intertrial interval. Let us assume that whenever such forgetting occcurs and the animal gains reaccess to the critical memory on the subsequent training trial, the consequential "practice" in accessing (retrieving) the memory facilitates subsequent access to the memory 24 hr later. Such practice in retrieving would seem less likely with massed training conditions as information concerning the prior trial would probably still reside in an active (or "working") state.

It was felt that before the implications of such a process could be explored, some basic assumptions should be tested empirically. If we view accessability of a memory as directly related to retention scores, two basic empirical questions emerge: (1) Does significant forgetting occur during the intertrial interval in these experiments? (2) If so, do the same variables that alter forgetting during the intertrial interval also alter the magnitude of the distributed-practice effect?

Bryan conducted a number of rather ingenious experiments to test this notion, but for our purposes they need not be described in detail. The empirical evidence simply did not provide much support for the hypothesis. In short, the greater benefit to retention that accompanied progressively longer intertrial intervals did not correspond very well to the diffferences in forgetting found after corresponding intervals following a single training trial. Also, variation in such factors as ambient temperature or potential sources of retroactive interference did not have the same effects on forgetting during the intertrial interval as on the distributed-practice effect itself. Finally, further tests based on the consequences of a reactivation treatment following a long intertrial interval also did not support the idea that "learning to retrieve" might account for the benefit to neonatal retention that accompanies distributed practice.

5. *Posttrial Processing*

A longer interval between trials provides, theoretically, more opportunity for the animal to process the events of that trial. Bryan conducted two experiments to determine if the introduction during the intertrial interval of events that might disrupt such hypothetical processing would reduce the retention benefit from distributed practice. In the first experiment the animals were merely handled every 60 sec during the intertrial interval. Neonates treated in this way showed unimpaired retention 24 hr later.

The second experiment employed a procedure analogous to that of Wagner, Rudy, and Whitlow (1973). The general strategy was to introduce a new conditioning episode during the intertrial interval. Bryan first determined that conditioning with only almond (odor) as CS+ and banana (odor) as CS− (or vice versa) does not alter the 7-day-old rat's preference for lemon compared to peppermint. Next, he gave the usual distributed conditioning trials with lemon and peppermint as alternative CSs, but for some animals, conditioning trials involving only almond and banana were introduced at certain points during the 30-min intertrial interval. The results indicated that retention 24 hr after conditioning of lemon versus peppermint was unaffected if the new task had been introduced at the very beginning of each intertrial interval. A slight disruption in this retention was found when the new task was introduced at the end of each intertrial interval, just prior to the next conditioning trial. With the conventional assumption that the importance of posttrial processing is greatest immediately after a trial and dissipates thereafter, it appears that the results of this experiment do not support an explanation based upon extra processing opportunities for animals in the distributed conditions.

6. *Summary and Comment*

This series of experiments began with the discovery that the benefit to long-term retention from distributed practice among rats about 20 days old does not seem to occur in infants only slightly younger (15 days old), although a similar effect does occur in much younger animals (7 days old). To be sure, the temporal dimensions defining the distributed practice effect among 7-day-old animals were quite different than those for the 20-day-olds (and it remains possible that given the "appropriate" temporal dimensions, the effect would be found in 15-day-olds). Yet, in view of the relative retention capacities of the 7- and 20-day-old animals, it is possible to see some reasonable correspondence between the temporal dimensions defining the phenomenon for these two age groups.

Regardless of our acceptance of this as evidence for an ontogenetic discontinuity at 15 days of age, however, a fundamental question is whether there are functional similarities or differences between the distributed-practice effects observed at age 7 and age 20 days. In terms of functional differences, retention by the 7-day-old seems sensitive to length of the intertrial interval, while that of the 20-day-old does not, but insensitive to contextual events occurring during the intertrial interval, while that of the 20-day-old seems importantly affected by them. However, functional similarities also are found: distributed practice benefits retention for the 20-day-old quite independently of its effect on degree of original learning (Coulter, 1979; Kessler, 1976; Spear, 1979) and, while it was difficult to entirely discount part of the benefit to retention among 7-day-olds as due to better learning by the distributed-practice animals, the effect on learning in these neonates seemed too small to account for the entire effect on retention. Also, Bryan found that the distributed-practice effect on retention among neonates did not seem due to differences in learning about the CS –, a conclusion shared by Kessler and Spear (1979) in tests of a similar design with animals 18–20 days of age. Finally, in testing hypotheses not previously tested with older immature animals, Bryan found no support for the notion that the facilitated retention in the neonates is due to either more effective posttrial processing or extra practice in memory retrieval provided by conditions of distributed practice.

At the end of this quite extensive series of elegant experiments conducted by Richard Bryan for his doctoral dissertation (I have not described all of them), a mechanism to account for the distributed-practice effect on neonatal retention remained elusive.

Perhaps the most significant aspect of this study is the remarkable robustness of the distributed-practice effect in neonates. Throughout some 35 thorough experiments and an extraordinary variety of experimental manipulations, significant 1-day retention measured by relative preference for the CS+ and CS– always occurred if practice was distributed but never if practice had been massed, with only three exceptions. For the first, Bryan found on one occasion that with a sufficient number of conditioning trials, slight but statistically significant retention was measured 24 hr after massed training; this would be interesting only if retention were not proportionally enhanced following a corresponding number of distributed-practice trials, a point not yet determined. The two other exceptions are potentially important: (1) Distributed conditioning trials did not yield significant retention 24 hr later on only one occasion—when the animals were left at room temperature during the intertrial interval (otherwise, unless explicitly cooled, ambient temperature during the intertrial interval was kept at about that present in the nest); (2) Slight retention was found 24 hr after massed conditioning when a reactivation treatment was introduced shortly before the retention test. The former result emphasizes physiological limitations of animals of this age that may interact with memory processing (regulation of body temperature), and the latter suggests that even with the 7-day-old pups, retention deficits may reflect difficulties in memory retrieval rather than loss of memory from storage.

VII. Summary and General Discussion

This contribution began from consideration of whether infantile amnesia arises from processes unique to immature animals or from processes common to animals of all ages that happen to operate with special effectiveness among immature animals. Unique processes causing forgetting might arise from the animals' immaturity during memory storage or from their growth between initial storage and later retrieval of a memory. A process that leads to forgetting among both immature and mature animals, but to which the former might be more susceptible, might be interference from conflicting memories.

Focusing on these three hypotheses of infantile amnesia—immaturity during memory storage, growth, and greater susceptibility to interference by immature animals—seemed logical. The last hypothesis has clear significance because there is virtually unanimous agreement that retroactive and proactive interference leads, in a quite ubiquitous fashion, to forgetting for an immense variety of organisms and learning episodes. The former two are important because theories of infantile amnesia can be categorized by whether they emphasize immaturity during memory storage or growth between initial storage of a memory and the need for its retrieval.

Although understanding of these factors remains fairly primitive, we noted some relatively direct evidence that infant rats are more suceptible to retroactive and proactive interference in forgetting than are adults and some indirect evidence that growth contributes to infantile amnesia.

A particular fact suggested, however, that the more important of the two possibly unique factors is immaturity during memory storage. This is the finding that for certain learning episodes—for certain kinds of information to be remembered—little infantile amnesia occurs. More generally, learning or retention for some episodes has seemed roughly equivalent for immature compared to mature animals. If the source of the more typical age-related deficits in remembering were growth within an animal, it would seem that infantile amnesia should occur rather uniformly for all kinds of episodes.

The primary topic of this paper was therefore memory storage during infancy, looking for factors that might lead to special competency in processing memories for some episodes but not others. It was hypothesized that immature animals might represent a given learning episode in terms of either fewer memory attributes or different attributes than adults. While storage of fewer attributes might have little bearing on initial learning and performance after a short retention interval, memory retrieval at a later date might depend upon redundancy in original storage. As to the immature animal's storage of different attributes, it is possible that the immature animal might store aspects of an episode that happen to be most readily forgotten. Either alternative would imply that given the "appropriate" type of learning episode, immature animals might show learning and retention equal or nearly equal to that of adults.

A test of these notions required consideration of task variables. It seemed reasonable to look for learning episodes involving events (i.e., stimuli) that commonly are processed by immature animals and simple episodes for which redundant events would play little role in retention; such episodes would seem to maximize retention by immature animals in comparison to that of adults and so perhaps not be accompanied by infantile amnesia. Although the data are not yet conclusive, they do suggest that young organisms store fewer and different memory attributes than adults store.

Surprisingly little is known empirically about any systematic influence of task variables on animal learning and retention. There has been important theoretical emphasis on such an influence, however. From the general recognition that different classes of animals might be disposed to learn different things about their environment, some theories have emphasized how species-specific response tendencies promote boundaries on the rate or probability with which certain tasks are learned (e.g., Bolles, 1970). Others have suggested that differential "preparedness" for the processing of certain episodes by different organisms may require quite different sets of principles to explain learning and retention than we have been used to (e.g., Seligman & Hager, 1972).

We can, however, learn something from the extensive empirical study of the effect of task variables on human verbal learning and retention. In particular, the history of this effort promotes caution in interpretation. For instance, in testing the influence of the meaningfulness of verbal materials on learning and retention, it became clear that the potential for confounding by correlated task characteristics (e.g., frequency of experience) was enormous (e.g., Underwood & Schulz, 1960) and that task variables having profound effects on learning may have negligible effects on retention (Underwood, 1972). Is it possible that the extraordinary infantile learning and retention observed with certain tasks is not because the task's components happen to match a special associative proclivity of the infant but instead is due to some correlated, possibly nonassociative feature of the task? On this basis we were led to consider features common to episodes found to be learned and remembered remarkably well by immature animals. Of special interest were those features often considered unimportant for the special associative requirements of the task, namely, contextual aspects of the environmental conditions surrounding the task.

Two extensive studies focused on the effect of having aspects of the home environment present during learning or a retention test. Generally speaking, stimuli from the home environment were found to have important effects on the behavior of immature animals engaged in learning, effects not found among mature animals. In some instances learning by immature animals was facilitated in the presence of home environmental stimuli, but in at least one general case, the conditioning of a taste aversion, learning was impaired by such stimuli. Both effects occurred in a seemingly lawful manner, although the precise mechanisms underlying the contextual influence of stimuli from the home environment remain obscure. However, one thing is clear: We must be cautious in interpreting unusually good learning by immature animals simply as a special "ethological fit" between the animal's stage of development and the particular content of the memory stored to represent an episode.

Other instances of extraordinary long-term retention by immature animals for certain kinds of episodes included those with distributed conditioning trials. While the processing of memories frequently has been especially effective when materials to be learned are presented in distributed fashion, there seemed no a priori reason to expect that this effect should be greater for immature than mature animals. However, the possibility seemed to demand a test.

Two thorough studies involving rats in the upper age ranges of infancy (18–20 days old) indicated that long-term retention by these animals benefited from distributed conditioning trials; these studies were somewhat ambiguous as to whether this benefit exceeded that for adults. A theory of the distributed-practice effect based on the limited capacities for information processing among immature animals received some preliminary support when tested experimentally. However, when a phenomenon having the same nominal characteristics—better retention with more widely distributed conditioning trials—was analyzed among more immature, neonatal rats (7 days old), a quite different set of explanatory principles seemed required. This was indicated both by the failure of certain manipulations to have a common effect on retention for the neonate and the older, infant animals but also by the observation that retention by animals of an intermediate age was quite unaffected by distribution of conditioning trials. It was as if one set of processes was responsible for the distributed practice effect in neonates, but as the animal advanced to the intermediate age it outgrew the influence of these processes and a new set of processes developed to account for the distributed practice effect among the older infants. Such a discontinuity in the ontogeny of processes responsible for retention and forgetting had been suggested earlier by Campbell and Spear (1972).

What of the theoretical alternatives of growth, immaturity during storage, and special infantile susceptibility to interference? Which of these is the best explanation of infantile amnesia? The evidence reviewed in the present contribution suggests that the better question should be "Which of these accounts for the greater portion of infantile amnesia?" because some support was registered for each. Unfortunately, at this point it is appropriate to return to the tired statement that we cannot yet know the answer to this question. The reason, too, is an old one: because the proper tests have not yet been conducted. There are extraordinary methodological difficulties in addressing any of these three theories because not only are growth and immaturity during storage naturally confounded, but related problems also exist in addressing the ontogeny of suceptibility to retroactive and proactive interference.

Although perhaps obvious, some of these methodological difficulties apply to the approach taken in the present paper and should be made explicit. First, it is apparent that level of maturity during memory storage and amount of subsequent growth prior to a retention test are quite confounded ordinarily. Essentially by definition, the more mature an animal at any point, the more subsequent growth must occur to attain maturity. One can deal with this analytically in either of two general ways. The direct approach is to hold constant or systematically vary rate of growth during a set interval after memory storage, perhaps by introducing certain hormonal manipulations. An indirect approach would be to manipulate those psychological factors that seem characteristic of the consequences of immaturity on memory storage. For example, on the basis of theory and empirical evidence, one might decide that the immature animal stores too few redundant memory attributes to support later retrieval and test this by systematic variation of age during memory storage and of the number of redundant contextual cues present in an episode that might conceivably be used for later retrieval. This latter strategy obviously is the one preferred in the present contribution. The attempts in my laboratory to influence learning and retention by direct hormonal manipulation of growth during a retention interval have met with limited success and, although such tests are probably necessary and worthwhile, the analytical problem of identifying the crucial consequences of the hormonal manipulation seems nearly overwhelming at present.

A problem associated with age-related susceptibility to conventional sources of forgetting, such as interference from conflicting memories, may also be apparent. This is that the interference produced by prior or subsequent storage of a conflicting memory is likely to depend on what is stored as the target memory, and this in turn may depend on the animal's degree of immaturity during storage. While not a great deal is known about the interaction between the content of a stored memory and its susceptibility to interference, some characteristics of retroactive and proactive interference lead one to suspect such a relationship: (1) the apparent influence of the similarity between the target and interfering memories and hence the probable value in storing redundant attributes that might help to differentiate the target memory; (2) the lesser interference effects found with higher degrees of learning the target memory, where "higher degree of learning" might itself reflect the acquisition of more redundant memory attributes or the selection of those more effective for memory retrieval; and (3) the recent suggestions that susceptibility to proactive interference may depend on the particular encoding (i.e., content of the stored memory) used in acquiring the target memory. Experimental segregation of the effects of immaturity on memory storage and susceptibility to interference will be difficult.

Finally, while the present approach toward understanding infantile amnesia has apparent difficulties, it does seem a shade more amenable to experimental analysis than our earlier framework in which the major alternatives were a psychological versus a physiological basis for infantile amnesia (Campbell & Spear, 1972). While this latter approach has been useful for experimental orientation to the problem, and while a rather artificial dichotomy of this kind may still be necessary to account for different characteristics of forgetting by neonates and older infants, it was of course clear from the beginning that differences between psychological and physiological factors cannot take us very far analytically, because they are fundamentally inseparable.

References

Adolph, E. F. *Origins of physiological regulations.* New York: Academic Press, 1968.

Alloway, T. M. Learning and memory in insects. *Annual Review of Entomology,* 1972, **17,** 43–56.

Allport, G. W. *Personality: A Psychological Interpretation.* New York: Holt, 1937.

Almli, C. R., & Fisher, R. S. Infant rat: Sensory motor ontogeny and effects of substantia nigra destruction. *Brain Research Bulletin,* 1977, **2,** 425–459.

Altman, J., & Bulut, F. G. Organic maturation and the development of learning capacity. In M. R. Rosenzweig & E. L. Bennett (Eds.), *Neural mechanisms of learning and memory.* Cambridge, Mass.: MIT Press, 1976.

Amsel, A. The ontogeny of appetitive learning and persistence in the rat. In N. E. Spear & B. A. Campbell (Eds.), *Ontogeny of learning and memory.* Hillsdale, N.J.: Lawrence Erlbaum Associates, 1979, in press.

Bach, M. J., & Underwood, B. J. Developmental changes in memory attributes. *Journal of Educational Psychology,* 1970, **61,** 292–306.

Berk, A. M. *Infantile amnesia, latent extinction, and stimulus generalization in infant and adult rats.* Unpublished doctoral dissertation, Brooklyn College, 1978.

Blass, E. M., Kenny, J. T., Stoloff, M., Bruno, J. P., Teicher, M. H., & Hall, W. G. Motivation, learning and memory in the ontogeny of suckling in albino rats. In N. E. Spear & B. A. Campbell (Eds.), *Ontogeny of learning and memory.* Hillsdale, N.J.: Lawrence Erlbaum Associates, 1979, in press.

Bower, G. H. A multicomponent theory of the memory trace. In K. W. Spence & J. T. Spence (Eds.), *The psychology of learning and motivation (Vol. I).* New York: Academic Press, 1967.

Brake, S. C. Discrimination training in infant, preweanling and weanling rats: Effects of prior learning experiences with the discriminanda. *Animal Learning and Behavior,* 1978, **6,** 435–443.

Campbell, B. A., & Alberts, J. R. Ontogeny of long term memory for learned taste aversions. *Behavioral and Neural Biology,* 1979, **25,** 139–156.

Campbell, B. A., & Coulter, X. Ontogeny of learning and memory. In M. R. Rosenzweig & E. L. Bennett (Eds.), *Neuromechanisms of learning and memory.* Cambridge, Mass.: MIT Press, 1976.

Campbell, B. A., Misanin, J. R., White, B. C., & Lytle, L. D. Species differences in ontogeny of memory: Indirect support for neural maturation as a determinant of forgetting. *Journal of Comparative and Physiological Psychology,* 1974, **87,** 193–202.

Campbell, B. A., & Raskin, L. A. Ontogeny of behavioral arousal: The role of environmental stimuli. *Journal of Comparative and Physiological Psychology,* 1978, **92,** 176–184.

Campbell, B. A., & Spear, N. E. Ontogeny of memory. *Psychological Review,* 1972, **79,** 215–236.

Coulter, X. The determinants of infantile amnesia. In N. E. Spear & B. A. Campbell (Eds.), *The ontogeny of learning and memory.* Hillsdale, N.J.: Lawrence Erlbaum Associates, 1979, in press.

Coulter, X., Collier, A. C., & Campbell, B. A. Long term retention of early Pavlovian fear conditioning in infant rats. *Journal of Experimental Psychology: Animal Behavior Processes,* 1976, **2,** 48–56.

Domjan, M., CS Preexposure in taste-aversion learning: Effects of deprivation and preexposure duration. *Learning and Motivation,* 1972, **3,** 389–402.

Domjan, M. Attenuation and enhancement of neophobia for edible substances. In L. M. Barker, M. R. Best, & M. Domjan (Eds.), *Learning mechanisms in food selection.* Tex: Baylor University Press, 1977.

Fuller, J. L., Easler, D. A., & Banks, E. M. Formation of conditioned avoidance responses in young puppies. *American Journal of Psychology,* 1950, **160,** 462–466.

Gleitman, H. Forgetting of long term memories in animals. In W. K. Honig & P. H. R. James (Eds.), *Animal memory.* New York: Academic Press, 1971.

Haroutunian, V., & Riccio, D. C. Effect of arousal conditions during reinstatement treatment upon learned fear in young rats. *Developmental Psychobiology,* 1977, **10,** 25–32.

Hasher, L., & Johnson, M. K. Interpretive factors in forgetting. *Journal of Experimental Psychology: Human Learning and Memory,* 1975, **1,** 567–575.

Kenny, J. T., & Blass, E. M. Suckling as an incentive to instrumental learning in preweanling rats. *Science,* 1977, **196,** 898–899.

Kessler, P. G. *Retention of early Pavlovian fear conditioning in infant rats: Effect of temporal variables in conditioning.* Unpublished doctoral dissertation, State University of New York at Stony Brook, 1976.

Kessler, P. G., & Spear, N. E. Distributed practice decreases infantile amnesia. In preparation, 1979.

Klein, S. B., & Spear, N. E. Influence of age on short term retention of active avoidance learning in rats. *Journal of Comparative and Physiological Psychology,* 1969, **69,** 583–589.

Leon, M., & Moltz, H. The development of the pheromonal bond in the albino rat. *Physiology and Behavior,* 1972, **8,** 683–686.

Lubow, R. E. Latent inhibition. *Psychological Bulletin,* 1973, **79,** 398–407.

Martin, L. T., & Alberts, J. R. Taste aversion to mother's milk: The age-related role of nursing in acquisition and expression of a learned association. *Journal of Comparative and Physiological Psychology,* 1979, **3,** 430–445.

Melkman, R., & Deutsch, C. Memory functioning as related to developmental changes in bases of organization. *Journal of Experimental Child Psychology,* 1977, **23,** 84–97.

Miller, R. R., & Berk, A. M. Retention over metamorphosis in the African claw-toed frog. *Journal of Experimental Psychology: Animal Behavior Processes,* 1977, **3,** 343–356.

Murphy, J. M., & Nagy, Z. M. Neonatal thyroxine stimulation accelerates the maturation of both locomotor and memory processes in mice. *Journal of Comparative and Physiological Psychology,* 1976, **90,** 1082–1091.

Nagy, Z. M. Development of learning and memory processes in infant mice. In N. E. Spear & B. A. Campbell (Eds.), *The ontogeny of learning and memory.* Hillsdale, N.J.: Lawrence Erlbaum Associates, 1979, in press.

Randall, P. K., & Campbell, B. A. Ontogeny of behavioral arousal in rats: Effect of maternal and sibling presence. *Journal of Comparative and Physiological Psychology,* 1976, **90,** 453–459.

Riccio, D. C., Hodges, L. A., & Randall, P. K. Retrograde amnesia produced by hypothermia in rats. *Journal of Comparative and Physiological Psychology,* 1968, **66,** 618–622.

Rosenblatt, J. S. The sensorimotor and motivation bases of early behavior and development of selected altricial mammals. In N. E. Spear & B. A. Campbell (Eds.), *The ontogeny of learning and memory.* Hillsdale, N.J.: Lawrence Erlbaum Associates, 1979, in press.

Rovee-Collier, C. Alleviated forgetting in 3-month old infants: Memory retrieval after direct reactivation. Paper presented at the meetings of the International Society for Developmental Psychobiology, St. Louis, November, 1978.

Rovee, C., & Fagan, J. Extended conditioning and 24-hour retention in infants. *Journal of Experimental Child Psychology,* 1976, **21,** 1–11.

Rudy, J. W., & Cheatle, M. D. Odor-aversion learning by neonatal rats. *Science,* 1977, **198,** 845–846.
Rudy, J. W., & Cheatle, M. D. Ontogeny of associative learning: Acquisition of odor aversions by neonatal rats. In N. E. Spear & B. A. Campbell (Eds.), *Ontogeny of learning and memory.* Hillsdale, N.J.: Lawrence Erlbaum Associates, 1979, in press.
Rudy, J. W., Rosenberg, L., & Sandell, J. H. Disruption of a taste familiarity effect by novel exteroceptive stimulation. *Journal of Experimental Psychology; Animal Behavior Processes,* 1977, **3,** 26–36.
Seligman, M. E. P., & Hager, J. L. (Eds.). *Biological boundaries of learning.* New York: Appleton, 1972.
Shapiro, S., & Salas, M. Behavioral response of infant rats to maternal odor. *Physiology and Behavior,* 1970, **5,** 815–817.
Smith, G. J., & Spear, N. E. Effects of the home environment on withholding behaviors and conditioning in infant and neonatal rats. *Science,* 1978, **202,** 327–329.
Smith, G. J. *A developmental study of the effects of noncontingent learning on subsequent learning and retention of a discrimination response.* Unpublished master's thesis, State University of New York at Binghamton, 1978.
Smith, G. J., Greenfield, R. J., & Spear, N. E. Effects of home environmental cues on learning a shock-escape spatial discrimination in neonatal rats. Paper presented at meetings of the Midwestern Psychological Association, Chicago, May 1979.
Smith, N. Effects of interpolated learning on the retention of an escape response in rats as a function of age. *Journal of Comparative and Physiological Psychology,* 1968, **65,** 422–426.
Spear, N. E. Forgetting as retrieval failure. In W. K. Honig & P. H. R. James (Eds.), *Animal memory.* New York: Academic Press, 1971.
Spear, N. E. Retrieval of memory in animals. *Psychological Review,* 1973, **80,** 163–194.
Spear, N. E. Retrieval of memories: A psychobiological approach. In W. K. Estes (Ed.), *Handbook of learning and cognitive processes* (Vol. 4). *Attention and memory.* Hillsdale, N.J.: Lawrence Erlbaum Associates, 1976.
Spear, N. E. *The processing of memories: Forgetting and retention.* Hillsdale, N.J.: Lawrence Erlbaum Associates, 1978.
Spear, N. E. Experimental analysis of infantile amnesia. In J. F. Kihlstrom & F. J. Evans (Eds.), *Functional disorders of memory.* Hillsdale, N.J.: Lawrence Erlbaum Associates, 1979.
Spear, N. E., & Campbell, B. A. (Eds.). *Ontogeny of learning and memory.* Hillsdale, N.J.: Lawrence Erlbaum Associates, 1979, in press.
Spear, N. E., Gordon, W. C., & Martin, P. A. Warmup decrement as failure in memory retrieval in the rat. *Journal of Comparative and Physiological Psychology,* 1973, **85,** 601–614.
Spear, N. E., & Parsons, P. Alleviation of forgetting by reactivation treatment: A preliminary analysis of the ontogeny of memory processing. In D. Medin, W. Roberts, & R. Davis (Eds.), *Processes in animal memory.* Hillsdale, N.J.: Lawrence Erlbaum Associates, 1976. Pp. 135–166.
Spear, N. E., & Smith, G. Alleviation of forgetting in neonatal rats. *Developmental Psychobiology,* 1978, **11,** 513–529.
Sullivan, M., & Rovee-Collier, C. Conditioning analysis of infant long-term memory. *Child Development,* 1979, in press.
Sussman, P. *Differential retention of components of avoidance learning by juvenile and adult rats.* Unpublished doctoral dissertation. Carleton University, Ottawa, 1978.
Tompkins, S. S. A theory of memory. In J. S. Antrobus (Ed.), *Cognition and affect.* Boston: Little, Brown, 1970.
Tulving, E. Episodic and semantic memory. In E. Tulving & W. Donaldson (Eds.), *Or-*

ganization of memory. New York: Academic Press, 1972.

Underwood, B. J. Attributes of memory. *Psychological Review*, 1969, **76,** 559–573.

Underwood, B. J. Are we overloading memory? In A. W. Melton & E. Martin (Eds.), *Coding processes in human memory*. Washington, D.C.: Winston, 1972.

Underwood, B. J., & Schulz, R. W. *Meaningfulness in verbal learning*. Philadelphia: Lippincott, 1960.

Wagner, A. R., Rudy, J. W., & Whitlow, J. R. Rehearsal in animal conditioning. *Journal of Experimental Psychology*, 1973, **97,** 407–426.

White, S. H., & Pillemer, D. B. Childhood amensia and the development of a sociallty accessible memory system. In J. F. Kihlstrom & F. J. Evans (Eds.), *Functional disorders of memory*. Hillsdale, N.J.: Lawrence Erlbaum Associates, 1979.

Zentall, T. R. Effects of context change on forgetting in rats. *Journal of Experimental Psychology*, 1970, **86,** 440–448.

LEARNED HELPLESSNESS: ALL OF US WERE RIGHT (AND WRONG): INESCAPABLE SHOCK HAS MULTIPLE EFFECTS[1]

Steven F. Maier and Raymond L. Jackson
UNIVERSITY OF COLORADO, BOULDER, COLORADO

I. Introduction

Organisms exposed to inescapable and unavoidable aversive events often show later deficits in learning to escape such events when escape is possible (see Maier & Seligman, 1976, for review). This phenomenon, which has been called the learned helplessness effect and the interference effect, has received a great deal of recent attention and many of its characteristics are now known. However, this contribution will not review the literature surrounding the learned helplessness effect. Its purpose is to explore the causes and explanations of this phenomenon, rather than all of its empirical characteristics, and to present new evidence bearing on these issues. That is, discussion will be limited to

[1]The preparation of this manuscript was supported by grant BNS 78-00508 from the National Science Foundation. We would like to thank Deborah Coon, Kurt Schlesinger, David R. Thomas, and K. Geoffrey White for helpful comments.

ISBN 0-12-543313-1

research and theorizing directed at uncovering the mechanisms which produce the basic learned helplessness effect. We will focus on what exposure to inescapable aversive events does to the organism so that it later performs poorly in escape learning tasks. A final goal will be to explore the implications of our work on learned helplessness for the psychology of learning in general.

II. Brief Review

Even though we will not review the learned helplessness literature in any general sense, it is useful to introduce the issues involved by briefly sketching some of the known facts so that the reader will have a feel for the generality and characteristics of the phenomena to be explained. The following is a list of the most salient features of the helplessness effect.

1. *Controllability.* Exposure to shock results in later failure to learn only if the organism is initially exposed to events which it cannot control. Thus, failure to learn to escape shock only occurs if the subject has first been exposed to inescapable and unavoidable shock; exposure to escapable shock (the subject controls shock termination) does not have this effect (Seligman & Maier, 1967). The fact that the organism's degree of control over the events presented determines whether interference with later learning will occur has become the central feature of learned helplessness. Both Maier and Seligman (1976) and Seligman (1975) have argued that an effect must be shown to be caused by the uncontrollability of the events involved before it can be classified as a learned helplessness effect.

2. *Immunization and Therapy.* If the organism experiences escapable shock before being exposed to inescapable shock, the interference with subsequent escape learning does not occur (Seligman & Maier, 1967). An initial exposure to controllable shock has such an immunizing effect even if it occurs in a situation different from that in which inescapable shock treatment and escape training later take place (Williams & Maier, 1977). The rat's first learning to escape shock by turning a wheel with its paws eliminated the interference with shuttlebox escape that would have been produced by exposure to inescapable shock in a restraining tube. An initial experience with uncontrollable shock does not produce immunization.

Further, forcibly exposing the subject to an escape contingency after exposure to inescapable shock eliminates subsequent escape-learning deficits (Seligman, Maier, & Geer, 1968). Again, such experience must be with controllable shock and can occur in a different situation than both inescapable shock treatment and escape testing and still produce a "therapy" effect (Williams & Maier, 1977). Thus, experience with controllable shock either before or after inescapable shock can prevent or eliminate the learned helplessness effect.

3. *Generality*. The interference effect has been demonstrated in a variety of species. Cats (Thomas, 1977), dogs (Overmier & Seligman, 1967), humans (Hiroto & Seligman, 1975), mice (Braud, Wepman, & Russo, 1969), and rats (Maier, Albin, & Testa, 1973) all show deficits in escape learning following inescapable shock exposure. It remains a matter of speculation whether the mechanisms involved are the same in all of these species. Moreover, a number of different aversive events and test tasks have been used. Escape decrements have been reported following exposure to inescapable electric shocks in cats, dogs, mice, and rats (Overmier & Seligman, 1967), following a forced water swim in rats (Altenor, Kay, & Richter, 1977), and following exposure to both inescapable loud noise and unsolvable anagrams in humans (Hiroto & Seligman, 1975). Furthermore, there are even suggestions that exposure to food which the subject cannot control interferes with the subsequent learning of responses that produce food (Bainbridge, 1973; Engberg, Hansen, Welker, & Thomas, 1973; Mullins & Winefield, 1977; Welker, 1976).

Deficits in performance following inescapable shock have also been found in a variety of different learning situations. Lever pressing (Seligman, Rosellini, & Kozak, 1975), nose pressing (Goodkin, 1976), shuttling (Maier *et al.*, 1973), water maze escape (Altenor *et al.*, 1977), button pressing, moving a lever back and forth to escape loud noise, and anagram solution in humans (Hiroto & Seligman, 1975) have all been used as test tasks.

Further, the inescapable and unavoidable aversive events and the escape learning test do not have to occur in identical or even very similar environments. In our laboratory inescapable shocks are typically administered by electrodes fixed to the tails of rats restrained in a small, cylindrical restraining tube. Under some conditions this treatment produces interference with learning to run back and forth in a large rectangular shuttlebox. In fact, the aversive events in the two phases of the experiment may not have to be the same. Altenor *et al.* (1977) found inescapable shock exposure in rats to produce deficits in learning to escape from water. Moreover, they found that forced swimming would subsequently interfere with shock escape learning. Rosellini and Seligman (1975) have shown that inescapably shocked rats are slow to learn to escape from a frustrating goal box in which expected food failed to occur. Even more remarkable, Goodkin (1976) has reported that exposure to food over which the organism has no control produces interference with learning to escape shock.

4. *Boundary Conditions*. Despite the impressive generality noted above,

a learned helplessness effect is not the invariant outcome of experiments which involve the delivery of uncontrollable aversive events. The kind of response used by the test task (Glazer & Weiss, 1976a; Maier *et al.*, 1973; Seligman & Beagley, 1975), the amount of feedback for escape responding (Maier, Jackson, Tomie, & Rapaport, 1975), the type of contingency involved (Maier & Testa, 1975), the shock intensity used during testing (Jackson, Maier, & Rapaport, 1978), and the time interval between preshock and testing (Jackson, Alexander, & Maier, 1979; Overmier & Seligman, 1967; Seligman & Groves, 1970) are all critical factors in determining whether a learned helplessness effect will occur. Various aspects of the inescapable shock procedure are also not without importance (Glazer & Weiss, 1976b; Kelsey, 1977; Maier & Jackson, 1977).

Elaboration and discussion of these factors is beyond the scope of the present paper. However, several points about these constraints on the helplessness effect should be noted here. Some have argued that because the occurrence of the interference effect depends on a variety of conditions it is a weak effect, or lacks generality, or is a trivial artifact. We disagree with such arguments. Most (if not all) psychological phenomena depend on a number of conditions and are modulated by many factors, but this does not mean that they have reduced stature. A phenomenon that has no limits and determining factors is usually one that has not been studied. For example, classical conditioning is not the inevitable outcome of the pairing of two stimuli. It will only readily occur with stimuli of certain intensities, with a restricted class of responses (some responses are difficult or impossible to condition), with certain CS–UCS intervals, if no other already conditioned stimuli are present, if the organism has not already experienced random presentations of the CS and UCS, etc. These facts do not suggest that classical conditioning is a weak phenomenon, lacks generality, or is an artifact.

The important question is whether one can make sense out of why the factors that modulate a phenomenon do so. It is in the course of coming to an understanding of these factors that one can realistically evaluate the scientific importance of a phenomenon. The conditions which modulate classical conditioning do seem to make theoretical sense and so the phenomenon is not viewed as suspect or trivial. Indeed, it is possible to view theory building as an attempt to make predictable the effects of factors which modulate a phenomenon. Later in this paper we will attempt to show that the variables which determine the learned helplessness effect make sense and are theoretically interpretable.

5. *Other Behaviors.* Escape learning is not the only class of behavior influenced by prior exposure to inescapable shock. For example, both

shock-elicited aggression (Maier, Anderson, & Lieberman, 1972) and social dominance in a food competition situation (Rapaport & Maier, 1978) are reduced by prior exposure to inescapable shock. Exposure to escapable shock does not have such effects. Further, uncontrollable aversive events produce greater symptoms of stress than do controllable ones (Weiss, 1968, 1971a; Weiss, Stone, & Harrell, 1970). This is true whether stress is measured by ulcer formation, weight loss, corticosteroid secretion, or central norepinephrine levels. Finally, Seligman (1975) has suggested that experiencing uncontrollable aversive events may lead to emotional depression. Thus, a broad range of behavior beyond escape response acquisition is influenced by the controllability of aversive events.

III. Why All the Controversy?

There is little agreement as to how to explain the learned helplessness effect. A large number of very different hypotheses have been proposed, each with supporting data and arguments. The literature is replete with papers attacking the other positions, defending a position, counterattacking, etc. This is a peculiar state of affairs, particularly when one considers the large number of empirical studies that have been published. Such studies should constrain theorizing and converge on a single theoretical position. Yet the explanation of the learned helplessness effect remains an issue of intense theoretical controversy (see, e.g., Anisman, 1975; Black, 1977; Bracewell & Black, 1974; Glazer & Weiss, 1976a, 1976b; Levis, 1976; Maier, 1977; Maier & Seligman, 1976; Seligman, 1975; Weiss, Glazer, & Pohorecky, 1975). This matter has produced such large disagreements and such intense and prolonged controversy that it might prove useful to consider why the explanation of the learned helplessness effect has been such a heated issue.

It is our feeling that the controversy arose as a reaction against the pretheoretical premises of the learned helplessness hypothesis offered by Maier and Seligman (Maier & Seligman, 1976; Maier, Seligman, & Solomon, 1969; Seligman, 1975; Seligman, Maier, & Solomon, 1971). Strong negative reactions occurred in part because the assertions of the learned helplessness hypothesis were incompatible with many traditional (S–R) assumptions of the psychology of learning. Thus, we believe that the disagreements concerning the explanation of the behavioral effects of prior exposure to inescapable shock can be viewed as a reflection of the larger "S–R" versus "cognitive" debate. We must, however, describe the hypotheses which have been offered to account for the interference effect before we can detail and defend this argument.

A. The Competing Explanations

1. *The Learned Helplessness Hypothesis*

The central assertion of the learned helplessness position (Maier & Seligman, 1976; Maier *et al.*, 1969; Seligman, 1975; Seligman *et al.*, 1971) is that organisms exposed to uncontrollable aversive events learn that these events are uncontrollable. That is, they learn that the events are independent of voluntary responses. Organisms could learn this by being sensitive to the conditional probability of an event occurring given that some response has been emitted, the conditional probability of that event occurring given that the same response has not been emitted, and the conjoint variation of these two probabilities. A given response exerts no control over an event when these two probabilities are equal. We assumed that when the organism learns that this equality obtains for a number of responses it then infers that no response will control the event; i.e., it comes to expect that the event is independent of its behavior. Thus, in the case of inescapable shock, we argued that the dog or the rat or the person learns that its responses are independent of shock termination and comes to expect that this will also be true in the future.

This still does not explain why the subject should be retarded in learning to escape in a new situation. Maier and Seligman argued that two mechanisms were responsible, one being emotional–motivational, and the other being cognitive–associative–perceptual. Maier and Seligman maintained that the acquisition of the expectation that shock and behavior are independent should reduce the organism's incentive to later attempt to escape. This notion was based on the assumption that such incentive is partly produced by the expectation that responding will lead to a reinforcing state of affairs. Second, it was argued that having learned response–outcome independence should interfere with the organism's propensity to associate or perceive the relationship between the new escape response and shock termination if a response should occur. We argued that having learned that responses and shocks are not correlated would interfere with learning that some response and shock is now correlated.

The idea of associative–perceptual interference becomes clearer if one considers what the helplessness hypotheses claims transpires during a helplessness-type experiment. First, consider the subject who is receiving inescapable shock. Some response undoubtedly will occur by chance just before shock terminates on some trial. However, the performance of this response on the next trial would not make shock terminate any sooner than it would otherwise. The subject might experience a number of such sequences in which the momentary contiguity between response and reinforcement is nothing more than a spurious relationship. Now consider the subject in the new situation where escape is possible. Suppose the animal is tested in a shuttlebox. If it jumps the hurdle and shock goes off, why should it attribute any significance to this pairing of events? The dog or rat has experienced many such pairings in the past, but the relation always proved unreliable. The mechanisms whereby such "generalized irrelevance" learning effects might occur will be discussed in Section VII. This set of conjectures is called the learned helplessness hypothesis.

2. *Learned Inactivity Hypotheses*

A number of investigators have argued that the inescapably shocked animal performs poorly in the escape learning test because it has learned to be inactive during inescapable shock exposure. This inactivity is directly incompatible with such responses as shuttling and lever pressing and would interfere with their performance. Unlike the helplessness hypothesis these hypotheses assert that motivation is not undermined and that there is not interference with what the organism learns from an exposure to the response–shock termination contingency during testing (but see Black, 1977, and a reply by Maier, 1977). They argue that there is simply mechanical incompatability between the inactivity response learned during inescapable shock and the test task response later required. Thus, the subject is viewed as less likely to respond, not as less likely to learn if it does respond. In contrast, the learned helplessness hypothesis asserts that the inescapably shocked subject will learn less than noninescapably shocked controls on a given trial even if it does respond and terminate shock.

The various learned inactivity hypotheses differ with regard to the mechanism whereby inactivity is acquired during inescapable shock treatment. Bracewell and Black (1974) proposed that the inescapable shock hurts more if the organism moves. This should have the effect of punishing movement, thereby decreasing its frequency. Glazer and Weiss (1976a, 1976b) believe that the onset of shock elicits a burst of movement which subsides after 3 or 4 sec. Since the duration of an inescapable shock has typically been 5 sec in our experiments, Glazer and Weiss maintained that the decrease in activity during shock is closely followed by shock termination. They argued that this should have accidentally reinforced activity reduction in the presence of shock. Activity subsided and this was always followed in a second or two by shock termination. Anisman, deCatanzaro, and Remington (1978) have recently made a similar argument. Levis (1976) has offered a somewhat more complex reinforcement process based on a two-process theory, but it does not differ in spirit from those above.

3. *Stress-Induced Inactivity*

Anisman (1975) and Weiss and his associates (Miller & Weiss, 1969; Weiss, 1971b; Weiss *et al.*, 1975, 1970) maintain that inescapable shock is a severe stressor and depletes neurochemicals necessary for the mediation of movement. Thus, the inescapably shocked organism performs poorly in an escape learning test because it cannot readily move enough to perform the designated response. Weiss has focused on norepinephrine as the depleted substance, while Anisman (1975) has argued for the additional involvement of cholinergic mechanisms. Glazer and Weiss (1976a, 1976b) have gone on to suggest that the neurochemical mechanism operates only when large numbers of intense inescapable shocks are used and that the inactivity reinforcement mechanism is operative when milder shocks are used.

B. Basic Underlying Assumptions

It should be apparent that the competing hypotheses differ quite radically in their basic outlook. The learned helplessness hypothesis explains the interference effect by invoking a series of processes that are clearly cognitive in nature and that are at variance with some traditional beliefs. The other explanations seem to have been offered in reaction to and as an alternative to the learned helplessness hypothesis. It is important to realize that they do not invoke processes and mechanisms beyond those traditionally assumed within an S–R framework. The learned inactivity views use only the effects of reinforcement and punishment of overt motor responses to account for subsequent performance deficits. The stress-induced inactivity views do not question any particular assumptions about the nature of learning.

This is not to imply that cognitive and S–R views are mutually exclusive and always clearly separable. In fact, it is not easy to specify the defining features of each. However, the two types of outlook do differ in flavor and emphasis. The learned helplessness hypothesis seems to be incompatible with five traditional S–R assumptions.

1. *Contiguity*

Until recent years contiguity has been one of the most fundamental and cherished principles of the psychology of animal learning. Almost all theorists have assumed that contiguity between events is critical for learning. Some have viewed contiguity as necessary but not sufficient (e.g., Hull, 1943) and some have viewed contiguity as both necessary and sufficient (e.g., Guthrie, 1935), but all have believed it to be of paramount importance. Classical conditioning theorists have differed with regard to whether CS–UCS or CS–UCR contiguity is of greater importance, but contiguity has still been the focus. Psychologists interested in operant conditioning (e.g., Herrnstein, 1966) have long maintained that contiguity between response and reinforcement is both necessary and sufficient to strengthen responses. This can be clearly seen in the concept of superstitious reinforcement. Here the delivery of a response-independent reinforcer is said to strengthen whatever response accidentally occurs shortly before the reinforcer. From this view the occurrence of a reinforcer always strengthens some response, it is just a matter of which response.

2. *Automatic Strengthening*

The principle of automatic strengthening is not unrelated to the contiguity assumption. It views the strengthening effect of contiguity and/or reinforcement as direct, inevitable, and independent of the cognitive activities of the organism. That is, contiguity/reinforcement has been viewed as sufficient for learning. The notion is that a CS–UCS pairing will of necessity produce an increment in the strength of an associative connection and that the occurrence of a reinforcer after a response will of necessity strengthen the response. The links are seen as being direct and simple.

3. *Simplicity of the Associative Process*

The traditional orientation has been that the associative process itself is quite simple. There may be complex performance rules and other factors might enter, but the basic hooking together process has been seen as being not very complex. It should be obvious that this viewpoint is not unrelated to contiguity and automatic strengthening.

4. *Breadth of Transfer*

Although not usually stated, it is typically assumed that what is learned about a given stimulus or response will remain specific to that stimulus or response. Only stimulus and response generalization along a dimension of physical similarity is generally allowed. Thus, what is learned is viewed as being able to produce behavioral effects under conditions that were not involved directly in training only to the extent to which generalization along hypothetical physical continua could occur. In the absence of such physical similarity transfer does not occur.

5. *Responses and Expectations*

Until recently most psychologists of animal learning have believed that what is learned in a classical conditioning or instrumental-learning situation is best characterized as a response (salivation, lever pressing, shuttling, etc.) rather than a representation of the environment and its contingencies. Transfer between situations was attributed to the mechanical interaction between the responses involved in the situations. If experience in one situation facilitated learning in another situation, then it was because the response learned in the first was compatible with the response required in the second. If experience in one situation interfered with learning in another situation, then it was because the response learned in the first was incompatible with (could not be performed at the same time as) the response required in the second.

These five factors constitute neither a unique nor an exhaustive treatment of what has usually been believed to be true of animal learning. However, it does help to clarify the manner in which the learned helplessness hypothesis departs from traditional beliefs. The helplessness hypothesis argues that exposure to response-independent shock leads to the development of an expectation or a representation of the independent relationship between responding and shock, rather than to a superstitiously reinforced motor response. What is learned is not seen as a reflection of the direct effects of chance contiguous relationships of behavior and outcome but is more like a concept developed by spurious relationships between various behaviors and reinforcement. That is, the expectation that responding and shock termination are independent is not viewed as being limited only to those responses that have occurred and have been found to be unrelated to shock termination during inescapable shock exposure. Maier and Seligman implicitly have assumed that the subject makes an inference to physically dissimilar responses after learning that a certain number are independent of shock termination.

Finally, the helplessness hypothesis presumes that the negative transfer to the escape testing phase is produced by this cognitive state rather than by any motor response which has been acquired.[2] Thus the learned

[2]The learned helplessness hypothesis does not, of course, deny that motor responses can be learned and produce transfer. It simply asserts that this is also true of cognitive states.

helplessness hypothesis departs from traditional notions concerning the very fundamental issue of how to describe what is learned and what leads to transfer (the learned helplessness hypothesis is, of course, not alone in raising these issues), while the alternative hypotheses support tradition. For them, motor responses are learned during inescapable shock and produce transfer effects to the testing situation.

The learned helplessness hypothesis also conflicts with the related contiguity–automatic strengthening–simplicity of associative processes assumptions. It argues that learning cannot be viewed as a simple product of the coincidence of response and reinforcer. Instead, it holds that the organism compares the probability of reinforcement in the presence and absence of responses. The simple temporal conjunction of response and reinforcement is not seen as sufficient to produce some sort of automatic strengthening. Rather, the organism is viewed as performing some sort of analysis of the causal structure of the environment. It further proposes that what is learned from a conjunction of the correct escape response in testing and shock termination will not be an automatic outcome of that conjunction. It will depend on the organism's prior representation of the relationship between responding and shock termination. Again, the other competing explanations do not make such assumptions.

In summary, it seems clear that the learned helplessness hypothesis departs from the usual view of learning in a number of fundamental ways. It is our belief that this is at least partly responsible for the controversy regarding the explanation of the learned helplessness effect. A phenomenon was investigated, a somewhat unusual explanation was offered, and others presented what they viewed as simpler and more parsimonious explanations which utilized existing mechanisms that did not require the modification of traditional views.

It might be noted that it is not unusual that those phenomena and theories which attract attention and controversy are ones that question long-established beliefs. This is easy to see in the learning and motivation area. Even a casual reading of the disciplines' journals will reveal that taste-aversion learning, autoshaping and related phenomenon, blocking, memory models, and questions about how events are represented, are receiving considerable attention. These all question long-standing beliefs. For example, taste-aversion learning attacks the notions of equipotentiality of stimuli and that CS–UCS contiguity is necessary for conditioning. Blocking questions whether contiguity is sufficient to produce conditioning; the work on memory models and on how events are represented investigates what is learned, etc. In addition to challenging traditional views, all have generated a considerable amount of theoretical controversy. It is our contention that the explanation of the learned helplessness effect is simply another instance of this phenomenon. We now turn to an exploration of these explanations.

IV. The Activity Deficit

All of the explanations of the learned helplessness effect discussed above predict that inescapably shocked subjects should later be less active than control subjects in the presence of shock. The learned inactivity and stress-induced inactivity hypotheses make this prediction directly. The learned helplessness hypothesis can account for an activity deficit in inescapably shocked organisms because it holds that the learning of response–shock termination independence should reduce the incentive to attempt to escape. Reduced incentive to escape might be expected to result in a reduction in movement during shock. It is thus surprising that there has not been a demonstration of such an activity decrement until quite recently.

Our first hint that inescapable shock might actually lead to an activity reduction in the presence of shock was the demonstration that the inescapable shock-induced shuttlebox escape-learning deficit in rats could be eliminated by using more intense shock during the escape training (Jackson *et al.*, 1978). In this experiment rats were either first given 80 1.0-mA, 5-sec inescapable shocks through electrodes attached to their tails while they were restrained in a tube, or were only restrained and given no shock. Escape/avoidance training in a shuttlebox occurred 24 hr later. Each trial began with a tone signal. Failure to respond led to the onset of shock 5 sec later, and shock remained until a response occurred. A trial terminated automatically if no response occurred within 35 sec of trial onset. A single crossing of the shuttlebox (FR-1) was required to terminate shock in the first five trials and two crossings (FR-2) were required in the remaining 25 trials. The rationale for this procedure is described in Maier *et al.* (1973).

Separate groups were tested with either .6 mA-, .8 mA-, or 1.0-mA intensity shock in the shuttlebox. Figure 1 shows the mean latency to complete the shuttling response for each of the groups. As is typical (Maier *et al.*, 1973; Maier & Jackson, 1977; Testa, Juraska, & Maier, 1974), there were no large group differences on FR-1 trials. However, a large learned helplessness effect emerged on FR-2 trials when testing was at .6 mA. The effect was somewhat diminished when testing was conducted with .8-mA shock and disappeared completely when testing was at 1.0 mA.[3] As is also apparent, the failure of a learned helplessness

[3]Investigators interested in studying the learned helplessness effect should not take these specific values too seriously as they will differ for different shock sources and test tasks.

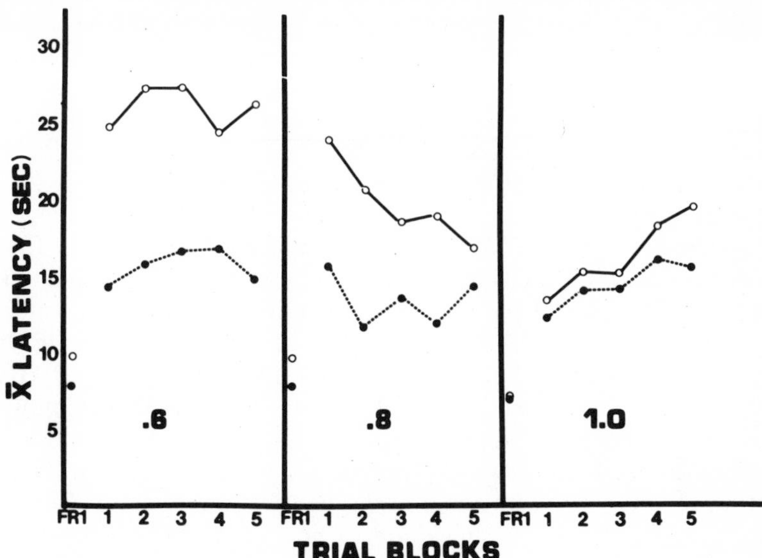

Fig. 1. Mean latency to escape shock across blocks of five shuttlebox escape trials as a function of the shock intensity used during testing. ○, Preshocked; ● restrained.

effect to appear at 1.0 mA is attributable to the effect of shock intensity on the preshocked rats. The performance of the preshocked rats improved with increasing shock intensity, while the performance of the restrained controls remained unchanged.

The most natural interpretation of these results is that inescapable shock reduces activity in the presence of shock and that this deficit is overcome by more intense shock. Certainly reduced activity makes more sense than an associative interference. There is no reason why more intense shock should directly counteract an associative deficit. However, it could do so indirectly. More intense shocks might sustain a higher level of unconditioned activity than do weak shocks, and the more activity a shock generates, the more likely it would be that an animal would repeatedly encounter the escape contingency. With a sufficient number of exposures to the contingency, even rats suffering associative deficits should come to learn. Thus, any of the hypotheses which have been advanced to explain the interfering effects of inescapable shock could predict that inescapably shocked rats would eventually acquire the escape response.

This reasoning led us to determine whether the unlearned frequency with which rats cross the shuttlebox twice (thus meeting the FR-2 contingency) varies as a function of shock intensity. This is preferable to measuring simple activity. A demonstration that inescapably shocked rats later emit less motor activity and that the inactivity is overcome by increased shock intensities would admit the possibility that the motor depression is not sufficient to produce decrements in shuttlebox crossings. Because the proposed consequences of the activity deficit is poor shuttlebox performance, it would still be necessary to show that the activity deficit is large enough to reduce shuttlebox crossings.

Thus we directly investigated whether inescapable shock reduces activity as assessed by unlearned shuttlebox crossing (Jackson *et al.*, 1978). Twenty-four hours after being restrained or receiving inescapable tail shock, rats were placed in the shuttlebox and given five FR-1 escape trials with the shock level set at either .6 or 1.0 mA. Following this, shocks were presented, but crossing the shuttlebox had no effect on shock. Shocks were 30 sec long and were not affected by the number of times the animal crossed the shuttlebox.

Figure 2 shows the number of times the animals crossed the shuttlebox two or more times across blocks of five trials. This is a measure of elicited activity in the presence of shock and of how often the subjects would encounter the escape contingency by means of simple elicited activity. It is clear that preshocked rats tested at .6 mA completed two or more crosses less frequently than did the restrained group tested at this intensity. However, at 1.0 mA both groups crossed more frequently and to the same degree. Thus, inescapable shock exposure does produce a later activity deficit in the presence of shock, and this deficit is overcome by increased shock intensities. These findings lend support to the hy-

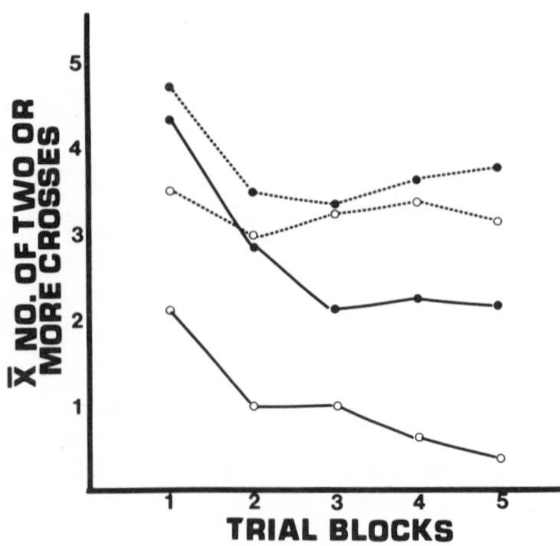

Fig. 2. Mean number of trials with two or more crosses across blocks of five trials. (●——●) Restrained, .6 mA; (○——○) preshocked, .6 mA; (●- - -●) restrained, 1.0 mA; (○- - -○) preshocked, 1.0 mA.

pothesis that the shuttlebox learned helplessness effect is attributable solely to a decrease in activity in the face of relatively mild electric shock; the unconditioned crossing data mirrored the escape response acquisition data. A learned helplessness effect only occurred under conditions that produced an activity decrement.

V. How Can the Explanations Be Discriminated?

It has already been noted that all of the hypotheses which have been advanced to account for the learned helplessness effect can account for the existence of an activity deficit, although it must be admitted that the learned activity and stress-induced inactivity views do so more naturally and directly than does the learned helplessness hypothesis. What distinguishes the learned helplessness hypothesis from the alternatives is the assertion that the organism learns act–outcome independence during exposure to inescapable shock and that this expectancy interferes with the organism's subsequent learning of response–shock termination relationships. That is, this position argues for the existence of associative interference in addition to any activity deficits which may occur. The inactivity hypotheses view the learned helplessness effect as representing a performance deficit; the learned helplessness hypothesis insists on both a true learning and a performance deficit.

The data just presented question whether it is necessary to assume the existence of an associative interference in order to account for the occurrence of the learned helplessness effect. It suggests that nothing need be assumed beyond an activity deficit produced by inescapable shock exposure. Thus, it is vitally important to inquire whether there exists any strong unambiguous evidence demonstrating an inescapable shock-produced associative deficit. This is the critical issue because it is the proposition that associative interference exists which distinguishes the learned helplessness hypothesis from its alternatives.

It is our feeling that there is no direct or clear evidence that demands the interpretation that exposure to inescapable shock produces a later deficit in the organism's tendency to associate its behavior and shock termination. There are findings which follow more naturally from the assumption of an associative interference than from only inactivity, but they can all be explained in a *post hoc* (and sometimes strained) fashion by inactivity theories (see, e.g., Levis, 1976). Thus the evidence is at best weak and indirect.

There is a simple reason why it has been difficult to provide evidence which clearly affirms or rejects the existence of an associative interference following inescapable shock exposure. The test tasks which have been used to assess the existence of a learned helplessness effect confound poor learning of escape and inactivity. In a typical animal study a rat is given inescapable shock and then tested in a shuttlebox or lever-press escape-learning situation. What is usually manipulated is some aspect of the inescapable shock, some aspect of the testing, the interval between them, the organism's previous experience, etc. What remains constant is the use of shuttling or lever pressing as the test task. However, poor shuttle or lever-press performance can be explained by reduced activity as easily as by poor learning. If an animal tends to be inactive, its performance on such tasks should suffer. So it only remains for the inactivity theorist to possess such sufficient cleverness to find a conceivable way in which the variables manipulated in the experiment might alter activity.

Moreover, matters are even more difficult. Inescapably shocked subjects frequently fail to respond at all on a given FR-2 shuttle or lever-press trial. Thus inescapably shocked and control subjects do not receive an equal number of exposures to the escape contingency. This further complicates any possible assessment of an associative interference using these tasks. How can one conclude that inescapably shocked subjects are performing poorly because of a reduced sensitivity to the escape contingency when they often fail to respond and are thus not exposed to the contingency? Add to this the fact that inescapably shocked and control subjects sometimes begin escape testing at different levels and the situation seems hopeless. How can one infer an associative deficit when performance differs from the very outset of the test?

VI. An Associative Deficit

A. Evidence

The foregoing discussion suggests the strategy of examining the effects of the controllability of an initial shock experience upon performance in an escape learning task that does not confound poor learning and decreased activity. That is, an experiment is needed which examines the effects of inescapable shock exposure on escape learning in a situation where decreased activity will not produce poor performance. Thus the learning task must be one in which response speed and level of learning are independent. Moreover, as we have seen, the task must also be one in which inescapably shocked rats do not begin testing at an inferior performance level and do not fail to respond.

A choice task in which shock is escaped by choosing the correct response from a number of alternatives seemed to provide an obvious way to meet these requirements. Here escape learning is assessed by the accuracy of the subject's choices rather than by response speed. High levels of activity should not necessarily lead to accurate choice performance and low levels of activity should not necessarily lead to inaccurate choices, provided enough activity is present for choices to occur. There is not an inevitable relation between response speed and accuracy, and, indeed, they may be independent. In any case, both response speed and choice accuracy can be measured and so their correlation can be assessed. Further, all animals should start at the same level of performance (chance responding) with regard to choice accuracy. The final requirement, an absence of failures to respond, seemed potentially surmountable by using a shock intensity sufficient to eliminate large activity differences (see page 168) and a very small apparatus such that not much movement would be needed for the subject to make a choice.

The most obvious task meeting the above specifications is a T maze. However, T mazes require that the subject be handled between trials, an undesirable feature. This led us to develop a Y-maze escape task. Each of the three 22.5-cm arms was at a 120° angle with respect to its neighbors and connected to a small central section in the shape of an equilateral triangle measuring 11.0 cm on a side. The animal only had to move about 12 cm into an arm of the maze to register a response, so very little running was required for the rat to choose one of the arms. Further, external stimulus cues were minimized. The arms were all identical and the maze was housed in a dark room so that extra maze cues could not easily be used. Thus, the rat had to learn a motor response, not to approach or avoid a particular set of external stimuli.

A trial began with the simultaneous onset of lights behind the end walls of the arms and 1.0-mA shock to the grids. This is an intensity sufficient to eliminate the inescapable shock-induced movement deficit, as measured by elicited shuttlebox crossings (Jackson, Maier, & Rapaport, 1978). The shocks and lights terminated if the rat entered the arm to the left of its position when the trial began. The animal spent the intertrial interval in darkness. However, if the rat moved into the arm to the right, a left turn from this arm was then required. If another right turn occurred, the rat then had to move into the arm to the left of this arm. Thus, a trial terminated only if a left turn was made and any number of incorrect choices (right turns) could occur before a correct response. Shock terminated automatically after 60 sec if a correct choice (left turn) had not occurred. The rat was free to move about the maze between trials. Its position at the beginning of a trial defined its starting point.

In our first experiment one group of rats was first inescapably shocked in restraining tubes and another group was only restrained. Twenty-four hours later both groups were given 100 escape-training trials in the Y maze as described above. The results of this experiment can be seen in Fig. 3, which presents the mean percent of trials on which one or more errors occurred across blocks of 10 trials. Initially both groups were as likely to choose the incorrect arm as they were to choose the correct response. However, the accuracy of the performance of the two groups quickly diverged. The preshocked rats had more trials on which at least one error occurred and improved less during the course of training than did the restrained controls. In fact, the performance of the preshocked subjects did not improve beyond chance until about 60 trials had occurred.

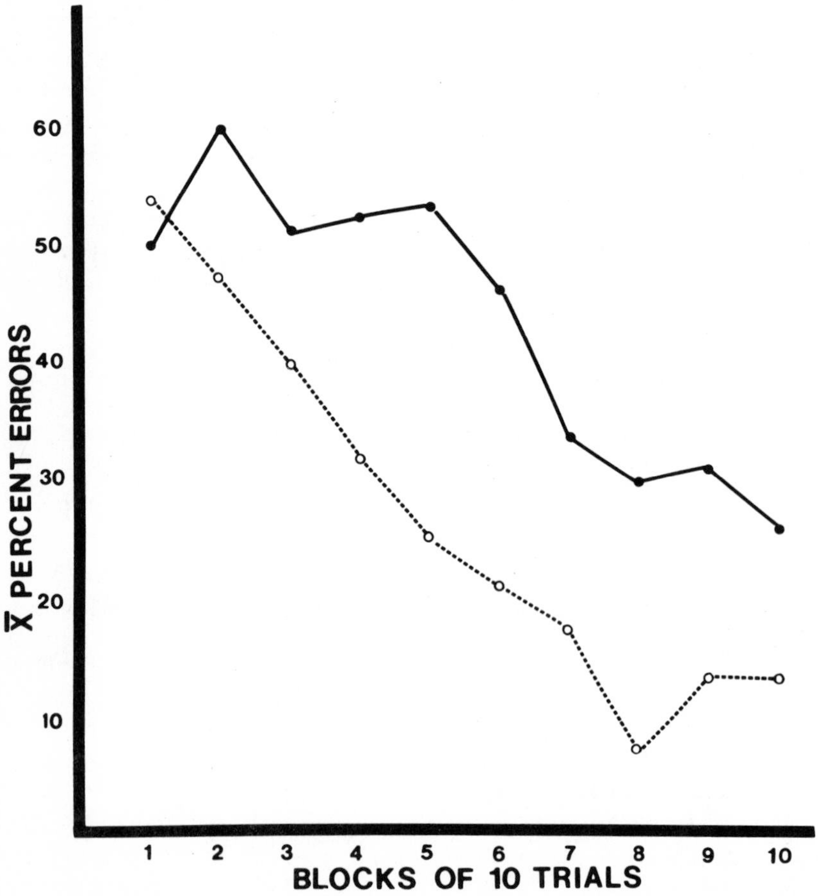

Fig. 3. Mean percentage of trials with one or more errors across blocks of 10 y-maze escape trials. ●, Preshocked; ○, restrained.

The difference between the preshocked and restrained groups was not caused by failures to respond as is the case in the shuttlebox. There were almost no failures to terminate a trial with a response. Only one subject in the preshocked group had any failures to respond, and this only on one trial. Thus, the error data indicated that preshocked rats made more errors than did the controls, not that they responded less often. They did not fail to respond and choose an arm of the maze, they simply chose incorrectly. Thus, the present data reveal an interference with learning under conditions in which the preshocked subjects are exposed to the correct contingency on every trial. The preshocked subjects continued to run and choose arms until a correct response finally occurred, but they simply made a large number of errors.

Even though the preshocked subjects responded on every trial, it is possible that they were slower to respond than the controls. Figure 4 presents the mean latency to complete the first response of a trial. Indeed, preshocked rats were slower to respond than the controls by about 1 sec (a statistically reliable difference). However, this small difference in response speed cannot be used to explain the inescapable shock-produced deficit in escape choice learning because a reliable correlation has not been obtained between response latency and choice accuracy, either including both groups ($r = +.12$) or just the preshocked group ($r = -.06$). The argument that response speed differences can account for choice accuracy differences requires a strong positive correlation between them.

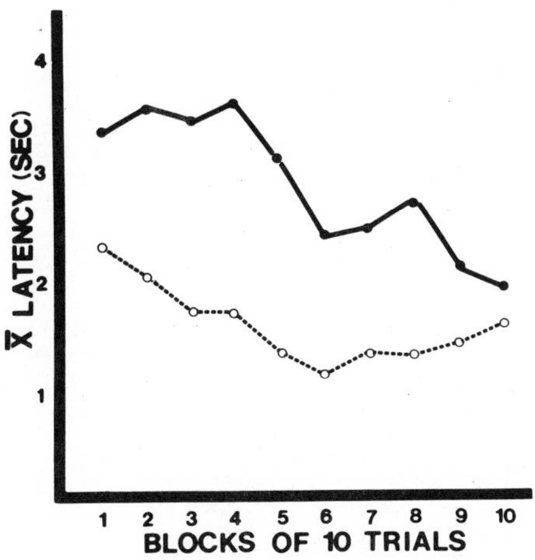

Fig. 4. Mean latency to complete the first response on a trial across blocks of 10 Y-maze escape trials. ●, Preshocked; ○, restrained.

Thus, it appears that the Y-maze choice escape task meets all of the requirements for the demonstration of a true associative deficit that cannot be explained by reduced activity. Inescapable shock exposure had only a small effect on activity as measured by the time to complete the first choice response. That the speed difference was so small is not surprising since the conditions of the experiment were arranged to minimize any activity deficits produced by exposure to inescapable shock. Our use of a small maze and a moderately high shock intensity were no doubt responsible. Further, the response speed measure did not correlate with choice accuracy. In addition, the groups began at the same level of performance and failures to respond did not occur (again because of the shock intensity and size of the maze). Thus, all groups were exposed to the escape contingencies equally often. The fact that exposure to inescapable shock still interfered with learning and produced poor choice performance strongly supports the existence of an associative deficit produced by exposure to inescapable shock.

However, the learned helplessness hypothesis requires that the associative deficit only develop in situations in which the subject has not had control over shock. The experiment just reported leaves open the possibility that the associative effect observed has been produced by simple shock exposure rather than the uncontrollability of the shock. Figure 5 shows the results of an experiment designed to investigate whether the Y-maze learning deficit was produced by the inescapability of the initial shocks or by shock per se. One group was first trained to escape shock by turning a wheel located in the front of a small box in which the animal was restrained. A second group received yoked inescapable shocks. Shocks began at the same time for both the escape and yoked subjects and terminated for both whenever the escape subject responded. Thus, both received the same durations and distributions of shocks, but the escape group had control over shock and the yoked group did not. A third group was merely restrained in the wheel turn boxes and did not receive shock. All groups were given 100 trials of Y-maze escape training 24 hr later. As is apparent from Fig. 5, the retarded Y-maze escape learning is produced by the inescapability of shock rather than by shock per se. The inescapably shocked rats were slower to learn than either the escapably shocked or the naive group. The latter two groups did not differ.

B. Possible Independence of the Associative and Activity Deficits: I. Shock Intensity

The evidence so far presented suggests that exposure to uncontrollable aversive events produces both an activity decrement and an associative interference with what the organism learns from an exposure to

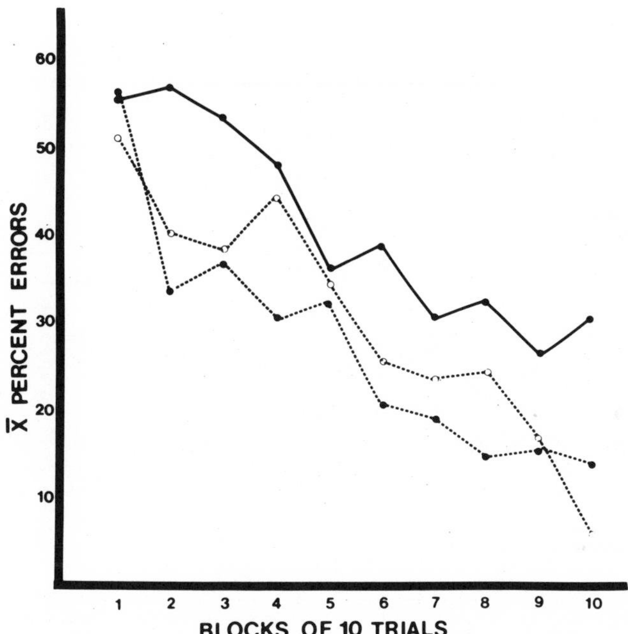

Fig. 5. Mean percentage of trials with one or more errors across blocks of 10 Y-maze escape trials. (●- - -●) Escape, (●——●) yoke, (○- - -○) naive.

response–shock termination contingencies. It also suggests that Y-maze escape learning, under the parameters employed, is primarily sensitive to the associative effect, while shuttlebox escape learning primarily reflects the activity effect. If this is true, then the influence of preshock on Y-maze performance should not be eliminated by treatments that eliminate the shuttlebox deficit by increasing activity. We have already noted that increasing the intensity of the shock used in the shuttlebox eliminates the helplessness effect and does so by improving the performance of inescapably shocked subjects. We argued that it did so by overcoming the activity deficit produced by inescapable shock. The learned helplessness hypothesis would not expect increased shock intensities to counteract the cognitive deficit produced by preshock. Thus, if the Y-maze task really does reflect an associative rather than an activity process, increases in shock intensity should not improve the performance of inescapably shocked rats as they do in the shuttlebox. Alternatively, if similar factors mediate the effects observed in the shuttlebox and Y maze, stronger shock should counteract the effects of inescapable shock.

The next experiment to be described investigated these possibilities.

Rats were inescapably shocked or restrained under our usual parameters and then given Y-maze escape training with either 1.0-, 1.6-, or 2.0-mA shock. Figure 6 shows the mean percent of trials with at least one error across blocks of 10 trials. While shock intensity had relatively little effect on the choice performance of preshocked rats, increases in shock intensity interfered with the performance of restrained subjects. The mean percent of trials with an error across all 100 trials was 43.5, 41.8, and 42.5 in the inescapably shocked rats tested at 1.0, 1.6, and 2.0 mA, respectively. Restrained rats had means of 30.4, 27.2, and 40.7, respectively.

The latencies to complete the first choice response are shown in Fig. 7. Inescapably shocked subjects were somewhat slower to respond than were restrained animals at 1.0 and 1.6 mA, while at 2.0-mA preshocked rats responded as rapidly as did controls. Again, there were no reliable correlations between response speed and accuracy. Even though an increase in shock intensity shortened response latencies it did not improve accuracy of choice. In fact, only at 2.0 mA was there an indication that shock intensity affected choice. Here strong shock interfered with the choice performance of restrained animals even though it produced short latencies.

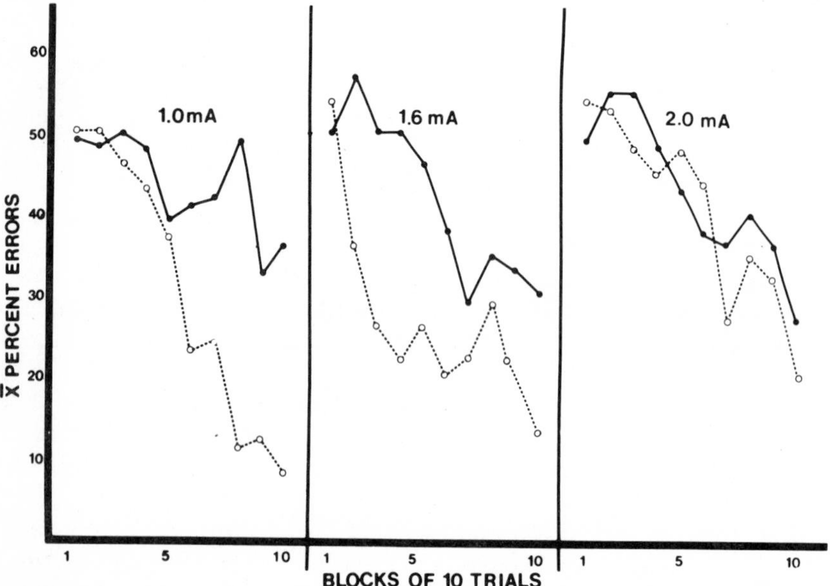

Fig. 6. Mean percentage of trials with one or more errors across blocks of 10 trials as a function of the intensity of shock used in the Y maze. ●, Preshocked; ○, restrained.

Three main findings emerge from this experiment: (1) Inescapably shocked subjects show a choice learning deficit relative to controls at 1.0 and 1.6 mA. This occurred despite the fact that 1.0 mA is sufficient to eliminate the shuttlebox learned helplessness effect. (2) Preshocked subjects were not retarded relative to controls when 2.0 mA was used. However, unlike the shuttlebox, this did not occur because the increased shock intensity improved the performance of preshocked subjects. Instead, the choice accuracy of the restrained controls deteriorated to the level of the preshocked subjects. It should be noted that a ceiling effect might have prevented the 2.0-mA shock from interfering with the choice performance of the preshocked subjects. The controls tested at 2.0 mA made an error on a mean of 40.7% of their trials. The preshocked rats tested at 1.0 mA had a mean of 43.5% of trials with an error. It might simply be difficult to perform at a poorer level on this task. This would make it unlikely that a difference between inescapably shocked and control subjects tested at 2.0 mA could be detected. (3) Increased shock intensity during testing decreased response latencies in both preshocked and restrained subjects, but this speed measure did not correlate with choice.

C. Implications

The experiments described in this section have a number of important implications. First, the findings indicate that exposure to inescapable shock produces two effects on Y-maze escape performance. Inescapably

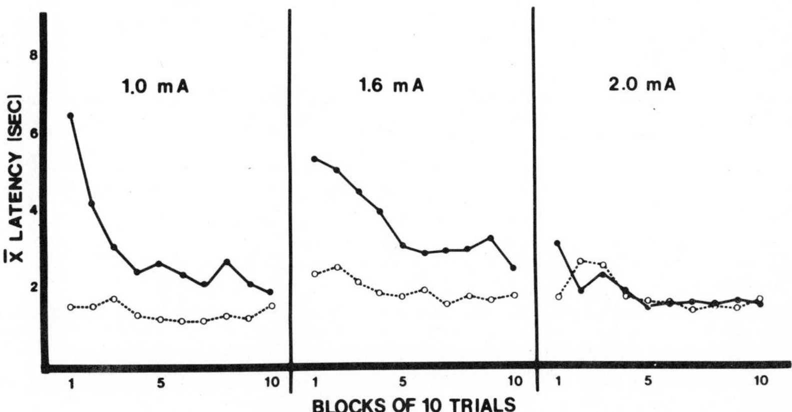

Fig. 7. Mean latency to complete the first response on a trial across blocks of 10 trials as a function of the intensity of shock used in Y-maze escape training. ●, Preshocked; ○, restrained.

shocked rats committed more errors than did escapably shocked or nonshocked controls when required to choose from among alternative responses. This strongly suggests that exposure to inescapable shock results in a decrement in the associability of behavior with shock termination. These data thus support the helplessness hypothesis' assertion that animals learn the independence of behavior and shock during exposure to uncontrollable shock. Also, inescapably shocked rats were slower to respond than were controls. This supports the notion that exposure to inescapable shock produces a later activity deficit.

The evidence for an associative deficit is particularly important because, as we have stated, it is the existence of an associative deficit that separates the learned helplessness hypothesis from its alternatives. We do not believe that the inactivity views are able to account for the deficit found in choice escape learning. Such explanations require that interference with escape learning be manifested in terms of less active responding in the presence of shock. However, we found that inescapable shock affected the accuracy of responding, not just the amount of responding. This eliminates the confounding inherent in prior shuttlebox and lever-press studies. In fact, inescapably shocked rats were more likely to make an error before terminating a trial with a correct response and thus emitted more movement than did controls.

As previously discussed (page 167), strong shock in a shuttlebox not only augments activity and thus the probability that inescapably shocked rats will encounter the FR-2 escape contingency, but it also eliminates the escape deficit typically observed. Also, relatively strong shock exerts its effect by facilitating the performance of preshocked subjects. However, strong shock did not improve the choice escape learning of inescapably shocked subjects in the Y-maze even though it did decrease their latency to respond. If strong shock simply increased the likelihood of running in the presence of shock and thereby eliminated the shuttlebox learned helplessness effect, it should not be surprising that strong shock decreased Y-maze response latencies but did not facilitate the escape learning of inescapably shocked subjects. Increases in response speed should not increase the unconditioned likelihood of turning left or right at the choice point. This pattern of data thus further supports the conclusion that the Y-maze escape deficit is associative in nature.

The shock intensity data also imply that Y-maze choice escape deficits and shuttlebox escape deficits are not mediated by the same factors. In both the shuttlebox and the Y-maze stronger shock led to faster responding, but it did not attenuate the effects of preshock on choice in the Y maze. If similar factors mediated the deficits observed in these two situations, then one might expect that when the latency to complete a response decreases, other indices of learning should also show improvement. Thus, while an activity decrement might be sufficient to account for inescapable shock-produced shuttlebox performance deficits, it is not sufficient as an account of the Y-maze choice deficit. The shuttlebox seems primarily sensitive to the activity effects of inescapable shock exposure, while Y-maze choice seems primarily sensitive to associative effects.

The facts that the activity deficit is overcome by increased shock intensities while the associative deficit is not, and the absence of a correlation between response speed and choice accuracy, suggest that these two effects of inescapable shock are somewhat independent (see Section VI, D for further support). This has important implications for the learned helplessness hypothesis. As the helplessness hypothesis is currently stated, associative and motivational deficits reflect the effects of the organism's retrieval of an expectancy about the effectiveness of its behavior. Thus this position would also seem to predict a positive correlation between indices of associative and motivational deficits. To the extent that choice accuracy and latency, respectively, provide measures of deficits in associative and incentive motivational processes, the failure to find a reliable correlation between these indices does not lend support to the motivational aspect of the helplessness hypothesis.

There are at least three related possibilities that might account for our failure to observe covariation in the latency and accuracy of performance. First, as the helplessness hypothesis suggests, changes in associative and incentive processes during testing may depend upon the retrieval of the set acquired during pretreatment. However, it could be argued that different and somewhat independent mechanisms are responsible for their respective effects on behavior. In other words, two different mechanisms may underlie activity and associative deficits, but both may require retrieval of the belief in response–outcome independence in order to affect behavior. If these mechanisms are in fact different, then it is conceivable that the correlation of motivational and associative processes would be low. Alternatively, it might be that motivational and associative deficits do not both depend upon the retrieval of a central state in order to be set into motion. Inescapable shock may produce associative effects like those described by the helplessness hypothesis. However, this associative effect may not be necessary to produce motivational/activity deficits. Motivational or activity deficits might be set in motion during exposure to inescapable shock by the learning that shock is uncontrollable. This deficit might thenceforth exist independently of the rearousal of the expectation that responding and shock termination are independent. However, the actual presence of this expectation during testing might be necessary for associative interference to occur.

A final possibility is that the associative deficit produced by inescapable shock exposure is a consequence of the sort of mechanism postulated by the learned helplessness hypothesis, while the activity deficit is produced by an entirely independent consequence of such treatment. After all, it is likely that inescapable shock has multiple effects. A stress-induced neurochemical depletion hypothesis is a viable candidate here. It is entirely possible that exposure to inescapable shock produces both act–outcome independence learning and neurochemical depletion. The former could be responsible for the observed associative deficit and the latter for the activity deficit. It should be noted that all of these possibilities agree that an associative deficit of the sort posited by the helplessness hypothesis is required to account for the error data reported in the present experiments. They differ in how closely they depend upon the retrieval of expectations concerning the efficacy of behavior in order to explain the activity deficit.

D. Possible Independence of the Associative and Activity Deficits: II. Time Course

The activity and associative effects of inescapable shock exposure should respond differently to variables other than shock intensity if they are really independent. That is, the shuttlebox and Y-maze escape learning learned helplessness effect should be differentially affected by variables other than shock intensity if the one reflects activity decrements while the other reflects decreases in the associability of responding and shock reinforcement.

One variable which might differentiate between associative and activity based deficits is the influence of the simple passage of time on performance. Whereas it can readily be argued that associative deficits should show substantial durability through time, activity deficits, particularly if produced by neurochemical factors, should more readily dissipate. This argument has previously been made by Weiss and his associates (e.g., Glazer & Weiss, 1976a; Miller & Weiss, 1969; Weiss *et al.*, 1975). In fact, Miller and Weiss first proposed a neurochemical depletion explanation of the interfering effects of inescapable shock because such effects do dissipate with time in dogs (Overmier & Seligman, 1967). If the activity deficit that seems to mediate performance in our shuttlebox is the consequence of some transient factor, then it might be anticipated that inescapable shock-produced interference with shuttlebox escape should dissipate as time passes. However, if poor performance in the Y maze is mediated by associative effects of inescapable shock exposure, such deficits should be substantially more durable.

In order to determine if deficits in shuttlebox escape learning dissipate with time in rats, rats were tested 24, 48, or 168 hr following exposure to inescapable shock. The results are shown in Fig. 8. As is readily apparent, the subjects tested 24 hr following inescapable shock showed a large learned helplessness effect, while those tested 48 or 168 hr after inescapable shock did not differ from restrained controls. Thus the shuttlebox learned helplessness effect dissipates in time.[4]

We have already argued that escape deficits in our shuttlebox reflect the amount of activity which is emitted during escape training. The main basis for this argument was that the shuttlebox learned helplessness effect only occurred under conditions in which inescapably shocked and

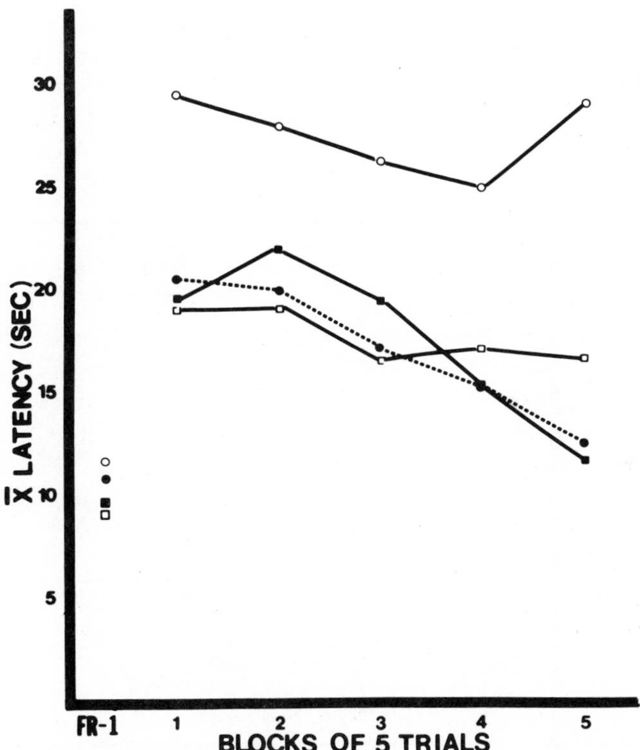

Fig. 8. Mean latency to escape shock across blocks five shuttlebox escape trials. Rats received preshock 24 (○, P24), 48 (□, P48), or 168 (■, P168) hours prior to shuttle escape training. Group R (●) was merely restrained 24 hr prior to training.

[4]It should be noted that other investigators (Glazer & Weiss, 1976a; Kelsey, 1977; Seligman, Rosellini, & Kozak, 1975) have found a more permanent effect under seemingly similar circumstances. See Jackson, Alexander, and Maier (1979) for a discussion of factors which may have produced these differing results.

control subjects were differentially active. Conditions that eliminated the differences in unconditioned activity also eliminated the helplessness effect. The same logic would suggest that unconditioned activity should follow the same time course as does the learned helplessness effect. If the shuttlebox learned helplessness effect is really produced by inescapable shock-induced inactivity, then the activity deficit should be present at 24 hr but not at 48 hr following inescapable shock treatment.

Figure 9 presents the results of an experiment designed to assess this possibility. Three groups of rats were inescapably shocked and then tested in a shuttlebox either 24, 48, or 168 hr later. A fourth group was merely restrained before testing and provided a baseline against which to gauge the degree to which unlearned crossing recovered with the passage of time. The shuttlebox test was one designed to measure unconditioned activity in the presence of shock. The rats received five trials of FR-1 training followed by 25 trials in which the crossing of the shuttlebox had no effect on shock—shock simply remained for 30 sec regardless of what the rat did. The figure shows how many times the various groups made two or more crosses during a trial. Again, this

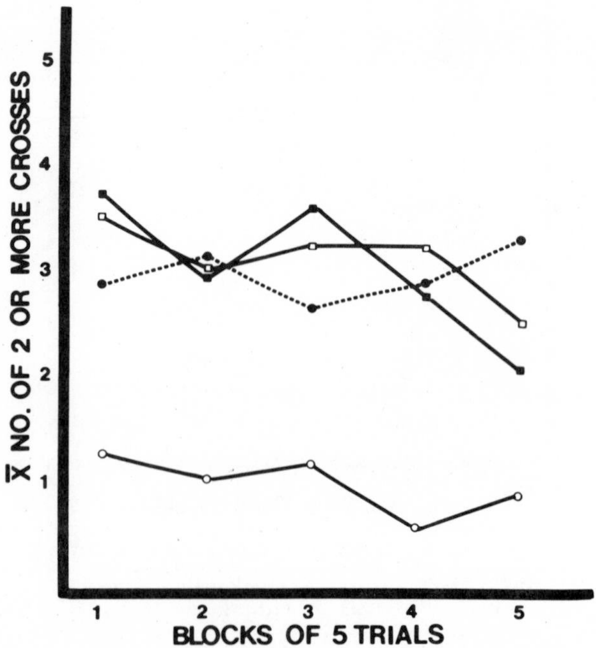

Fig. 9. Mean number of trials with two or more crosses. Rats were preshocked (P) or restrained (R) 24 or 168 hours prior to testing. (○——○) P24; (□——□) P48; (■——■) P168; (●- - -●) R.

particular measure is presented because it gives an indication of how many times the groups would have satisfied an FR-2 escape contingency on the basis of simple shock-elicited activity had an FR-2 contingency been in effect. It is easy to see that inescapably shocked subjects crossed less than did controls 24 hr after preshock, but that this depression in activity had fully recovered by 48 hr postshock. Thus activity and shuttlebox escape-learning deficits again covaried. Inescapably shocked rats crossed as frequently in the presence of shock as did unshocked controls 48 and 168 hr after inescapable shock. Such groups also acquired FR-2 escape responses in the previous experiment. Only the group tested 24 hr after inescapable shock crossed less frequently than did controls and only a group tested at this time interval showed deficits in FR-2 shuttlebox escape in the previous experiment. This close correspondence of activity and FR-2 escape-learning deficits as a function of time again supports the argument that the shuttlebox learned helplessness effect is mediated by an activity deficit. In addition, the fact that the shuttlebox learned helplessness effect dissipates suggests mediation by nonassociative processes.

However, the fact that interference with FR-2 escape dissipates with time does not necessarily mean that all effects of inescapable shock diminish over 48 hr. Instead, it may be that our shuttlebox task is insensitive to them. We have previously argued that inescapable shock produces an activity deficit as well as the learning that behavior is unrelated to outcome. Our data also suggest that the two effects may be somewhat independent of one another. It is conceivable that in the shuttlebox, activity masks what may be a fairly permanent associative deficit. It might well be impossible to detect any associative effects of the sort proposed by the helplessness hypothesis in a shuttlebox given that there is a very strong unlearned tendency to perform the FR-2 shuttle response.

If it is true that the failure to observe permanent effects of inescapable shock in the previous experiment reflects masking due to the recovery of the unlearned tendency to perform the required shuttle response, or the simple insensitivity of the shuttlebox to associative deficits, then examining the permanence of the effects of inescapable shock in tasks that are sensitive to associative deficits and in which activity does not determine performance is critical. We have previously argued that deficits in response accuracy in a Y-maze escape task cannot be readily attributed to inactivity. If it is the case that deficits in FR-2 shuttle escape dissipate because unlearned activity in the presence of shock recovers and masks more persistent associative effects, then durable effects of inescapable shock might be observed with Y-maze escape. This follows because our previous investigations of Y-maze escape learning indicate that deficits in choice accuracy in the Y maze seem to reflect associative rather than activity deficits. Our next experiment investigated this possibility.

Rats were either inescapably shocked or restrained and tested on the Y-maze choice escape-learning task either 24 or 168 hr later. The results can be seen in Fig. 10 which shows the mean percent of trials on which an error occurred across blocks of 10 trials. Here the escape learning deficit did not disappear even if a 168-hr interval intervened between inescapable shock exposure and escape learning testing. Further, the learned helplessness effect not only failed to disappear, but it did not even diminish in size. This result has two implications. First, it further supports the notion that exposure to inescapable shock has associative effects. This is because such effects are usually believed to dissipate in time only slowly (but see Maier & Seligman, 1976). Second, it adds to the body of evidence which supports the argument that exposure to inescapable shock has two effects which are largely independent and which are separately measured by shuttlebox and Y-maze choice per-

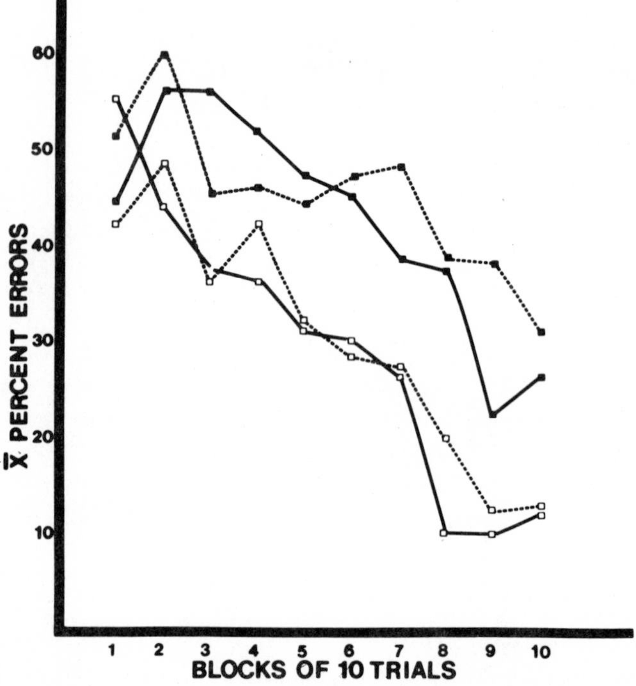

Fig. 10. Mean percentage of trials with one or more errors across blocks of 10 Y-maze escape trials. Rats were preshocked (P) or restrained (R) 24 or 168 hours prior to testing. (■——■) P24; (□——□) R24; (■- - -■) P168; (□- - -□) R168.

formance. This conclusion readily follows from the findings that the effects of inescapable shock on shuttlebox performance dissipated with time (activity deficit) but remained durable with regard to Y maze performance (associative deficit). These notions are further corroborated by the equivalent temporal functions found for shuttlebox escape performance and shuttlebox unconditioned activity.

VII. Possible Mechanisms Producing the Activity Deficit

In the previous section we argued that exposure to inescapable shock produces both associative and activity deficits, and that these two effects of uncontrollable aversive events might be somewhat independent and produced by different mechanisms. Thus we will inquire into the causes of these two separately.

A variety of hypotheses have already been encountered which can account for or predict that exposure to inescapable shock will lead to a later activity decrement in the presence of shock. Some have argued that exposure to inescapable shock leads to the learning of motor responses which interfere with movement in the presence of shock, either because movement is explicitly punished (Bracewell & Black, 1974) or because movement reduction is adventitiously reinforced (Glazer & Weiss, 1976a, 1976b). Others have argued that inescapable shock leads to a stress-induced depletion of neurochemicals necessary for movement. Adrenergic (Weiss *et al.*, 1975) and cholinergic (Anisman, 1975) mechanisms have both been implicated. Finally, it has been argued that inescapable shock leads to a decrement in the incentive to initiate responses to escape shock.

Unfortunately, each of these hypotheses encounters some difficulty in accounting for one or another aspect of the activity deficit. The learned inactivity views cannot readily account for the time course of the movement reduction produced by inescapable shock. Although learned motor responses can be forgotten, this usually requires more than 168 or 48 hr. It would seem that a learned motor response that is present 24 hr after uncontrollable shock should also be present 48 hr later. The learned helplessness explanation encounters similar difficulties. *Ad hoc* assumptions can be made (Maier & Seligman, 1976) which would allow the expectation that responding and shock termination are independent to be present 24 but not 48 hr after inescapable shock. Similarly, assumptions can be made (page 179) which would free the incentive reduction mechanism from the necessity that this expectation be either present or absent for its operation. However, the time course we have observed fits more naturally with a nonassociative process. This would suggest the neurochemical depletion hypotheses since it can be easily argued that the neurochemical substrate(s) recovers over time. However, these hypotheses also encounter difficulties. If the rat is made deficient in a substance that mediates movement, it should be less active than controls in nonshock as well as shock situations 24 hr after exposure to inescapable shock. Unfortunately, this does not seem to be the case. Chen and Amsel (1977), Rapaport and Maier (1978), and Rosellini and Seligman (1975) found running speed to obtain food reward in a runway to be unaffected by exposure to inescapable shock delivered 24 hr earlier. If a neurochemical necessary for the mediation of movement has been depleted, running speed should be reduced in appetitive as well as in aversive situations.

A. Habituation

The inability of existing hypotheses to gracefully account for the inescapable shock-produced activity deficit led us to think about other possible mechanisms. A mechanism was required which would dissipate in time and which would occur in the presence of shock but not in an appetitive situation. It is obvious that habituation to shock possesses the required characteristics. Habituation could easily dissipate with time and would only produce inactivity in the presence of the habituated stimulus. However, Maier and Seligman (1976) have presented a number of arguments against the simple notion that inescapably shocked subjects habituate to shock and that this produces the learned helplessness effect. Of course, we are here only considering habituation as a mechanism for the activity part of the learned helplessness effect. In fact, we will not propose habituation as the cause of even the activity deficit, but our current notion is sufficiently similar to habituation that we will review the points raised by Maier and Seligman (1976). Maier and Seligman noted seven facts that they felt were inconsistent with a habituation-based explanation of shuttlebox escape deficits.

1. Adaptation to repeated intense shock had not been demonstrated at that time.
2. Adaptation would be unlikely to persist for 24 hr.
3. The subjects in the dog helplessness experiments did not look as if they had adapted to shock. Maier and Seligman claimed "they howl, defecate, and urinate to the first shock presentations in the shuttlebox. On later trials, the dogs are passive; but they whimper and jerk with the shock" (p. 4). We have observed similar behavioral changes in rats.
4. Overmier and Seligman (1967) found that increasing the shuttlebox shock level for dogs from the usual 4.5 to 6.5 mA did not eliminate the interference effect.
5. Maier and Seligman argued that habituation should depend on the physical characteristics of the stimulus. Thus, any possible habituation should be equally produced by both escapable and yoked inescapable shocks, since they

are physically identical. Thus, the fact that the interference effect only follows exposure to uncontrollable shock is an embarrassment to a habituation explanation.

6. Prior exposure to escapable shock eliminates or reduces the interfering effects of subsequent experience with inescapable shock. There is no obvious reason why an initial exposure to escapable shock should prevent later inescapable shock from producing habituation.
7. Forcible exposure to the escape contingency eliminates the learned helplessness effect. There is no obvious reason why this should counteract any habituation that has developed.

B. Analgesia

While it seems unlikely that simple habituation to shock could bring about the interference effect, there are other means whereby the impact of shock could be reduced. It has long been supposed that powerful endogenous centrifugal controls exist and modulate the experience of pain. That is, nervous system mechanisms have been postulated which have an antinociceptive function (e.g., Melzack & Wall, 1965). It has recently been shown that focal electrical stimulation of medial brain stem structures, such as the nucleus raphe magnus, central periacqueductal gray, and caudal diencephalon, can produce profound analgesia. The analgesia produced by stimulation of these structures may last for several hours after the cessation of stimulation and can eliminate escape/avoidance behavior as well as spinal reactions to aversive stimuli (see Liebeskind & Paul, 1977, for review). Such data have been taken to indicate that these structures act in the endogenous regulation of pain (e.g., Liebeskind & Paul, 1977; Terenius, 1978).

Endogenous control over pain becomes particularly important for the present discussion in light of the fact that exposure to a variety of stressors can elicit analgesic reactions. Analgesia, as measured by the latency of a rat to flick its tail out of direct line with radiant heat, or to lick a paw heated on a hot plate, has been produced following footshock, exposure to stimuli paired with shock, swimming in 2°C water, rotation, and interperitoneal injection of hypertonic saline (Akil, Madden, Patrick, & Barchas, 1976a; Bodnar, Kelly, & Glusman, 1978a; Bodnar *et al.,* 1978b; Chance, Krynock, & Rosecrans, 1978a; Chance, White, Krynock, & Rosecrans, 1978b. Importantly, all of these stressors were also nominally inescapable; the animals could neither escape nor avoid these noxious events. This raises the possibility that exposure to uncontrollable aversive events may produce analgesia. If such analgesic reactions transfer to our shuttlebox test task, then it could be aruged that inescapably shocked rats are less active in the presence of shock because shock does not hurt as much as it might if they had not first received inescapable shock.

There is, however, a difficulty for this line of reasoning. Bodnar *et al.* (1978a) have shown that analgesia induced by swimming in 2°C water dissipates within 2 hr following swimming. Similarly, the analgesic effects of exposure to electric shock have also been shown to dissipate within this time period (Akil *et al.*, 1976a). Moreover, all the other studies which have reported stress-induced analgesia have assessed analgesia within an hour after the termination of stress. The fact that analgesia induced by exposure to inescapable events seems to dissipate so rapidly does not seem to encourage the speculation that analgesia may in part be responsible for changes in activity in our shuttlebox studies. We do not test behavior within an hour of inescapable shock. We test 24 hr later. If stress-induced analgesia is to account for our activity deficit, then it must be present 24 hr after inescapable shock exposure, but existing data would imply that animals should not be analgesic at this point in time.

However, our inescapable shock procedure differs in many ways from those used in studies reporting electric shock-induced analgesia. For example, we restrain our rats and deliver a 5-sec shock about once a minute through electrodes fixed to the animal's body, while the other studies typically apply shock through a grid floor to freely moving animals. Further, these shocks are usually about 1 sec long and occur much more frequently per unit of time than they do in our work. With these differences in mind, we decided to determine whether our inescapable shock procedure produced analgesia even 24 hr after the end of the stress session. While a variety of different analgesia measuring techniques exist, two seem most common. Both measures were used to provide the data which we will report.

One of these tests is called the hot plate test. Under this procedure, a rat is placed in a fairly large plastic box, the floor of which is copper. The metal plate is heated and maintained at a constant temperature. In our work we kept the hot plate at 50 ± .5°C, a relatively low temperature for such a test. The measure used to index pain sensitivity is the amount of time the animal spends on the plate before it licks a foot. We report only the latency to lick one of the rear feet because many of the animals reared up in the test apparatus and this effectively removes the front feet from the heat source.

The second commonly used test of sensitivity to painful events is called the tail-flick test. Here radiant heat is applied to the rat's tail. In our apparatus the energy source was a 250-W spotlight focused by a condenser lens to provide fairly localized heat to a point about halfway up from the tip of the rat's tail. The tail was placed over a photocell so that when it moved, the photocell would receive light and automatically terminate the heat. The animal was held by the experimenter so that its body was fairly well immobilized while its tail was free to move. The latency to flick the tail off of the photocell provided the measure of analgesia.

In our preliminary attempt to examine analgesia we exposed one group of rats to 80 fixed-duration inescapable shocks and merely restrained the control groups. The procedure was identical to that used in our previous work. Unfortunately, when we tested 24 hr later for analgesia with the hot plate test, we saw no hint of any difference between the groups. The shocked rats seemed as reactive as the group that had not been subjected to shock. If our inescapable shock procedure induced analgesia, the shocked animals seemingly had recovered to a normal level of sensitivity by the time we tested.

However, while it may be that the system(s) responsible for stress-induced antinociceptive reactions recovered to its baseline state within 24 hr, it still seemed possible that this system(s) might remain sensitized for some longer period of time. Thus, if the animals were reexposed to painful or fearful events while in this sensitized state, then the antinociceptive reaction might be rapidly recruited. In other words, we thought it possible that if exposure to inescapable shock predisposes animals to analgesic reactions 24 hr later, such reactions would not be observed unless the animals were exposed to more stress than that provided by the hot plate test.

In fact, data which we will now present do unequivocally support the idea that analgesia is produced by reexposure to the shock which occurs in the course of our normal shuttlebox procedure. Recall that our usual shuttlebox test procedure entails five FR-1 escape trials prior to the FR-2 trials that assess the helplessness effect. We reasoned that these five FR-1 trials might reinstate analgesic reactions. Thus, our next experiment examined paw lick latency as a function of two variables: (1) prior exposure to inescapable shock and, (2) whether or not the 5 FR-1 shuttle escape trials preceded the analgesia test.[5] Four groups of rats were employed. Two of these groups received 80 inescapable shocks as previously described. The remaining two groups were merely restrained in the restraining tubes and not shocked. Twenty-four hours later, one of the shocked (IE) groups and one of the restrained (RE) groups received five signaled FR-1 escape trials in a shuttlebox. The remaining two groups, I NO E and R NO E, were put in the shuttleboxes but were given no escape training or shock prior to the test for analgesia. The results of the analgesia test are shown in Fig. 11. Groups I NO E and R NO E, which did not receive FR-1 trials prior to analgesia testing,

[5]This experiment, and the subsequent experiments on analgesia, were conducted in collaboration with Deborah J. Coon.

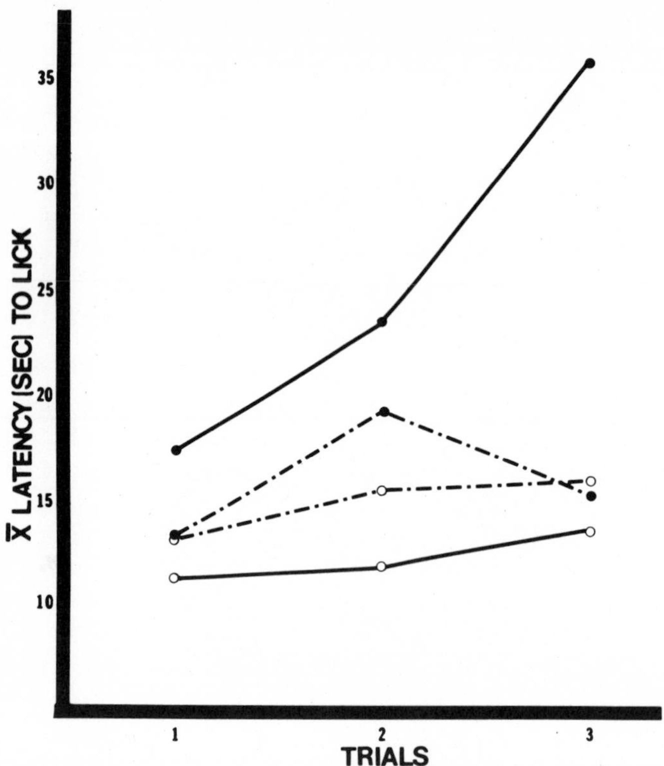

Fig. 11. Mean latency to lick a rear paw on each of three hot plate test trials. The rats received inescapable shock (I NO E, ●-·-●) or restraint (R NO E, ○-·-○) 24 hr before being tested on the hot plate. No escape training preceded testing in these two groups. The other groups received inescapable shock (IE, ●——●) restraint (RE, ○——○) and also received five shuttlebox escape trials immediately prior to the hot plate test.

licked a paw equally rapidly. Moreover, group RE did not respond differently from either of these two groups. Only group IE, which received both inescapable shock and FR-1 trials, responded slowly across the analgesia test trials. This group differed from all three of the other groups. Thus, analgesia is seen only in those rats which previously have received inescapable shock and which have then been reexposed to shock during the five FR-1 shuttle escape trials prior to analgesia testing. As our pilot work suggested, there was no evidence of analgesia in preshocked rats that were not reexposed to painful stimulation.

The long paw lick latencies seen in group IE were not due to the effects of FR-1 training per se. As is typical in our laboratory, preshocked and restrained rats performed equally well on the FR-1 trials. Therefore, the differences between groups IE and RE in their reactions to heat was not due to differences in the amount of shock received during FR-1 training. Moreover, inspection of the performance of the two restrained groups, one of which received FR-1s and the other of which did not, indicates that the FR-1 trials were not by themselves sufficient to induce analgesia. Thus, while the system responsible for stress-induced analgesia seems to have recovered to control levels within 24 hr after inescapable shock, our data indicate that it is sensitized and readily brought into operation by reexposure to stress. Therefore, inescapably shocked subjects are indeed analgesic during the FR-2 phase of our typical shuttlebox learned helplessness test.

It is conceivable that the paw lick data simply reflect the effects of inescapable shock on activity. Thus it would be important to assess analgesia using a test response that requires so little activity that it would seem unreasonable to invoke activity deficits as the mediating mechanism. The tail-flick test provides such a measure. The only activity required is a 5- to 7-mm deflection of the tail. No movements of the organism as a whole are required, and the body of the rat is, in fact, restrained. Only a twitch of the tail is required. Further, this movement in response to radiant heat is largely a spinal reflex (Dewey & Harris, 1975).

Thus we have replicated the previous experiment using the tail-flick test as the measure of analgesia. The procedure used in this experiment was identical to that used in the previous experiment except for the use of the tail-flick test apparatus. In this task a maximum trial duration of 20 sec was established in order to prevent tissue damage. The trial was automatically terminated if the animal did not respond within this time period. As Fig. 12 indicates, the results of the tail-flick test are in striking accord with those obtained with the hot plate measure. Only the inescapably shocked group that was reexposed to painful stimulation prior to the analgesia test showed any evidence of analgesia. This group reliably differed from all three of the other groups, which did not differ among themselves. Thus, these data suggest that inactivity in the presence of shock may be understood to be a consequence of inescapable shock-induced analgesia. Exposure to inescapable shock results in a greater propensity toward analgesic reactions. Obviously, reactivity to shock in the shuttlebox should be reduced if the painfulness of shock in the shuttlebox is lessened by endogenous pain control mechanisms.

However, in order to reasonably argue that inescapable shock-induced nociceptive change is responsible for the learned helplessness activity deficit, it is necessary to show that this analgesia has the same functional characteristics as does the activity learned helplessness effect. For example, if analgesia is to explain deficits in escape performance following

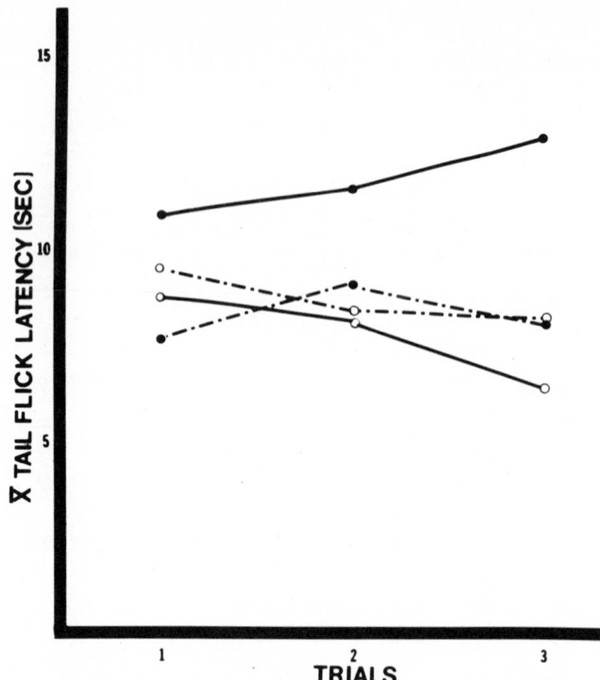

Fig. 12. Mean latency to flick the tail away from radiant heat on each of three trials. The group designations are identical to those used in Fig. 11.

inescapable shock exposure, then only exposure to inescapable shock should lead to analgesia. That is, rats that are initially exposed to shocks which they can escape or avoid subsequently learn in the shuttle escape task, while animals that receive an equivalent amount of inescapable shock subsequently fail to learn to escape. If analgesia is partly responsible for shuttle escape and activity deficits, it would follow that rats receiving escapable shocks should be less analgesic than rats receiving exactly the same amount and duration of inescapable shock. Thus, analgesia must be determined by the controllability of the shock.

We have completed the obvious study. Triads of rats were individually placed in one of three small boxes which had a wheel located on one wall. One rat could escape tail shocks by turning this wheel. The second rat was yoked to the first in such a way that it received an equivalent amount of shock on each trial but could not exert any behavioral control over the onset or offset of shock. The third rat was merely restrained in the box and not shocked. Testing was carried out 24 hr later using the tail-flick apparatus to measure analgesia. As before five FR-1 trials immediately preceded the analgesia test. Figure 13 shows the results of this experiment. Just as only inescapably shocked rats show escape deficits, only the yoked animals in this experiment were analgesic relative to the no-shock group. The escape-trained group, which received the same shock as did the yoked group, was not analgesic and these rats responded as rapidly as did the naive animals, which received no shock at all.

This is a very important finding. First, with regard to the effects of exposure to stressors on pain modulatory processes, the present study indicates that centrifugal mechanisms of pain control may be regulated by the psychological impact of the stressful event. The rats in the escape and yoked groups were given equal exposure to the same physical stimulus, yet only the yoked subjects became analgesic. The escape-trained subjects did not differ from rats that had not been previously shocked. While it has long been known that the controllability of stressors mitigates stress reactions in animals (e.g., Weiss, 1970a, 1970b, 1970c; Weiss

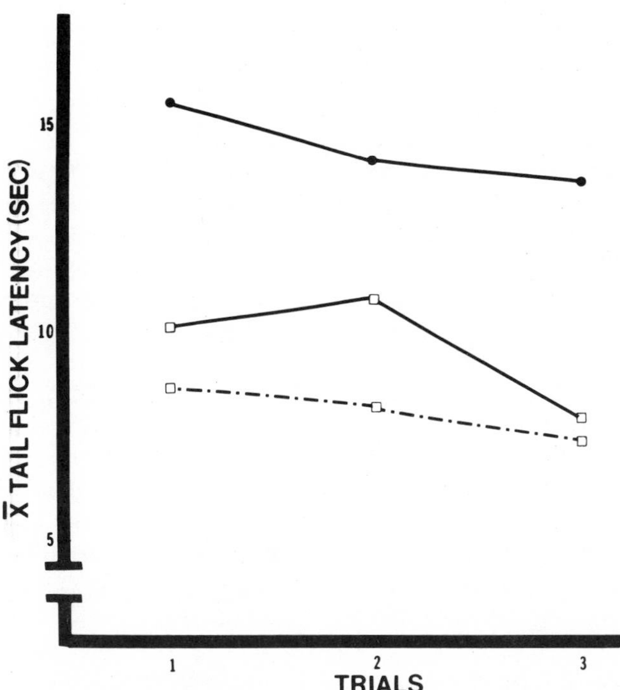

Fig. 13. Mean latency to flick the tail away from radiant heat on each of three trials as a function of whether rats had previously received escapable shock (escape, □—□), inescapable shock (yoke, ●—●), or no shock (naive, □–·–·□).

et al., 1970), this is the first demonstration that endogenous pain regulatory systems in animals are also sensitive to psychological manipulation.

Second, the present experiment demonstrates a necessary parallel between the effects of shock on shuttlebox escape performance and analgesia. Both are determined by the subject's control over shock. The yoke condition, which yields maximal shuttle escape performance deficits (Maier & Jackson, 1977), also yields the greatest degree of analgesia. Moreover, escape-trained subjects typically learn to perform the shuttle escape response as efficiently as do naive controls. The present study suggests that these two groups are also not differentially analgesic. Thus, there appears to be substantial correspondence between analgesia and escape performance as a function of the controllability of the pretreatment shock.

Another important characteristic of the helplessness activity and shuttlebox performance deficits are their time courses. The argument that these effects of inescapable shock are produced by the induction of an analgesia would be greatly strengthened by a demonstration of a similar time course for the inescapable shock-induced analgesia. As already discussed (page 181), the deleterious effects of inescapable shock on shuttlebox escape dissipated within 48 hr after inescapable shock. Moreover, the recovery in escape performance was paralleled by a recovery in unlearned activity (page 182). If changes in nociception mediate this activity change then we would expect that the sensitivity of the analgesia system to reinstatement by shock should also diminish within 48 hr of stress. Thus an experiment was run to evaluate this possibility. Rats were inescapably shocked or restrained and then given a tail-flick test either 24, 48, or 168 hr later. Five FR-1 shuttle escape trials preceded the tail-flick test. Figure 14 shows the results of this experiment. Again, there appears to be a parallel between changes in nociception and changes in escape deficits. Recall that we were unable to find any deficits in shuttlebox escape performance or activity 48 or 168 hr after inescapable shock. While still somewhat analgesic 48 hr after inescapable shock, the level of analgesia was less than observed 24 hr after shock. At 168 hr after inescapable shock rats were no longer analgesic.

So far we have shown that analgesia and the learned helplessness activity effect are similarly influenced by the same variables. Our argument that this analgesia is responsible for the activity deficit would be further strengthened by the demonstration of a direct relationship between nociception and escape performance. If high analgesia is responsible for low shuttle activity in the shuttlebox, then we should be able to obtain a substantial correlation between the two measures. We have completed such an experiment. Fourteen rats were first inescapably shocked and 24 hr later were placed in the shuttleboxes, where they

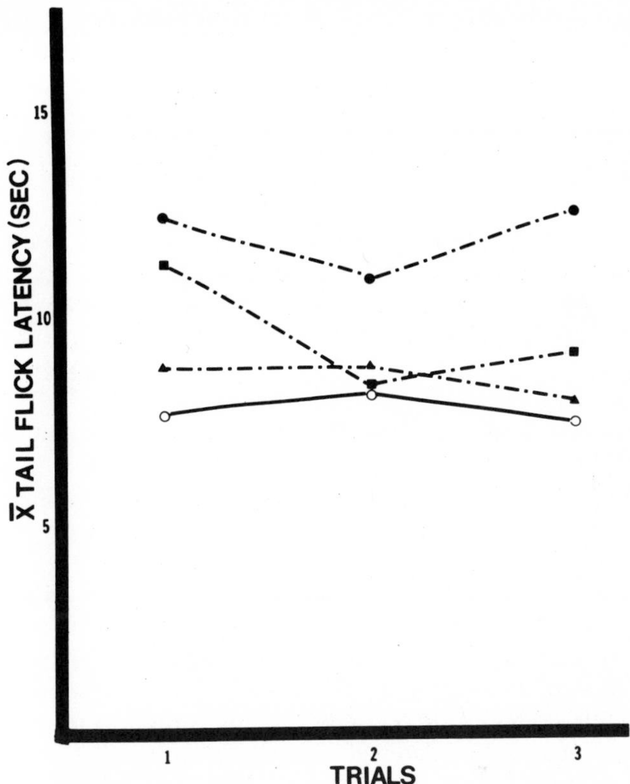

Fig. 14. Mean latency to flick the tail away from radiant heat on each of three test trials. Rats were preshocked 24 (P24, ● –·– ●), 48 (P48, ■ –·– ■), or 168 (P168, ▲–·–▲) hr prior to testing. Group R24 (○——○) was merely restrained 24 hr prior to testing.

received five FR-1 escape trials. They were then given two tail-flick analgesia test trials as previously described. Upon completion of analgesia testing, shuttlebox training resumed. However, crossing had no effect on shock. Shock was simply presented for 30 sec during which the total number of times the animal crossed the shuttlebox was recorded. Twenty-five of these trials were given. As we have previously noted, crossing in the absence of an escape contingency provides an index of the unlearned tendency to cross in the shuttlebox. The correlation between the total number of trials on which two or more crosses occurred and the mean tail-flick latency, while it was in the right direction, was not reliable ($r = -.34$). The failure of this relation to achieve significance does not necessarily contradict the notion that analgesia and shuttlebox activity are related. First, our sample is quite small and a certain amount of random variability in both our crossing and our analgesia measures might partly obscure the correlation. Second, the range of possible analgesia scores is severely truncated by the fact that trials automatically terminate within 20 sec if no response occurs. Moreover, there are similar constraints on the crossing measure of activity. Animals can either cross two or more times on a given trial or not. This limits the range activity of scores. Thus, in view of our small sample and the above constraints, it is not surprising that the correlation is unreliable.

However, another index of activity can be used which partly circumvents the problems associated with using the mean number of trials with two or more crosses measure. One could use the total number of times the animals crossed during testing as the measure of activity. With this measure scores can range from zero to some indefinite large number. It should also be noted that like the two or more crosses measure, the total number of crosses also reveals that preshocked rats are less active than controls (Jackson *et al.*, 1978) and also measures deficits in behaviors which are required for escape acquisition. Thus this measure also provides an index of activity deficits.

The correlation between the total number of times an animal crossed and its mean tail flick latency was $r = -.52$ ($p < .056$). This is an important result. It shows that our index of pain sensitivity successfully predicts the degree to which the animal emits those behaviors which are required during shuttle escape training. When animals tend to be analgesic, as indexed by long tail-flick latencies, they also shuttle back and forth in the shuttlebox less often. Thus, this finding supports the notion that inescapable shock-produced activity deficits are at least partly mediated by decrements in nociceptive processes.

It is important to note that these data vitiate many of the objections raised by Maier and Seligman when they explored the hypothesis that peripheral habituation to shock reduced the effectiveness of shock motivation and thereby led to poor performance. In fact, the first five of the seven objections (pages 186–187) disappear easily. We can now show that inescapable shock-induced deficits in nociception exist (point 1) and persist for at least 24 hr poststress (point 2). Further, it is not the case that simple exposure to the same physical shock stimulus induces equivalent changes in analgesia. Rather, analgesic reactions strongly depend upon psychological factors. Rats which can escape shock during initial training do not become analgesic 24 hr later, while rats which receive an equivalent amount of inescapable shock do (point 5). Thus, unlike a simple habituation notion, the data indicate that the mechanism responsible for analgesia is strongly affected by the psychological impact of the stressful event. It might also be noted that animals must be reexposed to shock in order to evidence any sign of analgesia when tested

24 hr after inescapable shock exposure. What is particularly important for explaining the shuttlebox learned helplessness effect is that the five FR-1 trials which ordinarily precede FR-2 training are sufficient to produce analgesia in inescapably shocked subjects. This suggests that analgesia increases during the course of FR-1 and early FR-2 trials. Perhaps, then, the observation that inescapably shocked dogs and rats react vigorously to shock initially and then become progressively more passive can be explained in terms of the recruitment of powerful analgesic processes over shuttle escape trials (point 3).

Finally, changes in nociception can, in principle, explain why increases in the intensity of shock had no effect on escape deficits in dogs (point 4). It is conceivable that sufficiently profound deficits in nociception might have been produced that even the most potent shocks applied in this study had little impact. While the analgesic argument is obviously *post hoc* and more than just a little speculative, it does have one virtue. It suggests that whether or not increases in shock intensity are effective in eliminating shuttlebox deficits may depend upon the level of analgesia that results from exposure to inescapable shock. In this regard it is worth noting that the analgesic effects we observe in rats are most clearly seen when we employ relatively low levels of heat in both the hot plate and tail-flick tests. Our hot plate was kept about 3°–5°C lower than the level that is commonly used, and we have adjusted our tail-flick apparatus so that our control animals have tail-flick latencies approximately 3–5 sec longer than those of roughly comparable controls in other laboratories. We did this because our early work indicated that higher heat levels could completely mask measurable analgesia. This suggests that inescapable shock may not induce extreme analgesia in rats—at least under our present conditions and shock parameters. If it does not, then it may not be quite so surprising that high shock intensity during shuttle escape training can eliminate escape deficits in preshocked rats (Jackson *et al.*, 1978). Obviously this possibility requires substantial empirical investigation before it can be taken too seriously. At this point we offer the argument more as an illustration of the potential explanatory power of the existence of shock-induced analgesia rather than as an illustration of its validity.

In sum, it appears to us that uncontrollable shock-induced analgesia fares far better than simple habituation as an explanation of activity deficits. In fact, it readily accommodates five out of the seven points raised by Maier and Seligman against habituation. The remaining two points, the effects of therapy and immunization on analgesia, remain to be investigated and the course of experimentation seems obvious.

It is also worth noting that the problems which we have argued to exist for the learned inactivity hypotheses as an explanation of the learned helplessness activity deficit do not apply to analgesia as an explanation of these activity deficits. Activity deficits dissipate within 48 hr. While this finding poses a challenge for associative explanations of the activity deficit, it is not problematic for the analgesia account. Empirically, we have shown that analgesia is substantially diminished within 48 hr and is undetectable under our current procedures within 168 hr. Thus, our data indicate that the system responsible for inescapable shock-induced analgesia is less labile 48 or more hours after inescapable shock than it is if only 24 hr have elapsed. Such a time course has never been demonstrated for a learned inactivity response.

Similarly, the major problem that exists for neurochemically based motor deficit hypotheses does not pose difficulties for an analgesia based account. Recall that we have argued (page 182) that such theories would expect movement decrements in situations that do not involve painful or fearful stimulation, but none have been found. If the animal is neurochemically unable to sustain extensive movement, the deficit should be obvious in both aversive and nonaversive tasks. However, analgesia is produced 24 hr after inescapable shock only if the animal is reexposed to shock. Thus in appetitive tasks the analgesia mechanism may not be switched in. Moreover, even if inescapably shocked animals are analgesic in non-shock-related tasks, it is not obvious that the simple fact of analgesia would render an animal less active in the absence of painful stimulation. Thus, we would argue that changes in nociception rather than learned inactivity or direct neurochemically linked motor deficits are at least partly responsible for inactivity in the presence of shock.

C. Mechanisms Underlying Inescapable Shock-Produced Analgesia

On the basis of the data and arguments presented in the previous section, it seems that inescapable shock-produced analgesia may mediate the resulting activity deficit. Thus, the mechanism(s) whereby analgesia is produced is of obvious interest. As previously noted, there is unequivocal evidence that endogenous centrifugal systems serve to modulate nociception. A particularly exciting body of research has recently emerged which indicates that a group of endogenous opiatelike substances, collectively called endorphins, may be vitally involved in the modulation of pain. These substances are found in both the brain (e.g., Hughes, 1975; Hughes, Smith, Kosterlitz, Fothergill, Morgan, & Morris, 1975) and the pituitary (e.g., Teschemacher, Opheim, Cox, & Goldstein, 1975).

It is not our intent nor does space allow us to thoroughly review the current information on endorphins. Such treatments are available to the reader in reviews by Frederickson (1977), Goldstein (1976), Snyder (1977), Terenius (1978), and in a recent book edited by Costa and Trabucchi (1978). What we shall attempt in this section is to provide some of the evidence which has been taken to imply that the endorphins are involved in the endogenous regulation of pain. Even more specifically here we will focus on the evidence which implicates the endorphins in stress-induced analgesic reactions.

A variety of different lines of evidence exists which are compatible with the idea that endorphins have a role in the production of analgesia. For one thing, they behave like opiate agonists. The biological effects of all opiate agonists are blocked by opiate antagonists, such as Naloxone and Naltrexone. These antagonists also block the activity of the endorphins (Goldstein, 1976). Furthermore, endorphins are observed in particularly high concentrations in the brain and spinal chord regions where opiates as well as focal electrical stimulation yield analgesia—the dorsal horn, substantia gelatinosa, central periaqueductal gray, and other regions in the mesolimbic portion of the brain. These data suggest that endorphins and analgesic agents, such as the opiates, may share common sites of action. Moreover, established similarities are not limited to sites of action. Endorphins may have physiological effects similar to those of morphine and like substances. For example, Wei and Low (1976) found that central infusion of endorphins induced analgesia and established tolerance to morphine. Moreover, the typical opiate withdrawal syndrome was elicited when the rats that had been chronically infused with endorphins were injected with Naloxone. Thus, the data strongly support the notion that the endogenously produced endorphins have many of the same characteristics as do manmade opiates, and, most importantly, these substances can induce analgesia.

Data such as that cited above have led to the proposition that the endorphins may be vitally involved in the centrifugal mechanisms of pain control (e.g., Liebeskind & Paul, 1977). Thus, it might be that the release of these substances is partly responsible for the analgesic reactions we observe following exposure to inescapable shock. Several further reports make this more than idle speculation. Akil *et al.*, (1976a) and Madden, Akil, Patrick, and Barchas (1976) found that exposure to inescapable footshock induced analgesia and elevated the level of endorphins found in the brain. Similar results have also been reported by Chance *et al.* (1978b). Moreover, Akil *et al.* demonstrated that the analgesic effects of the stressor could be partly reversed by Naloxone injections. Taken together, it seems clear that stress-induced analgesia may be at least partly subserved by the endorphins.

We have also attempted to determine if the analgesic reaction we observed following exposure to inescapable shock is dependent on the endorphins. Since Naloxone specifically antagonizes the action of these opiatelike substances we gave rats which had previously received inescapable shocks or restraint one 5 mg/kg dose of Naloxone 5 min before they received five shuttlebox escape-training trials and then another 5 mg/kg dose at the end of escape training. Although large, the dosage level of Naloxone we used was similar to that used by Akil *et al.* 1976a). We then tested the rats on both the hot plate and tail-flick devices. The results of these experiments are shown in Figs. 15 and 16. When the results from the rats that received a saline injection are examined, it is clear that exposure to inescapable shock induced analgesia. This rep-

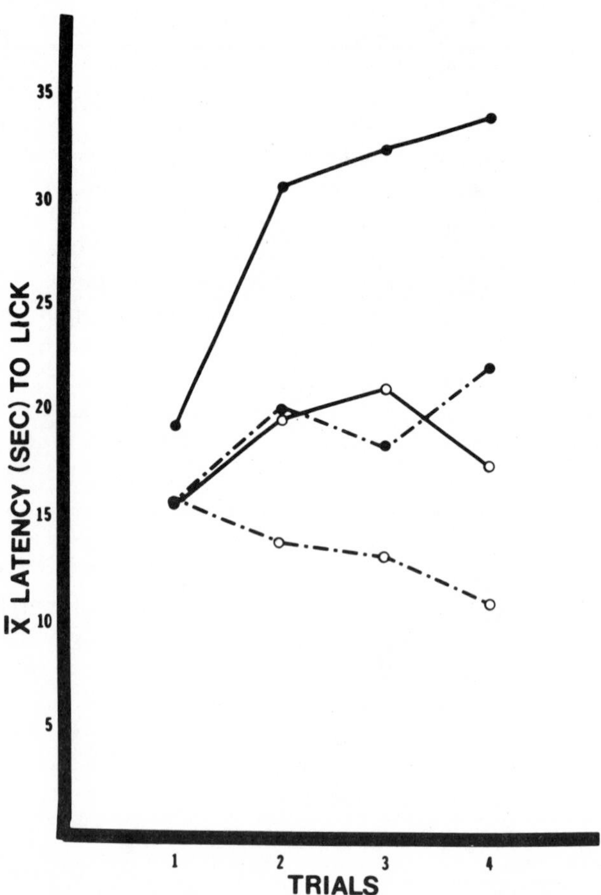

Fig. 15. Mean latency to lick a rear paw as a function of whether rats were previously inescapably shocked (P) or restrained (R) and injected with either naloxone (N) or saline (S) across four test trials. (●——●) PN; (○——○) RN; (●-·-●) PS; (○-·-○) RS.

licates our previous findings. However, Naloxone did not reduce the amount of measured analgesia. Rather, with both measures, Naloxone augmented the analgesic reaction in preshocked animals. To our knowledge, there are no other studies in which Naloxone leads to augmented analgesia.

We do not understand this result. It is replicable on two different measures and so it is apparently robust. All that can be said at this time is that these findings make it difficult to maintain that our analgesia effect is subserved by the endorphin system. If it were, then Naloxone should have diminished analgesia, not increased it. However, it should be noted that the effects of Naloxone on nociception are frequently

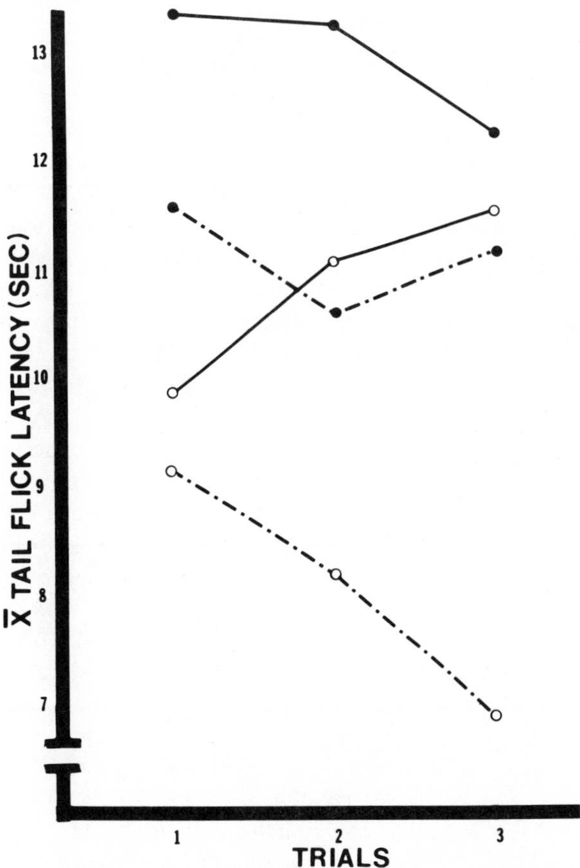

Fig. 16. Mean latency to flick the tail away from radiant heat as a function of whether the rats were previously inescapably shocked (P) or restrained (R) and injected with either naloxone (N) or saline (S) across three test trials. Key to curves is the same as in Fig. 15.

unclear and inconsistent. For example, Cheser and Chan (1977) found that Naloxone reversed shock-induced antinociception, while Hayes, Bennet, Newlon, and Moyer (1976) did not find such a Naloxone reversal. Neither Pert and Walter (1976) nor Yaksh, Yeung, and Rudy (1976) obtained Naloxone reversal of electrical stimulation-induced analgesia, while Akil, Mayer, and Liebeskind (1976b) did. Moreover, both of these analgesias are accompanied by increased endogenous opioid activity (e.g., Madden *et al.*, 1976). Thus, our failure to find that Naloxone reverses the present analgesia does not make the occurrence of the analgesia suspect nor does it conclusively rule out mediation by endogenous opioid systems.

D. Why Analgesia and Passivity?

We have demonstrated that exposure to inescapable shock predisposes an animal toward becoming analgesic when it subsequently encounters shock. We have also raised the possibility that such changes in sensitivity to painful events mediate the activity deficits reported by Jackson *et al.* (1978). Leaving aside the issue of whether the two are causally related, the fact that a rat exposed to inescapable shock becomes inactive and analgesic is rather curious. Why should the biological organization of the rat be such that its reactivity declines when it is exposed to intense trauma? The adaptiveness of such changes is not immediately apparent. Obviously, an animal which is inactive and experiencing less pain is probably less likely to be able to prevent the recurrence of the noxious event or even escape it.

However, let us consider the conditions under which the propensity toward analgesia has developed in our studies. Simple exposure to shock was not sufficient. Rather, analgesia followed only when the rat was exposed to shocks which it could not escape. Perhaps psychological and physiological changes that lessen the impact of the insult occur only when the organism experiences traumatic events with which it cannot or believes it cannot cope.

A number of investigators have argued that exposure to uncontrollable events can yield changes which are presumed to protect the organism from some of the deleterious effects of stressors. For example, such an idea was proposed by Frank (1953) and subsequently elaborated by Engel and his associates (e.g., Engel & Schmale, 1972). Engel's notions were based on observations of the reactions of infants and young children when they were confronted by such things as separation from their mother or an encounter with a stranger. Essentially, Engel noted two different stages in the child's reaction to these types of events. First, there was a period of struggling, crying, and other behaviors which seemed to be organized toward trying to produce a more desirable state of affairs in the situation. If these behaviors brought no relief the child's behavior changed radically. The coping attempts eventually terminated and the child became quiescent or even comatose. In this second stage, the child seemed to withdraw from the situation rather than actively attempting to cope with it. Similar behavioral patterns have been noted in adult concentration camp prisoners (Bettelheim, 1960).

It should also be noted that this pattern of behavior is not uniquely human. Kaufman and his associates (e.g., Kaufman, 1973) have observed the reactions of pigtail monkey infants to separation from their mothers and the pattern of behavior is strikingly similar to that seen in humans. Initially, the infant monkey emits distress calls and high levels of locomotor activity. Such behaviors would typically bring the infant back into contact with its mother if she were available. After a period of these activities the monkey withdraws; it sits quietly holding itself and is unresponsive to stimulation.

Engel argued that when an organism is in a set of circumstances in which a state of need is induced, it first attempts to restore homeostasis through what can be characterized as flight–fight behavioral patterns. However, if this activity fails, the organism enters what he terms a conservation–withdrawal reaction. This system of behavioral change is said to come into play when the fight–flight reactions threaten to or do exhaust the organism before relief is obtained. It is viewed as a means of minimizing the cost to the animal of being in a situation which it cannot modify. Engel argues that one aspect of the adaptive value of such an energy conserving mechanism is that it might permit the organism sufficient energy reserves to actively respond and take advantage of any subsequent changes in the conditions of the environment which would bring it relief.

A problem for the idea of conservation–withdrawal has always been the question of what is required to trigger the reaction—How does the biology of the organism anticipate its impending exhaustion? We would agree with Kaufman that such reactions may be a consequence of the establishment of the expectation that there is no relationship between behavior and outcome. Our rats only become passive and analgesic after exposure to inescapable shock. Escapable shock has no effect. Thus we would suggest that the passivity and analgesia we observe may be characterized as being aspects of the conservation–withdrawal syndrome described by Engel and Kaufman. This syndrome arises when repeated attempts to behaviorally cope fail and serves to minimize energy expenditure. Our data, however, suggest that while of some immediate benefit to the organism, conservation–withdrawal may prove costly in the long run. While becoming analgesic during inescapable shock would tend to minimize the impact of shock on the organism, it appears that a propensity toward later becoming analgesic in the presence of shock is established for at least 48 hr. This may subsequently reduce activity in the presence of shock and interfere with learning more efficient and beneficial solutions.

VIII. Possible Mechanism Producing the Associative Deficit

As we have previously noted, exposure to inescapable shock reduces activity in the presence of shock and, in addition, produces an associative deficit. In the previous section we have presented our current analysis of the mechanism(s) which produces the activity deficit. In this section we will discuss what is really at the heart of the helplessness hypothesis, the associative deficit. We now turn to a discussion of the associative deficits we believe are produced by exposure to inescapable uncontrollable aversive events.

The fact that rats which have previously received inescapable shock experience difficulty in learning which response out of a number of alternatives to choose in order to escape shock strongly argues for the existence of a true associative deficit. As already noted, inescapably shocked animals begin training at the same level of accuracy as controls, actively respond and terminate each trial with a correct response, and yet fail to learn as well as animals which did not previously receive inescapable shock. While incompatible with learned inactivity explanations of the interference effect, these results are interpretable from the learned helplessness hypothesis. The helplessness hypothesis asserts that during inescapable shock the animal learns that its behavior and shock termination are independent. This learning is then presumed to interfere with learning about the relationship between responding and shock in the test environment. However, even if one accepts the Y-maze choice results as firmly establishing the existence of an inescapable shock-produced associative deficit, a number of questions about the nature of this deficit remain. Two are particularly salient. The first is that, as currently stated, the helplessness hypothesis asserts that only the associability of responding and shock is diminished by exposure to inescapable shock. However, response–shock relationships are only one type of relationship which an organism may confront. Most of the test tasks which we have employed involve stimulus–shock relationships as well. We attempted to reduce the role of stimulus–shock contingencies in our Y-maze discrimination task. The maze was uniform in color and we hoped to minimize extramaze cues by making the animal spend the intertrial interval in darkness. Moreover, the task could not be performed efficiently on the basis of learning to approach one particular arm, etc. Superficially, then, it seems that our Y-maze task should emphasize response learning (left turn from present position). However, without too much imagination, one could imagine a number of ways that animals could utilize nonresponse cues to facilitate their performance. Perhaps, for example, they tend to follow whatever wall in the maze they happen to be closest to at the beginning of a trial. This would tend to put them closer to one of the two alternative arms in the maze at the moment of choice and could therefore bias the animal's selection. Moreover, despite our attempts to minimize them, other unknown intra- or extramaze cues may have been available and used in the animal's efficient solution of the Y-maze discrimination. These possibilities, by no means suggest that there is no response learning involved in our Y-maze task. All that is implied is that it is not easy to know whether the Y-maze associative deficit reflects interference with R–S learning, S–S learning, or both.

Thus, it is important to attempt to identify the locus of the associative interference effect. The Y-maze task cannot permit such analysis because response–shock and stimulus shock contingencies are not readily manipulable. A different task is required in order to analyze the nature of inescapable shock–induced associative deficits. Obviously, whatever analytical procedures are used in such investigations would also have to unconfound activity and associative deficits.

The second issue concerns exactly what the organism comes to expect after experiencing uncontrollable events. Mackintosh (1973, 1975a, 1975b) has argued that organisms learn that events which bear no predictive relationship to reinforcement are irrelevant, and that such learning diminishes their salience. As Mackintosh uses it, salience is an attentional construct. After sufficient experience with the nonpredictiveness of an event, he asserts that the organism simply ceases to attend to that particular event. Thus, when these events are subsequently placed in a predictive relationship with reinforcement, the learning of this relationship will be retarded.

Obviously, learned helplessness and learned irrelevance are rather similar hypotheses. The crux of both positions is that animals learn that events are unrelated and that such learning can interfere with subsequent learning. However, the two positions differ in the prediction of how broad such transfer should be. Irrelevance learning predicts that an animal should experience difficulty in associating only those events which it has previously experienced in a random relationship. This is because the animal presumably only ceases to attend to the particular events which have previously borne no relationship to reinforcement, or to others which physically resemble them. Its attention to other events should be undiminished. The helplessness hypothesis, in contrast, argues that as a result of sufficient experience with the independence between behavior and outcome, a generalized set to treat events which differ from those present during training as being independent may be acquired. This theoretical difference might be viewed as specific versus generalized irrelevance. The Mackintosh position holds that organisms only learn the irrelevance of specific responses and reinforcement; the learned helplessness position argues that something like a proposition about a larger class of responses emerges from sufficient specific irrelevance learning.

The specific irrelevance notion is certainly sufficient to account for the original shuttlebox interference effect. It need only be argued that components of the shuttling response occur during inescapable shock and are learned to be irrelevant to shock termination. However, our Y-maze interference effect is not so easily explained. A specific irrelevance notion would require the organism to emit responses during inescapable shock exposure that are more similar to turning one way than to turning the other way in the Y maze. For the specific irrelevance argument to work the organism would have to learn that some component of say "left" as opposed to "right" turning is irrelevant during exposure to shock while restrained in a tube. We cannot imagine what response an organism could make in a tube that is more similar to a correct than to an incorrect turn in a totally symmetrical maze. How could learning that some motor response is irrelevant make an organism more likely to turn one way than the other? Moreover, if a response bias was induced during inescapable shock, it should have been apparent during early Y-maze training trials. The fact that both inescapably shocked and restrained rats start at the same, chance level of performance weighs against such reasoning.

Thus it might appear that the data favor the learned helplessness view. However, an experiment by Baker (1976) provides support for the specific irrelevance position. In addition, his experiment provides a means for investigating the first issue noted above, namely, interference with R–S and S–S learning. Therefore, we will describe Baker's procedures and then present some further work of our own which has used his techniques. Baker trained rats to respond on a variable interval (VI) schedule for food reinforcement and then, while the animal continued to respond on the baseline schedule, some received a number of unsignaled, noncontingent, inescapable shocks. Next the animals received on-baseline discriminative punishment training. In this phase a warning signal was periodically presented during which response-contingent shocks occurred. Baker found that rats that were originally noncontingently shocked were slower to come to suppress responding to the cue than were rats which had not received prior shocks. Thus, the noncontingently shocked rats were slow to learn, even when slow learning entailed emitting relatively more rather than relatively less activity. It might be noted that such data seem to support the view that exposure to inescapable shock produces an associative deficit. Since failure to suppress means that the animals make more rather than fewer active responses, arguments based on direct transfer of incompatible motor responses which produce inactivity cannot account for the findings. Neither would neurochemical depletion explanations predict failure to learn in a situation where failure to learn is not reflected in reduced activity. Thus, Baker's procedure seems ideal for dissociating the effects of inescapable shock on associative processes from effects on activity or incompatible responses.

However, the implications of Baker's findings for the learned helplessness hypothesis and learned helplessness experiments are not completely clear. As discussed above, the learned helplessness hypothesis maintains that exposure to inescapable shock interferes with the acquisition of response–shock associations. Discriminative punishment involves two contingencies, a stimulus–shock and a response–shock contingency. Thus it is possible that the noncontingent shocks in Baker's study interfered with the acquisition of the stimulus–shock rather than the response–shock association. These possibilities could be examined by training noncontingently shocked rats on a task in which there is a contingency only between stimulus and shock. The failure of noncontingent shocks to retard such conditioned emotional response (CER) acquisition would constitute evidence that the noncontingent shocks in Baker's studies interfered with the acquisition of response-shock associations. Baker provided some groups with a CER acquisition test. However, he did so only for groups that had received a random mixture of noncontingent shocks and conditioned stimuli. Groups which had received only noncontingent shocks without random conditioned stimuli were not tested on CER acquisition. Thus, Baker's study leaves open the possibility that noncontingent shocks alone may interfere with CER acquisition as much as with signaled punishment. Therefore, Baker's data cannot be taken as evidence that exposure to inescapable shocks uniquely interferes with the acquisition of response–shock associations.

In addition, one can question the relationship between the Baker experiments and the typical learned helplessness experiment since many procedural and empirical differences exist. Two are particularly salient. First, learned helplessness effects are transsituational. Inescapable shocks are given in one situation and testing employs a different type of shock in a different situation. Baker gave inescapable shock in the Skinner box and the shocks were identical to those later used in discriminative punishment training. Thus it is not known whether inescapable shocks delivered in one situation would interfere with the acquisition of discriminative punishment suppression in a different situation.

Second, when inescapable shocks were delivered without the lever present, Baker failed to obtain subsequent interference with the acquisition of discriminative punishment suppression. Thus, although our investigations demonstrate transresponse interference, Baker's interference effect was response specific. Baker concludes that rats are capable of learning that a specific response and shock are independent but do not learn that responses in general and shock are independent, as maintained by the learned helplessness hypothesis.

In sum, while it seemed possible that Baker's procedures would allow us to disentangle deficits in response–shock from stimulus–shock learning, his data do not unequivocally do so. Moreover, the facts that his interference effect was response specific and his procedure was not transsituational leave open the question of specific versus generalized irrelevance.

While the issues of whether the interference with discriminated punishment could be obtained transsituationally and whether such interference was due to effects on response–shock or stimulus–shock learning could be addressed empirically, the apparent response specificity was more problematic. However, an examination of our respective procedures for administering inescapable shock suggested that Baker's findings could be easily reconciled with a more general learned helplessness view. Baker presented a total of 30 .5-sec, .25-mA shocks across 5 days. We typically present between 64 and 80 5-sec, 1-mA shocks. It would not be too surprising if general response outcome irrelevance learning requires more shock experience than does specific irrelevance learning. Thus we undertook an experiment (reported in Jackson *et al.*, 1978) in which we used Baker's testing procedures but delivered inescapable shock as in our other experiments. Four groups of rats were trained to press a lever for food on a variable-interval (VI) 60-sec schedule. Then two groups of rats received 80 5-sec, 1.0-mA shocks while confined in restraining tubes, while the other two groups were merely restrained. On the following day testing began. One of the shocked groups and one of the restrained groups received eight signaled punishment trials. A trial was marked by 3 min of white noise. During this cue a maximum of two shocks could occur. Once a shock was programmed to occur, it was delivered contingent upon the animal's next response. Thus, if the animal did not respond it could completely avoid all shocks. The remaining two groups of rats also received conditioning trials signaled by white noise, but for these animals shocks were not contingent upon their behavior. The shocks were delivered during the white noise as soon as they were programmed. It should be added that the number of shocks delivered were yoked to the punishment groups. Thus, while the first two groups were trained under conditions involving both response–shock and stimulus–shock relationships, the second pair of groups received training which involved only stimulus–shock contingencies. These two conditions allow us to evaluate the relative importance of these two types of relations in any effect of inescapable shock on suppression of lever pressing. To the extent that differences in the sensitivity to response–shock contingencies produce interference, only the preshocked group tested under discriminated punishment should differ from its control. The preshocked group tested under the noncontingent CER condition should not differ from its control because there is no explicit relationship between responding and shock under this set of circumstances. Here only a stimulus–shock relation is explicitly programmed. Conversely, if interference is produced by differences in sensitivity to stimulus–shock contingencies, then the preshocked groups should be less suppressed than their controls under both signaled punishment and CER conditions.

The results of this experiment are shown in Figs. 17 and 18. Figure 17 shows the CER data, while Fig. 18 depicts the signaled punishment results. Inspection of these data indicate that exposure to inescapable shock interfered with response–shock, but not with stimulus–shock learning. Only when there was an explicit contingency between responding and shock were preshocked rats slower to learn than controls. When only S–S contingencies were programmed, the two groups did not differ. Thus, these results lend support to the helplessness hypothesis view that exposure to inescapable, uncontrollable events subsequently makes it more difficult for the organism to associate its behavior with that outcome.

The results of this experiment also have implications for the specific–generalized irrelevance issue. Clearly, under our preshock condition the signaled punishment paradigm yields a generalized irrelevance result. Of course, it could be argued that components of lever pressing occur during inescapable shock exposure in the restraining tube. We cannot prove that this is not so. However, the burden of proof now falls on proponents of this argument.

This concludes our discussion of what we know about the manner in which the learned helplessness associative deficit occurs. It should be obvious to the reader that not much is yet understood. The two questions that we have explored have only been given very tentative answers and a considerable amount of further research will be required before these answers can be taken very seriously. Moreover, these two answers only

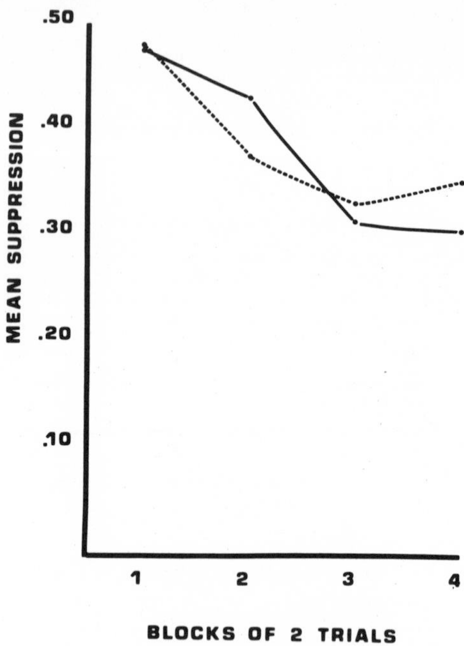

Fig. 17. Mean suppression ratios across blocks of two fear conditioning trials in which rats were previously inescapably shocked (•—•) or restrained (•· · ·•).

begin to confront the issue of the mechanism whereby the associative interference occurs. There are many obvious questions and possibilities. For example, does inescapable shock exposure produce an associative deficit by reducing the salience of behavior in shock situations or by operating on the associative process itself? That is, does exposure to inescapable shock influence the representation of the behavior(s) that is accessed by the associative linking mechanism or does it influence the linking mechanism itself? Does it perhaps reduce the likelihood that shock termination will initiate the processing of preceding behavioral sequences, etc.? We have no answers to these fascinating questions at the present time.

IX. Concluding Comments

It seems to us that the most important implication of the experiments which were reported here is that there may be two somewhat independent learned helplessness effects, not just one. In retrospect, it is not surprising that an event as potent and complex as exposure to inescap-

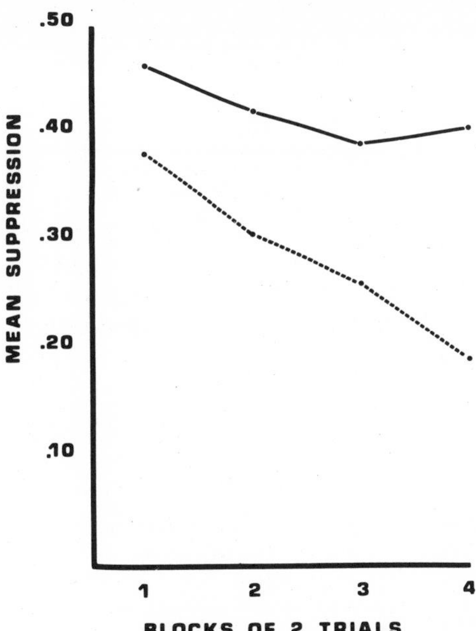

Fig. 18. Mean suppression ratios across blocks of two signaled punishment trials in which rats were previously inescapably shocked (•—•) or restrained (•· · ·•).

able shock has multiple effects, but the particular nature of the effects found may allow a measure of resolution to the conflicting views of the learned helplessness effect and, in addition, have important implications for our view of the learning process.

A number of papers have recently appeared which have presented evidence which it is claimed invalidates or mitigates against the learned helplessness hypothesis. The experiments reported have typically been inspired by inactivity hypotheses and show that inescapable shock exposure induces reduced activity in the presence of shock. For example, Anisman *et al.* (1978) have reported a very impressive series of experiments which demonstrate that inescapably shocked mice are later less active than controls and that manipulations designed to interfere with this activity reduction also reduce the shuttlebox learned helplessness effect. These data led Anisman *et al.* to conclude in favor of inactivity hypotheses and against a learned helplessness view.

However, the data presented here make it clear that the existence of an activity deficit does not mean that the mechanisms that make up the learned helplessness hypothesis do not exist. We agree that exposure to uncontrollable shock leads to inactivity in the presence of shock.

Further, we suggest that this is because the subjects have become analgesic. We also agree that the shuttlebox probably predominantly reflects this deficit. Shuttlebox escape is a task in which the level of performance should be readily influenced by the organism's propensity to run. Thus, in retrospect, it was a poor choice for the theoretical analysis of learned helplessness effects. At the same time, however, the data which have been reported here make it clear that the existence of an activity deficit does not weigh against the learned helplessness hypothesis. First, the learned helplessness hypothesis can itself explain reduced activity. Second, the learned helplessness hypothesis does not deny that exposure to inescapable shock has motoric effects. Rather, it asserts that the organism can learn act–outcome independence and that this expectation can reduce the organism's incentive to escape and can interfere with its associating other responses with that outcome. It seems to us that our Y-maze and signaled punishment experiments strongly support the conclusion that exposure to inescapable shock can produce an associative retardation (and by implication act–outcome independence learning) that is not interpretable in inactivity terms. Further, it is the potential associative effect of inescapable shock exposure that has the implications for the learning process that we previously described. Thus, we can easily accept the Anisman *et al.* data but still support the learned helplessness hypothesis. Indeed, our own data suggest that reduced activity may be largely responsible for the shuttlebox effect. Thus, everyone may have been correct. One way of putting this is that we may have been correct with regard to the organism's learning processes but wrong with regard to shuttleboxes. Perhaps others would not put it so kindly.

It might be worth noting that one series of experiments which attack the learned helplessness hypothesis cannot be accommodated as readily. Glazer and Weiss (1976a, 1976b) reported that shocks shorter than 5 sec will not produce a shuttlebox learned helplessness effect and that inescapable shock exposure did not interfere with the learning of a low-effort nose-poke escape response. In fact, it facilitated learning. These results are in keeping with their inactivity hypothesis.

With regard to the first finding, there certainly are conditions under which brief shocks produce a shuttlebox learned helplessness effect. For example, Kelsey (1977) has reported such a result. In our laboratory we investigated this question by giving groups of rats either 72 5-sec or 180 2-sec inescapable shocks. A control group was restrained for the same amount of time as the 180 2-sec group but was not shocked. These treatments were followed by our usual shuttlebox test 24 hr later. The results are shown in Fig. 19. Clearly, we were unable to replicate Glazer and Weiss' findings. The duration of inescapable shock had no effect. Whereas Glazer and Weiss found no escape deficits following shocks shorter than 5 sec, our effect is as strong with 2-sec preshock as it is

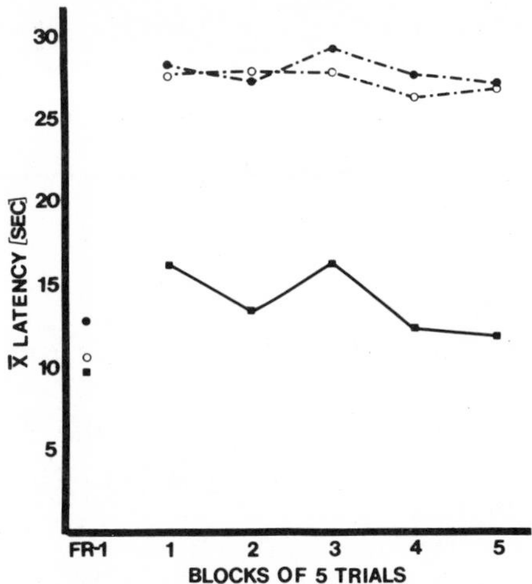

Fig. 19. Mean latency to escape shock across blocks of five shuttlebox escape trials. Rats had previously received 5-sec shock (P5" o- – -o), 2-sec shock (P2" o- – -o), or no shock (R, ■——■).

with 5-sec preshock. The reasons behind Kelsey's and our own failure to replicate Glazer and Weiss remain obscure. Glazer and Weiss' second finding is more troublesome and we can explain it only in a *post hoc* way. Our argument is based on an observation of the animal's behavior which is reported by Glazer and Weiss. It is important to know that their apparatus was a restraining tube with a conically shaped end with a small hole at its center. The rat could poke its nose through this hole and this response terminated shock. A small door covered the hole during the intertrial intervals and was lowered at the beginning of each trial. To quote from Glazer and Weiss,

"The basis for the superior performance of animals that had received inescapable shock was apparent on observation. The no shock animals were quite active between trials, frequently moving back and forth, struggling, and changing positions within the restraining tubes. The nosing response made by an animal in this group was a very discrete, active response. With the removal of the door over the hole, such an animal would thrust its head forward to complete a correct response, then jerk it back into the tube and resume its inter-trial activity. In contrast, the animals that had received inescapable shock remained immobile between trials, and, most significant, their nosing responses were more passive in nature. As trials progressed, such an animal would come to remain with its nose pressed against the door so that when the door was drawn back at the beginning of the trial its head followed the door forward, accomplishing a rapid correct response. Following this response, the door moved forward to cover the hole, simply pushing the animal's nose back into the tube for a similar correct response on the next trial" (Glazer & Weiss, 1976b, p. 205).

This quotation suggests a different interpretation from that proposed by Glazer and Weiss. Again, the question is not whether an activity decrement occurs, but whether it can entirely account for later learning decrements. The above quotation suggests that the performance of the inescapably shocked rats in the tube does not reflect learning. It suggests that the inescapably shocked rats simply laid their heads on the door and that the back and forth movement of the door produced what appears as rapid learning but may not be learning at all. The rat had its head on the door and simply fell into the hole when the door was drawn back. If the task does not reflect learning, the helplessness hypothesis is not embarrassed.

In concluding, we feel that the work reported in this paper should shift research in this area to a less polemical and perhaps more productive mode. As we have frequently noted, research concerning the interference effect has been characterized by an attack and counterattack style. The previous few paragraphs are a good example. Our demonstration of different consequences of exposure to uncontrollable shocks might reconcile several of the theoretical alternatives. There appear to be movement and associative effects, and it may be pointless to try and reduce one to the other. At this point the problem is to inquire into the mechanisms of these effects and how they interrelate.

References

Akil, H., Madden, J., Patrick, R. L., & Barchas, J. D. Stress-induced increase in endogenous opiate peptides: Concurrent analgesia and its partial reversal by naloxone. In H. Kosterlitz (Ed.), *Opiates and endogenous opiate peptides.* Amsterdam: Elsevier/North-Holland Biomedical Press, 1976. (a)

Akil, H., Mayer, D. J., & Liebeskind, J. C. Antagonism of stimulation-produced analgesia by naloxone, a narcotic antagonist. *Science,* 1976, **191,** 961–962. (b)

Altenor, A., Kay, E., & Richter, M. The generality of learned helplessness in the rat. *Learning and Motivation,* 1977, **8,** 54–62.

Anisman, H. Time-dependent variations in aversively motivated behaviors: Non-associative effects of cholinergic and catecholaminergic activity. *Psychological Review,* 1975, **82,** 359–385.

Anisman, H., deCatanzaro, D., & Remington, G. Escape performance deficits following exposure to inescapable shock: Deficits in motor response maintenance. *Journal of Experimental Psychology: Animal Behavior Processes,* 1978, **4,** 197–218.

Bainbridge, P. L. Learning in the rat: Effect of early experience with an unsolvable problem. *Journal of Comparative and Physiological Psychology,* 1973, **82,** 301–307.

Baker, A. G. Learned irrelevance and learned helplessness: Rats learn that stimuli, reinforcers, and responses are uncorrelated. *Journal of Experimental Psychology: Animal Behavior Processes,* 1976, **2,** 130–142.

Bettelheim, B. *The informed heart-autonomy in a mass age.* New York: Free Press, 1960.

Black, A. H. Comments on "Learned helplessness: Theory and evidence" by Maier and Seligman. *Journal of Experimental Psychology: General,* 1977, **106,** 41–44.

Bodnar, R. J., Kelly, D. D., & Glusman, M. Stress-induced analgesia: Time course of pain reflex alterations following cold water swims. *Bulletin of the Psychonomic Society,* 1978, **11,** 333–336. (a)

Bodnar, R. J., Kelly, D. D., Spiaggia, A., & Glusman, M. Stress-induced analgesia: Adaptation following chronic cold water swims. *Bulletin of the Psychonomic Society,* 1978, **11,** 337–340. (b)

Bracewell, R. J., & Black, A. H. The effects of restraint and noncontingent pre-shock on subsequent escape learning in the rat. *Learning and Motivation,* 1974, **5,** 53–69.

Braud, W., Wepman, B., & Russo, D. Task and species generality of the "helplessness" phenomenon. *Psychonomic Science,* 1969, **16,** 154–155.

Chance, W. T., Krynock, G. M., & Rosecrans, J. A. Antinociception following lesion-induced hyperemotionality and conditioned fear. *Pain,* 1978, **4,** 243–252. (a)

Chance, W. T., White, A. C., Krynock, G. M., & Rosecrans, J. A. Conditional fear-induced antinociception and decreased binding of [^{3}H]N-Leu-enkephalin to rat brain. *Brain Research,* 1978, **141,** 371–374. (b)

Chen, J. S., & Amsel, A. H. Prolonged, unsignaled, inescapable shocks increase persistance in subsequent appetitive instrumental learning. *Animal Learning and Behavior.* 1977, **5,** 377–385.

Chesher, G. B., & Chan, B. Footshock-induced analgesia in mice: Its reversal by naloxone and cross tolerance with morphine. *Life Sciences,* 1977, **21,** 1569–1574.

Costa, E., & Trabucchi, M. (Eds.). *Advances in biochemical psychopharmacology* (Vol. 18). New York: Raven, 1978.

Dewey, W. L., & Harris, L. S. The tail flick test. In S. Ehrenpreis & A. Neidle (Eds.), *Methods in narcotics research.* New York: Dekker, 1975.

Engberg, L. A., Hansen, G., Welker, R. L., & Thomas, D. R. Acquisition of key-pecking via autoshaping as a function of prior experience: "Learned laziness"? *Science,* 1973, **178,** 1002–1004.

Engel, G. L., & Schmale, A. H. Conservation-withdrawal. In *Physiology emotions and psychosomatic illness.* Amsterdam: Elsevier, 1972.

Frank, R. L. The organized adaptive aspect of the depression–elation response. In P. H. Hoch & J. Zubin (Eds.), *Depression.* New York: Grune & Stratton, 1953.

Frederickson, R. C. A. Enkephalin pentapeptides—A review of current evidence for a physiological role in vertebrate neurotransmission. *Life Sciences,* 1977, **21,** 23–42.

Glazer, H. I., & Weiss, J. M. Long-term and transitory interference effects. *Journal of Experimental Psychology: Animal Behavior Processes,* 1976, **2,** 191–201. (a)

Glazier, H. I., & Weiss, J. M. Long-term interference effect: An alternative to "learned helplessness." *Journal of Experimental Psychology: Animal Behavior Processes,* 1976, **2,** 201–213. (b)

Goldstein, A. Opioid peptides (endorphins) in pituitary and brain. *Science,* 1976, **193,** 1081–1086.

Goodkin, F. Rats learn the relationship between responding and environmental events: An expansion of the learned helplessness hypothesis. *Learning and Motivation,* 1976, **7,** 382–394.

Guthrie, E. R. *The psychology of learning.* New York: Harper, 1935.

Hayes, R. L., Bennett, G. J., Newlon, P., & Mayer, D. J. Analgesic effects of certain noxious and stressful manipulations in the rat. *Society for the Neurosciences Abstract,* 1976, **2,** 1350.

Herrnstein, R. J. Superstition: A corollary of the principles of operant conditioning. In W. K. Honig (Ed.), *Operant behavior: Areas of research and application.* New York: Appleton, 1966.

Hiroto, D. S., & Seligman, M. E. P. Generality of learned helplessness in man. *Journal of Personality and Social Psychology,* 1975, **31,** 311–327.

Hughes, J. Isolation of an endogenous compound from the brain with pharmacological properties similar to morphine. *Brain Research,* 1975, **88,** 295–308.

Hughes, J., Smith, J. W., Kosterlitz, H. W., Fothergill, L. A., Morgan, B. A., & Morris, H. R. Identification of two related pentapeptides from the brain with potent opiate agonist activity. *Nature (London),* 1975, **258,** 577–579.

Hull, C. L. *Principles of behavior.* New York: Appleton, 1943.

Jackson, R. L., Alexander J. H., & Maier, S. F. Learned helplessness, inactivity, and associative deficits: The effects of inescapable shock on response choice escape learning. Submitted for publication.

Jackson, R. L., Maier, S. F., & Rapaport, P. M. Exposure to inescapable shock produces both activity and associative deficits in the rat. *Learning and Motivation,* 1978, **9,** 69–98.

Kaufman, I. C. Mother–infant separation in monkeys: An experimental model. In J. P. Scott & E. C. Senay (Eds.), *Separation and depression.* Washington, D.C.: American Association for the Advancement of Science, 1973.

Kelsey, J. E. Escape acquisition following inescapable shock in the rat. *Animal Learning and Behavior,* 1977, **5,** 83–92.

Levis, D. J. Learned helplessness: A reply and alternative S–R interpretation. *Journal of Experimental Psychology: General,* 1976, **105,** 47–65.

Liebeskind, J. C., & Paul, L. A. Psychological and physiological mechanisms of pain. *Annual Review of Psychology,* 1977, **28,** 41–60.

Mackintosh, N. J. Stimulus selection: Learning to ignore stimuli that predict no change in reinforcement. In R. A. Hindle & J. Stevenson-Hinde (Eds.), *Constraints on learning.* New York: Academic Press, 1973.

Mackintosh, N. J. *The psychology of animal learning.* New York: Academic Press, 1975. (a)

Mackintosh, N. J. Blocking of conditioned suppression: Role of the first compound trial. *Journal of Experimental Psychology: Animal Behavior Processes,* 1975, **1,** 335–345. (b)

Madden, J., Akil, H., Patrick, R. L., & Barchas, J. D. Stress-induced parallel changes in control opioid levels and pain responsiveness in the rat. *Nature (London),* 1976, **265,** 358–360.

Maier, S. F. Competing motor responses: A reply to Black. *Journal of Experimental Psychology: General,* 1977, **106,** 44–46.

Maier, S. F., Albin, R. W., & Testa, T. J. Failure to learn to escape in rats previously exposed to inescapable shock depends on nature of escape response. *Journal of Comparative and Physiological Psychology,* 1973, **85,** 581–592.

Maier, S. F., Anderson, C., & Lieberman, D. A. Influence of control of shock on subsequent shock-elicited aggression. *Journal of Comparative and Physiological Psychology,* 1972, **81,** 94–100.

Maier, S. F., & Jackson, R. L. The nature of the initial coping response and the learned helplessness effect. *Animal Learning and Behavior,* 1977, **5,** 407–414.

Maier, S. F., Jackson, R. L., Tomie, A., & Rapoport, P. M. How to get learned helplessness in rats. Paper presented at the meeting of the Psychonomic Society, Denver, 1975.

Maier, S. F., & Seligman, M. E. P. Learned helplessness: Theory and evidence. *Journal of Experimental Psychology: General,* 1976, **105,** 3–46.

Maier, S. F., Seligman, M. E. P., & Solomon, R. L. Pavlovian fear conditioning and learned helplessness. In B. A. Campbell & R. M. Church (Eds.), *Punishment.* New York: Appleton, 1969.

Maier, S. F., & Testa, T. J. Failure to learn to escape by rats previously exposed to inescapable shock is partly produced by associative interference. *Journal of Comparative and Physiological Psychology.* 1975, **88,** 554–564.

Melzack, R., & Wall, P. D. Pain mechanisms: A new theory. *Science,* 1965, **150,** 971–979.

Miller, N. E., & Weiss, J. M. Effects of somatic or visceral responses to punishment. In B. A. Campbell & R. M. Church (Eds.), *Punishment and aversive behavior.* New York: Appleton, 1969.

Mullins, G. P., & Winefield, A. H. Immunization and helplessness phenomena in the rat in a non-aversive situation. *Animal Learning and Behavior,* 1977, **5,** 281–284.

Overmier, J. B., & Seligman, M. E. P. Effects of inescapable shock upon subsequent escape and avoidance learning. *Journal of Comparative and Physiological Psychology,* 1967, **63,** 28–33.

Pert, A., & Walter, M. Comparison between naloxone reversal of morphine and electrical stimulation induced analgesia in the rat mesencephalon. *Life Sciences,* 1976, **19,** 1023–1032.

Rapaport, P. M., & Maier, S. F. Inescapable shock and food-competition in rats. *Animal Learning and Behavior,* 1978, 6, 160–165.

Rosellini, R. A., & Seligman, M. E. P. Learned helplessness and escape from frustration. *Journal of Experimental Psychology: Animal Behavior Processes.* 1975, **1,** 149–158.

Seligman, M. E. P. *Helplessness: On depression, development and death.* San Francisco: Freeman, 1975.

Seligman, M. E. P. & Beagley, G. Learned helplessness in the rat. *Journal of Comparative and Physiological Psychology,* 1975, **88,** 534–541.

Seligman, M. E. P., & Groves, D. Non-transient learned helplessness. *Psychonomic Science,* 1970, **19,** 191–192.

Seligman, M. E. P., & Maier, S. F. Failure to escape traumatic shock. *Journal of Experimental Psychology,* 1967, **74,** 1–9.

Seligman, M. E. P., Maier, S. F., & Geer, J. The alleviation of learned helplessness in the dog. *Journal of Abnormal and Social Psychology,* 1968, **73,** 256–262.

Seligman, M. E. P., Maier, S. F., & Solomon, R. L. Unpredictable and uncontrollable aversive events. In F. R. Brush (Ed.), *Aversive conditioning and learning.* New York: Academic Press, 1971.

Seligman, M. E. P., Rosellini, R. A., & Kozak, M. Learned helplessness in the rat: Reversibility, time course, and immunization. *Journal of Comparative and Physiological Psychology,* 1975, **88,** 542–547.

Snyder, S. H. The brain's own opiates. *Chemical and Engineering News,* 1977, **55,** 25–35.

Terenius, L. Significance of endorphins in endogenous antinociception. In E. Costa & M. Trabucchi (Eds.), *Advances in biochemical psychopharmacology* (Vol. 18). New York: Raven, 1978.

Teschemacher, H., Opheim, K. E., Cox, B. M., & Goldstein, A. A peptide-like substance from the pituitary that acts like morphine. I. Isolation. *Life Sciences,* 1975, **16,** 1771–1776.

Testa, T. J., Juraska, J. M., & Maier, S. F. Prior exposure to inescapable electric shock in rats effects extinction behavior after the successful acquisition of an escape response. *Learning and Motivation,* 1974, **5,** 380–392.

Thomas, E., & DeWald, L. Experimental neurosis: Neuropsychological analysis. In J. D. Maser & M. E. P. Seligman (Eds.), *Psychopathology: Experimental models.* San Francisco:

Freeman, 1977.

Wei, E., & Low, H. Physical dependence on opiate-like peptides. *Science,* 1976, **193,** 1262–1263.

Weiss, J. M. Effects of coping responses on stress. *Journal of Comparative and Physiological Psychology,* 1968, **65,** 251–260.

Weiss, J. M. Effects of coping behavior in different warning signal conditions on stress pathology in rats. *Journal of Comparative and Physiological Psychology,* 1971, **77,** 1–13. (a)

Weiss, J. M. Effects of coping behavior with and without a feedback signal on stress pathology in rats. *Journal of Comparative and Physiological Psychology,* 1971, **77,** 22–30. (b)

Weiss, J. M. Effects of punishing the coping response (conflict) on stress pathology in rats. *Journal of Comparative and Physiological Psychology,* 1971, **77,** 14–21. (c)

Weiss, J. M., Glazer, H. I., & Pohorecky, L. A. Coping behavior and neurochemical changes: An alternative explanation for the original "learned helplessness" experiments. In *Relevance of the psychopathological animal model to the human.* New York: Plenum Press, 1975.

Weiss, J. M., Stone, E. A., and Harrell, N. Coping behavior and brain norepinephrine in rats. *Journal of Comparative and Physiological Psychology,* 1970, **72,** 153–160.

Welker, R. L. Acquisition of a free operant appetitive response in pigeons as a function of prior experience with response-dependent food. *Learning and Motivation,* 1976, **7,** 394–405.

Williams, J. L., & Maier, S. F. Transsituational immunization and therapy of learned helplessness in the rat. *Journal of Experimental Psychology: Animal Behavior Processes,* 1977, **3,** 240–253.

Yaksh, T. J., Yeung, J. L., & Rudy, T. A. An inability to antagonize with naloxone the elevated nociceptive thresholds resulting from electrical stimulation of mesencephalic central gray. *Life Sciences,* 1976, **18,** 1193–1198.

ON THE COGNITIVE COMPONENT OF LEARNED HELPLESSNESS AND DEPRESSION[1]

Lauren B. Alloy and Martin E. P. Seligman

UNIVERSITY OF PENNSYLVANIA
PHILADELPHIA PENNSYLVANIA

I. Introduction

In recent years, the concept of contingency has played an increasingly important role in theoretical accounts of learning. Contemporary learning theorists point to the role of objective contingencies among stimuli, outcomes, and responses as crucial determinants of animals' and humans' behavior in Pavlovian and instrumental-learning situations (Baum, 1973; Bindra, 1972; Bloomfield, 1972; Bolles, 1972; Catania, 1971; Church, 1969; Gibbon, Berryman, & Thompson, 1974; Kamin, 1968, 1969; Mackintosh, 1973, 1975; Maier & Seligman, 1976; Maier, Seligman, & Solomon, 1969; Premack, 1965; Prokasy, 1965; Rescorla, 1967, 1969c; Rescorla & Wagner, 1972; Seligman, 1975b; Seligman, Maier, & Solomon, 1971; Wagner, 1969; Wagner & Rescorla, 1972; Weiss,

[1]Preparation of this paper and the research reported were supported by National Science Foundation (SM-76 22871) and National Institute of Mental Health (MH 07284) Predoctoral Fellowships to L. B. Alloy and a National Institute of Mental Health grant (MH 10604) to M. E. P. Seligman. M. E. P. Seligman was a fellow at the Center for Advanced Studies in the Behavioral Sciences, Stanford, California during part of the preparation of this paper. L. B. Alloy is now at the Department of Psychology, Northwestern University, Evanston, Illinois, 60201. Thanks are due to Lyn Abramson, Aidan Alternor, Ronald Ehrman, and Joseph Volpicelli for many enlightening discussions on the topic of the perception of contingency.

ISBN 0-12-543313-1

1968a). Recent evidence also suggests that the presence and absence of contingencies between stimuli, responses, and outcomes has important emotional and physiological consequences as well. Aversive outcomes uncorrelated with antecedent stimuli may produce greater stress and anxiety than when predicted with prior stimuli (e.g., Azrin, 1956; Brimer & Kamin, 1963; Pervin, 1963; Weiss, 1968b). If allowed to choose, animals and humans opt for predictable aversive events over unpredictable ones (e.g., Badia, Suter, & Lewis, 1967; Lockard, 1963; S. M. Miller & Grant, 1979; Seligman & Binik, 1977). Similarly, aversive consequences that are not contingent on responses may produce more emotional distress (e.g., Hearst, 1965; Hokanson, DeGood, Forrest, & Brittain, 1971; S. M. Miller, 1979; Rodin & Langer, 1977; Schultz, 1976; Weiss, 1968a, 1971a, 1971b, 1971c) as well as more disruption of future problem solving behavior than response-contingent noxious outcomes (e.g., Hiroto & Seligman, 1975; Maier, Albin, & Testa, 1973; Seligman & Maier, 1967).

One learning theory to which the concept of contingency is central is learned helplessness (Maier & Seligman, 1976; Maier *et al.*, 1969; Seligman, 1975b; Seligman *et al.*, 1971). Learned helplessness argues that organisms actively form a subjective representation of the degree to which an outcome is dependent upon responses. This representation has been variously called a perception, belief, or expectation of control. Of particular interest to helplessness theory is the situation in which responses and outcomes are noncontingently related. In this case, the theory claims that the organism forms the expectation that the outcome will be independent of its behavior and that this expectation causes motivational, cognitive, and emotional deficits. The hypothesized motivational deficit is a reduced incentive for initiating voluntary responses, and the cognitive deficit is a reduced ability to learn future response–reinforcer contingencies. The emotional consequence of learning that aversive outcomes are independent of responding is anxiety followed by depression.

The learned helplessness theory occupies a special position in contemporary learning theory in two respects. First, it is cognitive. It is one of the few learning theories which postulates subjective representations of contingencies as a mediator between objective contingencies and behavioral effects (Bolles, 1972; Mackintosh, 1973; Tolman, 1932, are others). Second, it is unique among contemporary theories in explicitly proposing the same cognitive mechanism as an account for both human and animal maladaptive behavior. In this regard, it is similar to more traditional theories of learning (e.g., Guthrie, 1952; Hull, 1943; Skinner, 1938; Tolman, 1932).

In this chapter, we examine evidence bearing on the judgment of contingency in animals and humans as it bears on helplessness theory. We critically examine the findings offered in support of cognitive deficit in helpless animals and humans, with particular reference to the separation of this deficit from hypothesized motivation and activity deficits.[2] In addition, we present new data which bear directly on the existence of cognitive deficit, and we propose that the deficit stems either from perceptual or from expectational bias toward noncontingency. Finally, we conclude by questioning whether learned helplessness theory successfully integrates the animal and human data within a single theoretical framework.

II. The Concept of Contingency in Learning Theory

In this section we define the concept of contingency and present some examples of its importance in Pavlovian and instrumental conditioning.

A. Contingency and Pavlovian Conditioning

The traditional view of Pavlovian conditioning regards temporal contiguity between a conditional stimulus (CS) and an unconditional stimulus (US) as central to the establishment of conditioning. Recently, however, a number of authors have criticized this reliance on temporal contiguity or pairing as the sufficient condition for conditioning (e.g., Kamin, 1968, 1969; Premack, 1965; Prokasy, 1965; Rescorla, 1967). The crucial difference between the pairing and contingency views is that the former focuses solely upon the probability with which a US occurs in the presence of a CS, while the latter focuses upon both this probability and the probability with which the US occurs in the absence of the CS ($\overline{CS}$).

The distinction between the contiguity and contingency views is explicated more formally in Fig. 1, which presents the Pavlovian conditioning space.[3] The *x* axis, *p* (US/CS), represents the traditional contiguity dimension, the conditional probability of a US given a CS. At 1.0, the CS is always followed by a US (continuous reinforcement). At zero, the

[2]The reader should note that it is not our intention to provide an exhaustive survey of the experimental evidence supporting the learned helplessness theory. Rather, we present only those studies bearing directly on the existence of a cognitive deficit in helplessness. Readers interested in a more comprehensive examination of the evidence supporting learned helplessness theory are referred to Abramson, Seligman and Teasdale (1978b), Maier and Seligman (1976) and Seligman (1975b).

[3]See Gibbon, Berryman, and Thompson (1974) and Seligman, Maier, and Solomon (1971) for similar discussions of the Pavlovian and instrumental conditioning spaces.

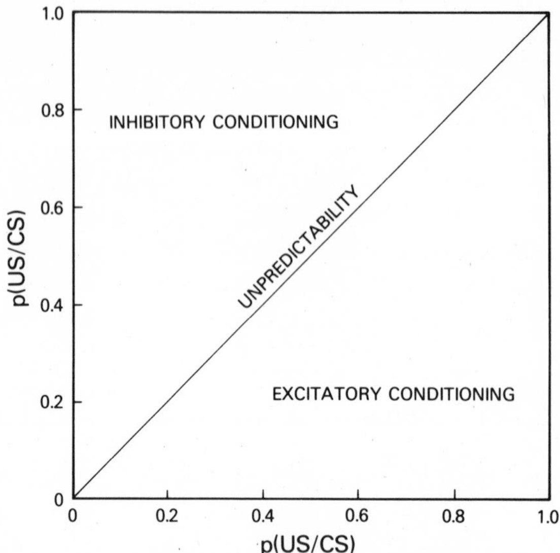

Fig. 1. The Pavlovian conditioning space. The ordinate and abscissa represent the relationships between CS and US. They are conditional probabilities, or stimulus contingencies, arranged by E. The 45° line represents a special condition, the unpredictability of Pavlovian reinforcement, because $p(\text{US/CS}) = p(\text{US}/\overline{\text{CS}})$. (From "Unpredictable and uncontrollable aversive events" by M. E. P. Seligman, S. F. Maier, and R. L. Solomon in *Aversive conditioning and learning* edited by F. R. Brush, New York: Academic Press, 1971. Copyright 1971 by Academic Press. Adapted by permission.)

CS is never followed by a US (extinction). According to the contingency view, one conditional probability is an incomplete description of the relations between a CS and a US about which organisms learn. Unconditional stimuli can also occur in the absence of a CS. An adequate description of contingency allows conjoint variation along both the x axis and the y axis, p (US/$\overline{\text{CS}}$), which represents the conditional probability of the US given the absence of the CS.

Seligman *et al.* (1971) define the concept of contingency and the notions of predictability and unpredictability within the Pavlovian conditioning space. A US is contingent upon a CS; i.e., it is predicted by that CS, if and only if,

$$p(\text{US/CS}) \neq p(\text{US}/\overline{\text{CS}}). \tag{1}$$

In contrast, a US is noncontingently related to a CS if it occurs with some fixed probability independent of whether or not the CS occurs; i.e., if and only if,

$$p(\text{US/CS}) = p(\text{US}/\overline{\text{CS}}). \tag{2}$$

When a US is independent of all CSs, it is said to be unpredictable. Within this framework, the degree of predictability or contingency between a CS and a US may be roughly indexed by the magnitude of the difference between the two conditional probabilities represented along the x and y axes.[4] Thus, degree of predictability is an attempt to capture the degree to which the CS provides information about the occurrence of the US.

In a series of highly influential papers, Rescorla (1967, 1968, 1969c) has argued that "true" Pavlovian conditioning is dependent upon the contingency, rather than upon the temporal contiguity between a CS and US. Whenever the probability of a US is greater in the presence of a CS than in its absence (positive contingency), the CS becomes a conditioned excitor (CS+). Instances of excitatory conditioning are represented by all points to the right of the 45° diagonal in Fig. 1. Rescorla (1967) has also pointed out that the concept of contingency has an important advantage over the contiguity view in that it allows one to distinguish between the mere absence of excitatory conditioning and the presence of active inhibitory conditioning. According to the contingency view, a CS becomes a conditioned inhibitor (CS−) whenever the US occurs more often in its absence than in its presence (negative contingency). Examples of inhibitory conditioning are represented by all points to the left of the 45° diagonal in Fig. 1. Finally, Rescorla (1967) postulates that when there is no contingency between CS and US (the 45° diagonal), neither excitatory nor inhibitory conditioning occurs. This last proposition is currently disputed (e.g., Ayres, Benedict, & Witcher, 1975; Benedict & Ayres, 1972; Bull & Overmier, 1968; Davis & McIntire, 1969; Keller, Ayres, & Mahoney, 1977; Kremer, 1974; Kremer & Kamin, 1971; Quinsey, 1971; Rescorla, 1968, 1972) but appears to be correct if animals are tested after conditioning asymptotes (Rescorla & Wagner, 1972).

A substantial body of evidence supports the contention that organisms are "sensitive" to both positive and negative contingencies (e.g., Dweck & Wagner, 1970; Hammond & Daniel, 1970; Moskowitz & LoLordo, 1968; Rescorla, 1968, 1969a, 1969b, 1969c; Rescorla & Wagner, 1972;

[4]This "difference in probability" metric is similar to that employed by Jenkins and Ward (1965). In addition, it is a close mathematical approximation to the phi coefficient (ϕ), the index commonly used in statistics to indicate degree of association between two events. S. M. Miller and Grant (1979) propose a ratio metric rather than a difference score to index degree of contingency, however. Space does not permit a discussion of the merits of the two indices.

Wagner & Rescorla, 1972). The paradigm demonstration of the dependence of Pavlovian conditioning on the degree of contingency between CS and US rather than on temporal contiguity is an experiment conducted by Rescorla (1968). Rescorla exposed 10 groups of rats to extensive conditioning involving different correlations between a tone CS and footshock. Test sessions followed in which the tone CS was repeatedly presented while the animals were bar pressing for food.

The results are graphed in Fig. 2. The data are presented in the form of suppression ratios $A/(A + B)$, where A equals the bar-pressing rate during the CS and B equals the rate in an equivalent interval prior to the CS. Thus, values close to zero indicate a high degree of conditioning and values close to 0.5 indicate little or no conditioning. Each panel of Fig. 2 shows the groups that received equivalent probabilities of shock during the tone (i.e., an equivalent number of CS–US pairings), but different shock probabilities in the absence of the tone. In each panel

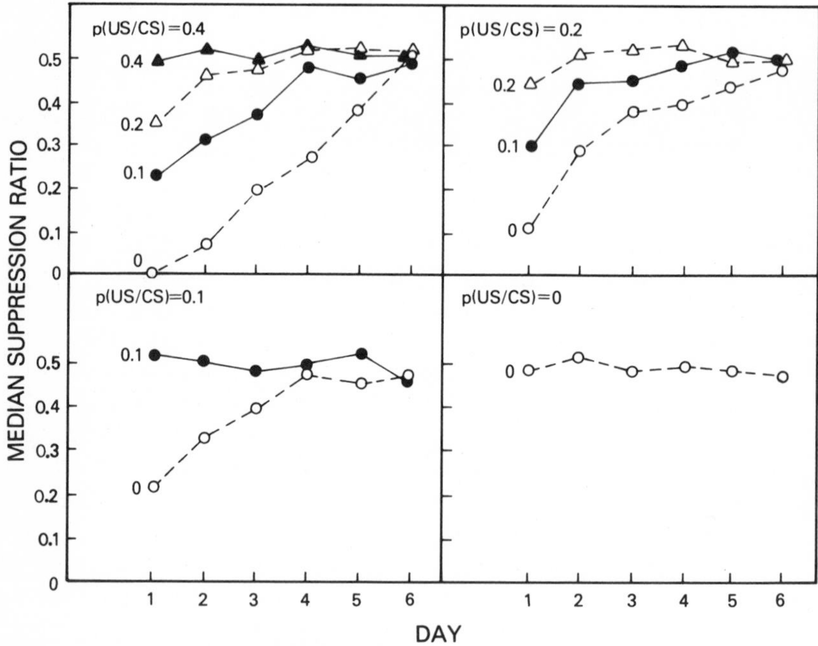

Fig. 2. Median suppression ratio for each group over the six test sessions. Within each panel, all groups have the same probability of US during CS; the parameter in each panel is the probability of US in the absence of CS. (From "Probability of shock in the presence and absence of CS in fear conditioning" by R. A. Rescorla, *Journal of Comparative and Physiological Psychology,* 1968, *66,* 1–5. Copyright 1968 by the American Psychological Association. Reprinted by permission.)

of the figure, conditioning decreased as the correlation between tone and shock decreased (i.e., as the probability of shock in the absence of the CS was increased). In addition, those groups which were exposed to equal shock probabilities in the presence and absence of the tone (zero contingency) showed almost no conditioning. Rescorla's experiment provides convincing evidence that the contingency between a CS and US and not simply the number of pairings can determine conditioning in Pavlovian experiments.

B. Contingency and Instrumental Conditioning

The traditional view of instrumental learning, like that of Pavlovian conditioning, treats temporal contiguity between response and reinforcer as the essential determinant of conditioning. According to this view, a reinforcer strengthens any response which precedes it, whether or not the reinforcer occurs in the absence of the response. However, just as recent evidence has required a revision of the contiguity view in favor of contingency within Pavlovian conditioning, theorists of instrumental learning have also paid increasing attention to the concept of contingency (e.g., Baum, 1973; Bloomfield, 1972; Catania, 1971; Church, 1969; Gibbon *et al.*, 1974; Maier *et al.*, 1969; Seligman *et al.*, 1971; Weiss, 1968a). For example, Seligman *et al.* (1971) argued that instrumental learning is adequately explained only in terms of conjoint variations in two response–outcome probabilities: the conditional probability of an outcome given the occurrence of a response, $p(O/R)$, and the conditional probability of that outcome given the absence of that response, $p(O/\bar{R})$.

Figure 3 represents the instrumental conditioning space. The x axis is the traditional contiguity dimension, $p(O/R)$, and the y axis is the probability of the outcome in the absence of the response, $p(O/\bar{R})$. Points to the right of the 45° diagonal represent instances of reward training if the outcome is appetitive and punishment if the outcome is aversive. Points to the left of the 45° diagonal are instances of omission (appetitive outcome) or avoidance (aversive outcome) training.

Seligman *et al.* (1971) define the concepts of controllability and uncontrollability within this two-dimensional space. An outcome is contingent upon or controlled by a response whenever its occurrence depends on whether or not the response occurs. That is, a response stands in a relation of control to an outcome, if and only if,

$$p(O/R) \neq p(O/\bar{R}). \tag{3}$$

In contrast, when a response does not effect an outcome, the outcome is independent of the response. Specifically, an outcome is independent of a response, if and only if,

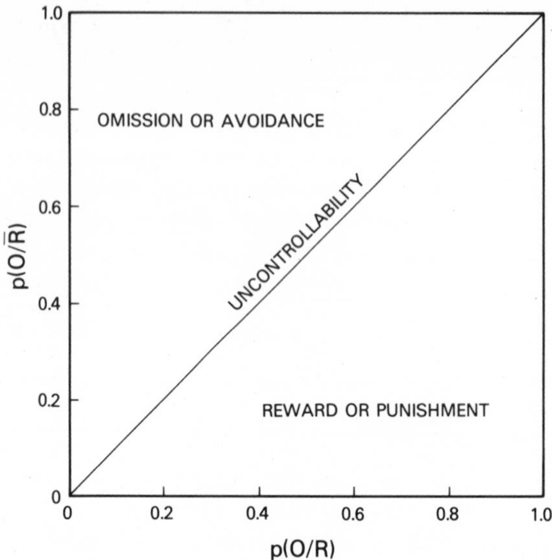

Fig. 3. The instrumental conditioning space. The ordinate and abscissa represent the relationships between S's response and an outcome. They are conditional probabilities, or response contingencies, arranged by E. The 45° line represents a special condition, when the outcome is uncontrollable because $p(\mathrm{O/R}) = p(\mathrm{O}/\bar{\mathrm{R}})$. (From "Unpredictable and uncontrollable aversive events" by M. E. P. Seligman, S. F. Maier, and R. L. Solomon in *Aversive conditioning and learning* edited by F. R. Brush, New York: Academic Press, 1971. Copyright 1971 by Academic Press. Adapted by permission.)

$$p(\mathrm{O/R}) = p(\mathrm{O}/\bar{\mathrm{R}}). \tag{4}$$

When this is true of all voluntary responses, the outcome is said to be uncontrollable.[5] Degree of control may be roughly indexed by the arithmetic difference in the conditional probability of outcome given the presence versus the absence of the response.

We know of no instrumental-learning experiment which demonstrates the inadequacy of the contiguity view as elegantly as the Pavlovian experiment conducted by Rescorla (1968). However, the need for the concept of contingency in instrumental learning theory became increasingly apparent as evidence accumulated that the presence versus absence of a contingency between responses and outcomes had vastly different consequences for behavior. For example, Weiss (1968a) reported two experiments in which two groups of rats were trained to escape and

[5]In line with the Seligman, Maier, and Solomon (1971) discussion, Alloy and Bersh (1979) have extended the concept of control within the instrumental conditioning space to include characteristics of the outcome other than its probability of occurrence.

avoid tailshocks. One group of rats (experiment 1) was trained to escape and avoid tailshock by jumping up onto a platform, while the other group (experiment 2) could escape and avoid tailshock by pressing a copper plate with its nose. Two additional groups of rats received tailshocks which were noncontingently related to all of their responses. These animals were yoked to the rats which could escape and avoid and, thus, they received an identical number and pattern of shocks. Weiss found that the yoked rats which received uncontrollable shocks gained less weight, drank less, defecated more, and developed more stomach ulcers than rats which were able to control shock.

Perhaps the most dramatic instance of the differential effects of controllable and uncontrollable outcomes and, thus, the greatest impetus for a contingency view of instrumental learning is the learned helplessness phenomenon and the theory proposed to account for it.

III. Learned Helplessness

A. The Phenomenon

Let us consider two experiments.

In one experiment (Seligman & Maier, 1967), three groups of dogs were given experience in a Pavlovian hammock. Dogs in one group, the escape group, received 64 unsignaled shocks, which they could escape by pressing a panel located on either side of their heads. A yoked group received shocks identical in number, duration, and pattern to the shocks delivered to the escape group. The yoked and escape groups differed only with respect to the contingency between responses and shocks. While panel pressing terminated shock for the escape group, it had no effect on shock for the yoked group. A naive control group received no shocks in the hammock. Twenty-four hours later, dogs in each of the three groups were given 10 trials of two-way shuttlebox escape/avoidance training in which the requisite response was a jump over a barrier.

Figure 4 shows the median latency of barrier jumping, on each of the 10 trials, for each of the three groups. Dogs in the yoked group were much slower to escape than dogs in the escape or naive group, which did not differ from each other. The behavior of the dogs in the yoked group was qualitatively different from that of the other two groups, as well as quantitatively different. Six of the eight dogs in the yoked group failed to escape shock on every trial. Initially in the shuttlebox, the yoked dogs behaved exactly as did the dogs in the naive and escape groups: They ran around frantically, urinated, defecated, and howled. However, as shock continued, they stopped running and instead lay down "passively" and whimpered. On later trials, they made no escape movements

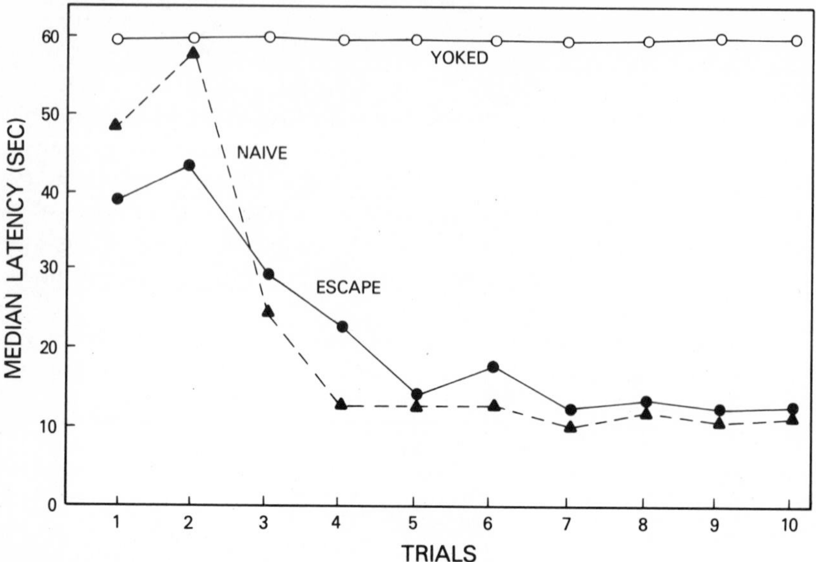

Fig. 4. Median escape latency in a shuttlebox for dogs given escapable, yoked inescapable, or no shock in a harness. (From "Unpredictable and uncontrollable aversive events" by M. E. P. Seligman, S. F. Maier, and R. L. Solomon in *Aversive conditioning and learning* edited by F. R. Brush, New York: Academic Press, 1971. Copyright 1971 by Academic Press. Reprinted by permission.)

at all. A few yoked dogs actually would jump the barrier and successfully terminate shock; yet on subsequent trials they returned to taking the shock. In contrast, dogs in the naive and escape groups would scramble over the barrier during the initial shock. On subsequent trials, these dogs would jump the barrier more and more quickly. The results of the Seligman and Maier experiment indicate that it was not shock per se that led to the yoked dogs' failure to escape, since dogs in the escape group received an equivalent amount of shock, but exposure to shocks that could not be controlled.

The second experiment to consider produces analogous findings in humans. Using the triadic design of Seligman and Maier (1967), Hiroto (1974) compared three groups of college students: an "escapable" group, which received experience with 110-db, 3000-Hz tones that they could terminate by button pressing; an "inescapable" group, which received experience with the tones noncontingently related to button pressing; and a "no-tone" group, which received no tones. All groups were subsequently tested for escape and avoidance of the tones on a human analog to a two-way shuttlebox. The appropriate escape/avoidance response in the test task was moving a knob across the shuttlebox. Paralleling the results of Seligman and Maier, Hiroto found that students who had received noncontingent tones, as compared to students receiving contingent or no tones, were slower to escape, failed to escape more often, and required more trials to reach a criterion of three consecutive escapes once a successful escape had occurred.

These two experiments illustrate the debilitating effects of uncontrollable aversive outcomes. People and animals who are exposed to outcomes which occur independently of their responses become "helpless." They exhibit passivity and are impaired in learning future responses to control reinforcement. Below, we describe the theory proposed by Maier *et al.* (1969) and Seligman *et al.* (1971) to explain this phenomenon.

B. Description of the Theory

The basic proposition of the learned helplessness theory is that organisms which experience outcomes that occur independently of any instrumental responses form an expectation that there will be no contingency between their behavior and the outcome in the future. This expectation produces three effects: motivational, cognitive, and emotional.

The motivational effect is reflected in greater difficulty initiating voluntary responses relative to escape or naive groups and is the consequence of the expectation that outcomes are uncontrollable. If an organism expects that its responses will not affect some outcome, then the likelihood of emitting such responses decreases. (See Bolles, 1972, for a more extended discussion of expectations and incentive motivation.) Thus, the yoked dogs in the Seligman and Maier (1967) experiment failed to respond in the face of shock because they had previously acquired the expectation that shock termination would be independent of their responses.

The cognitive effect consists of greater difficulty in learning that future responding and outcomes are dependent than the escape and naive groups and is also viewed as a consequence of the expectation that outcomes will be independent of responses. According to helplessness theory, learning that an outcome is unrelated to responses proactively interferes with future learning that the outcome is now dependent upon responses. Thus, the yoked dogs in the Seligman and Maier (1967) experiment and the inescapable noise subjects in the Hiroto (1974) experiment failed to follow one successful escape response with another because they had trouble learning that responding would terminate the aversive outcome. Finally, the learned helplessness theory claims that increased stress and depressed affect are also the result of learning that aversive outcomes are noncontingently related to responses (see Maier & Seligman, 1976; Seligman, 1975b, for reviews of the data supporting the motivational, cognitive, and emotional deficits).

It is important to emphasize that the learned helplessness theory involves three stages, the mediating one being cognitive.

1. Objective contingency →
2. Subjective representation of the contingency (perception → expectation) →
3. Behavior

In its commerce with the environment, an organism is provided with information about the objective degree of contingency between outcomes and its responses. This information is processed and transformed into a subjective representation of the degree of contingency.

This subjective representation must involve at least two steps: first, the perception, or registration, of the immediately present or past contingency, followed by the formation of an expectation about future contingency. The step from perception to expectation will be influenced by already extant expectations, beliefs, knowledge, and perhaps most importantly, attributions. A recent reformulation of the theory (Abramson, Seligman, & Teasdale, 1978b) adds the additional step of attribution formation between the perception → → expectation of contingency link. Attribution of the cause of noncontingency to stable and global factors (or conversely, of contingency to unstable and specific factors) will increase the probability that an expectation biased toward noncontingency will occur more often in the future and in a wide variety of situations. Because we have recently reviewed the attributional evidence elsewhere, we shall concentrate on perceptual and expectational evidence (Abramson *et al.*, 1978b).

It is important to recognize that the cognitive mediation consists of two steps, not one, and helplessness theory until recently has failed to make this distinction clear. The net cognitive result of experience with uncontrollable outcomes is to make learning future response–outcome dependencies more difficult than for organisms that have had experience with controllable outcomes or no relevant experience. The final step in this process must be an expectation biased toward response–outcome noncontingency. Such a biased expectation could itself result from bias at either of the two steps: *(a)* If perception of present contingency is unbiased, but expectation of future contingency is biased by past experience with noncontingency, the resultant expectation will be biased toward noncontingency. The most obvious source of a biased expectational process is the global, stable attributional style for noncontingency (or conversely, the specific, unstable attributional style for contingency) discussed by Abramson *et al.* (1978b) *(b)* The expectational mechanism may be unbiased, but the earlier perceptual process may be biased toward detecting noncontingency when contingency is actually present. The most obvious source of a perceptual bias toward noncontingency is attentional. If either the salience of the feedback from responding (Mackintosh, 1975) decreases after response-independent outcomes or the salience of the relationship between outcomes and responding decreases, seeing response–outcome contingencies will be retarded. We shall not discuss an attentional mechanism of the perceptual bias further, since the relevant experiments have not been done. (For example, will an external stimulus paired with shock termination in the same situation in which responding is independent of shock termination be a more effective blocker of subsequent Pavlovian conditioning with a shock termination US than relevant control stimuli?) or *(c)* Both steps *(a)* and *(b)* could occur. Most evidence about the cognitive deficit does not tease these possibilities apart, but there are at least one animal study (Maier & Testa, 1975) and two human studies (Abramson, Alloy, & Rosoff, 1979; Alloy & Abramson, 1979) that do, and we shall discuss them below. Where possible, however, it is important to recognize that demonstration of a cognitive deficit is relatively gross and in principle could be refined into demonstration of a perceptual or an expectational (or attributional) bias.

A note on our terms is necessary here:

> *Cognitive deficit* is a term used to denote interference with learning response–outcome contingencies, which does not stem from motivational, activity, or emotional factors. Synonymous with "associative deficit," associative interference, and cognitive interference. The cognitive deficit is an inference, not a direct observation: All that is directly observed is the fact that organisms fail to respond after successful responding; that this failure does not stem from motivational, activity, or emotional deficits is a theoretical inference from relevant experimental observations.
>
> *Perceptual bias* is a tendency to see ongoing and past response–outcome contingencies as noncontingent. It is one of the possible mechanisms or processes which could explain the cognitive deficit.
>
> *Expectational bias* is a tendency to expect that future response–outcome contingencies will be noncontingent. It is also one of the possible mechanisms or processes which could explain the cognitive deficit.
>
> *Attributional bias* is a tendency to attribute the cause of helplessness to global and stable factors and nonhelplessness to specific and unstable factors. It is a likely mechanism for producing the expectational bias defined above.

Let us illustrate how these mechanisms might proceed. An individual has had a prior history of uncontrollable shock. He now receives three trials of controllable shock, which he turns off with a sequence of button presses, but on trial 4 he fails to emit the sequence. Assume that this is the deficit is cognitive. (1) If he has acquired a perceptual bias toward noncontingency, he will be less likely than the relevant comparison groups, to see that his button pressing on trials 1–3 turned off shock, and therefore, he will be less likely to expect that button pressing will turn off shock on trial 4. This weaker expectation decreases the probability of response initiation on trial 4. (2) If he has no perceptual bias, but only an expectational bias produced by an attributional bias, the following sequence might occur: During prior uncontrollable shock, the individual perceives that responding and relief are noncontingently related. Any preexisting attributions about the causes of responding contingently producing relief should be rendered less global and less stable by virtue of experience in which responding is, in at least this place and time, independent of relief. Following trial 3 in the new situation, he perceives as accurately as comparison groups that the sequence of button pressing produced relief on trials 1–3. However, since he attributes the cause of this contingency to less stable and global factors, his expectation that responding will again produce relief on trial 4 is weaker, and response initiation on trial 4 is less probable. ("I know that the response worked on trials 1–3, but will the contingency be the same or will I be able to do the sequence again?")

Historically, helplessness theory has been ambiguous about the process producing the cognitive deficit. Sometimes uncontrollability was alleged to produce a cognitive (associative) deficit which was perceptual, interfering with seeing that responding and outcomes were contingent (now and in the past); at other times it was expectational, interfering with expecting that responding and outcomes are contingent (in the future).[6] At any rate, mere exposure to objective uncontrollability is not sufficient to render an organism helpless; rather, the organism must form the expectation that future outcomes will be uncontrollable in order to exhibit helplessness. Conversely, an organism can show a helplessness effect without being exposed to objective noncontingency; it can

[6]The two authors disagree about the ambiguity of the theory in the past. Alloy believes that helplessness theory was not ambiguous in stating that a helpless organism's expectation of no control produced a cognitive deficit consisting of difficulty in perceiving, not expecting, contingency between responses and outcomes. On Alloy's view, the animal data described below support the cognitive (read perceptual) deficit and the human data do not support the cognitive (perceptual) deficit. Seligman would like to accept Alloy's view, since he believes that "truth arises more surely out of error than out of confusion," but cannot since he believes the theory was ambiguous. He cites the following quotations as examples of the mechanism sometimes seeming like a perception, sometimes like an expectation.

Expectation.

. . . This learning not only reduces the probability of response initiation to escape

merely come to expect erroneously that events will be uncontrollable. So it is the subjective representation of uncontrollability that directly influences the organism's behavior and leads to the motivational, cognitive, and emotional components of helplessness.

Learned helplessness theory has received much experimental support and the phenomenon has been demonstrated in several species across a wide variety of situations (see Maier & Seligman, 1976, for review). Perhaps the broadest application of the learned helplessness theory has been its proposal as a model of human depression (W. R. Miller, Rosellini, & Seligman, 1977; Seligman, 1975a, 1975b; Seligman, Klein, & Miller, 1976). Learned helplessness and naturally occurring depression appear to share many common symptoms: passivity or lowered response initiation, negative cognitive set or a belief in the inefficacy of responding, emotional distress, reduced aggression, loss of appetite and libido, and an implicated role of norepinephrine depletion (e.g., Seligman, 1975b). In brief, the helplessness theory claims that depressed people, like helpless people and animals, are characterized by the expectation that important outcomes and responding will be independent and this expectation is hypothesized to cause the major motivational, cognitive, and emotional symptoms of depression.

---

shock, but also inhibits the formation of the response–relief association if S does make an escape or avoidance response. (Seligman, Maier, & Geer, 1968, p. 261)

Perception.

Uncontrollability may retard the perception of control. (Maier & Seligman, 1976, p. 13)

Expectation.

Response–outcome independence is learned actively and, like any other active form of learning, interferes with learning about contingencies that contradict it. (Seligman, 1975b, p. 51)

Perception.

Depressives should tend to perceive reinforcement as more response independent than nondepressives. (W. R. Miller & Seligman, 1973, p. 62)

Alloy believes these quotations are random with respect to the issue at hand and believes that they all imply perceptual interference. Seligman believes that learning theory's stern proscription of the future tense (the organism expects that shock termination will be independent of responding) contributed to the prior ambiguity. He (and his learning theoretic collaborators) could not bring themselves to use the future tense in describing the mechanism (resulting in such awkward utterances as "the expectation that responding and outcomes are independent"). If the future tense had been appended to expectation earlier, a distinction between perceptual bias now and expectational bias about the future would have emerged earlier. The interested and scholarly reader should get out from behind his laboratory bench, go to the library, and decide for himself. In either case, the distinction between perceptual and expectational bias is a useful elaboration of the theory and we will continue to employ this distinction in the rest of this contribution.

C. Testing the Theory

We believe that any thorough test of the learned helplessness theory involves three parts. First, the three components of helplessness (motivational, cognitive, and emotional) must be demonstrated ideally in isolation from one another. Second, it must be shown that these three components result from the cognitive representation of uncontrollability. Finally, it must be determined if the cognitive deficit results from biased perception, attribution, or expectation.

In the remainder of this chapter we discuss the notion of subjective representation of contingencies and critically review the evidence for a cognitive deficit in helplessness and depression. We focus on the cognitive component because it lies at the heart of helplessness theory and distinguishes this theory from other noncognitive theories of learning. Specifically, we examine helplessness theory's prediction that helpless and/or depressed animals and humans have more difficulty in learning the relationship between their responses and an environmental outcome, when such a contingency exists, than nonhelpless and nondepressed organisms do, and less difficulty learning a contingency does not exist when it actually does not.

IV. Subjective Representation of Contingency

Essential to the helplessness view is the notion that men and animals represent objective stimulus–or response–outcome contingencies cognitively, in the form of perceptions and expectations. Current experimental knowledge does indeed suggest that organisms are sensitive to the presence and absence of correlations between stimuli and/or responses and outcomes, in the sense that their behavior is often a function of such contingencies (see Section II). While contemporary learning theorists are in general agreement about the need for a concept of contingency in theoretical accounts of learning, the role of subjective representations of contingencies in such learning is still the subject of much debate. Within the realm of Pavlovian conditioning, for example, Rescorla and Wagner (1972) have developed a molecular theoretical formulation to account for the functional relation between conditioning and CS–US correlations which does not invoke a concept of contingency with subjective reality. Rescorla (1972) eschewed subjective representation of contingencies because it required postulating an organism capable of calculating a running correlation coefficient. The Rescorla and Wagner (1972) model employed a more traditional and simpler contiguity mechanism to explain the finding that occasional pairings of CS and US in the absence of a correlation are not sufficient to produce conditioning. Their analysis assumes that the organism learns nothing about the actual relationship between CS and US during uncorrelated presentations of the two. Mackintosh (1973), however, as did Seligman (1969) and Maier and Seligman (1976), proposed that lack of correlation is represented cognitively by the subject.

A. In Humans

What are the sufficient criteria for demonstrating the subjective reality of contingency? In humans, we might consider the ability to quantify accurately the objective degree of contingency between two stimulus events or between responses and an outcome as sufficient for inferring a cognitive representation of that contingency. Several investigators have used this criterion to examine people's perception of contingency. It is important to note that such experiments focus on perception of contingency, not on expectation, or extrapolation of such a perception to the future.

Jenkins and Ward (1965), for example, developed a promising method for assessing human capacities for cognitive representation of contingencies. Jenkins and Ward (1965, experiment 1) presented subjects with a series of contingency problems in an instrumental-learning situation. For each problem, subjects were given 60 trials on which a choice between two responses (button 1 and button 2) was followed by one of two possible outcomes (score or no score). The contingency problems differed with respect to both the degree of contingency which actually existed between responses and outcomes and the frequency with which the score outcome occurred. All subjects received five problems, two in which responses and outcomes were contingently related and three in which responses and outcomes were noncontingently related. In addition, subjects received some problems in which the desired outcome (score) occurred frequently and some in which it occurred rarely. The experiment was run under several conditions. Under one condition ("score" instructions), the subject was instructed to obtain the score outcome as often as possible. In the other condition ("control" instructions); the subject was instructed to learn how to produce each outcome at will on any trial. In addition, subjects were either active participants in the task or merely spectators. At the end of each of the five problems, subjects in all conditions were asked to rate, on a 0 to 100 scale, the degree of control (contingency) which the responses exerted over the outcomes. In their study, Jenkins and Ward used the definition of degree of control described previously (Section II, B), i.e., the magnitude of the difference between the conditional probability of the score outcome given the occurrence of response 1 versus the conditional probability of the score outcome given the occurrence of response 2.

Surprisingly, Jenkins and Ward (1965) found that their subjects were often grossly inaccurate in judging contingencies. Specifically, regardless of the actual degree of contingency, subjects' ratings of degree of control correlated highly only with the number of successful trials (i.e., the number of trials on which the desired outcome appeared) and were totally unrelated to the objective degree of control. Importantly, they did not perceive lack of contingency. This was true for spectators as well as actors and for the "control" condition as well as the "score" condition.

In another experiment, Jenkins and Ward (1965, experiment 3) attempted to improve the accuracy of subjects' ratings of control by providing a small amount of pretraining. Subjects received two pretraining problems and were given the correct judgments for these problems in advance. In one of the problems there was no contingency, while in the other there was a high degree of contingency. (In the crucial condition, subjects received pretraining examples chosen so that the number of successes would not vary with the correct values for judged control.) The results of this experiment were again surprising. Although pretraining broke up the correlation between subjects' ratings and number of successes, subjective rating of control still did not show a significant correlation with objective degree of control.

Based on these results, Jenkins and Ward (1965) argued that people do not have an abstract concept of control which entails the core concept of contingency. Similar conclusions have been reached by Smedslund (1963), Chapman and Chapman (1967), and Starr and Katkin (1969) based on their own findings of illusory correlation in the diagnostic setting (see also Langer, 1975; Wortman, 1975). For example, Smedslund (1963) stated "normal adults with no training in statistics do not have a cognitive structure isomorphic with correlation." These results and the conclusion based upon them are a problem for learned helplessness theory. If people do not have an abstract concept of contingency, how then can an expectation of noncontingency develop and interfere with learning future contingencies?

Alloy and Abramson (1979) postulated that Jenkins' and Ward's (1965) failure to find accurate judgments of contingency may be due to a particular aspect of their experimental procedure. In Jenkins' and Ward's study, subjects were presented with two response buttons, R_1 and R_2. Jenkins and Ward calculated the objective degree of contingency in each of their problems by comparing the probability of the outcome when R_1 occurs to the probability of the outcome when R_2 occurs. Jenkins and Ward did not take into account the probability of the outcome when no response (neither R_1 nor R_2) was made, and this probability was always zero. The fact that trials were self-initiated in the Jenkins and Ward experiments increases the likelihood that subjects did, in fact, consider this third conditional probability. If the subjects in their experiments were "computing" the conditional probability associated with no response in addition to the two conditional probabilities associated with R_1 and R_2, then degree of contingency would, in fact, correlate with number of successes. Also, total lack of contingency would never be obtained. In other words, Alloy and Abramson (1979) suggested that subjects in Jenkins' and Ward's experiments may have arrived at their judgments of contingency by comparing the probability of the outcome's occurrence when they made no response with some average of the probability of the outcome's occurrence when they performed R_1 and R_2. Since the probability of the outcome when no response was made was zero, this difference would, in fact, be closely related to the actual number of successes the subject received. Alloy and Abramson argued that if their analysis was correct, subjects in the Jenkins and Ward study were employing an appropriate concept of contingency.

Finally, in their own series of experiments, Alloy and Abramson demonstrated that people can quantify accurately the objective degree of response–outcome contingency across a wide range of the instrumental contingency space (see Section V, B, 3 for a detailed description of the Alloy and Abramson experiments).[7] Finally, it is important to recognize that all these experiments infer perception of contingency from judgment of contingency, and that they do not measure perception of contingency directly.

B. In Animals

At least under some conditions, people may have a subjective representation of contingency which is isomorphic with objective contingency. Do animals form cognitive representations of contingency which mirror objective contingencies? While it is difficult, and perhaps impossible, to demonstrate convincingly that animals have cognitive representations of objective contingencies, Killeen (1978) has developed a procedure which is at least relevant. Since his experiment uses contingency as a discriminative stimulus, it bears on perception of ongoing noncontingency, as opposed to expectation of future noncontingency.

[7]Further support for the Alloy and Abramson (1979) analysis has been provided by Jenkins (1978). Jenkins directly compared judgments of contingency in a response–no-response versus a response 1–response 2 condition. Subjects' judgments of contingency were accurate only in the former condition.

Killeen (1978) examined pigeons' ability to discriminate between response-dependent and response-independent stimulus change in a signal detection framework. Killeen trained four pigeons to peck a central white key, followed by one of two side keys after the center key darkened, to obtain food. Each center key peck the pigeon made had a probability of 0.05 of darkening the center key and illuminating the side keys. In addition, a computer generated "pseudopecks" at the same rate as the pigeon's pecking, with each pseudopeck also having a probability of 0.05 of darkening the center key and lighting the side keys. The pigeon's task was to decide whether the stimulus change was dependent on his last peck or independent of that peck. Pigeons indicated their decision by pecking the right-side key for response-dependent and the left-side key for response-independent darkening of the center key. Correct choices were rewarded with food and incorrect choices were followed by a brief time-out. Killeen delivered unequal amounts of food for correct choices to the left and right keys as a means of varying the payoff ratio associated with deciding "response dependent" versus "response independent."

The results indicated that the pigeons were highly sensitive to the contingencies, as sensitive, in fact, as human observers who were watching them. Both the birds and the humans were correct on approximately 80% of the trials. In addition, the birds were able to maximize their reinforcement by biasing their responses as a function of the payoff ratio. It appeared, however, that the pigeons' accuracy in discriminating response-dependent from response-independent stimulus change was based on the delay between a response and key darkening, since response-dependent changes immediately follow a peck, while independent ones need not. The probability of false alarms (deciding response dependent when stimulus change is actually response independent) increased as the interval of time between a response and noncontingent key darkening shortened, and the majority of false alarms occurred when a response-independent stimulus change occurred between 0.5 and 2.0 sec of a pigeon's response. Thus, Killeen's experiment may indicate only that pigeons can perceive time adequately, not contingency.

Killeen's (1978) basic signal detection experiment would provide a more convincing demonstration of perception of contingency in animals with a major modification. The mean time intervals between a peck and a response-dependent stimulus change and between the last computer generated pseudopeck and a response-independent stimulus change must be equated. With this modification, discrimination could not be based on elapsed time between stimulus change and the last peck, but would have to be based on the relative probabilities of stimulus change given the presence versus absence of a peck; that is, on contingency.

So our discussion of the subjective reality of contingencies suggests that humans may indeed form perceptual representations of contingencies which mirror objective contingencies, but there is as yet too little evidence for perceptual representations of contingencies in animals.

The learned helplessness theory claims that one of the major effects of cognitive representations of response–outcome noncontingency is that it interferes with learning response–outcome contingencies. Evidence demonstrating the existence of such interference would be consistent with the notion of subjective contingency, although it would not uniquely imply such cognitive representation. (See Black, 1977, for an example of a noncognitive, competing motor response theory of cognitive deficit.) In the next section, we critically examine the evidence for a cognitive deficit in helplessness and depression.

V. Empirical Evidence for the Cognitive Deficit of Helplessness

As noted earlier (Section III, C), an adequate test of the cognitive component of learned helplessness theory ideally requires the demonstration of this component in isolation from the response initiation component. Historically, it has been difficult to demonstrate the existence of the cognitive deficit in helpless animals and humans independently of the response initiation deficit. The data of early helplessness studies usually confounded the two deficits. This problem, of course, is not unique to helplessness theory; for the separation of performance effects from those of learning has traditionally been a thorny problem in learning theory (e.g., Tolman, 1955). Recently, however, investigators of animal and human helplessness and depression have become more concerned with developing methods that can tease apart the two components.

In addition to response initiation deficits, motor activity effects of experience with uncontrollable outcomes also need to be separated from the cognitive deficit of helplessness. Critics of the learned helplessness theory have proposed a variety of hypotheses which involve differences in activity level or learned motor patterns as explanatory mechanisms for the debilitating effects of uncontrollable outcomes. It should be noted that these hypotheses only attempt to account for animals' failure to learn to escape and avoid shock following exposures to inescapable shock, not for other animal data or any of the human data. However, motor activity explanations in the spirit of these hypotheses also could be proposed for the helplessness effect seen in other animal contexts and in humans.

One group of these motor activity hypotheses argues that exposure to inescapable shock produces a motor response that is incompatible with the test response and therefore competes with it. Bracewell and Black (1974), for example, suggested that movement is punished during exposure to inescapable shock. In a subsequent shuttlebox test, "holding still" transfers and competes with shuttling. Anisman and Waller (1973) argue that experience with inescapable shock induces "freezing" as the dominant response in the animal's repertoire, and such freezing competes with the occurrence of active escape and avoidance responding in the subsequent escape/avoidance task. Levis (1976), proposing a more complex mechanism, has also argued that behavior incompatible with shuttling is acquired during exposure to inescapable shock. Glazer and Weiss (1976a, 1976b) and Anisman, deCatanzaro, and Remington (1978) maintain that inactivity develops during experience with inescapable shock due either to adventitious reinforcement by shock termination during inescapable shock exposure (Glazer & Weiss, 1976a, 1976b) or to a decreased tendency for shock to maintain vigorous motor activity over prolonged periods (Anisman *et al.*, 1978). These competing motor response hypotheses all claim that either a learned or an elicited skeletal response is responsible for subsequent failure to escape and avoid. A second pair of hypotheses maintains that inescapable shock produces depletion of a neurochemical necessary for the occurrence of movement (Anisman, 1975; Weiss, Glazer, & Pohorecky, 1976). According to these two hypotheses, inescapably shocked animals fail to acquire active escape/avoidance responses because they simply cannot move around enough. All of the motor activity explanations have in common the fact that they indirectly affect learning by limiting the amount of contact that an animal has with the escape contingency. Any data consistent with helplessness theory which are also consistent with these alternative motor activity explanations do not provide unconfounded evidence for cognitive deficit.[8]

Consequently, in our review and analysis of the cognitive component of helplessness we abide by the following ground rules. Experimental data are regarded as providing support for the cognitive deficit if there is evidence to indicate that (1) these data are the result of differential experience with uncontrollability and (2) that they are not consistent with explanations based on either a lowered response initiation deficit or a motor activity deficit. We wish to note that some findings consistent with a response initiation or motor activity deficit are not in themselves inconsistent with the learned helplessness theory. The learned help-

[8]It is not our intention to review data directly supporting the motor activity explanations of the helplessness interference effect. The interested reader is referred to Anisman, deCatanzaro, and Remington (1978), Bracewell and Black (1974), Glazer and Weiss (1976a, 1976b), Levis (1976), and Weiss, Glazer, and Pohorecky (1976) for presentation of this evidence and to Maier and Seligman (1976) for a critique.

lessness theory, of course, predicts response initiation deficits as a consequence of an expectation of no control, and insofar as lower activity results from lower response initiation, such data are not decisive. In addition, there are many routes to poor escape performance (e.g., the animals could sprain an ankle) and evidence for a motor activity deficit resulting from exposure to inescapable shock does not imply that the effects of uncontrollability postulated by helplessness theory do not also exist. (3) Since, as we now see it, the "cognitive deficit" could stem from either biased perception or biased expectation, we will highlight any evidence which distinguishes between perceptual and expectational bias. Most evidence, however, is not fine grained enough to bear on this distinction.

A caveat is in order. We feel a bit uncomfortable talking about perceptions and expectations in animals because such entities are a bit less observable than stimuli, responses, and reinforcers, which are themselves not directly observable. We are more uncomfortable ascribing attributions to animals because they are even more inferential and may require a level of cognitive complexity which animals do not have, and most importantly because no operational definitions exist for attributions in animals. Thus, we will speak of the "cognitive deficit" as a whole in reviewing the animal literature.

A. Evidence from Animal Studies

1. *The Early Dog Experiments*

The behavioral observation that dogs exposed to unavoidable and inescapable electric shocks in a Pavlovian harness not only refrained from emitting escape responses in a subsequent shuttlebox escape/avoidance task, but also failed to follow one successful barrier jump with another provided the original basis for inferring an associative deficit in helpless animals (Overmier & Seligman, 1967; Seligman & Maier, 1967, described in Section III, A). Seligman and Maier (1967) reasoned that while simple failure to respond in the face of shock suggests a lack of motivation, failure to follow one successful escape response with another suggests that the dogs did not perceive the relationship between termination of the shock and the occurrence of their own response. This behavioral observation does not provide unique support for such a cognitive deficit. The motivational deficit alone could account for failure to follow one successful escape response with another. An animal that has a reduced tendency to initiate voluntary responses is, probabilistically speaking, less likely to emit two or more consecutive escape responses.

Seligman and Maier (1967, experiment 2) found that dogs could be "immunized" against the deleterious effects of uncontrollable shocks by prior experience with controllable shocks. In this experiment, the immunized group of dogs received escape/avoidance training in a shuttlebox in phase I followed later by phase II training with inescapable shocks in the Pavlovian harness. A second group of dogs only received phase II training, while a third group only received phase I training. Following this pretraining, all groups were tested for escape/avoidance performance in the shuttlebox, and the immunized group was not debilitated.

The Seligman and Maier immunization experiment does not provide an unconfounded demonstration of the cognitive deficit. The immunization effect may have been due to the prior acquisition of the specific shuttling response used in the test for helplessness rather than to the dogs' initial control over shock, since prior escape training and subsequent escape testing both involved the same task. Motor activity explanations could argue that such specific response training strengthened shuttling sufficiently to overcome the interfering effects of inactivity or other incompatible motor responses. Subsequent experiments using rats demonstrated cross-situational immunization effects, thus unconfounding initial control over an aversive outcome with prior acquisition of the test task response (Maier & Rhoades, cited in Maier & Seligman, 1976; Seligman, Rosellini, & Kozak, 1975; Williams & Maier, 1977). Cross-situational immunization seems inconsistent with the motor activity explanations because prior experience with control should not prevent the establishment of inactivity or some other competing response during exposure to uncontrollable shock. However, cross-situational immunization does not provide unconfounded support for the cognitive component of helplessness; prior experience with control may have its effect by preventing lowered response initiation rather than by proactively interfering with learning that shock is uncontrollable. Indeed, Volpicelli, Altenor, and Seligman (1979) have presented data which indicate that prior escapable shock increases rats' persistence during subsequent exposure to inescapable shock.

Two of the early helplessness studies in dogs were designed to test the helplessness hypothesis versus incompatible motor response alternatives. Overmier and Seligman (1967) found that dogs exposed to inescapable shock while paralyzed by curare showed as large an interference effect during subsequent testing as dogs not given curare. Since curare immobilizes the skeletal–motor musculature, these results disconfirm any competing motor response account which relies on active movement during initial exposure to inescapable shock (e.g., Bracewell & Black, 1974; Glazer & Weiss, 1976a, 1976b). They do not, however, rule out neurochemically mediated or fear-mediated motor activity deficits (e.g., Anisman, 1975; Anisman & Waller, 1973; Levis, 1976; Weiss, *et al.*, 1976).

Maier (1970) conducted a study in which he explicitly reinforced an incompatible motor response during pretraining with escapable shock. One group of dogs (passive escape) was restrained in the Pavlovian hammock and had panels pushed to the top and sides of their heads. They could terminate shock by not touching any of the panels for a specified period of time from the point of shock onset; i.e., by holding still or freezing. Another group of dogs received inescapable shock in the hammock, identical in number and pattern to those received by the passive escape group. A third group received no shocks. Following pretreatment, all groups were tested for two-way shuttle escape/avoidance. Maier reasoned that if inescapable shock produces interference with subsequent escape and avoidance because it produces inactivity or some other incompatible motor response, then the passive escape group should escape at least as poorly as the yoked group. The helplessness theory makes the opposite prediction. In contrast to the yoked dogs, the passive escape dogs should learn that they have control over shock in the hammock, albeit by being passive; thus, they should eventually learn to shuttle. This is exactly what happened. The dogs in the yoked group predominantly failed to acquire shuttling and the no-shock controls escaped normally. The passive escape group, trained to hold still in the presence of shock, was slow to acquire shuttling, but all dogs did eventually learn. Although the Overmier and Seligman (1967) and Maier (1970) experiments may not be accounted for by the competing motor response hypotheses, they provide no independent evidence that the interference effect observed is the result of cognitive interference rather than lowered response initiation caused by an expectation of no control.

The same argument can be advanced about the studies showing reversibility of learned helplessness. Seligman, Maier, and Geer (1968) showed that failure to escape could be eliminated in dogs by dragging the dogs back and forth across the shuttlebox during shock until they began to respond on their own. Seligman *et al.* argued that this dragging "therapy" was effective because it forcibly exposed the dogs to the escape/avoidance contingency and therefore, disconfirmed the initially acquired expectation that shock termination was independent of responses. An alternative view is that dragging works because it breaks up inactivity or some other competing motor pattern. However, in an analogous therapy experiment in rats, Seligman *et al.* (1975) showed that random dragging of rats around the box was not as effective in breaking up the interference effect as dragging which exposes the animal to the response–relief contingency. Although the Seligman *et al.* (1975) experiment supports the hypothesis that therapy works because it exposes a helpless animal to the response–relief contingency, it does not provide unconfounded support for the cognitive as opposed to the response initiation deficit. Forced exposure to the escape contingency could increase the tendency to initiate responses. Seligman *et al.* (1968) argued that the finding that so many forced exposures to the contingency were required (20–50 in their experiment) before dogs responded on their own confirmed the notion that the initial learning interfered with the formation of a response–relief association, but this finding may only attest to the great strength of the motivational deficit. (See also our discussion above for the failure to observe consecutive successful escape responses.)

2. *The Rat Experiments*

Since the original dog experiments, the helplessness interference effect has been studied in fish, cats, mice, rats, monkeys, and man. The majority of animal helplessness studies, however, have used rats as subjects. Due to the large number of these studies, we have chosen to examine only a small subset of these experiments. In particular, we discuss those experiments which have been claimed specifically by proponents of the helplessness theory to provide support for the existence of associative or cognitive interference in helplessness.

Several rat helplessness experiments have shown that the nature of the escape response employed in the test task for helplessness is a crucial determinant of whether the interference effect is obtained. Maier *et al.* (1973) found that across a wide range of parameters, rats exposed to uncontrollable shocks do not perform worse than controls on a shuttlebox escape/avoidance task if the response required to terminate shock is one crossing of the box (FR-1). However, if the response requirement was increased to two crossings of the shuttlebox (FR-2), rats previously exposed to inescapable shock did show an interference effect. Similarly, Seligman and Beagley (1975) found that inescapably shocked rats would acquire an FR-1 lever-press response to terminate shock, but not an FR-3 lever press.

Maier *et al.* (1973) argued that the reason inescapable shock interferes with the acquisition of FR-2 but not FR-1 shuttling is that FR-1 shuttling is a high-probability initial response to shock in the rat and may, in fact, be elicited. They found that rats required to cross the shuttlebox once responded as rapidly on the first trial as after 30 trials; i.e., there was no acquisition curve. Helplessness theory postulates that experience with uncontrollability will interfere only with "voluntary," not reflexive, responses. Therefore, even if inescapably preshocked rats do have difficulty in associating shock termination with their responses, the strong tendency of rats to cross the shuttlebox rapidly in response to shock will mask this deficit. In addition, this tendency to cross rapidly in response to shock will insure that inescapably preshocked rats are exposed to the

FR-1 contingency enough times to learn, even if associative interference would have been present. The FR-2 shuttling response, however, is not an elicited response to shock and, in addition, provides a more difficult contingency between crossing and shock termination than does FR-1 shuttling. Thus, the cognitive interference produced by learning that shock is uncontrollable might be evident in the FR-2 procedure.

The motor activity deficit hypotheses can also explain why inescapable shock does not debilitate FR-1 escape. The competing motor response explanations (e.g., Anisman & Waller, 1973; Bracewell & Black, 1974; Glazer & Weiss, 1976a, 1976b; Levis, 1976) could argue that a competing response acquired during exposure to inescapable shock is strong enough to interfere with FR-2 shuttling, but not with the highly elicited FR-1 response. In addition, animals are exposed to more shock in the FR-2 procedure than in the FR-1 procedure, and this might potentiate a competing response. Alternatively, the neurochemical depletion variants of the motor activity deficit hypothesis (Anisman, 1975; Weiss *et al.*, 1976) could argue that rats exposed to inescapable shock have enough neurochemical reserves to support only a limited amount of activity: one crossing of the shuttlebox, but not two crossings.

Maier and Testa (1975) conducted two experiments in which they pit the helplessness theory's cognitive interference explanation against the motor activity (and response initiation) account of FR-2 performance. Maier and Testa observed that the two classes of explanations focus on different features of the FR-2 shuttlebox procedure as the crucial determinant of the interference. The motor activity deficit (and response initiation) hypotheses point to the effortfulness of the FR-2 response and/or the greater amount of shock experienced by the rats. The cognitive interference hypothesis, in contrast, emphasizes the difficulty of learning the dependency of shock termination on shuttlebox crossing in an FR-2 procedure.

Maier and Testa attempted in two different ways to determine which of these two aspects of the FR-2 procedure is crucial for interference. In the first of two experiments, they simplified the contingency between shuttlebox crossing and shock termination, while maintaining the high effortfulness and greater amount of shock exposure inherent in the FR-2 procedure. They presented a 1-sec interruption of shock following the first crossing of the FR-2 to both inescapably preshocked and nonshocked rats. They argued that this interruption should not have an appreciable effect on either the extent of shock exposure or the effortfulness of the FR-2 response, but it would make the response–shock termination relationship easier to perceive. Inescapable shock retarded FR-2 acquisition only when there was no interruption of shock after the first response of the FR-2. When shock was interrupted, the inescapably shocked rats performed as rapidly as did nonshocked controls. Maier and Testa claimed that this experiment unconfoundedly demonstrated the cognitive deficit of helplessness, since the only apparent difference between the inescapably shocked groups which did and did not show an interference effect was the perceptibility of the response–shock termination contingency to which they were exposed.

In their second experiment, Maier and Testa (1975) tried to produce a learned helplessness interference effect by arranging a less perceptible contingency between shuttling and shock termination while keeping the effortfulness of the response and the duration of shock low. They made the contingency less perceptible by interposing a 1- or 3-sec delay between FR-1 crossing of the shuttlebox and shock termination. Thus, the requisite response was not more effortful than the usual FR-1 task, which does not yield an interference effect, but like the FR-2 procedure, which does produce interference, it contained a degraded contingency between crossing and shock termination. Delay of either 1 or 3 sec retarded acquisition of FR-1 shuttlebox escape behavior in rats which previously experienced inescapable shock but had no effect on the behavior of rats which had not previously experienced inescapable shock. Further, Maier and Testa claimed that this was not explained by the longer durations of shock of the delay procedure, since an inescapably preshocked, nondelayed group with the extra amount of shock did not show poorer performance of the FR-1 response. In a similar experiment, Kelsey (1977, experiment 3) also found that increasing the difficulty of the escape contingency in the test task (by reducing exteroceptive feedback) enhanced the interference effect caused by prior inescapable shocks. Maier and Testa concluded that the perceptibility of the contingency between the escape response and shock termination is more important than is either the effortfulness of the escape response or the extent of shock exposure in producing an interference effect in rats, and therefore, the interference effect must be at least partially due to the cognitive deficit.

Although the Maier and Testa (1975) investigation is probably the most frequently cited study in support of the cognitive deficit in helplessness, their results do not provide a wholly unambiguous demonstration of this deficit. The Maier and Testa findings can be explained in terms of a motor activity deficit or the response initiation deficit postulated by learned helplessness theory. In Maier's and Testa's first experiment, inescapably shocked rats may have successfully performed two shuttlebox crossings when shock was briefly interrupted because the break in shock overcame reduced activity or reduced response initiation by eliciting the second crossing, not because it made the contingency between crossing and shock termination easier to perceive. In other words, the break in shock may have transformed the FR-2 response into two FR-1 responses. Maier *et al.* (1973) demonstrated that inescapable shock does not interfere with the acquisition of high-probability FR-1 responses. Alternatively, the inescapably shocked rats may have failed to perform as well as the nonshocked controls in the FR-1 with delay procedure (Maier & Testa, 1975, experiment 2) due to lowered activity or response initiation induced by the longer shock duration inherent in the procedure. That is, the long shock durations received by the preshocked animals on each shuttlebox test trial as a result of the delay could act as discriminative stimuli which reinstate an inactivity response learned during prior exposure to inescapable shock (e.g., Anisman *et al.*, 1978; Glazer & Weiss, 1976a, 1976b). Maier and Testa (experiment 2) included a group of preshocked rats tested with no delay as a control for the added shock duration. These rats received an amount of shock in the shuttlebox equivalent to the preshocked group that had the delay. However, this group does not adequately control for the discriminative function of long shocks on each shuttlebox trial because these control animals received all of the added shock in 10 separate inescapable shock trials which occurred before the FR-1 escape contingency was introduced. According to the present account, it is the added shock duration on each test trial which makes the trial more similar to the shocks received during pretreatment and, thus, allows these test trials to function as discriminative stimuli for the previously acquired inactivity response. A similar explanation can be advanced for Kelsey's (1977) findings.

While we doubt that either of these noncognitive accounts is true, and we realize that these objections are strained, we believe that the cognitive deficit is not definitively demonstrated in the Maier and Testa studies. Except for the Maier and Testa studies, all of the animal evidence for a cognitive deficit does not bear on the question of whether the bias is perceptual or expectational. The animals could fail to initiate responses after experience with the FR-1 with delay contingency either because they did not perceive the contingency or because they did not expect the contingency to obtain on future trials. We cannot think of an expectational bias explanation of the Maier and Testa studies, however. FR-1 with a delay should be more vulnerable to a perceptual bias toward noncontingency than FR-1 with no delay; but why should it be more difficult to extrapolate an accurate perception of the FR-1 delay contingency to the future?

Another class of helplessness experiments which putatively support the cognitive deficit is studies demonstrating the generality of the interference effect produced by uncontrollability. Several investigators have shown that interference transfers across different training and testing conditions (e.g., Altenor, Kay, & Richter, 1977; Braud, Wepman,

& Russo, 1969; Goodkin, 1976; Rosellini, 1978; Rosellini & Seligman, 1975). Altenor *et al.* (1977) and Braud *et al.* (1969) found inescapable shock to interfere with the learning of a response to escape from cold water. Rosellini and Seligman (1975) reported that inescapable shock interfered with the learning of a hurdle-jump response to escape frustration. Goodkin (1976) found that exposure to noncontingent food interfered with the acquisition of a response to escape and avoid shock, while Rosellini (1978) reported the complementary effect: Exposure to inescapable shock interfered with the acquisition of a response to obtain food. While these studies support the notion that animals exposed to uncontrollable outcomes form a generalized expectation of response–reinforcer independence, they provide no special evidence that this interference results from a cognitive deficit rather than through reduced response initiation.

To this point, we have examined a large number of animal helplessness studies and have yet to find definitive evidence for a cognitive deficit, unconfounded by a motivational or activity deficit. The major problem is that both cognitive and activity or response initiation deficit accounts predict that the animal should be slow to respond. We believe that in order to isolate the cognitive deficit from these other deficits, helplessness experiments must employ one of the following two strategies: (1) equate the helpless group with its appropriate controls for the occurrence of the requisite response, or (2) use a design in which effects due to lowered activity or response initiation would be in a direction opposite to those predicted by cognitive deficit.

Testa, Juraska, and Maier (1974) reported an experiment which employed the first of these two strategies. In phase 1 of the experiment, rats were exposed to escapable (E); yoked, inescapable (Y); or no-shock (N) in a wheel-turn box. Rats in group E received 64 shocks which they could terminate by the first one-quarter turn of a wheel after the onset of shock. Each member of group Y was yoked for the number and duration of shocks to one of the members of group E, while each rat in group N was simply restrained in the wheel-turn box for a period of time equal to its E–Y pair. Twenty-four hours after this pretreatment all rats were given 30 FR-1 escape/avoidance acquisition trials in the shuttlebox, followed by 30 trials of escape/avoidance extinction with inescapable shock. Testa *et al.* reasoned that since the three groups had previously been shown not to differ on FR-1 responding (Maier *et al.*, 1973; Seligman & Beagley, 1975), any differences observed during extinction would reflect the operation of cognitive factors.

All rats rapidly acquired the FR-1 shuttlebox response and there were no differences between groups. In the extinction phase, group Y responded at a lower level than did groups E and N, which did not differ from each other. Testa *et al.* explained these results by arguing that the association between crossing the shuttlebox and shock termination was not as strong in the inescapably shocked rats as in the escapably shocked and nonshocked rats due to their previously acquired expectation of response–shock independence, and thus, they extinguished more rapidly during inescapable shock. Although the design of the Testa *et al.* experiment can in principle isolate the effects of the cognitive component of helplessness, their particular experiment does not do this unambiguously. Rapid extinction in inescapably shocked rats may reflect response initiation or activity deficits that go undetected during FR-1 acquisition because of a ceiling effect. That is, the elicited nature of FR-1 shuttling (Maier *et al.*, 1973) may produce an equivalent level of escape in E, Y, and N rats despite the fact that Y rats are less likely than these other rats to initiate voluntary responses.

Volpicelli *et al.* (1979, experiment 3) conducted an experiment which is similar in conception to the Testa *et al.* (1974) study but cannot be explained in terms of activity or response initiation deficits. In their experiment, rats were randomly assigned to an escape (E), yoked (Y), or naive (N) group. During pretreatment, group E received 10 FR-1 escape trials followed by 50 FR-2 trials in the shuttlebox. Group Y animals received the identical pattern of shock as their E counterparts. Group N animals were simply placed in the shuttlebox without shock presentations. Twenty-four hours after pretreatment, each animal received 20 shock escape trials in a lever-press box. A 3-sec delay was imposed between the FR-1 response requirement and shock termination. If the rat failed to respond in 30 sec, shock was automatically terminated, so that the maximum amount of shock animals could receive in the test task was 500 sec. In the previous experiment of the series (experiment 2) Volpicelli *et al.* had demonstrated that the E and N groups do not differ on the number of lever-press responses emitted when exposed to continuous inescapable shock for up to 500 sec, while group Y animals emit significantly fewer responses. The use of continuous inescapable shock permits a test of differential activity or response initiation among groups without any possibility of adventitious response–shock termination pairings occurring to confound the measure of response initiation.

The results of the Volpicelli *et al.* experiment 3 are presented in Fig. 5. As can be seen in the figure, group E escaped faster than Group N ($p < .05$), which in turn escaped faster than group Y ($p < .05$). While the interference effect shown by the yoked rats may be attributed to response initiation or motor activity deficits due to the reduced tendency of these rats to respond during continuous inescapable shock (experiment 2), the facilitation shown by rats in group E cannot be explained in this manner. Groups E and N responded equally during continuous shock.

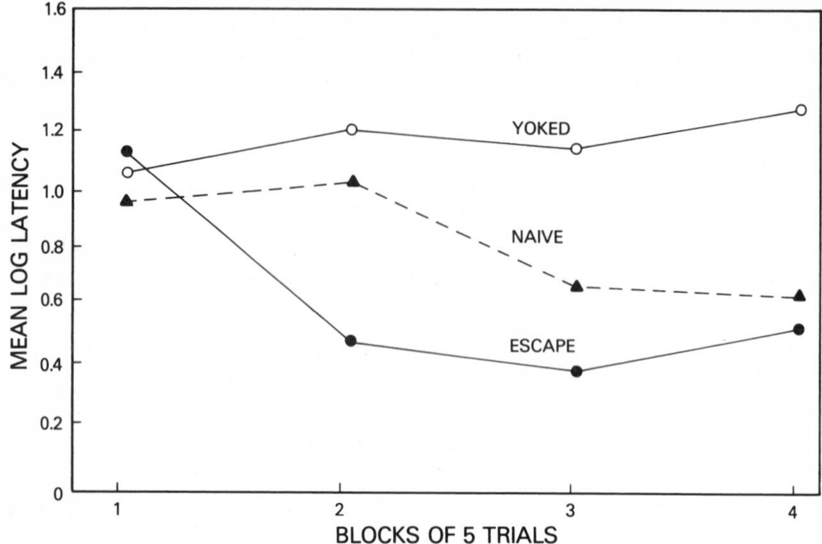

Fig. 5. Mean log FR-1 with delay escape latency in a lever press box for rats previously given escapable, yoked inescapable, or no shock in a shuttlebox. (Volpicelli, Altenor, & Seligman, 1979). (The "escape" and "naive" rats were previously equated for activity.)

We believe that the results of the Volpicelli *et al.* study come close to demonstrating cognitive facilitation in helplessness unconfounded by response initiation or motor activity factors. It is possible, however, that the E and N groups responded at the same high rate in experiment 2 because of a ceiling effect, and that more activity or response initiation in the E group was masked. As noted earlier (Section III, C), facilitation of learning response–reinforcer dependence produced by prior experience with controllable outcomes provides evidence for the cognitive component of helplessness theory just as interference caused by prior experience with uncontrollable outcomes does.

Unambiguous demonstration of cognitive interference in animal helplessness can be provided by studies which oppose the effects of the response initiation and cognitive deficits. Baker (1976) has recently reported a series of experiments which uses this strategy. Baker presented rats with unsignaled, inescapable shocks while they lever pressed on a variable interval (VI) schedule for food. In the second phase of the experiment, the animals received on-baseline discriminative punishment training involving periodic presentation of a warning signal (CS) during which shocks occurred contingent upon responding. Baker found that inescapably shocked rats were slower to suppress responding than were nonshocked rats. These data provide unconfounded support for a cognitive deficit produced by inescapable shock. Since failure to suppress means that the rats make more rather than fewer active responses, lowered response initiation or transfer of incompatible motor responses which produce inactivity predicts that inescapably shocked rats will respond less, not more, as they do. Similarly, neurochemical depletion-induced inactivity does not predict failure to learn under conditions in which poor learning is indexed by enhanced activity.

Jackson, Maier, and Rapaport (1978), however, have criticized the Baker (1976) investigation on several grounds. First, Jackson *et al.* noted that Baker's interference effect was response specific, while helplessness experiments typically show interference across responses: Baker failed to obtain interference if prior exposure to noncontingent shocks occurred without the lever present. Baker also gave discriminative punishment training to rats in the same box and with the same kind of shock as they had received in the prior phase. Learned helplessness effects, however, are usually demonstrated transsituationally. Thus, Baker's findings may not provide strong support for the learned helplessness theory because evidence was found only for "specific irrelevance" learning rather than for "general irrelevance" learning. Finally, Jackson *et al.* argued that Baker's findings do not show whether inescapable shock interferes with the perception or expectation of response–shock or stimulus–shock contingencies. The learned helplessness theory maintains that exposure to uncontrollable outcomes interferes only with the acquisition of response–outcome dependencies. The discriminative punishment procedure used by Baker, however, involves both a stimulus–shock and a response–shock contingency. Baker attempted to determine which of these two contingencies was involved by testing another group of noncontingently shocked rats on a task which involved only a stimulus–shock contingency (i.e., CER acquisition). Unfortunately, Baker only tested groups on CER acquisition which had received random presentations of both CSs and noncontingent shocks and not rats which had received noncontingent shocks alone. Hence, Jackson *et al.* maintain that Baker's data do not show that exposure to uncontrollable shocks unconfoundedly interferes with the perception or expectation of response–shock dependency.

To unconfound this, Jackson *et al.* (1978, experiment 4) repeated Baker's basic design but tested rats previously exposed to inescapable shocks or simple restraint on both signaled punishment and CER acquisition. In phase 1, rats were trained to press a lever for food reinforcement. During each of the last three sessions of phase 1, a white-noise CS was presented twice to reduce any unconditioned suppression to the cue. On the following day, the animals were matched for lever-press rate and unconditioned suppression to the CS and assigned to one of two groups ($n = 16$). One group received 80 unsignaled inescapable shocks in restraining tubes, while the second group was restrained without shocks. Twenty-four hours later, the animals were returned to the lever-press chambers and half of each group was trained on either discriminative punishment or CER acquisition. In the discriminative punishment test, a maximum of two shocks could occur during each 3-min CS presentation. The CS was divided into 18 10-sec intervals and shocks were randomly programmed in any two of these intervals. A programmed shock was delivered contingent upon the next lever press. Thus, an animal could receive anywhere from zero to two shocks per trial depending on its behavior. In the fear conditioning test, shocks were presented independently of lever presses.

The results of the Jackson *et al.* experiment are graphed in Fig. 6. The data are presented in the form of suppression ratios $A/(A + B)$, where A = the number of responses made during the CS, and B = the number of responses made in the 3-min period prior to the CS. Thus, a suppression ratio of 0 indicates maximum suppression and a ratio of 0.5 indicates no suppression. The left panel of Fig. 6 shows the data for the discriminative punishment test and the right panel shows the data for the CER test. Jackson *et al.* found no reliable differences in the

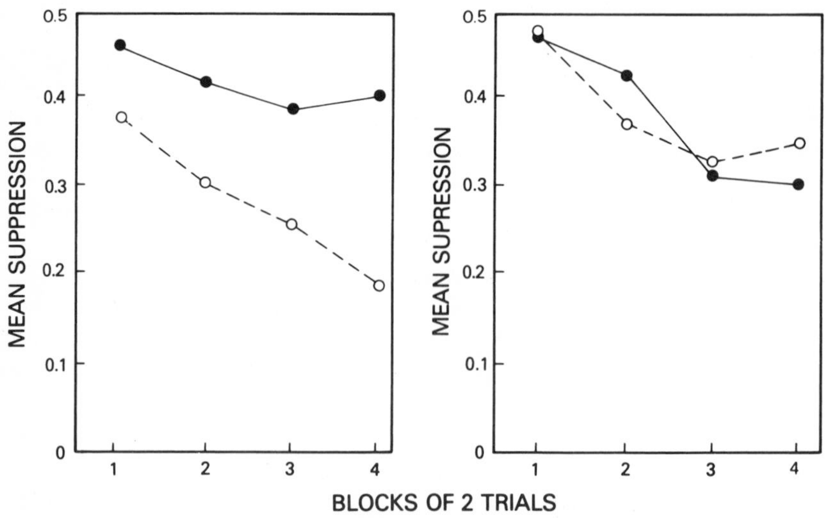

Fig. 6. Mean suppression ratio for preshocked (•——•) and restrained (○– – –○) rats across blocks of two trials during discriminative punishment conditioning (left) and CER conditioning (right). (From "Exposure to inescapable shock produces both activity and associative deficits in the rat" by R. L. Jackson, S. F. Maier, and P. M. Rapaport, *Learning and Motivation*, 1978, *9*, 69–98. Copyright 1978 by Academic Press. Adapted by permission.)

baseline rate of responding in either test condition. As can be seen in the figure, inescapably shocked rats suppressed significantly less to the CS than did restrained controls in the discriminative punishment test but did not differ from the controls in the fear conditioning test. The results of the Jackson *et al.* experiment demonstrate that exposure to inescapable shock produces transsituational interference with response–outcome learning, but not stimulus–outcome learning. Their data provide clear support for the cognitive deficit postulated by learned helplessness theory, uncontaminated by response initiation or motor activity deficits.

We have one reservation about both the Jackson *et al.* and Baker studies: the lack of an escape group. As the studies stand, the results could be produced by more physical stress in the inescapably shocked group, since no group was run which received the same shock escapably.

In an unpublished investigation, Alloy and Ehrman (1979) also provided clear-cut evidence for cognitive interference following inescapable shock. However, the interference they observed affected Pavlovian conditioning, rather than instrumental learning. That is, in two experiments, Alloy and Ehrman found that experience with response–shock independence modifies subsequent learning of stimulus–shock contingencies.

In their first experiment, Alloy and Ehrman examined the effects of preexposure to escapable, inescapable, or no shocks on the acquisition of fear to a CS presented in a truly random control (TRC) procedure. A TRC procedure consists of the presentation of a CS and a US in a random relation to each other. According to the contingency view of Pavlovian conditioning (e.g., Rescorla, 1967), a TRC procedure should produce no conditioning, since there is no contingency between CS and US. However, recent evidence suggests that TRC procedures sometime lead to conditioning. Naive animals are likely to show excitatory conditioning in an uncorrelated procedure if learning is still preasymptotic (Keller *et al.*, 1977; Rescorla, 1972) and if the overall probability with which the CS or US occurs is high (Kremer & Kamin, 1971; Rescorla, 1972). Based on an extension of the learned helplessness theory, Alloy and Ehrman predicted that rats exposed to inescapable shock would show less excitatory conditioning to a CS presented in a TRC procedure than naive or escapably preshocked rats under conditions where such excitatory conditioning is typically found (i.e., less than asymptotic exposure to the TRC and high probability of the US). They reasoned that animals which have learned that their responses and reinforcement are noncontingently related may be more likely to detect future instances of noncontingency, even between a stimulus and reinforcement (Section III,C; see also Testa *et al.*, 1974, for similar predictions). This prediction is based on the view that feedback from responding is a Pavlovian stimulus event.

Experiment 1 consisted of four phases. In the first phase, water-deprived rats were trained to lick a drinking tube for sucrose solution on a continuous reinforcement (CRF) schedule. During the last session of phase 1 two 20-sec CS presentations served to habituate the rats to the CS. The CS was a 1000-Hz, 70-db tone. On the following day, phase 2 began. The rats were divided into three groups (n = 16) matched for unconditioned suppression to the CS and baseline licking rate. Rats in the escapable shock (E) group received 60 1.0-mA shocks in a shuttlebox which they could terminate by performing an FR-1 crossing response for the first 10 trials and an FR-2 response for the remaining 50 trials. Rats in the inescapable shock (I) group were yoked to members of group E for number and duration of shocks, while rats in the no-shock (N) group were merely restrained in the shuttlebox for a period of time equal to that of their E–I partners. Following helplessness training, all rats received one baseline recovery day in the drinking tube boxes and then received phase 3 training in a third chamber. In phase 3, all rats received a TRC schedule in which the tone CS and shock US were randomly presented. For half of the rats in each of the three groups, the $p(\mathrm{US/CS}) = p(\mathrm{US}/\overline{\mathrm{CS}}) = 0.5$ and for the other half the $p(\mathrm{US/CS}) = p(\mathrm{US}/\overline{\mathrm{CS}}) = 0.1$. In addition, half of the rats in each group received 2 days of TRC training and half received 4 days of TRC training. After 2 more days of baseline recovery, all rats were tested for suppression to the tone in the drinking tube boxes. Testing consisted of two presentations of the 20-sec CS over four extinction sessions.

Figure 7 shows the results of this experiment. The data are presented in the form of mean suppression ratios collapsed over the four test sessions. Small suppression ratios indicate considerable conditioning, whereas values near 0.5 indicate no conditioning. There were no reliable differences among the three groups in baseline licking rate on any of the recovery days or during the pre-CS periods of the test days (Fs < 1). As can be seen in Fig. 7, rats exposed to the TRC schedules for 2 days showed greater suppression than rats exposed to the TRC schedules for 4 days ($F = 14.3, p < .01$; compare the left and right panels). In addition, rats exposed to the 0.5–0.5 TRC suppressed more than rats exposed to the 0.1–0.1 TRC ($F = 7.0, p < .05$). These two findings were expected on the basis of previous work with the TRC (e.g., Rescorla, 1972). The important finding was that the groups effect was highly reliable ($F = 5.9, p < .01$). Inescapably shocked rats showed significantly less conditioning than escapably shocked or nonshocked rats ($p < .01$), which did not differ from each other.

This experiment may be interpreted as positive transfer between

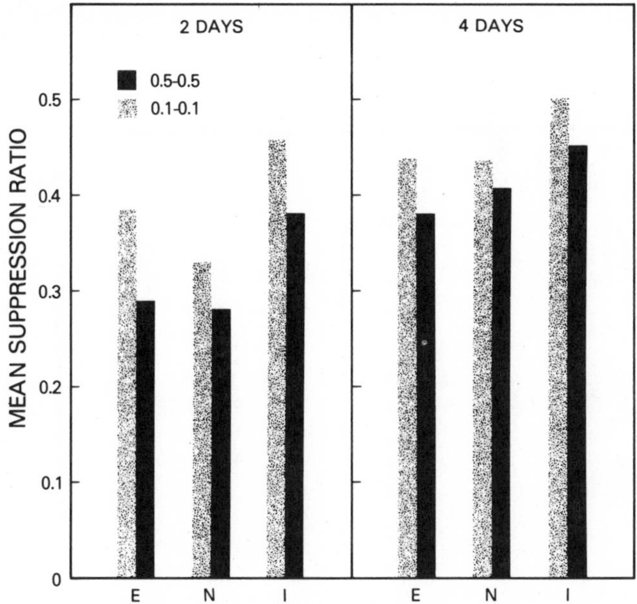

Fig. 7. Mean suppression ratios collapsed over test sessions for rats previously given escapable (E), yoked inescapable (I), or no shock (N). The rats were exposed to either a 0.5–0.5 tone–shock TRC procedure or to a 0.1–0.1 tone–shock TRC procedure for either 2 days (left) or 4 days (right). (Alloy & Ehrman, 1979.)

learning response–outcome independence and learning stimulus–outcome independence. Inescapably shocked rats may show less conditioning because they have greater difficulty in assocating the chance pairings of tone and shock which occur in the TRC. If this is correct, rats exposed to inescapable shock also should show less conditioning when there is a contingency between tone and shock.

Alloy and Ehrman (1979) conducted a second experiment to test this possibility. This experiment was identical to the first experiment in all respects, with the exception of the conditioning phase: All shocks that occurred in the absence of the tone CS were eliminated. Thus, animals in experiment 2 were exposed to one of two classical conditioning contingencies in which the probability of the US given the CS was either 0.5 or 0.1 and the probability of the US given no CS was zero.

The data from experiment 2 are presented in Fig. 8 as mean suppression rations collapsed over the six test sessions. Again, as in experiment 1, there were no differences among the E, I, and N groups in licking rate during either the recovery days or the pre-CS periods of the test days. Rats suppressed more after 4 days of conditioning than after 2

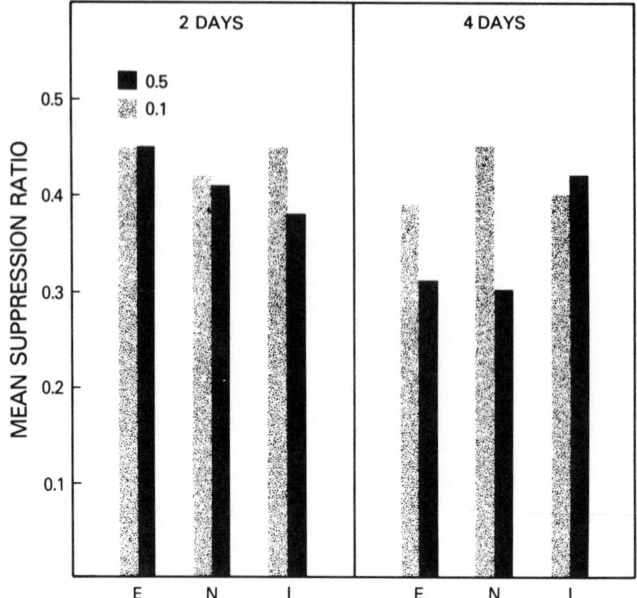

Fig. 8. Mean suppression ratios collapsed over test sessions for rats previously given escapable (E), yoked inescapable (I), or no shock (N). The rats were exposed to either a 0.5 tone–shock contingency or to a 0.1 tone–shock contingency for either 2 days (left) or 4 days (right). (Alloy & Ehrman, 1979.)

days ($F = 9.6, p < .001$) and with a 0.5 CS–US contingency than with a 0.1 CS–US contingency ($F = 11.2, p < .001$). The finding of import was again the comparison among groups. Statistical analysis indicated that the three groups differed only in the 4-day, 0.5 CS–US contingency condition ($F = 3.5, p < .05$). In this condition, group I rats showed significantly less conditioning to the CS than group E or N rats (ps $< .05$), which did not differ from each other.

The results of the Alloy and Ehrman experiments taken together provide evidence for a very broad cognitive deficit in learned helplessness. The data suggest that learning about response–shock independence produces difficulty in learning stimulus–shock associations. These findings cannot be interpreted in terms of a response initiation or motor activity deficit, since interference occurred in a situation where active responding plays no part (i.e., Pavlovian conditioning). Moreover, within the test for conditioning, response initiation and activity deficits would lead inescapably shocked rats to show less frequent licking during the CS rather than more frequent licking as compared to naive and escape rats. It should be pointed out that Jackson *et al.* (1978) failed to find any effect of inescapable shock on subsequent CER acquisition. There are many procedural differences between the Jackson *et al.* and Alloy and Ehrman studies which could account for the discrepant results, but perhaps the most important is the different CS–US contingencies used. Jackson *et al.* presented rats with a 1.0 correlation between tone and shock in their CER acquisition experiment, while Alloy and Ehrman used a degraded correlation. A 1.0 contingency may be so easy to perceive that inescapably shocked animals condition as well as naive or escapably shocked animals—a ceiling effect.

In summary, clear evidence exists for a cognitive deficit following inescapable shock in rats, which is not confounded by lower response initiation or activity. Inescapably shocked rats learn degraded contingencies poorly, even when effortfulness is low; they learn punishment contingencies poorly; and they learn Pavlovian noncontingency better and Pavlovian contingency worse than escapably shocked or nonshocked rats. With the exception of Maier and Testa (1975), this evidence does not, however, tease apart perceptual bias from expectational bias. The majority of these results could follow from either a bias to perceive noncontingency, a bias to expect future noncontingency, or both.

What experiments remain to be done in the exploration of a cognitive deficit in animals?: (1) Further convergent validation for such a deficit should be sought; (2) further experiments which tease apart perceptual from expectational bias should be attempted (e.g., are helpless rats better able to use response–outcome independence as a discriminative stimulus?); (3) the mechanism of perceptual and/or expectational bias toward noncontingency must be further delineated. Does inattention to response feedback or relationships between feedback and outcomes exist in helpless rats?

B. Evidence from Human Studies

In examining the evidence for a cognitive deficit in animals, we had to consider both response initiation and motor activity deficits as alternative explanations for any particular set of findings. In reviewing the status of the cognitive deficit in helpless and depressed humans, however, we need be concerned with the separation of this component only from the response initiation component. Competing motor response explanations become implausible in the human helplessness studies. As with the animal helplessness phenomenon, the isolation of the cognitive deficits in helpless and depressed humans is difficult. Early human helplessness studies relied on the relatively indirect method of examining people's performance on instrumental-learning tasks to infer difficulty in learning response–outcome dependencies. Later studies attempted to develop more direct methods of assessing the cognitive deficit.

1. *Instrumental Performance Experiments*

Early investigators of human helplessness noted that people exposed to inescapable noise, like dogs exposed to inescapable shocks, often failed to follow one successful escape response with another during the test task for helplessness (Hiroto, 1974; Hiroto & Seligman, 1975; Klein, Fencil-Morse, & Seligman, 1976; Klein & Seligman, 1976; W. R. Miller & Seligman, 1975). These investigators developed a quantitative index of the degree to which people exposed to uncontrollable outcomes failed to profit from successful response–outcome sequences. For each individual, the average conditional probability of an escape response on a trial given a successful escape response on the previous trial was computed. Typically, this conditional probability was lower for individuals previously exposed to uncontrollable events than for individuals previously exposed to controllable or no events and also for depressed individuals as compared to nondepressed individuals (Hiroto, 1974; Hiroto & Seligman, 1975; Klein *et al.*, 1976., Klein & Seligman, 1976; W. R. Miller & Seligman, 1975). As argued above (Section V, A, 1), these results do not provide unconfounded evidence for the cognitive deficit in helpless or depressed people. They could be explained by a response initiation deficit alone.

Several investigators have used a patterned anagrams task as an alternate index of the cognitive deficit in helplessness and depression (e.g., Benson & Kennelly, 1976; Gatchel & Proctor, 1976; Hiroto & Seligman, 1975; Klein *et al.*, 1976; W. R. Miller & Seligman, 1975; Price, Tryon, & Raps, 1978; Willis & Blaney, 1978). For example, in the Hiroto and Seligman (1975) study, three groups of college students received escapable, inescapable, or no noise followed by 20 anagrams, each scrambled five-letter words. Since there was a pattern to the anagrams, all could be solved by an identical rearrangement of letters. Solution of three consecutive anagrams within 15 sec was taken as evidence that the subject "discovered the pattern." The results showed that subjects who first experienced inescapable noise required more trials to discover the pattern than those who received escapable or no noise (see also W. R. Miller & Seligman, 1975). Similar findings have been reported for unsolvable discrimination problems (e.g., Hiroto & Seligman, 1975; Klein *et al.*, 1976). In addition, depressed individuals are also slower to discover the pattern than nondepressed controls (W. R. Miller & Seligman, 1975; Willis & Blaney, 1978).

The interpretation of the anagram pattern results is difficult. Difficulty in detecting a pattern in anagrams does not necessarily reflect an underlying difficulty in expecting or perceiving anything about the relationship between one's responses and outcomes. Intuitively, difficulty in seeing patterns in anagrams seems no more intimately related to the specific cognitive deficit postulated by learned helplessness theory than it does to a more generalized intellectual impairment (Costello, 1978). A second problem concerns the separation of the cognitive and motivational deficits in the anagrams task. A measure of the trials required to discover a pattern in anagrams seems subject to lowered response initiation. If a helpless or depressed person generates fewer hypotheses about letter order, difficulty in discovering the pattern will follow. The instrumental performance experiments, then, do not provide an unconfounded demonstration of the cognitive deficit in helplessness.

2. *Chance-Skill Experiments*

W. R. Miller and Seligman (1973) developed a superficially more promising method for isolating the cognitive component of learned helplessness and depression. This method was based on the assumption that the helplessness cognition that responses and outcomes are independent was similar to Rotter's (1966) concept of external locus of control. Rotter suggested that "internals" tend to perceive outcomes as under their control and "externals" tend to perceive outcomes as not under their control. Some support for the similarity between the helplessness concept and external locus of control was provided by Hiroto's (1974) finding that externals who were subjected to inescapable noise were significantly poorer at escaping noise in a new situation than internals exposed to inescapable noise.

In examining the locus of control concept, Rotter and his associates (James, 1957; James & Rotter, 1958; Phares, 1957; Rotter, Liverant, & Crowne, 1961) used tasks in which success appeared to be determined by either chance or skill. They demonstrated that verbalized expectancies for future success are affected by reinforcements on previous trials. Reinforcements on previous trials have a greater effect on expectancies for future success when people believe reinforcement is dependent upon responses (skill determined) than when they believe reinforcement is independent of responses (chance determined). So, the amount of expectancy change over trials appeared to measure belief in response–reinforcer dependence.

W. R. Miller and Seligman (1973) argued that depressed individuals should believe reinforcement to be more response independent than nondepressed individuals in skill tasks (where reinforcement is actually response dependent) if depressives' expectations of no control interfere with future perceptions of control as postulated by learned helplessness theory. Thus, Miller and Seligman predicted that depressed college students would exhibit smaller expectancy change following success and failure than nondepressed students in skill tasks. In chance tasks (where responding and reinforcement are actually independent), both depressed and nondepressed students were predicted to perceive reinforcement to be response independent and, thus, to show similar small expectancy changes following success and failure. It should be noted that this second prediction is different from the one we have made above (Section III, C). We believe that nondepressed individuals should be less likely to perceive or expect response–outcome independence because of their expectation of control, unless the task is too obviously chance.

Miller and Seligman found that depressed students gave smaller expectancy changes than nondepressed students on a skill task, while the groups did not differ on a chance task, as predicted. Similar findings have been reported for depressed students by Klein and Seligman (1976), W. R. Miller and Seligman (1976), and W. R. Miller, Seligman, and Kurlander (1975) and for hospitalized unipolar depressives by Abramson, Garber, Edwards, and Seligman (1978a). In addition, nondepressed students given prior experience with uncontrollable noise show an expectancy change pattern in chance and skill tasks similar to depressives (Klein & Seligman, 1976; W. R. Miller & Seligman, 1976). [See, however, McNitt & Thornton (1978), O'Leary, Donovan, Kruger, and Cysewski (1978), Smolen (1978), and Willis and Blaney (1978) for alternative findings and Seligman (1978) for a comment on these discrepant findings.] Based on these results, W. R. Miller and Seligman (1973, 1976) and Klein and Seligman (1976) inferred that helpless and depressed individuals had acquired a generalized expectancy of response–outcome independence which interfered with perceiving that their responses would produce outcomes.

The chance–skill method as an assessment of the cognitive deficit in helpless and depressed humans has two complications. The first concerns its assumption that external locus of control and the expectation of independence between responses and outcomes are conceptually similar. Abramson *et al.* (1978b) recently argued that the expectation of response–outcome independence and external locus of control are orthogonal. They distinguish between cases of "personal" helplessness, in which people attribute the independence between their responses and outcomes to internal factors, and cases of "universal" helplessness, in which people attribute the independence between their responses and outcomes to external factors.

The second complication concerns the relationship between expectancy changes and beliefs about control. Recent developments in attribution theory (Weiner, 1974; Weiner, Frieze, Kukla, Reed, Rest, & Rosenbaum, 1971; Weiner, Heckhausen, Meyer, & Cook, 1972; Weiner, Nierenberg, & Goldstein, 1976) suggest that sizes of expectancy changes are indices not of perception of response–outcome contingency, but of the attributional dimension of stability. According to Weiner and colleagues, people give large expectancy changes when they attribute outcomes to stable factors (factors expected to be present in the future) and small expectancy changes when they attribute outcomes to unstable factors (factors not expected to be presented in the future). Thus, since it is found that depressed and helpless subjects give smaller changes after both success and failure, attribution theorists would infer that they make more unstable attributions for both success and failure.

Much of the skill/chance data confirm a cognitive deficit which is expectational rather than perceptual: (1) The basic data are derived from subjects' opinions about how they expect to do on the next trial, not how they perceived what they did on the last trial. (2) After success, helpless and depressed subjects show smaller expectancy changes in skill, suggesting an unstable attribution for response-contingent outcomes. Unstable attributions for success are consistent with an expectational bias, rather than a perceptual bias, in helplessness and depression (see Section III, B), and are also consistent with common verbalizations of depressed subjects, such as "I know I did it right that time, but I'm not sure I can do the same thing again." Since attributions have not been directly measured in these studies, however, this argument is at present only inferential. (3) Helpless and depressed students on post-experimental questionnaires rate skill as playing as large a role in a person's performance on the skill task as nonhelpless and nondepressed students, despite the fact that their expectancy changes are smaller (Klein & Seligman, 1976; W. R. Miller & Seligman, 1976; W. R. Miller *et al.*, 1975). This suggests that they perceive response–outcome dependence but do not necessarily believe it will recur in the future. There is, however, a major inconsistency in the skill/chance data for such an expectational bias. After failure, depressed and helpless subjects change less. This suggests an unstable attribution for failure (as well as success), but an expectational bias toward noncontingency requires stable (and global) attributions for failure and unstable (and specific) attributions for success (see Seligman, Abramson, Semmel, & von Baeyer, 1979). So the skill/chance data provide some inconsistent support for the existence of an expectational bias in helplessness and depression.

To this point, our analysis of the evidence claimed to demonstrate a cognitive deficit in humans suggests that no methodology has yet assessed this deficit unconfoundedly. In the next section, we describe a method developed by Alloy and Abramson (1979) which may provide a more adequate test of the cognitive component of helplessness and depression. This method attempts to assess perceptions of present control, not expectations of future control.

3. *Judgment of Contingency Experiments*

Unlike earlier, relatively indirect attempts to measure the cognitive component of helplessness and depression, Alloy and Abramson (1979) asked people to actually quantify the degree of contingency between their responses and an outcome. Contingency learning problems consisted of a series of 40 trials on which the subject made one of two possible responses (pressing a button or not pressing a button) and received one of two possible outcomes (a green light or no green light). At the end of the series of trials, the subject was asked to judge on a 0 to 100 scale the degree of contingency or control which existed between button pressing and green light onset. In these judgment of contingency studies, the objective contingency between responses and green light was indexed by the difference between the *p*(green light onset/press) and the *p*(green light onset/no press) (see Section II, B).

The judgment of contingency task developed by Alloy and Abramson provides an assessment of the perceptual step of the cognitive deficit, unconfounded by the response initiation deficit. In these studies, failure to perceive the degree of contingency between one's responses and green light onset cannot be ascribed to a lower tendency to emit the relevant responses. The relevant responses were simple and required little or no effort: pressing a button or not pressing a button. Moreover, subjects were instructed to sample these two responses fairly equally and analysis of their sampling patterns in all of the experiments described below indicated that they did so.

In a series of four experiments, Alloy and Abramson (1979) presented depressed and nondepressed college students with one of a series of contingency problems.[9] Assume that the cognitive deficit is produced by a bias in the perceptual step, rather than the attributional–expectational step, and that depressed individuals are biased toward perceiving noncontingency. It follows that depressed individuals will perceive response–outcome contingencies less readily and noncontingencies more readily than nondepressed individuals.

In the first experiment, Alloy and Abramson examined depressed

[9]Depression was assessed by the Beck Depression Inventory (Beck, 1967). Reliability and validity studies for this inventory are reported by Alloy and Abramson (1979).

and nondepressed students' perceptions of contingent response–outcome relationships. Students were presented with one of three problems, in which the actual degree of control over green light onset was either 25%, 50%, or 75%. The problems were counterbalanced for whether pressing or not pressing the button produced the higher percentage of green light onset. In addition to differing on degree of contingency, the three problems were also designed to differ on overall percentage of "reinforcement" (i.e., overall frequency of green light onsets), since previous work (e.g., Jenkins & Ward, 1965) suggested that this variable was often a better predictor of people's judgments than objective contingency. In particular, the percentage of reinforcement for the problems was negatively correlated with the degree of contingency. The second experiment was identical to the first with the exception that students were asked to judge degree of control for one of two problems in which responses and green light onset were noncontingently related. In one problem, green light onset occurred on 25% of the trials independent of responses, while in the other problem, green light onset occurred on 75% of the trials independent of responses.

Figure 9 presents judgments of control in experiments 1 (right panel) and 2 (left panel) as a function of the actual contingency. As can be seen in the figure, depressed and nondepressed students' judgments of control did not differ in the contingent problems and were highly accurate. Indeed, in experiment 1, judgments of control correlated significantly with actual degree of control ($r = .56, p < .001$) for both depressed and nondepressed students. In contrast, depressed and nondepressed students' judgments differed for the noncontingency problems of experiment 2. Nondepressed students judged that they had more control in the noncontingent–75% reinforcement problem than the depressed students ($p < .05$).[10] When green light onset was noncontingently related to pressing in the 25% condition, both groups accurately detected lack of relationship between responses and outcomes. So nondepressed subjects show an "illusion of control" in the high-density, noncontingent problem.

In two additional experiments, Alloy and Abramson examined judgments of control in situations which were more like the "real world," in that they involved affectively positive or negative outcomes. Students were assigned to one of two conditions in which green light onset gained or lost money. In the "win" condition, students gained a quarter each time the green light came on and in the "lose" condition, they lost a quarter each time the green light did not come on. The experiments differed in the actual degree of contingency between responses and green light. In experiment 3, green light onset occurred on 50% of the

[10]This effect was much stronger in nondepressed females than in nondepressed males.

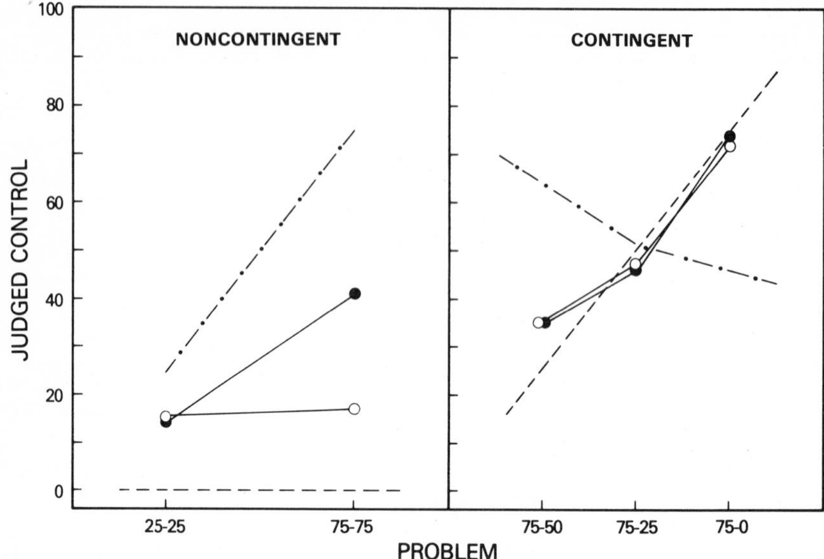

Fig. 9. Judged control for depressed (D, ○) and nondepressed (ND, ●) students as a function of problem type in experiment 1 (right) and experiment 2 (left). For comparison, actual degree of control (ACON, – – –) and actual percentage of reinforcement (ARF, –•–) are also shown as a function of problem type. (From "Judgment of contingency in depressed and nondepressed students: Sadder but wiser?" by L. B. Alloy and L. Y. Abramson, *Journal of Experimental Psychology: General,* 1979, in press, Copyright 1979 by the American Psychological Assocation. Adapted by permission.)

trials and was noncontingently related to responses (0% control). In experiment 4, green light onset was contingently related to responses (50% control).

Figure 10 presents the results for experiments 3 (left panel) and 4 (right panel). In the noncontingent problems of experiment 3, nondepressed students judged that they had more control in the "win" condition than in the "lose" condition ($p < .001$), while depressed students' judgments did not differ between the two conditions. In addition, nondepressed students judged that they had more control than did depressed students in the "win" condition ($p < .001$), but not in the "lose" condition. Similarly, in the contingent problems of experiment 4, nondepressed students judged that they had less control in the "lose" condition than in the "win" condition ($p < .001$) and less control than did depressed students in the "lose" condition ($p < .01$).[11]

[11]See Abramson and Alloy (1979) for the real-world implications of these errors in judging contingencies.

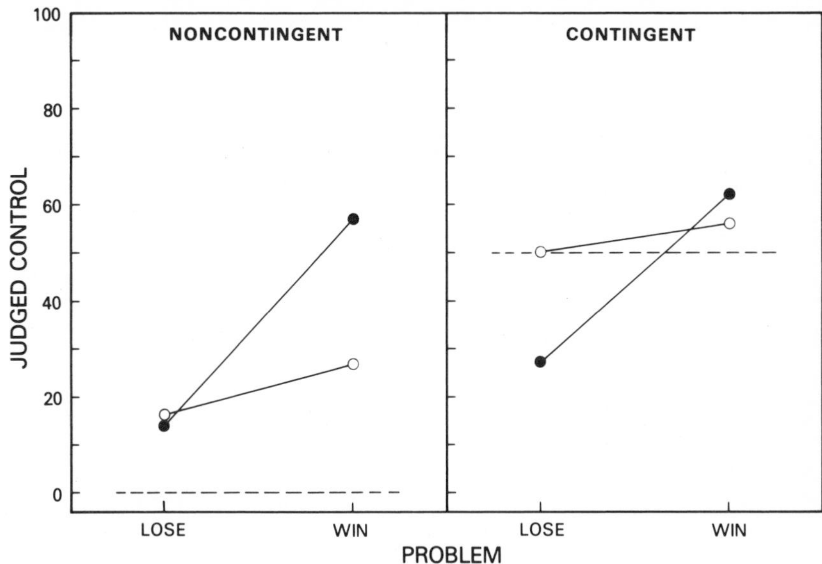

Fig. 10. Judged control for depressed (D, ○) and nondepressed (ND, ●) students as a function of problem type in experiment 3 (left) and experiment 4 (right). For comparison, actual degree of control (ACON, – – –) is also shown as a function of problem type. (From "Judgment of contingency in depressed and nondepressed students: Sadder but wiser?" by L. B. Alloy and L. Y. Abramson, *Journal of Experimental Psychology: General,* 1979, in press. Copyright 1979 by the American Psychological Association. Adapted by permission.)

What are the implications of these four experiments for the cognitive deficit in depression? *(a)* Experiment 1, which finds no difference between depressed and nondepressed groups on contingent problems, offers evidence against perceptual bias toward noncontingency in the depressed group. *(b)* Experiment 2, which finds that the depressed group perceives noncontingency more readily than the nondepressed group, supports the hypothesis that there will be a net difference between depressed and nondepressed students on judgment of noncontingency. It is fascinating, however, that the distortion from reality lies in the nondepressed group, which perceives control even when none is present, while the depressed group is accurate. [This finding does not support Beck's (1967) view of depression.] *(c)* Experiments 3 and 4 also provide no evidence of a perceptual bias in depressed subjects. The results from these experiments may be consistent with the hypothesis that nondepressed subjects defend their self-esteem by believing they have control when winning and believing they have no control when losing, while depressed subjects do not defend their self-esteem. This possibility leads to two interpretations of experiments 3 and 4 which have different implications for helplessness theory. First, the presence or absence of motivation to maintain self-esteem may produce a reporting bias and, thus, no firm conclusion may be possible as to what the underlying perceptions actually are before the reporting step takes place. Alternatively, motivation to preserve self-esteem might affect the detection of contingencies, not reporting bias (Erdelyi, 1974). If this is the case, then the helplessness theory's explanation of the cognitive deficit is inadequate, and more generally, the signal detection view in which motivation and perception are regarded as independent factors is inadequate (Green & Swets, 1966).

The findings of the four experiments, then, are mixed: they provide some possible confirmation of perceptual bias (experiment 2), some clear disconfirmation (experiment 1), and some findings which do not allow certain inference about perceptions (experiments 3 and 4).

Abramson *et al.* (1979) provided further evidence that depressed individuals are perceptually accurate and can make nonbiased judgments of contingency. Depressed and nondepressed students were given a judgment of contingency problem in which they could exert 75% control over green light onset with a time-dependent response. For half of the students in each group, the controlling response was a press of the button within the first 2 sec of a 5-sec interval. For the other half, the controlling response was a button press in the last 2 sec of the 5-sec interval. In addition, students were run under one of two conditions. In a "self-generated" (SG) condition, students were required to generate potential controlling responses themselves. In the "experimenter-generated" (EG) condition, a small pool of potential responses (including the correct one) to be tested was generated for them. The EG condition controls for the effects of lowered response initiation. If depressives have difficulty in perceiving the relationship between the controlling response and green light onset they should underestimate the degree of control in both conditions. If, however, they are merely less likely to generate responses (response initiation deficit) but perceive accurately, they should underestimate degree of control only in the SG condition.

The results of this experiment are shown in Fig. 11, which presents judgments of control for depressed and nondepressed students as a function of condition. The pattern of the data is clear. Nondepressed students accurately judged that they had approximately 75% control in both conditions. Relative to nondepressives, depressed students underestimated the degree of control in the SG condition ($F = 8.8, p < .01$), but not in the EG condition ($F < 1$). Self-generation, per se, did notcause the distortion in depressed subjects, since those who generated a sufficient number of hypotheses (including the correct one), judged control accurately. The Abramson *et al.* experiment, then, provides further evi-

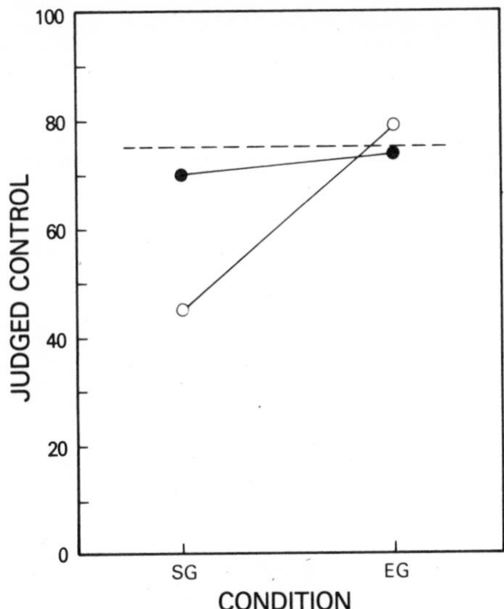

Fig. 11. Judged control for depressed (D, ○) and nondepressed (ND, ●) students in the self-generated (SG) and experimenter-generated (EG) conditions. Actual degree of control (ACON, – – –) is also shown for comparison. (Abramson, Alloy, & Rosoff, 1979.)

dence against a perceptual deficit in depressed individuals. Depressives do not distort response–outcome contingencies when they have had sufficient opportunity to perceive these contingencies.

If, as the Alloy and Abramson (1979) and Abramson *et al.* (1979) experiments suggest, depressed individuals do not have difficulty perceiving contingent relationships between their responses and outcomes, why do they perform so poorly on instrumental-learning tasks? One possibility is that it is the expectational step, not the perceptual step, of the cognitive representation of contingency that is biased toward noncontingency. If this were so, depressives should tend to expect that outcomes will be noncontingent in the future even though they perceive that they are contingent now. Such an expectation would lower response initiation. The chance–skill data provide some support for this, and additional support for this notion is provided by Seligman *et al.* (1979).

Seligman *et al.* (1979) found evidence that supported biased attributions in depression, independent of perceptual processes. Depressed and nondepressed college students were asked to imagine vividly 12 situations that might occur to them; e.g., "A friend asks you to help and you turn him down," "You give a report in front of a class and it goes badly." Six were success situations, six failures. They were then asked to name the most likely cause and to quantify whether *(a)* the cause was due more to the student himself (internal) or to circumstances or other people (external); *(b)* the cause would always be present when the situation recurred (stable) or never be present again (unstable); or *(c)* the cause would affect many situations (global) or just this situation (specific). They found that for failure (helplessness) situations, depressed people give more global, stable, and internal causes (all $ps < .001$) and for success (nonhelplessness) situations, depressed people give more unstable and external causes ($ps < .01$).

What are the implications of having such an attributional style? According to Abramson *et al.* (1978b), attributions form the mediating step between perceptions and expectations. An individual who attributes an instance of response–outcome independence to stable and global factors or an instance of response–outcome dependence to unstable and specific factors should be less likely to expect response–outcome dependence in the future and in other situations. Thus, the attributional style found for depressives by Seligman *et al.* (1979) may serve to bias expectations of failure or of noncontingency in the direction of permanence and pervasiveness and increase the likelihood of expecting future failure.

What experiments remain to be done in assessing the cognitive deficit in human helplessness and depression? (1) Some concrete account of the smaller expectancy changes after failure on skill tasks needs to be articulated and tested. (2) Depressed and helpless attributions must be measured and manipulated in the context of the chance–skill, judgment of contingency, and the usual helplessness paradigms. (3) The parallel judgment of contingency experiments should be carried out in helpless, nondepressed subjects. (4) Convergent validation of an expectational bias must be sought.

VI. Conclusion

We have reviewed a large number of studies relevant to the existence of the cognitive deficit postulated by learned helplessness theory. We have formally defined the concept of contingency and have presented some examples of the kinds of experiments which have led contemporary learning theorists to the conclusion that the concept is important for learning theory. Learning theorists are in general agreement that the degree of contingency between stimuli and outcomes or between responses and outcomes is a central determinant of Pavlovian and instrumental conditioning. While most learning theories argue that postulating underlying cognitive mechanisms in animals is unnecessary, learned helplessness is one of the few theories which maintains that cognitive representation of contingencies is the crucial mediator between objective contingencies and behavior. The theory postulates that organisms exposed to response–outcome independence will have more difficulty learning later response–outcome dependencies than naive organisms or organisms first exposed to response–outcome dependence and that such a learning deficit stems from "cognitive" or "associative" interference. We have distinguished between two mechanisms—biased perceptions of present contingencies toward noncontingency and biased expectations of future contingencies toward noncontingency—either or both of which would account for observed interference in learning.

It has required experimental ingenuity to isolate and test the cognitive deficit apart from the response initiation deficit postulated by the theory or from alternative motor activity explanations. Several recent animal and human experiments, however, have done so. The evidence from the animal studies supports the existence of the cognitive deficit of helplessness theory. Animals exposed to outcomes which are independent of their responses have difficulty in learning that outcomes are later contingent upon their responses, and this difficulty does not stem from lowered response initiation, lowered activity, or incompatible responses. However, the animal studies, for the most part, do not tease apart perceptual from expectational mechanisms of interference. This evidence is consistent with the conclusion that objective contingencies have subjective reality for animals.

Evidence from the human experiments is less clear. While helpless and depressed humans show a similar pattern of deficits on instrumental tasks as helpless animals (they fail to respond, or respond and revert to not responding), that this is cognitive, rather than motivational or emotional, has yet to be demonstrated. Some of the human experiments attempt to separate expectational from perceptual mechanisms of interference. These studies do not support the existence of a perceptual bias in depression and helplessness. Depressed individuals do not have difficulty perceiving that their responses control outcomes. In fact, they are surprisingly accurate. Some evidence, however, suggests the existence of an expectational bias. Depressed individuals, unlike nondepressed individuals, make global and stable attributions for failure, and such an attributional style may increase the probability that future outcomes will be expected to be noncontingent.

In conclusion, helplessness theory has, in the past, attempted to integrate the animal and human data by focusing on a single cognitive deficit—the difficulty that helpless organisms have learning about subsequent response–outcome contingencies. We suggest that the theory has been inarticulate about the process underlying this deficit, and that difficulty learning later response–outcome contingencies could stem from either, or both, of two processes: perceptual bias to see present relationships as noncontingent, or expectational bias to see future relationships as noncontingent. The present state of animal research strongly indicates that helpless animals have trouble learning later contingencies but has not yet isolated whether the deficit is perceptual or expectational. The present state of human research tends less strongly to indicate that depressed and helpless humans have trouble learning later contingencies. We suggest that this is more likely to result from an expectational bias since we have found evidence against a perceptual bias, but we have found evidence for the relevant attributional bias. Whether animals and humans who experience uncontrollable outcomes arrive at their cognitive deficits by the same underlying process remains to be demonstrated.

References

Abramson, L. Y., & Alloy, L. B. Judgment of contingency: Errors and their implications. In A. Baum & J. Singer (Eds.), *Advances in environmental psychology.* (Vol. 2). Hillside, N.J.: Lawrence Erlbaum Associates, 1979, in press.

Abramson, L. Y., Alloy, L. B., & Rosoff, R. Depression and the role of complex hypotheses in the judgment of response-outcome contingencies. Submitted to the *Journal of Abnormal Psychology,* 1979.

Abramson, L. Y., Garber, J., Edwards, N. B., & Seligman, M. E. P. Expectancy changes in depression and schizophrenia. *Journal of Abnormal Psychology,* 1978, **87,** 102–109. (a)

Abramson, L. Y., Seligman, M. E. P., & Teasdale, J. D. Learned helplessness in humans: Critique and reformulation. *Journal of Abnormal Psychology,* 1978, **87,** 49–74. (b)

Alloy, L. B., & Abramson, L. Y. Judgement of contingency in depressed and nondepressed students: Sadder but wiser? *Journal of Experimental Psychology: General,* 1979, in press.

Alloy, L. B., & Bersh, P. J. Partial control and learned helplessness in rats: Control over shock intensity prevents interference with subsequent escape. *Animal Learning and Behavior,* 1979, in press.

Alloy, L. B., & Ehrman, R. N. Instrumental to Pavlovian transfer. Learning about response-reinforcer contingencies affects subsequent acquisition of stimulus-reinforcer contingencies. In preparation, 1979.

Altenor, A., Kay, E., & Richter, M. The generality of learned helplessness in the rat. *Learning and Motivation,* 1977, **8,** 54–62.

Anisman, H. Time-dependent variations in aversively-motivated behaviors: Nonassocative effects of cholinergic and catecholaminergic activity. *Psychological Review,* 1975, **82,** 359–385.

Anisman, H., deCatanzaro, D., & Remington, G. Escape performance following exposure to inescapable shock: Deficits in motor response maintenance. *Journal of Experimental Psychology: Animal Behavior Processes,* 1978, **4,** 197–218.

Anisman, H., & Waller, T. G. Effects of inescapable shock on subsequent avoidance performance: Role of response repertoire changes. *Behavioral Biology,* 1973, **9,** 331–355.

Ayres, J. J., Benedict, J. O., & Witcher, E. S. Systematic manipulation of individual events in a truly random control in rats. *Journal of Comparative and Physiological Psychology,* 1975, **88,** 97–103.

Azrin, N. H. Some effects of two intermittent schedules of immediate and nonimmediate punishment. *Journal of Psychology,* 1956, **42,** 3–21.

Badia, P., Suter, S., & Lewis, P. Preference for warned shock: Information and/or preparation. *Psychological Reports,* 1967, **20,** 271–274.

Baker, A. G. Learned irrelevance and learned helplessness: Rats learn that stimuli, reinforcers, and responses are uncorrelated. *Journal of Experimental Psychology: Animal Behavior Processes,* 1976, **2,** 130–142.

Baum, W. M. The correlation-based law of effect. *Journal of the Experimental Analysis of Behavior,* 1973, **20,** 137–153.

Beck, A. T. *Depression: Clinical, experimental, and theoretical aspects.* New York: Harper, 1967.

Benedict, J. O., & Ayres, J. J. Factors affecting conditioning in the truly random control procedure in the rat. *Journal of Comparative and Physiological Psychology,* 1972, **78,** 323–330.

Benson, J. S., & Kennelly, K. J. Learned helplessness: The result of uncontrollable reinforcements or uncontrollable aversive stimuli? *Journal of Personality and Social Psychology,* 1976, **34,** 138–145.

Bindra, D. A unified account of classical conditioning and operant training. In A. H. Black & W. F. Prokasy (Eds.), *Classical conditioning II: Current theory and research.* New York: Appleton, 1972.

Black, A. H. Comments on "Learned helplessness: Theory and evidence" by Maier and Seligman. *Journal of Experimental Psychology: General,* 1977, **106,** 41–44.

Bloomfield, T. M. Reinforcement schedules: Contingency or contiguity? In R. M. Gilbert & J. R. Millenson (Eds.), *Reinforcement: Behavioral analysis.* New York: Academic Press, 1972.

Bolles, R. C. Reinforcement, expectancy, and learning. *Psychological Review,* 1972, **79,** 394–409.

Bracewell, R. J., & Black, A. H. The effects of restraint and non-contingent pre-shock on subsequent escape learning in the rat. *Learning and Motivation,* 1974, **5,** 53–69.

Braud, W., Wepman, B., & Russo, D. Task and species generality of the "helplessness" phenomenon. *Psychonomic Science,* 1969, **16,** 154–155.

Brimer, C. J., & Kamin, L. J. Disinhibition, habituation, sensitization and the conditioned emotional response. *Journal of Comparative and Physiological Psychology,* 1963, **56,** 508–516.

Bull, J. A., III, & Overmier, J. B. Additive and subtractive properties of excitation and inhibition. *Journal of Comparative and Physiological Psychology,* 1968, **66,** 511–514.

Catania, A. C. Elicitation, reinforcement, and stimulus control. In R. Glaser (Ed.), *The nature of reinforcement.* New York: Academic Press, 1971.

Chapman, L. J., & Chapman, J. P. Genesis of popular but erroneous psychodiagnostic categories. *Journal of Abnormal Psychology,* 1967, **72,** 193–204.

Church, R. M. Response suppression. In B. A. Campbell & R. M. Church (Eds.), *Punishment and aversive behavior.* New York: Appleton, 1969.

Costello, C. G. A critical review of Seligman's laboratory experiments on learned helplessness and depression in humans. *Journal of Abnormal Psychology,* 1978, **87,** 21–31.

Davis, H., & McIntire, R. W. Conditioned suppression under positive, negative, and no CS-US contingency. *Journal of the Experimental Analysis of Behavior,* 1969, **12,** 633–640.

Dweck, C. S., & Wagner, A. R. Situational cues and correlation between conditioned stimulus and unconditioned stimulus as determinants of the conditioned emotional response. *Psychonomic Science,* 1970, **18,** 145–147.

Erdelyi, M. H. A new look at the new look: Perceptual defense and vigilance. *Psychological Review,* 1974, **81,** 1–25.

Gatchel, R. J., & Proctor, J. D. Physiological correlates of learned helplessness in man. *Journal of Abnormal Psychology,* 1976, **85,** 27–34.

Gibbon, J., Berryman, R., & Thompson, R. L. Contingency spaces and measures in classical and instrumental conditioning. *Journal of the Experimental Analysis of Behavior,* 1974, **21,** 585–605.

Glazer, H. I., & Weiss, J. M. Long-term and transitory interference effects. *Journal of Experimental Psychology: Animal Behavior Processes,* 1976, **2,** 191–201. (a)

Glazer, H. I., & Weiss, J. M. Long-term interference effect: An alternative to "learned helplessness." *Journal of Experimental Psychology: Animal Behavior Processes,* 1976, **2,** 201–213. (b)

Goodkin, F. Rats learn the relationship between responding and environmental events: An expansion of the learned helplessness hypothesis. *Learning and Motivation,* 1976, **7,** 382–393.

Green, D. M., & Swets, J. A. *Signal detection theory and psychophysics.* New York: Wiley, 1966.

Guthrie, E. R. *The psychology of learning* (rev. ed.). New York: Harper, 1952.

Hammond, L. J., & Daniel, R. Negative contingency discrimination: Differentiation by rats between safe and random stimuli. *Journal of Comparative and Physiological Psychology,* 1970, **72,** 486–491.

Hearst, E. Stress induced breakdown of an appetitive discrimination. *Journal of the Experimental Analysis of Behavior,* 1965, **8,** 135–146.

Hiroto, D. S. Locus of control and learned helplessness. *Journal of Experimental Psychology,* 1974, **102,** 187–193.

Hiroto, D. S., & Seligman, M. E. P. Generality of learned helplessness in man. *Journal of Personality and Social Psychology,* 1975, **31,** 311–327.

Hokanson, J. E., DeGood, D. E., Forrest, M. S., & Brittain, T. M. Availability of avoidance behaviors in modulating vascular-stress responses. *Journal of Personality and Social Psychology,* 1971, **19,** 60–68.

Hull, C. L. *Principles of behavior.* New York: Appleton, 1943.

Jackson, R. L., Maier, S. F., & Rapaport, P. M. Exposure to inescapable shock produces both activity and associative deficits in the rat. *Learning and Motivation,* 1978, **9,** 69–98.

James. W. H. *Internal versus external control of reinforcement as a basic variable in learning theory.* Unpublished doctoral dissertation, Ohio State University, 1957.

James, W. H., & Rotter, J. B. Partial and one hundred percent reinforcement under chance and skill conditions. *Journal of Experimental Psychology,* 1958, **55,** 397–403.

Jenkins, H. M. *The concept of contingency.* Colloquium presented to the Department of Psychology, University of Pennsylvania, April 1978.

Jenkins, H. M., & Ward, W. C. Judgment of contingency between responses and outcomes. *Psychological Monographs,* 1965, **79**(1, Whole No. 594).

Kamin, L. J. "Attention-like" processes in classical conditioning. In M. R. Jones (Ed.), *Miami symposium on the prediction of behavior: Aversive stimulation.* Miami: University of Miami Press, 1968.

Kamin, L. J. Predictability, surprise, attention and conditioning. In B. A. Campbell & R. M. Church (Eds.), *Punishment and aversive behavior.* New York: Appleton, 1969.

Keller, R. J., Ayres, J. J., & Mahoney, W. J. Brief versus extended exposure to truly random control procedures. *Journal of Experimental Psychology: Animal Behavior Processes,* 1977, **3,** 53–65.

Kelsey, J. E. Escape acquisition following inescapable shock in the rat. *Animal Learning and Behavior,* 1977, **5,** 83–92.

Killeen, P. R. Superstition: A matter of bias, not detectability. *Science,* 1978, **199,** 88–90.

Klein, D. C., Fencil-Morse, E., & Seligman, M. E. P. Depression, learned helplessness, and the attribution of failure. *Journal of Personality and Social Psychology,* 1976, **33,** 508–516.

Klein, D. C., & Seligman, M. E. P. Reversal of performance deficits and perceptual deficits in learned helplessness and depression. *Journal of Abnormal Psychology,* 1976, **85,** 11–26.

Kremer, E. F. The truly random control procedure: Conditioning to the static cues. *Journal of Comparative and Physiological Psychology,* 1974, **86,** 700–707.

Kremer, E. F., & Kamin, L. J. The truly random control procedure: Associative or non-associative effects in rats. *Journal of Comparative and Physiological Psychology,* 1971, **74,** 203–210.

Langer, E. J. The illusion of control. *Journal of Personality and Social Psychology,* 1975, **32,** 311–328.

Levis, D. J. Learned helplessness: A reply and an alternative S-R interpretation. *Journal of Experimental Psychology: General,* 1976, **105,** 47–65.

Lockard, J. S. Choice of a warning signal or no warning signal in an unavoidable shock situation. *Journal of Comparative and Physiological Psychology,* 1963, **56,** 526–530.

Mackintosh, N. J. Stimulus selection: Learning to ignore stimuli that predict no change in reinforcement. In R. A. Hinde & J. Stevenson-Hinde (Eds.), *Constraints on learning.* New York: Academic Press, 1973.

Mackintosh, N. J. A theory of attention: Variations in the associability of stimuli with reinforcement. *Psychological Review,* 1975, **82,** 276–298.

Maier, S. F. Failure to escape traumatic shock: Incompatible skeletal motor response or learned helplessness? *Learning and Motivation,* 1970, **1,** 157–170.

Maier, S. F., Albin, R. W., & Testa, T. J. Failure to learn to escape in rats previously exposed to inescapable shock depends on nature of escape response. *Journal of Comparative and Physiological Psychology,* 1973, **85,** 581–592.

Maier, S. F., & Seligman, M. E. P. Learned helplessness: Theory and evidence. *Journal of Experimental Psychology: General,* 1976, **105,** 3–46.

Maier, S. F., Seligman, M. E. P., & Solomon, R. L. Pavlovian fear conditioning and learned helplessness. In B. A. Campbell & R. M. Church (Eds.), *Punishment.* New York: Appleton, 1969.

Maier, S. F., & Testa, T. J. Failure to learn to escape by rats previously exposed to inescapable shock is partly produced by associative interference. *Journal of Comparative and Physiological Psychology,* 1975, **88,** 554–564.

McNitt, P. C., & Thornton, D. W. Depression and perceived reinforcement: A reconsideration. *Journal of Abnormal Psychology,* 1978, **87,** 137–140.

Miller, S. M. Controllability and human stress. In M. E. P. Seligman & J. Garber (Eds.), *Human helplessness: Theory and application.* New York: Academic Press, 1979, in press.

Miller, S. M., & Grant, R. P. The blunting hypothesis: A theory of predictability and human stress. In S. Bates, W. S. Dockens, K. G. Gotestam, L. Melin, & P. O. Sjoden (Eds.), *Trends in behavior therapy.* New York: Academic Press, 1979, in press.

Miller, W. R., Rosellini, R. A., & Seligman, M. E. P. Learned helplessness and depression. In J. D. Maser & M. E. P. Seligman (Eds.), *Psychopathology: Experimental models.* San Francisco: Freeman, 1977.

Miller, W. R., & Seligman, M. E. P. Depression and the perception of reinforcement. *Journal of Abnormal Psychology,* 1973, **82,** 62–73.

Miller, W. R., & Seligman, M. E. P. Depression and learned helplessness in man. *Journal of Abnormal Psychology,* 1975, **84,** 228–238.

Miller, W. R., & Seligman, M. E. P. Learned helplessness, depression, and the perception of reinforcement. *Behaviour Research and Therapy,* 1976, **14,** 7–17.

Miller, W. R., Seligman, M. E. P., & Kurlander, H. M. Learned helplessness, depression, and anxiety. *Journal of Nervous and Mental Disease,* 1975, **161,** 347–357.

Moskowitz, A., & LoLordo, V. M. Role of safety in the Pavlovian backward fear conditioning procedure, *Journal of Comparative and Physiological Psychology,* 1968, **66,** 673–678.

O'Leary, M. R., Donovan, D. M., Kruger, K. J., & Cysewski, B. Depression and perception of reinforcement: Lack of differences in expectancy change among alcoholics. *Journal of Abnormal Psychology,* 1978, **87,** 110–112.

Overmier, J. B., & Seligman, M. E. P. Effects of inescapable shock upon subsequent escape and avoidance learning. *Journal of Comparative and Physiological Psychology,* 1967, **63,** 23–33.

Pervin, L. A. The need to predict and control under conditions of threat. *Journal of Personality,* 1963, **31,** 570–585.

Phares, E. J. Expectancy change in chance and skill situations. *Journal of Abnormal and Social Psychology,* 1957, **54,** 339–342.

Premack, D. Reinforcement theory. In D. Levine (Ed.), *Nebraska Symposium on Motivation* (Vol. 13). Lincoln: University of Nebraska Press, 1965.

Price, K. P., Tryon, W. W., & Raps, C. S. Learned helplessness and depression in a clinical population: A test of two behavioral hypotheses. *Journal of Abnormal Psychology,* 1978, **87,** 113–121.

Prokasy, W. F. Classical eyelid conditioning: Experimental operations, task demands, and response shaping. In W. F. Prokasy (Ed.), *Classical conditioning.* New York: Appleton, 1965.

Quinsey, V. L. Conditioned suppression with no CS-US contingency in the rat. *Canadian Journal of Psychology,* 1971, **25,** 69–82.

Rescorla, R. A. Pavlovian conditioning and its proper control procedures. *Psychological Review,* 1967, **74,** 71–79.

Rescorla, R. A. Probability of shock in the presence and absence of the CS in fear conditioning. *Journal of Comparative and Physiological Psychology,* 1968, **66,** 1–5.

Rescorla, R. A. Conditioned inhibition of fear resulting from negative CS-US contingencies. *Journal of Comparative and Physiological Psychology,* 1969, **67,** 504–509. (a)

Rescorla, R. A. Establishment of a positive reinforcer through contrast with shock. *Journal of Comparative and Physiological Psychology,* 1969, **67,** 260–263. (b)

Rescorla, R. A. Pavlovian conditioned inhibition. *Psychological Bulletin.* 1969, **72,** 77–94.(c)

Rescorla, R. A. Informational variables in Pavlovian conditioning. In G. H. Bower (Ed.), *The psychology of learning and motivation* (Vol. 6). New York: Academic Press, 1972.

Rescorla, R. A., & Wagner, A. R. A theory of Pavlovian conditioning: Variations in the effectiveness of reinforcement and nonreinforcement. In A. R. Black & W. F. Prokasy (Eds.), *Classical conditioning II.* New York: Appleton, 1972.

Rodin, J., & Langer, E. J. Long-term effects of a control-relevant intervention with the institutionalized aged. *Journal of Personality and Social Psychology,* 1977, **35,** 897–902.

Rosellini, R. A. Inescapable shock interferes with the acquisition of an appetitive operant. *Animal Learning and Behavior,* 1978, **6,** 155–159.

Rosellini, R. A., & Seligman, M. E. P. Learned helplessness and escape from frustration, *Journal of Experimental Psychology: Animal Behavior Processes,* 1975, **1,** 149–158.

Rotter, J. B. Generalized expectancies for internal versus external control of reinforcement. *Psychological Monographs,* 1966, **80**(1, Whole No. 609).

Rotter, J. B., Liverant, S., & Crowne, D. P. The growth and extinction of expectancies in chance controlled and skilled tasks. *Journal of Psychology,* 1961, **52,** 161–177.

Schultz, R. Effects of control and predictability on the physical and psychological well-being of the institutionalized aged. *Journal of Personality and Social Psychology,* 1976, **33,** 563–573.

Seligman, M. E. P. Control group and conditioning: A comment on operationism. *Psychological Review,* 1969, **76,** 484–491.

Seligman, M. E. P. Depression and learned helplessness. In R. J. Friedman & M. M. Katz (Eds.), *The psychology of depression: Contemporary theory and research.* New York: Wiley, 1975. (a)

Seligman, M. E. P. *Helplessness: On depression, development, and death.* San Francisco: Freeman, 1975. (b)

Seligman, M. E. P. Comment and integration. *Journal of Abnormal Psychology,* 1978, **87,** 165–179.

Seligman, M. E. P., Abramson, L. Y., Semmel, A., & von Baeyer, C. Depressive attributional style. *Journal of Abnormal Psychology,* 1979, in press.

Seligman, M. E. P., & Beagley, G. Learned helplessness in the rat. *Journal of Comparative and Physiological Psychology,* 1975, **88,** 534–541.

Seligman, M. E. P., & Binik, I. The safety signal hypothesis. In H. Davis and H. M. B. Hurwitz (Eds.), *Pavlovian—Operant interactions.* Hillside, N.J.: Lawrence Erlbaum Associates, 1977.

Seligman, M. E. P., Klein, D. C., & Miller, W. R. Depression. In H. Leitenberg (Ed.), *Handbook of behavior modification and behavior therapy.* Englewood Cliffs, N.J.: Prentice-Hall, 1976.

Seligman, M. E. P., & Maier, S. F. Failure to escape traumatic shock. *Journal of Experimental Psychology,* 1967, **74,** 1–9.

Seligman, M. E. P., Maier, S. F., & Geer, J. The alleviation of learned helplessness in the dog. *Journal of Abnormal Psychology,* 1968, **73,** 256–262.

Seligman, M. E. P., Maier, S. F., & Solomon R. L. Unpredictable and uncontrollable aversive events. In F. R. Brush (Ed.), *Aversive conditioning and learning.* New York: Academic Press, 1971.

Seligman, M. E. P., Rosellini, R. A., & Kozak, M. Learned helplessness in the rat: Reversibility, time course, and immunization. *Journal of Comparative and Physiological Psychology,* 1975, **88,** 542–547.

Skinner, B. F. *The behavior of organisms.* New York: Appleton, 1938.

Smedslund, J. The concept of correlation in adults. *Scandinavian Journal of Psychology,* 1963, **4,** 165–173.

Smolen, R. C. Expectancies, mood, and performance of depressed and nondepressed psychiatric inpatients on chance and skill tasks. *Journal of Abnormal Psychology,* 1978, **87,** 91–101.

Starr, B. J., & Katkin, E. S. The clinician as an aberrant actuary: Illusory correlation and the incomplete sentence blank. *Journal of Abnormal Psychology,* 1969, **74,** 670–675.

Testa, T. J., Juraska, J. M., & Maier, S. F. Prior exposure to inescapable electric shock in rats effects extinction behavior after the successful acquisition of an escape response. *Learning and Motivation,* 1974, **5,** 380–392.

Tolman, E. C. *Purposive behavior in animals and men.* New York: Century, 1932.

Tolman, E. C. Principles of performance. *Psychological Review,* 1955, **62,** 315–325.

Volpicelli, J. R., Altenor, A., & Seligman, M. E. P. Learned mastery in the rat. In preparation, 1979.

Wagner, A. R. Stimulus selection and a "modified continuity theory." In G. H. Bower & J. T. Spence (Eds.), *The psychology of learning and motivation* (Vol. 3). New York: Academic Press, 1969.

Wagner, A. R., & Rescorla, R. A. Inhibition in Pavlovian conditioning: Application of a theory. In R. A. Boakes & S. Halliday (Eds.), *Inhibition and learning.* New York: Academic Press, 1972.

Weiner, B. (Ed.). *Achievement motivation and attribution theory.* Morristown, N.J.: General Learning Press, 1974.

Weiner, B., Frieze, I., Kukla, A., Reed, L., Rest, S., & Rosenbaum, R. M. *Perceiving the causes of success and failure.* Morristown, N.J.: General Learning Press, 1971.

Weiner, B., Heckhausen, H., Meyer, W., & Cook, R. E. Causal ascriptions and achievement behavior: A conceptual analysis of locus of control. *Journal of Personality and Social Psychology,* 1972, **21,** 239–248.

Weiner, B., Nierenberg, R., & Goldstein, M. Social learning (locus of control) versus attributional (causal stability) interpretations of expectancy of success. *Journal of Personality,* 1976, **44,** 52–68.

Weiss, J. M. Effects of coping response on stress. *Journal of Comparative and Physiological Psychology,* 1968, **65,** 251–260. (a)

Weiss, J. M. Effects of predictable and unpredictable shock on development of gastrointestinal lesions in rats. *Proceedings of the 76th Annual Convention of the American Psychological Association,* 1968, 263–264. (b)

Weiss, J. M. Effects of coping behavior in different warning signal conditions on stress pathology in rats. *Journal of Comparative and Physiological Psychology,* 1971, **77,** 1–13. (a)

Weiss, J. M. Effects of coping behavior with and without a feedback signal on stress pathology in rats. *Journal of Comparative and Physiological Psychology,* 1971, **77,** 22–30. (b)

Weiss, J. M. Effects of punishing the coping response (conflict) on stress pathology in rats. *Journal of Comparative and Physiological Psychology,* 1971, **77,** 14–21. (c)

Weiss, J. M., Glazer, H. I., & Pohorecky, L. A. Coping behavior and neurochemical changes: An alternative explanation for the original "learned helplessness" experiments. In G. Serban & A. King (Eds.), *Animal models in human psychobiology.* New York: Plenum, 1976.

Williams, J. L., & Maier, S. F. Transituational immunization and therapy of learned helplessness in the rat. *Journal of Experimental Psychology: Animal Behavior Proceses,* 1977, **3,** 240–252.

Willis, M. H., & Blaney, P. H. Three tests of the learned helplessness model of depression. *Journal of Abnormal Psychology,* 1978, **87,** 131–136.

Wortman, C. B. Some determinants of perceived control. *Journal of Personality and Social Psychology,* 1975, **31,** 282–294.

A GENERAL LEARNING THEORY AND ITS APPLICATION TO SCHEMA ABSTRACTION[1]

John R. Anderson and Paul J. Kline

CARNEGIE-MELLON UNIVERSITY,
PITTSBURGH, PENNSYLVANIA

and Charles M. Beasley, Jr.

YALE UNIVERSITY
NEW HAVEN, CONNECTICUT

I. Introduction

We are interested in understanding learning. For many years learning theory was practically synonymous with experimental psychology; however, its boundaries have shrunk to such an extent that they barely overlap at all with those of modern cognitive psychology. Cognitive psychologists, by and large, concern themselves with a detailed analysis of the mechanisms that underlie adult human intelligence. This analysis has gone on too long without adequate attention to the question of how these complex mechanisms may be acquired. In an attempt to answer this question, we have adopted one of the methodological approaches of modern cognitive psychology: Results of detailed experimental analysis of cognitive behaviors are elaborated into a computer simulation of

[1]This research is supported by contrast N00014-77-0242 from the Office of Naval Research and grant NIE-G-77-0005 from the National Institute of Education. Some of the ideas presented developed out of discussion with David Nicholas and, particularly, Pat Langley.

ISBN 0-12-543313-1

those behaviors. The simulation program provides new predictions for a further experimental testing, the outcomes of which is then used to modify the simulation, and the whole process then repeats itself.

Our computer simulation is called ACT. The ACT system embodies the extremely powerful thesis that a single set of learning processes underlies the whole gamut of human learning—from children learning their first language by hearing examples of adult speech to adults learning to program a computer by reading textbook instructions.

In this paper we will give a general overview of the ACT learning theory and describe its application to research on abstraction of schemas. Elsewhere we have provided somewhat more technical discussions of the ACT system and described its application to other domains (Anderson, 1976; Anderson, Kline, & Beasley, 1977; Anderson, Kline, & Beasley, 1980; Anderson, Kline, & Lewis, 1977).

A. The ACT System

In ACT, knowledge is divided into two categories: declarative and procedural. The declarative knowledge is represented in a propositional network similar to semantic network representations proposed elsewhere (Anderson & Bower, 1973; Norman & Rumelhart, 1975; Quillian, 1969). While the network aspects of this representation are important for such ACT processes as spreading activation, they are not important to the current learning discussion. For present purposes we will consider ACT's declarative knowledge as a set of assertions or propositions and ignore the technical aspects of its network representation.

ACT represents its procedural knowledge as a set of productions. The ACT production system can be seen as a considerable extension and modification of the production systems developed at Carnegie-Mellon University (Newell, 1972, 1973; Rychener & Newell, 1978). A production is a condition–action rule. The condition is an abstract specification of a set of propositions. If a set of propositions which meets this specification can be found in the data base the production will perform its action. Actions can both add to the contents of the data base and cause the system to emit observable responses.

ACT's productions can only have their conditions satisfied by active propositions. ACT's activation mechanism is designed such that the only propositions active are those that have recently been added to the data base or that are closely associated to propositions which have been added. Propositions are added to the data base either through input from the environment or through the execution of productions. Thus, this activation system gives ACT the property of being immediately responsive to changes in its environment or in its internal state.

ACT's basic control structure is an iteration through successive *cycles*, where each cycle consists of a production selection phase followed by an execution phase. On each cycle an APPLYLIST is computed which is a probabilistically defined subset of all of the productions whose conditions are satisfied by active propositions. The probability that a production will be placed on the APPLYLIST depends on the strength *(s)* of that production relative to the sum *(S)* of the strengths of all the productions whose conditions mention active elements; that is, this probability varies with *s/S*. As will be seen in a later section (II.C), this strength reflects just how successful past applications of this production have been. Thus, one component of the production-selection phase consists of choosing out of all the productions which could apply those which are the most likely to apply successfully. Further discussion of the details of production selection and execution is best conducted in the context of an example.

B. An Example of a Production System

Table I presents a set of productions for adding two numbers.[2] Let us consider how this production set would apply to the addition problem of 32 + 18. We assume this problem is encoded by a set of propositions which may approximately be rendered as:

The goal is to add 32 and 18
32 begins with a 2
The 2 is followed by a 3
32 ends with this 3
18 begins with an 8
The 8 is followed by a 1
18 ends with this 1

The above propositions encode the digits from right to left as is required by the standard addition algorithm.

The condition of production 1 (P1) in Table I is satisfied by making the following correspondences between elements of the condition and propositions in the data base:

The goal is to add *LV number*1 and *LV number*2	=	The goal is to add 32 and 18

[2]The productions presented in this paper are translations of the formal syntax of the implemented productions into (hopefully) more readable prose. The reader interested in the actual implementation details may request listings of the implemented versions and examples of their operation.

*LV number*1 begins with a *LV digit*1 = 32 begins with a 2

*LVnumber*2 begins with a *LVdigit*2 = 18 begins with a 8

In making these correspondences, the variables *LVnumber*1, *LVnumber*2, *LVdigit*1, and *LVdigit*2 are bound to the values of 32, 18, 2, and 8, respectively. The *LV* prefix indicates that these are local variables and can be bound to anything. Since they only maintain their binding within the production, other productions are not constrained to match these variables in the same way. The action of P1, "the subgoal is to add *LVdigit*1 and *LVdigit*2," becomes, given the values of the variables, an instruction to place the proposition, "The subgoal is to add 2 and 8," into the data base. This serves as a cue to productions that will actually add 2 and 8.

After the execution of P1 the first element of the condition of production 2 (P2) is satisfied:

The subgoal is to add *LVdigit*1 and *LVdigit*2
= The subgoal is to add 2 and 8

The remaining condition of P2 matches a proposition in the data base about integer addition:

LVsum is the sum of *LVdigit*1 and *LVdigit*2 = 10 is the sum of 2 and 8

The action of P2 adds to the data base "The subgoal is to put out 10."

The next production to apply is P5 which is matched as follows:

The subgoal is to put out *LVsum* = The subgoal is to put out 10
The subgoal is to add *LVdigit*1 and *LVdigit*2
= The subgoal is to add 2 and 8
LVsum is greater than 9 = 10 is greater than 9
LVsum is the sum of *LVdigit*3 and 10 = 10 is the sum of 0 and 10

The action of P5 writes out 0 as the first digit in the answer, places a proposition in the data base, "The subgoal is to do the next digits after 2 and 8," to the effect that this column is finished, and sets a carry flag.

It is worth considering why no other production besides P5 can apply. All the conditions of production P3 match, but P5 contains all the conditions of P3 plus two additional propositions. Because its condition contains more elements, P5 is applied rather than P3. This illustrates the principle of specificity—if two productions match but the condition of one of them is a subset of the condition of the other, then the production with the larger number of conditions (the more specific one)

TABLE 1

A Set of Productions for Adding Two Numbers

P1:	IF	the goal is to add *LVnumber*1 and *LVnumber* 2
		and *LVnumber*1 begins with a *LVdigit*1
		and *LVnumber*2 begins with a *LVdigit*2
	THEN	the subgoal is to add *LVdigit*1 and *LVdigit*2
P2:	IF	the subgoal is to add *LVdigit*1 and *LVdigit*2
		and *LVsum* is the sum of *LVdigit*1 and *LVdigit*2
	THEN	the subgoal is to put out *LVsum*
P3:	IF	the subgoal is to put out *LVsum*
		and the subgoal is to add *LVdigit*1 and *LVdigit*2
	THEN	write *LVsum*
		and the subgoal is to add the digits after *LVdigit*1 and *LVdigit*2
P4:	IF	the subgoal is to put out *LVsum*
		and the subgoal is to add *LVdigit*1 and *LVdigit*2
		and there is a carry
		and *LV sum*1 is the sum of *LV sum* plus 1
	THEN	write *LVsum*1
		and the subgoal is to do the digits after *LVdigit*1 and *LVdigit*2
		and remove the carry flag
P5:	IF	the subgoal is to put out *LVsum*
		and the subgoal is to add *LVdigit*1 and *LVdigit*2
		and *LVsum* is greater than 9
		and *LVsum* is the sum of *LVdigit*3 and 10
	THEN	write *LVdigit*3
		and the subgoal is to.do the next digits after *LVdigit*1 and *LVdigit*2
		and set the carry flag
P6:	IF	the subgoal is to put out *LVsum*
		and the subgoal is to add *LVdigit*1 and *LVdigit*2
		and there is a carry
		and *LVsum* is greater than 9
		and *LVsum* is the sum of *LVdigit*3 and 9
	THEN	write *LVdigit*3
		and the subgoal is to do the digits after *LVdigit*1 and *LVdigit*2
P7:	IF	the subgoal is to put out the digits after *LVdigit*1 and *LVdigit*2
		and the *LVdigit*1 is followed by a *LVdigit*3
		and the *LVdigit*2 is followed by a *LVdigit*4
	THEN	the subgoal is to add *LVdigit*3 and *LVdigit*4
P8:	IF	the subgoal is to add the digits after *LVdigit*1 and *LVdigit*2
		and the goal is to add *LVnumber*1 and *LVnumber*2
		and *LVnumber*1 ends with the *LVdigit*1
		and *LVnumber*2 ends with the *LVdigit*2
	THEN	the goal is satisfied

will apply instead of the production with fewer conditions (the more general one). Productions P4 and P6 do not apply because there is no carry into the first column. One might wonder why P1 or P2 does not apply again since their conditions were satisfied once by data-base elements that have not been changed. The current version of the ACT production system does not allow production conditions to match twice to exactly the same data-base propositions. This constraint serves to avoid unwanted repetitions of the same productions and thus some of the danger of infinite loops.

Production 7 (P7) applies next, adding "The subgoal is to add 3 and 1" to the data base so that the next column can be added. Production 2 next applies, finds the sum, and adds "The subgoal is to put out 4" to the data base. Production 4 adds the carry to *LVsum* and writes out the second digit of the answer, 5. Production 8 then applies, noting that the problem is finished.

This example illustrates a number of important features of the ACT production system.

1. Individual productions act on the information in long-term memory. They communicate with one another by entering information into memory.
2. Productions tend to apply in sequences, where one production applies after another has entered some element into the data base. Thus the action of one production can help evoke other productions.
3. The condition of a production specifies an abstract pattern of propositions in the data base. The more propositions that a condition requires in its pattern, the more difficult it is to satisfy the condition. Similarly, the more a condition relies on constants instead of variables to describe its pattern, the more difficult it is to satisfy that condition.

II. Learning in ACT

ACT can learn both by adding propositions to its data base and by adding productions. It can also learn by modifying strengths of propositions and productions. We will concentrate here on the learning that involves productions. Production learning tends to involve the more significant events of cognitive restructuring. It is also through production learning that ACT accounts for schema abstraction.

Productions can be added to the data base in one of two ways. They can be added by deliberate designation, as in the encoding of instructions, or they can be encoded by spontaneous restructuring of productions in response to experience. We will discuss two varieties of spontaneous restructuring: generalization and discrimination. There is another spontaneous process, strengthening, which adjusts strengths of productions in response to their record of success. Our discussion of learning will be divided into three subsections—one to describe deliberate designation, another to describe generalization and discrimination, and a third to describe the mechanisms of strength adjustment.

A. Designation

Productions can designate the creation of other productions in their action just as they can designate the creation of a propositional structure. We will illustrate the basic idea with an example. Consider how ACT might assimilate the following rules defining various types of expressions in the programming language LISP (adapted from Weissman, 1967, Chap. 2):

1. If an expression is a number it is an atom.
2. If an expression is a literal (a string of characters) it is an atom.
3. If an expression is an atom it is a *S*-expression.
4. If an expression is a dotted pair, it is an *S*-expression.
5. If an expression begins with a left parenthesis, followed by an *S*-expression, followed by a dot, followed by an *S*-expression, followed by a right parenthesis, it is a dotted pair.

After receiving this instruction ACT will have the sentences expressing these rules represented in its data base. However, this representation, by itself, does not allow it to perform any of the cognitive operations that would normally be thought of as demonstrating an "understanding" of these rules. In order to obtain such an understanding, a means of integrating these rules into ACT's procedural knowledge is required. Since these rules have the form of conditionals (antecedent implies consequent), they can be translated in a fairly straightforward manner into the condition–action format of productions. Table II illustrates four ACT productions for performing such a translation.[3] Production 9 (P9) handles the antecedents of the first four conditionals. For example, P9 matches the segment "If an expression is a number . . ." of rule 1 by binding *LVword* to the word "number" and *LVconcept*1 to the concept @NUMBER that ACT considers underlies that word. Its action is to save the proposition "An object is a @NUMBER" for the condition of a new production.

[3]These productions and some others in this paper embody some clearly oversimplified notions about language comprehension; a more adequate treatment would only distract attention from the learning processes which are the matters of present interest, however. For a discussion of language processing within the ACT framework see Anderson, Kline, and Lewis (1977). (One complication necessary to any complete analysis of language comprehension is, nevertheless, being observed in some of the examples in this paper—the distinction between words and the concepts underlying them.)

TABLE II

A SET OF PRODUCTIONS FOR ENCODING RULES ABOUT LISP EXPRESSIONS

P9:	IF	there is a sentence beginning: "IF an expression is a *LVword* . . ." and *LVconcept* is the concept for *LVword*
	THEN	save "an object is a *LVconcept*" for a new condition
P10:	IF	the sentence ends: ". . . it is a *LVword*" and *LVconcept* is the concept for *LVword* and *LVcondition* is the saved condition
	THEN	BUILD IF *LVcondition* THEN it is a *LVconcept*
P11:	IF	there is a sentence beginning: "IF an expression begins with a *LVword* . . ." and *LVconcept* is the concept for *LVword*
	THEN	save "IF an object begins with an *LVconcept* . . ." for a new condition and *LVconcept* is the last concept
P12:	IF	the sentence continues: ". . . followed by a *LVword*" and *LVconcept* is the last concept and *LVconcept*1 is the concept for *LVword*
	THEN	add the *LVconcept*1 is before a *LVconcept*" to the new condition and *LVconcept*1 is the last concept

Production 10 (P10) is responsible for actually building the productions encoding these rules. It obtains the actions of these new productions from its own processing of the consequent parts of the rules, while the conditions of these new productions have already been identified, so P10 only needs to retrieve them. For example, in the case of rule 1, P10 applies after P9, matching the remainder of the sentence ". . . it is an atom." The local variables *LVword* and *LVconcept* receive values of "atom" and @ATOM, respectively, in the process of matching. The action of P10 builds the production:

```
P13:      IF  an object is a @NUMBER
        THEN  it is an @ATOM
```

Production 13 is the mechanism by which ACT can actually make the inferences authorized by rule 1.

Productions 11 (P11) and 12 (P12) are responsible for processing such complex conditionals as rule 5. Production 11 processes the first "begins" phrase and P12 each subsequent "followed by" phrase. After the antecedent of the conditional has been entirely processed, production P10 will apply to the process of consequent and the designate a production. If the case of rule 5 this production would be:

P14: IF an object begins with @LEFT-PARENTHESIS
and the @LEFT-PARENTHESIS is before a @*S* EXPRESSION

and the @*S*-EXPRESSION is before a @DOT
and the @DOT is before a @*S*-EXPRESSION
and the @*S* EXPRESSION is before a @RIGHT-PARENTHESIS
THEN it is a @DOTTED-PAIR

This designation process serves in any learning situation as the initial means of introducing productions into the system. Once productions are introduced, the generalization and discrimination processes can operate to create new productions. The designating productions in Table II are quite sophisticated. However, one can also propose much more primitive designating productions. For instance, it would not be unreasonable to propose that a child has the following production which encodes a simple principle of reinforcement:

P15: IF *LVevent* occurs just before ACT performs *LVaction*
and *LVaction* is followed by reinforcement

THEN BUILD IF *LVevent*
THEN *LVaction*

B. Generalization and Discrimination

It is the ability to perform successfully in novel situations that is the hallmark of human cognition. For example, *productivity* has often been identified as the most important feature of natural languages, where this term refers to the speaker's ability to generate and comprehend utterances never before encountered. Traditional learning theories are generally considered inadequate to account for this productivity and ACT's generalization abilities must eventually be evaluated against this same standard.

1. *Generalization*

While it is possible for ACT to designate new productions to apply in situations where existing ones do not, this kind of generalization requires having designating productions that correctly anticipate future needs. It is plausible that ACT could have such designating productions to guide its generalizations in areas in which it possesses some expertise. However, there are many situations where it would be unreasonable to assume such expertise. For this reason, ACT has the ability to create new productions automatically that are generalizations of its existing productions. This ability, while less powerful than the ability to designate generalizations, is applicable even in cases where ACT has no reliable expectations about the characteristics of the material it must learn.

We will use an example from the schema abstraction literature to illustrate ACT's automatic generalization mechanism. Figure 1 illustrates

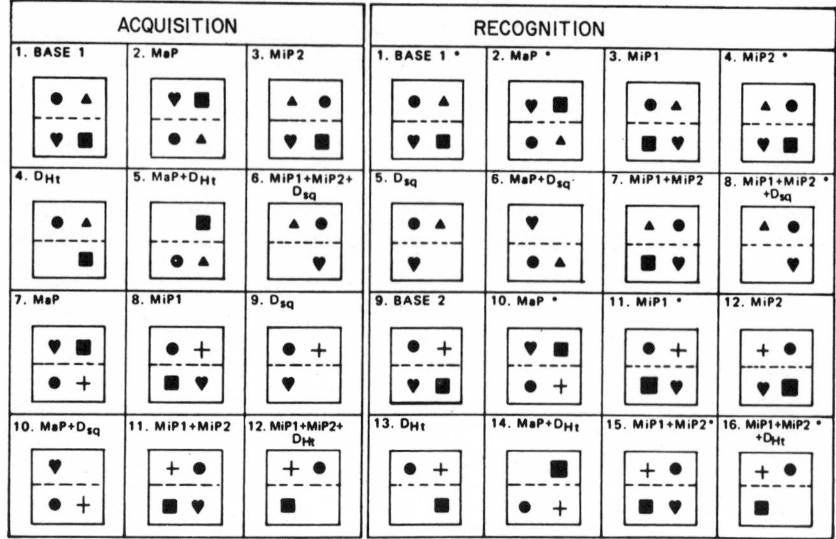

Fig. 1. The material used in Franks and Bransford (1971). Copyright 1971 American Psychological Association. Reprinted by permission.

the stimuli from experiments 3 and 4 of Franks and Bransford (1971). The 12 figures on the left-hand side of the figure were presented to subjects for study. We will assume that subjects designate productions to recognize each stimulus. So for the first stimulus item subjects would designate the following production:

P16: IF a *triangle* is to the right of a *circle*
and a *square* is to the right of a *heart*
and the first pair is *above* the second pair
THEN this is an instance of the study material

For the third stimulus the following production would be designated:

P17: IF a *circle* is to the right of a *triangle*
and a *square* is to the right of a *heart*
and the first pair is *above* the second pair
THEN this is an instance of the study material

From these two productions a generalization can be formed that captures what these two productions have in common. This involves deleting terms on which the two productions differ and replacing these terms by local variables. Thus, we have the following generalization:[4]

[4]As discussed elsewhere (Anderson, Kline, & Beasley, 1979), there can be many different maximal common generalizations. In this case there is another maximal common generalization besides P18. This generalization preserves the information that there is a *triangle* and a *heart* in both stimuli but consequently looses information about the position of the shapes. This generalization could be rendered in our approximate syntax as:

P18: IF a *LVshape*1 is to the right of a *LVshape*2
and a *square* is to the right of a *heart*
and the first pair is *above* the second pair
THEN this is an instance of the study material

This generalization can be thought of as an attempt on ACT's part to arrive at a more general characterization of the study material. Note that ACT's generalization mechanism needs only two examples to propose a generalization.[5] This generalization does not replace the original two; instead, it coexists with them as an alternate means of characterizing the stimulus set. Which production will actually produce the response depends on the strength mechanism that is described in Section II, C.

Restrictions are needed on how many elements can be deleted in making a generalization. Consider ACT's representation for the sixth stimulus from the Franks and Bransford set:

P19: IF a *circle* is to the right of a *triangle*
and a *heart* is to the right of a *blank*
and the first pair is *above* the second pair
THEN this is an instance of the stimulus material

If we allowed this stimulus to be generalized with stimulus 1 (P16) we would get the following generalization:

P20: IF a *LVshape*1 is to the right of a *LVshape*2
and a *LVshape*3 is to the right of a *LVshape*4
and the first pair is *above* the second pair
THEN this is an instance of the stimulus material

This production will accept any array of geometric objects as an instance of the study material. While it is conceivable that any possible array may be an experimental stimulus, this seems too strong a generalization to make just on the basis of these two examples. Therefore, a limit is placed on the proportion of constants that can be replaced by variables. In the current system no more than half of the constants in the production with least constants can be replaced by variables in a generalization. The terms that ACT considers constants are italicized

---

IF there is a *triangle*
and there is a *heart*
and a *square* is to the right of a *heart*
and the second pair is below another pair
THEN this is an instance of the study material

In our simulations we will be working with the first generalization.

[5]This feature of generalization (two instances to make a generalization) fits well with the following observation about inductions which has been attributed to George Miller (by E. Smith, personal communication): "Suppose one person comes into your office and says, 'I cannot make our appointment. I am going to Brazil.' A second person comes into your office and says, 'Could you teach my class for me, I am going to Brazil.' You immediately ask the question, 'Why is everyone going to Brazil?'

in P16, P17, and P19. There are five constants in each of these productions. Production 18 is an acceptable generalization from P16 and P17 because it only involves replacement of two of the constants. Production 20 is not an acceptable generalization from P16 and P19 because it involves replacement of four of the five constants.

Even with this restriction on the proportion of constants deleted it is likely that unacceptably many generalizations will be formed. A realistic simulation of an adult human's entire procedural knowledge would require hundreds of thousands of ACT productions. Under these circumstances it would be disastrous to attempt to generalize all possible pairs of productions. ACT only attempts to form generalizations when a new production has been designated. Although no potential generalizations would be missed if a generalization were attempted for each possible pairing of this newly designed production with existing productions, an enormous computational cost would be required even under this scheme. For this reason generalizations are attempted only for pairings of newly designated productions with the productions on the APPLYLIST. Since a production is on the APPLYLIST only if the constants it references are active and it has met a strength criterion (see p. 279), this implies that attempts to generalize will be restricted to productions that are relevant to the current context and that have enough strength to indicate a history of past success.

2. *Discrimination*

Even with these restrictions placed on it, ACT's generalization mechanisms will produce productions that are overgeneralizations of the desired production. However, given our goal of a psychologically realistic simulation, such overgeneralizations on ACT's part are actually desirable since it can be shown that people make similar overgeneralizations. For example, children learning language (and, it appears, adults learning a second language, see Bailey, Madden, & Krashen, 1974) overgeneralize morphemic rules. Thus, a child will generate "mans," "gived," etc. ACT will do the same. It is also possible that productions will be directly designated in overgeneral form. Thus, for instance, ACT might generate the following rule for predicting rice growing:

P21: IF the climate of *LVplace* is warm
and there is ample rainfall in *LVplace*
THEN *LVplace* can grow rice

This rule is over general in that it fails to specify that the terrain be flat.

To correct overgeneralizations ACT must create more discriminative productions. A production can be made more discriminative either by adding clauses to the condition or by replacing variables by constants.

So production 22 (P22) serves as a discrimination of P21 by the addition of a clause:

P22: IF the climate of *LVplace* is warm
and there is ample rainfall in *LVplace*
and the terrain is flat in *LVplace*
THEN *LVplace* can grow rice

Such a discriminative production does not replace P21 but rather coexists with it. Because of the specificity principle described earlier (pp. 280–282), P22 will apply rather than P21 if both are selected for application.

It is possible for ACT to directly designate such productions to correct overgeneral ones. However, just as in the case of designated generalizations, the existence of the required designating productions is plausible only for domains in which ACT already possesses some expertise. In such domains, ACT could possess the knowledge required to debug its own errors intelligently, but in the majority of cases it will rely on its automatic discrimination mechanism.

ACT's automatic discrimination mechanism requires that it have examples of both correct and incorrect application of a production. This raises the issue of how ACT can get feedback on the operation of its productions. Productions place new propositions into the data base and emit observable responses; either of these actions can be declared incorrect by a human observer or by ACT itself. In the absence of such a declaration an action is considered correct. That is, the only distinction made by the discrimination mechanism is between error feedback and its absence. Since the way in which ACT declares that the action of a production is incorrect is to apply another production that makes such a declaration as part of its own action, arbitrarily complex ACT computations can be performed to decide the correctness of any particular action.

The discrimination mechanism will only attempt to discriminate a production when it has both a correct and an incorrect application of that production to compare. Basically, this algorithm remembers and compares the variable bindings in the correct and incorrect applications. By finding a variable that has had different bindings in these two applications, it is possible to place restrictions on that variable that would prevent the match that has led to the unsuccessful application while still permitting the match that has led to the successful application. Although we have explored other ways of restricting this variable, in the simulations of schema abstraction that are discussed in Section III a new production was formed from the old production simply by replacing the variable by the constant it was bound to during the successful application.

As an example of a discrimination process, we will consider a categorization experiment from Medin and Schaffer (1978). We will focus on two instances they presented from category A. One was two large red triangles and the other was two large blue circles. From these two examples, ACT would designate the following categorization productions:

P23: IF a stimulus has two large red triangles
THEN it is in category A

P24: IF a stimulus has two large blue circles
THEN it is in category A

From these two ACT would form the following generalization:

P25: IF a stimulus has two large *LVcolor LVshapes*
THEN it is in category A

However, this turned out to be an overgeneralization. To be in category A the stimulus had to be either red or a circle or both. Thus, the counterexample was presented of two large blue triangles which was a stimulus in category B. Generalization P25 misapplied in this circumstance. By noting what distinguished the circumstances of correct application of generalization P25 from the circumstances of incorrect application, both of the following productions would eventually be formed by the discriminative mechanism. These productions will always produce correct classifications.

P26: IF a stimulus has two large red *LVshapes*
THEN it is in category A

P27: IF a stimulus has two large *LVcolor* circles
THEN it is in category A

These productions were formed from P25 by replacing one of its variables by the binding that variable had during a successful application (i.e., an application to a stimulus that was actually from category A). As an aside, these two productions illustrate how ACT can encode disjunctive concepts by the use of multiple productions.

C. Production Strength

When a new production is created by the designation process there is no assurance that its condition is really the best characterization of the circumstances in which its action is appropriate. For this reason, generalization and discrimination processes exist to give ACT the opportunity to evaluate alternative conditions for this action. It is the responsibility of ACT's strength mechanisms to perform the evaluation of these competing productions.

Through experience with the ACT system we have created a set of parameters that appear to yield humanlike performance. The first time a production is created (by designation, generalization, or discrimination) it is given a strength of .1. Should that production be recreated, its strength is incremented by .05. Furthermore, a production has its strength incremented by .025 every time it applies or a production consistent with it applies. (One production is considered consistent with another if its condition is more general and its action is identical.) Finally, whenever a production receives error feedback its strength is reduced by a factor of ¼ and the same happens to the strength of all productions consistent with it. Since a multiplicative adjustment produces a greater change in strength than an additive adjustment, "punishment" of an error is more effective than strengthening of a correct response.

Note that productions are created out of what might be considered a "reinforcing" event. That is, the designation of a production occurs because for some reason ACT considers this to be a "good" rule. Generalization occurs in response to a designation event—that is, generalizations are found by comparing designated productions with productions on the APPLYLIST. Since designation and generalization can lead to an increase in strength and negative feedback leads to a decrease in strength, the ACT strength mechanism can be seen to have a principle of reinforcement built into it. There is also a principle of exercise—a production gains strength just by applying. This principle is motivated by the observation that behaviors become more reliably evoked and rapidly executed by sheer exercise.

Both decrements and increments in strength are inherited by more general productions. This means that if a more general production is created it can rapidly gain strength even if it does not apply or is not recreated.

It is important to understand how production strength affects performance and how it interacts with specificity. Recall that a production's strength determines the probability that it will apply. If s is the strength of a production and S the total strength of all productions selected, the probability of that production being chosen on a cycle for application is $1 - e^{-bs/S}$, where b is a parameter currently set at 15. Of course, if a production is not applied one cycle and the circumstances do not change, it can apply on a later cycle. Thus, strength affects both the latency and reliability of production application.

While selection rules based on strength can make some of the required choices among competing productions, it is clear that strength cannot be the sole criterion. For example, people reliably generate irregular plurals (e.g., "men") under circumstances in which the "add s" rule for regular plurals is presumably also applicable. This reliable performance is obtained despite the fact that the productions responsible for generating regular plurals are applied much more frequently than those for irregulars and therefore should be much stronger. ACT's solution to the problem of exceptions to strong general rules relies on the specificity-ordering principle to decide which productions on the APPLYLIST it should actually execute. This principle accounts for the execution of a production generating an irregular plural since its condition presumably contains all of the requirements for generating the regular plural and must, in addition, make reference to the specific noun to be pluralized.

The precendence of exceptions over much stronger general rules does not imply that exceptions always apply, however. In order to benefit from the specificity-ordering principle, exceptions must first have achieved the amount of strength necessary to be placed on the APPLYLIST. Furthermore, because the amount of strength necessary depends on the strengths of the other productions that could apply, the stronger a general rule is, the more strength its exceptions need in order to apply reliably. This property of the ACT model is consistent with the fact that words with irregular inflections tend to have high frequencies of ocurrence.

Production strength is an important way in which ACT differs from other computer-based learning systems (e.g., Anderson, 1977; F. Hayes-Roth & McDermott, 1976; Sussman, 1975; Vere, 1977; Waterman, 1974; Winston, 1970). The learning within all these systems has an all-or-none character that ACT would share if creating new productions were its only learning mechanism. Our hope is that strength mechanisms modulate the all-or-none character of production creation in a way that enables ACT to cope with the kind of world that people have to cope with—a world where data are not perfectly reliable and contingencies change in such a way that even while one is being cautious occasional errors will still be made.

D. Review of Critical Assumptions

It is worthwhile, as a review, to state what the critical assumptions are which underlie the ACT learning model.

1. Productions can be designated by other productions.
2. When a production is designated, an attempt will be made to generalize it with all the productions on the APPLYLIST.
3. Generalization occurs by replacing constants on which two productions differ by variables.
4. A generalization of two productions will be formed if they have the same action and if no more than half of the constants in the production with the least constants are replaced by variables in forming the generalization.
5. If a production has a record of both a correct and incorrect application, a discrimination will be formed.
6. A discrimination is formed by filling in one variable of the production with the value that variable had during its correct application but did not have during its incorrect application.

7. Upon creation productions are given strength of .1.
8. Upon an attempt to recreate a production its strength is increased by .05.
9. Every time a production is applied, its strenght is increased by .025.
10. When any of events 7, 8, or 9 occurs, a strength increment of .025 is inherited by all consistent productions.
11. If a production is found to misapply, its strength is decreased by ¼ as is the strength of all consistent productions.
12. If S is the total strength of all productions selected and s is the strength of a particular selected production, the probability of its being applied if it matches is $1 - e - 15s/S$
13. If two productions on the APPLYLIST both match the data and one is more specific, the more specific production will apply.

III. Applications to Schema Abstraction

There is a growing literature concerned with the process by which subjects form concepts by detecting regularities among stimuli (e.g., Franks & Bransford, 1971; B. Hayes-Roth & Hayes-Roth, 1977; Neumann, 1974; Posner & Keele, 1970; Reed, 1972; Reitman & Bower, 1973; Rosch, & Mervis, 1975). This literature is often referred to as studying prototype formation, but for various reasons we prefer to refer to it as studying schema abstraction.

There are a number of features of this research area that distinguish it from the related research area that is often called concept formation: In the concept formation literature the concept that is to be discovered is usually quite simple (e.g., "red and a triangle") and subjects are often able to verbalize the hypotheses they are considering at any point. In contrast, the concepts used in the schema abstraction literature may be quite complex. For example, these concepts might be defined in terms of a linear discriminant function (e.g., Reed, 1972) or solely by a listing of the exemplars (e.g., Medin & Schaffer, 1978). Subjects will often emerge from such experiments without being able to verbalize the criteria they are using to correctly classify instances. Their instructions may even suggest that they should avoid formulating explicit hypotheses and should simply study the instances one by one. Within the ACT framework there is a corresponding distinction between forming a concept by the action of a general set of productions for hypothesis testing versus forming a concept by the action of the automatic learning mechanisms of generalization, discrimination, and strengthening.

Our intention in the rest of this paper is to show that ACT's automatic learning mechanisms have a straightforward application to schema abstraction. In outline, this application is as follows: For each instance presented, ACT designates a production that recognizes and/or categorizes that instance alone. Generalizations occur through the comparison of pairs of these productions. If feedback about the correctness of these generalizations is provided, then the discrimination process can be evoked. Our working definition of a concept will be this set of designations, generalizations, and discriminations. It turns out that such sets of productions nicely capture the family resemblance structure that has been claimed for natural categories (e.g., Rosch & Mervis, 1975). It also turns out that ACT simulations can account for the results of various experiments in the literature on schema abstraction.

A. Franks and Bransford: Illustration of Basic Phenomena

We have already introduced (Fig. 1) the material used by Franks and Bransford in one of their experiments on schema abstraction. Subjects studied the 12 pictures on the left of Fig. 1 twice and then were transferred to a recognition phase in which they had to give recognition ratings of the 16 figures on the right of Fig. 1, plus six other figures, called noncases, which violated the rules under which the cases were generated. The 16 test cases in Fig. 1 were generated by applying zero, one, two, or three transformations to the base figures. Half of these 16 were actually studied and half were not. While Franks and Bransford do not report subjects' performance for each stimulus, they do report that confidence ratings for recognition generally decreased with the number of transformations and was lowest for the noncases.

We attempted to simulate the Franks and Bransford experiment by having ACT go through propositional encodings of the items in the study set twice, designating a recognition production for each stimulus it saw.[6] Then at test ACT was again presented with propositional encodings of the stimuli and the production which applied (if any) was noted. Sufficient generalization had occurred so that most of the stimuli were recognized by at least one of the productions.

A critical question was how to map the production selected onto a confidence rating that the response chosen was correct. We assumed that ACT's confidence would be a function of the number of constants in the condition of the selected production (and therefore an inverse function of the number of variables). This procedure for assigning confidence will be used throughout this paper. This is a reasonable procedure for assigning confidence, since the more constants in the recognizing production the closer it is to an encoding of an actual test item.

[6]The simulations were not performed with the general purpose ACT simulation program, but with a special purpose simulation which runs about 10 times faster. This special simulation does not have all the general computational features of ACT. Rather, it is especially designed to allow us to follow only the interaction of strengthening, discrimination, and generalization.

In the extreme, if the stimulus is recognized by a production with no variables the subject can be sure that the item has been studied since a production with no variables is an encoding of a study item.

Note that this procedure for assigning confidence implicitly weights the strength of productions as well as their number of constants. Since strength of productions determines whether a production is selected, the stronger the productions that can classify an instance, the more of these productions that will be selected and, thus, the more likely it is that a production with many constants will be selected. This increased probability of selecting a production with many constants translates quite directly into an increase in the probability of a high confidence rating because of ACT's preference for applying the most specific productions that have been selected. We have given some thought to the possibility that strength should have more than an implicit role in assigning confidence. That is, confidence could have been assumed to a joint function of number of constants in a production that applies and the strength of that production. Considering a production's strength in assigning confidence could be justified by the fact that strength reflects the production's past success in classifying instances and therefore it should predict how successful the current application will be. We have not used this more complex procedure for assigning confidence mainly because we have been able to account for all the results using just the number of constants.

Consider again production 16 (on page 286) which encodes the first item in the stimulus set:

P16: IF a *triangle* is to the right of a *circle*
and a *square* is to the right of a *heart*
and the first pair is *above* the second pair
THEN this is an instance of the study material

The five constants that can be replaced by variables are italicized. If this production applied, ACT would assign a confidence rating of 5 to its recognition of that stimulus. If all five constants were replaced by variables, we would have a production that would recognize anything and if this applied we would assign a confidence of 0. For shorthand, we will denote the production above as ATCSH where each letter is the first letter of one of the constants (i.e., *above, triangle, circle, square, heart*). Variables will be denoted by hyphens. Therefore, production P18 (on p. 287) would be denoted A--SH.

To obtain predictions for this experiment we ran 10 ACT simulations. Each simulation involved giving ACT a study phase and then following this with five passes through the test material. Since the process of production selection is probabilistic, ACT's rating varied from one test to another. Altogether we obtained 50 ratings for each test stimulus and the data we report are based on averages of these 50 ratings. The practice of having five test trials for each study represents a departure from the Franks and Bransford experiment. However, since the study phase was relatively expensive in computational terms, it made sense to get as many data as possible from each study phase that was stimulated.

The numbers that were obtained from these simulations depend on the rather arbitrary values for the strengthening parameters that were detailed earlier (p. 292).[7] It is currently impractical and probably premature to perform a search of the parameter space to determine the best fitting parameters. For this reason, we have used these arbitrary values for all of the simulations that are reported here and have had to be content to predict the relative ordering of conditions rather than their exact values.

The test stimuli identified as base or zero transformation (1.9 on the right side of Fig. 1) were given a mean rating of 1.66 (i.e., mean number of constants in matching productions); the test stimuli (2–5, 10–13) identified as one transformation away from the base were rated 1.24; the stimuli (6, 7, 14, 15) identified as two steps away were rated 1.11; the stimuli (8, 16) three steps away were value 1.13; and the noncases were rated .65. This corresponds to Franks and Bransford's report of an overall correlation between closeness to base and rating. (Franks and Bransford do not report the actual ratings.)

Neumann (1974) performed a replication of Franks and Bransford and he did report mean ratings for each of the five categories of test stimuli. Subjects assigned ratings of +1 to +5 to the stimuli that they thought they recognized, and assigned ratings of −1 to −5 to stimuli they did not recognize. Their ratings averaged 2.79 for base stimuli, 2.18 for one-transformation stimuli, .49 for two-transformation stimuli, .90 for three-transformation stimuli, and −.26 for noncase stimuli. While the ordering of ACT's scores corresponds perfectly to the ordering of Neumann's mean ratings, a comparison of the exact values is not meaningful because the scales are different. Some monotonic transformation is required to convert the ACT scores which are based on the number of constants in the recognizing production into the −5 to +5 confidence scale used by Neumann's subjects. If the transformation from ACT match score to confidence were linear, there should be a strong correlation between the two measures. In fact, the

[7]One additional parameter besides those discussed earlier is required. If ACT had all of the productions that would be needed to account for a subject's total procedural knowledge, some of these, although irrelevant to the schema abstraction task, would be selected anyway and their strengths would contribute to S in assumption to 12 (p. 293). For all of the simulations reported in this paper, the contribution of such irrelevant productions to S was set to 20.

correlation is .927, suggesting such a linear transformation may not be that far from the truth.

This experiment does not provide a particularly telling test of the ACT learning model, but it is a good introduction in that it serves to illustrate that ACT can account for one of the basic phenomena of schema abstraction—namely, that confidence falls off with distance from the stimuli that are the central tendency of the category. Subsequent experiments will deal with the issue of whether the details of ACT's abstraction process correspond to the details of human abstraction.

To help understand how ACT accounts for preference for central stimuli, such as 1 or 9, consider Fig. 2, which compares the specificity network around test stimulus 1 during one of the 10 simulations (part a) with the specificity network around test stimulus 8 (part b). The links in this network go down from general productions to their more specific variants. In our notation, test stimulus 1 is ACTHS (i.e., above, circle left of triangle, heart left of square) and test stimulus 8 is ATCBH (B stands for blank). Both were presented twice during study and so have strength .15. However, ACTHS is more similar to other stimuli and so has entered into more generalizations. Hence, there is a denser network above ACTHS. (Actually, the network around ACTHS is even denser than Fig. 2 shows, but we have eliminated some of the generalizations to make the figure easier to read.) ATCBH differs from all other stimuli on at least two dimensions. Consequently, there are no one-variable productions above ATCBH. However, there are two one-variable productions (ACT-S and -CTHS) above ACTHS with a combined strength of .40. ACTBH does have two two-variable productions above it (A-C-H and ATC- -), but their combined strength of .325 is still much less than the combined strength of 1.475 possessed by the four two-variable productions above ACTHS (A- -HS, -CT-S, -C-HS, AC-H-; only three of these are illustrated). A similar picture is obtained when we look at the three- and four-variable generalizations: There are two three-variable productions above ATCBH (A- - -H and A-C- -) with strength 1.025; but there are six three-variable productions above ACTHS (A- - -S, - - -HS, -C- -S, -C-H-, AC- - -, A- -H-; only four of these are illustrated) with total strength of 3.4. Finally, ATCBH was involved in no four-variable generalizations, while ACTHS is involved in three (- - - -S, -C- - -, - - -H-) with total strength of 3.25. Table III, part (a), summarizes these comparisons.

Under some approximating assumptions, it is possible to derive the expected match values from these strengths. Assume that if an n-variable production is selected which matches the stimulus, it will apply in preference to all $(n + 1)$-variable productions. This assumption is an approximate realization of ACT's specificity ordering. Let $Q_{i,s}$ be the prob-

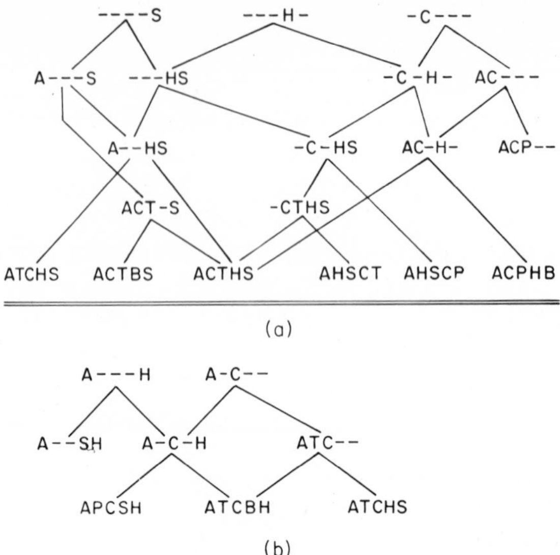

Fig. 2. (a) The specificity network around stimulus 1 (ACTHS). (b) The specificity network around stimulus 8 (ATCHS).

TABLE III

Analysis of the Differences between the Stimuli ACTHS and ATSBH

	ACTHS	ATSBH
a. Strengths of classifying productions with different numbers of variables		
0 variables	.150	.150
1 variable	.400	—
2 variables	1.475	.325
3 variables	3.400	1.025
4 variables	3.250	—
	ACTHS	ATCBH
b. Probabilities of selecting productions with different numbers of variables		
Q_0	.062	.062
Q_1	.158	—
Q_2	.469	.130
Q_3	.767	.356
Q_4	.752	—
	ACTHS	ATCBH
c. Probabilities of applying productions with different numbers of variables		
P_0	.062	.062
P_1	.148	—
P_2	.371	.122
P_3	.321	.290
P_4	.073	—

ability of at least one i-variable production being selected for stimulus S. The probability $P_{i,s}$ that one of the i-variable productions will be the one that applies to classify stimulus S is:

$$P_{i,s} = Q_{i,s}\,[1 - \sum_{i=0}^{i-1} P_{i,s}]. \tag{1}$$

That is, the probability that an i-variable production will be the one to apply is the probability that an i-variable production is selected times the probability that no more discriminative production is also selected. The expected rating for stimulus S is:

$$R_s = \sum_{i=0}^{4} (5 - i)P_{i,s}. \tag{2}$$

By the end of this experiment, the total strength of all productions, relevant and irrelevant, was about 35. Therefore, according to assumption 12 in Section II,D, if $t_{i,s}$ is the strength of all of the productions matching S that have i variables, then the probability of at least one being selected is:

$$Q_{i,s} = 1 - e^{-15t_{i,s}/35.} \tag{3}$$

From Eq. (3) we can derive the probabilities of selecting productions with various numbers of variables and these are given in part (b) of Table III.

From these values we can calculate by Eq. (1) the probabilities of applying an i-variable production, $P_{i,s}$, subject to the specificity restriction. These probabilities are given in part (c) of Table III. Substituting these values into Eq. (2) yields the expected confidence ratings:

$$R_{\text{ACTHS}} = 2.730$$
$$R_{\text{ATSBH}} = 1.256$$

In actual fact, the rating difference between zero-transformation stimuli, such as ACTHS, and four-transformation stimuli, such as ATSBH, is considerably less than this expected difference. This can be shown to be due to the following fact: If two productions are selected that match a stimulus and neither has a condition that is a subset of the other, the one to apply is determined probabilistically by relative strength and not by the number of nonvariable condition elements. Thus, unlike our analysis, it is not always the production with the least number of variables that applies. For instance, if - - -H- and ACT-S are both selected, the more variabilized - - -H- may apply because neither production is above the other in the specificity network. Nonetheless, the above analysis does illustrate in approximate terms why zero-transformation stimuli get better ratings than the noncentral stimuli.

B. Hayes-Roth and Hayes-Roth: Variation of Instance Frequency

One of the interesting features of the ACT simulation of the Franks and Bransford experiment is that the ratings of the three-transformation stimuli are predicted to have slightly higher ratings than the two-transformation stimuli; this prediction has been confined in the data of Neumann. ACT makes this prediction because both of the three-transformation stimuli have been presented for study, while only one of the four two-transformation stimuli has been studied. It is weak memory for the instances that have been studied which gives the three-transformation stimuli this slight advantage. The Franks and Bransford paradigm has not been systematically studied for instance memory, but the ACT simulation predicts a weak advantage for studied stimuli over comparable nonstudied stimuli.

B. Hayes-Roth and Hayes-Roth (1977) report a study, one function of which was to obtain data relevant to the issue of memory for instances. They presented subjects with three-attribute descriptions of people. One attribute was age and could have values 30, 40, 50, or 60. Another was education and could have values junior high, high school, trade school, or college. The third was marital status, which could have values single, married, divorced, or widowed. Subjects were also given proper name and hobby but these dimensions were not relevant. Thus, a subject might hear the description "John Doe, 30 years old, junior high education, single, plays chess." Subjects' task was to learn to classify these individuals as members of club 1, members of club 2, or members of neither club.

The four values of each dimension will be represented symbolically by the numbers 1–4. The assignment of the symbolic values 1–4 to the values of each dimension was randomized for each subject. In our discussion we will refer to stimuli by these numbers. Thus "111" might refer to "40 years, high school, single." The rules determining assignment of individuals to clubs were as follows:

1. If one of values was a 4, the individual belonged to neither club.
2. If there were more 1s than 2s and no 4s the individual was assigned to club 1.
3. If there were more 2s than 1s and no 4s the individual was assigned to club 2.
4. If there were as many 1s as 2s the individual was assigned with a 50% probability to club 1 and with 50% probability to club 2.

Thus, 1s were diagnostic of club 1, 2s were diagnostic of club 2, 3s were "don't cares," and 4s disqualified club membership. A prototypical member of club 1 would be 111 and a prototypical member of club 2 would be 222. These prototypes were never presented.

We will assume that for each individual encountered, subjects designated a production mapping that individual's features into a prediction about club membership. So, for instance, a subject might form the following production:

IF a person is 40 years old
and he has gone to high school
and he is single
THEN he is a member of club 1

Or, more symbolically, we will represent this production as 111 → 1.

Hayes-Roth and Hayes-Roth varied the frequency with which various exemplars were studied and Table IV shows these frequencies. A study trial consisted of first presenting the subject with an exemplar, asking him to classify it, and then providing feedback as to the correctness of the classification. In the case of equivocal exemplars, such as 132, the subject was given feedback half the time specifying club 1 and half the time specifying club 2. The feedback aspect to this experiment is a significant difference from the Franks and Bransford experiment. Negative feedback will lead to the evocation of ACT's discrimination mechanism, which was silent during the earlier simulation.

Table IV also indicates which items were tested. Subjects were first asked to categorize each of the stimuli and then they were asked to decide whether each of the stimuli had been studied or not. The rec-

TABLE IV

INITIAL CLASSIFICATION EXEMPLARS AND TEST ITEMS[a]

Exemplar	Club	Number of initial classifications	Tested for recognition and final classification
112	1	10	Yes
121	1	10	Yes
211	1	10	Yes
113	1	1	Yes
131	1	1	Yes
311	1	1	Yes
133	1	1	Yes
313	1	1	Yes
331	1	1	Yes
221	2	10	Yes
212	2	10	Yes

(*continued*)

[a]In B. Hayes-Roth and Hayes-Roth (1977). Copyright 1977 Academic Press. Reprinted by permission.

TABLE IV (Continued)

Exemplar	Club	Number of initial classifications	Tested for recognition and final classification
122	2	10	Yes
223	2	1	Yes
232	2	1	Yes
322	2	1	Yes
233	2	1	Yes
323	2	1	Yes
332	2	1	Yes
132	Either	10	Yes
321	Either	10	Yes
213	Either	10	Yes
231	Either	0	Yes
123	Either	0	Yes
312	Either	0	Yes
111	1	0	Yes
222	2	0	Yes
333	Either	0	Yes
444	Neither	0	Yes
411	Neither	1	No
422	Neither	1	No
141	Neither	1	No
242	Neither	1	No
114	Neither	1	No
224	Neither	1	No
441	Neither	1	No
442	Neither	1	No
144	Neither	1	No
244	Neither	1	No
414	Neither	1	No
424	Neither	1	No
134	Neither	1	No
234	Neither	1	No
413	Neither	1	No
423	Neither	1	No
341	Neither	1	No
342	Neither	1	No
124	Neither	1	No
214	Neither	1	No
412	Neither	1	No
421	Neither	1	No
241	Neither	1	No
142	Neither	1	No
143	Neither	1	No
243	Neither	1	No
314	Neither	1	No
324	Neither	1	No
431	Neither	1	No
432	Neither	1	No

ognition judgment was assigned a confidence from 1 to 5, as was the categorization judgment.

Table V gives the mean recognition ratings as well as mean categorization ratings for seven different classes of stimuli. The recognition ratings were averages formed by weighting rejection confidences negatively and acceptance confidences positively. The categorization ratings were averages formed by weighting negatively the confidences ascribed to incorrect category assignments and weighting positively the confidences ascribed to correct category assignments.

The first class in Table V is formed from two prototypes which were never in fact studied. They receive the highest categorization rating and a relatively high recognition rating, indicating that subjects have extracted the central tendency of this set. The second class consists of the nonprototypes that have received 10 study trials each. They have the highest recognition ratings, reflecting their high degree of exposure,

TABLE V

RECOGNITION AND CLASSIFICATION FROM B. HAYES-ROTH AND HAYES-ROTH (1977) COMPARED TO ACT'S MATCH SCORES

	Recognition		Classification	
	Subject's degree of confidence	ACT's degree of match	Subject's degree of confidence	ACT's degree of match
1. Nonpracticed Prototypes (111,222)	1.00	.94	2.61	.94
2. Much practiced Nonprototypes (112,121,211, 221,212,122)	2.53	1.46	2.34	.86
3. Little practiced close-to-prototype (113, 131, 311, 223, 232, 322)	.03	.70	2.27	.70
4. Little practiced far-from-prototype (133, 313, 331, 233, 323, 332)	−2.25	.42	2.01	.41
5. Much practiced equivocal (132, 321, 213)	1.34	1.25	—	—
6. Nonpracticed equivocal (231, 123, 312)	−.93	.46	—	—
7. Nonpracticed anti-prototypes (333, 444)	−2.52	.07	—	—

and the second highest categorization rating. They get higher recognition ratings than the third class, which is closer to (or as close to) the prototype. This reflects some residual instance memory. The third class perhaps can be regarded as closer to the prototype than the second because its members have "don't care" elements rather than an element that directly violates the category's prototype. The third class is clearly closer to the prototype than the fourth, whose members have two "don't care" items. The third and fourth classes have one exposure of each member, but the third class receives a higher rating reflecting the fact it is closer to the prototypes. The fifth class is equivocal between the two categories and probably is further from either prototype than are classes 3 or 4. Still it is given higher recognition ratings than classes 1, 3, or 4, reflecting its greater exposure. However, it does get a lower rating than class 2 despite the fact that members have the same frequency of exposure. This may be due to distance from prototye or the equivocal response assignment in study. Categorization ratings are not meaningful for class 5 nor are they for classes 6 or 7. Class 6 is just as equivocal as class 5 but was never studied so it receives lower recognition ratings. The lowest recognition ratings are reserved for class 7, which contains nonpresented instances composed of all 3s or all 4s.

There are two features to emphasize about these data. First, ratings are influenced by a rather complex mixture of frequency of exposure and closeness to prototype. Second, the rank orderings of the recognition and classification data are not identical. Therefore, these data should provide a challenging test for the ACT simulation program.

Simulation

This experiment was simulated with the same parameter settings as the Franks and Bransford experiment. The one significant difference was that ACT was given feedback about the correctness of its classifications. This meant that productions would not simply increase in strength with every application but would either increase or decrease in strength depending on their success in classification. Providing feedback also meant that it was possible for ACT to compare variable bindings on successful applications in order to produce more discriminative versions of its overgeneral productions. A study session consisted of passing through 132 classify-then-feedback trials presented in random order. After this, the 28 test stimuli were presented in random order five times. This whole procedure was repeated 10 times. The data we report are averaged from the 50 test trials given to each stimulus.

As in the Franks and Bransford experiment, recognition confidence was based on the number of constants in the production that recognized the stimulus. In this experiment that number would vary from 1 to 3.

A value of 0 was assigned if no production was evoked to categorize the stimulus. These mean match scores are reported in Table V. The classification scores were taken by weighting negatively the confidences of incorrect classifications and weighting positively the confidences of correct classifications and ignoring the confidences of classifications to the "neither club" category. Class 2 received a classification rating that was much lower than its recognition rating. This reflects the application of productions assigning the stimuli to the wrong category. Such productions were formed through the generalization process. For example, generalizing 121 → 1 with 321 → 1 would yield the production of -21 → 1 which would misclassify the instance 221.

The general hypothesis is that the ACT scores will be monotonically and perhaps linearly related to the obtained ratings. The monotonic hypothesis is clearly confirmed in Table V in that ACT perfectly predicts the rank ordering of the seven recognition scores and the rank ordering of the four classification scores. The linear hypothesis also fares quite well—a correlation of .968 is obtained for the recognition scores and one of .948 for the classification scores.

Hayes-Roth and Hayes-Roth present a model for their data which is quite similar to the ACT model. (We discuss similarities to other models in Section III,D of this paper.) They derive a set of pairwise comparisons among conditions which their model better predicts than any of a large class of categorization models. ACT's predictions correspond exactly with those of Hayes-Roth and Hayes-Roth on these pairwise conditions. However, the ACT model is more powerful than theirs, predicting the complete ordering of conditions, and offers a possibility of assigning an interval scale to that ordering. They are unable to do this on the basis of their model, but it is something that falls out of a theory which has a computer simulation.

One important aspect of the ACT simulation of this experiment is its prediction of better performance on the class 5 stimuli than on the class 3 stimuli, despite the fact that both types of stimuli have been presented equally frequently. The reason for this is the equivocal nature of the response assignment for class 5 which results in punishment of the productions that classify these stimuli and the consequent weakening of these productions. Most of the ACT predictions for the experiments under discussion rely on the generalization mechanism or discrimination and generalization in concert. This, however, is an instance of a result which depends solely on the discrimination mechanism.

C. Medin and Schaffer: Effects of Interitem Similarity

An interesting series of experiments has been performed by Medin and Schaffer (1978) who show that, under some circumstances, how typical an instance is considered of a category depends not on how close it is to the central tendency of the instances in the category but on how close it is to specific instances in the category. Particularly important is whether there are any category members which are very similar to this instance. Their experiments are also interesting because they report data on the time it takes to learn to make a classification.

They presented subjects with stimuli that took one of two values on four dimensions: color (red or blue), form (circle or triangle), size (large or small), and number (1 or 2). As in the Hayes-Roth and Hayes-Roth experiment these stimuli are best referred to abstractly with the numbers 0 and 1 for the values on each dimension. Values were randomly assigned to numbers for each subject. Thus, for one subject a 1101 might be a single small red circle. Subjects had to learn to classify these as members of a category A or category B. The material was always designed so that 1111 was the central tendency for category A and 0000 was the central tendency for category 2.

1. *Experiment 1*

Table VI illustrates the material for experiment 1. The A training stimuli were designed so that for each dimension there were two training stimuli that had values of 1 on that dimension. The B training stimuli were similarly designed so that two 0 values could be found for each dimension. Thus, the A prototype would be 1111 and the B prototype would be 0000. Subjects were trained in categorizing the material until they had correctly categorized all six twice in a row or until 20 trials through the six items expired. Table VI reports the mean number of errors made on each stimulus in achieving criterion. Then subjects were given transfer trials in which they saw the six old stimuli plus six new ones and had to judge the category of each stimulus. The categorization judgments were made on a three-point scale varying from 1 = guess to 3 = high confidence. Medin and Schaffer transformed these scores to a six-point scale where 1 = high confidence wrong and 6 = high confidence correct. Subjects made categorization judgments shortly after study and after a week's delay. The mean scores, averaged over the immediate delay tests as reported by Medin and Schaffer, are in Table VI. A value of 3.5 reflects chance performance.

new stimuli. They predicted higher performance on the A transfer stimuli than on the B transfer stimuli even though the stimuli were all equally similar to their prototypes. They made this prediction because the A transfer stimuli agree in three positions with two of the study items (0111 with 1111 and 0101; 1101 with 1111 and 0101; 1110 with 1111 and 1010), while the B transfer stimuli agree in three positions

TABLE VI

STIMULI USED IN EXPERIMENT 1 OF MEDIN AND SCHAFFER (1978), NUMBER OF ERRORS ON TRAINING STIMULI, CLASSIFICATION CONFIDENCES, AND ACT SIMULATION

	Errors in original learning		Final categorization	
	Data	ACT	Data	ACT's match
A training stimuli				
1111	3.6	2.1	4.8	2.38
1010	4.7	3.8	4.6	2.28
0101	4.4	3.6	4.8	2.20
B training stimuli				
0000	3.1	3.3	5.2	2.79
1011	4.9	6.6	4.5	.81
0100	3.8	3.3	4.9	2.65
A transfer stimuli				
0111			4.3	1.22
1101			4.4	1.26
1110			3.6	1.57
B transfer stimuli				
1000			3.5	.00
0010			4.0	.00
0001			3.2	.00

with only one study item (all with the prototypical 0000). Moreover, each of the B transfer stimuli agrees in three positions with an A study stimulus (1000 with 1010; 0010 with 1010; 0001 with 0101). The Medin and Schaffer predictions were verified.

ACT simulations of this experiment were performed with the same parameter settings as the previous experiments. Each simulation involved training ACT to criterion or until the 20 trials were up. Then, five test passes through the 12 items were administered to get classification ratings for each item. The strength of each production was then reduced by 50% to simulate the loss of strength with a week's delay and five more ratings were obtained for each stimulus. Ten such simulations were performed. Therefore, the ACT match ratings are calculated on 100 ratings per stimulus. The number of constants in the classifying production (weighted positively for correct classification and negatively for incorrect ones) was again taken to be ACT's confidence rating. Table VI gives ACT results in terms of trials to criterion and mean match ratings. The ACT trials to criterion provide a good, but not perfect, rank order correlation (r = .89) with the actual data. Similarly, the ACT match scores provide a good, but not perfect, rank order correlation (r = .88) with the actual classification ratings. The linear correlation between the match scores and actual rating scores ($r = .83$) is again fairly high, suggesting the possibility of a linear transformation of one into the other. Note that in simulating this experiment, unlike those of Franks and Bransford or Hayes-Roth and Hayes-Roth, ACT has the more demanding task of predicting the data obtained for individual stimuli. The less than perfect correlations may reflect this but they may also reflect that both the data points it is trying to predict and its own estimates of those data points tend to be less reliable than in previous simulations.

One consequence of the small number of stimuli in this experiment is that it is possible to consider the total set of classifying productions that are generated by ACT's automatic learning mechanisms. Figure 3 illustrates the condition sides of the A-response productions (top) and the B-response productions (bottom) arranged according to their specificity ordering. The 1111 and 0101 A-response productions generalize to form the -1-1 production, and the 1111 and 1010 productions generalize to form the 1-1- production. This last production can misapply in training and match the 1011 B stimulus. This mistake can evoke the discrimination process and so give rise to the 1-10 and 111- productions, which discriminate between the successful and unsuccessful contexts of application of the 1-1- generalization. These discriminations did not appear in all the simulation runs because they depended on a particular sequence of events happening and ACT sometimes reached learning criterion before this sequence was complete.

As for the B-response productions, there is only one generalization: 0000 and 0100 can combine to form 0-00. Note that another generalization could be formed, from 0000 and 1011, which would be -0- -. However, this generalization would involve replacing more than 50%

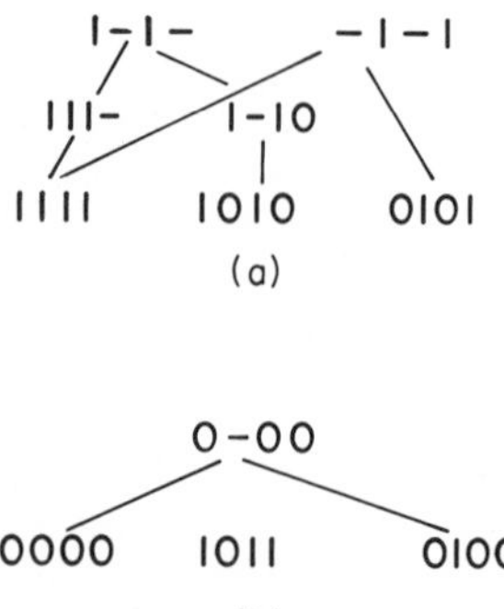

Fig. 3. (a) The specificity network of A productions. (b) The specificity network of B productions.

of the constants by variables; so this generalization is not allowed because the productions it would merge are just too dissimilar. Note that none of the productions in Fig. 3 can match the B transfer stimuli. This accounts for their low rating. In contrast, at least one of the A generalizations matches each of the A transfer stimuli: -1-1 matches 0111 and 1101, while 1-1-, 1-10, and 111- all match 1110. This accounts for the higher rating of the A transfer stimuli. Medin and Schaffer had constructed the material so that the A transfer stimuli would be closer to study items than the B transfer stimuli. The consequence in ACT is that the A transfer stimuli are closer to a number of generalizations that arose from the study elements.

2. *Experiments 2 and 3*

Medin and Schaffer used very similar procedures for experiments 2 and 3. As in experiment 1 there were four dimensions with two values on each. However, in these experiments there were more study and test stimuli. Experiment 2 used the same geometric stimuli as experiment 1, while experiment 3 used Brunswik faces that varied in the dimensions of nose size, mouth height, eye separation, and eye height. There were two procedural differences between these two experiments and the first one. First, the criterion for terminating the study phase was one correct response to all nine study stimuli or 16 total passes through the material (32 passes in experiment 3). The second procedural difference was that there was no delayed test at the end of a week.

The ACT simulation was basically the same as for experiment 1 with two changes to reflect the procedural changes. First, we used the criterion of one correct pass or 20 total passes (a compromise between the 16 in experiment 2 and the 32 in experiment 3). Second, there was no attempt to simulate performance at a delay since Medin and Schaffer did not collect such data.

Table VII presents the data from the two experiments and from the ACT simulation. Transfer stimuli were classified as A or B by Medin and Schaffer according to a linear discriminant function calculated to separate the A and B training stimuli. In general, subjects learned more slowly in experiment 3 with the faces than in experiment 2 with the geometric stimuli. This may be due to the fact that the face material had distracting irrelevant dimensions. In any case, we used just one simulation run of ACT to fit both sets of data. As discussed earlier, our concern is to be able to reproduce the ordinal trends in the data, and not to perform the kind of parameter search required to get exact fits.

Again the prototype of category A is 1111 and for category B it is 0000. Medin and Schaffer were particularly interested in the contrast

TABLE VII

STIMULI USED IN EXPERIMENTS 2 AND 3 OF MEDIN AND SCHAFFER (1978), NUMBER OF ERRORS ON TRAINING STIMULI, CLASSIFICATION CONFIDENCES, AND ACT SIMULATION

	Experiment 2		Experiment 3		ACT	
	Errors	Rating	Errors	Rating	Errors	Match score
A training stimuli						
1110	4.9	4.8	5.5	5.2	2.6	1.88
1010	3.3	5.4	4.2	5.2	1.7	2.30
1011	3.2	5.1	2.8	5.1	1.7	1.92
1101	4.8	5.2	11.9	4.7	1.9	1.58
0111	4.5	5.2	8.2	4.1	1.9	1.60
B training stimuli						
1100	5.5	5.0	15.2	4.3	6.2	1.22
0110	5.2	5.1	12.9	4.1	5.3	.74
0001	3.9	5.2	6.6	5.1	4.0	1.02
0000	3.1	5.5	4.4	5.2	1.5	2.02
A transfer stimuli						
1001		3.7		4.0		.70
1111		5.3		5.2		1.70
0101		3.3		2.5		.64
0011		4.1		2.7		.72
B transfer stimuli						
1000		4.4		3.7		.24
0010		4.1		2.7		.22
0100		4.9		4.8		1.40

between the A training stimuli 1110 and 1010. While 1110 is closer to the A prototype than 1010, 1010 is closer to the A training instances. For example, the only A training stimulus that 1110 is one feature removed from is 1010, and it is this close to two of the B stimuli, 1100 and 0110. By contrast, 1010 is one feature removed from the two A training stimuli 1110 and 1011 and there are no B training stimuli one feature distant. As Medin and Schaffer predicted, performance was higher on 1010 when measured either by the number of errors on training trials or by the subsequent classification ratings. ACT predicts this because a 1-10 generalization will be formed from the 1110 and 1010 combination and a 101- generalization will be formed from the 1010 and 1011 combination which will help classify 1010. In contrast, there is only one three-item generalization (101-) to classify 1011, and there is a B generalization (e.g., -1-0) that will misclassify the 1110 stimulus.

In general, ACT does a good job of predicting the rank orderings of the error data. ACT's rank ordering correlates .88 with the ordering in experiment 2 and .80 with that in experiment 3. It is worth noting that the rank orderings of experiments 2 and 3 only correlate .85 with each other. So ACT is doing about as well as can be expected without introducing a lot of additional machinery about the salience of individual dimensions. As for rank orderings of classification data, ACT's match scores correlate .79 with experiment 2 and .89 with experiment 3. The two experiments only correlate with each other at r = .77. Another test was performed of the hypothesis that the ACT match scores were related to the confidence ratings by a linear transformation. The correlations between the actual ratings and ACT's match scores were .73 for experiment 2 and .81 for experiment 3.

3. *Experiment 4*

The final experiment we simulated was experiment 4 from Medin and Schaffer, which used geometric stimuli again. The materials for this experiment are illustrated in Table VIII. Subjects were given a maximum of 16 passes through the material to achieve the criterion of one perfect recall. ACT was run given the same 16 trial limit. Table VIII also presents the data from the experiment and from the ACT simulation.

Again a linear discriminant function was calculated to separate A from B training stimuli and then used to classify the transfer stimuli. Again 1111 would be regarded as the prototype for the A stimuli and 0000 for the B stimuli. Despite this, Medin and Schaffer predicted that subjects would display better performances on a number of A stimuli than on their B counterparts—0110 better than 1001, 0111 better than 1000, 1101 better than 0010, 1011 better than 0100, and 1111 than 0000. As can be seen, ACT makes these same predictions. Medin and Schaffer made these predictions on the basis of the number of other stimuli similar to the favored A instances. ACT makes these predictions because if there are a large number of similar stimuli, generalizations will be made. These predictions are supported by the data except for the 0110 versus 1001 contrast.

The correlation between the rank order of ACT errors and the rank order of the data is fairly high (r = .62). The rank order correlation with classification ratings and ACT match scores is somewhat higher (r = .79). Again as a test of a linear relation we performed a correlation between the actual ratings and match scores. This correlation was even higher (r = .83).

4. *Summing up the Medin and Schaffer Experiments*

Medin and Schaffer designed their experiments to show the inadequacies of an independent cue theory which creates a prototype out of the modal values on each dimension and assigns rank orderings ac-

TABLE VIII

STIMULI USED IN EXPERIMENT 4 OF MEDIN AND SCHAFFER (1978), NUMBER OF ERRORS ON TRAINING STIMULI, CLASSIFICATION CONFIDENCES, AND ACT SIMULATION

	Experiment 4		ACT	
	Errors	Rating	Errors	Rating
A training stimuli				
0110	5.1	4.5	4.5	1.64
1110	3.8	4.7	1.4	1.96
0111	4.1	5.0	1.4	2.04
1010	4.3	5.1	4.6	1.98
1101	4.9	4.8	3.2	2.02
1011	4.3	5.1	3.9	1.90
B training stimuli				
1001	5.0	4.8	5.4	1.18
1000	5.6	4.3	4.2	1.86
0010	5.8	4.3	7.0	1.36
0011	4.9	4.5	7.4	1.76
0100	4.8	4.4	6.6	.94
A transfer stimuli				
1111		4.6		1.76
0101		3.8		.66
1100		3.6		.40
B transfer stimuli				
0000		4.4		1.62
0001		3.9		.94

cording to distance from these prototypes. Their data clearly refute such a model and indicate that subjects are sensitive to similarities among individual instances. Fortunately, ACT lines up with Medin and Schaffer in predicting this result. Medin and Schaffer's theory is that subjects only store instances and that ratings are particularly influenced by what instances are close to a test instance. ACT's ratings are also influenced by what instances are close to a test instance because these result in generalizations that will classify the test instance.

Medin and Schaffer derived predictions from their theory and compared these with predictions from an independent-cue-prototypes model. Rank order correlations were reported between these models and their data. It is interesting to compare the correlations of these two models with ACT. The three sets of rank order correlations are reported in Table IX experiments 2, 3, and 4 (Medin and Schaffer do not report correlations for experiment 1). There are two remarks that need to be made about interpreting these data. First, Medin's and Schaffer's correlations concern percent correct classification, while ACT's previously reported classification correlations have concerned confidence ratings. The ratings and percent correct are not perfectly correlated. We chose

TABLE IX

RANK ORDER CORRELATIONS BETWEEN CORRECT CLASSIFICATION, PREDICTIONS FOR INDEPENDENT-CUE MODEL, PREDICTIONS OF MEDIN AND SCHAFFER (1978) CONTEXT MODEL, ACT WITH ZERO DEGREES OF FREEDOM, AND ACT WITH FOUR DEGREES OF FREEDOM

	Independent cue model	Medin and Schaffer	ACT	ACT and four parameters
Experiment 2	.79	.81	.58	.78
Experiment 3	.89	.92	.79	.94
Experiment 4	.41	.72	.67	.74

to report correlations with ratings because this measure tended to be more informative. For instance, if one compares two stimuli in the Medin and Schaffer experiments with identical percent correct classification, one studied and the other not, the studied one will tend to receive higher mean confidence. Averaging over 10 nonstudied stimuli and 17 comparable studied stimuli with mean correct identification of 81%, the nonstudied stimuli were rated 4.60 and the studied stimuli 4.83.

ACT predicts this because some of the studied stimulus judgments will result from the application of the production that was designated to classify just that stimulus. In contrast, all judgments for the nonstudied stimuli result from the application of generalizations. Application of a designated production results in higher confidence than application of a generalization because the designated production has no variables. This dissociation between confidence and percent correct is not predicted by the other models.

A second remark is that the independent-cue model and the Medin–Schaffer context model estimated separate parameters for the salience of each dimension. This allows them to account for variation among dimensions—both real and random. The impact of this is clear in experiment 2 versus experiment 3. These two experiments have the same structure. The independent-cue and context theories disply rank order correlations of about .8 with the data of experiment 2 and about .9 with experiment 3. However, the two experiments only correlate with each other .69 in rank order of percent correct classification.

ACT's correlations are uniformly below those of the Medin and Schaffer context model. They are also below the independent-cue model, except for experiment 4 which was explicitly designed to discriminate maximally between the independent-cue model and the Medin and Schaffer theory. It needs to be emphasized, however, that ACT's predictions were done without any parameter search and without any parameters for cue salience. Thus, in ACT we are using a zero-parameter model to fit the data, while the context model had four parameters and the independent-cue model have five parameters.

One atheoretical way to give ACT four degrees of freedom is to identify for it the best four conditions and only require it to predict the ordering of the remaining 12 conditions. This was done in the last column of Table IX. Now ACT correlates better than either model in experiments 3 and 4 and is only slightly worse than the other models in experiment 2. Given that ACT did this well with the addition of four totally atheoretical parameters, we suspect that an ACT model that estimated separate parameters for the salience of each of the four dimensions would do at least as well as the Medin and Schaffer model in accounting for the data.

D. Comparison of ACT with Other Models

There are three basic types of models for schema abstraction. One type proposes that subjects learn a single characterization of the central tendency of the category. A frequent suggestion is that they distinguish a particular instance (it need not be one they have actually seen) as the prototype for the concept. Other instances are members of the category to the extent that they are similar to this prototype. This class of models would include Franks and Bransford (1971), Bransford and Franks (1971), Rosch and Mervis (1975), Posner and Keele (1970), and Reed (1972). In order to account for the effects of instance frequency demonstrated by Hayes-Roth and Hayes-Roth, the prototypes would have to be augmented by some memory for the individual instances studied. However, it is much more difficult for prototype models to accommodate the results of Medin and Schaffer which indicate that subjects are sensitive to similarities among individual instances.

A second class of theories are those that propose that subjects store individual instances only and make their category judgments on the basis of the similarity between the test instance and the stored instances. Among the theories in this class is the Medin and Schaffer theory. A difficulty for the Medin and Schaffer version of the store-instances-only model was the low correlation found by Hayes-Roth and Hayes-Roth between recognition and classification. They found that the prototypes received the highest classification ratings but the frequently presented nonprototypes received the highest recognition ratings. This suggests that information is acquired both about the instances and about their more abstract characteristics.

In a certain sense, any results that can be accounted for by a theory that says that subjects store abstractions can also be accounted for by a theory that says subjects only store instances. A store-instance-only theory could always be proposed that went through a test process equivalent to calculating an abstraction from the stored instances and making a judgment on the basis of the abstraction. However, a difficulty for the instance model is the frequent phenomena of subjects reporting verbally the existence of abstract characterizations or prototypes (e.g., Reed, 1972).

The third class of models is that which proposes that subjects store cooccurrence information about feature combinations. ACT is an instance of such a model, as are those proposed by Reitman and Bower (1973), B. Hayes-Roth and Hayes-Roth (1977), and one aspect of Neumann's (1974) model. These models can potentially store all subsets of feature combinations. Thus, they store instances as a special case. The Hayes-Roth and Hayes-Roth experiment showed this model has advantages over many versions of the instance-only or prototype models. However, the Medin and Schaffer version of the instance-only model can accommodate their results.

It is very difficult to find empirical predictions that distinguish ACT from the various other feature-set models. Perhaps it would be best to regard them as equivalent, given the current state of our knowledge, and simply conclude that subjects respond in terms of feature sets. However, there are a number of reasons for preferring ACT's version of the feature-set model. First, it is a fully specified process model. As Medin and Schaffer argue, it is often difficult to see in any detail how some of the feature-set models apply to particular paradigms or produce particular results.

Second, ACT has a reasonably efficient way of storing feature sets. It only stores those subsets of properties and features that have arisen because of generalization or discrimination rather than attempting to store all possible subsets of features from all observed instances. While it seems as if there should be empirical consequences of these different ways of storing feature sets, our efforts to find them have not been successful. However, if there is very little difference in behavior, that would seem to be all the more reason to prefer the more efficient storage requirements of ACT.

Third, it needs to be emphasized that the ACT learning mechanisms were not fashioned to account for schema abstraction. Rather they were designed in light of more general considerations about the nature of the rules that need to be acquired and the information typically available to acquisition mechanisms in real world situations. We were particularly concerned that our mechanisms should be capable of dealing with acquisition of language and of rules for making inferences and predictions about one's environment. The mechanisms were designed to be robust (in being able to deal with many different rules in many different situations) and efficient. Their success in accounting for schema abstraction represents an independent confirmation of the learning theory.

Before concluding, we would like to discuss one characteristic of feature-set models which may seem unappealing on first encounter. This is the fact that they store so many different characterizations of the category. ACT may not be so bad as some of the other theories, but still having a set of productions for recognizing instances of a category seems far less economical than having a single prototype. However, the remark that needs to be made is that natural categories defy economical representations. This has been stressed in discussions of their family resemblance structure by Wittgenstein (e.g., Wittgenstein, 1953) and more recently by Rosch (e.g., Rosch & Mervis, 1975). The important fact about many natural categories (e.g., games, dogs) is that there is no set of features that defines the category, nor is there a prototypical instance that functions as a standard to which all other category members must be compared. However, these categories do not seem to be unstructured; they are not merely a list of instances. The introspections of one of us (J.A.) suggest that for him the category of dogs has subclasses that include the following:

a. *"The very large dogs, with short noses, and floppy ears,"* which include the St. Bernards, Newfoundlands, and mastiffs
b. *"The medium to large dogs with relatively long hair, and floppy ears,"* which include the spaniels, setters, and some of the other retrievers
c. *"The short and hairy dogs"* which include such breeds as the pekinese and toy terriers
d. *"The large, multicolored dogs, with medium hair, and pointed ears,"* which include the German shepherds and huskies.

The portion of each description in quotation marks gives the physical features that seem to characterize that subclass. There are several things to notice about these feature-set descriptions. First is that certain features are left unspecified; for example, subclass a makes no reference to coloration or hair. The implication is that these subclasses of the larger dog category are not defined by prototypes either. A second observation is that the feature-set descriptions overlap in complex and relatively unsystematic ways. For example, while there is a tendency for size to distinguish the subclasses, subclass b overlaps with subclass d on this feature so that large dogs are in both subclasses. Other features, such as ear type, serve to distinguish some subclasses (viz., subclass d from subclasses a and b), fail to distinguish others (viz., subclass a from subclass b), and are irrelevant for still others (viz., subclass c). Feature-set models such as ACT seem uniquely suited to explain the complex, overlapping, and only partially specified feature structures of natural categories.

REFERENCES

Anderson, J. R. *Language, memory and thought.* Hillsdale, N.J.: Lawrence Erlbaum Associates, 1976.

Anderson, J. R. Induction of augmented transition networks. *Cognitive Science,* 1977, **1,** 125–157.

Anderson, J. R., & Bower, G. H. *Human associative memory.* Washington, D.C.: Winston, 1973.

Anderson, J. R., Kline, P. J., & Beasley, C. M. *A theory of the acquisition of cognitive skills* (ONR Tech. Rep. 77-1). New Haven, Conn.: Yale University, 1977.

Anderson, J. R., Kline, P. J., & Beasley, C. M. Complex learning processes. In R. E. Snow, P. A. Federico, & W. E. Montague (Eds.), *Aptitude, learning, and instruction: Cognitive process analyses.* Hillsdale, N.J.: Lawrence Erlbaum Associates, 1980.

Anderson, J. R., Kline, P. J., & Lewis, C. A production system model for language processing. In P. Carpenter & M. Just (Eds.), *Cognitive processes in comprehension.* Hillsdale, N.J.: Lawrence Erlbaum Associates, 1977.

Bailey, N., Madden, D., & Krashen, S. D. *Is there a "natural sequence" in adult second language learning?* New York: English Language Institute and Linguistics Department, Queens College and the Graduate Center, City University of New York, 1974.

Bransford, J. D., & Franks, J. J. The abstraction of linguistic ideas. *Cognitive Psychology,* 1971, **2,** 331–350.

Franks, J. J., & Bransford, J. D. Abstraction of visual patterns. *Journal of Experimental Psychology,* 1971, **90,** 65–74.

Hayes-Roth, B., & Hayes-Roth, F. Concept learning and the recognition and classification of exemplars. *Journal of Verbal Learning and Verbal Behavior,* 1977, **16,** 321–338.

Hayes-Roth, F., & McDermott, J. Learning structured patterns from examples. *Proceedings of the Third International Joint Conference on Pattern Recognition,* 1976, 419–423.

Medin, D. L., & Schaffer, M. M. A context theory of classification learning. *Psychological Review,* 1978, **85,** 207–238.

Neumann, P. G. An attribute frequency model for the abstraction of prototypes. *Memory & Cognition,* 1974, **2,** 241–248.

Neumann, P. G. Visual prototype formulation with discontinuous representation of dimensions of variability. *Memory & Cognition,* 1977, **5,** 187–197.

Newell, A. A theoretical exploration of mechanisms for coding the stimulus. In A. W. Melton & E. Martin (Eds.), *Coding processes in human memory.* Washington, D.C.: Winston, 1972.

Newell, A. Production systems: Models of control structures. In W. G. Chase (Ed.), *Visual information processing.* New York: Academic Press, 1973.

Norman, D. A., & Rumelhart, D. E. *Explorations in cognition.* San Francisco: Freeman, 1975.

Posner, M. I., & Keele, S. W. Retention of abstract ideas. *Journal of Experimental Psychology,* 1970, **83,** 304–308.

Quillian, M. R. The teachable language comprehender. *Communications of the ACM,* 1969, **12,** 459–476.

Reed, S. Pattern recognition and categorization. *Cognitive Psychology,* 1972, **3,** 382–407.

Reitman, J. S., & Bower, G. H. Storage and later recognition of exemplars of concepts. *Cognitive Psychology,* 1973, **4,** 194–206.

Rosch, E., & Mervis, C. B. Family resemblances: Studies in the internal structure of categories. *Cognitive Psychology,* 1975, **7,** 573–605.

Rychener, M. D., & Newell, A. An instructible production system: Basic design issues. In D. A. Waterman & F. Hayes-Roth (Eds.), *Pattern-directed inference systems.* New York: Academic Press, 1978.

Sussman, G. J. *A computer model of skill acquisition.* New York: American Elsevier, 1975.

Vere, S. A. Induction of relational productions in the presence of background information. *Proceedings of the Fifth International Joint Conference on Artificial Intelligence, Boston,* 1977, 349–355.

Waterman, D. A. *Adaptive production systems* (CIP Working Paper No. 285). Pittsburgh: Psychology Department, Carnegie-Mellon University, 1974.

Weissman, C. *LISP 1.5 Primer.* Belmont, Calif.: Dickenson, 1967.

Winston, P. H. *Learning structural descriptions from examples* (Artificial Intelligence Laboratory Project AI-TR-231). Cambridge, Mass.: MIT, 1970.

Wittgenstein, L. *Philosophical investigations.* New York: Macmillan, 1953.

SIMILARITY AND ORDER IN MEMORY[1]

Robert G. Crowder

YALE UNIVERSITY, NEW HAVEN, CONNECTICUT

The goal of this work is to clarify two related issues in human memory theory—how to represent in a general way the effects of similarity on serial memory and how to understand the distinction between item and order information. A central phenomenon for both issues is the interaction first documented by Horowitz (1961) showing that high intralist similarity facilitates item memory but inhibits order memory. The conclusion below will be that this interaction is less of a puzzle than it first seems and that the item versus order distinction is not particularly fundamental. However, before we explain the arguments that favor this conclusion, we shall pause to consider some background.

I. Similarity, the All-Purpose Memory Tool

Our interest in similarity as a factor in memory is only a manifestation of a remarkably stable preoccupation with similarity effects that spans

[1]This research was supported by Grants MH26623 from the National Institutes of Mental Health and BNS77-07062 from the National Science Foundation. I acknowledge happily the contribution of Virginia Walters to the planning, execution, and analysis of the experiments reported here. John Golden assisted ably with programming schedules of stimulus lists. Alice F. Healy made many useful suggestions, including the application of sophisticated guessing theory which was tested in experiments 8 and 9. Finally, I want to thank the Psychology Department of the University of Melbourne for providing me with a congenial setting in which to write this report.

THE PSYCHOLOGY OF LEARNING AND MOTIVATION, VOL. 13

ISBN 0-12-543313-1

wide periods of history and differences in theoretical fashions. Experimental manipulation of similarity among learning materials has been the strategy of choice from the earliest evolution of interference theory (see Crowder, 1976, Chaps. 1 & 8), to information-theoretic models of memory (Aborn & Rubenstein, 1952; Miller, 1958), to information-processing models (Conrad, 1964; Posner & Konick, 1966), to more recent organizational and processing-depth approaches (Craik, 1978; Tulving & Pearlstone, 1966). Craik (1978) has recently suggested, for example, that the benefits of deep processing come from the fact that the deeper levels permit more breadth of elaboration, resulting in more distinctive, that is, less similar, memory traces.

Thus, attention to similarity effects is a recurrent theme across widely divergent styles of theorizing about memory. It is time we try formulating statements about similarity that are not parochial with respect to these shifting styles. We shall be especially concerned here with the ostensibly different effects of intralist similarity on item and order information and also with whether different kinds of similarity—semantic and phonological—operate in the same way.

A. Item and Order Information

In list memory experiments, where the target of performance is recalling a set of items in the order of presentation, item information is indexed by the number of list members included somewhere on the response protocol; order information is, of course, indexed by the placement of these items in either their relative or their absolute list positions. A test of free recall is at face value a pure measure of item information. The most transparent support for the item–order distinction is that people sometimes can correctly place an item in the proper list but cannot locate it within that list. This common sense distinction touches on issues of substance when we extend the empirical criteria for item and order information to the level of hypothetical memory processes.

In interference theory, the distinction between response availability and associative learning (Underwood, Runquist, & Schulz, 1959) is one clear version of the item–order distinction from the context of paired-associate methodology. However, the theoretical identification of response availability with associations between the stable experimental context to response terms (McGovern, 1964) gives basic priority to the associative relationship.

The first firm statements about item and order information were made during the first wave of British work on short-term memory and information processing: Brown (1958) and Crossman (1961) tried to understand the basic facts of memory span from an information-theoretic point of view. They both suggested that the uncertainty, in bits, of sequential aspects of memory series was larger than that of the items themselves. Crossman was particularly responsible for the idea, to which we shall return later, that item information increases slowly with list length, whereas order information increases rapidly and is, in fact, the performance limiting factor.

There are three possible positions on the theoretical relation between item and order information—that they are separate and independent, that order information is derivative from item information, and that item information is derivative from order information. Murdock (1974, 1976) has most enthusiastically promoted the theoretical distinction between item and order information. Without quite openly declaring himself for true independence, he points to variables whose effects are in opposite directions for item measures and for order measures of performance. This dissociation is just what one needs to bolster a theoretical separation of the two and the empirical status of this dissociation will be one major focus of the present paper. Bjork and Healy (1974) have found evidence for formal independence of "acoustic confusion errors" and transposition errors and have concluded (p. 95) that ". . . each can occur independently of one another and that they reflect the loss of different types of information."

Shiffrin and Cook (1978) have proposed a model with explicitly separated machinery for item and order information. In their associative model, item bonds stand for the types of information that specify items and relational bonds specify their order relative to one another. Shiffrin and Cook decided with reluctance that, in view of their data, complete independence of item and order information was not likely; however, their preferred modification of the independence assumption (that loss of one type of bond accelerates loss of any other bond) does little to neutralize their view that items and their ordering are separately represented.

At this point, I digress to raise two distinctions, which are related to the issues of concern here but which will not be explored further in the interests of space: First, some writers (e.g., Lee & Estes, 1977; Shiffrin & Cook, 1978) have sought to distinguish memory for position from memory for order. Second, there has been an effort among the same theorists to assign mechanisms for item and order memory to either short- or long-term storage. These two issues, important as they are, do not need to be settled before serious attention is given to the item–order distinction.

Theories that propose ordered receptacles, or bins, for the storage of information make the claim that item information is primary and order information derivative. Wickelgren (1977) has termed these theories *nonassociative* and Conrad's (1965) model is a well-known example. Conrad wanted to explain the occurrence of order transpositions, which seem on the surface to be perfect evidence for separate storage of order information. By establishing an association between the occurrence of phonological confusions and transpositions, Conrad argued that the item loss was primary and the apparent order loss followed as the coincidence of two item errors. Bjork and Healy (1974) showed later, however, that a more scrupulous partitioning of errors led to conclusions different from those based on data such as Conrad's.

The contention that item information is secondary to order information is more widely held. Wickelgren's (1965, 1977) *associative theory* proposes that items are stored phonemically, with associations built both within an item (among its constituent phonemes) and in the forward direction between phonemes in adjacent items. Several arguments are presented in Wickelgren (1977) favoring this type of model over the nonassociative, or bin, type of model. Order information is basic to item information, in Wickelgren's model, inasmuch as an item, say, a particular syllable, is assumed to be represented by forward, adjacent associations between phonemes.

Estes' hierarchical coding model (Estes, 1972) is another example of deriving item information from a more fundamental set of assumptions about order information. In this system, the main connections are between constituents at one level and their control elements at a higher level. Thus, a letter representation might subordinate two or three phoneme representations. Short-term storage, within this system, is produced by a synchronous recycling between a superordinate control element and the lower level constituents subsumed under it—as between the name of a letter and its constituent phonemes. The position of any element in the sequence of recycling elements is maintained, on the average, except as the individual cycle times are subject to random perturbation, which increases as time elapses since the whole sequence was set up.

The heart of Estes' (1972) position on the present issue is found in how this fundamentally sequential format for short-term storage can produce item errors. There are two mechanisms: In one, phonemes from adjacent items exchange to produce illegal or impossible phoneme sequences; for example, if the interior phonemes in the sequence . . . FG . . . exchanged, the two resulting items would not be letter names at all. The second source of item errors in Estes' system is wholesale or partial exchanges between the memory material (often letters) and the interpolated distractor materials (often digits). Thus, it is no problem for a short-term storage format whose "moving parts" all involve order information to produce the classic symptom of loss of item information, an omission.

In the long-term storage assumptions of Estes' (1972) theory, it is proposed that there are forward inhibitory associations produced between items subsumed under the same control element. These form as a consequence of rehearsal and they freeze, as it were, the current status of the reverberatory process described above. There will be more to say on this in Section III, A, 1.

The model of Sperling and Speelman (1970) also represents items in short-term storage as strings of phonemes. Their essential argument is that item information represents no new theoretical commodity beyond order information. Any excess performance, when scoring is by a free-recall criterion rather than an ordered-recall criterion, can be attributed to possibilities for guessing which may vary with the properties of the vocabulary used in testing. In other words, these authors deny that the concept of item information is useful at all. This attitude is expanded with approval in the next section.

B. No Fundamental Difference between Item and Order Information

The point has been made elsewhere (Crowder, 1976, Chap. 12) that item and order information could not really be different in a fundamental theoretical sense: In virtually all experiments on memory, and in most real life situations as well, the items being remembered are thoroughly familiar units composed of even more familiar subunits. What sense does it make to speak of whether the subject knows the word KANGAROO after it appears on a list? Of course he knows it. We are using the term "item information" to cover whether he knows that it has occurred in a particular time and a particular place—often the most recent list given him in the laboratory.

However, that is also what we mean by order information—that KANGAROO has occurred in a particular location, perhaps between HARPSICHORD and LINGUIST on the most recent list. In one case information specifies when an item has occurred relative to other lists, and in the other case it specifies when an item has occurred relative to other items within a given list; one is coarse grained and the other fine grained, but they are hardly fundamentally different types of information.

C. The Crucial Role of Similarity

Why, then, all the fancy machinery that has been proposed to account for item and order information separately? An excellent reason would be evidence, at the empirical level, for a functional dissociation of the two. Three such dissociations have been advanced in earlier work: Fuchs (1969), Estes (1972), and Healy (1974) have all noted that measures of item and order information show different serial position functions, the latter bowed and symmetrical and the former monotonic increasing. This difference falls naturally out of Estes' model and must be considered a major source of support for that model. However, it can hardly be held up as a fundamental dissociation of item and order information, for Estes' theory embraces the view that item information is only a derivative manifestation of changes in ordering.

The second proposed dissociation (Bjork & Healy, 1974) is that item and order information (error types based on these) show different rates of decay in short-term storage, order information deteriorating faster than item information. This sort of evidence serves to dissociate different performance measures within the context of one data base, which is what Bjork and Healy were trying to do, but it cannot be used to advance the theoretical distinction. If order and item information were simply coarse- and fine-grained order information, one would expect the fine grained to be lost first, for example.

The third dissociation of item and order information is more serious: Conrad (1965) and Murdock (1974) have both remarked that what we really need is a variable that exerts opposite effects on item and order measures of performance, to begin our argument for a theoretical separation. The interaction identified above with Horowitz (1961)—that high intralist similarity facilitates item memory but inhibits order memory—satisfies this criterion and we begin now with a brief review of other instances of the interaction.

Studies of paired-associate learning show some divergent results with regard to whether high intralist similarity uniformly facilitates response integration and retards associative learning (see summaries in Hall, 1971, p. 134; Saltz, 1971, p. 186). Horowitz first displayed the interaction starkly. He had people learn either highly similar lists of trigrams (the items VXF, XVS, FSV, SFX, XFV, FXS, VSX, SVF, VFS, FVX, SXV, and XSF) or lists formed of dissimilar items (QSZ, KXW, MRV, WQJ, VKH, ZMQ, HWS, FVX, JZR, XHF, SJM, RFK). Some subjects learned the 12-item list by a free-recall criterion and others learned by a method of order reconstruction (12 items were given them on cards and subjects placed the cards in order). In recall under free-recall instructions there was a large initial advantage of high-similarity lists, which tended to weaken with later trials. Ordering was much worse for the high-similarity list, consistently through practice. Horowitz thought the advantage of high similarity for free recall was due to chance guessing but he did not attempt to evaluate this hypothesis against the rate of extralist intrusions.

Wickelgren (1965) presented six-item lists for ordered recall from either vocabularies high in phonological similarity (B, C, D, T, G, and so on) or low in phonological similarity. Wickelgren devised statistically independent measures of item recall and of position recall and found that similarity enhanced the former and impaired the latter. The net effect of similarity, when position recall and item recall were combined in the conventional ordered-recall criterion ("items in correct position" score), was negative.

Watkins, Watkins, and Crowder (1974) replicated the Wickelgren finding with lists of common words varied in phonological similarity (BUD, CUB, TUCK, BUG, and so on, versus BEAD, CAB, TAKE, BEG, and so on). They found free recall higher for the high-similarity lists but ordered recall (combining item and position information as these are understood) poorer for high-similarity lists.

Murdock and vom Saal (1967) used the Brown–Peterson method for measuring short-term memory for words. Triads of words presented for memory on a trial were either high in conceptual similarity or not, with conceptual similarity defined as coming from the same category (RED, GREY, BLUE). They found the net effect of similarity on ordered recall to be positive but there were higher rates of transpositions in the high-similarity condition. They termed the interaction "the category effect."

These experiments form the immediate background for experiments 1, 2, and 3.

II. Semantic Similarity and Ordered Recall

A. Experiment 1

The studies reviewed above make a case for a serious dissociation of item and order information with respect to similarity effects. The first experiment sought to generalize this dissociation.

Figure 1 shows the main result of Watkins *et al.* (1974) with regard to similarity effects. A special feature of their experiment was a test of Horowitz's guessing hypothesis as an explanation of the free-recall advantage for high similarity. Watkins *et al.* began with a collection of 10 pools of phonologically similar words. To form lists for the free-recall phase of their study, they randomly selected 12 of the 14 words within a phonologically similar set for the high-similarity condition, and 12 unrelated words from different 14-item sets for the low-similarity condition. If subjects were guessing in the high-similarity condition, they should often hit on one of the two words excluded from the list. Because such intrusions almost never occurred, in fact, we may rule out a simple guessing explanation of the free-recall similarity advantage. The paucity of intrusions observed by Watkins *et al.* fits with other reports (Roediger, 1974; Tulving & Pearlstone, 1966) that subjects only rarely respond with words from outside the experimental context, even when strong retrieval

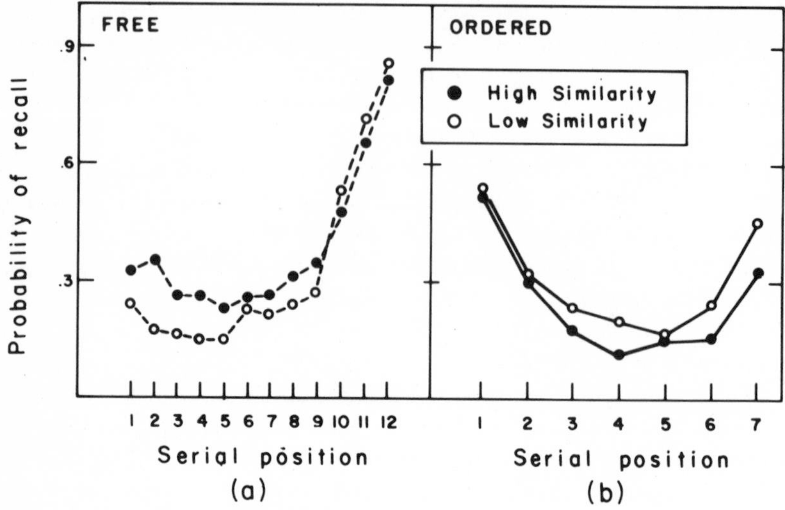

Fig. 1. Free (a) and serial recall (b) as a function of serial position and phonological similarity. (After Watkins, Watkins, & Crowder, 1974.)

cues would seem to encourage such importations. Guessing may have been the agency for Horowitz's (1961) free-recall similarity advantage but we need to look elsewhere for a general explanation of the result.

The impairment in ordered recall for high-similarity lists was not unexpected in light of previous reports, beginning with Conrad and Hull (1964). At a low level of analysis, the results of Fig. 1 demonstrate the dissociation of item and order information and thus tend to encourage the distinction between them. At a higher level, there is a responsibility to account for the interaction theoretically. As Watkins *et al.* observed, there is no difficulty accounting for either the facilitation or inhibition by itself; it is less trivial to explain the two effects with the same framework.

Watkins *et al.* (1974) chose to work within the perturbation model of Estes (1972). In free recall, they observed, loss of item information would be caused mainly by timing errors that exchange phonemes among adjacent items. When all the words in the list rhyme, as in their high-similarity lists, exchanges of vowel sounds have no adverse effect on performance (CUB BUD and so on). With low-similarity lists, exchange of vowels could produce anomalies that would appear as item loss (COB BID, for example).

In ordered recall, Watkins *et al.* observed that the phonologically heterogeneous lists contain more reliable cues to ordering than the homogeneous lists; in the low-similarity condition, a given pair of items has order information in the vowels as well as in the consonants. For the consonant–vowel–consonant items they used, a complete transposition could occur on the basis of one-third fewer phoneme exchanges with the high-similarity lists than with the low-similarity lists. This explanation for the similarity decrement in ordering is similar to Wickelgren's (1965) statement that order is "better replicated" in the low similarity materials.

Most of the modifications introduced by Lee and Estes (1977) make little difference to the derivations in question here. The new theory is explicit that basic memory capacity is the same for high- and low-similarity lists and that similarity decrements in order recall are introduced by mechanisms at the time of recall. The basic idea is that retained phonemes from adjacent and similar letters produce mutual inhibition in retrieval. For example, the similar constituents of the letter C and Z, in adjacent positions, tend to produce an effort to recall both simultaneously, an inhibition that would be reduced if the two similar items were spaced farther apart. There is not space here to fully review the Lee and Estes proposal and argue whether its new assumptions are really necessary extensions of the 1972 model. Locating the similarity decrement in the retrieval phase as they do, however, does make it difficult to explain why the similarity decrement disappears with filled retention intervals; if the decrement is produced during recall of similar letters, it should make no difference whether this recall act is immediate or delayed. A review of the evidence on this point is found in Crowder (1979).

Whatever differences remain among these explanations for similarity effects in free recall and in ordered recall, they resemble one another in being firmly fixed at the phonological level. What if it were shown that similarity at the phonological level behaves no differently from similarity at the semantic level? Such a demonstration, which was one purpose of experiment 1, would show at least that the hypotheses we have been reviewing here are too narrow. At most, we should have to worry whether it would even be possible to state these hypotheses in more general form.

1. *Method*

In a between-groups design, 12 subjects heard five lists of 10 semantically similar nouns. The other 12 subjects heard five lists of semantically dissimilar nouns. Instructions were for ordered recall and scoring was both by an ordered criterion and a free-recall criterion.

a. Subjects. The subjects were 24 Yale undergraduate and graduate students serving either for pay or for credit toward introductory psychology.

b. Procedure. The experimenter, who had formal training in speech and phonetics, read each list aloud at a rate of one word every 2 sec in a monotone voice. At the end of each list, subjects were to write down the words in the order of presentation. The collections of words that were received by a subject were controlled, as indicated below; however, both the order of lists and of words on each list were determined randomly and independently for each subject.

c. Materials and Design. One hundred words were chosen to conform to a 10 × 10 array in which the words within a row all came from the same semantic class (States of the Union, types of fish, types of trees, and so on) but words within the same column were all different by this criterion. This matrix of words is shown in the Appendix at the end of this contribution. Ten lists with high similarity, the rows of the matrix, and 10 lists with low similarity, the columns, were defined by this matrix. Across the experiment, these 20 lists were used equally often, guaranteeing that similarity comparisons were free from confounding with words.

Of the 12 subjects who received high-similarity lists, half received lists defined by the first five rows of the matrix and the other half received those in the second five rows. Likewise, of the other 12 subjects, who got low-similarity lists, half received the first five columns and half received the last five columns.

2. *Results*

The main results of experiment 1 are shown in Fig. 2, which gives correct recall as a function of serial position for the two similarity conditions and for the two scoring criteria. The ordered-recall data show a large effect of serial position and a complex effect of similarity: In the early serial positions, there is some advantage for high similarity but this reverses, to show a similarity decrement, for the later serial positions. This pattern was evident in an analysis of variance with similarity and position as factors. Besides the large main effect of serial position, there was no main effect of similarity ($F < 1.0$); however, the interaction of similarity with position was statistically significant, $F(9, 198) = 2.36$, $p < .01$. Thus, there was not a straightforward similarity decrement in ordered recall.

Free-recall scoring gives credit for items if they appear anywhere in the recall protocol. These results are shown in the dashed lines of Fig. 2. There was a reliable advantage for high similarity, by this criterion, $F(1, 22) = 4.67$, $p < .05$. The interaction between similarity and position

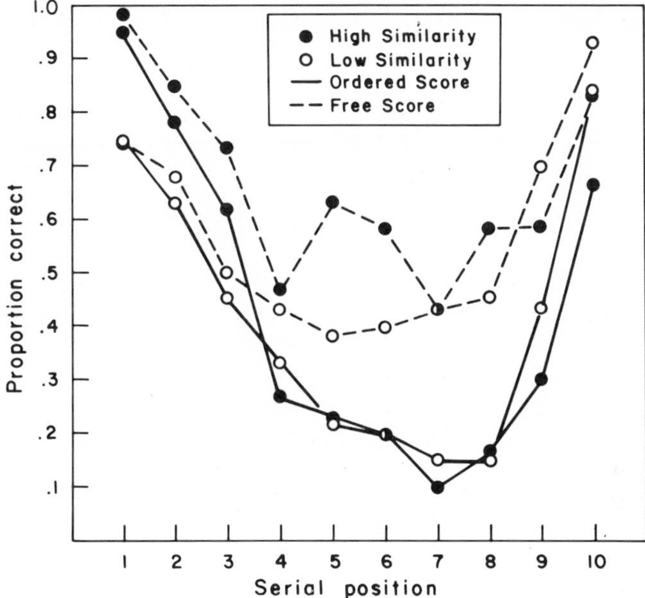

Fig. 2. Ordered recall scored by an ordered criterion (solid lines) and by a free-recall criterion (dashed lines) as a function of semantic similarity (experiment 1, nouns).

was also reliable, $F(9, 198) = 2.73, p < .005$, indicating that the similarity advantage was stronger earlier in the list than later.

3. *Discussion*

Experiment 1 did not produce the interaction that had been anticipated on the basis of the Watkins *et al.* (1974) result shown in Fig. 1 and on the basis of the Horowitz (1961) interaction. High similarity did facilitate free-recall performance but there was not a similarity impairment for ordered recall. It can be argued that ordered recall is a combination of item information and order information and that therefore ordering, as such, must have been hurt by high similarity in order to bring the facilitation in item information back to zero in ordered recall. However, the fact remains that with phonological similarity ordered recall is sharply impaired and this did not happen with semantic similarity. Furthermore, Murdock and vom Saal (1967) found the same result in their study of short-term retention as a function of semantic similarity. They observed overall better ordered recall for homogeneous trigrams than for heterogeneous trigrams; it was only in the conditional probability of a transposition that similarity was inhibitory.

One possibility for these discrepancies is that semantic and phonological similarity are subject to different principles. Ordered recall is invariably damaged by phonological similarity but enhancement of item recall by phonological similarity is weak and inconsistent across experiments (Lee & Estes, 1977). In contrast, semantic similarity produces here a robust item advantage in free recall but only a weak and inconsistent decrement in ordered recall.

A less interesting possibility is that the lists in experiment 1 were not as strong a manipulation of similarity as were those used by Watkins *et al.* This proposition is nearly impossible to test. However, experiment 2 was an effort to see if the results would be changed by a more plausible definition of semantic similarity than common category membership.

B. Experiment 2

Most experiments on intralist semantic similarity rely on category membership as the similarity criterion. Thus, GARTER and OVERCOAT are defined as similar because they are both articles of clothing. Although these two words are indeed more similar than either is to ENZYME, there is hardly any possibility of substituting one for the other, which could be one criterion of semantic similarity. In experiment 2, adjectives were used in the same experimental design exactly as that of experiment 1. Adjective materials permitted selection of list members more nearly synonymous (ANXIOUS, AFRAID, FEARFUL, and so on) than were the nouns

1. *Method*

The method of experiment 2 was the same as that of experiment 1 in all ways except a matrix of 100 adjectives was used instead of nouns (see Appendix), and there were 16 subjects in each group rather than 12.

2. *Results*

Figure 3 shows the main results in the same format as that used in Fig. 2. For ordered recall, there was neither a main effect of similarity nor an interaction with position, Fs = 1.04 and 1.11, respectively. By the free-recall criterion, there was a large main effect favoring high similarity, $F(1, 30) = 19.65, p < .0001$. The interaction was not reliable.

3. *Discussion*

The results for adjectives were very similar to those for nouns—a large advantage of high similarity in item information but no similarity

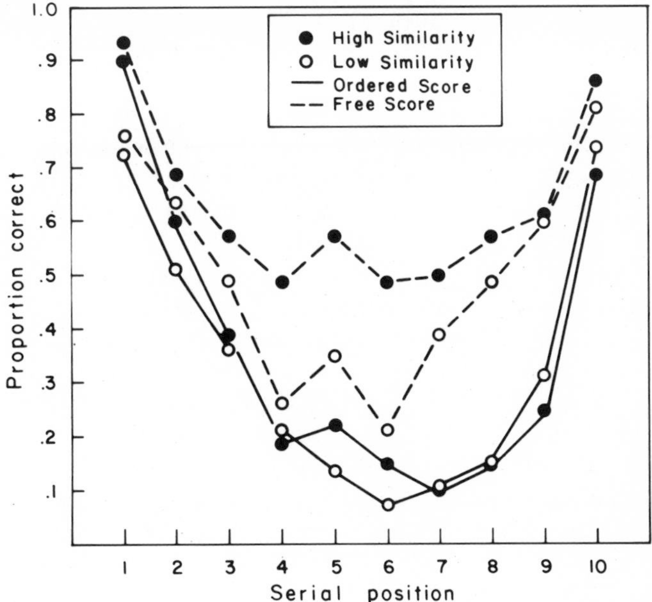

Fig. 3. Same as Fig. 2 except semantic similarity was defined within lists of adjectives (experiment 2).

decrement in ordered recall. Again, it can be argued that if similarity had no effect, lowering ordering, there should have been a net positive effect of similarity on ordered recall. However, it is preferable to show the similarity decrement on ordering directly, without having to presume the item–order distinction that is under question in this paper.

C. Experiment 3

To show a decrement for high similarity in memory for ordering, experiment 3 employed a reconstruction task similar to that used by Horowitz (1961). Subjects were given cards with the list items randomized and were asked to place them in the proper serial order. Item information was assessed at the end of the session in a test of final free recall.

1. *Method*

a. Design and Materials. In experiment 3, both the 100 nouns from experiment 1 and the 100 adjectives from experiment 2 were used as materials. Each of 40 subjects received a total of 20 lists, either all of the similar noun lists and all of the dissimilar adjectives or, alternatively, all of the dissimilar noun lists and all of the similar adjective lists (that is, all the rows of one 10×10 matrix in the Appendix and all the columns of the other one). The order of these two blocks of lists was balanced against both the similarity and the part of speech manipulations.

b. Procedure. Once a subject was assigned to a particular order of receiving adjectives and nouns and of similarity conditions, the order of the 10 word groups within a condition (that is, the order of the 10 rows or columns of the matrices in the Appendix) was determined randomly. Furthermore, the words within each list were randomized individually for each subject. The conditions of presentation were just the same as in experiments 1 and 2; however, the test procedure was different. After each list, the subject received a shuffled deck of 10 cards containing the items he had just heard. He was then given a minute to place these in their correct order. Following the twentieth of these episodes, the subject was given as long as he wanted for final free recall of all words on all lists; this final free-recall test was not anticipated by the instructions. The subjects were 40 students from the same source as in the earlier studies.

2. *Results*

The main results are shown in Fig. 4, which gives proportion of correct initial ordering to final free recall separately for the two similarity conditions. These data show the Horowitz interaction clearly, with a regular similarity decrement in immediate reconstruction of order and a similarity facilitation in final free recall. However, an analysis of variance on the order-reconstruction data showed no reliable effect beyond the serial position effect. A comparable analysis of the free-recall data did show that the advantage of similarity was reliable, $F(1, 19) = 8.16$, $p = .01$. The effect of serial position was also reliable in this analysis, $F(9, 171) = 12.17$, $p < .01$, which is more or less interpretable as a primacy effect (or, if one wishes, negative recency).

3. *Discussion*

The data on final free recall provide a slightly new witness to the advantage of high intralist similarity in remembering item information. However, the ordering data from experiment 3 still fail to give us a reliable similarity decrement. In view of the consistency across interior serial positions with which there was an apparent similarity decrement, it would be perilous to accept the null hypothesis with much conviction.

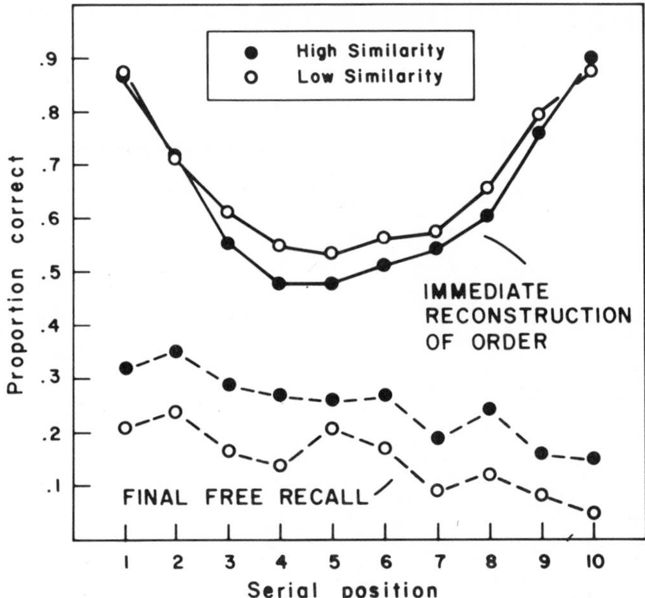

Fig. 4. Immediate reconstruction of order and final free recall as a function of semantic similarity and serial position (experiment 3).

However, rather than trying to squeeze the impression of reliability from the data of Fig. 4, we replicated the study with a slightly different procedure.

D. Experiment 4

It is arguable that the subjects of experiment 3, expecting to be tested for reconstruction of order, adopted an encoding strategy specially designed for that type of test. Since they were not expecting to have to reproduce the items in full, the subjects might have tended to rely on first-letter cues for getting access to the order of items, for example. Against this conjecture is the large similarity advantage which appeared in final free recall; this must mean there was some semantic coding. However, the general point remains that the test method, as anticipated by subjects, might have affected the potency of the similarity manipulation. Experiment 4 was conducted under conditions that would not allow such anticipation—subjects heard the lists in the same way as before but were not informed until the time of test whether they were responsible for reconstructing the order or for free recall of the items.

1. *Method*

The experimental design was much the same as that of experiment 3, with the following changes: 20 subjects from the same source were used in experiment 4. Lists were shortened from 10 to eight items. This was to check on the conclusions of Watkins *et al.* (1974) that extralist intrusions are vanishingly rare even in high-similarity lists and could not, therefore, explain the similarity advantage in free recall.

After each input list was read to him, the subject drew a token from a pile in front of him, each token informing him whether the test was to be one of immediate reconstruction of order or one of immediate free recall. In the former case, the experimenter provided an appropriate deck of cards; if free recall was called for, a blank sheet of paper was provided.

2. *Results*

Figure 5 shows the outcome of experiment 4, with nouns and adjectives combined. The ordering data look very similar to those in Fig. 4 and show a similarity decrement. In the analysis of variance based on the similarity by serial position crossing, the main effect of similarity was statistically significant by a one-tailed but not by a two-tailed test, $F(1, 19) = 3.04$, $p < .05$, one tailed. The interaction was not reliable ($F = 0.19$).

In view of the strong prior expectation of a similarity decrement with these materials, and considering the close replication of this effect across experiments 3 and 4, we are justified in a strong inference from the directional test.

The free-recall data show much the same pattern seen earlier in *(a)* free-recall scoring of the data from experiments 1 and 2, and *(b)* final free recall of words initially tested by reconstruction of ordering (experiment 3). Both the main effect of similarity and its interaction with position were statistically significant, $F(1, 19) = 5.23$, $p < .05$, and $F(7, 133) = 2.38$, $p < .05$, respectively. The interaction of similarity and position which appears here and in some of the other data sets is not especially interesting; there is little room for a similarity effect when performance is constrained at the ceiling in primacy and recency regions of the list.

Experiment 4 thus demonstrates within one design the Horowitz interaction. The overall proportions correct, collapsing over serial position, went from .551 to .619 as similarity was changed from high to low in the ordering task. Corresponding proportions in the free-recall task were .752 and .653. An analysis of variance based on this breakdown showed the interaction to be highly significant, $F(1, 19) = 9.88$, $p < .01$.

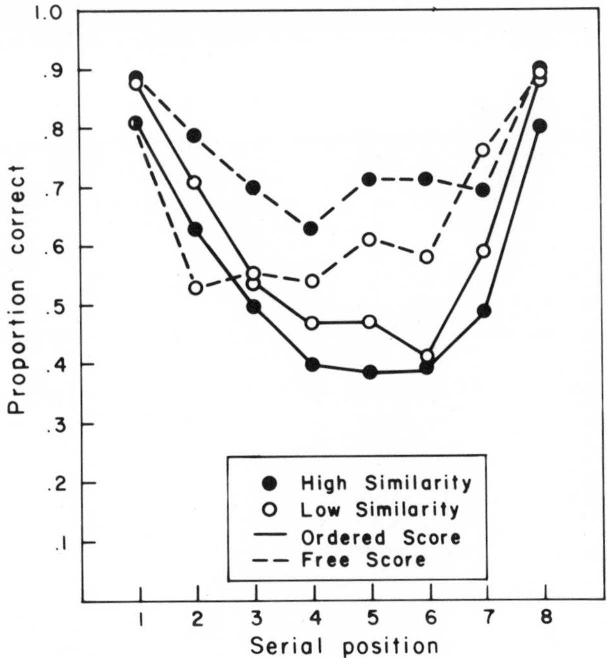

Fig. 5. Immediate ordering and immediate free recall as a function of semantic similarity and serial position. Instructions for ordering or free recall came only after the list had been presented (experiment 4).

Free recall was easier than ordering, $F(1, 19) = 21.35$; however, there was no overall effect of similarity.

As in the study by Watkins *et al.* (1974), intrusions were a rarity. In the low-similarity condition there were 32 intrusions and in the high-similarity condition there were 24.

E. Comments on Experiments 1–4

On balance there is no denying that the interaction between similarity and item–order performance measures occurs for semantic similarity as well as phonological similarity. The interaction is directly evident in Figs. 4 and 5; it is implied in Figs. 2 and 3, where the large advantage for high similarity in item recall must have been neutralized by an opposite tendency in order memory such that the two balanced out to no effect in ordered recall.

The main difference here, and in the other studies that have been done on this problem, is that the balance of item and order information seems different for phonological and semantic similarity: In semantic similarity studies it is easy to get facilitation in free recall but difficult to show impairment in ordered recall of the same lists. In phonological similarity experiments, it is just the opposite. This result is anticipated by the Murdock and vom Saal (1967) experiment, with word trigrams in the Brown–Peterson method, where the net effect of similarity on ordered recall was positive, when similarity was defined by category membership.

The fact that two grossly different manifestations of intralist similarity should have essentially similar patterns of interaction in memory for items and memory for order leads us to wonder whether theories of similarity effects that are couched in phonological terms can be applied to the semantic results. The Sperling and Speelman (1970) theory of similarity effects is probably most vexed by the results of experiments 1–4. Their hypotheses are based on a phonemic-string representation, the predictability of item-recall scores from ordered-recall scores, and guessing in high-similarity lists. The contention that item scores carry no new information beyond position (ordered-recall) scores is particularly suspect in the present context. Here, there was essentially no difference as a function of similarity in ordered-recall scoring but a large difference in item (free-recall) scoring. Nor was there evidence for guessing in experiment 4.

The Wickelgren (1965, 1977) notions fare somewhat better. His forward interphonemic associations must be replaced with comparable associations among semantic features, but the logic transfers directly. If a word concept can be decomposed into connotative and denotative semantic features, it is reasonable that a string, such as LOATHSOME ODIOUS REPUGNANT, contains a common element to which the distinguishing features all get attached, just as the string BDP contains the common vowel sound /i/. In contrast, the string LOATHSOME CLEVER DELICIOUS is less likely to have such a common feature, similarly to the phonological representations of the string BLW. The relative difficulty of memory for order in the high-similarity materials, of either kind, comes from the fewer distinctive cues for order when successive items overlap in many features than when they do not overlap. The explanation of an item-recall advantage for high similarity is that the common features will serve as retrieval cues for all the items and they are sure to be retained themselves. Wickelgren's hypothesis on this last point is not a version of guessing—the cuing from a common semantic or phonological feature of high-similarity lists takes place among the episodic memory structures produced by the list and not within semantic memory.

The Watkins *et al.* (1974) application of Estes' (1972) theory is similarly translatable into the domain of semantic similarity, substituting semantic features for phonological units. Indeed, the explanation for why order information shows a similarity disadvantage is essentially identical in the Estes and the Wickelgren accounts.

Thus, the first four experiments of this series suggest that we have been taking too restricted a view of similarity effects in list memory. It is necessary to generalize our theories of these effects so that they will accommodate semantic as well as phonological similarity. We now turn to another aspect of the item versus order problem.

III. List Length and Item versus Order Learning

A. The Neo-Malthusian Hypothesis

Anyone who wishes to separate item and order information must concede that ordered recall includes a contribution from both. Experiments 5–7 were designed to explore one hypothesis for how this joint contribution works in ordered recall. The particular focus was on how the balance of item and order information in ordered recall might change as a function of how long the memory lists are. The hypothesis of interest, which was first stated clearly by Crossman (1961), is that item information grows more slowly with series length than order information. Our interest in this hypothesis can be motivated by reference to some disparate findings, as follows.

In ordered recall of word trigrams with high or low semantic similarity, Murdock and vom Saal (1967) observed a net positive effect of similarity. Subsequent performance analyses showed, of course, that this was the result of facilitation in item recall and inhibition in order recall. In experiments 1 and 2 here, however, there was no convincing net main effect of semantic similarity, even though similarity was defined by category membership in the former study, as it had been in the Murdock and vom Saal study. There are many differences in procedure between the two demonstrations, including especially that the short lists have to be tested following a period of distractor activity in order for subjects to make any errors. Disregarding these inherent differences, why should there be a net positive effect with the short lists and no effect with the longer lists? (In other, unpublished research, I have occasionally found a net positive effect of phonological similarity on recall of trigrams in the Brown–Peterson task, which contrasts with the universal finding of inhibition with span length items.)

Crossman's (1961) hypothesis was that item information grows proportionately to the list length, n, whereas order information grows proportionately to n factorial. Each new item adds a constant amount of item information but it has an accelerating effect on the accumulation of order information. The argument is not changed by the fact that Crossman had in mind a logarithmic proportionality; any reasonable assumption leads to the arithmetic growth of item information and the geometric growth of order information with list length.

If ordered recall depends on the complexity of both item and order information, acting jointly, and if item information is facilitated by similarity and order information inhibited, it follows that the net effect will turn increasingly negative with longer lists. This derivation is tested formally in experiments 5, 6, and 7.

Redundancy of Order Representation

Of course, the assumption that item information grows with n and order information with $n!$ entails the prior assumption that order is represented redundantly. Logically, order could be specified by $n - 1$ connections between adjacent items. However, Ebbinghaus (1885/1964), Hull (1935), Estes (1972), and Wickelgren (1977) have all, for vastly different reasons, chosen the redundant format for representing order in their associative systems. In one way or another, they all stipulate that not only is A ordered relative to B and B relative to C, but also A is ordered relative to C. This property of associative models for lists is plausible in light of evidence found by Rundus (1971) that early positions are rehearsed in temporal contiguity with later positions.

In Estes' (1972) theory, order information is held in two formats, corresponding to short- and long-term storage. We emphasized the short-term mechanism, the "vertical" recycling between a constituent and its control element, in the discussion above and now we turn briefly to the long-term mechanism. Because of the perturbation in timing that characterizes the short-term system, some less precarious format is obviously necessary. The assumption is that if rehearsal is possible, adjacent and remote forward associations will be formed among constituents subordinate to the same control element. Furthermore, these associations are assumed to be inhibitory, in contrast to the vertical associations, which are excitatory. In recall, the function of the horizontal connections is to prevent the most superordinate elements from excitating simultaneous recall of all their subordinate elements at the same time; only the least inhibited, or leftmost, element will be realized overtly, after which it becomes refractory for a time, to allow a left to right responding. Crowder (1976, Chaps. 7 & 12) can be consulted for more details on this theory.

The important point is that Estes proposes that the difficulty of a list, in ordered recall, depends on the total number of associations in the memory structure, both vertical excitatory ones and also horizontal inhibitory ones. The relative numbers of these depend on what subgroupings are formed during the rehearsal process. If a series of six items is ungrouped, there will be six excitatory connections between the items and a common control element; the number of inhibitory assocations would then be 15, or, in general, $[(n - 1) + (n - 2) + \ldots + 1]$. The total difficulty is indexed in this case at $6 + 15 = 21$. If the same list were subdivided into two subgroups of three, there would be eight excitatory connections—two from the highest superordinate leading to control elements for the two subgroups, and another three from these latter control elements to the terminal items within each subgroup; the same representation would entail seven inhibitory connections, one relating the control elements for the two subgroups and then three within each subgroup. Performance should be better with grouping, in this instance.

As list length increases, the relative growth of item (vertical, excitatory) and order (horizontal, inhibitory) information depends on the groupings employed by the subject. If a grouping size of three is consistently used at all levels of the hierarchy, both types of association will grow just in pace with each other, for a grouping of three always has the same number of vertical and horizontal associations. If groupings of two were used, item information would grow faster than order information with list length. If any grouping size larger than three were used, however, then the order associations would escalate faster than the item associations.

This dependence of difficulty on grouping size is a striking accomplishment for the Estes (1972) theory, Wickelgren (1967) having shown that three is empirically the optimal grouping unit in serial memory. Our interest here is to return with these observations to the neo-Malthusian hypothesis we have drawn from the Crossman (1961) observation. The result is that Estes' theory joins Crossman's in predicting faster growth of order than item information, with list length, provided rehearsal leads to groupings greater, on the average, than three. This will be indeterminant with ordinary experimental methods, of course, so it is probably best to take the Crossman and Estes formulations as examples of a class of theories that anticipate differential changes in item and order difficulty as list length is increased. If this neo-Malthusian hypothesis has merit, the length–difficulty relationship should then be steeper for high than low intralist similarity materials. This is because similarity seems to have a negative effect on order information and, if order information assumes a larger and larger role with longer lists, the net effect should turn negative faster with the similar materials.

B. Experiments 5–7

Experiments 5, 6, and 7 all had essentially the same design: Performance was compared for lists with high or low intralist similarity at five different list lengths. In experiment 5, semantic similarity was varied with lengths from six through 10. In experiment 6, semantic similarity was again varied, but the lengths were increased to the range nine through 13. In experiment 7, the similarity manipulation was phonological, using the shorter range of lengths (6–10). The three studies will be presented together and since their outcomes were anticlimactic, they will be discussed in summary form.

1. Method of Experiment 5

The materials were the two 10 × 10 arrays of words (adjectives and nouns) used in experiments 1–4. Every subject heard 20 lists, one block of 10 lists with nouns (either high or low similarity) and the other with adjectives at the other similarity level, with their order counterbalanced across subjects. Order of lists was uniform but subjects received individually randomized words.

Once the design was constructed as to which type of materials occurred in what order for groups of subjects, two lists of each type (nouns, adjectives, similar, dissimilar) were truncated to a length of six items, two more to seven items, and so on for the five lengths. Since the lists were presented in uniform order, different schedules of truncation across these lists were employed for different subgroups of subjects, unconfounding list length with particular words. There were 40 subjects, 20 told to recall in serial order and 20 told to recall the items in any order.

2. Method for Experiment 6

Experiment 6 was exactly the same in design as experiment 5 except for changes required by increasing the range of list lengths from 6–10 to 9–13. Some additional words had to be generated to produce the longer lists, of course.

3. Method for Experiment 7

Phonological similarity, rather than semantic similarity, was varied in experiment 7. A 10 × 10 matrix of nouns and adjectives, mixed, was derived for this purpose and is shown in the Appendix. Only the six stop consonants were used as consonant sounds. The vowel sounds were uniform within a row of the matrix. Similar and dissimilar lists were defined by taking either rows or columns of this array. Each of 40 subjects heard 20 lists, 10 similar lists and 10 dissimilar lists; thus, unlike in the earlier studies, subjects heard each word twice, once in the high- and once in the low-similarity context. In all other respects this study was similar to experiment 5.

4. *Results*

The results of these three experiments will be displayed together. However, there are several scoring criteria, and these will be taken up separately.

a. Ordered Recall. For the subjects who were asked to recall lists in order of presentation, we are interested in some measure that takes into account both item and order information. The first such evaluation to be considered is the simplest—the number of list items recalled in their proper position, which we have been calling ordered recall.

However, in these studies the subject was not constrained to recall exactly n items or to indicate with place savers where he drew a blank. This required something other than a ruthless position by position strategy for scoring. The measure of ordered recall used here was derived by counting in from both the beginning and end of the recall protocol until the first error in either direction was reached and adding together the number of correct recalls from both starting points.

Figure 6 shows the results in terms of this measure of ordered recall. If the neo-Malthusian hypothesis were true, we should expect to see a sharper length–difficulty relation with high than with low similarity. Such an interaction was not evident visually or statistically for either data set with semantic similarity varied; neither was it evident for that with phonological similarity varied. Overall there was no effect of conceptual similarity on ordered recall: in experiment 5, $t(19) = -.15$ and in experiment 6, $t(19) = 0.24$, both ts nonsignificant. In experiment 7, where phonological similarity was varied, ordered recall was much better for the low-similarity strings than for the high-similarity strings.

Experiments 5 and 7, therefore, produced an interaction between the similarity criterion, semantic or phonological, and the degree of similarity, high or low. These two studies used different words and a different experimental design, so to document the interaction it was necessary to calculate a net similarity difference for each subject and then to compare these two distributions between experiments. In experiment 5, subjects made an average of 3.76 more correct responses in the high- than in the low-similarity condition, whereas in experiment 7, this difference was 9.30 in the opposite direction, $t(38) = 3.17, p < .005$.

b. P scores. Horowitz (1961) suggested that Kendall's P might be a

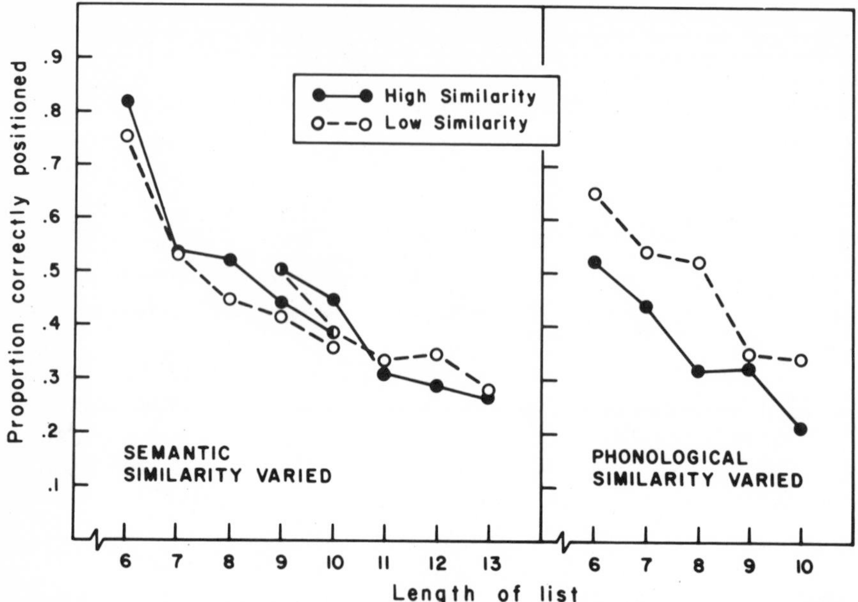

Fig. 6. The relation between list length and proportion of correctly positioned elements (ordered recall) as a function of semantic similarity (experiments 5 and 6) and of phonological similarity (experiment 7).

useful measure of ordered recall in studies with different list lengths. Here we use a measure based on *P:* For a stimulus of length *n,* the number of ordered pairs of items is $[(n - 1) + (n - 2) + \ldots + 1]$; we shall define our version of *P* as the proportion of these that appear in recall. For a list, ABCDEF, a recall of ACBFD would give a *P* score of $8/15 = .53$. This, too, is a compromise between credit for item and order information.

The data from experiments 5, 6, and 7, measured in *P* scores, are shown in Fig. 7. The breakdown is identical to that in Fig. 6. As with ordered recall, there is no indication here of a sharper length–difficulty function for the high- than for the low-similarity condition. Combining lengths, high-similarity facilitated performance in experiment 5, $t(19 = 2.53, p < .05$, and in experiment 6; however, the latter difference was not statistically reliable, $t(19) = 1.68$. With phonological similarity, in experiment 7, there was a reversal of this difference, with low similarity superior, $t(19) = 2.57, p = .02$.

The two experiments on semantic similarity, experiments 5 and 6, reveal no reliable net effect in Fig. 6, with ordered recall, but they do in Fig. 7, with the *P* scores. Evidently the latter measure places relatively

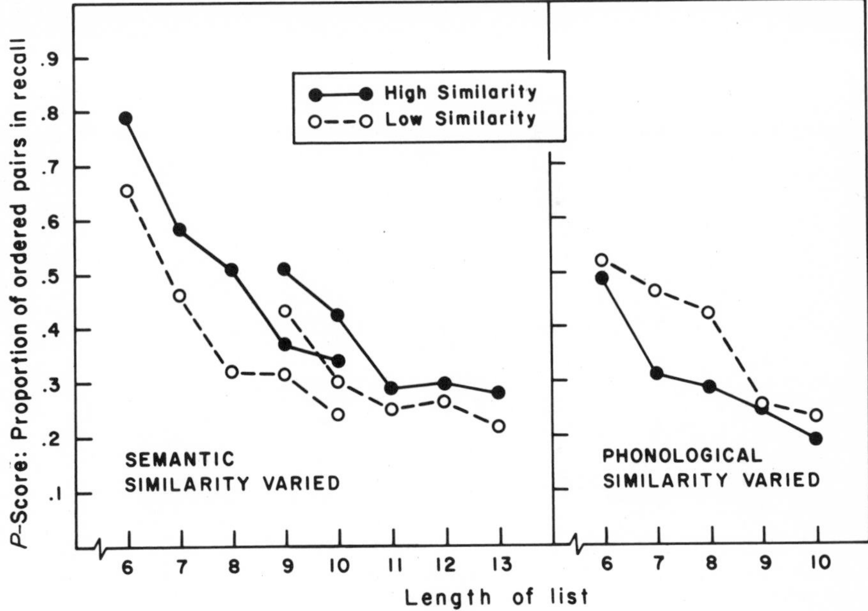

Fig. 7. Same as Fig. 6 except the performance measure (*P* score) is the proportion of correctly ordered pairs (experiments 5, 6, and 7).

more weight in whatever component of performance is facilitated by high similarity. To check that this was not a chance occurrence in these studies, data from experiment 1 were reanalyzed in terms of the *P* measure. Whereas there was no net effect of similarity on straight ordered recall, $t(22) = 0.29$, there was a similarity advantage for the *P* score, $t(22) = 2.54$, $p = .02$. If one chooses to attribute the facilitative effect to item information, then this means that *P* weights item information more than ordered recall. The more general lesson is not to place too much weight on results obtained with only one of several possible theoretically motivated performance measures.

As with the data of Fig. 6, there was a cross-experiment interaction between the net effect of similarity and the type of similarity involved. On a 0–1 scale, semantic similarity facilitated performance by an average of .1179 in experiment 5, whereas phonological similarity inhibited performance by an average of .0821 in experiment 7, $t(38) = 3.49$, $p < .01$.

c. Free Recall. For completeness, the free-recall data are shown in Fig. 8. These data contain no surprises, for it has never been in question that similarity aids free recall. This effect was only marginal for phonological similarity here, $t(19)$ z 1.85 p) .10 by a two-tailed test.

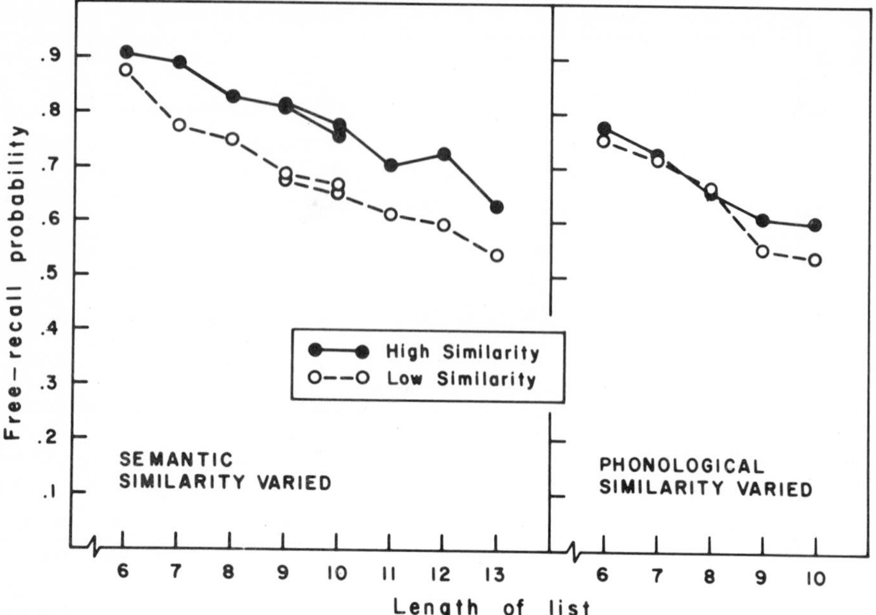

Fig. 8. Probability of correct free recall as a function of list length and of semantic (experiments 5 and 6) or phonological (experiment 7) similarity.

5. *Discussion of Experiments 5–7*

The main reason for doing the last three experiments was to test the neo-Malthusian hypothesis of a steeper length–difficulty relation for high- than for low-similarity lists. There was not the remotest comfort for this hypothesis, when either the standard ordered-recall measure was used or the proportional *P*-score.

One curiosity raised by these data can only be mentioned here in passing: Measures traditionally thought to combine item and order information (Figs. 6 and 7) show a positive effect for semantic similarity and a negative effect for phonological similarity. One might be tempted to conclude from this that the two kinds of similarity behave differently but, of course, experiments 1–4 have established that the qualitative effects are comparable. This all suggests that whatever factor it is that facilitates item recall for high-similarity lists is stronger in the semantically similar lists than in the phonologically similar lists. This, in turn, is consistent with the only marginal reliability of the free-recall (Fig. 8) facilitation by high phonological similarity. I turn next to one hypothesis for what this facilitative factor might be.

IV. Another Look at the Guessing Hypothesis

Earlier research (Watkins *et al.*, 1974; see also experiment 4 in this paper) has established that blatant guessing cannot be used to account for the similarity advantage in free recall. Intrusion errors of items arbitrarily left off the lists are vanishingly rare in these studies. Yet a modification of the perceptual theory called *sophisticated guessing* could still handle the phenomenon.

The sophisticated guessing hypothesis assumes that knowledge of intralist structure ("all words rhyme with the vowel sound in HOG") combines with partial memory information about particular items to enhance recall. For another example, consider that the subject has encoded that all words on a list of adjectives are fear related; if there is also some information that a list item contained the letter X, the subject might be able to recall ANXIOUS. Correct recall of this sort would not really be guessing and would not result in the sorts of intrusions we invited in earlier studies by leaving words off the list. Yet if the sophisticated guessing mechanisms lay behind the similarity advantage in free recall, there would be no inherent similarity effect on item information. This, in turn, would simplify our thinking about item and order information because there would no longer be any cause for worrying about the interaction uncovered by Horowitz (1961).

Experiments 8 and 9

If the sophisticated guessing hypothesis were true, as presented above, then a recognition test of pure item information should show no similarity difference. In the appropriate test, the subject would be faced with choosing between ANXIOUS and FEARFUL after receiving a list of fear-related adjectives; only one of these two items would have actually occurred on the list, and so knowledge of list structure would be no help. Experiments 8 and 9 differed only in whether the type of similarity varied was semantic or phonological, respectively, and they will be described in parallel.

1. *Method for Experiments 8 and 9*

The stimuli were based on 13 × 13 matrices in which words within a row were approximately synonymous (experiment 8) or homonymous (experiment 9). The former words are just those used in experiment 6 and the phonologically controlled words were expanded from those used in experiment 7. A subject received only one level of similarity, either all 13 high-similarity lists or 13 low-similarity lists. The lists presented were all nine items long, four items having been randomly selected for deletion on an individual basis. In testing, there were four forced-choice tests containing two alternatives; in each pair, one word from the list was paired with one of the four that had been withheld from that list. The location of "old" items was balanced against serial position across subjects but this factor was not analyzed.

The stimulus lists were read aloud by the experimenter at a one word per second rate, preceded by the signal READY. Immediately following the last item on the list, subjects began working on a Scrabble-cubes task in which they had 1 min to construct as many words as possible from a haphazard throw of letter cubes. They calculated their own scores after a minute and then had another try and a second calculation of their scores. This double-distractor task took about 3 min. At this point, the subjects were shown the four two-choice memory tests, one at a time, for recognition ratings. They indicated first which of the two items they thought was the old one and then rated their confidence in this choice on a three-point scale. There were 52 Yale students in experiment 8 and another 52 in experiment 9.

2. *Results*

In both experiments, each subject had 13 lists, either all similar or all dissimilar, of which four items on each were tested. The first analysis is in terms of mean errors out of these 52 forced-choice tests for each subject. The next analysis establishes that choosing another criterion from the six-point scale (derived from confidence ratings) does not alter the conclusion that similarity had no effect. The final analysis displays the response distributions across the six-point scale.

a. Results of Experiment 8. Out of 52 opportunities for error, the 26 subjects in the high-similarity group made an average of 9.19 (s.d. = 4.51) and the low-similarity group made an average of 8.73 (s.d. = 4.29), which is not a reliable difference $t(50) = 0.378$. This analysis defines an error as choosing the old and new responses incorrectly, whatever the confidence rating. In terms of the six-point scale, in other words, we have just split at the 3-to-4 point. In a second analysis we consider to be in error any response other than the highest confidence in a correct old/new choice (that is, a 5-to-6 split on the scale). Mean errors, by this strict definition, were 24.38 for the high-similarity group and 26.04 for the low-similarity group, $t(50) = 0.698$. These two contrasts span error rates of from about 17% to about 50% (9/52 to 25/52) and so there can be no claim that either ceiling or floor effects were responsible for the null finding.

A power analysis was conducted on the 3-to-4 split to place the null finding in statistical context. If we say that a difference of 2.0 words (out of 52) is a reasonable difference to have expected, by a directional test, then experiment 8 had a power of .921 to reject a truly false null hypothesis. This is smaller than a 4% performance difference and it is not unreasonable to have anticipated this large an effect in light of the other studies in this series. (The power of experiment 8 to detect a one-word effect was .390.)

b. Results of Experiment 9. Using the 3-to-4 split in the response scale, the high-similarity group made an average of 11.11 errors (s.d. = 4.46) and the low-similarity group made 10.31 (s.d., = 5.27), a difference that was far from statistical reliability, $t(50) = 0.596$. Redefining an error at the 5-to-6 point in the rating scale, the high-similarity group made fewer errors than the low-similarity group (20.81 versus 24.33), a result that was just barely reliable by a directional test, $t(50) = 1.692, p < .05$. This last outcome can be discounted: Notice that it is in the opposite direction to the result obtained with the 3-to-4 split; with the extremely strict criterion, the subjects who had high similarity materials responded with more caution, apparently, than those with low-similarity materials. The same thing happened in experiment 8, where the high-similarity group made more errors, slightly, with the moderate criterion and fewer with the strict criterion.

Figure 9 shows this criterion effect in both studies. This figure contains frequency distributions for both studies across the six response categories. In both distributions, but especially in that of experiment 9 with phonological similarity, there is a tendency for high similarity to reduce the occurrence of "6" responses. This difference, we have seen, was reliable in the phonological study but not in the semantic study. However, in both experiments there is a compensatory tendency for high-similarity subjects to place more responses in the low confidence but correct categories. Apparently, highly similar materials are more damaging to confidence than they are to accuracy.

The conclusion of experiment 9, that similarity has no effect on item memory, was backed up by the same power analysis as was that of experiment 8. Considering again that a mean difference of 2.0 words is a reasonable alternative hypothesis, the power of experiment 9 to reject a false null hypothesis is .895 (the power against a one-word difference is .358).

3. *Discussion of Experiments 8 and 9*

The conclusion that item information shows no similarity effect in recognition conflicts with the conclusion of Murdock (1976, experiment 1) on the same question. In Murdock's study, subjects received three-word trigrams and were tested following 3, 9, or 18 sec of numerical distractor activity. In a test of recognition for item information, the subject had

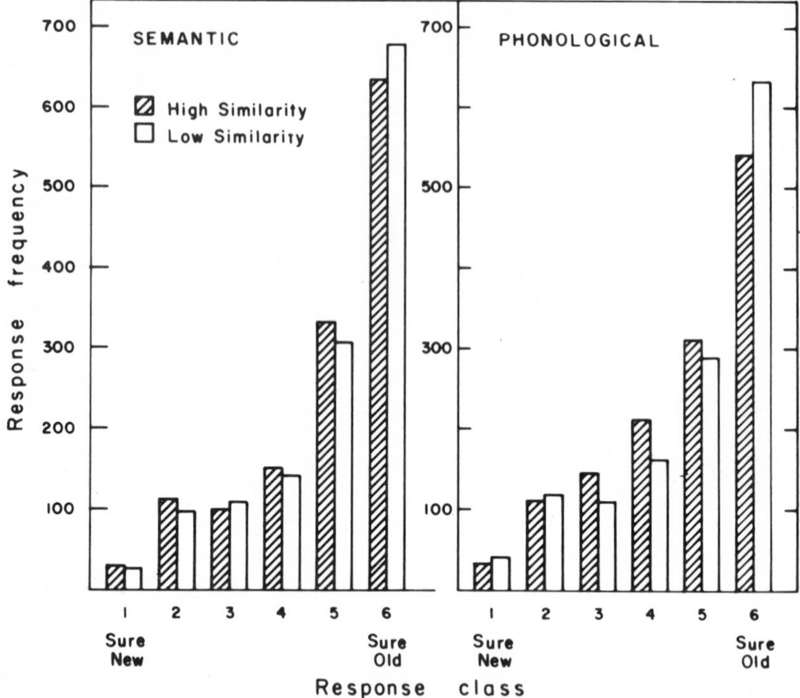

Fig. 9. Frequency distribution of confidence ratings as a function of type of similarity varied (semantic in experiment 8, left panel, and phonological in experiment 9, right panel) and level of similarity.

to pick the three presented words from among six alternatives. These six words were either all from the same category or not. There was a higher proportion of words recognized in the high-similarity condition (.907) than in the low-similarity condition (.885). The significance of the difference was tested by a sign test and showed reliability at the .05 level.

It is not clear what accounts for the difference between Murdock's results and those offered here. One possibility is that the complexity of Murdock's experimental design induced his subjects to subordinate item to order information. On a random half of the trials, the subject was asked to recall the three words from that trial and on the other half he recognized the correct words from among three distractors. In either case, the next job was to reconstruct the order of the items. In the present studies, however, the subject never saw more than one level of similarity and he was never tested for anything other than item information.

Murdock's study notwithstanding, our best conclusion is that similarity is not effective in changing recognition memory for pure item information, whether similarity is varied semantically or phonologically. A true effect small enough to have gone undetected in experiments 8 and 9 is numerically uninteresting with comparison to the robust similarity effects observed in Figs. 1–5 on recall. The most obvious explanation for why similarity helps recall of item information so much and does not help recognition of item information is the sophisticated guessing hypothesis: A fragmentary memory trace, itself too sketchy to support recall, is supplemented with memory for list structure (similarity) to narrow down the possible recall candidates. When both recognition alternatives conform to the structure, there is no basis for facilitation.

V. General Discussion

There are two major empirical conclusions from this series of experiments. First, the results of experiments 1–4 argue that semantic similarity affects performance in list memory situations much in the same way as does phonological similarity. This means investigators should formulate explanations for these effects in terms that transcend particular manipulations of similarity. Second, the last two studies show that the facilitation of high intralist similarity for item information, such as in free recall, does not occur with recognition tests of item information. This result may be understood with reference to the sophisticated guessing hypothesis and it has a major implication for the distinction between item and order information, as follows.

It will be recalled that we began with the struggle to unravel the empirical and theoretical distinctions between memory for items and memory for their order. It turned out that the single major empirical result demanding such a distinction was the dissociation of item and order information in experiments on intralist similarity. Now it appears that there is a bit less to this dissociation than it first seemed. Similarity does not after all have opposite effects on item and order information once we have removed the facilitation due to sophisticated guessing. Instead, similarity has no effect on item information as such.

This pattern of findings offers considerable comfort to the assertion made above that item and order information must, at heart, be similar in format, each locating a well-known item with respect to its temporal–spatial occurrence. Why, then, we may ask, should it be true that the fine-grained occurrence information (order information) is damaged by intralist similarity but the coarse-grained occurrence information (item information) is not? This, too, turns out to be much less of a problem than it seems: The difficulty in retention of item information is locating a word with respect to a particular list, almost always the most recent list as opposed to earlier lists in the same context. The kind of similarity that should be inhibitory for these list-discrimination memories is similarity among successive lists learned in the same context, not similarity within any single one of them. Thus, it should be semantic or phonological relationships spanning lists N and $N + 1$ that produce item–information decrements; similarity within any individual list would be irrelevant to list discrimination. Anderson and Bower (1972) have shown dramatic inhibition from interlist similarity. The buildup and release of proactive inhibition in short-term memory can be understood from the same perspective.

In remembering order information, however, the discrimination that is crucial is between items' temporal assocations within the list. In both cases, in other words, similarity operates the same way but it is defined across a different aggregate of events—across lists in the case of item information and across items within lists in the case of order information. It remains to work out the mechanism for similarity effects exactly, in terms of the sorts of theories explained in the earlier pages of this report. However, the job is now perhaps slightly simplified by our conclusions that *(a)* all similarity effects appear to operate in the same way, and *(b)* similarity seems to have uniform effects on item and order information once these are defined with respect to the proper scale.

Appendix

NOUNS FOR EXPERIMENT 1

CALIFORNIA	TEXAS	MARYLAND	FLORIDA	ILLINOIS
SHARK	HERRING	CATFISH	PERCH	SALMON
BIRCH	MAPLE	ELM	DOGWOOD	SPRUCE
ROSE	TULIP	CARNATION	DAISY	VIOLET
MARY	SUE	ANN	JANE	JUDY
FLY	ANT	BEE	MOSQUITO	SPIDER
CARROT	PEA	CORN	BEAN	POTATO
CAR	BUS	AIRPLANE	TRAIN	TRUCK
ROBIN	SPARROW	CARDINAL	EAGLE	CROW
PIANO	DRUM	TRUMPET	VIOLIN	CLARINET
VIRGINIA	PENNSYLVANIA	MAINE	OHIO	INDIANA
TUNA	GOLDFISH	SWORDFISH	COD	FLOUNDER
WILLOW	CEDAR	PALM	OAK	POPLAR
ORCHID	PANSY	DAFFODIL	GERANIUM	LILY
CAROL	BARBARA	LINDA	JOAN	NANCY
BEETLE	WASP	MOTH	FLEA	TERMITE
TOMATO	LETTUCE	SPINACH	CELERY	SQUASH
BICYCLE	BOAT	WAGON	BIKE	TAXI
CANARY	HAWK	WREN	PARROT	PIGEON
FLUTE	GUITAR	OBOE	TUBA	HARP

ADJECTIVES FOR EXPERIMENT 2

CHILDLIKE	IMMATURE	INNOCENT	NAIVE	TRUSTFUL
HATEFUL	CONTEMPTIBLE	ABHORRANT	DETESTABLE	LOATHSOME
QUICK	FAST	SPEEDY	RAPID	SWIFT
SMALL	SLIGHT	MINIMAL	LEAST	LITTLE
OLD	ELDERLY	AGED	SENILE	ANCIENT
JOVIAL	MERRY	HILARIOUS	JOLLY	MIRTHFUL
WILD	SAVAGE	UNCIVILIZED	TURBULENT	STORMY
STRANGE	ODD	EERIE	ALIEN	MYSTERIOUS
IDSRESPECTFUL	INSULTING	SCORNFUL	RUDE	DERISIVE
SIMPLE	ARTLESS	TENDER	UNRIPE	UNSOPHISTICATED
DISGUSTING	REPUGNANT	ODIOUS	DISTASTEFUL	OBNOXIOUS
FLEET	HASTY	PROMPT	AGILE	NIMBLE
TRIFLING	MINOR	TRIVIAL	PETTY	MINUTE
NOBLE	FOREMOST	CHIEF	PRINCIPAL	ILLUSTRIOUS
ARCHAIC	ANTIQUE	OBSOLETE	VENERABLE	DODDERING
EXUBERANT	AMUSING	ELATED	JOYFUL	JOCULAR
CRAZY	CRUDE	RAW	PRIMITIVE	UNRESTRAINED
UNFAMILIAR	FOREIGN	PECULIAR	UNNATURAL	WIERD
SARCASTIC	CONTEMPTUOUS	INSOLENT	IRREVERENT	DISDAINFUL

MATERIALS USED FOR EXPERIMENT 7

CAULK	BOUGHT	TALK	BOG	AWE
BITE	PIE	KITE	DIE	BUY
KEEP	BEAK	PEA	KEY	DEED
CUB	TUB	BUT	DUG	TUG
COD	TOP	COB	GOD	GOT
DIG	KICK	DID	DIP	PIT
DEAD	GET	BED	DECK	PEP
BACK	GAB	CAD	DAD	CAP
POKE	TOAD	GOAT	DOUGH	CODE
PAID	GATE	TAKE	DATE	PAY
DOG	PAW	TAUT	OUGHT	CAUGHT
GUIDE	PIPE	TIED	TIE	TYPE
PEAT	EAT	TEA	DEEP	BEAT
CUP	BUCK	DUCK	PUP	BUG
POP	COT	DOCK	POT	DOT
BIT	BIG	TIP	KID	PICK
BEG	BET	PET	PECK	DEBT
CAB	TACK	BAD	GAP	PAD
COKE	COPE	COAT	BOAT	TOE
CAPE	BAIT	BAKE	TAPE	CAKE

References

Aborn, M., & Rubenstein, H. Information theory and immediate recall. *Journal of Experimental Psychology,* 1952, **44,** 260–266.

Anderson, J. R., & Bower, G. H. Recognition and retrieval processes in free recall. *Psychological Review,* 1972, **79,** 97–123.

Bjork, E. L., & Healy, A. F. Short-term order and item retention. *Journal of Verbal Learning and Verbal Behavior,* 1974, **13,** 80–97.

Brown, J. Some tests of the decay theory of immediate memory. *Quarterly Journal of Experimental Psychology,* 1958, **10,** 12–21.

Conrad, R. Acoustic confusions in immediate memory. *British Journal of Psychology,* 1964, **55,** 75–84.

Conrad, R. Order errors in immediate recall of sequences. *Journal of Verbal Learning and Verbal Behavior,* 1965, **4,** 161–169.

Conrad, R., & Hull, A. J. Information, acoustic confusion, and memory span. *British Journal of Psychology,* 1964, **55,** 429–432.

Craik, F. I. M. *Depth of processing and aging in memory.* Paper presented at the George W. Talland Memorial Conference on Aging and Human Memory, Boston, July 1978.

Crossman, E. R. F. W. Information and serial order in human memory. In C. Cherry (Ed.), *Information theory.* London: Butterworth, 1961.

Crowder, R. G. *Principles of learning and memory.* Hillsdale, N.J.: Lawrence Erlbaum Associates, 1976.

Crowder, R. G. Audition and speech coding in short-term memory. In J. Requin (Ed.), *Attention and performance* (Vol. 7). Hillsdale, N.J.: Lawrence Erlbaum Associates, 1979.

Ebbinghaus, H. E. *Memory: A contribution to experimental psychology.* New York: Dover, 1964. (Originally published in 1885.)

Estes, W. K. An associative basis for coding and organization in memory. In A. W. Melton & E. Martin (Eds.), *Coding processes in human memory.* Washington, D.C.: Winston, 1972.

Fuchs, A. H. Recall for order and content of serial word lists in short-term memory. *Journal of Experimental Psychology,* 1969, **82,** 14–21.

Hall, J. F. *Verbal learning and retention,* Philadelphia: Lippincott, 1971.

Healy, A. F. Separating item from order information in short-term memory. *Journal of Verbal Learning and Verbal Behavior,* 1974, **13,** 644–655.

Horowitz, L. M. Free recall and ordering of trigrams. *Journal of Experimental Psychology,* 1961, **62,** 51–57.

Hull, C. L. The conflicting psychologies of learning—A way out. *Psychological Review,* 1935, **42,** 491–516.

Lee, C. L., & Estes, W. K. Order and position in primary memory for letter strings. *Journal of Verbal Learning and Verbal Behavior,* 1977, **16,** 395–418.

McGovern, J. B. Extinction of associations in four transfer paradigms. *Psychological Monographs,* 1964, **78**(16, Whole No. 593).

Miller, G. A. Free recall of redundant strings of letters. *Journal of Experimental Psychology,* 1958, **56,** 485–491.

Murdock, B. B., Jr. *Human memory: Theory and data.* Hillsdale, N.J.: Lawrence Erlbaum Associates, 1974.

Murdock, B.B., Jr. Item and order information in serial short-term memory. *Journal of Experimental Psychology: General,* 1976, **105,** 191–216.

Murdock, B. B., Jr., & vom Saal, W. Transpositions in short-term memory. *Journal of Experimental Psychology,* 1967, **74,** 137–143.

Posner, M. I., & Konick, A. W. On the role of interference in short-term retention. *Journal of Experimental Psychology,* 1966, **72,** 221–231.

Roediger, H. L., III. Inhibiting effects of recall. *Memory & Cognition,* 1974, **2,** 261–269.

Rundus, D. Analysis of rehearsal processes in free recall. *Journal of Experimental Psychology,* 1971, **89,** 63–77.

Saltz, E. *The cognitive bases of human learning.* Homewood, Ill.: Dorsey Press, 1971.

Shiffrin, R. M., & Cook, J. R. Short-term forgetting of item and order information. *Journal of Verbal Learning and Verbal Behavior,* 1978, **17,** 189–218.

Sperling, G., & Speelman, R. G. Acoustic similarity and auditory short-term memory: Experiments and a model. In D. A. Norman (Ed.), *Models of human memory.* New York: Academic Press, 1970.

Tulving, E., & Pearlstone, Z. Availability versus accessibility of information in memory for words. *Journal of Verbal Learning and Verbal Behavior,* 1966, **5,** 381–391.

Underwood, B. J., Runquist, W. A., & Schulz, R. W. Response learning in paired-associate lists as a function of intralist similarity. *Journal of Experimental Psychology,* 1959, **58,** 70–78.

Watkins, M. J., Watkins, O. C., & Crowder, R. G. The modality effect in free and serial recall as a function of phonological similarity. *Journal of Verbal Larning and Verbal Behavior,* 1974, **13,** 430–447.

Wickelgren, W. A. Acoustic similarity and retroactive interference in short-term memory. *Journal of Verbal Learning and Verbal Behavior,* 1965, **4,** 53–61.

Wickelgren, W. A. Rehearsal grouping and hierarchical organization of serial position cues in short-term memory. *Quarterly Journal of Experimental Psychology,* 1967, **19,** 97–102.

Wickelgren, W. A. *Learning and memory,* Engelwood Cliffs, N.J.: Prentice-Hall, 1977.

STIMULUS CLASSIFICATION: PARTITIONING STRATEGIES AND USE OF EVIDENCE

Patrick Rabbitt

UNIVERSITY OF OXFORD, OXFORD, ENGLAND

I. Introduction

Human beings do not make a different response to each new stimulus they encounter. Rather, they make the same response to various patterns of sensory input which are usually discriminable from each other, and which sometimes may appear to have no characteristics in common. In other words, people distinguish between categories of stimuli rather than between unique events. The question of how they do so has been dealt with from a variety of theoretical standpoints. Approaches include the mathematical (set theory, group theory, theory of combinations), the philosophical (e.g., Frege, 1958; Strawson, 1959; Wittgenstein, 1956), formal linguistics (e.g., Katz & Fodor, 1963; Ross, 1974), psycholinguistics (e.g., Anderson & Bower, 1973; Collins & Quillian, 1969; Meyer,

THE PSYCHOLOGY OF LEARNING AND MOTIVATION, VOL. 13

ISBN 0-12-543313-1

1970; Morton, 1970; Rips, Shoben, & Smith, 1973; Rosch, 1973; Smith, Shoben, & Rips, 1974), and information theory (e.g., Garner, 1962, 1974). A review of this literature would be a formidable task for a group of talented specialists. The present paper has a much more modest aim, namely, to consider the contribution of reaction time and visual search experiments to our understanding of how alternative classifications of stimulus materials are made in different situations.

If we consider how any information-processing system can categorize inputs, we find that two factors will determine efficiency of performance. First, there is the particular way in which the system partitions the stimulus set in order to achieve a given categorization. Experimental paradigms are typically designed to generate particular ways of partitioning will resemble a taxonomy of experimental design. However, this is not the whole story for, as we shall see, subjects sometimes adopt strategies which are not logically optimal for the tasks they are given, and they also appear to change strategies as they become more practiced.

A second factor which determines efficiency in categorization tasks is the physical evidence on which classifications are based. A second possible taxonomy of stimulus classification might be based on the different kinds of relationships within and between sets of complex signals which subjects use in order to discriminate among them.

These two factors will mutually influence one another, since the selection and use of physical evidence as a basis for a particular classification will be partly determined by the partitioning strategies which subjects use. Furthermore, both factors will be modified by practice. Improvement on classification tasks may be described as the gradual progression from inferior to optimal partitioning strategies, and from more to less inconvenient or redundant systems of evidence.

II. Partitioning of Stimulus Sets

We shall first consider the various ways in which sets of signals can possibly be partitioned, the ways in which different partitioning schemes are forced on subjects by different experimental paradigms, and the relative efficiency with which subjects can use these different schemes.

A. Type A Partitioning: Simple "All Go"

Simple "all go" is conceptually the simplest type of partitioning of stimuli which can occur. All stimuli are treated as a single class, the same response being made whatever stimulus occurs, and no response being made if no stimulus occurs.

The experimental paradigm designed to investigate this sort of partitioning is the classic simple reaction time task, termed the a-reaction task by Donders (1869). The subject is asked to make a single response when a stimulus occurs and no response otherwise. For example, he may be asked to press a key when he hears a tone. Logically, it would not appear to matter whether tones were identical or not since the subject is not required to discriminate between them. However, as we shall see, in practice there appear to be important differences between tasks employing one or several stimuli.

B. Type B Partitioning: Complex "All Go"

Here again the subject responds to all stimuli, but in the complex all go case different responses are given to different stimuli or subsets of stimuli. Thus, the total stimulus set is divided into several classes, each consisting of one or more stimuli, and each class requiring a different response.

The experimental paradigm which appears to correspond to this partitioning is the classic choice reaction time paradigm, termed the b-reaction task by Donders (1869).

C. Type C Partitioning: "Go–No Go"

Go–no go partitioning differs from types A and B in that there is a class of stimuli to which the subject does not respond. This nonresponse class may consist of one or more stimuli. The remaining set of one or more stimuli constitutes the positive class to which a single response is made.

We will argue that, contrary to Donders' (1869) assumptions, this partitioning typically is adopted in the classic c-reaction task, where subjects are presented with a set of stimuli and only required to respond to one of them.

III. Evidence for Partitioning in Different Experimental Paradigms

A. Simple Reaction Time Paradigm

We have argued that in simple reaction time tasks, when several different stimuli are used, subjects can perform adequately by adopting a type A partitioning and treating all stimuli as instances of a single class. However, there is evidence that, although they need not, subjects in this type of task may test sensory input in a way adequate to determine which of the possible signals has occurred. P.M.A. Rabbitt, Margaret Clancy, and S.M. Vyas (unpublished observations) found that, as least early in practice, subjects in a simple reaction time task made finer discriminations than were necessary. Five groups of subjects were presented with 1, 2, 4, 8, or 16 different types of tone and required to press a key when they heard a tone. All stimuli were pure tones in the range 500–2000 Hz. A total of 1000 trials was given. When only the first 50 trials were considered, it was found that reaction time *(RT)* increased significantly with signal set size, and all differences between groups were significant. In contrast, for the last 50 trials in the series, all groups were equally fast, with no apparent effect of signal set size on *RT*.

Why and how does practice remove the effect of set size? Pending further evidence a tenable hypothesis is that one of the things that changes is the way in which the signal sets are partitioned. Early in practice it seems that subjects find it necessary to process sufficient information to discriminate between all possible signals and consequently the task becomes harder as the signal set size increases. Late in practice they no longer do this but only process information sufficient to discriminate any auditory signal presented by the experimenter from all other environmental events. In other words, improvement in RT with practice does not simply mean that subjects carry out the same functional operations faster and more accurately. They rather develop and use a new strategy of signal classification.

B. Choice Reaction Time Paradigm

Von Merkel (1885) was the first to show that, in a choice reaction where a single stimulus corresponds to each response, time paradigm *RT* increases logarithmically with the number of different signals and corresponding responses. This result was independently replicated by Hick (1952) and Hyman (1953). In his classic paper on the rate of gain of information, Hick (1952) suggested that the best fitting equations for his data were of the form $RT = \log_2 N$, where N is signal set size. This encouraged him to propose an information theoretic model based on the assumption that subjects progressively dichotomize the signal ensemble until the current signal is located. Note that this, like many of Hick's profoundly original insights, anticipates current models of perceptual categorization. A subject is first assumed to decide to which half of an ensemble the signal belongs (e.g., on which side of a linear display it is located), and next to decide to which half of that subset it belongs, and so on, until identification is complete. Thus, if this hypothetical succession of contingent dichotomizations were arrested before it was completed (as could occur with tachistoscopically presented signals), a subject might be able to say that the signal was a member of a particular category of signals before he could say which particular member of the total signal ensemble it was. Models assuming that subjects can recognize the category to which a signal belongs before they can identify it completely are now increasingly common (e.g., Gleitman & Jonides, 1976; Jonides & Gleitman, 1976), and will be discussed in Section III, F.

Another of Hick's (1952) insights concerns the fact that in this sort of task subjects have to withold responses when no signal occurs, as well as to select responses to signals. He regarded this as an extra choice, equivalent to any other of the serial contingent binary choices he assumed subjects to make. This led him to test, and prefer, the fit of equations of the type $RT = k \cdot \log_2 (N + 1)$ allowing for this additional partitioning. The notion that subjects need to distinguish environmental stimuli, not planned by the experimenter, from experimental stimuli is one to which we shall return.

These two points show that, even in this apparently simple task of one-to-one mapping, a variety of different schemes for partitioning signal sets are logically possible, that each such scheme has implications for functional models of classification processes, and that tests between functional models imply tests between hypothetical schemes of partitioning.

We must also consider the effects of practice in this type of task. Mowbray and Rhoades (1959) showed that, after sufficient practice, variations in set size from two to eight signals ceased to affect *RT*. Related findings by Kristofferson (1977) and Rabbitt, Cumming, and Vyas (1979a), to be discussed in Section III, F, strongly suggest that extensively practiced subjects improve performance by shifting from less good to optimal signal partitioning strategies.

When subjects are required to respond to sets of stimuli rather than individual stimuli, logically they need to discriminate between signal sets but not within them. It is necessary to process enough information to distinguish every signal in set *X* from every signal in set *Y*, but not to process further information to identify individual signals as particular members of these sets. However, it is possible that in practice no such economy of information processing can be achieved so that subjects cannot recognize signals as members of classes without also completely identifying them as individual members of the total signal ensemble.

P. M. A. Rabbitt, Margaret Clancy, and S. M. Vyas (unpublished observations) demonstrated that under appropriate conditions, either of these possibilities might apply. Subjects responded to pure tones using two schemes of many-to-one mapping. In the easy mapping condition, they made one response (a keypress) to all tones of 800 Hz and below, and another response to all tones of 900 Hz and above. In this condition,

RT remained constant when the number of tones in each response set was increased from one to four. In this easy mapping condition, the mutual discriminability of tones within each response set did not affect *RT,* i.e., *RT* was as fast when tones within each set differed by 25 Hz or 50 Hz as when they differed by 100Hz. In the difficult mapping task subjects were required to make one response to each of two "interleaved" sets of tones on an equal interval scale. For example, they might be asked to press one key to 400, 600, 800, and 1000 Hz, and the other to 500, 700, 900, and 1100 Hz. In this condition, *RT* increased logarithmically with the number of tones in the total ensemble, just as it does in tasks in which one-to-one signal-to-response mapping is employed (e.g., Hick, 1952). Further, when intervals between tones were reduced to 50 Hz, *RT* and errors increased dramatically. The mapping rules thus determine the way in which signal sets must be partitioned. The total number of signals which may occur is less important than the number of distinctions which must be made to partition them. Apparently in the easy mapping condition subjects consider each signal in relation to a single reference point on the frequency continuum with which they are concerned; i.e., they consider whether any tone is higher or lower than a critical frequency. The number of possible signals in each set, and their mutual discriminability within each set, does not matter in this case. In the difficult mapping condition, mapping rules do not allow signals to be judged in relation to a common reference point and they must be judged in relation to each other. Effects of signal set size and of mutual discriminability are similar to those in tasks in which a signal has to be identified as a particular member of a total ensemble.

As in other experimental paradigms, practice on this sort of task changes the nature of the relationship between *RT* and signal ensemble size. In straightforward two-choice many-to-one signal classification tasks, early in practice *RT* increases with the size of the signal ensemble (Pollack, 1963; Rabbitt, 1962), whereas late in practice very large ensemble increases cause little or no increase in *RT* (Pollack, 1963; Rabbitt, 1959). When the signal ensemble has to be divided into six or more response sets there is a multiplicative interaction between the number of signals in each set and the number of sets employed (Pollack, 1963; Rabbitt, 1959; Rapoport, 1959). This relationship is also affected by practice and it may be that even with large numbers of response sets variations in ensemble size cease to affect *RT* if sufficient practice is given.

C. Donders' c-Reaction Task and Related Paradigms

It did not occur to Donders (1869) that stimulus partitioning in his b-reaction and c-reaction tasks might differ. He assumed that in both cases subjects identified all signals as particular members of a total ensemble, i.e., that they discriminated between five sets of one signal each. He argued that the tasks differed in that in the b-reaction task the subject had to choose between five possible responses, whereas in the c-reaction task he had to only make a response if one particular stimulus had occurred. On this rationale, Donders used the difference in *RT* between the two tasks as an estimate of time taken to select one of five responses. Donders' interpretation of these tasks was to go unchallenged for over 100 years.

The possibility ignored by Donders was that, rather than identifying each individual stimulus in the c-reaction task, subjects might discriminate signals into two sets of one ("go") and four ("no go"), while being obliged to discriminate them into five sets in the b-reaction task. P. M. A. Rabbitt, Margaret Clancy, and S. M. Vyas (unpublished observations) investigated this possibility. Matched pairs of subjects experienced identical sets of stimuli in b-reaction and c-reaction paradigms. Each paradigm was tested in an easy and a difficult condition. In the easy condition, subjects discriminated between three tones, 100-Hz apart, within the range 500–1500 Hz. The b-reaction group made one response to the center tone (e.g., 700 Hz) and a different response to either of the other tones (e.g., to 600 and 800 Hz). The c-reaction group responded only to one tone (e.g., 700 Hz) and ignored the other two tones. In the difficult condition, subjects were given five tones 100-Hz apart in the same range, the b-reaction group again giving one response to the center tone and a different response to other tones, and the c-reaction group responding only to the center tone. In both easy and difficult conditions the central, critical stimulus occurred on 50% of trials. For each group the measurement of interest was *RT* to the central critical stimulus. As might be expected, the b-reaction condition which required a choice between two responses resulted in longer *RT*s than the c-reaction condition. The point of interest was whether equivalent increases in *RT* occurred as signal set size increased in both tasks. Over the first 50 trials critical signal *RT* increased as the number of signals rose from three to five. However, this increase was significantly greater in the b-reaction than in the c-reaction task. Over trials 101 to 200, *RT*s in the c-reaction task remained constant whether three or five signals were presented, but *RT*s in the b-reaction task were longer in the difficult than in the easy condition. Over trials 401 to 500, *RT*s in both tasks were unaffected by signal set size.

In both tasks there is no logical reason why *RT* to the critical signal should increase with signal set size since in both cases the same number of cutoffs (one higher and one lower) serves to discriminate between sets in both easy and difficult conditions. The fact that, early in practice,

RT to the critical signal increases with ensemble size emphasizes two things. First, signal partitioning tasks cannot be regarded as tasks in which independent S–R links are set up between each signal and each response appropriate to it. The entire context of discriminations within the signal set determines *RT* to any signal. Second, this context of discriminations is different for b-reaction and c-reaction paradigms, since variations in ensemble size have different effects. This latter point is particularly evident as practice proceeds. After 100 trials, set size does not affect *RT* in the c-reaction task but still affects *RT* in the b-reaction task. Later in practice these differences disappear.

It seems that Donders' assumptions are not tenable, and that early in practice b-reaction and c-reaction involve different strategies of partitioning the stimulus set.

D. Visual Search Tasks

Visual search tasks are logically equivalent to signal classification tasks, since subjects scan displays to identify one or more categories of target items among a further category of irrelevant background items. For example, a subject may be shown an array of letters and numbers and be asked to press a button if he detects the letters A or B. This would seem to call for a type C partitioning. Neisser (1963) and Neisser, Novik, and Lazar (1963), using a visual search paradigm, found that early in practice the rate at which subjects could scan and reject members of a constant set of background items on a display varied with the size of the target set. Later in practice, scanning rates remained constant whether target sets contained one or 10 symbols. This is reminiscent of findings by Rabbitt (1959) and Pollack (1963) in choice reaction time tasks.

When subjects make a different response to each target signal in a visual search task a new situation arises. Theoretically, subjects may treat the task as one in which they classify signals on the display into $N + 1$ sets, N sets to be responded to, and one set to be ignored (where N is the number of different simuli to which different responses are required). Alternatively, subjects may initially classify items on a display into two sets, all target or all background, in order to locate any target item. They may then make a second classification to assign a located target to the appropriate one of N possibilities. By analogy with results from choice reaction time experiments, we might suppose that if the subjects use the first partitioning strategy the time taken to scan and reject background items should increase as some multiplicative function of the number of sets into which symbols must be partitioned (i.e., $N + 1$) and the total ensemble of target and background signals. This is much what has been found when subjects are unpracticed (Kaplan & Carvellas, 1965; Kaplan, Carvellas, & Metlay, 1966; Rabbitt, 1962, 1964; Shepherd, 1965). However, practice changes this picture. Rabbitt *et al.* (1979a) practiced a subject for 30 days on this type of visual search task. After this amount of practice he scanned background items equally rapidly whether he was searching for two or for eight targets. However, further data analysis suggested that he took longer to identify a target item, once he had located it, if it was one of eight possible targets rather than only one of two. This suggests that improvement of visual search with prolonged practice may occur because subjects gradually learn to partition sets of signals in new and more efficient ways. The fact that early in practice scanning time to reject background letters increases with target set size suggest that, at this level, subjects classify signals into *N* target classes plus one background class. Data from experiment III of this series suggest that, after 30 days of practice, a subject can learn to speed scan by making two successive classifications, first locating targets by a two-choice (target/no target) type C partitioning, and only then by identifying each target he locates by a *N*-choice procedure (type B partitioning). This argument resembles that proposed by Gleitman and Jonides (1976) and Jonides and Gleitman (1976) to account for subjects' ability to make fast discriminations between the highly familiar stimulus sets of letters and digits.

E. The Distinction between Type A and Type C Partitioning

So far we have drawn a sharp distinction between type A and type C partitionings. However, it may be asked whether logically they are distinct. Simple reaction time experiments investigating type A partitioning have been described as situations in which either a stimulus occurs, in which case the subject responds, or nothing happens, in which case he does nothing. However, the subject is not in a sensory vacuum when no stimuli are presented. Although the experimenter does not deliberately introduce extraneous stimuli, various environmental events may occur in any stimulus modality and the subject must learn not to respond to these. This argument is reminiscent of Hick's (1952) suggestion that in choice reaction time tasks subjects must decide whether or not a signal has occurred, as well as deciding which stimulus a given signal is. When we compare partitionings A and C it is apparent that the distinction between a "noncritical signal" and a "nonsignal event" is arbitrary. "Noncritical signals" are distractors deliberately introduced by an experimenter and arranged to be similar to critical signals. "Nonsignal events" are other, unplanned, incidental events which might occur while the subject is performing the task. The fuzziness of this distinction means that our separation of A and C partitionings rests uneasily on the relative discriminability of critical signals from distractors and from other, incidental, events both in terms of their physical properties and in terms of whether they occur at moments when critical signals are expected.

P. M. A. Rabbitt and S. M. Vyas (unpublished observations) arranged a demonstration to clarify some of these issues. Four groups of subjects were given brief (100-signal) *RT* tasks. Two groups performed while incidental, noncritical signal events were presented, and two without such events. Distractors were loud (75-db) and brief (300-msec) tones varying from 500 to 2000 Hz, delivered from a loudspeaker 2 feet from the subject's head. In each condition, one group performed an a-reaction (simple reaction time) task, and the other a c-reaction task. All subjects responded to digits presented visually every 10 sec precisely. In the a-reaction task only the digit 8 appeared and subjects responded to it as fast as possible. In the c-reaction task 6, 7, 8, and 9 all appeared equally often but subjects only responded to the digit 8. Each of the groups in the distraction condition experienced 20 tones during their tasks. Onset times of tones were unpredictable and identical for both groups. On 10 occasions tones occurred at precisely the moment when a signal was due. When this happened no digit signal occurred. On the remaining 10 occasions tones occurred not less than 3 sec before or after a signal was due.

The effects of distractors on *RT* and on errors were compared across the two tasks. For the a-reaction task it seemed that the occurrence of distractors increased *RT* early in practice, but that subjects adapted to them successfully as practice continued. For the first 25 trials mean *RT* was slightly but significantly longer (by about 25 msec) for the distracted group. For the remaining 75 trials there was no difference between conditions. In contrast, for the c-reaction task, there was no sign that the occurrence of auditory distractors affected *RT* at any stage of practice.

In both tasks, subjects sometimes made errors by responding when a distractor tone occurred but no signal was present. In the a-reaction task subjects made 32 such errors. Of these errors 26 occurred when a distractor tone coincided with the moment when a signal was expected. In the c-reaction task subjects only made eight errors of this kind. Four of these occurred when a distractor coincided with the expected onset of a signal.

Obviously tone signals and digit displays are easily discriminable events. Nevertheless confusions sometimes occur and, in a-reaction tasks at least, tone distractors increase *RT* early in practice. What is more interesting is that if subjects have to make a complex discrimination between digits rather than simply to respond to signal onset, they appear to be able to ignore distractors more easily.

The partitioning of signal sets necessary in a c-reaction task, at least early in practice, seems to bring about a mobilization of attentional resources which allows subjects to discriminate more easily between signal and nonsignal events. Thus, though the distinction between type A and type C partitionings of signal sets is logically "fuzzy," it does seem to usefully capture differences in task demands which have consequences for the efficiency of human selective attention.

F. Partitioning Strategies in Sequential Tasks

Our analysis of stimulus partitioning has so far ignored the possibility of strategies which depend on the sequential properties of stimulus displays. We have implicitly assumed that whatever partitioning the subject adopts he treats each stimulus as independent from those preceding it. There is, however, evidence that this is not so, but that subjects are able to adopt strategies which depend on sequential information.

Bertelson (1963) suggested that during continuous self-paced choice–response tasks, subjects compare each new signal to a memory trace of its immediate predecessor. If the new signal and trace match, the same response can rapidly be repeated and *RT* is very fast, a phenomenon known as "the repetition effect" (Bertelson, 1961, 1963, 1965). It is assumed that if the new signal does not match the trace then a further, more complex, analysis is necessary to determine which new signal has appeared.

Jordan, Rabbitt, and Vyas (1977) and Rabbitt, Jordan, and Vyas (1979b) found that this hypothesis explained results they obtained in a two-choice *RT* task in which subjects classified complex displays with redundant components. Critical signals were the symbol plus (+) and minus (−) which appeared in random order with equal probability against red, amber, or green circular colored patches. When both symbol and patch color were repeated in successive displays (e.g., red + after red +) *RT* was faster than when the symbol was repeated but display color changed (e.g., red + after green +), even though in both cases a repetition of the same response was called for. This suggested that subjects first make a rapid, holistic match to compare each new display against a memory trace of the last. If successive displays match in all respects, they can immediately repeat the response they have just made. If they do not match, the new display must be analyzed further to determine which critical symbol is present.

Rabbitt, Cumming, and Vyas (1977) found evidence for a similar process in a visual search task in which subjects had to detect a target letter among background letters. Performance was particularly rapid when the same target letter occurred on successive displays. Once again it seems that an initial fast comparison detects constancy or change, the response being repeated if constancy is detected. A further more elaborate analysis occurs only if change is detected.

In terms of the signal partitioning strategies we have discussed, these successive contingent decisions could be described as a type C partitioning (repeat of target = "go"; change = "no go"), with a type B partitioning (dividing stimuli into classes wth appropriate responses) contingent on the no go outcome of the first stage.

Recent work on visual search suggests that subjects improve their performance with practice partly because they learn to make two-stage contingent C–B decisions rather than using a single-stage type B partitioning. Gleitman and Jonides (1976) and Jonides and Gleitman (1976) suggest that when subjects search for members of one overlearned class of symbols (e.g., letters) among another overlearned class (e.g., digits) they can use a two-stage decision process, first scanning to discover whether any target letter is present and, once target location is determined, then processing it further to discover which letter it is. Rabbitt *et al.* (1979a) found that when a single subject was practiced at search for a particular subset of target letters among a particular subset of background letters for a period of 30 days he began by using a type B partitioning and progressed to a more efficient C–B two-stage partitioning strategy, in which he first scanned the display to decide whether or not each symbol was a target, only proceeding to identify the stimulus further when he had located a target.

So far we have considered the abstract properties of schemes by which signal sets may be partitioned, without considering the various relationships between signals which may be used to classify them into sets. We have looked at how subjects partition signal sets and now move on to consider the various kinds of evidence which they use in order to do so.

IV. Types of Evidence Used in Classification

A. Critical Discriminating Features

A simple demonstration of how subjects may use a critical discriminating feature to divide stimuli into sets was made by Green and Anderson (1956). They used a visual search paradigm in which subjects search for members of a positive set of symbols embedded among others. Speed of performance in such tasks is usually proportional to the number of different shapes between which subjects must discriminate, more complex discriminations slowing down search. Green and Anderson showed that if symbols were of different colors, and if subjects were told the color of the target symbol, then search time was proportional only to the number and variety of symbols of that color on the display. Knowledge of this critical cue allowed them to inspect further only those symbols of the correct color. Background symbols of different colors were apparently scanned and rejected without further processing to determine their shape.

Neisser (1963) similarly demonstrated that if all target symbols on a display share a particular critical feature (e.g., curved lines) which is not possessed by any background symbols (e.g., when all background stimuli are constituted of straight lines), visual search is especially fast and accurate. Rabbitt (1967) showed that subjects trained to discriminate between a particular set of background symbols showed negative transfer when required to look for the same target symbols among a new background set. This indicates that improvement of signal classification with practice partly depends upon discovery and use of particular critical cues optimal for distinguishing between sets of complex signals. Rabbitt (1967) further showed that if the same cues (e.g., curved rather than straight lines) were adequate to discriminate target symbols from either set of background symbols, no such negative transfer occurred.

Rabbitt *et al.* (1979a) have shown that such specific, critical cue systems learned over 2000 trials may be retained and are available to improve performance on visual search for as long as 4 weeks without intervening practice.

At first sight, these data suggest an attractively simple model for the internal representations of sets of categories of signals, cognate to that implicit in feature counting and classification machine systems such as Pandemonium (Selfridge & Neisser, 1960). However, not all data can be accounted for by such a model. Rabbitt *et al.* (1979a) found that, when subjects were given 20–30 days practice at discriminations between a specific target and a specific set of background symbols they no longer showed any negative transfer when required to search for the same targets among new background symbols. Kristofferson (1977) reports similar results in a classification task of the kind used by Sternberg (1975) using a fixed memory set. In both of these experiments improvement with practice occurred which could not simply be due to learning of optimally nonredundant critical cues common to all targets and not possessed by background items. Extended practice must teach subjects to base their discriminations on other kinds of evidence.

B. Classification by Different Rules: AND, OR, NAND, and NOR Classification Principles

It is seldom the case that all complex stimuli in one set possess one particular common feature, while complex stimuli in other sets all lack this feature (so that a type C partitioning is possible) or share some other common feature (so that a type B partitioning is possible). More typically distinctions between sets of complex stimuli must be made in terms of the presence or absence of two or more critical elements. If we consider decisions made on the basis of two elements, X and Y, there are four possible ways in which these in combination can be used to identify signal sets.

1. AND combinations. Members of a set of complex stimuli are identified by the joint occurrence of two elements X and Y.
2. OR combinations. Members of a set of complex stimuli are identified by the occurrence of either X or Y.
3. NAND combinations. Members of a set of complex stimuli are identified by the absence of both X and Y.
4. NOR combinations. Members of the set are identified by the absence of X or by the absence of Y.

It might seem that, functionally, OR and NOR combinations are equivalent since in either case sets are identified by the presence of one element and the absence of another. This is not the case. Neisser (1963) and Neisser *et al.* (1963) showed that search of displays for the absence of a letter was much slower and less accurate than search for the presence of the same letter. P. M. A. Rabbitt, M. R. Anderson, and S. M. Vyas (unpublished observations) have investigated cases where subjects have searched displays of five letters to classify them in terms of AND, OR, NAND, and NOR combinations of two target letters. With extended practice OR conditions gave fastest classification times, AND were next fastest, and NAND and NOR were very slow indeed. Evidently, there were very marked functional differences in strategies for classification of displays in terms of presence or absence of elements, despite the apparent equivalence of OR and NOR conditions in these experiments. These differences persisted with practice and subjects apparently continued to follow classification schemes described in task instructions in spite of their inconvenience. The marked differences between these conditions emphasizes that we still know very little about the ways in which people handle combinations of evidence from different stimulus characteristics in classification tasks. Until more data are available our models for classifications of complex stimuli will remain tentative.

C. Classification by Abstract Relationships

So far we have tacitly assumed that particular signals, or features of complex signals, have corresponding internal representations in the nervous system and that complexes or aggregates of these internal representations make up internal representations of sets of classes. The experiments described above suggest that this might sometimes be the case. However, with complex stimuli, such as patterns, it is not usually the presence or absence of particular critical features which defines a class of stimuli. Distinct generative rules exist from which one class of patterns rather than another can be derived. In discriminating between patterns, subjects seem to recognize and use differences in the relationships between component elements or features rather than differences in the particular elements or features themselves.

P. M. A. Rabbitt and S. M. Vyas (unpublished observations) provided a demonstration of how subjects use relationships between stimulus features to facilitate classification. To maintain comparability with other experiments, sets of equally loud pure tones were used. Two conditions of a choice reaction time task were compared. In both conditions, subjects made one response to a set of four tones at equal intervals on a frequency scale (i.e., 400, 600, 800, and 1000 Hz). One group of subjects (regular condition made their other response to another set of tones also at 200-Hz intervals on the frequency scale (i.e., 450, 650, 850, 1050 Hz). The other group (irregular condition) made their other response to a set of tones separated by unequal intervals along the frequency scale (i.e., 450, 550, 700, and 950 Hz). Note that the discriminations required between adjacent frequencies are as coarse, or coarser, in the irregular condition as in the regular condition. Nevertheless, even after 200-trials practice, subjects in the regular condition responded faster and more accurately than subjects in the irregular condition. Within the irregular condition, subjects responded faster to the regular than to the irregular tone set.

There have been many demonstrations that people learn to discriminate between sets of signals by deriving and using rules, rather than by learning invariant critical features (e.g., for dot patterns: Posner and Keele, 1968, 1969; for spatial position: Duncan, 1977, 1978). Such classification systems go beyond the physical evidence present on a display. In terms of a useful, recently developed terminology we may say they are "resource driven" or "memory driven," being based on rule structures which are not intrinsic to displays but which represent abstract "hypotheses" developed by subjects. In contrast simpler systems based on feature identification are "data driven" or "bottom up" systems of classification, using intrinsic physical properties of displays (Bobrow & Norman, 1975).

D. Detection of Change or Constancy in Serial Tasks

We have already discussed how, in serial tasks, subjects may compare holistically each presented stimulus with a memory trace of its predecessor. All models of signal recognition in two-choice tasks have assumed that subjects accumulate and assess evidence from each stimulus until they are certain that it represents an instance of one or the other class (cf. Audley, 1960; 1973; Audley & Pike, 1965; Laming, 1968; Vickers, 1970). However, Fletcher and Rabbitt (1978) found that this is not necessarily the case, and that classification strategies can be based solely on detection of constancy or change.

Subjects were asked to make one response to the letter A, and another to B. As soon as they responded to the display the next display occurred. Very occasionally, instead of A or B, a random dot pattern ("hash") of the same size appeared. These rare events were explained to subjects as machine failures and they were instructed to respond as soon as possible with either key to remove a "hash" and obtain the next display. Early in practice subjects responded to "hashes" by repeating a response made to the previous stimulus. These responses were very slow. Late in practice they invariably responded to "hashes" by making the alternate response to that made to the last stimulus. Such responses were typically as fast as responses to valid displays. This effect does not occur in tasks in which subjects make different responses to three or more symbols. Fletcher and Rabbitt (1978) conclude that in fast serial two-choice tasks subjects learn to improve their performance by ceasing to identify each display as a particular event different from others. They respond, instead, to transitions between successive displays, repeating the same response if there is no change and alternating responses when change occurs. Note that, in this case, change in any feature of a display is adequate evidence for alternation. This is quite different from systems of optimization which employ critical, rather than redundant, features of complex stimuli, as in Section IV A and IV B, above.

E. Establishing Boundary Conditions

1. *Number of Class Boundaries Involved in a Classification*

We have seen that when signals can be ordered along a continuum (e.g., tones of equal loudness ordered in frequency) subjects find it easy to partition them into two classes on either side of a single cutoff point (e.g., above and below 700 Hz). Partitioning requiring more cutoff points becomes progressively more difficult. P. M. A. Rabbitt, Margaret Clancy, and S. M. Vyas (unpublished observations) demonstrated this in a two-choice task. The stimuli were eight tones of 500, 600, 700, 800, 900, 1000, 1100, and 1200 Hz. In the simplest, one-cut, condition one response was made to tones of 800 Hz and lower frequencies and a different response to tones of 900 Hz and higher frequencies. In the three-cut condition one response was made to tones of 500, 600, 900, and 1000 Hz and the other to tones of 700, 800, 1100, and 1200 Hz. In the seven-cut condition, one response was made to 500, 700, 900, and 1100 Hz, and the other to 600, 800, 1000, and 1200 Hz. Reaction time and errors increased sharply with the number of cuts necessary to discriminate the signals into two sets. Note that at least two different factors must be considered in explanations of such effects. The first is the possibility that subjects' internal representations of signals are organized in terms of ordered continua. Classifications required by experimenters may demand more or fewer cuts along these continua and so be more or less difficult for subjects. In this experiment the continuum was self-evident, but the possibility should not be dismissed that there may be continua which subjects use in classification which are not evident to experimenters.

A second factor is that when signals are actually ordered along a continuum of physical difference, such as frequency, intensity, or spatial position, the number of discriminations along that continuum will, actually, increase with the number of cuts which a classification requires. In the experiment described above, the number of discriminations necessary between signals increased steadily with the number of cuts which had to be imposed to classify them.

2. *Distance from Class Boundary*

We have argued that in many-to-one stimulus–response mappings subjects may adopt the economical strategy of discriminating between stimulus sets but not within them. If this occurs, then it is likely that distance of a given stimulus from the class boundary will be related to the efficiency with which the subject processes that stimulus. P. M. A. Rabbitt, Margaret Clancy, and S. M. Vyas (unpublished observations) demonstrated such boundary effects in a task in which subjects responded to series of tones, using one hand to respond to 500, 600, 1100, and 1200 Hz, and the other to respond to 700, 800, 900, and 1000 Hz. The *RT*s to tones at set boundaries (i.e., 600, 700, 1000, and 1100 Hz) were significantly longer than to other tones. Evidently subjects learned not to discriminate every tone from all other tones but discriminated tones in terms of distance from critical frequency boundaries between sets.

3. *Distance from Typical Exemplars of Classes*

Recent discussions of semantic judgments have raised the possibility that meaning classes are organized in terms of relative distance from paradigmatic exemplars (Rips *et al.*, 1973; Rosch, 1973; Smith *et al.*, 1974). By analogy, we might expect to find similar effects in cases where subjects have to form internal representations of simple signals in order to categorize them in choice response tasks.

P. M. A. Rabbitt, Margaret Clancy, and S. M. Vyas (unpublished observations) arranged a simple demonstration of effects of familiar versus unfamiliar exemplars of sets, as well as of the effects of distance from paradigmatic exemplars. Subjects discriminated between the same two sets of tones as in the previous experiment. Although the two sets of tones occurred equally frequently, one stimulus within the second set (800 or 900 Hz) occurred more frequently than the others. Overall, *RT* was faster to this second set, containing one especially frequent exemplar, than to the first set, where all tones occurred with equal probability. As might be expected, when individual stimuli were considered it was found that *RT* was fastest to the especially frequent tone (800 or 900 Hz). It seems that common exemplars of tone sets are more rapidly recognized than rare exemplars. Particularly interesting was the finding that when the 800-Hz tone occurred most frequently *RT*s to the adjacent 700-Hz tone were faster than to the distant 1000-Hz tone. When the 900-Hz tone was the most frequent this difference was reversed. It seems that biasing the occurrence of one signal within a set not only reduces *RT* to that particular signal but also reduces *RT* to signals adjacent in some conceptual series. A possible inference is that subjects form mental representations of sets of items in which particularly frequent signals serve as exemplars, and other signals are judged in terms of their relative distance from these exemplars as well as their relative distance from set boundaries.

F. Classifications Made Independently of Input Characteristics: Response Classes

We have discussed how subjects may use sensory evidence to partition stimulus sets. However, partitioning is not always based on the physical characteristics of stimuli, or even on abstract relationships between physical characteristics. Consider stimuli such as a picture of a cat, the printed word "c–a–t," and a tape recording of mewing. These stimuli are readily classified into a single set, although their physical characteristics have nothing in common. They are grouped together because they evoke the same response from the subject. A useful general model for word recognition proposed by Morton (1970) distinguishes between structures which analyze physical input (analyzers) and other structures which may be activated by many different kinds of input (logogens).

The different stimuli listed above would all activate the central logogen corresponding to the word "cat" and so are all implicitly recognized as members of the same category or response class.

Later adaptations of this model by Keele (1973) and Posner and Snyder (1975) assume that activation of this central common structure (logogen) can also imply associated analytic structures (pathways) which are activated by stimulus input. The fact that subjects can more rapidly identify one representation of a letter if they have previously recognized another version of the same letter is interpreted as evidence for this hypothesis. Similar hypotheses have been used to explain how recognition of one word (e.g., "nurse") can facilitate subsequent recognition of a conceptually associated but physically distinct word (e.g., "doctor").

Learned response categorizations can determine efficiency at visual search and related tasks, independently of the physical characteristics of the stimuli and the particular partitioning adopted. Karlin and Bower (1976) and Henderson (1976) showed that subjects were more efficient at visual search if all target words belonged to one defined noun class and all background words belonged to another. Fletcher and Rabbitt (1976) and Fletcher (1979) have found that word lists are most efficiently categorized when all words in at least one category are semantically related to each other. Indeed in these experiments efficiency of categorization depends more on semantic relationships within response sets than on graphemic similarities between words to be categorized.

When response sets are very familiar, classification time can be more strongly affected by response set boundaries than by stimulus discriminability. A classic experiment by Fitts and Switzer (1962) showed that unpracticed subjects discriminate faster between pair of digits adjacent in the number series (e.g., 1 and 2) than between equally discriminable digits widely separated in the number series (e.g., 2 and 7). Their explanation is that in the latter case subjects take time to become accustomed to the fact that intermediate digits will not occur, while in the former case the boundaries of the population within which they must discriminate are conceptually better delimited. An experiment by Marcel (1976) shows the reverse effect. If subjects are required to class together groups of adjacent digits (e.g., 1 to 4, 5 to 8, etc.), responses are slower to numbers at class boundaries (e.g., 4, 5) than to other numbers, even though stimulus discrimination on the basis of physical characteristics is not a problem.

G. Relationships between Stimulus and Response Classifications

There are three basic relationships possible between classifications of stimuli and classifications of the responses made to them.

First, there is a simple case where a different response is made to each of a set of physically different stimuli. Here stimulus and response classifications completely coincide, but it is important to note that effects due to mutual discriminability of stimuli are quite distinct from effects due to difficulties of selection between responses. For example, in Fitts and Switzer's experiments, *RT* might independently be affected by relative discriminability of digits (e.g., 3 and 5 as against 3 and 1) and relative familiarity of response set boundaries.

Second, the same response may be made to each of many different stimuli. As we have seen, in such many-to-one stimulus–response mapping situations, mutual discriminability of signals and possible classifications of signals in terms of critical common features, or in terms of abstract relationships between features, have effects which may be quite distinct from confusions due to the ways in which response classification systems are ordered.

The third and most interesting case occurs when two or more different responses are made to the same stimulus. The most common example is that of homonyms and homophones. A single written word may have more than one meaning [e.g., "live" (to exist) and "live" (alive)], and a single spoken word may have several graphemic representations associated with different meanings (e.g., "no" and "know"). A single word may have more than one meaning even when phonemic and graphemic codes correspond [e.g., "safe" (free from danger) and "safe" (strongbox)]. Experiments using symbols have suggested two ways in which classification time may be affected in this sort of situation.

First, as Fraisse (1969) points out, subjects may access some responses to a symbol more rapidly than others. His French subjects responded faster when naming the same symbol "zero" or "o" than when naming it "circle."

Second, subjects may select more rapidly between responses from two different cognitive categories than between responses from the same cognitive category. Jonides and Gleitman (1972) found that the symbol "o" was located more rapidly among letters when searched for as "zero" rather than as "o," and faster among digits when searched for "o" rather than "zero." Since stimulus features are constant, these differences must be due to response-based classification.

V. Summary

We have looked at stimulus classification from two angles. First, we have considered possible ways in which subjects may partition a given set of stimuli. Three main types of partitioning are described: type A, in which all stimuli are treated as an undifferentiated class to which a response is made; type B, in which stimuli are grouped in separate classes with a different response for each class; and type C, where a negative class of stimuli, to which no response is made, is differentiated from a positive class, to which a response is made. Four main conclusions concerning stimulus partitioning may be listed.

1. More than one type of partitioning is possible in many experimental tasks, and different partitionings are associated with different levels of efficiency.
2. Subjects do not always adopt the most appropriate partitioning for the task which they are given, and consequently experimenters' assumptions about the processes underlying classifications their subjects make may not be justified.
3. Although it can be argued that type A and type C partitionings are not logically separate, there is empirical support for maintaining the distinction between them.
4. In tasks in which the same signal can occur twice in succession, subjects may adopt a very efficient two-stage classification, which involves a C-type partitioning followed by a B-type partitioning contingent on a no-go outcome of the first partitioning. Two-stage classifications may also occur in visual search tasks when subjects are highly practiced.

A second way of examining stimulus classification is in terms of the types of evidence which subjects use to classify signals into sets. The following points emerged from this analysis.

1. Subjects may use individual stimulus features, simple combinations of features (AND, OR, NAND, and NOR combinations), or more abstract patterns of relationships between stimuli as a basis for classification.
2. Against traditional models of stimulus processing, we have presented evidence that in sequential tasks subjects may respond on the basis of whether successive stimuli are constant or not, without analyzing them further.
3. Number of class boundaries involved in a classification, distance of a given stimulus from a class boundary, and distance from typical exemplars of the class will affect ease of classification.
4. Some classifications may be made independently of the physical characteristics of stimuli, being based rather on the responses elicited by stimuli.

An important general conclusion to emerge concerns the effect of practice in stimulus classification tasks. It is commonly assumed that when subjects improve this represents increasing efficiency at performing one set of operations necessary to do the task. We have presented evidence to show that this may not be the case but that, rather, subjects may improve because they learn to adopt more efficient strategies, either by using a more appropriate stimulus partitioning or by basing their classification on a less redundant set of evidence than they used initially.

References

Anderson, J. R., & Bower, G. H. *Human associative memory.* Washington, D.C.: Winston, 1973.

Audley, R. J. A stochastic model for individual choice behaviour. *Psychological Review,* 1960, **67,** 1–15.

Audley, R. J. Some observations on theories of choice reaction time: Tutorial review. In S. Kornblum (Ed.), *Attention and performance IV.* New York: Academic Press, 1973.

Audley, R. J., & Pike, A. R. Some alternative stochastic models of choice. *British Journal of Mathematical and Statistical Psychology,* 1965, **18,** 207–225.

Bertelson, P. Sequential redundancy and speed in a serial two-choice responding task. *Quarterly Journal of Experimental Psychology,* 1961, **12,** 90–102.

Bertelson, P. S–R relationships and reaction times for new versus repeated signals in a serial task. *Journal of Experimental Psychology,* 1963, **65,** 478–484.

Bertelson, P. Serial choice reaction time as a function of response versus signal-and-response repetition. *Nature (London),* 1965, **206,** 217–218.

Bobrow, D. G., & Norman, D. A. Some principles of memory schemata. In D. B. Bobrow & A. M. Collins (Eds.), *Representation and understanding: Studies in cognitive science.* New York: Academic Press, 1975.

Collins, A. M., & Quillian, M. R. Retrieval time from semantic memory. *Journal of Verbal Learning and Verbal Behavior,* 1969, **8,** 240–247.

Donders, F. C. Over de snelheid van psychische processen. Onderzoekingen gedaan in het Physiologisch Laboratorium der Utrechtsch Hoogeschool, 1868–1869. *Tweede Reeks,* 1869, **II,** 92–120.

Duncan, J. Response selection rules in spatial choice reaction tasks. In S. Dornic (Ed.), *Attention and performance VI.* Hillsdale, N.J.: Lawrence Erlbaum Associates, 1977.

Duncan, J. Response selection in spatial choice reaction: Further evidence against associative models. *Quarterly Journal of Experimental Psychology,* 1978, **30,** 429–440.

Fitts, P., & Switzer, G. Cognitive aspects of information processing I. The familiarity of S–R sets and subsets. *Journal of Experimental Psychology,* 1962, **63,** 321–329.

Fletcher, C. Ph.D. Thesis in preparation. University of Oxford (1979).

Fletcher, C. (B.), & Rabbitt, P. M. *Categorization and visual search.* Paper presented at the meeting of the Experimental Psychology Society, Durham, England, July 1976.

Fletcher, C. (B.), & Rabbitt, P. M. The changing pattern of perceptual analytic strategies and response selection with practice in a two-choice reaction time task. *Quarterly Journal of Experimental Psychology,* 1978, **30,** 417–427.

Fraisse, P. Why is naming longer than reading? In W. Koster (Ed.), *Attention and performance II.* Amsterdam: North-Holland Publ., 1969.

Frege, G. *The foundation of arithmetic.* Oxford: Blackwell, 1958.

Garner, W. R. *Uncertainty and structure as psychological concepts.* New York: Academic Press, 1962.

Garner, W. R. *The processing of information and structure.* Potomac, Md.: Lawrence Elrbaum Associates, 1974.

Gleitman, H., & Jonides, J. The cost of categorization in visual search: incomplete processing of targets and field items. *Perception & Psychophysics,* 1976, **20,** 281–288.

Green, B. F., & Anderson, L. K. Colour coding in a visual search task. *Journal of Experimental Psychology,* 1956, **51,** 19–24.

Henderson, L. *Semantic effects in visual search through word lists for physically defined targets.* Paper presented at the annual general meeting of the British Psychological Society, York, England, 1976.

Hick, W. E. On the rate of gain of information. *Quarterly Journal of Experimental Psychology,* 1952, **4,** 11–26.

Hyman, R. Stimulus information as a determinant of reaction time. *Journal of Experimental Psychology,* 1953, **45,** 188–196.

Jonides, J., & Gleitman, H. A conceptual category effect in visual search: 0 as a letter or as a digit. *Perception & Psychophysics,* 1972, **12,** 457–460.

Jonides, J., & Gleitman, H. The benefit of categorization in visual search: Target location without identification. *Perception & Psychophysics,* 1976, **20,** 289–298.

Jordan, T. C., Rabbitt, P. M. A., & Vyas, S. M. Response times to stimuli of increasing complexity as a function of aging. *British Journal of Psychology,* 1977, **68,** 189–201.

Kaplan, I. T., & Carvellas, T. Scanning for multiple targets. *Perceptual and Motor Skills,* 1965, **21,** 239–243.

Kaplan, I. T., Carvellas, T., & Metlay, W. Visual search and immediate memory. *Journal of Experimental Psychology,* 1966, **71,** 488–493.

Karlin, M. B., & Bower, G. H. Semantic category effects in visual word search. *Perception & Psychophysics,* 1976, **19,** 417–424.

Katz, J. J., & Fodor, J. A. The structure of semantic theory. *Language,* 1963, **39,** 170–210.

Keele, S. W. *Attention and human performance.* Pacific Palisades, Calif.: Goodyear, 1973.

Kristofferson, M. W. The effects of practice with one positive set in a memory scanning task can be completely transferred to a new set. *Memory & Cognition,* 1977, **5,** 177–186.

Laming, D. R. J. *Information theory of choice reaction times.* New York: Academic Press, 1968.

Marcel, A. J. Negative set effects in character classification: A response–retrieval view of reaction time. *Quarterly Journal of Experimental Psychology,* 1976, **29,** 31–48.

Meyer, D. E. On the representation of retrieval of stored semantic information. *Cognitive Psychology,* 1970, **1,** 242–300.

Morton, J. A functional model for memory. In D. A. Norman (Ed.), *Models of human memory.* New York: Academic Press, 1970.

Mowbray, G. H., & Rhoades, M. V. On the reduction of choice reaction times with practice. *Quarterly Journal of Experimental Psychology,* 1959, **11,** 16–23.

Neisser, U. Decision time without reaction time: Experiments in visual scanning. *American Journal of Psychology,* 1963, **76,** 376–385.

Neisser, U., Novik, R., & Lazar, R. Searching for ten targets simultaneously. *Perceptual and Motor Skills,* 1963, **17,** 955–961.

Pollack, I. Speed of classification of words into superordinate categories. *Journal of Verbal Learning and Verbal Behavior,* 1963, **2,** 159–165.

Posner, M. I., & Keele, S. W. On the genesis of abstract ideas. *Journal of Experimental Psychology,* 1968, **77,** 353–363.

Posner, M. I., & Keele, S. W. Retention of abstract ideas. *Journal of Experimental Psychology,* 1969, **83,** 304–308.

Posner, M. I., & Snyder, C. R. R. Facilitation and inhibition in the processing of signals. In P. M. A. Rabbitt & S. Dornic (Eds.), *Attention and performance VI.* New York: Academic Press, 1975.

Rabbitt, P. M. A. Effects of independent variations in stimulus and response probability. *Nature (London),* 1959, **183,** 1212.

Rabbitt, P. M. A. *Perceptual discrimination and the choice of responses.* Unpublished doctoral dissertation, University of Cambridge, 1962.

Rabbitt, P. M. A. Ignoring irrelevant information. *British Journal of Psychology,* 1964, **55,** 403–414.

Rabbitt, P. M. A. Learning to ignore irrelevant information. *American Journal of Psychology,* 1967, **80,** 1–13.

Rabbitt, P. M. A., Cumming, G. C., & Vyas, S. M. An analysis of visual search, entropy and sequential effects. In S. Dornic (Ed.), *Attention and performance VI.* Potomac, Md.: Lawrence Erlbaum Associates, 1977.

Rabbitt, P. M. A., Cumming, G. C., & Vyas, S. M. Improvement, learning and retention of skill at visual search. *Quarterly Journal of Experimental Psychology,* 1979, in press. (a)

Rabbitt, P. M. A., Jordan, T. C., and Vyas, S. M. Attentional priming in serial, self-paced choice–response tasks. In preparation, 1979. (b)

Rapoport, A. A study of disjunctive reaction times. *Behavioral Science,* 1959, **4,** 229–315.

Rips, L. J., Shoben, E. J., & Smith, E. E. Semantic distance and the verification of semantic relations. *Journal of Verbal Learning and Verbal Behavior,* 1973, **12,** 1–20.

Rosch, E. On the internal structure of perceptual and semantic categories. In T. E. Moore (Ed.), *Cognitive development and the acquisition of language.* New York: Academic Press, 1973.

Ross, J. R. Three batons for cognitive psychology. In W. B. Weiner & D. S. Palermo (Eds.), *Cognition and the symbolic process.* Hillsdale, N.J.: Lawrence Erlbaum Associates, 1974.

Selfridge, O. T., & Neisser, U. Pattern recognition by machine. *Scientific American,* 1960, **203,** 60–68.

Shepherd, R. D. Classification time and class complexity in inspection tasks. *Occupational Psychology,* 1965, **38**(2), 87–97.

Smith, E. E., Shoben, E. J., & Rips, L. J. Structure and process in semantic memory: A featural model for semantic decision. *Psychological Review,* 1974, **81,** 214–241.

Sternberg, S. Memory scanning: New findings and current controversies. *Quarterly Journal of Experimental Psychology,* 1975, **27,** 1–32.

Strawson, P. F. *Individuals.* London: Methuen, 1959.

Vickers, D. Evidence for an accumulator model of psychophysical discrimination. *Ergonomics,* 1970, **13,** 37–58.

von Merkel, J. Die zeitlichen Verhaltnis der Willensthatigheit. *Philsophische Studien,* 1885, **2,** 73–127.

Wittgenstein, L. [Remarks on the foundations of mathematics.] G. H. von Wright, R. Rhees, & G. E. M. Anscombe (Eds.), *Remarks on the foundations of mathematics* (G. E. M. Anscombe, trans.). Oxford: Blackwell, 1965.

IMMEDIATE MEMORY AND DISCOURSE PROCESSING[1]

Robert J. Jarvella

MAX-PLANCK-GESELLSCHAFT, NIJMEGEN, THE NETHERLANDS
AND
THE ROCKEFELLER UNIVERSITY, NEW YORK, NEW YORK

I. Introduction

This paper is about people's immediate memory for ordinary English connected discourse. In continuous listening and reading situations, it is common for us to remember exactly only the most recent bits of the message to which we are attending. Within experimental psycholinguistics, there is now a modest yet seemingly coherent body of findings which touch on and explore this general phenomenon. A major conclusion which can be drawn is that significant aspects of linguistic struc-

[1]This research was supported in part by a grant from the U.S. National Institute of Education to the Rockefeller University, and a grant from the Stiftung Volkswagenwerk, Hannover, to the Max Planck Gesellschaft.

ISBN 0-12-543313-1

ture are mirrored in what we can accurately recall. The organization being reflected in such data is most plausibly an outcome of natural processing on the discourse which has just taken place. My general purpose here is to bring the available findings on this subject together in one place and interpret them as a whole.

The strategy I will adopt is simple. First, I will try to define the topic a little better. Then, I will pose, in a summary way, the questions that have been asked in this research and give some hints of what may be their answers. Next, I will try to provide a general psychological framework for viewing the work. Then, the studies and results themselves will be discussed in greater detail. I will end with a few concluding remarks. Most of my points will fall into two partially overlapping groups. For expository convenience, I have made a distinction between findings for clauses and sentences treated as wholistic entities, on the one hand, and results for between-clause and between-sentence relations, on the other. (The two overlap because clauses cooccur and are interrelated within sentences.)

For a theory of discourse processing, a distinction between basic structural units and between relations among these (or their parts) may also be of some heuristic value. The distinction, however, is a relative one unless basic units can be established, since language appears to be essentially relational (the units are defined by relations). I do not really have what can be called a theory to propose here, but rather a view toward such a theory.

A. A Definition of Discourse

This paper is about English connected discourse and its immediate memory. Let me explain what I mean by connected discourse.

We all have an intuitive idea of what connected discourse is, but let us try to be a little more explicit. By connected discourse, I mean a coherent, extended linguistic message having the following properties:

a. It consists mainly of meaningful, grammatical, often quite complicated sentences.
b. The sentences are interrelated by content thematically and by structure textually.
c. The sentences occur from left to right and one after the other, either in speech or in writing.
d. The overall message sequence fulfills usual (i.e., conventional) requirements on talking about something at length.

It seems clear that most printed language (practically any book or article) and much spoken language based on it (such as speeches, lectures, drama) will fit this definition. So will some spontaneous use of language (for an up to date summary of the many contemporary views of discourse within linguistics, see Dressler, 1978). The language that I am concerned with is English, however, though some of the results may apply to other languages as well. Nearly all of the studies of the kind to be reviewed simply have been done in English. Above all, the discourses that were used were intended to provide a natural context for looking at processing of smaller, more uniform segments and text relations. The passages are described in detail later.

Discourse becomes a subject of possible psychological interest whenever someone attends to or conceptualizes it in some way. When it is heard or read, for example, or later if it is reflected on or thought about. However, why study immediate memory? Immediate memory for discourse is interesting because discourse is initially experienced over time from left to right and from bottom to top, and our basic information-processing mechanisms should lead us to isolate and relate events described in discourse as they occur in actual time. In this situation the memory which is sustained can cast light on the boundaries of our immediate understanding. At any point during a discourse, there should be a rough temporal correspondence between our understanding of what is happening at that point and how what is happening is described. Examining memory for what discourse says, almost as soon as it is heard or read, is a way of seeing how we may use linguistic structure to get behind a text to the ideas being expressed.

From the data with which I will be concerned, I think I can make a plausible argument that certain aspects of structure play a central role in this process. I am afraid that I cannot show exactly how they do so, however. Natural language is an instrument of great refinement and sensitivity. Though Chomsky (1975) has recently characterized it as a cognitive structure itself, we have little precise knowledge of just how language is realized psychologically. I will here review some data for immediate recall of segments of discourse and try to suggest something about the basic representational structures formed. The actual relation between speech processed and its mental form I presume to be far more intricate, abstract, and tantalizing than what I am able to propose on the basis of one kind of experiment. My observations are limited to very short-term memory for the surface form of discourse, inferred from words recalled that actually have been heard; they try to make at least limited sense using these retrospective reports of a process that ordinarily works without self-consciousness. As a consequence, I will have less to say about the language mechanism in our heads or its actual operations than about its state at a few capturable moments.

B. An Opening Dialog

In this section, I will summarily review the questions we will be asking and try to give them some simple answers. In the next section, I will put them into perspective. First, let us consider just sentences in discourse and their constituent clauses. Our dialog will run something like this:

Q. Is only the most recent sentence which is attended to in running discourse usually capable of being remembered?
A. Yes, to a large extent that is true.
Q. Well, is its most recent clause then especially well recalled?
A. Very clearly so.
Q. But, if the measure is the overt recall of clauses, doesn't this perhaps exaggerate the differences found?
A. No, the effects are easily replicated, and very potent, even when recognition memory is tested.
Q. So, memory for the segments of discourse corresponding to the most recent sentence and clause is clearly favored in both recall and recognition. Does performance also suggest some qualitative difference?
A. Yes, the word-recall curves over serial positions suggest this. The most recent segment tends to be recalled as a whole, while recall of previous ones tends to break down, with their recall curves being characteristically U shaped over serial position.
Q. Well, how rapidly does recall for a clause or sentence normally deteriorate as further material is presented and processed?
A. Processing as little as two words into the next segment can seriously depress recall, and bring out the U-shaped curve, for segments on either level.
Q. Does prosody contribute to these recency effects when the discourse is heard?
A. The sentence effect appears to be enhanced by both normal pause and intonation. The clause effect is equally apparent with or without these prosodic features in the stimulus.
Q. What if the discourse is read?
A. Under limited conditions where discourse is presented visually, both effects are also obtained in very strong forms.
Q. Are comparable effects to be found for children and adults?
A. Developmental studies do show basic similarities to experiments using college students as subjects, but also some curious differences.

Now consider some of the questions that can be raised in the same situation about processing dependencies between two clauses or two sentences:

Q. First, is the forgetting of a previous sentence or clause simply a consequence of hearing further speech? That is, will hearing any following speech segment seriously depress recall?
A. That is certainly not the case. Rather, forgetting seems to depend on how actively the following segment is processed. If this is, for example, an instruction to recall what has just preceded it, the effect of hearing it is quite minimal and seems to be of a different order.

Q. But in more ordinary cases, does memory for a constituent succeeded by further speech also depend on what follows it?

A. In that case there is usually more forgetting of the earlier phrase, but this effect seems to depend on a number of factors. One segment can be related to the next in several ways. These affect how quickly and how much of a sentence or clause is forgotten in the following speech context.

Q. What happens, for example, when an earlier segment grammatically supports a later one?

A. Anaphora and ellipsis are both examples of grammatical phenomena which can operate across sentence and clause boundaries and have been shown to affect memory. When one of these devices is used following a fully explicit segment, for example, the part of the segment it refers back to, and sometimes all of it, can still be recognized and recalled quite well.

Q. So, immediate memory for clauses and sentences heard in discourse depends partly on what happens in the just following context.

A. Yes. If a following segment is largely independent and explicitly expresses primarily new or unrelated information, the preceding one's form is more quickly forgotten.

Q. And what happens in the reverse case, where, for instance, the first clause in a sentence depends on the second one?

A. When a subordinate clause begins a sentence, both it and the full sentence may be better recalled when the sentence is finished.

Q. What if discourse is made fully meaningless? If subjects are prevented from interpreting segments at all, is forgetting for them even more accelerated?

A. Yes, and this is particularly true for a previous segment.

Q. And what if text is made only partially nonsensical, so that the links between consecutive segments cannot be exploited?

A. Then forgetting of either a previous or an immediate normal constituent is promoted. Experiments on distorted discourse bear on both kinds of issue—the integrity of segments and their interconnections.

Q. So immediate memory is sensitive to and modulated by a range of contextual dependencies as well as different constituent types.

A. This conclusion seems supported by the available data. And such a general statement alone seems to do justice to them.

The questions and answers comprising this dialog will be posed and explored at greater length in this paper. Before I review the research, however, I want to provide a psychological perspective for viewing it.

II. The Notion of a Processing Structure

Psychologists who study language processes are faced with a common and sometimes elusive problem of description. Because they collect language data and vary in how they do so linguistically, they need to use at least general concepts and terms of linguistic analysis. Unlike linguists, however, it is their primary task to describe not the structure of language but the mind of the language user. The linguistic and the psychological concepts in their research have quite different status. The former are descriptive, the latter presumably also explanatory. To use linguistic concepts with a psychological interpretation may sometimes be an acceptable shorthand, but we need to be clear that we are talking about mental structures and processes when we do so.

The problem comes up, as it inevitably must, in the study of discourse processing. It is necessary to describe what is presented and what is perceived or recalled in linguistic terms, but to interpret what has happened in psychological terms. The following discussion is partly motivated by this concern.

The central issue in this research is the very short-term representation of a running language message. From a purely linguistic point of view, and for purpose of description, this will have to do with the message's form and content. Take the following example, from Westrup's *Introduction to Musical History:*

> We can best understand the particular problems of the history of music by considering the nature of history in general. It is not merely a chronicle. The historian tries to treat events in an orderly sequence, to see patterns without imposing them, to study causes, results, and interactions of events, and finally to make all of this interesting and stimulating to the reader. If we accept these four objectives, there is no need to argue whether history is a science or an art. It is both—a science involving method and an art involving creative skill in presentation. (Westrup, 1963, p. 11)

The passage consists of a series of sentences and various relations within and between them. From what we have already said, it can be expected that someone reading this paragraph from left to right will process each sentence and clause largely as a whole but also relate it to context. On reading "It is not merely a chronicle," both processes may come into play: The previous sentence may become difficult to remember, but part of it—"history in general"—is the antecendent of and needed to interpret the anaphor "it." Likewise, consider the following sentence, in which a string of objectives is outlined. Reading each of the complement clauses ("to treat . . . , to see . . . ," etc.) may in turn downwardly limit recall for the one before it. However, the clauses are at the same time linked together by ellipsis and conjunction and are complements of the same verb. So our memory for the "historian's trying" may be quite good even at the end of the sentence, 35 words later. Or consider the beginning clause of the next sentence: "If we accept these four objectives." Even after the rest of the sentence is read, this clause may be remembered quite well. It is a subordination and gives a premise we may need to keep in mind in order to evaluate the conclusion following it. One of these phenomena linking segments is in the next sentence as well: the anaphoric use of "it."

The above is a brief description of some of the things in the passage which should, so to speak, catch our eye. Both sentence and clause recency and certain interrelations which override or modulate them should be forthcoming. However, it is not really sufficient to limit our discussion to linguistic structures and relations. The empirical consequences of discourse organization on immediate recall are just a beginning. We need to work away from them, toward a more psychological description. To start with, there is a need for a concept that can capture the essence of the internal representation of discourse as this occurs. The general notion I will try to elaborate I will call a *processing structure.*

A. The Natural Course of Language Processing

Consider the problem of representing discourse in very general terms. Linguistic structure in a message is not just given but must be imposed. It is by building up the internal representation that we obtain an understanding of what some piece of discourse says and means. Usually, this must be done a little at a time, from left to right as more is heard or read. Apparently, moreover, two aspects of this processing are very basic. First, though discourse physically may be quite continuous, each new clause or sentence is worked on somewhat independently from what preceded it. Second, however, each such part does build onto the rest, perhaps usually most of all upon that part which has just come before. So the psychological process at any moment will tend to be focused around that part of the representation currently being formed and its clearest relation to the prior text.

A processing structure may be thought of as simply the short-term representation of some part of a discourse. Above all, it is a mental structure in the sense just mentioned. It might be the structure that is currently being built, the one to which it is contextually related, or perhaps at a higher level, both together. In memory, there will usually only be one segment being built at any one time and, potentially, another which it extends or branches off from in some way. This processing at a linguistic level has a correspondence in our awareness of what events are being described and how they are related. The representations are quite fleeting; as we track a discourse, the passage of events (and non-events—see Grimes, 1975) which we are aware of in the description is in rapid flux.

B. Why Sentences and Clauses?

Sentences and their clauses are natural linguistic segments for describing events, actions, states, processes and, in general, for expressing any judgment predicating something of something else (including another judgment). As we have suggested, the experiments to be reviewed indicate that sentences and clauses, and some relations between them, are represented, or dealt with, in a way having clear consequences on immediate recall. As they are being processed, these segments tend to be remembered very accurately and largely as wholes; after they are processed, this manner of representation quickly transfers to the next segment and whether the first is still remembered or not depends largely on what else is said.

Both the representation and its function are of interest here. The representation must integrate several kinds of linguistic information: phonetic, syntactic, and semantic. This much we know from linguistics. Discourse processing, however, is a continuous process, making either linguists' or our own conventional notions of clause or sentence seem out of place. However, though its development obviously depends on the order of input and processing events, there is reason to believe that the representation formed for given segments is unified. In the short term, I think it is now fairly evident that this is organized around surface grammatical form. If one wishes to import phonetics and semantics into this representation, as I think we must, it should perhaps be viewed not as interpreted (though for meaning it is this) but as highly bonded. This is meant to imply not that all processing is parallel and interactive but merely that a single representation is formed from which results understanding (meaning, not semantics).

Second, from the brief mention of results above, it is apparent not only that processing structures are developed by degrees but that they change in character as they decay or as further processing ensues. This is not a feature of ordinary linguistic descriptions and depends both on segments' recency and certain grammatical and perhaps other linkages which may join them. As a result, there seem to be different degrees of fullness of the representations that are currently available for use.

C. The Function of Processing Structures

When listeners consciously attend to a language message, their immediate aim is usually to understand it. This aim is served by building up processing structures for its parts, which are superceded as more speech is analyzed. Since our understanding often seems to be almost immediate, the fleetingness of these short-term representations seems especially worth looking into. Information from speech that is grouped or built up during listening and retained or lost after intervals of no more than a few seconds may cast light on basic processes by which discourse is divided or held together.

What, however, is the function of memory in these processes? Processing discourse is apparently an activity during which attention is held on or near the forward boundary of time. Perhaps only when it is diverted is the most recent speech less actively processed. However, short-term memory could easily provide a buffer of temporary products of processing; it would seem wasteful to expend its resources on speech which is barely analyzed, or on fully computed output either. If memory is instrumental rather than incidental to this process, then, its function should be motivated by the normal course of processing itself. Perhaps the reason for short-term memory for segments is that processing structures that are formed further guide and constrain processing themselves, as well as resulting from it. Thus, their short-term retention would be functional rather than residual.

The principle of maintaining a short-term representation of very recent discourse processed appears to confer several advantages. Alternatively, it may operate somewhat differently in the two sets of cases with which we are concerned. If one makes a distinction between processing within segments and between them (that is, apprehending their relations), two subprinciples appear to emerge which together seem to play a role in nearly all of the results to be reviewed. One I will call the *principle of awaiting completion,* which is a kind of analog to obtaining perceptual closure. The other I will call the *principle of maintaining continuity,* which is a kind of function permitting bridges to be built between different linguistic segments. Suppose the two principles apply about as follows. First, once a processing structure is begun, it guides the assimilation of further speech which naturally falls into it. The structure is largely maintained until it is complete, when most decisions concerning it become final. Second, the continued retention of a structure may then serve the more transitional function, as a reference point for the construction of that following it. This may, for example, not only use the content of the residual structure as context but depend directly on it grammatically for its interpretation. The two principles are similar to one another in that they each tie processing which has already occurred to that which is about to occur. Only the level and type of constraint being carried forward may be different. Memory is thus seen as being organized by the processes of segmenting and building interpretations of discourse on several levels.

D. The General Research Paradigm

It is of most interest to determine how processing structures are built up, are sustained, and at some critical point start to break down. In practice, we are forced to ask when, or under what conditions, speech seems to be integrated into a largely unified psychological structure, and what linguistic devices which are subject to manipulation foster or help supercede this tendency. This has been inferred in the present experiments by stopping the discourse and examining subjects' immediate memory—usually via verbatim recall of some of what was just heard. Thus, an attempt is made to halt the ongoing process temporarily to check on the current contents of memory.

The connected discourse for which memory was studied was principally narrative, documentary-style writing of the kind one might find in major stories in the common press. The textual materials used in most of my experiments were adapted, for example, from stories appearing in out of date copies of *The Nation*. In a few cases, extended excerpts of dialog taken from old radio plays were also used, and in one special case, largely narrative episodes were selected from books written for children. In studies by other investigators which I review, the textual materials used also fit the loose definition of discourse given above.

In my studies reviewed here, the general strategy was to "plant" specially constructed test segments at or near the ends of sections of these discourses. The test endings were meaningful and made good continuations of the text preceding them. The resulting pieces of discourse, including these final segments, ranged considerably in length but were never shorter than four or five sentences or so long as to take more than a minute or two to read aloud. Generally, they were read aloud, as normally as possible, tape recorded, and played back for listeners to hear.

The listeners, usually tested in small groups, were asked to attend to the discourse normally, as if someone were telling them a story. A subsequent test of listening comprehension to be given was emphasized as reason to listen normally to what was said. These tests called for subjects to either answer a series of true–false questions about the passages or write a summary of what had happened in them. During a discourse, whenever a special section came to an end, subjects were asked to remember some of what had just been said. The particular task requirements varied to some extent, but it was always stressed that the test segment of interest should be recalled, or compared with a recognition item given, as exactly as possible, word for word. In experiments using oral recall, a sufficient pause was left between the end of one section of discourse and the beginning of the next for subjects to respond. When subjects wrote their answers, they were provided with a test booklet for each passage heard, and the tape recording was stopped during tests. In recognition studies, and a few using prompted recall, the tape was stopped, and subjects turned a page in their booklet to see the test information printed there.

We might, before going farther, ask whether the general method is likely to succeed in telling us what we want from it. Two limitations come to mind and should be explicitly recognized. The first concerns the naturalness of the task, and whether it elicits performance that can be considered typical. Our practice has been to present a discourse message for subjects to understand, and only occasionally interrupt it to test their memory for what was just presented. We know that they are able to accurately answer questions or write a detailed summary about what happens in such a story after it is over. Nevertheless, listeners may attend to superficial detail more carefully in this setting than they do normally. In that sense, the results found would present a somewhat generous view of what people can remember; the effects of segmentation into processing structures as memory units might be exaggerated.

A second limitation is perhaps more serious. The kind of test conducted has looked backward, retrospectively, at segments that have already received substantial processing. One can probably safely assume that a speech-processing structure can only be formed during a critical period relatively synchronous with the speech it circumscribes, and that the period during which it can provide support for further speech processing later is also limited. Accordingly, the procedure we use is aimed at looking for both what the structures are and how, depending on their interrelations, they supplant or coexist with each other in memory. Basically, we try to draw a clear boundary between good memory (verbatim recognition and recall), and poor memory. However, the measures gained do not show how extensive processing must be for a structure as it is being built. Put simply, the experiments are studies of remembering, however immediate, not of perception. The memory data provide fairly convincing evidence of the processing structures, and some of their interdependencies. However, the data leave uncertain many details of the formation and the dissolution of processing structures.

The two following sections review the experimental literature on immediate memory for discourse in English. Both published and previously unpublished studies are included. Where I am partly or fully responsible for some work, the experiment is given with a number and, if it has been previously reported, with a reference to the original source.

As mentioned, the work to be considered falls into two categories. The first has to do with sentences and clauses taken more or less as processing structures; the second has to do with some of the relations between pairs of sentences and clauses. In the first category, the work examined sentence and clause recency in several test situations. Most of these studies used one basic set of materials. (An appendix containing these can be found in Jarvella, 1970b). While materials limitation restricts the generality of the results somewhat, it also permits results to be compared when task requirements, mode or conditions of presentation, and the like were varied. The general results have also been replicated elsewhere. In the second category of experiments, the materials used were more heterogeneous.

III. Studies of Sentence and Clause Recency

A. Experiments I–IV: Recall of Spoken Discourse

The common materials referred to were two 1500-word narrative discourse passages. Sixteen matched pairs of test items were constructed, half for each passage. The items were constructed to meet the requirements that, within each matched pair, both members ended in the same sequence of (primarily high-frequency) words, but that the sequence fell into two different syntactic configuations, SHORT–LONG and LONG–SHORT. The critical sequence was always two sentences long and made up of three clauses seven, six, and seven words in length, as follows:

	Clause		
SHORT–LONG	[Context]	[Previous	Immediate]
LONG–SHORT	[Context	Previous]	[Immediate]

Only the initial context clauses were different. As the brackets suggest, within each pair, the SHORT–LONG context clause was intended as short sentence, causing the following previous and immediate clauses to fall together in a long sentence. The other context clause was intended to cause the following previous clause to fall together with it in a long sentence, leaving the immediate clause as a short sentence by itself. The previous and immediate clauses were the same for both members of test pairs. The following is an example:

Short sentence and then a long one:	
Context:	"The confidence of Kofach was not unfounded.
Previous:	To stack the meeting for McDonald,
Immediate:	the union had even brought in outsiders."
Long sentence and then a short one:	
Context:	"Kofach had been persuaded by the international
Previous:	to stack the meeting for McDonald.
Immediate:	The union had even brought in outsiders."

Several different types of test items were integrated into the passages together with dummy filler items at staggered intervals ranging from every 50 to 250 words. Two versions of the passages were formed, each containing four SHORT–LONG and four LONG–SHORT test items and the same number of filler items, in a semirandom order. The passages were recorded for presentation by reading them out loud with normal intonation at a rate of about four syllables (2.5 words) per second. Following each test item, a test pause was left.

The four experiments were conducted using somewhat different recall requirements. Both written and oral ordered recall and two kinds of prompted written recall of the ends of test segments were tried. In experiment I (Jarvella, 1971, experiment I), subjects were instructed:

> Your task will be to write down as much of the end of the passage just immediately preceding the interruption as you can remember. We are interested in learning how much of the immediately preceding speech you can remember exactly, word-for-word. It is important that you reproduce as exactly as possible what you have just heard. Your written answer should go right up to and include the last word you heard just before the pause.

In experiment II (Jarvella, 1971, experiment II), subjects were given the first word of the identical sequence (the thirteenth word from the end) as a prompt after each test item and told to write down just the speech that had followed it, up to and including the last word heard. In experiment III (Jarvella, 1972, Fig. 1c), the same task as in experiment I was used, but with oral rather than written recall. In experiment IV (Jarvella, 1972, Fig. 1d), subjects were prompted by 200- and 600-Hz tone cues after each test segment to write down only the previous or the immediate sentence heard. As in the other experiments, stress was placed on reproducing speech heard as exactly as possible. It was emphasized in all cases that the meaning of the material in the passages should be grasped. Listening comprehension for each passage was tested by a series of true–false questions. Almost all of these questions were correctly answered by all subjects tested. The four experiments used 24, 20, 16, and 48 subjects, respectively. As in later studies, the subjects were native speakers of American English about 18–20 years old. The data are summarized in Table I, where it can be seen that at both sentence and clause levels the closer a segment was to the end of what was heard, the better it was recalled. Let us consider these results in turn.

1. Sentence Recency.

In these four experiments, the final sentence heard was recalled quite well, and far better than the sentence just before it. The immediate sentence was also remembered more as a single unit than the previous one. Table I shows two recall measures, the first based on mean number of words recalled over serial positions within clauses, the second on mean number of clauses for which all words were recalled, irrespective of order. (Ordered recall of the words in sentences is highly correlated

TABLE I

PERCENT RECALLED OF SPOKEN DISCOURSE SEGMENTS

Condition, measure, and segment	Experiment I	II	III	IV
SHORT (sentence)–LONG (sentence)				
Word recalled				
Contest	29	—	12	58
Previous	81	84	77	74
Immediate	96	97	92	96
Clauses recalled				
Context	12	—	7	29
Previous	54	63	54	44
Immediate	86	87	71	82
LONG (sentence)–SHORT (sentence)				
Words recalled				
Context	47	—	31	54
Previous	50	62	32	52
Immediate	96	95	86	98
Clauses recalled				
Context	21	—	8	25
Previous	20	34	15	18
Immediate	84	84	72	95

with this measure.) First, consider just the critical middle clause. Averaged across the four studies shown, 79% of the words from this clause was recalled when (in SHORT–LONG) it formed part of the immediate sentence, as opposed to only 49% of the words when (in LONG SHORT) it was part of the previous sentence. Similarly, all of the words in the critical clause were recalled 54% of the time when it was in the final sentence, versus just 22% of the time when it was not. In all experiments, these differences were highly significant (p) .001) by both subjects and items. Second, the joint probability of recalling both the previous and immediate clauses, and the conditional probability of recalling the previous one given recall of the immediate one, were far higher for SHORT–LONG—.50 and .56, respectively—than for LONG–SHORT—.16 and .19—where they were not. The serial-position functions for recall were also very different in the two cases; these are considered below, in Section III, C, however.

2. *Clause Recency*

Like the immediately heard sentence, the clause heard last in these discourse segments was much better recalled than the one just preceding it. The more relevant condition here is SHORT–LONG, where the two clauses were part of the same sentence. Averaged across the four experiments, 95% of the words in the immediate clause were recalled (versus 79% for the previous clause). Perhaps more significantly, however, perfect verbatim recall was often limited to the final clause. In SHORT–LONG, in 82% of instances, all of its words were correctly recalled together (versus 54% in the nonfinal clause). Again, these differences were highly significant statistically in all experiments. Again, as will be treated later, the recall over serial-positions functions were different in the two cases.

In these studies, clause recency was partly confounded with the content of clauses and with the way in which they joined to form a sentence. Where clause order, content, and sentence structure have been more rigorously controlled (e.g., Jarvella & Herman, 1972), however, basically the same results have been found. That study, and some others (Jarvella, Snodgrass, & Adler, 1978) have found, however, that recall is somewhat better in the final clause when it is the only clause of the final sentence heard. Experiment IV, where the sentence to be recalled was immediately prompted, also shows this trend (see Table I). This difference need not reflect better verbatim representation of the final clause when it is a sentence by itself, however, since recalling the earlier clause first in the other condition can interfere with, and delay, recalling the later one. This seems a plausible explanation, since the second clause is actually sometimes forgotten by children when they try to recall the whole sentence in such a task (Jarvella, 1976; Tyler & Marslen-Wilson, 1978).

Thus, although largely accessible to recall, the linguistic information even in immediate sentences heard in discourse is often less than perfectly remembered, even in their most recent clause. In the Jarvella and Herman study, over 700 immediately heard sentences contained errors when recalled. About 60% of these errors involved lexical substitutions, 30% deletions, and 10% some addition. There were practically no errors made where the lexical material in sentences was recalled with a largely different surface structure than the one presented. However, a sizable number of errors involved full subject and predicate phrases, and 15% involved full clauses. Major constituent errors of these kinds were predominantly located in recall of previous clauses; about twice as many occurred in these clauses as in the sentences' final or only clauses.

3. *Cross-Study Comparisons*

What is the reason for conducting four studies as similar as experiments I–IV in the first place? One reason was that experiment I revealed a response bias for listeners to recall just the last sentence they heard, or at least to recall this sentence first. Experiment II showed that the sentence and clause recency effects could still be obtained if the same point for beginning left-to-right recall of the final sequence was used.

Still, if sentences were the main organizing structures in memory, the immediate sentence effect there might have been due partly to requiring entry into the middle of the previous sentence in LONG–SHORT. However, experiment IV, which cued recall of the sentences, showed that accuracy for only the short ones (in both positions) was increased by this technique. The two-clause sentences were remembered about as before. The point of experiment III, in contrast, was partly to examine oral recall itself and partly to see if processing differences could be detected between the two ears. While in the other studies subjects were tested in groups, here they were tested individually and heard the materials monaurally. Oral recall for the nonfinal sentence heard suffered in comparison with the other three studies, but subjects hearing the materials in their right ear were better in remembering the first clause of both kinds of longer sentences.

B. Experiment V: Recognition of Discourse Segments

From experiments like those reviewed above, it was tempting to conclude that "the most recently heard clause and sentence (of discourse) are organized as speech processing structures in memory" (Jarvella, 1971, p. 415). However, the testing of immediate recall for completed, normally spoken, segments of these kinds by itself cannot really justify this conclusion. Too many factors remained unexplored. One of the questions was whether recall as a technique itself led largely to the results found. For example, was the organization found imposed during processing of the discourse or during the production of a response? One way to rule out the latter explanation is to conduct a similar study of recognition memory, where listeners simply judge whether sentences shown immediately after discourse segments repeat them. In fact, the general findings reported above, as well as some to be reviewed later, have been replicated using recognition memory tasks of this type. As a rule, this has been done by using as test material sentences which are highly similar to the original ones heard and based on either formal changes made in them or common errors made in recall.

The first recent experiment of this kind was done by Sachs (1967). Sachs located the critical sentences at the very end of discourse passages, or 80 or 160 syllables earlier. Test sentences were then presented which were identical to these, changed in form, or changed in meaning. When the critical sentence immediately preceded the test, subjects were usually (80–90% of the time) correct in their judgments as to whether it was repeated, and they made these judgments with high confidence. When there was intervening speech, however, subjects did better and were more confident in noticing meaning changes than in noticing whether the sentence's form was maintained when meaning was largely preserved.

Sachs' (1967) experiment makes the major point that the form of a sentence originally perceived may be "stored only for the short time necessary for comprehension to occur" (p. 437). However, it is difficult to say how closely comprehension and accurate verbatim memory for recent discourse were really approached. Sentences were taken to be the relevant processing units, but no attempt was made to see if, say, an earlier clause of a sentence just heard, or any linguistic segment completed less than 30 sec earlier, was also relatively difficult to remember exactly. In other studies, using recognition rather than recall as a task, we have been able to replicate both the results reported above for experiments I–IV, and some later ones regarding relations between sentences and clauses.

The first study, experiment V here, was done in collaboration with Amy Adler and Lisa Rosen, and it employed the same listening materials as reviewed above. The recognition test items were constructed by choosing characteristic errors in recall and working these into the sentences used in the recognition test. For example, the form of one SHORT–LONG item was "For Taylor, getting this signature was difficult. To obtain permission to travel abroad, a trip to Washington would be necessary." Across subjects, a change was introduced in each of the three clauses, as follows:

Context:	For Taylor, *obtaining* this signature was difficult.
Previous:	To *get* permission to travel abroad, a trip to Washington would be necessary.
Immediate:	To obtain permission to travel abroad, a trip to Washington would be *needed*.

These, along with the three complementary changes in the LONG–SHORT version (those in the final two clauses being identical to these), defined six conditions. (The previous dummy test items were re-presented exactly as heard.) The different versions of the sentences were typed onto the top of test sheets. Along the bottom, subjects checked whether they thought the sentence shown was exactly the same or somehow different from the one being cued and rated the confidence of their judgment on a five-point scale (5 = very confident, 1 = very unconfident).

Each of 48 subjects received two or three recognition items of each of the six kinds. For each form, responses were obtained for eight different subjects. Subjects heard a tone signal following each recorded test item, once for the immediate sentence and twice for the previous one. They then turned over to and completed the relevant test page in their booklet, including marking any specific change they noticed in the sentence shown. The task was explained both by clear instructions and an example:

The rain in Spain falls/fell mainly on the plain

After each recorded passage, subjects were asked to write a summary of what had happened in it. Nearly all subjects were able to write a clear account of both passages; the data from the few who could not were discarded.

The results of this experiment are summarized in Table II. In general, it can be seen that, as for experiments I–IV, subjects were more accurate the nearer the sentence or clause which they had to remember was to the end of the test segment. In this case, they were better in noticing that something was changed, in identifying exactly what was different, and more confident in their judgments. For all three measures, the differences are very large. For both subjects and items analyses on the percent correct measure, the immediate clause was better remembered than both the previous and the context clauses ($p < .001$ for each). Moreover, the previous clause in SHORT–LONG, where it was part of the final sentence, was remembered better ($p < .05$) than the previous clause in LONG–SHORT, where it was not. Thus, false recognitions occurred significantly less often for the immediate than for the previous constituents of both types.

C. Memory within Sentence and Clause Units: Serial Position Effects

We have seen that both the last sentence and last clause heard in running discourse seem to hold a privileged place in listeners' immediate memory. Of these two levels, the final clause tends to be remembered in a far more verbatim form, with performance verging on error-free reproduction and recognition. A previous clause from the same final sentence is remembered less confidently and less accurately. The decreasing memory for the just previous sentence is still greater.

Conclusions of this kind are supported not only by relative levels of recall for clauses and sentences as wholes. As well, the recall function over serial positions seems to be qualitatively different for the final and nonfinal segments in each case. By the time a full constituent at the clause or sentence level is heard, the clause or sentence preceding it is quite difficult to remember, and this shows in especially poor recall for items near the middle of the segment. Over serial positions, the recall function becomes strikingly U shaped.

The recall data for experiment I are shown plotted over serial positions in Fig. 1. It can be seen there that the words-recalled function is

TABLE II

RESULTS FOR EXPERIMENT V: RECOGNITION MEMORY

Condition and measure	Clause position: Context	Previous	Immediate
SHORT–LONG			
Percent correct judgments	48	59	85
Mean confidence when correct	2.7	4.2	4.5
Number of corrections			
a. Attempted	32	51	80
b. Successful	21	40	72
LONG–SHORT			
Percent correct judgments	45	41	95
Mean confidence when correct	2.6	2.6	4.8
Number of corrections			
a. Attempted	26	30	97
b. Successful	12	9	93

fairly flat only in the final clause. It is bowshaped in the previous clause of the final sentence, and both previous sentences show a single U-shaped curve. In experiment I, the following differences between serial positions were all significant (Jarvella, 1970b) at the .02 significance level by both subjects and items:

a. In the long previous sentence, words in the first and last three serial positions were more accurately recalled than words in the seven middle positions.
b. In the short previous sentence, words in the first two and last two serial positions were better recalled than those in the middle three positions.
c. In the previous clause os the long final sentence, words in the first and last positions were better recalled than those adjacent to them, and these were recalled better than those in the two center positions.

In a similar experiment in which listeners were asked to recall final sentences of discourse made up of two eight-word clauses, Marslen-Wilson and Tyler (1976) also found significant quadratic components to such curves. It seems clear that the primary analysis of the material in these phrases was completed by the time recall was tested; the clauses and sentences were processed as wholes in some sense; for previous segments, the processing structures formed had begun to lose their integrity as the new segments were heard.

D. EXPERIMENT VI: HOW FAST DOES FORGETTING OCCUR?

Perhaps the most striking feature of the serial-position curves shown in Fig. 1 is the rise in recall to a peak at the beginning of the final sentence and clause heard. That memory is anchored around these points is also suggested by the corresponding increase in responses which

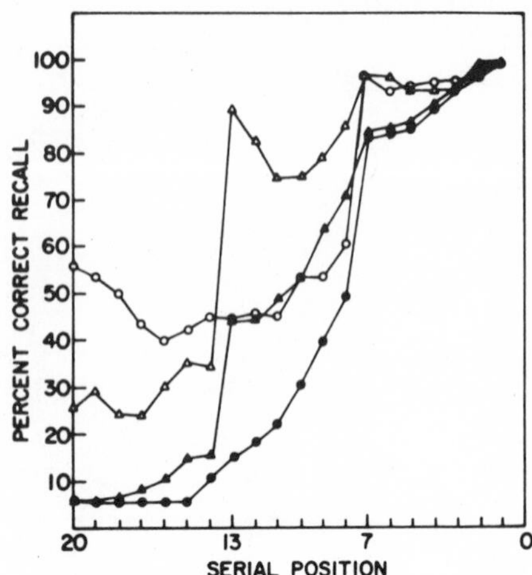

Fig. 1. Serial position curves for word recall and cumulative running memory span in SHORT–LONG (△, ▲) and LONG–SHORT (○,●) conditions in experiment I. (From Jarvella, 1971.)

are perfectly correct from that point on. This is shown by the curves plotted for the running memory span. However, the falling away of verbatim memory for the now previous segments can only be roughly inferred from these data. What is especially unclear is the rate at which the representation of those segments was being lost. To be sure, the results set a kind of upper limit of one clause or seven words of further speech for the amount of forgetting we can suppose to have occurred. We clearly need to look for a lower limit, however, closer to the time at which a segment is initially presented. One way of doing this is to observe what happens to recall of a segment as only small increments of further speech have been processed. At the same time, we might look at what happens for memory within this further segment as increased amounts of it are heard. These were the general aims of the next experiment to be described (Jarvella *et al.*, 1978, experiment I).

There are several hints of what might happen in the results of earlier studies. This is especially true of two of the earliest studies that were conducted in this series. In the first case (Jarvella, 1970a), discourse was interrupted four or seven words following the last major constituent boundary, and subjects were instructed to recall the last seven words they had heard. Where the constituent boundary occurred four words before the interruption, recall in the preceding three positions averaged only 78% correct, as opposed to almost perfect recall found in all other positions in both conditions. Thus, in that case, recall of the previous segment was depressed after only four words of further speech.

In another case (Jarvella & Herman, 1972), the length of one- and two-clause immediate sentences, and of previous sentences heard in discourse, was left to vary relatively freely. There was little relation found between the length of either kind of immediate sentence, or the previous one, and how well they were recalled. The one-clause, final sentences were as short as three words, the two-clause ones 9–15 words long, and the previous sentences were as long as 20 words. As in the experiments reported above, rather than length, per se, the crossing of a boundary between segments was a much better predictor of success or failure in recall.

In the present experiment, the amount of speech following a completed sentence or clause was systematically varied. Using the same listening materials as in experiments I–V, the test items were cut back and presented without their final clause at all, or with part, most, or all of it present. For instance, for the example cited above about union affairs, in SHORT–LONG the segment now ended either at "McDonald," without the final clause, or ended at one of the three locations indicated by the lines below:

> "To stack the meeting for McDonald
> the union had even brought in outsiders."
> ________
> ________________
> ___________________________________

The first clause of the other final sentences in SHORT–LONG was similarly followed by zero, two, four, or all seven words of the second clause. In the other version of each item, in LONG–SHORT, the first sentence was followed either by no further speech, or by two, four, or all seven words of the short final sentence.

Eight balanced versions of the passages, each containing two items of each kind, were constructed and presented to listeners in taped recorded form. There were 64 subjects. During each passage, recall of the test sentences was prompted at the end of test items using tone signals; from the actual experimental items, only the LONG sentences were cued. Subjects were instructed to write down the sentence being prompted as accurately as possible, word for word. Following each passage, they were asked to write a summary of what happened in it.

Figure 2 shows percent correct recall over serial positions for the final sentences heard in the SHORT–LONG condition. The clause boundary lies between the sixth and seventh words. When the first clause was the last speech heard, recall for it was highly accurate (95% correct) and the serial-position curve was fairly flat. As the following clause was heard, recall of the now in fact previous clause decreased progressively. With two more words heard, accuracy dropped to 85% correct, with four to 76%, and with all seven to 71%. Interestingly, the only significant decrease observed between adjacent curves shown was between no further speech heard and the first two words of the following clause ($p < .01$). Second, it is evident from Fig. 2 that accuracy of recall in the first clause became bow shaped over serial positions, as the second clause was heard, and rose sharply at the clause boundary. However, whether two, four, or all seven words of the second segment were heard, accuracy in recalling that second segment remained about the same (from 91% to 93%). Thus, each clause was apparently processed as a largely independent structure, almost as it was heard.

For the nonfinal sentences from the LONG–SHORT condition, results were quite comparable. Recall averaged 77%, 58%, 52%, and 37% correct, respectively, when the long sentences in this condition were followed by zero, two, four, and all seven words of the final short sentences. Again, the only stepwise difference that was significant was between no further speech heard and the first two words of the following segment ($p < .01$). For both clauses and sentences, then, hearing only two words of a further constituent was sufficient for recall of the previous one to drop off dramatically.

E. Experiments VII and VIII: Prosodic Factors in Discourse Memory

The clause and sentence recency effects found in the studies reviewed above were found for discourse produced in a normal and natural manner of speaking. A question that can be raised about them is to what extent are they a function of processing which is dependent on prosodic cues? Narrative discourse, for example, is usually read aloud with some pause between sentences. This might aid their segmentation by the listener. In view of this possibility, two further studies, done in collaboration with Lisa Rosen and Amy Adler, were conducted bearing specifically on the contribution of prosodic factors to these effects. In a limited way, these studies looked at the effects of rhythm, pause, and intonation contour. The results of these studies, together with one by Marslen-Wilson and Tyler (1976, experiment II), appear to support the conclusion that as sentences in text are made more phonetically degenerate, the clause effect is strengthened and the sentence effect weakened. Prosodic cues do enhance segmentation, but the clause effect itself is robust.

In the Marslen-Wilson and Tyler study, subjects first listened to a normal prose passage, and then to one in which the passage's words were replaced by others of the same form class and these were scrambled into a random order. Both passages were read at a rate of 160 words per minute, the normal one with a normal intonation pattern, the random word-order one with an approximation to this. The test "sentences"

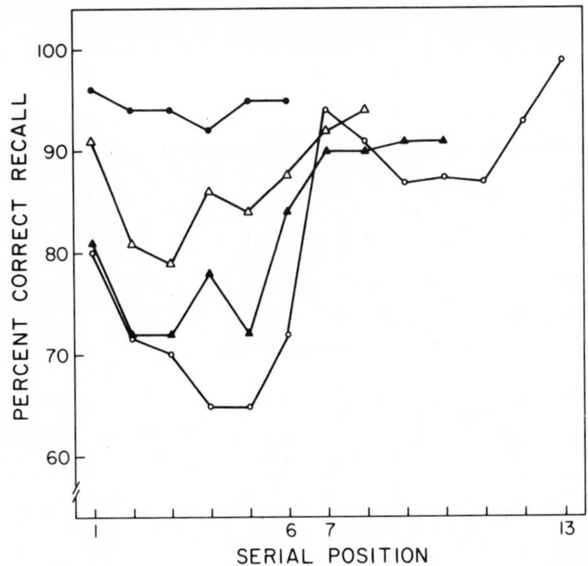

Fig. 2. Word recall by serial position in SHORT–LONG in experiment VI: ●, first clause only; △, plus two words; ▲, plus four words; ○, plus all seven words of second clause. (From Jarvella, Snodgrass, & Adler, 1978.)

consisted of two eight-word clauses. In the normal prose condition the data were not reported, but in a parallel study using the same material the usual clause recency effect was found: 86% of the words (using an ordered-recall criterion) in the final clause were recalled, versus 79% in the previous one. In the random word-order condition, subjects were able to recall 68% of the words in the most recent "clause" but only 6% of those in the less recent one. When recall of the earlier "clause" was prompted by giving subjects its first word, recall for it did not improve. Thus, subjects were able to use prosody alone to segment and remember the last segment of prose deprived of its grammatical structure and meaning (essentially grouped sets of unrelated words). The grouping observed for such segments in the Marslen-Wilson and Tyler experiment, however, does not point to such effects in normal prose processing. These were looked at in the two experiments described below.

To effectively reduce the cues to discourse structure supplied by prosody, it is necessary to control the rhythm of the speech, its intonation or pitch contour, and the occurrence of pauses. In our two studies, this was done by presenting the speech in a monotone at a constant rate. The speaker making the stimulus tapes read aloud at a rate of one syllable per half second with a flat pitch contour. The materials were shortened versions of the two narrative passages used previously. In experiment VII, the speaker was allowed to breathe between the two final sentences in the test items; this occurred randomly in about half the cases. In experiment VIII, there were no such breathing pauses (or other hesitations) in the period needed to say the final 20 words, i.e., the entire test sequence of interest. Instructions emphasized verbatim recall of just the last part of the segments, as in previous experiments. To ensure that subjects listened to the sense of the stories, they were required to write a summary of them after they were heard. In experiment VII there were 16 subjects, in experiment VIII, 24 subjects.

Taken together, the two experiments suggest that hesitation and other aspects of speech prosody each influence listeners' segmentation of discourse into successive sentences. This is indicated by two results in particular. First, in experiment VII, recall of the previous clause heard was generally better when a hesitation fell just before or after it, separating the two sentences. In the SHORT–LONG condition, about one third more words were remembered in the previous clause when it was preceded by a pause. In LONG–SHORT, about one-fourth more words in the previous clause were remembered when it was followed by a pause. The effect of the hesitations separating the two sentences was spread throughout the clause but was especially prominent at its beginning and end.

The second result is from experiment VIII and further suggests that prosody contributed to the sentence recency effect found earlier. The data for word recall are plotted by serial position in Fig. 3. It can be seen that there is little difference between the SHORT–LONG and the LONG–SHORT curves in any of the three most recent clauses heard. For context, previous, and immediate clauses, the percentages of words recalled in SHORT–LONG were 91%, 53%, and 32%, respectively. In LONG–SHORT, they were 88%, 47%, and 34%, respectively. There is a sentence recency effect to be sure: the relatively small difference in recall of previous clauses was significant ($p < .025$), and recall of the clauses in this position in SHORT–LONG appears anchored from their first word, where the curves diverge most strongly. The effect is really slight with respect to previous experiments, however.

Partly as a consequence of the weakening of the sentence recency effect, however, the clause recency effect appears to be stronger than ever in these studies. It was the most salient effect in both experiments. Averaged over SHORT–LONG and LONG–SHORT, word recall in the final two clauses was 44% and 87%, respectively, in experiment VII, and 50% versus 89% in experiment VIII. One of the problems in these experiments which we should keep in mind, however, is that the discourse was heard at only about one-half normal speech rate. We did not have the technical facilities to double the speed of the recording and maintain a sufficiently intelligible signal. If there is a real-time limit to short-term memory for discourse, this experiment should bring it out. That a sen-

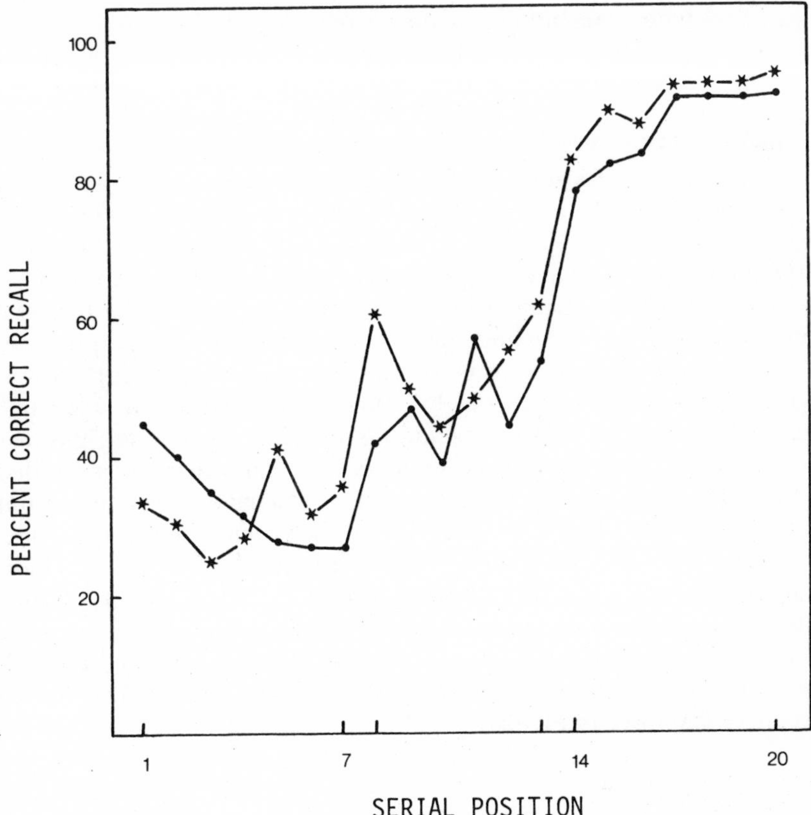

Fig. 3. Word recall by serial position in experiment VIII in SHORT–LONG (*) and LONG–SHORT (○) conditions.

tence recency effect was still obtained under such circumstances is perhaps worth remembering, though of course the effect for clauses is the one which stands out.

F. Experiment IX: Recall of Read Discourse

A further way of investigating the effects of the way discourse might be spoken on its representation in immediate memory is to change modality of presentation itself. More generally, it is of interest to know if the kind of immediate sentence and clause effects we have been exploring can also be found in some reading situations. Apparently, they do hold for reading, at least where discourse is presented to, and presumably processed by, subjects from left to right. In such highly controlled circumstances, we have used the running presentation–immediate recall type of technique to look at both oral and silent reading of discourse. Here it is the silent reading tasks, with oral recall at test interruptions, which are pertinent. Two such experiments, done in collaboration with Judy Orasanu and Lisa Rosen, will be described, one at this point and one later.

The first study was done to see if the clause and sentence recency effects found in the listening studies would be replicated when discourse passages were read. Subjects were presented with the shortened versions of the same two narrative passages used in the studies of prosodic factors. The passages were presented in capital letters on a computer terminal using normal punctuation and spacing, but in such a way that phenomenally, a window appeared to be passing over and revealing the text in each line shown from left to right. The window was seven characters wide and was moved forward by adding one character to the right and deleting one from the left every 50 msec. Two blank spaces were added to the right-hand side of each line before carriage return to permit subjects to sweep their eyes back to the beginning of the next one. Previous studies of reading in these circumstances had shown that most adult readers can read such a message orally making only a minimal number of errors. It translates into a presentation rate of about three words per second, which is also in the normal speech range. The following is an example of what the display might have looked like at successive 100-msec intervals:

```
A TRIP
  TRIP TO
    IP TO W
      TO WAS
        O WASHI
          WASHING
            SHINGTO
              INGTON
                GTON WO
                  ON WOUL
                    WOULD
                      OULD BE
                        LD BE N
                          BE NEC
                            E NECES
                              NECESSA
                                CESSARY
```

At the end of each test item, the screen went blank and subjects were asked to orally repeat as much of the very end of the segment that had been presented as they could remember. Subjects were trained prior to the study to read text presented in this manner aloud. During the test passages they read silently. After each passage, they were required to summarize what had happened in it.

Results for verbatim recall showed very strong sentence and clause recency effects. In fact, these were as great in magnitude as in any of the studies on listening. In SHORT–LONG, word recall in the context, previous, and immediate clauses averaged 4%, 39%, and 85% correct, respectively. In LONG–SHORT, it averaged 11%, 15%, and 88% correct, respectively. Thus, over twice as much of the material in previous clauses was remembered when these were in the final sentence heard; over twice as much again was recalled from the clause following these and heard last. It was generally only this final clause that was recalled with high accuracy: Word recall increased across the within-sentence clause boundary from 40% to 81% correct. Taken across both conditions, more than half of all responses had a running memory span of seven words, or exactly clause length. In about two thirds of cases, all the words in final clauses were recalled together.

It is thus apparent from this study that the sentence and clause read last in discourse presented from left to right are also represented as structures in memory. The effects are not modality specific. Rather, they result from a process common to listening and reading.

G. Experiment X: Developmental Aspects of Sentence and Clause Recency

The recency effects for sentences and clauses have also been investigated using child subjects. Although relatively few studies of this kind have been done with children, and those studies have looked at additional factors in recall, the results generally appear to be consistent with findings for adults. In this section, three such studies will be reviewed (Jarvella, 1976; Tyler & Marslen-Wilson, 1978a, 1978b). All three will also be considered in section IV, on effects of processing dependencies between clauses and sentences.

In the first study (Jarvella, 1976), called experiment X here, a total of 72 children over three grade levels were tested. The average age of the groups in years and months was 6,8; 8,8; and 10,8. Parts of two novels for children were adapted for use in the experiment. As presented, each contained nine sections ranging from 50 to 150 words in length. At the end of each section were two five-word clauses, which in some cases fell together into the same sentence and in others into two different short sentences. The stories were tape recorded in two different versions, with tones inserted at the ends of test segments to signal oral recall.

The subjects were instructed that they would hear a story told to them in several parts. After each part, the person telling the story would sound a horn. It would then be the child's turn to talk and to say back what he had just heard. The children were instructed to say back just "the last thing or two" they had heard, using the same words as the storyteller. No other linguistic concepts were introduced. Each child then heard one version of one of the stories, with the first item counted as practice. During the experiment, if a child reported only one of the two final clauses heard, the other was prompted by asking what had been said just before or after the one that was mentioned.

The main developmental finding of interest here was that the youngest children tended to recall just the final clause heard, while the older children tried to recall both clauses. The 7-year-olds, even with prompting, repeated nothing from more than one-third of the earlier clauses heard, but they fully recalled nearly two-thirds of the following, final clauses. The older children, however, usually tried to recall both clauses spontaneously, in the order in which they had occurred. In 90% of cases, they did recall some of the first clause. This trend held for both the short sentences and the long ones. However, recall of the first clause was also partly a function of whether it was a separate sentence. Across ages, this clause was recalled more poorly when it was a separate sentence. For the two short sentences, word recall pooled over age was 62% in the first clause and 83% in the second clause. For the long sentences, it was 73% in the first clause and 76% in the second. Similarly, the full short sentences were recalled 30% and 72% of the time, respectively, and the two clauses in the longer sentences, 54% and 47%, respectively.

The Tyler and Marslen-Wilson Studies

Tyler and Marslen-Wilson (1978a) presented a total of 30 5-, 7-, and 11-year-old children a normal prose passage whose segments ended in two-clause sentences. For the 5-year-olds, the sentences were 10 words in length, and for the two older groups, 14 words long. The children were told that, whenever the story stopped, they should tell the experimenter "the last sentence you heard, exactly . . . as you heard it."

In experiment X, the U-shaped serial-position curves within clauses typically found for adults were already apparent in 7-year-olds. In this later study, however, where still younger subjects were examined, such U-shaped functions were found for the normal prose only from this age upwards (hence, also only on the longer 14-word sentences). The performance of the 5-year-olds was best fitted with a single quadratic curve, covering the full sentence, not a double-bowed curve. Tyler and Marslen-Wilson, on this basis, proposed that, for the younger children, the sentences were represented in memory in such a way that the syntactic information in either clause failed to influence the recall curve; what did affect recall was the meaning of the speech heard.

In their second developmental study, Tyler and Marslen-Wilson (1978b) conducted one study using 20 Dutch children and another using 40 English children. In each case, half of the children were 5 years old and the other half 7 years old. The sentences ending test segments of the stories used were again two clauses in length, this time 12 words for the younger subjects and 14 words for the older ones. As indicated by double-bowed serial-position curves, the first study did find clausal segmentation in the 5-year-olds, especially for particular sentences, as well as for the 7-year-olds. The second study was reported mainly as an analysis of errors. At both ages, a substantial number of errors occurred in which the earlier clause in the final sentences was fully omitted in recall. From *post hoc* analyses of the relation of these clauses to prior context, and from other errors, Tyler and Marslen-Wilson argued that in many of these cases it is plausible that the clauses not recalled had been processed and integrated with the speech preceding them.

IV. Processing Dependencies between Sentences and Clauses

The findings reported above suggest that clauses and sentences are partly processed as independent information structures in discourse. This processing works iteratively as more discourse is taken in. General effects of retroactive interference in short-term memory, at the level of whole linguistic segments or full constituents, are a consequence. Thus, each further sentence or clause which is constructed overrides in some sense the continued representation of the one before it. In the current section, we will have a look at some of the factors which may retard this process, and then at some which may speed it up.

While segment by segment processing seems to be a quite basic routine in handling discourse, true for different kinds of sentences and clauses, it is evidently not the only process working at that level. In short, it takes too little account of the question of continuity between segments. Relations between sentences are important in discourse, and the relatedness of clauses within a sentence in fact predicts the kind of sentence recency effect that was established for previous clauses heard. The remembering for immediate constituents in discourse, and forgetting of previous ones, seems to be a product of maintaining continuity as well as achieving partial, complete analyses of what is said.

We thus need to go beyond the recency function per se and explore some effects of linguistic context. As suggested earlier, the representation of a prior segment heard or read might be seen as helping guide processing of a current one, serving as a basis for its interpretation.

And, on its side, the current structure being formed may be seen not only as "working off" the previous one, but in some cases even allowing its interpretation. For real discourse, we will consider examples of both kinds. On the one hand, some studies of coreference between segments will be reviewed which suggest that a processing structure can be used as a linguistic or conceptual bridge to what follows it, such as when this segment is an appendage which is grammatically abbreviated. On the other hand, there are such cases as cataphora, backward pronominalization, and other right-to-left constraints across major phrase boundaries, where holding a previous structure in memory after it is heard may be needed to fully understand it. The illustration we will use to suggest this is memory for complex sentences beginning with subordinate clauses. In both types of phenomena, a higher level processing link that encompasses both segments is implied. In this sense, the relations between clauses in sentences and between pairs of full sentences differ from each other only in degree.

We will also need to look at certain questions of discourse content and I will, in fact, begin with one. In linguistics, the meaning of, e.g., sentences is taken to be a joint function of their form and their content. The same is presumably true for the meaning acquired in understanding. Until now, I have had little to say about this, and, in fact, I will not have much to say about it here either. If form and content are taken to be different parts of a processing structure, they must be considered to be highly integrated parts, perhaps inseparable ones. However, linguistic segments on both the sentence and the clause level, and the structural relations that we will take up here, have a content side to them. Often psycholinguists have attempted to manipulate form and content independently, artificially drawing them apart.

The formation of a processing structure for a segment can evidently be accomplished even when its meaning is opaque, but such a structure can as a result have little function as part of a discourse representation. When a wedge is driven between sentence form and content by constructing and presenting subjects with text that is complete nonsense, the effects on recall are inhibitory rather than facilitative. Several studies reviewed at the end of this section have shown that the meaningless parts are not remembered once constructed and inhibit memory for normal segments with which they would be interpreted.

A. Experiment XI: The Text Relevance of Final Segments

One initial question that can be raised about the recency effects is to what extent immediate segments heard "write over" or simply mask previous ones from memory. In other words, is hearing a short final clause or sentence sufficient cause for the one just before it to become difficult to remember accurately? If memory depends as well on the interrelations between successive parts of a discourse message, this is certainly false. Most of the experiments described in the remaining part of the paper support that view. One method to collect relevant data is to make whatever further speech is heard completely irrelevant to the message itself. This was done in the following experiment (Jarvella *et al.*, 1978, experiment II) by appending recall instructions to the end of test segments of discourse.

The listening materials in experiment XI were the full 1500-word versions of the same two narrative passages described above. The SHORT–LONG and LONG–SHORT items were equally spread over two versions of the passages as before. Each version was then recorded in three forms. In one form, the discourse segments were read aloud, separated only by test pauses, as in experiment I. In a second, a clause was always appended to the final sentence saying:

"and now write down this sentence."

In a third form, a sentence of the same length was added just after the final sentence from the discourse saying:

"Now write down the last sentence."

A total of 64 adult subjects were tested. For the straight narrative versions of passages, subjects were instructed to write down in their test booklets the last sentence they had heard before a pause, word for word. In the two other conditions, subjects were told to write down the last sentence going up to, but not including, the final instructions. After each passage was heard, subjects answered a series of true–false questions about it.

Recall of the final sentence of test items (minus the instruction, if any) was scored as in previous experiments. Figure 4 shows the corresponding serial-position curves found. There were two obvious, but also obviously different, effects of clause and sentence recency. The first of these is that less of the earlier clause of the long sentences (in SHORT–LONG) was recalled (86% of words correct) than either the later clause of these sentences (92% correct) or the final clause (in LONG–SHORT) presented as a single sentence (96% correct). In each case, the difference was significant beyond the .001 level.

Second, recall of the sentences as a whole (short and long both) was slightly but consistently worse when they were followed by instructions than by silence. For clause instructions, the difference was significant at .05, for sentence ones at .001. What is perhaps most striking about Fig. 4, however, is that neither the sentence nor the clause instructions

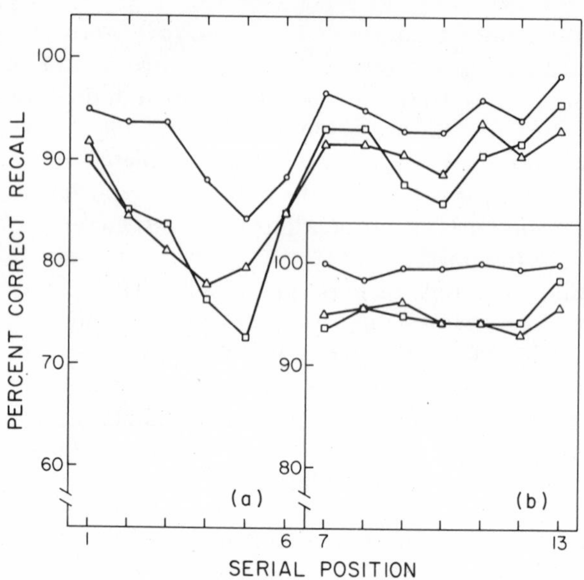

Fig. 4. Word recall by serial position (a) in 13-word and (b) 7-word final sentences in experiment XI: ○, no further speed heard ▲, plus clause instruction; □, plus sentence instruction. (From Jarvella, Snodgrass, & Adler, 1978.)

that were added to test segments very much affected the shape of the recall functions. Compared with the clause recency effect for the same material shown in Figs. 1–3, as well as that in Fig. 4a, the effect of the additional clause heard in Fig. 4b was very slight—just a fine decrease in accuracy throughout the clause, and no apparent bowing in the middle. Moreover, the same kind of very reduced effect can be seen in recall of the two-clause discourse sentences. In contrast with the long previous sentences (in LONG–SHORT) shown in Fig. 1, here the sentences recalled can at best be described as having double-bowed curves. Hearing the instructions afterward did little to change this. It thus appears from these data that other processing of immediately heard segments than called for by the instructions leads to the forgetting normally observed for the ones just preceding them. That further processing is processing relevant to the representation of the immediate discourse message.

B. Experiments XII and XIII: Coreference and Discourse Structure

One of the things that happens when we talk about something at any length is that it gets mentioned a number of times. Language, however, provides a useful economy of expression for these cases. Several clauses and sentences can corefer to the same thing without all of them mentioning it explicitly. Overtly, therefore, what is said is much less repetitive than it would otherwise need be. Thus, in our sample passage illustrated at the beginning of this paper, the pronoun "it" was used several times as an anaphor after an antecedent had been provided in the context preceding it; there was also a case of multiple ellipsis where a series of actions were all attributed to what a historian tries to do. Such cases are examples of a widespread phenomenon. If we know that the Smiths are going to a party and the Joneses are going to a party, and it is relevant to mention both, we might say "The Smiths are going to a party, and so are the Joneses" (using the anaphor "so"), or "The Smiths are going to a party. The Joneses are, too" (using ellipsis). If a particular festive gathering is established by context, which is the same for both families named, we can simply say (by further ellipsis) "The Smiths are going, the Joneses too." Then the second segment depends on the first for "are going" and both on the previous context for "to the party."

It seems likely that for these constructions to work we need to be able to maintain a good idea of their earlier part throughout them. In other words, we may have to be able to access the structure of one or more preceding segments to form a processing structure for a current one. In a sense, we have to remember implicitly what is not given overtly. In the next two studies (Jarvella, 1973), this kind of rough hypothesis was examined experimentally. Subjects were asked to recall in one experiment, or recognize in the other, either of the final two sentences they had heard in a recorded dialog. There were three conditions. In one case, the more recent speech heard—namely, the following sentence or clause—was partly coreferential with the one of interest, and grammatically abbreviated in one of the ways just mentioned. In a second case, the coreferential part was repeated fully. In a third, the final segment was fully novel. Recall and recognition were looked at for both the critical phrase (the ones implied or repeated) and remaining portions of the sentences containing them.

Twelve sets of test items were developed for each of the two sentence positions. The following gives an example of each kind:

Critical phrase in previous sentence:		
		I suppose *the reflected headlights probably blinded him.*
	Overt coreference	Don't you think the reflected headlights probably blinded him?
	Implicit coreference	Don't you think so?
	No coreference	Weren't we both lucky?
Critical phrase in immediate sentence:		
		I want to hear this saddening account detailed,
	Overt coreference	and I will hear this saddening account detailed, too
	Implicit coreference	and I will, too.
	No coreference	before something tragic happens.

When the critical phrase was part of the previous sentence, this sentence was prompted for recall or recognition. When it was part of the final sentence, it was prompted. As in these examples given, the number of words in the following context was equal for implicit and no coreference. The test items were integrated into segments of dialog between a man and a woman adapted from four radio plays. Three balanced versions of the dialog were constructed, each with four items of the six kinds. The recall subjects' task was to write down the sentence being prompted verbatim, from left to right. For the recognition subjects, test booklets were constructed on the basis of common errors made in recalling the sentences, as in experiment V. On turning to a test page, it was the subjects' task to read the sentence, decide if it was in the same form as one of those heard, rate the confidence of their judgment on a three-point scale (very confident, confident, not confident), and identify any change they noticed in the printed form. Four of the 24 test items were printed as they had been heard. The others were presented with small changes. The changes usually involved substitution, deletion, or addition of one word. When an item was presented changed, the change could fall either in the critical phrase, or the surrounding context. Across subjects, changes of both kinds were tested for all items. In all, 112 subjects in nine groups were tested, one recall group for each version of the materials recorded, and two on recognition.

In general, the data obtained for recall and recognition were quite comparable, as they were in experiments I–IV and V. Moreover, the same trends in the data were obtained for both immediate and previous sentences heard. In Table III, they appear pooled over both sentences.

For experiment XII, on recall, the measure shown is the percent of segments that were remembered exactly as heard—either full sentences, the critical phrase, or the portion remaining. Significant differences be-

TABLE III

EXPERIMENTS XII–XIII: COREFERENCE

Task segment	Type of coreference		
	Implicit	Overt	None
Recall (Experiment XII)			
Full sentences	39	35	18
Critical phrases	59	74	36
Remaining part	65	59	53
Recognition (Experiment XIII)			
Unchanged items	98	80	82
Critical phrase changed	51	58	41
Remaining part changed	61	44	44

tween conditions were found for the sentences as whole and for each of their subparts. For full sentences, no coreference led to significantly worse ($p < .01$) recall than either implicit or overt coreference. For critical phrases, recall was higher with overt than with implicit coreference (p) .05), and with implicit coreference than none (p) .01). For the remaining part of the sentence, recall was better with implicit coreference than with either overt or none (p) .05).

For experiment XIII, on recognition, the measure shown in the table is percent correct recognition judgments. Again, significant differences were found for all three sentences parts. For correct same judgments, accuracy was greater with implicit coreference than either overt or no coreference ($p < .05$). For correct different judgments, when critical phrases had been changed, repeated coreference was superior to implied ($p < .05$) and this in turn was superior to none at all ($p < .01$). When the change was elsewhere, there were more correct different judgments for implicit than for either overt or no coreference (p) .025). Finally, as in experiment V, response confidence was closely related to recognition accuracy.

Coreference in Children's Memory for Discourse

Some further support for these findings comes from experiment X. In that study the final segments of discourse presented to children 7–11 years old were two five-word clauses (plus a conjunction when present). The two clauses were also partly coreferential or not, as seen in the following pair of examples:

First clause	Second clause
Willy was a curious mouse.	He was born that way. *or* The music was getting louder.
Homer looked at the job	that he was about to finish. *or* for the process was about finished.

In each case, the first clause was the same, and this was followed across subjects by two endings, one partly coreferential with it, the other not. Individual subjects were presented discourse in which the test items had either all coreferential endings or all noncoreferential endings.

At all three age levels, more words were recalled from the coreferential items ($p < .025$). The children also recalled about 10% more full clauses and 40% more full sentences when coreference was present. The advantage for coreference was found for all sentence constructions tested: two short sentences, compound sentences, and complex ones. The results suggested, moreover, that subjects were able to process the second clause without forgetting the first at an earlier age when coreference was present to link them. At age 7, an overall clause and sentence recency effect was obtained both with and without coreference; at age 9, only without it; and at age 11, neither with nor without it.

Finally, Tyler and Marslen-Wilson (1978b, experiment II) have reported partly similar results. The test sentences they presented to children at the end of discourse segments also contained two clauses. From a content analysis of these materials, Tyler and Marslen-Wilson partitioned the items into categories where (roughly) the first clause was informationally more related to the context or to the second clause. They then analyzed their data accordingly. They found, among other things, that *(a)* there were more meaning-changing errors in clauses which reported mainly new events, *(b)* more previous clauses were omitted from what was recalled if the following clause reported a new event, and *(c)* there were more "integration errors"—where clauses were fused or inferences made between them—when two clauses described the same event.

Results such as these, combined with the ones reported for coreference, anaphora, and ellipsis, suggest that listeners usually maintain some continuity in memory between successive segments of discourse heard. It is when a current sentence or clause is fully explicit—contains primarily new information and needs to be processed most independently—that the most forgetting of the one just preceding it occurs.

C. Experiment XIV: Subordination

As in the case of anaphora and ellipsis, with subordination some information relevant to a clausal segment is often not given explicitly. In English, for example, many such clauses begin without an overt subject or a finite verb, for example: "After seeing . . . ," "To get . . . ," "Breaking away . . . ," etc. When one of these clauses occurs first in a sentence, the relevant contextual information often comes afterward rather than before. In one of our examples above, for instance, a test sentence began "To stack the meeting for McDonald." In order for us to understand this clause, we need to know who stacked the meeting, and in the particular discourse that information was provided only in the following clause. It is also the case that pronominalization conventionally operates from main to subordinate clauses. When a subordinate clause with an anaphoric pronoun begins a sentence, we may not learn its referent until a later clause heard, as in "When he left, John took along an umbrella." Perhaps above all, however, sentences which begin with subordinations are generally not complete until some main clause is given.

When a subordination falls within a main clause, as a nominalized subject or as a relative clause embedded in the subject, it may need to be retained as the predicate is processed, perhaps causing the full sentence to be held in memory together. Experiment XIV was concerned largely with whether sentences beginning with subordinations which depend on, or are part of, or which interrupt main clauses in these ways would in fact be retained more verbatim in contrast to ones which begin with full main clauses and whose subordinations come later. It was generally the case in experiments I–IX that previous clauses of long final sentences were better recalled when the sentences had subordinate–main clause order.

In this experiment (Jarvella & Herman, 1972), the sentences ending segments of heard connected discourse consisted of either a main clause, or a subordinate clause, or the main clause preceding the subordinate clause, or the subordinate clause preceding the main one. Across groups of subjects, all four types of ending were used for each of 48 test items. The following set of endings is one example:

Main:	It seems natural to his followers
Subordinate:	That Castro was involved in the uprising.
Main–Subordinate:	It seems natural to his followers that Castro was involved in the uprising.
Subordinate–main:	That Castro was involved in the uprising seems natural to his followers.

The test items were of various types and lengths. They were integrated into four narrative passages adapted from new stories from the 1950s. Each of 45 subjects received 12 items of each kind. Subjects were told they would hear some recorded passages read to them, should listen carefully to the speech, and, whenever the passage stopped, should write down as much of the very end of the text as they could remember verbatim, up to and including the last word. After each passage, they answered a set of true–false questions about what had happened in it.

We will be concerned here only with the findings relevant to differences between the two types of clauses and the two clause orders. On both word and clause recall measures, main clauses were remembered better than subordinate clauses ($p < .05$), and previous clauses within a final sentence were remembered worse than final clauses or single-clause sentences ($p < .001$). This second finding, however, was far more significant for main than for subordinate clauses. In the long, two-clause sentences, more full subordinate previous clauses were remembered than main ones (73% vs. 70%), and more main immediate clauses were remembered than subordinate ones (79% vs. 73%). Similarly, the two-clause sentences were better recalled when they had subordinate–main clause order (63% correct) than when they had main–subordinate clause order (56% correct) ($p < .025$). Qualitatively, there were two further asymmetries: in the two-clause sentences, there were relatively far more errors involving full phrases in the previous than the immediate position with main–subordinate clause order; there were more subordination marking errors in sentences with this clause order.

Some Complementary Results from Experiment X.

Similar results for clause types and order have been found in the developmental studies reported above. In experiment X, the two-clause sentences presented to children consisted of either two main clauses (i.e., they were compound sentences) or a main and a subordinate clause. The latter complex sentences included ones with main clause-first order and others with subordinate-first order. The following gives an example for each:

Main–main:	He never acted like this, and dinner was really good tonight.
Main–subordinate:	Willy listened with both ears, trying not to miss anything.
Subordinate–main:	When he had found the paints, the tubes were completely new.

Each subject received two items of each kind.

The clauses in the compound sentences were recalled fully about 10% more often than the main clauses in the complex sentences. In the complex sentences, the main clauses were completely recalled 20% more often than the subordinate clauses ($p < .01$). In this regard, it is worth noting that more main than subordinate clauses were also remembered by the younger children in the earlier study reported by Tyler and Marslen-Wilson (1978a).

In experiment X, the order of clauses in the complex sentences also seemed to lead to the same kind of findings in the experiment with adults. Four findings suggesting this were:

1. The main clause advantage was obtained principally in the most recent clause position (fully one-third more main than subordinate clauses were deleted in the less recent one).
2. When the basic subject–verb content of both clauses was recalled, errors in recalling the conjunction (which was not otherwise scored) occurred in 26% of main–subordinate responses but only 12% of subordinate–main ones.
3. Seven-year-olds omitted 35% of all clauses from main–subordinate sentences but only 15% of those in subordinate–main ones. In the less recent position, 40% of main clauses were omitted—the same percent as of separate sentences.
4. Eleven-year-olds recalled only 31% of full main–subordinate sentences but 41% of subordinate–main ones.

It thus appears that sentence form was recalled more verbatim when subordinations occurred at the beginning than at the end of final sentences heard. The 7- and 9-year-olds, in fact, remembered substantially more of the clauses in subordinate–main sentences incompletely (50% vs. 32%), but fewer of them fully (39% vs. 46%). In contrast to the deletion of main clauses in first position, their responses in subordinate-first sentences tended to be more fragmentary throughout. This again suggests that the sentences were processed more as wholes.

D. Some Further Dependencies on Sentence Content

A general implication that can be drawn from the experiments reviewed in this paper is that the tighter the linguistic relation between (especially) consecutive segments of discourse, the more likely it is that they will both be able to be immediately remembered. In this final part of the review, two studies will be summarized in which the same conclusion can be drawn from discourse which is fully or partly meaningless. The first study, by Marslen-Wilson and Tyler (1976, experiment I), was done using a kind of pseudodiscourse, which seems semigrammatical but has no identifiable meaning. The second study, by my colleague Judy Orasanu at Rockefeller University, combined normal prose and distorted prose in order to look at interactive effects in memory between them.

1. The Marslen-Wilson and Tyler Experiment

In their experiment, Marslen-Wilson and Tyler presented listeners first with a normal discourse passage and then with either a "syntactic prose" passage—where all the words in the normal version were randomly replaced by other words of the same form class and frequency—or the syntactic prose passage in which the word order was further scrambled. The technique used was the same as in most of the experiments on listening reported here, but where subjects were asked to write down as much as they could of just the last sentence (for the normal prose) heard. On nonfiller items, the speech presented just before test interruptions always consisted of two eight-word clauses joined in a sentence. The recall protocols were scored by counting as correct only words recalled in which correct serial order was maintained.

The results found are shown plotted over serial position in Fig. 5. As can be seen, clause "1" was recalled relatively much more poorly than clause "2" in the syntactic than the normal prose condition, and in the random word-order than the syntactic prose condition. Taken over word positions, recall in the two classes, respectively, was 79% and 86% for the normal prose, 43% and 75% for the syntactic prose, and, as reported

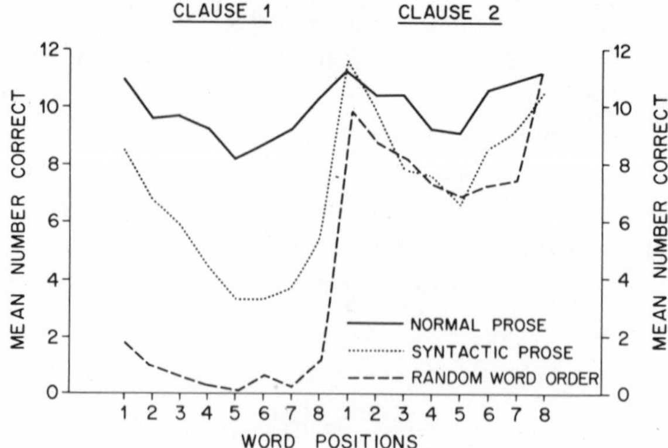

Fig. 5. Word recall over serial position in the three prose conditions examined by Marslen-Wilson and Tyler. (From Marslen-Wilson & Tyler, 1976.)

previously, 6% and 68% for the case where only prosody linked the two segments. Obviously, there is much more difference between conditions in recalling the less recent than the more recent segment. A similar difference has been found by Orasanu (1979) in some studies for recall of normal and distorted clauses in normal discourse. It seems apparent from these results that prosodic, syntactic, and semantic information all contribute to the extreme accuracy found for the final clause of normal prose heard. In the nonfinal clause, syntactic form still has a role to play, perhaps leading mainly to the bowed serial-position curves, but content now plays a much stronger role. This is, of course, what we would expect if understanding is a function of forming a full representation of a sentence, and if partial representations are formed and assimilated cyclically, clause by clause.

2. *The Orasanu Experiments*

In recent studies Orasanu (1979) has looked at reading of discourse where one of the final segments seen before recall is tested may be distorted. It is either made anomalous, as in Marslen-Wilson and Tyler's studies, or made ungrammatical by scrambling word order, or both anomalous and ungrammatical. The discourse was presented under the same conditions reported in experiment IX, from left to right on a standard CRT computer terminal with a frame width of seven visual characters at a rate of about 180 words per minute. The following gives an example of a case where a normal previous clause could be followed by another normal clause, an anomalous one, or a scrambled word-order version of this:

Clause 1:	A trip to Washington would be needed
Clause 2:	
Normal	In order to obtain permission to leave
Anomalous	In power to express festival to run
Random anomalous	Power to in run express in festival

The anomalous clauses were formed as in Marslen-Wilson and Tyler; the discourse passages and test items were approximately as in experiments I–IX, except that only two-clause final sentences were tested and these were changed so that each clause contained seven words.

The most reliable result is that the anomalous clause interfered with recall of the normal clause preceding it. With a normal following clause, about 56% of the words in the clause of interest were recalled, as opposed to only 43% when followed by an anomalous clause. If a normal or anomalous clause preceded a normal final clause, the latter was recalled 71% and 62% correctly, respectively. An interesting point that this study makes is that, in both cases, the inability to link a normal clause with an anomalous one—to interpret them as a whole—is a plausible explanation for the retroactive and proactive interference observed for memory of the normal clause. Part of the forgetting of the anomalous material in the Marslen-Wilson and Tyler study, especially in the previous clause, may be a result of a similar process.

V. Final Summary and Remarks

From the first few experiments reported here, we were led to believe that the immediate clause and sentence of discourse were being organized as speech-processing structures in immediate memory. One of the results of this processing was that the previous sentence and clause became rather poorly recalled when this was attempted, though recall was reasonably structured for them as seen by U-shaped serial-position curves. These effects were found in a number of different recall settings and in a recognition memory task as well. Experiment VI showed that the U-shaped recall curves that were apparently prototypic of this kind of performance appeared almost as soon as further relevant speech was processed. Experiments VII and VIII showed that the sentence recency effect, where more than just one clause of a sentence had been heard, was facilitated by normal prosody: Without prosodic cues to sentence structure, the clause recency effect was far stronger. Experiment IX, however, showed that the sentence and clause recency effects were easily replicable using visual presentation of text.

The second set of results showed that the forgetting of a previous clause or sentence heard or read in discourse was a function of the linguistic context. Forgetting was not simply a consequence of hearing further speech, since experiment XI showed that final sentence or clause instructions has only a marginal effect.

In experiments XII and XIII, it was shown that, if the speech following a segment in discourse was largely coreferential with it, the segment could often be remembered explicitly afterward. Novel content in the following segment, in contrast, had the reverse effect. Some studies of subordination then showed that a complex sentence may be processed and remembered more largely as a whole when it begins with a nonmain clause which depends on the following context. And in some studies reviewed in which sentence meaning was sometimes made incomprehensible, it was shown that interpretable content has a greater effect in remembering the previous clause of a sentence than the immediate one.

For both the sentence and the clause recency effects, and for those of context, some developmental data were also reported. These data generally also suggested that sentences and clauses were structural units in this kind of immediate memory, that memory depends in the same way on such factors as coreference and subordination and on content generally. The more two segments were related, the more likely it was that they would be processed and remembered together.

References

Chomsky, N. *Reflections on language.* New York: Pantheon, 1975.

Dressler, W. U. (Ed.). *Trends in textlinguistics.* Berlin: de Gruyter, 1978.

Grimes, J. E. *The thread of discourse.* The Hague: Mouton, 1975.

Jarvella, R. J. Effects of syntax on running memory span for connected discourse. *Psychonomic Science,* 1970, **19,** 235–236. (a)

Jarvella, R. J. *The immediate recall of connected speech.* Unpublished doctoral dissertation, University of Michigan, 1970. (b)

Jarvella, R. J. Syntactic processing of connected speech. *Journal of Verbal Learning and Verbal Behavior,* 1971, **10,** 409–416.

Jarvella, R. J. Speech processing memory. In C. P. Smith (Ed.), *1972 Conference on Speech Communication and Processing.* New York: Institute of Electrical and Electronics Engineers, 1972.

Jarvella, R. J. Co-reference and short-term memory for discourse. *Journal of Experimental Psychology,* 1973, **98,** 426–428.

Jarvella, R. J. Children's short-term memory for discourse. In W. von Raffler Engel & Y. Lebrun (Eds.), *Baby talk and infant speech.* Amsterdam: Swets & Zeitlinger, 1976.

Jarvella, R. J., & Herman, S. J. Clause structure of sentences and speech processing. *Perception & Psychophysics,* 1972, **11,** 381–384.

Jarvella, R. J., Snodgrass, J. G., & Adler, A. P. Memory for on-going discourse. In A. M. Lesgold, J. W. Pellegrino, S. D. Fokkema, & R. Glaser (Eds.), *Cognitive psychology and instruction.* New York: Plenum, 1978.

Marslen-Wilson, W., & Tyler, L. K. Memory and levels of processing in a psycholinguistic context. *Journal of Experimental Psychology: Human Learning and Memory,* 1976, **2,** 112–119.

Orasanu, J. *Effects of text distortion on text memory.* Paper presented at the meeting of the Eastern Psychological Association, Philadelphia, 1979.

Sachs, J. S. Recognition memory for syntactic and semantic aspects of connected discourse. *Perception & Psychophysics,* 1967, **2,** 437–442.

Tyler, L. K., & Marslen-Wilson, W. Some developmental aspects of sentence processing and memory, *Journal of Child Language,* 1978a, **5,** 113–129.

Tyler, L. K., & Marslen-Wilson, W. Understanding sentences in context: some developmental studies. *Papers and reports on child language development,* XV. Stanford, California: Stanford University, 1978b.

Westrup, J. *An introduction to musical history* (2nd Ed.). London: Hutchinson, 1973.

SUBJECT INDEX